☝ **W9-BVU-313**

1001 Chocolate Treats

1001
Chocolate
Treats

GREGG R. GILLESPIE

PHOTOGRAPHS BY PETER BARRY

BLACK DOG
& LEVENTHAL
PUBLISHERS
NEW YORK

Published by

Black Dog & Leventhal Publishers, Inc.
151 West 19th Street
New York, NY 10011

Distributed by

Workman Publishing Company
708 Broadway
New York, NY 10003

Designed by Martin Lubin Graphic Design

Manufactured in the United States of America

Library of Congress Catalging-in-Publication Data
   1001 chocolate treats / Gregg R. Gillespie.
        p.   cm.
   Includes index.
   ISBN 1-884822-86-X
   1. Cookery (Chocolate)   2. Chocolate   I. Title
TX767,05G554   1996
641.6'374--dc20   96-27502
                                         CIP

ISBN: 1-884822-86-X

h g f e d c b a

ACKNOWLEDGMENTS

When I started writing this book and putting the recipes in proper order, I found I couldn't do it alone. The project was almost too large for me, one assistant and two computers. Beacause of their hard work I would therefore like to thank the many people who helped me with the birth of this book.

First I would like to thank my research assistant Gordon Allan who kept me from going crazy when everything looked as if it would fall apart. Then there is Mrs. Neleta Paré of Klamath Falls, Oregon who gave so freely of her time and expertise. I must not forget Stacy, Carol, Heidi, Katie, and Shelli; or the chocoholic of the crowd —Kelli —Thanks gang for your willingness, and yes, even eagerness to give me feedback on the goodies you tasted.

Then there is the single most important person in my life and in the life of this book: Pamela Horn, my editor. Through it all she has been a mentor and constant consultant. Without her, I don't where I would be. She has always been ready to offer a soothing word or a stern criticism. When I became irritated or too big for my britches, she always seemed to be there to put me in my place. Together we have proven the generation gap doesn't exist. Pam, you're the greatest, I just hope I haven't been too much of a pain in the backside over these many months.

Before any of this could happen, there was J.P. Leventhal, and yes even the Black Dog, Tess. Without J.P.'s acceptance of me and my projects none of this could have happened in the first place. J.P., I will always be eternally grateful.

As always, a special thanks to Martin Lubin for his creative and thoughtful design. His wisdom and patience helped to produce an extraordinary result.

Thank you to Peter Barry. Peter has taken an impossible subject and task, and made the images jump off the page into your kitchens.

Thanks to the food stylists Clare Breen, Wendy MacDonald, and Jacqueline Bellefontaine for their hard work and beautiful creations.

Special thanks to Isabelle Vita, Karen Berman, and Alice Thompson for their editorial help, knowledge, and willingness to immerse themselves in chocolate for a few months.

Thanks to James Worrell for the cover photograph. Thanks to Andrea Stupka for the use of her hand.

CONTENTS

Introduction 8

102 Hints for Baking 9

Chocolate and Cocoa 12

Ingredients 15

Equipment 16

About the Chapters 19

Beverages 19
Cakes 19
Candy 20
Cookies 20
Ice Cream 21
Pies and Tarts 21
Puddings 21
Quick Breads 21
Tortes 21
Miscellaneous Chocolate 22
Frostings, Icings, and Sauces 22
Garnishes and Decorations 22

Recipes:

Beverages 23

Cakes 33

Candy 165

Cookies 197

Ice Cream 243

Pies and Tarts 257

Puddings 291

Quick Breads 331

Tortes 365

Miscellaneous Chocolate 383

Frostings, Icings, and Sauces 393

Garnishes and Decorations 419

Reference section 425
Cake Pan Sizes and Servings 425
Ingredients Equivalency Charts 426
Temperature Equivalencies When Making Syrups and Candies 431
High-Altitude Baking 431
Weights and Measures 432

Index 433

INTRODUCTION

For many people, chocolate is a legal addiction. That is why this book and many others have been written about chocolate. Everyone is continually looking for new and different ways to serve and eat the fruit of the cacao tree. In this work, I will not investigate the history of chocolate or how it is manufactured. This is a book about how to prepare chocolate in an unbelievable number of ways.

I don't believe such a variety of chocolate recipes has ever been gathered together between two covers. Never before has a book offered so many different and easy ways to enjoy the taste of chocolate.

I have endeavored to make every recipe in this book as simple as possible, yet still exciting. There are many recipes that are easy enough for a beginner and there are others that are a challenge even for the more experienced baker or cook.

There is one thing you should always keep in mind when trying a new recipe —everyone has to learn his or her trade one step at a time. You may not produce the greatest chocolate pie the first time out, but perhaps after the second, third, or fourth time you will. To put in another way, practice makes perfect.

If every basic chocolate cake recipe in this book was used as a base for every frosting, icing, glaze, or sauce, the possibilities for chocolate cakes would be almost endless. I don't know for sure the ultimate number of combinations of the recipes in this collection, but it surely exceeds tens of thousands, maybe even more.

GREGG R. GILLESPIE

102 HINTS FOR BAKING

1 Always read the recipe over at least once before starting.

2 Always use the very best ingredients you can afford.

3 Flour is the primary ingredient in baking and you should always have good quality flour on hand.

4 Unless stated otherwise, the oven should always be preheated before the item is placed in it.

5 Unless stated otherwise, it is assumed you will have the rack in the center position. If you are baking with more than one rack, remember the rack closest to the heat will have the greatest chance of browning or burning.

6 Completely cool a baking pan or baking sheet before reusing it.

7 Different oven controls react in different ways, therefore most baking temperatures given in recipes are suggestions only.

8 Unless stated otherwise, all ingredients should be at room temperature.

9 To measure ⅛ a teaspoon, first measure out ¼ a teaspoon, then remove half of what you have measured out.

10 To measure honey, molasses or corn syrup, first lightly grease or oil the inside of the measuring device.

11 The measurement of nuts in recipes is usually considered whole. If a recipe calls for "½ cup of walnuts, ground," measure out ½ cup of the larger pieces and then grind them into smaller pieces. If it calls for ground walnuts, grind the nuts before measuring.

12 To prevent brown sugar from hardening, place a damp piece of cloth or paper towel in a small plastic bag, punch all over with a needle, and place in airtight container with the sugar.

13 When mixing in flour, do not add it all at once. It is best to add half of the flour and mix it in and then mix in the remainder, a little at a time.

14 If you are adding flour and liquids alternately, be sure the flour is the first and last ingredient added.

15 Store flour in an airtight container.

16 It is always best to sift flour before measuring, if a recipe calls for sifted flour.

17 Never use an aluminum bowl to beat egg whites. Copper is considered best, glass or ceramic are the next best to use.

18 When beating egg whites until stiff, the bowl and beaters must be clean and free of any grease or oil, or the egg whites can deflate.

19 It is best to use unsalted butter for baking. Remember that plain butter and margarine all contain salt. If you are going to use these products, the salt measurement in the recipe should be reduced. Butter-flavored shortening contains salt, but it is the best substitute for butter because of its blending and cooking qualities.

20 If butter is used in place of vegetable shortening, the amount of butter should be at least one quarter more than the amount of shortening.

21 Use regular stick margarine or butter, do not use the whipped, spread, or tub type, unless instructed to do so by the recipe.

22 For rich European-style pastries, use only butter.

23 When an alcoholic beverage is used to plump dried fruit, do not discard it after draining. It can be saved to use again or for flavoring in another recipe.

24 To chop sticky dried fruit, heat the knife or food chopper blades before using them.

25 When using dried herbs, the flavor may be brought out if you soak them in hot water for a few minutes.

26 Check liquid measures at eye level in a glass measuring cup.

27 When measuring with the standard measuring spoon, use a knife or spatula as a straight edge across the top.

28 Ovens should be preheated 12 to 20 minutes before using.

29 Shelled and unshelled nuts can attract insects. Store unshelled nuts in the refrigerator. Shelled nuts should be kept in the freezer.

30 Heat a lemon in a microwave for a few seconds before you squeeze it. It will produce more juice.

31 Always test for doneness after the minimum baking time. If a recipe tell you to bake something for 10 to 12 minutes, check it after 10 minutes.

32 To cream any mixture by hand, use the back of a large spoon until the mixture is soft and smooth.

33 When you stir, use a circular motion, not a beating motion or an over and under motion.

34 When a recipe says to beat in ingredients, use quick strokes in an over and under motion. Don't forget, when you are beating the mixture you will be adding air to it.

35 Do not melt chocolate in pieces smaller than 1-inch square over direct heat. Melt them in a pan or dish set over a pot of hot water.

36 It is best to cream butter by itself before adding the sugar.

37 Unless stated otherwise, use double acting baking powder.

38 For the very delicate butter-type cookies, use butter to grease the baking sheets.

39 To keep fruits and nuts from settling to the bottom of baked goods, dredge them in flour before adding them the batter.

40 A dark metal pan or baking sheet will bake faster than a shiny metal pan.

41 Glass containers cook baked goods faster than metal ones.

42 If baking more than one item in the oven at a time and using more than one shelf, stagger them rather than place them directly over each other. Be sure to allow for space between the item and the oven sides, back, and top for circulation of heat.

43 The best way to treat a first-degree burn from the oven or stove is to place ice cubes on it. Then check with a first aid guide or consult your doctor.

44 To rid pots and pans of flour wash them in warm water.

45 Egg whites should always be whipped at room temperature.

46 Always start to whip egg whites on a low speed and slowly increase the speed.

47 Dry wines are not compatible for use with fruit juices in baked goods, but sweet wines work very well.

48 Some ceramic bowls and dishes have a surface glaze that contains lead. After a short time, plastic tends to loose it surface shine and will absorb food and soap odors. For these reasons, it is best to use a metal or glass bowl.

49 It is not necessary to wash a flour sifter after each use. Simply place it in a plastic bag and tie it tightly closed.

50 When separating eggs, do it over a small bowl. Do not separate them over a bowl containing other recipe ingredients.

51 When making muffins, grease the muffin pans, rather than using paper baking cups. They will retard the muffins from rising.

52 Be careful not to stir muffin mixture when spooning the mixture into the pan, it will affect the finished product. Spoon the mixture only from the edge of the bowl.

53 When making doughnuts, if older dough is used to make the doughnuts, it will increase the frying time.

54 When making doughnuts, undermixed dough will usually produce a finished product that is rough in appearance. Overmixed dough will result in tough doughnuts.

55 If too much water is used in making a pie or pastry dough, the baked crust will be tough.

56 If milk is used in making pie or pastry dough, the crust will be less crisp.

57 Unless instructed otherwise, shortening should always be chilled when blended into the dough.

58 To reduce the unwanted juices in fruit pies, sprinkle cookie or cake crumbs over the bottom of the crust in the pie pan before adding the fruit.

59 For variations in fruit pies, spread a thin layer of pastry cream on the bottom, before the fruit is added.

60 To make an attractive fruit pie, save the best-looking slices of fruit for the top. Chop all of the fruit that is to go underneath the slices.

61 In open-face pies, when using hard fruit such as apples or pears, precook the fruit before adding to the pie. If you do not, the pie crust will cook before the fruit, and the bottom will be soggy.

62 After an open-faced fruit pie has been baked, brush the top fruit with a dessert glaze.

63 A greased baking sheet will cause puff pastry to spread. Line the pan with parchment paper in place of greasing.

64 If puff pastry is removed from the oven too soon, it may collapse.

65 Too much flour on a rolling surface can cause a pastry dough to become tough.

66 When rolling a pastry dough, use flour-dusted waxed paper. It won't be necessary to use as much flour.

67 Most pastry dough for pies should be rolled to a thickness of 1/8 inch.

68 One way to avoid soggy bottom crusts in pies is to place the bottom of the pie pan closer to the heat; bake the pie on the lowest rack in the oven.

69 Do not add hot fillings to unbaked pie crusts.

70 When making a pie filling, always add the sugar or lemon juice after the filling has been heated and thickened.

71 Pumpkin pie filling should be allowed to stand untouched for 30 minutes before being poured into the pie shell.

72 When preparing cream-style pies, do not use too much unflavored gelatin or the filling will be rubbery.

73 Do not use raw, uncooked pineapple or papaya with gelatin. Precook it first.

74 On the average, it should take from 8 to 10 minutes to properly cream butter and sugar using the slow or medium speed of a hand-held electric mixer. Do not use high speed to cream the two ingredients.

75 When melted chocolate is added to a batter, add it immediately after creaming the fat and sugar and before any eggs or liquid.

76 On average, it takes no less than 5 minutes to beat eggs into a cake batter.

77 When adding dry ingredients to cake batters, do it one third at a time, alternating with half of the liquids, beginning and ending with the dry ingredients.

78 Usually beaten egg whites are the last ingredient added to a cake batter.

79 Slightly warmed eggs can be beaten to a greater volume than cold ones.

80 Too hot an oven will cause a cake to set unevenly with a humped center. Too cool an oven causes poor volume and texture.

81 Unless instructed otherwise, always cool cake layers completely before assembling and icing.

82 Excessive crowns (humps) on cakes should be sliced off with a serrated knife before icing.

83 When assembling a cake, where the filling is different from the frosting, do not spread the filling over the edge of the cake.

84 In warmer climates, substitute fondant icings for buttercream icings.

85 When making cookies, remember that most crisp cookies are made from very stiff doughs.

86 A high sugar content in a cookie dough increases the chance of excessive spreading while baking.

87 Using fine grain sugar in cookie doughs will decrease the chance of spreading.

88 A large amount of baking soda in a cookie dough causes spreading, as does over creaming of the sugar and fat.

89 There is a greater chance of a cookie dough spreading if the oven temperature is too low.

90 In most cookie baking, the degree of doneness is indicated by the color of the baked cookie.

91 When making pudding, if the milk is scalded before being added it will reduce the cooking time.

92 Leftover cakes and other baked desserts can be dried as you would dry bread crumbs and used as a garnish on other dessert items and baked goods. Chocolate cake is particularly good for this. Leave the cake out in the air for 24 to 36 hours, or until it becomes very hard. Then crush or pulse into a fine crumb using hand grinder or food processor.

93 Don't rely only on baking times for checking the doneness of cakes. To test if a cake is finished baking, always check the look, smell, sound, and feel. It will pull slightly away from the sides of the pan, it will have a distinct aroma, the sounds of air bubbles popping in the cake will have slowed, and it will spring back when gently touched.

94 Always start to check for doneness with a cake about 10 minutes before the recommended baking time has passed.

95 Unless stated otherwise, most cakes should be cooled for 5 to 10 minutes in the pan set on a wire rack before inverting onto a wire rack or plate to finish cooling.

96 When a cake is to be frozen or stored in the refrigerator, always wrap it securely in waxed paper and then in a plastic wrap or aluminum foil. Large selfsealing plastic bags are ideal for this purpose.

97 Be sure the icing, frosting, or garnish that is placed on a cake complements the flavor of the cake.

98 Cheesecakes will often crack on the top if they are cooked in too hot an oven.

99 Even in the best recipes in the world, chocolate is a very difficult ingredient to work with. Be sure you understand it before you try to work with it. (See Chocolate and Cocoa Section.)

100 When adding a lot of liquids to melted chocolate, stir fast and add the liquid all at once.

101 If chocolate stiffens or thickens, heating alone will not thin chocolate.

102 When cutting marshmallows, use scissors by dipping them in hot water, and they will not stick to the blade.

CHOCOLATE AND COCOA

Both chocolate and cocoa are edible ingredients produced from the cacao bean. After the beans are picked they are fermented, roasted, and ground. The end product is known as chocolate liquor. Included in the liquor is the yellow fat called cocoa butter. Once obtained, there are six types of food products or ingredients that can be processed from the chocolate liquor: cocoa or what we know as unsweetened cocoa powder, bitter chocolate, sweet chocolate, milk chocolate, cocoa butter, and finally white chocolate.

Cocoa is a dry powder. It is what is left after most of the cocoa butter has been removed from chocolate liquor. *Dutch processed cocoa powder* is a product that has been processed with alkali and is usually slightly darker in color. The flavor is more delicate and it is more easily dissolved in liquids, such as hot water or milk. Dutch processed cocoa is usually neutral or slightly alkaline and will not react with baking soda in a recipe. Therefore baking powder must be used as the leavening agent in a recipe.

When baking with cocoa, if not enough baking powder is used in the recipe the finished product can range in color from light tan to a dark brown depending on the amount of cocoa powder added. If too much baking powder is used, the color will be a reddish-brown and this is usually only desirable in a devil's food cake.

It is important to remember that there are differences between various brands of cocoa powder, including Dutch processed cocoa powders. Should it be necessary to switch from one brand of cocoa powder to another, it is recommended to experiment first to see if you will have the same results.

Non-Dutch processed cocoa powder is usually called natural cocoa and is more acidic. When it is used to make cakes and other baked goods it is possible to use baking soda as part of the leavening. All cocoa powders will keep for an extended period of time if stored in airtight containers with moistureproof covers.

One thing to remember is that cocoa powder also contains starch, and starch will tend to absorb the moisture in a batter. So, if you want to add cocoa powder to a yellow cake recipe to make it a chocolate cake, the amount of flour should be reduced to compensate for the added starch.

Bitter chocolate or *unsweetened chocolate* as it is also known, is the same as chocolate liquor. It contains no sugar and is bitter to the taste. For a chocolate liquor to be classified as unsweetened it must contain 50 to 58 percent cocoa butter. There are several qualities of unsweetened chocolate on the market. The least expensive brands have usually removed most of the cocoa butter and replaced it with a coconut oil or inexpensive vegetable shortening.

Sweet chocolate is unsweetened chocolate that has sugar

added and the cocoa butter has been adjusted in varying proportions. If the amount of sugar is low, then it may be referred to as semisweet. If the sugar is less than for semisweet, it will be called bittersweet. In both cases it must contain at least 35 percent chocolate liquor and the sugar content will range from 35 to 50 percent. At the same time a product labeled sweet chocolate may contain as little as 15 percent chocolate liquor.

When using sweet chocolate as a candy coating, the chocolate must be prepared by a process called tempering. This is nothing more than melting the chocolate without letting it get too hot, then reducing the temperature to a predetermined acceptable level, and rewarming it a second time. There are less expensive chocolates available for this procedure. They have had part of the cocoa butter replaced with vegetable shortening or coconut oil. They are easier to handle and they don't require tempering. The products are usually sold under the names of Chocolate Coating, Cake Coating, Candy Coating, and even Baking Chocolate. Read the label carefully to determine if the product is right for you.

Milk chocolate is like sweet chocolate only milk solids have been added. Although it may be purchased in edible bar forms, it is also used to coat various other types of candies. Because of its low taste factor it is seldom melted and incorporated into baked goods.

Cocoa butter is the fat that is pressed out of the chocolate liquor during processing. It is seldom available in supermarkets and its primary use is in bake shops and candy making facilities where it is used for thinning coating chocolate.

White chocolate isn't really a chocolate in that it contains no chocolate liquor. Usually it is made from cocoa butter (and that is where the name chocolate is derived from), sugar, and milk solids. It is used for making candies, decorations, and occasionally to make frostings for baked goods. A less expensive type and variety of this product is readily available. It is often called almond bark.

Chocolate should be stored in a cool, dry place with a constant temperature between 60 to 75 degrees. The key word is dry; the humidity should not be more than 50 percent. When refrigerated, chocolate must be wrapped tightly in an airtight bag or container. If it is left unwrapped it can absorb moisture that will condense when the chocolate is removed from the refrigerator. It can also absorb unwanted odors from other items in the refrigerator. Most chocolate, if kept tightly wrapped, can keep in the refrigerator for 6 months or more, but it is advised that the chocolate be used as soon after purchasing as possible. Some experts say that chocolate cannot be kept in the freezer. Those who say it can be frozen, say it can keep up to 4 months with no change in the flavor or texture.

On occasion a candy bar or baking chocolate will have a grayish white film, like a mold on the surface. This is called "bloom." Bloom usually develops when chocolate has been exposed to fluctuations in temperature. While bloom may look unattractive, it is safe to eat. If the chocolate is melted, it will loose the bloom.

It is easy to become confused when substituting cocoa for chocolate. The primary difference between cocoa and unsweetened chocolate is that cocoa has much less cocoa butter. Usually extra vegetable shortening or oil will be necessary when substituting cocoa powder for chocolate. There is one problem in using regular shortening as a replacement for cocoa butter. Shortening has about twice the shortening power of cocoa butter. Because of all the various cocoa powders available, there is no single substitution ratio for all of them. Most brands of cocoa powder do include substitution directions on their packaging, so check the label.

MELTING CHOCOLATE

The melting of chocolate is critical to the success of a recipe and there are many ways that chocolate can be melted. Always grate, chop, or shave chocoate before melting it. When heating chocolate, use a metal spoon and stir frequently in a circular motion until the chocolate is melted and smooth. Do not use an over and under motion with the spoon because this might add air to the chocolate. Any of the following methods can be used, but the first two are highly recommended.

1 Hot-Water Bath Method: Place the chocolate in a clean dry metal bowl or top of a double boiler. Place over a larger bowl or pan that contains hot water. The water should not be boiling. When the chocolate starts to melt, use a metal spoon and stir in a circular motion. (It may be necessary to hold one edge of the bowl while stirring.) After the chocolate is completely melted and smooth, remove from the water and set aside until ready to use. If the chocolate is to be used for dipping, leave it over the warm water. It may be necessary to refresh the warm water before you are ready to use the chocolate. While this method is usually the slowest, there is less chance of scorching the chocolate.

2 Double Boiler Method: Place the chocolate in the top of the double boiler, being sure the pan is dry and free of any moisture. Place water in the bottom pan. Place the top pan with the chocolate in it into the bottom pan and place over low heat. Stir constantly until the chocolate is melted. Do not allow the water in the bottom pan to touch the top pan as this could overheat the chocolate. Do not place a cover on the top pan as moisture might collect inside of the cover and drop into the chocolate. If this happens the chocolate might sieze and thicken. If a single drop of moisture falls into the chocolate, carefully lift the drop out with a metal spoon. When the chocolate is melted, remove the top pan from the bottom one and set aside until ready to use. If the chocolate is to be used for dipping, leave the top pan over the bottom pan off the burner. The water in the bottom pan must be kept lukewarm. When the water cools, replace it with warm water.

3 Direct Heat Method: Place the chocolate in a small saucepan and working quickly over low heat, stir constantly until the chocolate is melted and smooth. This method is very fast but has a greater chance of failure. Chocolate burns at such a low temperature that unless you are very experienced with melting chocolate, this method is not recommended.

4 Microwave Method: Place the chopped chocolate in a small microwave safe bowl and microwave, uncovered, on medium power for 1 to 2 minutes. Remove from the microwave and stir with a metal spoon. The chocolate will not become liquid while in the oven. As a matter of fact it will retain its shape until stirred. It will be shiny when it is ready to be stirred. If after the first heating the chocolate hasn't melted sufficiently or is a little lumpy, return it to the oven for another 20 to 30 seconds. It is recommended that medium power be used until you have become accustomed to melting chocolate in a microwave.

TEMPERING CHOCOLATE

The more one gets into the wonderful world of chocolate, the more they will hear the term tempering. The most important use for tempered chocolate is in candy making, for dipping or coating other items. It is really a very simple procedure, but at the same time one of the most important. It only involves three steps: melting, tempering, and rewarming.

In the melting step the chocolate is melted using one of the above methods. Stir the chocolate gently and use a thermometer to check the temperature frequently. Immerse the bulb of the thermometer completely in the chocolate, being careful that it does not touch the pan. Let sit

for 1 minute before taking a reading. During this process, the temperature of the chocolate is raised to 115 to 118 degrees. (NOTE: it is important to remember that not all chocolate is alike and the manufacturers of various chocolates will recommend different temperatures for their chocolate. One European manufacturer recommends that its chocolate be melted at 122 degrees.)

In the tempering step, cooling or precrystalling occurs. After the chocolate is melted, it is removed from the heat, set in a cool place, and stirred constantly but slowly so no air is incorporated until it reaches 78 to 79 degrees on a thermometer. Although most manufacturers of chocolate recommend a slow cooling, pastry chefs will usually speed up the process by setting the pan or bowl containing the hot chocolate over a larger container of cold water.

By the time the chocolate has cooled to the proper temperature, it is too thick for dipping or other uses and must be warmed and melted a second time. The chocolate is rewarmed using one of the above melting methods until the temperature of the chocolate is 86 to 88 degrees. Rewarming is the most important step. At no time should the chocolate be allowed to rise above the recommended temperature. If it does, the process will have to be repeated all over again.

Some additional tips for melting and tempering chocolate are:

1 First and foremost, do not allow any water, even a drop, to come into contact with the chocolate.

2 If the pan or bowl you are using to melt or temper chocolate is too thin, it might transfer heat too fast and subsequently burn the chocolate.

3 Do not rush to melt the chocolate by increasing the temperature. If you do, it might curdle and thicken. If this does happen, add a little vegetable shortening. Do not add butter or margarine.

4 Do not substitute semisweet or milk chocolate for unsweetened chocolate in a recipe.

5 When working with melted or tempered chocolate use a wooden spoon or metal spatula.

6 When working with tempered chocolate, the work area should be cool; 65 to 68 degrees is the ideal temperature.

7 In hot or warm weather, if the chocolate seems too thick, the addition of melted wax will help the chocolate resist the heat. One-half ounce of melted wax should be sufficient for ½ pound of chocolate.

PREMELTED CHOCOLATE

Premelted unsweetened chocolate was introduced into the baking market a few years ago. It is used as a convenient alternative to blocks of chocolate that are subsequently chopped or grated and then melted. Premelted unsweetened chocolate is a mixture of unsweetened cocoa powder and vegetable oil that is sealed in premeasured servings in a foil pouch. It is used primarily for flavoring in cakes, cookies, and other baked goods.

INGREDIENTS

Sometimes it is very difficult to know what ingredients to stock in a kitchen and this is even more so when it comes to baking ingredients. For those who do not know what they might need to make the recipes in this book, below are two lists. The first is a list of bare essentials. The second is a wish list. It lists items that could be used, but are not always available. It is a list for those who can go into the kitchen and prepare a recipe from memory, and for the homebaker who, when he or she runs out of one item, will try another.

ESSENTIALS

all-purpose flour
almond extract
almonds
baking soda
butter or margarine
cake flour
chocolate extract
shredded or flaked coconut
cream cheese
cream of tartar
dark or light brown sugar
double acting baking powder
Dutch processed cocoa
    powder
graham crackers
granulated sugar
ground allspice
ground cinnamon
ground cloves
ground ginger
ground nutmeg
ladyfingers
large eggs
lemon extract
milk
powdered sugar
rolled oats
salt
semisweet chocolate

semisweet chocolate chips
unflavored gelatin
unsweetened chocolate
vegetable shortening
walnuts

FULL LIST

all-purpose flour
almond extract
almonds
Amaretto liqueur
apricot liqueur
baking soda
banana extract
banana instant pudding
butter-flavored margarine
butter or margarine
buttermilk
butterscotch chips
cake flour
cashew nuts
cherry liqueur
chocolate instant pudding
chocolate extract
chocolate wafer cookies
coconut milk
flaked and shredded coconut
coffee liqueur
cornstarch
cream cheese
cream of tartar
crème de cacao
dark brown sugar
double acting baking powder
Dutch processed cocoa
    powder
graham crackers
Grand marnier
granulater sugar
green crème de menthe
ground allspice
ground cinnamon
ground cloves
ground ginger
ground nutmeg
hazelnuts
instant coffee
ladyfingers
large eggs
lemon extract

light brown sugar
Liquore Galliano
macadamia nuts
mayonnaise
milk
miniature chocolate chips
miniature marshmallows
marshmallow creme
mint chocolate chips
molasses
orange extract
parafin wax
peanut butter
peanut butter chips
peanuts
pecans
pine nuts
pistachio nuts
powdered sugar
praline liqueur
raspberry extract
rolled oats
salt
semisweet chocolate
semisweet chocolate chips
sour cream
sprinkles
Triple Sec
unflavored gelatin
unsalted butter
unsweetened chocolate
vanilla extract
vanilla instant pudding
vegetable oil
vegetable shortening
walnuts
white chocolate chips
white chocolate or almond
    bark
white crème de menthe
whole wheat flour
yogurt

In addition to the above lists, there are a few nonfood items that are essential: waxed paper, parchment paper or pan liner papers, aluminum foil, paper doilies, assorted cake boards, extra-large plastic bags.

EQUIPMENT

Below is a list of the items you will need to prepare the recipes in this book. You may have learned long ago how to get along without certain things. However, I find that using the right equipment will produce the best results.

There really is only one basic rule when purchasing kitchen equipment: purchase the best you can afford. If the top of the line is not in your price range, it is worth the time and trouble to save to purchase the best. It has been said that more fingers have been cut by inexpensive knives than any other thing in the world.

Angel food cake pan: This is also called a tube pan. It is available in a round or square shape. It may or it may not have a removable bottom and it is designed to be placed upside down resting on the tube section when cooling the cake.

Aluminum foil: As a handy item to cover and seal bakery items, aluminum foil is one of the best. It is available in at least two sizes. One 10 to 12 inches long and the other 18 to 24 inches long.

Baking sheets: Also called cookie sheets. I recommend the type that are a flat sheet of metal that may have the edge at one end raised.

Baking tray or sheet pans: Large metal pans used for anything from cookie baking to cookie display in a show case. Not usually found in the home kitchen, but recommended. They come in two sizes: full sheet pans are 18 x 26 inches, and half sheet pans are 18 x 13 inches.

Beater: (Rotary or electric) The older style rotary beater, often referred to as an egg beater, has many uses when you are baking. Although an electric beater is faster, the average homebaker has a tendency to overbeat, especially when it comes to beating egg whites and yolks. See Whisks.

Bowls: Bowls in various sizes are a must. They can be made of ceramic, baked enamel on metal, copper, aluminum, or stainless steel. There are differences of opinion between bakers as to which is best. The one point all bakers agree on is that copper is the best bowl to use when whipping eggs. The essential bowls to own are a 1-pint mixing bowl, a 1½-quart mixing bowl, and a 3-quart mixing bowl.

Bowl Scraper: This is basically the same thing as a rubber spatula except there is no handle. It is usually very thin and flat. It can be found in kidney shape and rectangular.

Brushes: Any store that sells kitchen utensils will sell brushes for the kitchen, but most are too coarse for use in baking. The best place to purchase a pastry brush is in the paint department. When a paint brush is purchased, care should be taken to see that it is cleaned and sterilized before using.

Bundt pan: A pan that has a center tube and is molded in an elegant design for decorative cakes and desserts.

Cake or icing comb: Also known as a decorating comb or comb scraper, this helpful tool is used to form swirls and grooves in the frosting on the top and sides of a cake. Usually this tool is used after the frosting has been applied and before any other decoration is put on a cake.

Cake pans: There are many sizes and they come in round, square, and rectangular shapes. The pans you will need for the cakes in this book are: three 8-inch round layer cake pans, three 9-inch round layer cake pans, one 12-inch round layer cake pan, one 8-inch square cake pan, one 9-inch square pan, one 13 by 9 by 2-inch baking pan, and one 26 by 18-inch sheet pan.

Cake rack: A round wire rack used to invert cakes onto to cool. See Wire rack.

Cake tester: This tool can be a little wooden toothpick, a bamboo skewer, or a professional cake tester that is made of stainless steel with a plastic hook at one end to use as a handle. It is used to insert into a cake to check if the cake is baked.

Candy thermometer: See Thermometer.

Cardboard rounds or cake trays: These are usually available at any store that sells baking supplies or in stores that sell craft supplies. The boards are usually nothing more than a piece of cardboard cut into specific shapes and coated on one side with a foodproof material. Cakes are placed on them to make it easier to handle them after they have been frosted and or decorated.

Chopping board: This item is included only because when one uses a counter for chopping or cutting there might be a tendency to scratch or mar an expensive counter top.

Cookie cutters: Cutters made of plastic, ceramic, and metal that are used to cut dough or a baked item into various shapes. These are also used to cut decorative items out of chocolate to place on cakes.

Custard cups: These small bowls are called custard cups or ramekins, and are used for puddings and custards. You will the need 4-ounce size.

Grater: There are several varieties of this implement available, ranging from the very inexpensive plastic to the very expensive gourmet models. Some have just one size grating holes while others have two or more.

Double boiler: A 2- or 3-quart is recommended. The utensil consists of a pan placed directly on the burner, in which water is held and heated. The top portion is a rounded pan that fits onto the top of the bottom pan.

Flour sifter: With today's new milling methods for flours, it is questionable if this device is still recommended. The only ingredient that I use that seems to need sifting is powdered sugar. Look for a 5-inch flour sifter.

Jelly roll pan: This is a shallow baking pan, much like a baking tray, except the sides are seldom higher than 1 inch. Many bakers will use a baking tray in place of a jelly roll pan.

Loaf pan: This is used for yeast breads, quick breads, and loaf cakes. You will need one 9 by 5 by 3-inch loaf pan, and an 8 by 4 by 2½ inch loaf pan.

Knives: Many cooks and bakers prefer the French Chef's knives. They are made of carbon or stainless steel. The carbon knives stay sharp much longer, but must be keep scrupulously clean. You will need a bread knife with serrated edge, a chopping knife with a 7-inch pointed blade, a palette knife or spatula with a 7-inch blade for frosting cakes, and a fruit or vegetable knife with a 4-inch blade (some fruits and vegetables will stain carbon knives).

Measuring utensils: Measuring devices are the single most important utensil in the kitchen. They are available in metal, glass, plastic, and ceramic. If the plastic ones are selected, they should be replaced at least once every two years because of wear and the tendency of the plastic to absorb flavors after a period of time. For measuring liquids use glass measuring cups. For dry use the plastic or metal. You will need one set of glass US standard measuring cups, 1 cup, 2 cup, 4 cup sizes. One set of plastic or metal US standard measuring cups, 1 cup, ¾ cup, ½ cup, ⅓ cup, ¼ cup size. One set of US standard measuring spoons: ¼ teaspoon, ½ teaspoon, 1 teaspoon, 1 tablespoon.

Muffin Pan: This is used for baking cupcakes, rolls and muffins. They come in a variety of sizes. They are also known as cupcake pans. You will need pans that will make a dozen 2½-inch muffins and a dozen 3-inch muffins.

Pancake Turner: See Turner.

Paper Cone: A piece of parchment paper is cut into a small square. It is rolled into a cone and filled. The top is folded over and the tip of the cone is cut off. The cone is usually used for piping small intricate designs, flower stems, or for writing, or even for drizzling glaze or icing over the tops of cakes.

Paper products: Items you will need include: Non-stick cooking paper or parchment paper, plastic bags of varying sizes, plastic wrap, paper towels, and waxed paper

Pastry Bag: A waterproof cone used for piping decorations on cakes, and filling pastries. Different style tips are fitted on the end. You will need one medium-sized star tip and three plain round tips, ¼ inch, ½ inch, and ⅜ inch.

Pastry blender: A device used for cutting fats into dry ingredients. Many people prefer to cut the fat into the dry ingredients with an electric mixer.

Pastry wheel: A device with a wheel on one end used for scoring the edges of pies and baked goods.

Pie pans: These are usually made of glass, glass ceramic, dull metal, aluminum, or stainless steel. You will need two 8- or 9-inch pie pans.

Rolling pin: Traditionally made of wood, they are available in a variety of sizes and designs. This more than anything else in the kitchen is a matter of personal preference.

Saucepans: A 1-pint, a 1½-pint, and 3-quart are recommended.

Spatulas: These come in rubber or plastic. It is recommended that only heavy-duty spatulas be used. The thin plastic type break easily.

Spoons: Traditionally, spoons for baking should be made of wood. You will need a 9-inch spoon, 12-inch spoon, and 14-inch spoon. Also one large metal spoon and a 14-inch slotted spoon.

Springform Pan: This baking pan has a side section that can be completely removed without harming or disturbing the item inside. You will need a 9-inch and a 10-inch pan.

Strainers: An invaluable utensil when you need to strain seeds out of a fruit puree or broken egg shells from eggs. You will need a 6-inch fine screen strainer and a standard strainer for sifting dry ingredients.

Soufflé dishes: Usually made of glass or porcelain, they are straight sided and come in a variety of sizes. You will need a 1½-quart soufflé dish.

Tart or flan pan: A fluted round pan with a removable bottom. This is also known as a quiche pan.

Thermometer: When baking, there are three thermometers that may be required. The first is a dough thermometer for measuring the temperature of the prepared dough while rising and before baking. The fat thermometer is used to measure the heat in a fat kettle before frying. Then there is the candy thermometer, also called the sugar thermometer. The candy thermometer is an absolute must when preparing all sorts of candies. A candy thermometer can be used with chocolate, but because of its bulkiness and the low temperatures that chocolate reaches, a dough thermometer may be used as well.

A candy thermometer is a long paddle-shaped instrument with the glass tube of the thermometer in its center. On the back is a clip that can be fastened onto the side of a pan. There is an inexpensive model of the candy thermometer where the calibrated thermometer sits in a glass tube with a small glass ball at the end filled with metal beads. In the middle of the tube is an adjustable clip for attaching to the side of a pan. Always be careful to keep the bottom portion of the glass tube from touching the pan as you may get an innaccurate reading.

Turner: There are many shapes and sizes for turners, each designed for a specific task while cooking. Turners may be plain and solid, slotted, or are rounded. A turner will lift and remove food from a hot surface, or transfer foods from one place to another.

Whisks: Usually small metal balloon whisks used for beating egg whites. Ideally the balloon portion of the whisk will fit the curve of the mixing bowl. You will need one 6-inch whisk and one 10- to 12-inch whisk.

Wire rack: A useful item on which baked goods are placed to cool. It allows for a circulation of air around all sides. See Cake rack.

ABOUT THE CHAPTERS

BEVERAGES

At one time, the use of chocolate in beverages was more popular than coffee. All over Europe, chocolate houses that catered to the rich were the only ones that could afford the delicate taste and flavor of chocolate.

One of the things to remember when making the hot chocolates is to be sure to whip the cream or milk vigorously before adding the chocolate, and whip again just before it is poured into a cup. Whipped cream will not be needed as a topping. In order to achieve the intense concentrated chocolate flavor desired in chocolate drinks, it is recommended that Dutch processed cocoa be used.

CAKES

It doesn't matter if you are preparing a cake just for yourself or for a whole group of people, the way the cake looks and tastes must be pleasing for it to be a success. But when others are involved you especially don't want to be embarrassed by a sheet cake that looks like a saddle or a mountain ski run.

These disappointments are the reason many people are hesitant to try new recipes. Failures can be kept to a minimum by following the recipe directions exactly as written. See also my 102 Hints for Baking for some additional tips. Most people will take short cuts when cooking. However, baking cakes does not permit that. Ingredients must be measured precisely, mixing directions followed exactly, and oven temperatures must be accurate.

Have you ever wondered why a cake didn't rise or why a cake split down the middle? Here are some common problems found in cakes and possible causes for them. As you can see, not all of the problems are easy to diagnose. The source of the trouble with a cake can be caused by one or more of the causes listed.

PROBLEMS AND POSSIBLE CAUSES

CAKE DID NOT RISE:

1 Improper mixing.

2 Overbeating the batter.

3 Too much liquid.

4 The pan was too large.

5 Not enough baking powder or baking soda.

6 Oven too cool. Preheat 20 to 25 minutes and use an oven thermometer

CAKE IS VERY HEAVY:

1 Batter mixed too slowly after the liquid was added.

2 The flour had too much gluten in it. Use the flour recommended in the recipe.

3 Too much fat.

4 Not enough baking powder. Improper measuring.

5 The oven was not hot enough. Preheat the oven for 20 to 25 minutes and use an oven thermometer.

6 The oven was too hot.

CAKE TEXTURE IS COARSE:

1 Batter not beaten enough.

2 Batter beaten too much.

3 Too much sugar.

4 Too much baking powder or baking soda.

CAKE WAS DRY:

1 Not enough liquid.

2 Not enough fat.

3 Too much flour.

4 Too much baking powder.

5 The oven was too hot. Use an oven thermometer.

6 Cake overbaked.

CAKE FELL:

1 Pan too small for the amount of batter.

2 Too much baking powder or baking soda.

3 Too much sugar.

4 Too much fat.

5 Cake was underbaked.

6 Oven too hot.

7 Oven too cool. Preheat the oven 20 to 25 minutes and use an oven thermometer.

8 Oven didn't maintain temperature while baking. Check with a repair person.

CAKE LAYER IS SOGGY:

1 Too much liquid.

2 Batter was overbeaten.

3 Batter was underbeaten.

4 Oven temperature too cool. Preheat the oven 20 to 25 minutes and use an oven thermometer.

TOO MUCH SHRINKAGE:

1 Batter was overbeaten.

2 Too much liquid.

CAKE MOUNDED ON TOP:

1 Baking pan was too small.

2 Oven temperature was too hot. Use an oven thermometer.

3 Batter was overbeaten.

4 Too much liquid.

CAKE NOT LEVEL ON TOP:

1 Pans not properly spaced in oven.

2 Oven didn't maintain temperature while baking. Check with a repair person.

3 Oven rack or pan wasn't level.

4 Too much flour.

CAKE STICKS IN PAN:

1 Pan not properly greased and floured.

2 Cake cooled in pan for too long a period.

TOP OF CAKE WAS STICKY:

1 Too much liquid in batter.

2 Too much sugar.

3 Cake underbaked.

CAKE CRACKED ON TOP:

1 Oven too hot.

2 Batter overmixed.

3 Flour had too much gluten. Use flour recommended in recipe.

4 Pan too deep for cake batter.

CANDY

The environment in the room used when dipping or coating with chocolate should be free of humidity, cooking odors, and have a constant circulation of air, although no direct drafts are advisable. In order to obtain an attractive high gloss and even color in chocolate dipped candies, an even cooling is essential. For this reason it is not advisable to dip or coat candies with chocolate on a sunny warm day, unless the work room is air conditioned; 60 to 70 degrees is the best temperature to work in.

On average, six to seven dozen centers may be dipped from a single pound of melted chocolate. Chocolate dipped fresh fruits should be eaten the same day they are prepared.

Some important temperatures to note for the various elements of the candy-making process are:

60 to 70 degrees: Temperature of the room in which candy is being made.

Just below 185 degrees: Water temperature in the bottom of the double boiler to melt the chocolate.

96 to 110 degrees: Temperature to which melted chocolate registers.

Cold tap water: Water temperature in the bottom of double boiler when cooling chocolate.

85 degrees: Water temperature in bottom of double boiler when holding chocolate during dipping.

83 degrees: Temperature of melted chocolate when starting dipping.

The following trouble shooting chart may be helpful when making chocolate candy:

PROBLEMS AND POSSIBLE CAUSES

GREY OR STREAKED CHOCOLATE:

1 Fluctuating room temperature.

2 Too much humidity in the room or the atmosphere.

3 Dipping in the line of a draft in the room.

4 Dipping centers were too cold when dipping started.

6 Dipped chocolates were cooled too slowly.

A BROAD BASE APPEARED ON THE CHOCOLATE AFTER DIPPING:

1 Dipping while the chocolate was too warm.

2 Excess dip chocolate not removed after dipping.

STICKY SPOTS APPEAR ON COATING:

1 Creams from the center leak due to improper dipping.

COOKIES

Cookies are the easiest item to bake. There is probably no more universal baked good we eat than a cookie. With few exceptions, there are very few categories of food that are as old as the cookie. Although they were prepared with only barley flour and honey, the ancient Egyptians made small round cakes four thousand years before the common era.

The only thing to remember about making the cookies in this book is to follow the recipe. There are two important words when making cookies: crispy and chewy (or soft). Most people do not usually like crispy cookies, preferring instead to have them chewy.

A crisp cookie will usually have a high ratio of fat to sugar, and a low moisture content. Usually the dough will be rolled out very thin, more like a cracker than a cookie. Baking time will be extended beyond what might be considered normal for other cookies, and the most important thing—the moisture content of the cookie will be low.

A chewy cookie will usually have a high portion of eggs, a high level of sugar and liquid, and the amount of fat in the cookie will be low or non-existent.

The easiest cookies to make are the bar cookies. These recipes generally have only a few instruction steps. The most difficult are those that must be prepared and then deposited onto a baking sheet or tray using a pastry bag. In between these two, the formed cookies and drop cookies offer no challenge to the experienced homemaker. As a matter of fact, most recipes for making cookies that can be found on ingredient packages are for the drop cookies.

ICE CREAM

It has been said that ice cream is America's favorite dessert. If this is true, then in this book we have taken ice cream and added America's favorite addiction: chocolate.

Ice cream is a combination of milk products to which a sweetener has been added. All ice creams are stirred or beaten while freezing. In these recipes, chocolate or vanilla or almond extracts are added as flavorings. Other additions include crushed nuts, chopped fruits, raisins, and/or candies.

PIES AND TARTS

If the average homebaker were asked which item receives the most complaints, the majority would say pie crusts. Because of this reason, a whole commercial industry has arisen: ready made pie crusts. Today most people prefer to simply purchase a prepared pie crust, and bake it. What could be better than that? Nothing, unless you want to eat pieces of cardboard. Yes, cardboard. For that is what the commercial pie crusts taste like.

The secret to making a great pie crust is water, time, and practice. When you are making a pie crust it is important not too add too much water. When the water is added and not absorbed instantly, do not become impatient and add a little more water, and a little more, until you have added more than double what you should have. Allow time for the small amount of water that is needed to be absorbed. Finally, practice is what most

of us lack. If you made a pie crust every day for a month you would be very proficient in making pie crusts and they would always be worth eating.

PUDDINGS

In this book we are interested in the sweet puddings which also include custards, mousses, and creams.

When using pasteurized milk in the preparation of a pudding, it is not necessary to scald it, although the scalding of the milk will reduce the preparation time. The standard procedures for making most custard, creams, and puddings are well outlined and should be followed precisely.

QUICK BREADS

When people hear the term "quick bread" many think of sweet loaves or dessert bread, such as nut bread or cranberry bread. While these sweet baked goods fall into the "quick bread" category, they encompass only a portion of it. Quick breads offer the home baker the greatest range of easy-to-make baked goods. The category of quick breads also includes biscuits, coffee cakes, corn breads, doughnuts, flat breads, sweet loaves, muffins, pancakes, popovers, scones, and waffles. We have tried to represent as many variations of quick breads as possible. What we have provided are an ample number of chocolate flavored or chocolate based goods to make this a most interesting section.

TORTES

A frequently asked question is: What is a torte? (Also called torta and toren.) One definition is: a rich cake made with as little flour as possible but usually containing all of the other major ingredients found in a cake. Tortes are usually multilayered and filled with all types of cream, fruits, preserves, etc.

Since the amount of flour in a torte is very minimal to none, the substitution is usually made with crumbs that are not too finely ground, and nuts, or a meal that is dry.

There are several things to remember when making a torte:

1 The nuts should never be ground in a food processor. This will bring out the oil in the nuts and could ruin the whole product. Crushing in a small hand operated food mill, or chopping into fine pieces using a sharp knife is preferred. Do not crush with a rolling pin as this too will bring out the oils in the nuts.

2 The pastry of a torte is usually very delicate and to make it easy to remove after baking, a springform pan is used.

3 Although torten can be eaten as they are when they come out of the oven, many cooks and bakers prefer to stack up multiple layers of the delicate discs and layer thick heavy cream and fruit in between them. They may also be decorated as are cakes, spreading the buttercream, or heavy whipped cream, over the sides and top.

MISCELLANEOUS CHOCOLATE

The items that comprise the miscellaneous chocolate section include recipes that do not fit exactly into any of the other categories in the book. The recipes may be a hybrid of a few chapters or really stand out on their own, and therefore we have the miscellaneous chocolate section.

FROSTINGS, ICINGS, AND SAUCES

We have tried to include in this book the largest and most varied collection of frostings, icings, sauces, glazes, and toppings imaginable. If you are preparing to make one of the recipes and do not have the ingredients to prepare the frosting or topping recommended for that recipe, then choose a substitute that you feel would complement the recipe. This is an opportunity for the baker to get creative and experiment.

Spreading a frosting, icing, glaze, or sauce can be messy. Many cooks use an apron of paper placed around the cake to prevent this. It is nothing more than cutting strips of waxed paper, or even a clean brown paper bag. The strips should be 2 to 3 inches wide and 12 to 14 inches long (depending on the size of the cake). The strips are placed under the edge of the cake on all four sides, to create a square of paper between the cake to be frosted and the plate the cake is sitting on. After frosting the cake these paper strips are removed and the cake plate is left clean and ready to serve from.

Throughout the recipes in the book there are frequently baking notes warning about the use of raw eggs. The toppings that use raw eggs should always be kept refrigerated, and only used for up to three days after making it (check baking notes for specific instructions). When using cream as a topping, frosting or filling, it too should be kept under refrigeration at all times. The same holds true when using fresh fruit and cheeses.

GARNISHES AND DECORATIONS

The garnishes and decorations in this book are designed to make the food more appealing and desirable to eat, and are also edible themselves. These range from all kinds of chocolate in many forms to edible flowers.

On the market there are a whole series of edible decorations made by commercial companies. They are usually available only through cake decorating outlets. They consist of a wide range of flowers made from eggs and cornstarch, and there are other decorations made from a basic sugar and water formula. These commercially manufactured items have very little taste.

Edible flowers and greens offer a wide variety of garnish items. They can be used in their natural state or molded to specific shapes. Do not use any living flowers or leaves that have not been thoroughly washed. Inquire with a florist or nursery as to whether a particular flower or leaf is fit to eat or come into contact with food. All of the flowers mentioned in this book are considered safe to eat, but even then, caution should be taken. The general rule is, almost all herbs can be used. If using herbs, use the leaves to garnish the cake, pie, or pudding and discard it afterwards. The best flowers used for decorations in these chocolate recipes are: mums, pansies, and violets.

Chrysanthemum—Morifolium also known as Mums Mums are an all time favorite for both garden and home. They have edible flowers with a tangy, bitter taste. The variety and color combinations and the availability all year round makes them a very favorable decoration on chocolate baked goods. Select flowers on the day they are newly opened. Be sure to wash and dry the blooms before using.

Viola x Wittrockiana—also known as the Pansy Nothing more need be said about the pansy except to be sure fresh blooms are picked and that the flowers be throroughly washed and dried before use.

Violets These flowers make a wonderful sugar called violet sugar. When using the blooms make sure they are thoroughly washed and dried.

Beverages

1 ■ BRAZILIAN ICED CHOCOLATE

MAKES 6 TO 8 SERVINGS
CHILL TIME: *20 minutes*

4 cups milk
2 ounces unsweetened chocolate, grated or finely chopped
¼ cup granulated sugar
1 cup hot strong brewed coffee
1 cup chocolate ice cream, softened
½ cup Chocolate Whipped Cream (see page 406)

1 In a medium saucepan, heat the milk until bubbles form around the edges. Remove the pan from the heat.

2 In a large saucepan, over low heat, melt the chocolate, stirring until smooth. Add the sugar and coffee; beat in the hot milk. Over medium heat, cook for 10 minutes. Remove from the heat. Cover and refrigerate 20 minutes, or until completely chilled.

3 Just before serving, beat in the ice cream until blended. Pour into individual cups and garnish with a dab of chocolate whipped cream.

2 ■ CAFÉ LIÉGEOIS

MAKES 2 TO 4 SERVINGS
CHILL TIME: *3 hours*

3 cups chocolate ice cream, softened
2 tablespoons mocha-flavored instant coffee powder
¼ cup coffee liqueur
⅓ cup heavy cream
1 teaspoon crème de cacao

1 In a medium bowl, combine the ice cream, coffee powder, and liqueur. Spoon the mixture into 4 large wine glasses and chill in the freezer for 2 to 3 hours, or until just set.

2 Meanwhile, in a small bowl, using an electric mixer, on high speed, whip the heavy cream and crème de cacao until soft peaks form. Fill a pastry bag fitted with a star tip and pipe a large rosette on the top of each dessert. Serve immediately.

3 ■ CHILLED EUROPEAN COFFEE

MAKES 2 TO 4 SERVINGS
CHILL TIME: *30 to 40 minutes*

3 cups cold very strong brewed coffee
1 ounce unsweetened chocolate, grated or finely chopped
¼ cup granulated sugar
1 cup heavy cream or half-and-half
Ice for chilling and serving

1 Pour the coffee into a 1½-quart pitcher.

2 In a small saucepan, over a medium heat, combine the chocolate, sugar, and cream. Bring to a boil, stirring constantly. Remove from the heat and set pan in a larger pan filled with ice and water. When cooled, pour into the prepared pitcher. Add ice and serve.

4 ■ CHOCOLATE BERRY COOLER

MAKES 2 TO 4 SERVINGS

¼ cup fresh berries
1 tablespoon Dutch processed cocoa powder
1½ tablespoons granulated sugar
1½ cups milk
½ cup seltzer water, chilled
1 cup whipped topping
Fresh berries for garnish

1 In the container of a blender, combine the berries, cocoa powder, and sugar, blending on high speed for 10 seconds. Add the milk and seltzer and blend on low speed for 10 seconds. Pour into tall glasses and serve with a large dollop of whipped topping and garnish with fresh berries.

BAKING NOTES: The berries can be of any variety in season, such as raspberries or blackberries. Frozen berries can be substituted if they are thawed and well drained. If using frozen berries, garnish with chocolate curls (see page 422) or a sprinkling of chocolate wafer cookie crumbs.

1   2   3   4

5 ■ CHOCOLATE COFFEE PUNCH

MAKES 32 SERVINGS OR 8 QUARTS

½ cup instant coffee powder
2 cups granulated sugar
3 quarts hot water
½ gallon milk
½ cup Chocolate Syrup I (see page 406)
2 tablespoons crème de cacao or 1 tablespoon chocolate extract
1 gallon chocolate ice cream

1 In a large pan, stir the coffee powder, sugar, and water over high heat until blended and the sugar dissolves. Do not boil. Mix in the milk and chocolate syrup until blended. Stir in the crème de cacao. Pour mixture into a serving bowl.

2 Add the ice cream by scoopfuls into the punch and stir gently. Serve.

6 ■ CHOCOLATE DRINK

MAKES 8 TO 12 SERVINGS

2 cups milk
¼ cup granulated sugar
¼ cup Dutch processed cocoa powder
1 package (3.4 ounces) chocolate instant pudding mix
1 teaspoon chocolate extract
8 ice cubes
Fresh mint sprigs for garnish

1 In the container of a blender, combine the milk, sugar, cocoa powder, and pudding mix. Blend on high speed for 15 to 20 seconds. Add the chocolate extract and ice. Blend until the ice is crushed and immediately pour into chilled glasses. Garnish with the mint sprigs and serve.

7 ■ CHOCOLATE EGGNOG

MAKES 6 SERVINGS
CHILL TIME: *30 minutes*

4 large eggs, separated
⅔ cup Dutch process cocoa powder
¼ cup plus 2 tablespoons granulated sugar
2 cups milk
¼ cup rum
Ground nutmeg or cinnamon for garnish

1 In a small bowl, using an electric mixer, on high speed, beat the egg yolks until foamy.

2 In a medium saucepan, over low heat, blend the cocoa, ¼ cup of the sugar, the milk, and beaten egg yolks. Cook, stirring constantly, until the mixture thickens and coats the back of a spoon. Remove from the heat. Chill for 30 minutes.

3 In a medium bowl, using an electric mixer on high speed, beat the egg whites and the remaining 2 tablespoons of sugar until stiff peaks form. Fold in 3 tablespoons of the cooled cocoa mixture and the rum. Then fold the egg white mixture back into the cocoa mixture. Pour into mugs, sprinkle with ground nutmeg or cinnamon, and serve.

8 ■ CHOCOLATE MILK SHAKE

MAKES 2 SERVINGS

3 tablespoons Chocolate Syrup I (see page 406)
1 pint chocolate ice cream
¾ cup milk
Sliced fresh kiwifruit or peaches in season for garnish

1 Place all of the ingredients except the fruit in the container of a blender, cover tightly, and blend on high speed until smooth. Immediately pour into glasses, and serve garnished with a slice of fruit.

BAKING NOTES: Any flavor of ice cream that complements the chocolate syrup can be used. For extra flavor add a few drops of almond extract or peppermint extract.

6

7

5

8

9 ■ CHOCOLATE MINT COLA

MAKES 12 TO 15 SERVINGS

2 cans (12 ounces each) cola beverage, chilled
1½ cups seltzer water
1 cup Chocolate Syrup I (see page 406)
1 tablespoon chocolate extract
3 drops peppermint extract
Ice for chilling
½ cup heavy cream
2 tablespoons granulated sugar

1 In a large serving bowl, combine the cola, seltzer, chocolate syrup, and the chocolate and peppermint extracts. Add a few ice cubes or place the bowl in a tray or larger bowl filled with ice cubes to chill.

2 In a medium bowl, using a wire whisk, whip the cream and sugar until soft peaks form. Serve the cola with the whipped cream on the side.

10 ■ CHOCOLATE MINT COOLER

MAKES 2 SERVINGS

1 cup cold strong brewed coffee
¼ cup Cocoa Syrup I (see page 407)
2 tablespoons crème de menthe
1 cup shaved ice
2 scoops chocolate ice cream
Fresh mint sprigs for garnish

1 In the container of a blender, combine the coffee, syrup, and crème de menthe. Blend on low speed for 10 seconds.

2 Fill two chilled tall glasses with ½ cup shaved ice each. Pour the syrup mixture over the top and stir to blend. Top each with 1 scoop chocolate ice cream and garnish with a mint sprig.

BAKING NOTE: For best results, make your own chocolate syrup, although a store-bought syrup is acceptable.

11 ■ CHOCOLATE SHAKE

MAKES 4 SERVINGS

1 pint chocolate ice cream
2 cups milk
¼ cup Grand Marnier
Chocolate Whipped Cream for garnish (see page 406)
Grated chocolate or chocolate curls for garnish

1 In the container of a blender, combine the ice cream, milk, and Grand Marnier. Blend on low speed for 30 to 40 seconds, or until smooth. Pour into 4

large chilled wine glasses. Garnish with dollops of the chocolate whipped cream and sprinkle the grated chocolate over the top.

BAKING NOTES: More ice cream can be added to make the mixture thicker.

12 ■ CHOCOLATE SODA

MAKES 1 SERVING

¼ cup Chocolate Syrup I (see page 406)
1 tablespoon milk
2 large scoops of chocolate ice cream
¾ to 1 cup chilled seltzer water
Whipped cream or whipped topping for garnish
Ground hazelnuts or walnuts for garnish
1 maraschino cherry for garnish

1 In a tall soda glass, combine the syrup and milk. Stir vigorously. Gently drop in the ice cream. Pour in enough seltzer water to fill the glass. Top with whipped cream, sprinkle with nuts, and top with the cherry.

BAKING NOTES: To prevent the seltzer from foaming up and running out of the glass, pour slowly.

10 12 9

13 ■ CHOCOLATE SPIKE

MAKES 1 SERVING

¾ cup milk
1½ tablespoons Chocolate Syrup II
  (see page 406)
⅛ teaspoon ground nutmeg
⅛ teaspoon ground cloves
⅛ teaspoon ground cinnamon
1 large scoop of chocolate ice cream

1 Place all of the ingredients together in the container of a blender and pulse on and off 30 to 40 seconds, until blended and smooth. Pour into a glass and serve at once.

14 ■ CHRISTMAS COFFEE PUNCH

MAKES 20 SERVINGS OR 5 QUARTS
PREPARATION TIME: *4 to 6 minutes*

1¼ cups granulated sugar
1 gallon strong brewed coffee
1½ teaspoons crème de cacao or
  coffee liqueur
2 pints chocolate ice cream,
  softened
1 pint heavy cream, whipped
Fresh mint sprigs for garnish

1 In a large bowl, blend the sugar and coffee. Stir in the crème de cacao. Add the ice cream and mix until blended Gently fold in the whipped cream. Serve at once, garnishing each serving with a sprig of fresh mint.

15 ■ CINNAMON COCOA

MAKES 4 TO 6 SERVINGS

¼ cup Dutch processed cocoa
  powder
¼ cup granulated sugar
¼ teaspoon ground cinnamon
⅛ teaspoon salt
1 cup water
3 cups milk
1 teaspoon chocolate extract

1 In a medium saucepan, over medium heat, combine the cocoa powder, granulated sugar, cinnamon, salt, and water. Using a wire whisk, beat until thick and hot. Do not boil. Stir in the milk and chocolate extract. Remove from the heat.

2 Using an electric mixer on medium speed, beat until foamy. Pour into warmed cups and serve immediately.

BAKING NOTES: For a richer cocoa, use half-and-half instead of milk. Ground nutmeg or allspice can be substituted for the cinnamon, or omit the spice and serve with a stick of cinnamon in each cup.

16 ■ COCOA IN A MUG

MAKES 1 SERVING

1 cup milk
1 tablespoon Dutch processed
  cocoa powder
1 tablespoon granulated sugar
Miniature marshmallows for
  garnish

1 In a saucepan, heat the milk until bubbles form around the edges. Stir in the cocoa powder and sugar and serve with miniature marshmallows on top.

17 ■ COCOA-N-HONEY

MAKES 2 TO 4 SERVINGS

⅓ cup Dutch processed cocoa
  powder
2 tablespoons granulated sugar
3 tablespoons honey
¼ cup water
3½ cups milk
½ teaspoon chocolate or vanilla
  extract

11
13
14
15
16
17

1 In a saucepan, over medium heat, stirring constantly, bring the cocoa powder, sugar, honey, and water to a rolling boil. Add the milk and chocolate extract and heat until bubbles form around the edges. Pour into cups and serve.

BAKING NOTES: To change the flavor of this beverage, substitute ½ teaspoon of any other flavor of extract for the chocolate or vanilla extract.

18 ■ FRENCH CHOCOLATE

MAKES 4 TO 6 SERVINGS
CHILL TIME: *40 minutes*

2 ounces semisweet chocolate, grated or finely chopped
¼ cup light corn syrup
2 tablespoons crème de cacao
¼ teaspoon chocolate or vanilla extract
1 cup heavy cream
3 cups milk
Frsh mint leaves for garnish

1 In a small saucepan, over low heat, melt the chocolate, stirring until smooth. Stir in the corn syrup and crème de cacao until blended. Remove from the heat and stir in the chocolate extract. Transfer to a medium bowl, cover, and chill 30 to 40 minutes, or until thickened.

2 In a medium bowl, using an electric mixer on medium speed, whip the cream until soft peaks form. Gently stir into the chocolate mixture.

3 In a medium saucepan, heat the milk until bubbles form around the edges.

4 To serve, spoon 3 to 5 tablespoons of the chocolate cream mixture into each cup and fill with hot milk. Stir well and garnish each serving with a mint leaf.

19 ■ HAWAIIAN SHAKE

MAKES 4 SERVINGS

1 cup coconut milk (see Baking notes)
1 cup unsweetened pineapple juice
½ cup Chocolate Syrup I (see page 406)
2 teaspoons white Okolehao Liqueur or coconut extract
1 cup chocolate ice cream
Papaya and/or pineapple wedges for garnish

1 Chill 4 tall glasses in the freezer for 30 minutes.

2 In the container of a blender, combine the coconut milk, pineapple juice, chocolate syrup, and Okolehao. Blend on high speed for 10 to 12 seconds, or until smooth. Add the chocolate ice cream and blend for 5 seconds. Immediately pour into the prepared glasses. Garnish with a papaya or pineapple wedge on the side of each glass.

BAKING NOTES: Coconut extract can be substitued for the liqueur, but the flavor of the shake will be different. Omit the liqueur if serving to children. Coconut milk can be found canned in specialty food stores or supermarkets.

20 ■ HOT CHOCOLATE I

MAKES 4 SERVINGS

1 cup water
2 ounces unsweetened chocolate, grated or finely chopped
3 tablespoons granulated sugar
3 cups milk

1 In a medium saucepan, bring the water to a boil. Add the chocolate and stir until the chocolate is melted and the mixture is smooth. Add the sugar. Bring to a boil and simmer for 3 minutes. Remove from the heat and stir in the milk. Heat until bubbles form around the edge of the pan. Remove from the heat. Cool slightly. Using a wire whisk, beat vigorously until light and fluffy. Serve immediately.

BAKING NOTES: The secret of this hot chocolate is the beating after it has been cooked. To prepare Iced Chocolate: Prepare as above and let cool completely after beating. Serve over cracked ice in tall glasses and garnish with a sprig of mint. Or

18

20

19

pour the prepared hot chocolate into a cocktail shaker, add ½ cup light cream and 4 or 5 ice cubes. Shake until frothy and pour at once into tall glasses. To prepare Brazilian Hot or Iced Chocolate: Prepare as directed above substituting 1 cup very strong brewed coffee for the water in the recipe.

21 ■ HOT CHOCOLATE II

MAKES 1 SERVING

3 tablespoons Dutch processed cocoa powder
½ cup milk
½ cup water
Granulated sugar to taste

1 In a small saucepan, stir the cocoa and milk until blended. Bring to a boil and stir in the water. Return to a boil. Remove from the heat, stir in sugar to taste, and serve.

BAKING NOTES: This recipe originally appeared in *Mrs. Beeton's Book of Household Management* dated 1861.

22 ■ HOT CHOCOLATE EUROPEAN STYLE

MAKES 3 SERVINGS

¼ cup heavy cream
2 cups boiling water
1 cup hot strong brewed coffee
½ cup Chocolate Syrup I (see page 406)
Grated chocolate for garnish

1 In a small bowl, using an electric mixer on high speed, whip the cream until soft peaks form.
2 In a pitcher, stir the water, hot coffee, and chocolate syrup until blended. Place 1 tablespoonful of whipped cream in each cup and pour the hot mixture over the top. Garnish with a sprinkling of grated chocolate and serve.

BAKING NOTES: For best results, do not reheat the hot coffee mixture.

23 ■ HOT CHOCOLATE MOCHA

MAKES 1 TO 2 SERVINGS

1 cup hot strong brewed coffee
½ cup heavy cream
¼ cup semisweet chocolate, grated

1 In a small saucepan, heat the coffee and cream until bubbles appear around the edge of the pan. Remove from the heat. Stir in the chocolate until melted. Serve in warmed mugs.

24 ■ HOT RUM WITH CHOCOLATE

MAKES 4 TO 6 SERVINGS

1 quart milk
½ cup Chocolate Syrup II (see page 406)
½ cup dark rum
½ cup heavy cream
2 tablespoons granulated sugar

1 In a medium saucepan, heat the milk over medium heat until bubbles form around the edges. Stir in the chocolate syrup and rum. Remove from the heat.
2 In a small bowl, using a wire whisk, whip the cream and sugar until soft peaks form. Spoon tablespoonfuls into each cup. Pour the hot chocolate over the top and serve.

25 ∎ INSTANT HOT COCOA MIX

MAKES 36 SERVINGS OR 9 QUARTS

1 box (8 quart size) non-fat powdered milk
16 ounces Dutch processed cocoa
  powder
1 jar (7 ounces) non-dairy creamer
2 cups powdered sugar
1/2 teaspoon salt
Miniature marshmallows or
  whipped cream for garnish

1 In a large bowl, combine the
powdered milk, cocoa powder,
creamer, powdered sugar, and
salt. Store in an airtight container in a dry place.

2 To make 1 serving: Place 1 cup
boiling water in a blender and
add 3 tablespoons of the hot
cocoa mix. Blend on high for 5
to 10 seconds, or until smooth.
Serve with miniature marshmallows or a dab of whipped cream
on top.

BAKING NOTES: To prepare the
hot cocoa by hand, in a small
bowl, whisk 3 tablespoons hot
cocoa mix with 1 cup boiling
water until smooth.

26 ∎ IRISH CREAM I

MAKES 6 SERVINGS

1 cup heavy cream, whipped to soft
  peaks
4 large eggs
1 cup Irish whisky
2 tablespoons instant coffee powder crystals
2 tablespoons Chocolate Syrup I
  (see page 406)
1 can (14 ounces) sweetened condensed milk
2 tablespoons crème de cacao
2 tablespoons granulated sugar

1 In a medium bowl, using an
electric mixer on high speed,
beat the cream until soft peaks
form.

2 In a cup, combine the coffee
powder and chocolate syrup.

3 In a large bowl, using an electric mixer on high speed, beat
the eggs until they are thick and
light-colored. Beat in the
whisky. Beat in the coffee powder mixture. Beat in the con-

densed milk, crème de cacao,
and sugar. Fold in the whipped
cream. Pour into an airtight container and seal. Keep refrigerated until serving.

BAKING NOTES: Owing to the
raw eggs in this recipe, keep
refrigerated at all times.

27 ∎ IRISH CREAM II

MAKES 8 SERVINGS

1 cup Irish whisky
1 cup heavy cream
1 can (14 ounces) sweetened condensed milk
1 tablespoon Chocolate Syrup II
  (see page 406)
2 large eggs
1/2 cup coconut liqueur

1 In the container of a blender,
combine the whisky, cream, and
milk. Blend on medium speed
for 18 to 20 seconds. Blend in the
chocolate syrup. Blend in the
eggs, one at a time, mixing well
after each addition. Stir in the
coconut liqueur.

2 Store in an airtight container
in the refrigerator until ready to
use, up to 7 days.

BAKING NOTES: Owing to the
raw eggs used in this recipe,
keep refrigerated at all times.

28 ∎ MEXICAN-STYLE COFFEE

MAKES 1 SERVING

1 1/2 teaspoons Chocolate Syrup I
  (see page 406)
1/2 cup fresh brewed espresso
1 tablespoon heavy cream,
  whipped
Grated nutmeg for garnish
  (optional)

1 Spoon the chocolate syrup
into the bottom of a cup and
pour the hot espresso over it.
Top with the whipped cream,
sprinkle with nutmeg if desired,
and serve.

26

27

25

29 ■ MEXICAN-STYLE HOT CHOCOLATE I

MAKES 20 SERVINGS OR 5 QUARTS

3 sticks cinnamon
2½ cups water
1 gallon milk
1 cup granulated sugar
½ cup Dutch processed cocoa powder
5 ounces unsweetened chocolate, grated or finely chopped
1 tablespoon cornmeal
Cinnamon sticks for garnish

1 In a large saucepan, over a medium heat, bring the cinnamon sticks and 2 cups of the water together to a boil. Reduce the heat to low and simmer for 5 minutes. Remove the cinnamon sticks and and stir in the milk and sugar. Return to a rolling boil. Stir in the cocoa powder and chocolate and cook over low heat for 10 minutes.

2 In a small bowl, dissolve the cornmeal in the remaining ½ cup of water and add to the chocolate mixture. Serve warm with cinnamon sticks a for garnish.

BAKING NOTES: This is the perfect recipe for a festive holiday party.

30 ■ MEXICAN-STYLE HOT CHOCOLATE II

MAKES 2 TO 4 SERVINGS

2 large egg whites
2 ounces semisweet chocolate, grated or finely chopped
2 cups milk
2 to 4 sticks cinnamon

1 In a small bowl, using an electric mixer on high speed, beat the egg whites until stiff peaks form.

2 In a saucepan, over a low heat, melt the chocolate, stirring constantly. Add the milk and cinnamon sticks. Bring the mixture to a boil, remove from the heat, and discard the cinnamon sticks. Using a wire whisk, whisk in the egg whites until the mixture is foamy. Serve at once.

31 ■ MOCHA COFFEE

MAKES 2 TO 4 SERVINGS

5 ounces semisweet chocolate, grated or finely chopped
4 cups milk
2 tablespoons instant coffee powder
2 tablespoons honey
1 teaspoon crème de cacao or vanilla extract
2 to 4 cinnamon sticks for garnish

1 In a saucepan, over a low heat, melt the chocolate, stirring until smooth. Stir in the milk, coffee powder, and honey. Cook until bubbles form around he edges. Remove from the heat and stir in crème de cacao. Immediately pour into serving cups and place a cinnamon stick in each cup.

BAKING NOTES: For best results, use crème de cacao rather than vanilla extract. Or, substitute hazelnut or coffee liqueur for the crème de cacao.

28
29
30
31

32 ■ MOCHA MILK SHAKE

MAKES 2 TO 4 SERVINGS

2 cups milk
²/₃ cups instant cocoa mix
1 teaspoon instant coffee powder
2 cup chocolate ice cream, softened

1 In the container of a blender, combine all of the ingredients. Blend on low speed for 10 to 15 seconds, until smooth. Pour into chilled glasses and serve at once.

33 ■ PEPPERMINT PATTY

MAKES 8 SERVINGS

1 cup heavy cream
4 cups milk
³/₄ cup Dutch processed cocoa powder
1¹/₂ cups peppermint schnapps
Fresh mint sprigs for garnish

1 In a medium bowl, using an electric mixer on medium speed, beat the cream until soft peaks form. Chill until ready to use.

2 In a saucepan, heat the milk over low heat until bubbles form around the edges. Place 2 cups of the milk in the container of a blender. Add the cocoa powder and blend on high until combined. Blend in the remaining 2 cups milk and peppermint schnapps. Pour into warmed cups or glasses. Top with a dab of the whipped cream and garnish with a sprig of mint.

34 ■ SPICED HOT COCOA

MAKES 6 SERVINGS

¹/₂ cup Dutch processed cocoa powder
¹/₃ cup granulated sugar
¹/₂ teaspoon ground cinnamon
¹/₄ teaspoon ground nutmeg
¹/₂ cup hot water
3¹/₂ cups milk
1 teaspoon chocolate extract
1 teaspoon crème de cacao

1 In a large saucepan, stir the cocoa powder, sugar, spices, and hot water until smooth and blended. Bring to a boil over medium heat, and simmer for 2 to 3 minutes. Add the milk and heat until bubbles form around the edges. Remove from the heat. Add the chocolate extract and crème de cacao. Using a wire whisk, beat until foamy. Serve hot.

35 ■ THREE BRIDGES HOT CHOCOLATE

MAKES 4 TO 6 SERVINGS

¹/₄ cup Dutch processed cocoa powder
¹/₄ cup granulated sugar
2 cups milk
2 cups heavy cream
1 teaspoon coffee liqueur
Pinch ground nutmeg
Sprigs of mint for garnish

1 In a saucepan over low heat, combine the cocoa powder, sugar, and milk. Using a wire whisk, beat until the sugar is dissolved. Stir in the cream, liqueur, and nutmeg and simmer until bubbles form around the edges. Remove from the heat. Using an electric mixer on high speed, beat until thickened and foamy. Immediately pour into warm cups and serve with a sprig of mint on top.

BAKING NOTES: As an added variation, place a dab of chocolate whipped cream (see page 406) and then the mint.

32   33   34   35

Cakes

36 ■ 20-MINUTE FROSTED CHOCOLATE CAKE

YIELD: *12 to 15 servings*
BAKING TIME: *25 minutes*

BUTTERMILK CAKE

1/2 cup butter or margarine
1/2 cup canola oil
1 cup water
1 teaspoon vanilla or chocolate extract
2 cups granulated sugar
2 cups all-purpose flour
2 large eggs
1/2 cup buttermilk
1 teaspoon baking soda

COCOA FROSTING

1/4 cup butter or margarine
1/4 cup Dutch processed cocoa powder
6 tablespoons heavy cream
2 cups powdered sugar

1 Position a rack in the center of the oven and preheat the oven to 350 degrees. Lightly grease a 13 by 9-inch pan.

2 To make the cake, in a large saucepan, over medium heat, combine the butter, oil, water, and vanilla extract and bring to a boil. Remove from the heat. Using an electric mixer on medium speed, immediately beat in the sugar and then the flour. Beat in the eggs, buttermilk, and baking soda, blending until smooth. Pour the mixture into the prepared pan.

3 Bake for 20 to 25 minutes, or until a cake tester inserted into the center comes out clean. While the cake is baking, make the frosting. Frost the cake as soon as it comes out of the oven.

4 To make the frosting, in a medium saucepan over medium heat, mix the butter, cocoa powder, and cream and bring to a boil. Remove from the heat. Stir in the powdered sugar until blended. Spread the frosting over the top of the hot cake. Cool in the pan on a wire rack. Cut into servings.

37 ■ ALMOND FUDGE CAKE

YIELD: *16 servings*
BAKING TIME: *70 minutes.*

3 ounces unsweetened chocolate, grated or finely chopped
2 cups all-purpose flour
1 (3.4 ounces) package chocolate instant pudding mix
3/4 cup semisweet chocolate chips
1 teaspoon baking powder
1/4 teaspoon cream of tartar
1/2 teaspoon salt
1 1/2 cups slivered almonds
1/2 cup butter or margarine, at room temperature
1 1/3 cups granulated sugar
2 large eggs
3/4 cup sour cream
1 teaspoon almond extract
1 teaspoon amaretto
1 cup Chocolate Frosting V (see page 400)

1 Position a rack in the center of the oven and preheat the oven to 350 degrees. Lightly grease and flour a 10-inch tube pan.

2 To make the cake, melt the chocolate (see page 13). Remove from the heat.

3 Combine the flour, pudding mix, chocolate chips, baking powder, cream of tartar, and salt.

4 Sprinkle 3/4 cup of the almonds in the bottom of the prepared pan.

5 In a large bowl, using an electric mixer on medium speed, beat the butter and sugar until fluffy. Beat in the eggs. Beat in the sour cream, almond extract, and amaretto. Pouring it in a thin stream, beat in the melted chocolate. Beat in the dry ingredients. Fold in the remaining 3/4 cup almonds. Pour the mixture into the prepared pan.

6 Bake for 60 to 70 minutes, or until a cake tester inserted into the center comes out clean. Cool in the pan on a wire rack.

7 Make the frosting.

8 Invert the cake onto a serving plate. Spread the frosting on the top and sides of the cake.

38 ■ ALMOND FUDGE FRUITCAKE

YIELD: *16 servings*
BAKING TIME: *120 minutes*

CAKE

5 ounces unsweetened chocolate, grated or finely chopped
2 cups all-purpose flour
1 tablespoon baking powder
1 1/2 cups dates, pitted and chopped
1 1/2 cups candied fruit, finely diced
1 1/2 cups whole blanched almonds, chopped

½ teaspoon salt
¾ cup butter or margarine, at room temperature
1 cup granulated sugar
3 large eggs

TOPPING

1 tablespoon brandy
Coffee Hard Sauce (see page 408)
Thinly sliced kiwi fruit for garnish

1 Preheat the oven to 300 degrees. Grease and flour a 10-inch Bundt or tube pan.

2 Melt the chocolate (see page 13). Remove from the heat.

3 Combine the flour, baking powder, dates, fruit, almonds, and salt.

4 In a large bowl, using an electric mixer on medium speed, beat the butter and sugar until fluffy. Beat in the melted chocolate. Beat in the eggs. Gradually blend in the dry ingredients. Scrape the batter into the prepared pan.

5 Bake for 1½ to 2 hours, or until a cake tester inserted into the center comes out clean. Immediately invert the cake onto a wire rack covered with aluminum foil. Drizzle the brandy over the top of the hot cake. Wrap in the foil and cool completely.

6 Make the hard sauce.

7 Transfer the cake to a serving plate. Fill a pastry bag fitted with a star tip with the hard sauce and pipe fancy designs around the top and lower edge of the cake. Garnish with thinly sliced kiwifruit.

39 ■ AMARETTO-FLAVORED CHOCOLATE CHEESECAKE

YIELD: *16 servings*
BAKING TIME: *120 minutes*
CHILL TIME: *90 minutes*

CRUST

1 cup graham cracker crumbs
¼ cup Dutch processed cocoa powder
2 teaspoons granulated sugar
¼ cup butter, melted

FILLING

8 ounces unsweetened chocolate, grated or finely chopped
16 ounces cream cheese, at room temperature
½ cup granulated sugar
3 large eggs
1 cup sour cream or plain yogurt
⅓ cup amaretto
1 teaspoon chocolate extract
1 teaspoon almond extract

TOPPING

2 ounces semisweet chocolate, grated or finely chopped
2 tablespoons butter or margarine
½ cup heavy cream
1 tablespoon powdered sugar
2 teaspoons amaretto
¼ cup sliced almonds
Maraschino cherries for garnish
Fresh mint leaves for garnish

1 Position a rack in the center of the oven and preheat the oven to 300 degrees. Lightly grease the bottom and sides of a 10-inch springform pan.

2 To make the crust, in a medium bowl, using a slotted wooden spoon, combine the graham cracker crumbs, cocoa powder, and sugar. Mix in the melted butter to form an even, crumbly mixture. Press onto the bottom and 1 inch up the sides of the prepared pan.

3 To make the filling, melt the chocolate (see page 13). Remove from the heat.

4 In a large bowl, using an electric mixer on medium speed, beat the cream cheese and sugar until the mixture is thick and smooth. Beat in the eggs, one at a time, beating well after each addition. Stir in the sour cream, melted chocolate, amaretto, and the chocolate and almond extracts. Carefully pour the mixture over the prepared crust.

5 Bake for 1 hour, or until firm. Turn off the oven and leave the cheesecake undisturbed in the oven for 1 hour. Remove from the oven and refrigerate 30 minutes or until completely chilled.

6 To make the topping, in a small saucepan, over low heat, melt the chocolate and butter, stirring until smooth. Spread the mixture over the cheesecake and chill for 1 additional hour.

7 In a medium bowl, using an electric mixer on medium speed, beat the cream and powdered sugar until the mixture forms stiff peaks. Fold in the amaretto.

8 To assemble, remove the side from the springform pan and carefully place the cheesecake on a serving plate. Fill a pastry bag fitted with a large star tip with the whipped cream and pipe a decorative design over the chocolate topping. Garnish with maraschino cherries and mint leaves.

40 ■ AMAZING CHOCOLATE CAKE

YIELD: *12 to 15 servings*
BAKING TIME: *45 minutes*

3 ounces unsweetened chocolate, grated or finely chopped
2 cups all-purpose flour
2 teaspoons baking soda
1 can (8 ounces) beets
½ cup butter or margarine, at room temperature
2½ cups packed light brown sugar
3 large eggs
2 teaspoons vanilla extract
½ cup buttermilk
1½ cups Cocoa Honey Frosting (see page 407)

1 Position a rack in the center of the oven and preheat the oven to 350 degrees. Lightly grease a 13 by 9-inch pan.

2 Melt the chocolate (see page 13). Remove from the heat.

3 Combine the flour and baking soda.

4 Drain the beets and reserve the juice. In a blender or food processor, puree the beets to a smooth puree.

5 In a large bowl, using an electric mixer on high speed, beat the butter and brown sugar until fluffy. Beat in the eggs. Beat in the vanilla extract and melted chocolate. Beat in the

buttermilk. Gradually blend in the dry ingredients. Fold in the pureed beets and the reserved juice. Pour the mixture into the prepared pan.

6 Bake for 40 to 45 minutes, or until a cake tester inserted into the center comes out clean. Cool in the pan on a wire rack.

7 Make the frosting.

8 Spread the frosting over the top and sides of the cake.

41 ■ AMORE —THE ITALIANO LOVE CAKE

YIELD: *16 servings*
BAKING TIME: *35 minutes*
CHILL TIME: *20 to 30 minutes*

CAKE

1¼ cups powdered sugar, sifted
1 cup cake flour
15 large egg whites (1½ cups)
1½ teaspoons cream of tartar
1½ teaspoons vanilla extract
¼ teaspoon almond extract
¼ teaspoon salt
1 cup granulated sugar

FILLING AND TOPPING

½ cup amaretto
1 pint pistachio ice cream, softened
1 pint chocolate ice cream, softened
2 cups heavy cream
1 cup (6 ounces) semisweet chocolate chips for garnish

1 Position a rack in the center of the oven and preheat the oven to 375 degrees.

2 To make the cake, combine the powdered sugar and cake flour.

3 In a large bowl, using an electric mixer on high speed, beat the egg whites, cream of tartar, vanilla extract, almond extract, and salt until well mixed and soft peaks form. Beat in the sugar, a little at a time, and beat until stiff but not dry. With a rubber spatula, fold in the dry ingredients until the flour is just incorporated. Pour the mixture into an ungreased 10-inch tube pan, shaking the pan lightly.

4 Bake for 30 to 35 minutes, or until the top springs back when touched and is golden brown. Invert the pan onto a bottle or funnel and cool completely.

5 To assemble, using a serrated knife, cut the cake into 3 layers. Sprinkle each of the layers with some of the amaretto. Place one layer on a serving plate. Spread the pistachio ice cream on the bottom layer and top with the second layer. Spread the chocolate ice cream on the second layer and top with the third layer. Freeze the cake for 20 to 30 minutes, or until set.

6 Meanwhile, to make the topping, in a chilled bowl, using an electric mixer on medium speed, beat the heavy cream and the remaining amaretto until it forms soft peaks. Spread on the top and sides of the cake. Return to the freezer.

7 Meanwhile, in a small saucepan, over low heat, melt the chocolate chips, stirring until smooth. Line a baking sheet with aluminum foil. Pour the melted chocolate onto the prepared pan, spreading it ¼ inch thick. Let chocolate set for 15 minutes. Using an oiled heart-shaped cookie cutter, cut out hearts. Place them on top of the cake. Keep cake in the freezer until ready to serve.

42 ■ APPLE CHOCOLATE CAKE

YIELD: *16 servings*
BAKING TIME: *45 minutes*

3 cups diced apples
2 cups plus 1 tablespoon all-purpose flour
1 cup granulated sugar
1 cup (6 ounces) semisweet chocolate chips
½ cup ground walnuts
1 teaspoon baking soda
1½ teaspoons ground cinnamon
½ teaspoon ground nutmeg
1 cup canola oil
2 large eggs
2 teaspoons vanilla or almond extract
1 recipe Chocolate Glaze II (see page 401)

1 Position a rack in the center of the oven and preheat the oven to 350 degrees. Lightly grease a 10-inch Bundt pan. Sprinkle 1½ cups of the diced apples in the bottom of the pan.

2 Combine two cups of the flour, the sugar, chocolate chips, walnuts, baking soda, and spices.

3 In a large bowl, using an electric mixer on medium speed, beat the oil, eggs, and vanilla extract until blended. Using a wooden spoon, gradually stir in the dry ingredients. The batter will be slightly lumpy. Carefully spoon into the prepared pan.

4 In a small bowl, dust the remaining 1½ cups diced apples with the remaining 1 tablespoon flour. Toss to coat. Sprinkle the apples on top of the batter in the pan.

5 Bake for 40 to 45 minutes, or until a cake tester inserted into the center comes out clean. Cool in the pan on a wire rack for 10 minutes. Invert onto the rack to cool completely.

6 Meanwhile, make the chocolate glaze. Drizzle the glaze over the top of the cake, allowing it run down the sides.

43 ■ APPLE CHOCOLATE CHEESECAKE PIE

YIELD: *8 to 10 servings*
BAKING TIME: *45 minutes*
CHILL TIME: *60 minutes*

COCOA PASTRY CRUST

2 cups all-purpose flour
½ cup Dutch processed cocoa powder
6 tablespoons sugar
¼ teaspoon salt
1 cup butter-flavored vegetable shortening
2 teaspoons chocolate extract
4 tablespoons ice-cold water

FILLING

½ cup cream cheese, at room temperature
2 tablespoons granulated sugar
1 large egg
1½ teaspoons amaretto
1 can (21 ounces) apple pie filling (dry pack)

TOPPING

1 large egg white, beaten
Granulated sugar for sprinkling

1 Position a rack in the center of the oven and preheat the oven to 400 degrees.

2 To make the crust, in a large bowl, combine the flour, cocoa powder, sugar, and salt. Using a pastry blender or two knives scissor fashion, cut in the vegetable shortening to make a crumbly mixture. Combine the chocolate extract and water. Sprinkle the water mixture over the top and mix with a fork until the dough is just moist enough to hold together. Cover and chill for at least 1 hour, or overnight.

3 On a lightly floured surface, roll out about half of the dough into an 11-inch circle. Line a 9-inch pie pan with the crust. Roll out the remaining dough for the top crust, setting it aside until ready to use.

4 To make the filling, in a small bowl, using an electric mixer on medium-high speed, beat the cream cheese, sugar, egg, and amaretto until smooth.

5 To assemble, fill the crust in the pie pan with the canned apples, spreading them evenly over the bottom. Pour the filling mixture over the top. Moisten the edges of the bottom crust

and place the top crust over the filling. Crimp or flute the edges if desired and poke the top crust twice with the tines of a fork. Brush with the beaten egg white and sprinkle with sugar.

6 Bake for 40 to 45 minutes, or until the top looks very dry. Cool in the pan on a wire rack for 15 to 20 minutes.

44 ■ APPLESAUCE CHOCOLATE CAKE

YIELD: *12 servings*
BAKING TIME: *35 minutes.*

CAKE

2 cups all-purpose flour
1/2 cup Dutch processed cocoa powder
1 tablespoon baking powder
1/2 teaspoon baking soda
1 teaspoon ground cinnamon
1/2 teaspoon salt
1/2 cup vegetable shortening
3/4 cup granulated sugar
1 large egg plus 1 large egg yolk
1 1/4 cups sweetened applesauce

FROSTING AND GARNISH

2 large egg whites
1 2/3 cups powdered sugar
6 tablespoons chilled water
1/8 teaspoon cream of tartar
1 tablespoon green crème de menthe
1 kiwifruit, thinly sliced
1/2 cup green glacé cherry halves

1 Position a rack in the center of the oven and preheat the oven to 350 degrees. Lightly grease and flour two 8-inch round cake pans.

2 To make the cake, combine the flour, cocoa powder, baking powder, baking soda, cinnamon, and salt.

3 In a large bowl, using an electric mixer on high speed, cream together the shortening and sugar until fluffy. Beat in the egg and egg yolk. Stir in the applesauce. Gradually blend in the dry ingredients. Divide the mixture evenly between the prepared pans.

4 Bake for 30 to 35 minutes, or until a cake tester inserted into the center comes out clean. Cool in the pans on wire racks for 10 minutes. Invert onto the racks and cool completely.

5 To make the frosting, in the top of a double boiler over simmering water, combine the egg whites, powdered sugar, water, and cream of tartar. Beat with a hand-held electric mixer on medium-high speed until the mixture forms soft peaks. Remove the top of the double boiler from the pan of simmering water and fold in the crème de menthe.

6 To assemble, using a serrated knife, trim the rounded tops off the cakes. Place one of the cakes on a serving plate. Spread some of the frosting on the top and place the second layer on top of the frosting. Using all of the remaining frosting, spread an even layer over the top and sides of the cake. Decorate with the kiwifruit and green glacé cherries.

41

44

CAKES ■ 38

45 ■ APRICOT-FILLED CHOCOLATE ROLL

YIELD: *12 to 16 servings*
BAKING TIME: *15 minutes*
CHILL TIME: *2 hours*

FILLING

1/2 pound dried apricots, finely diced
2 cups water
2 tablespoons lemon extract
1/2 cup granulated sugar
3 tablespoons apricot liqueur
1 teaspoon fresh lemon juice

CAKE ROLL

4 ounces unsweetened chocolate, grated or finely chopped
4 ounces semisweet chocolate, grated or finely chopped
1/3 cup coffee liqueur
1 teaspoon chocolate extract
1 teaspoon vanilla extract
7 large eggs, separated, plus 1 large egg white
3/4 cup granulated sugar

TOPPING

1/2 cup heavy cream
2 tablespoons Dutch processed cocoa powder for garnish

1 To make the filling, in a medium saucepan, combine the apricots, water, and lemon extract and cook over medium heat until the fruit is just tender. Stir in the sugar and cook until the sugar is dissolved. Using a pastry blender or a fork, mash the fruit. Mix in the apricot liqueur and lemon juice. Cover and chill for 2 hours.

2 Position rack in center of the oven and preheat the oven to 350 degrees. Grease a 15½ by 10½-inch jelly roll pan. Line the bottom of the pan with waxed paper. Grease and flour the paper.

3 To make the cake roll, melt the chocolates (see page 13), stirring until smooth. Stir in the coffee liqueur. Remove from the heat.

4 In a medium bowl, using an electric mixer on high speed, beat the egg yolks until thick and light-colored. Slowly beat in the melted chocolate.

5 In a large bowl, using an electric mixer on high speed, beat the egg whites until soft peaks form. Beat in the sugar until stiff but not dry. Fold one-third of the egg whites into the chocolate mixture, then fold the chocolate mixture back into the remaining egg whites. Pour the mixture into the prepared pan and spread evenly.

6 Bake for 10 minutes, reduce the oven to 300 degrees, and bake for 5 minutes. Remove from oven, cover with a damp, not wet, cloth, and cool on a wire rack for 1 hour.

7 To make the topping, in a small bowl, using an electric mixer on high speed, whip the heavy cream until soft peaks form.

8 To assemble, run a knife around the sides of the cake to losen it from the pan and invert onto a towel on a flat surface. Remove the pan and waxed paper. Spread the apricot filling evenly over the top of the cake, leaving a 1-inch border around the edges. Starting on one of the long sides, carefully roll up the cake jelly-roll fashion. Transfer to a platter, seam-side down. Fill a pastry bag with the whipped cream and pipe over the top of the cake. Sprinkle with the cocoa powder.

BAKING NOTES: This rolled cake can be decorated in many ways: Chocolate Ganache can be spread over the top and it can be garnished with Chocolate Leaves; Chocolate Cream Frosting can be used and sprinkled with Chocolate Cake Crumbs; or a coating chocolate can be poured over the cake to seal it in a layer of chocolate, and then it can be decorated with icings and garnishes. (See Frostings and Garnishes.)

46 ■ BAKED FUDGE CAKE

YIELD: *12 to 15 servings*
BAKING TIME: *25 minutes*

4 ounces unsweetened chocolate, grated or finely chopped
1/3 cup butter or margarine
2 large eggs
1 cup granulated sugar
1/2 cup all-purpose flour
1/2 cup chopped walnuts
1 teaspoon chocolate extract
Pinch of salt
1½ to 2 cups Chocolate Fudge Frosting II (see page 401)

1 Preheat the oven to 350 degrees. Lightly grease a 13 by 9-inch pan. Line the bottom of the pan with greased waxed paper.

2 In the top of a double boiler, over simmering water, melt the chocolate and butter, stirring until smooth. Remove from heat.

3 In a large bowl, using an electric mixer on high speed, beat the eggs until thick and light-colored. Beat in the sugar. Beat in the chocolate mixture. Stir in the flour, walnuts, chocolate extract, and salt. Scrape the mixture into pan and spread evenly.

4 Bake for 20 to 25 minutes, or until a cake tester inserted into the center comes out clean. Cool in the pan on a wire rack for 10 minutes. Invert onto a platter to cool completely.

5 Make the frosting. Spread the frosting over the top and sides of the cake.

47 ■ BANANA SPLIT CAKE

YIELD: *12 to 15 servings*
BAKING TIME: *5 minutes*
CHILL TIME: *2 hours*

CRUST

1²/₃ cups graham cracker crumbs
1/4 cup granulated sugar
1/3 cup vegetable shortening

FILLING

4 medium bananas, sliced
1 cup (6 ounces) semisweet chocolate chips
1 pint fudge ripple or chocolate ice cream, softened

TOPPING

1⅓ cups evaporated milk
1 cup (6 ounces) semisweet choco-
    late chips
½ cup butter or margarine
½ teaspoon vanilla or chocolate
    extract
1 cup heavy cream
2 tablespoons chopped pecans for
    garnish
¼ cup fruit cocktail, well drained,
    for garnish

1 Position a rack in the center of the oven and preheat the oven to 375 degrees. Lightly grease a 13 by 9-inch pan.

2 To make the crust, in a medium bowl, combine the crumbs and sugar. Using a pastry blender, cut in the shortening until it forms a crumbly mixture. Press onto the bottom of the prepared pan.

3 Bake for 5 minutes, or until golden brown. Cool on a wire rack.

4 To make the filling, cover the baked crust with the sliced bananas in a single layer. Sprinkle with the chocolate chips and spread the ice cream over the top. Chill in the freezer for 1 hour.

5 To make the topping, in a saucepan, over a medium heat, combine the milk, chocolate chips, and butter. Bring to a boil, reduce heat to low, and simmer for 5 minutes, or until mixture thickens slightly. Remove from the heat and stir in the vanilla extract. Cool completely. Spread over the chilled ice cream layer and freeze for 1 hour.

6 In a medium bowl, using an electric mixer on medium-high speed, beat the cream until soft

peaks form. Spread the whipped cream over the top of the cake and garnish with the nuts and fruit. Serve immediately.

BAKING NOTES: For a special occasion, make the dessert in a fancy oven-proof bowl or in a springform pan. Chocolate whipped cream (see page 406) can be used in place of the plain whipped cream.

48 ■ BITTERSWEET CHOCOLATE CUPCAKES

YIELD: *9 servings*
BAKING TIME: *18 minutes*

½ cup plus 6 tablespoons heavy
    cream
2 tablespoons butter or margarine
1 tablespoon Dutch processed
    cocoa powder
8 ounces unsweetened chocolate,
    grated or finely chopped
2 large eggs
¼ cup granulated sugar
¼ cup ground pecans
1 teaspoon chocolate extract
1½ cups Chocolate Glaze IV (see
    page 401)
Chocolate ice cream (optional)

1 Position a rack in the center of the oven and preheat the oven to 350 degrees. Lightly grease and sprinkle with sugar nine 2½-inch muffin-pan cups.

2 In a medium saucepan, heat ½ cup of the cream, the butter, and cocoa powder over medium heat, stirring until smooth and bubbles form around the edges. Remove from the heat and stir in the chocolate. Set aside to cool slightly.

3 In a medium bowl, using an electric mixer on high speed, beat the eggs and sugar until thick and light-colored.

Beat in the remaining 6 tablespoons cream. Beat in the pecans and chocolate extract. Pour in the chocolate mixture in a thin stream, stirring until blended. Spoon into the prepared muffin-pan cups, filling each cup two-thirds full.

4 Bake for 15 to 18 minutes, or until a cake tester inserted into the center of a cupcake comes out clean. Cool in the pan on a wire rack for 10 minutes. Invert onto the rack and cool completely.

5 Meanwhile, make the chocolate glaze.

6 Place the cupcakes on individual serving plates and spoon the chocolate glaze over the tops. Serve with chocolate ice cream on the side, if desired.

49 ■ BLACK-BOTTOM CUPCAKES

YIELD: *12 servings*
BAKING TIME: *25 minutes*

FILLING

8 ounces cream cheese, at room
    temperature
⅓ cup granulated sugar
1 large egg
1 cup (6 ounces) semisweet choco-
    late chips

46

48

CUPCAKES

3 cups all-purpose flour
1/2 cup Dutch processed cocoa powder
2 teaspoons baking soda
1 teaspoon salt
2 cups granulated sugar
2/3 cup canola oil
2 cups water
2 tablespoons cider vinegar

1 Position a rack in the center of the oven and preheat the oven to 350 degrees. Place paper baking cups in twelve 2-inch muffin-pan cups.

2 To make the filling, using an electric mixer on medium speed, beat the cream cheese, sugar, and egg until smooth. Fold in the chocolate chips.

3 To make the cupcakes, combine the flour, cocoa powder, baking soda, and salt.

4 In a large bowl, using an electric mixer on medium speed beat the sugar, oil, water, and vinegar until combined. Gradually stir in the dry ingredients. Fill the prepared muffin cups one-third full. Spoon heaping teaspoonfuls of the cream cheese mixture onto the chocolate batter in each cup.

5 Bake for 20 to 25 minutes, or until the tops spring back when touched. Remove from the pan to a wire rack to cool.

50 ■ BLACK FOREST CHEESECAKES

YIELD: *24 servings*
BAKING TIME: *25 minutes*
CHILL TIME: *45 minutes*

24 chocolate wafer cookies
1 1/4 cups granulated sugar
1/3 cup Dutch processed cocoa powder
2 tablespoons all-purpose flour
16 ounces cream cheese, at room temperature
3 large eggs
1 cup sour cream or chocolate flavored yogurt
1/2 teaspoon almond extract
1/2 cup heavy cream
1 can (14 ounces) cherry pie filling

1 Position a rack in the center of the oven and preheat the oven to 325 degrees. Line twenty-four 3-inch muffin-pan cups with aluminum foil baking cups. Place a cookie in the bottom of each cup.

2 Combine the sugar, cocoa powder, and flour.

3 In a large bowl, using an electric mixer on medium-high, beat the cream cheese until smooth. Beat in the dry ingredients. Beat in the eggs, one at a time, beating well after each addition. Beat in the sour cream and almond extract. Spoon the mixture into the prepared pans, filling each cup three-fourths full.

4 Bake for 20 to 25 minutes, or until set and firm to the touch. Cool in the pan on racks for 10 minutes. Remove from pans to finish cooling.

5 Meanwhile, in a medium bowl, using an electric mixer on high speed, whip the cream until stiff peaks form. Spread a tablespoon of the whipped cream over the top of each cooled cupcake. Chill 30 to 45 minutes, or until ready to serve. Place a dab of the cherry pie filling in the center of the whipped cream just before serving.

BAKING NOTES: For a variation, use any type of preserved fruit or fruit compote in place of the cherry pie filling.

37

47

42

49

51 ■ BLACK RUSSIAN CAKE

YIELD: *16 servings*
BAKING TIME: *50 minutes*

2 cups cake flour, sifted twice
1 package (2.9 ounces) chocolate instant pudding mix
1 tablespoon baking powder
1/2 teaspoon salt
1/2 cup butter or margarine, at room temperature
1 1/4 cups granulated sugar
1 cup evaporated milk
1/4 cup Kahlúa
1/4 cup vodka
4 large egg whites
Powdered sugar for dusting

1 Position a rack in the center of the oven and preheat the oven to 350 degrees. Lightly grease and flour a 10-inch Bundt or tube cake pan.

2 Combine the flour, pudding mix, baking powder, and salt.

3 In a large bowl, using an electric mixer on medium-high speed, beat the butter and sugar until light and fluffy. Beat in the milk. Beat in the Kahlúa and vodka. Gradually blend in the dry ingredients.

4 In a medium bowl, using an electric mixer on high speed, beat the egg whites until they form soft peaks. Gently fold the beaten egg whites into the butter mixture. Pour mixture into the prepared pan.

5 Bake for 45 to 50 minutes, or until a cake tester inserted into the center comes out clean. Cool in the pan for 10 minutes. Invert onto a wire rack and cool completely. Transfer to a serving plate and dust with powdered sugar.

52 ■ BROWN AND WHITE CHOCOLATE ROLL

YIELD: *12 to 16 servings*
BAKING TIME: *15 minutes*
CHILL TIME: *15 minutes*

FILLING

1 1/2 cups heavy cream
1 cup (6 ounces) white chocolate chips
6 ounces semisweet chocolate, grated or finely chopped
3 tablespoons coffee liqueur

CAKE ROLL

6 large eggs, separated
1/2 cup granulated sugar
1 teaspoon vanilla extract
1/4 cup powdered sugar for dusting
1 1/4 cups fresh strawberries, thinly sliced
Whole fresh strawberries for garnish

1 Position a rack in the center of the oven and preheat the oven to 350 degrees. Lightly grease a 17 1/2 by 11 1/2-inch jelly-roll pan. Line the pan with waxed paper and lightly grease the paper.

2 To make the fillings, in a saucepan, over a low heat, warm the cream until bubbles form around the edges. Remove from the heat. Add the white chocolate chips and stir until smooth. Set aside at room temperature.

3 Melt the semisweet chocolate (see page 13). Remove from the heat and add the liqueur all at once, whisking with a wire whisk until blended. Set aside at room temperature.

4 To make the cake, in a large bowl, using an electric mixer on high speed, beat the egg whites until stiff but not dry.

5 In another large bowl, using an electric mixer on medium speed, beat the egg yolks until they are thick and light-colored. Beat in the granulated sugar. Beat in the vanilla. Fold in the egg whites. Scrape the mixture into the prepared pan and spread evenly.

6 Bake for 12 to 15 minutes, or until set and a cake tester inserted into the center comes out clean. Cover with a damp, not wet, cloth and cool on a wire rack for 15 minutes

7 On a flat surface, place two 20-inch strips of waxed paper, overlapping 1 inch in the center. Dust the powdered sugar over the paper. Invert the cake onto the powdered sugar. Remove the pan and peel the waxed paper off the bottom of the cake.

8 With an electric mixer on high speed, beat the white chocolate mixture until smooth. On high speed, beat the dark chocolate mixture until smooth.

52

54

9 To assemble, spread an even layer of the white chocolate over the cake, leaving a ½-inch border around the edges. Carefully spread the dark chocolate mixture over the top of the white chocolate. Place a layer of the sliced strawberries over the top of the dark chocolate layer. Starting with one of the long sides, carefully lift the cake edge up with the waxed paper, and roll up the cake jelly-roll fashion. Place the cake seam-side down on a serving platter and chill for 15 minutes, or until ready to serve. Garnish with the whole strawberries.

BAKING NOTES: This is a great dessert to serve to guests. For a variation, spread an even layer of Ganache I (see page 410) on the platter before placing the roll on it. Then frost the top and ends of the roll. Fill a pastry bag with additional ganache and pipe large rosettes around the bottom edges of the roll. Garnish with chocolate-covered strawberries, chocolate leaves, and sliced strawberries.

53 ▪ BROWNIE PEANUT BUTTER CHEESECAKE

YIELD: *16 servings*
BAKING TIME: *47 minutes*
CHILL TIME: *Overnight*

CRUST

3½ ounces semisweet chocolate, grated or finely chopped
¼ cup butter or margarine
½ cup all-purpose flour
⅛ teaspoon baking powder
2 large eggs
1 cup packed light brown sugar
1½ teaspoons chocolate extract

FILLING

12 ounces cream cheese, at room temperature
1 cup packed light brown sugar
3 large eggs
½ cup sour cream or yogurt
1⅓ cups creamy peanut butter

TOPPING

¾ cup sour cream or yogurt
2 teaspoons granulated sugar

½ cup creamy peanut butter
Small apricot roses for garnish (see page 420)

1 Position a rack in the center of the oven and preheat the oven to 350 degrees. Lightly grease and flour a 9 or 10-inch springform pan.

2 To make the crust, in the top of a double boiler over simmering water, melt 3 ounces of the chocolate and the butter, stirring until smooth. Remove from the heat.

3 Combine the flour and baking powder

4 In a medium bowl, using an electric mixer on medium speed, beat the eggs until thick and light-colored. Beat in the brown sugar until well blended. Beat in the melted chocolate, chocolate extract, and remaining ½ ounce grated chocolate. Gradually stir in the dry ingredients, mixing just until blended. Spread 1 cup evenly onto the bottom of the prepared pan. Chill the remaining crust mixture.

5 Bake for 15 to 17 minutes, or until firm. Cool in the pan in the refrigerator for 15 to 30 minutes.

6 Meanwhile, to make the filling, in a large bowl, using an electric mixer on medium speed, beat the cream cheese and brown sugar until smooth. Beat in the eggs and sour cream. Beat in the peanut butter.

7 To prepare the pan, use a spatula to spread the remaining chilled crust mixture evenly around the insides of the pan. To make this easier, set the pan on its side and roll it, spreading at the same time. Pour in the filling mixture.

8 Bake 25 to 30 minutes, or until the filling is firm, spreading the topping on the cheesecake about 3 minutes before removing from the oven.

9 Meanwhile, to prepare the topping, in a small bowl, using an electric mixer on medium speed, mix the sour cream, sugar, and peanut butter until smooth. Spread evenly over the top of the cake in the oven 2 to 3 minutes before it is removed.

Cool on a wire rack for 1 hour. Place in a plastic or paper bag and chill overnight.

10 Remove the side of the pan and garnish with the small apricot roses. Cut the cake into narrow wedges and serve.

54 ▪ BROWNSTONE CHOCOLATE CAKE

YIELD: *10 to 12 servings*
BAKING TIME: *60 minutes*

2 ounces unsweetened chocolate, grated or finely chopped
1 cup boiling water
1 teaspoon amaretto
2 cups all-purpose flour
1 teaspoon baking soda
¼ teaspoon salt
3 large eggs
½ cup sour cream or yogurt
¼ cup butter or margarine, at room temperature
1¾ cups packed light brown sugar
1⅔ cups Custard Filling (see page 409)
¾ cup Strawberry Glaze (see page 416)
Sliced fresh strawberries or chocolate-dipped strawberries for garnish

1 Position a rack in the center of the oven and preheat the oven to 350 degrees. Lightly grease and flour a 9 by 5-inch loaf pan.

2 In a small bowl, combine the chocolate and boiling water, stirring until chocolate is melted and smooth. Add the amaretto.

3 Combine the flour, baking soda, and salt.

4 In a medium bowl, using an electric mixer on medium speed, beat the eggs, sour cream, and chocolate mixture until smooth.

5 In a large bowl, using an electric mixer on medium-high speed, beat the butter and brown sugar until fluffy. In three additions, mix in the dry ingredients, alternating with the chocolate mixture, beginning and ending with the dry ingredients. Scrape the mixture into the prepared pan and spread evenly.

6 Bake for 55 to 60 minutes, or until a cake tester inserted into the center comes out clean. Cool completely in the pan on a wire rack.

7 Make the custard filling and strawberry glaze.

8 To assemble, using a serrated knife, slice the cake in half horizontally. Place the bottom layer on a serving platter and spread with the custard filling. Top with the second layer and pour strawberry glaze over the top. Garnish with the sliced strawberries or strawberries dipped in chocolate.

55 ■ BUTTERCREAM RIBBON CHOCOLATE FUDGE CAKE

YIELD: *12 to 15 servings*
BAKING TIME: *60 minutes*

FILLING

8 ounces cream cheese, at room temperature
¼ cup granulated sugar
1 large egg
3 tablespoons milk
2 tablespoons butter or margarine, at room temperature
1 tablespoon cornstarch
½ teaspoon vanilla extract

CAKE

4 ounces unsweetened chocolate, grated or finely chopped
2 cups all-purpose flour
1 teaspoon baking powder
½ teaspoon baking soda
¼ teaspoon salt
½ cup butter or margarine, at room temperature
2 cups granulated sugar
2 large eggs
1⅓ cups milk
1 teaspoon chocolate extract
1½ cups Chocolate Buttercream (see page 395)

1 Position a rack in the center of the oven and preheat the oven to 350 degrees. Lightly grease a 13 by 9-inch pan.

2 To make the filling, in a medium bowl, using an electric mixer on medium-high speed, beat the cream cheese, sugar, and egg until smooth. Beat in the milk, butter, cornstarch, and vanilla extract. Set aside.

3 Melt the chocolate (see page 13). Remove from the heat.

4 To make the cake, combine the flour, baking powder, baking soda, and salt.

5 In a large bowl, using an electric mixer on medium-high speed, beat the butter and sugar until light and fluffy. Beat in the eggs, one at a time. Beat in the melted chocolate. Beat in the milk and chocolate extract. Gradually blend in the dry ingredients. Spread half of this chocolate evenly on the bottom of the prepared pan. Spread filling mixture over the top. Spread the remaining half of the chocolate mixture over the filling.

6 Bake for 55 to 60 minutes, or until a cake tester inserted into the center comes out clean. Cool completely in the pan.

7 Make the frosting.

8 Spread the frosting over the top of the cake.

BAKING NOTES: For a more decorative touch, invert the cake onto a wire rack to cool. Transfer to a serving platter and frost the top and sides. Garnish with fruit and candies.

56 ■ CARAMEL FUDGE CAKE

YIELD: *12 to 15 servings*
BAKING TIME: *45 minutes*

CARAMEL FILLING

1 package (14 ounces) caramels
½ cup butter or margarine
1 can (14 ounces) sweetened condensed milk
1 cup chopped pecans

FUDGE CAKE

2 cups all-purpose flour
1 teaspoon ground cinnamon
½ teaspoon salt
1 cup water
¼ cup buttermilk
1 teaspoon baking soda
½ cup butter or margarine
½ cup canola oil
¼ cup Dutch processed cocoa powder
2 large eggs
2 cups granulated sugar
1 teaspoon vanilla or almond extract

1 Position a rack in the center of the oven and preheat the oven to 350 degrees. Lightly grease and flour a 13 by 9-inch pan.

2 To make the filling, in a saucepan over low heat, melt the caramels and butter. Remove from the heat and stir in the condensed milk until well blended.

3 To make the cake, combine the flour, cinnamon, and salt.

4 In a small bowl combine the water, buttermilk, and baking soda.

5 In a small saucepan, over low heat, combine the butter, oil, and cocoa powder, stirring until smooth. Remove from the heat and cool slightly.

6 In a large bowl, using an electric mixer on medium speed, beat the eggs and sugar. Beat in the vanilla extract and cocoa mixture. In three additions, blend in the dry ingredients, alternating with the buttermilk, beginning and ending with the dry ingredients. Spread one-half of the batter into the prepared baking pan.

7 Bake for 15 minutes. Remove from the oven. Immediately spread the caramel filling over the top. Spread the remaining cake batter on top of the caramel.

8 Bake for 30 minutes, or until a cake tester inserted into the top half of the cake comes out clean. Cool in the pan on a wire rack. Cut into squares.

55

BAKING NOTES: For a festive occasion, serve with Raspberry Sauce (see page 416).

57 ■ CHERRY CHOCOLATE CAKE

YIELD: *12 to 15 servings*
BAKING TIME: *40 minutes*

2 cups all-purpose flour
1 package (3.4 ounces) chocolate instant pudding mix
1 tablespoon baking powder
½ teaspoon salt
4 large egg whites
½ cup butter or margarine, at room temperature
1¼ cups granulated sugar
1 cup evaporated milk
1 can (21 ounces) cherry pie filling
1¼ cups Mocha Whipped Cream Frosting (see page 414)

1 Position a rack in the center of the oven and preheat the oven to 350 degrees. Lightly grease a 13 by 9-inch pan.

2 Combine the flour, pudding mix, baking powder, and salt.

3 In a medium bowl, using an electric mixer on medium-high speed, beat the egg whites until they form soft peaks.

4 In a large bowl, using an electric mixer on high speed, beat the together the butter and sugar until light and fluffy. Beat in the milk. Gradually blend in the dry ingredients. Fold in the cherry pie filling. Fold in the beaten egg whites. Pour the mixture into the prepared pan.

5 Bake for 35 to 40 minutes, or until cake springs back when gently touched. The cake will look dry. Cool in the pan on a wire rack.

6 Make the frosting. Spread the frosting over the top of the cake.

58 ■ CHOCOLATE ALMOND CAKE I

YIELD: *12 servings*
BAKING TIME: *25 minutes*
CHILL TIME: *1 hour*

CAKE

4 ounces unsweetened chocolate, grated or finely chopped
¼ cup butter or margarine
⅔ cup granulated sugar
½ cup whole almonds
3 tablespoons cornstarch or arrowroot
3 large eggs, separated
¼ teaspoon cream of tartar
2 tablespoons Grand Marnier

TOPPING

¾ cup heavy cream
1½ teaspoons granulated sugar
1½ teaspoons Grand Marnier
1½ ounces semisweet chocolate, grated or finely chopped
1½ teaspoons Cocoa Sugar for garnish (see page 407)

1 Position a rack in the center of the oven and preheat the oven to 350 degrees. Lightly grease a 9-inch round cake pan. Line bottom of pan with a round of waxed paper.

2 To make the cake, in the top of a double boiler over simmering water, melt the unsweetened chocolate and butter, stirring until smooth. Remove from the heat.

3 In a blender or food processor, grind the sugar and almonds. In a small bowl, combine the almond mixture and cornstarch. Stir in the melted chocolate.

4 In a small bowl, using an electric mixer, beat the egg whites and cream of tartar until stiff but not dry.

5 In a medium bowl, using an electric mixer on medium speed, beat the egg yolks until thick and light-colored. Beat in the Grand Marnier. Fold in the chocolate mixture, stirring just until blended. Fold in the beaten egg whites, stirring until no white streaks remain. Pour the mixture into the prepared pan.

6 Bake for 20 to 25 minutes, or until a cake tester inserted into the center comes out clean. Cool for 5 minutes in the pan on a wire rack. Invert onto the wire rack and remove the waxed paper. Invert the cake onto a serving platter and refrigerate for 30 minutes

7 Meanwhile, to make the topping, using an electric mixer on medium-high speed, whip the cream until it starts to thicken. Add the sugar and continue beating until firm peaks form. Fold in the Grand Marnier. Spread the whipped cream over the top and sides of the cake and sprinkle with cocoa sugar. Chill for 20 to 30 minutes before serving.

56

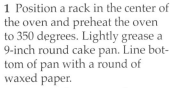

59 ■ CHOCOLATE ALMOND CAKE II

YIELD: *16 servings*
BAKING TIME: *35 minutes*

CHOCOLATE ALMOND CAKE

½ cup ground almonds
4 ounces semisweet chocolate, grated or finely chopped
2 ounces unsweetened chocolate, grated or finely chopped
½ cup butter or margarine
¼ cup heavy cream
5 large eggs, separated
1 cup powdered sugar
Pinch of salt
6 tablespoons amaretto
1 tablespoon instant espresso powder
1 tablespoon cornstarch
1 teaspoon almond extract

TOPPINGS

¾ cup brandy
½ cup seedless raspberry preserves
6 ounces semisweet chocolate, grated or finely chopped
¼ cup heavy cream
1 teaspoon instant espresso powder
3 tablespoons canola oil

1 Position a rack in the center of the oven and preheat the oven to 350 degrees. Lightly grease and flour a 10-inch springform pan. Line the bottom of the pan with waxed paper and grease the paper.

2 To make the cake, in a saucepan, over low heat, combine the almonds, chocolates, butter, and cream, stirring until smooth. Remove from the heat.

3 In a large bowl, using an electric mixer on medium-high speed, beat the egg yolks until thick and light-colored. Beat in ½ cup of the powdered sugar.

4 In another large bowl, using an electric mixer with clean beaters on high speed, beat the egg whites and salt until foamy. Add the remaining ½ cup powdered sugar and beat until stiff but not dry.

5 Gradually stir the chocolate mixture into the egg yolks. Stir in the amaretto, espresso powder, cornstarch, and almond extract. Fold in one-third of the whites and then fold all of the mixture into the egg whites.

Scrape the mixture into the prepared pan and spread evenly.

6 Bake for 35 minutes, or until a cake tester inserted into the center of the cake comes out slightly moist. Cool in the pan on a wire rack for 10 minutes. Invert onto a serving plate and remove the waxed paper.

7 For the toppings, in a small saucepan, warm the brandy. Pour evenly over the top of the cake.

8 In the saucepan, warm the preserves slightly. Spread in a thin layer over the center of the top of the cake.

9 In the top of a double boiler over simmering water, melt the chocolate with the cream and espresso powder, stirring constantly until smooth. Stir in the oil. Spoon the mixture over the area without preserves around the edge of the cake and let the excess drip down the sides to form a pool around the base of the cake.

60 ■ CHOCOLATE ALMOND TEA CAKE

YIELD: *16 servings*
BAKING TIME: *55 minutes*

1 cup cake flour, sifted twice
1 cup (6 ounces) semisweet chocolate chips
¾ cup (4 ounces) ground almonds
⅓ cup granulated sugar
1 tablespoon finely grated orange zest
1 teaspoon baking powder
½ teaspoon ground cardamom
½ cup butter or margarine, at room temperature
½ cup packed light brown sugar
1 large egg yolk plus 3 large eggs
¾ teaspoon almond extract
2 tablespoons heavy cream
3 tablespoons powdered sugar for garnish
1 cup sliced almonds for garnish

1 Position a rack in the center of the oven and preheat the oven to 325 degrees. Grease and flour a 10-inch springform pan.

2 Combine the flour, chocolate chips, almonds, granulated sugar, orange zest, baking powder, and cardamom.

3 In a large bowl, using an electric mixer on medium-high speed, beat the butter and brown sugar until smooth and fluffy. Beat in the egg yolk and almond extract. Beat in the whole eggs, one at a time. In three additions blend in the dry ingredients, alternating with the cream, beginning and ending with the dry ingredients. Scrape the mixture into the prepared pan and spread evenly.

4 Bake for 50 to 55 minutes, or until a cake tester inserted into the center comes out clean. Cool in the pan on a wire rack for 5 minutes. Remove the sides of the pan. Dust the top with powdered sugar and sprinkle with sliced almonds. Serve warm or at room temperature.

BAKING NOTES: While this cake does not require any additional garnish, edible flowers will add color and enhance its appearance for special occasions.

61 ■ CHOCOLATE AMARETTO CAKE

YIELD: *16 servings*
BAKING TIME: *40 minutes*

1 box (18½ ounces) German chocolate cake mix
1 cup sour cream or chocolate-flavored yogurt
½ cup butter or margarine, at room temperature
½ cup amaretto
3 large eggs
1 cup (6 ounces) semisweet chocolate chips
1 cup Apricot Glaze (see page 394)
1 recipe Chocolate Whipped Cream (see page 406)

1 Position a rack in the center of the oven and preheat the oven to 350 degrees. Lightly grease and flour a 10-inch Bundt pan.

2 In a large bowl, using an electric mixer on medium speed, beat the cake mix, sour cream, butter, amaretto, and eggs until smooth. Fold in the chocolate chips. Pour the mixture into the prepared pan.

3 Bake for 35 to 40 minutes, or until a cake tester inserted into the center comes out clean. Cool in the pan on a wire rack for 10 minutes. Invert onto the rack to cool completely.

4 Meanwhile, make the apricot glaze. Drizzle over the top of the cake, allowing the excess to drip down the sides. Serve with chocolate whipped cream on the side.

62 ■ CHOCOLATE AMARETTO CHEESECAKE

YIELD: *12 servings*
BAKING TIME: *90 minutes*
CHILL TIME: *overnight*

1 recipe Chocolate Cookie Crumb Crust (see page 267)
4 ounces unsweetened chocolate, grated or finely chopped
4 ounces semisweet chocolate, grated or finely chopped
2 tablespoons amaretto
1 1/2 tablespoons instant espresso powder
1 teaspoon almond extract
24 ounces cream cheese, at room temperature
1 cup sugar
3 large eggs
1 1/2 cups sour cream or chocolate-flavored yogurt
Fresh mint sprigs and chocolate curls for garnish

1 Make the chocolate wafer cookie crumb crust. Press into the bottom and halfway up the sides of a 9-inch springform pan. Chill until ready to use.

2 Melt the chocolates (see page 13). Remove from the heat.

3 In a cup, combine the amaretto, espresso powder, and almond extract.

4 In a medium bowl, using an electric mixer on medium speed, beat the cream cheese until smooth. Add the sugar and eggs, beating well until smooth. Beat in the melted chocolate. Stir in the amaretto mixture. Fold in the sour cream. Carefully pour the mixture into the prepared pan.

5 Bake for 60 minutes. Turn off the oven and leave the cheesecake undisturbed with the oven door slightly open for 30 minutes. Cool in the pan on a wire rack. Chill over night. Remove the side of the pan and garnish with mint sprigs and chocolate curls.

63 ■ CHOCOLATE AMBROSIA CAKE

YIELD: *12 servings*
BAKING TIME: *25 minutes*

2 cups cake flour
1 1/2 teaspoons baking powder
1/2 teaspoon baking soda
3 ounces unsweetened chocolate, grated or finely chopped
1/2 cup butter-flavored vegetable shortening
1 1/4 cups packed dark brown sugar
1 teaspoon Ambrosia liqueur
2 large eggs
1 cup milk
1 1/2 cups Cocoa Honey Frosting (see page 407)

1 Position a rack in the center of the oven and preheat the oven to 350 degrees. Lightly grease and flour two 8 or 9-inch round cake pans.

2 Combine the flour, baking powder, and baking soda. Sift two times.

3 Melt the chocolate (see page 13). Remove from the heat.

4 In a large bowl, using an electric mixer on high speed, beat the vegetable shortening and brown sugar until fluffy and smooth. Beat in the liqueur. On low speed beat in the eggs, one at a time, beating well after each addition. By hand stir in the melted chocolate. In three additions blend in the dry ingredients, alternating with the milk, beginning and ending with the dry ingredients. Pour the batter into the prepared pans.

5 Bake for 20 to 25 minutes, or until a cake tester inserted into the center comes out clean. Cool in the pan on a wire rack for 10 minutes. Invert onto the rack to cool completely.

6 Make the frosting.

7 To assemble, place one of the cake layers on a serving plate. Spread evenly with some of the frosting and top with the second layer. Spread frosting on the top and sides of the cake.

62

63

CAKES ■ 48

64 ■ CHOCOLATE ANGEL FOOD CAKE I

YIELD: *16 servings*
BAKING TIME: *65 minutes*

CAKE

1¾ cups granulated sugar
1 cup cake flour
¼ cup Dutch processed cocoa
  powder
15 large egg whites (1½ cups)
½ teaspoon salt
1½ teaspoons cream of tartar
1 teaspoon coffee liqueur
¼ teaspoon chocolate extract

FROSTING

3 tablespoons powdered sugar
2 tablespoons Dutch processed
  cocoa powder
1 cup heavy cream
½ teaspoon crème de cacao
Chocolate Curls or Chocolate
  Leaves (see page 422) for garnish

1 Position a rack in the center of the oven and preheat the oven to 325 degrees.

2 To make the cake, in a medium bowl, combine the sugar, cake flour, and cocoa powder. Sift two times.

64

3 In a large bowl, using an electric mixer on high speed, beat the egg whites and salt until foamy. Sprinkle the cream of tartar over the top and continue beating until stiff but not dry. Fold in the dry ingredients, blending until just mixed. Fold in the coffee liqueur and chocolate extract. Scrape the mixture into an ungreased 10-inch tube pan, and spread evenly.

4 Bake for 60 to 65 minutes, or until a cake tester inserted into the center comes out clean. Invert the pan onto a wire rack or stand it on its tube and cool completely. Remove the cake from the pan and place on a serving plate.

5 Meanwhile, to make the frosting, combine the powdered sugar and cocoa powder.

6 In a medium bowl, using an electric mixer on medium-high speed, beat the cream to soft peaks. Fold in the dry ingredients. Fold in the crème de cacao. Chill well before using.

7 Place the cake on a serving plate and spread the chocolate whipped cream frosting over the entire cake and garnish with chocolate curls or chocolate leaves.

BAKING NOTES: The cake can also be split into layers and filled. Using a serrated knife, cut the cake horizontally into three layers. Use the chocolate whipped cream as a filling and sprinkle cocoa sugar over the top (see page 407).

66

65 ■ CHOCOLATE ANGEL FOOD CAKE II

YIELD: *16 servings*
BAKING TIME: *60 minutes*

¾ cup cake flour
¼ cup Dutch processed cocoa
  powder
13 large egg whites
1¼ cups granulated sugar
1 teaspoon cream of tartar
1 teaspoon vanilla extract
1 tablespoon powdered sugar for
  dusting

1 Position a rack in the center of the oven and preheat the oven to 350 degrees.

2 In a small bowl, combine the cake flour and cocoa powder. Sift two times.

3 In a large bowl, with an electric mixer on medium speed, beat the egg whites until foamy. Beat in the sugar, cream of tartar, and vanilla and whip until stiff but not dry. Gradually fold in the dry ingredients, mixing only until blended. Pour the batter into a 10-inch ungreased tube pan and spread evenly.

4 Bake for 55 to 60 minutes, or until a cake tester inserted into the center comes out clean. Invert the pan on its tube or onto the legs on the pan. Cool completely in the pan.

5 Remove the cake from the pan and place on a serving platter. Dust with the powdered sugar.

67

66 ■ CHOCOLATE APPLE CAKE

YIELD: *12 to 15 servings*
BAKING TIME: *35 minutes*

3/4 cup milk
1 1/2 teaspoons baking soda
1 cup all-purpose flour
1 cup whole wheat flour
1/4 cup Dutch processed cocoa powder
1 1/2 teaspoons ground cinnamon
3/4 teaspoon ground cloves
3/4 teaspoon ground nutmeg
1/8 teaspoon salt
1 1/2 cups granulated sugar
2 large eggs
2 cups finely chopped apples
1/2 cup chopped walnuts
3/4 cup chopped raisins
1 recipe Chocolate Rum Sauce (see page 404)

1 Position a rack in the center of the oven and preheat the oven to 350 degrees. Lightly grease and flour a 13 by 9-inch pan.

2 In a cup, combine the milk and baking soda.

3 Combine the flours, cocoa powder, spices, and salt.

4 In a medium bowl, using an electric mixer on high speed, beat the sugar and eggs until sugar is dissolved. Beat in the eggs. Beat in the milk mixture. Gradually blend in the dry ingredients. Fold in the apples, walnuts, and raisins. Scrape the mixture into the prepared pan and spread evenly.

5 Bake for 30 to 35 minutes, or until a cake tester inserted into the center comes out clean. Cool in the pan on a wire rack.

6 Make the chocolate rum sauce. Spread the sauce on the top of the cake. Cut into squares.

BAKING NOTES: For a festive occasion, garnish each serving with a strawberry half and mint sprig.

67 ■ CHOCOLATE BANANA CAKE I

YIELD: *16 servings*
BAKING TIME: *60 minutes*

1 1/4 cups all-purpose flour
1/2 cup Dutch processed cocoa powder
1 teaspoon baking powder
1/2 teaspoon baking soda
1/4 teaspoon salt
1 banana, diced
1 tablespoon finely grated orange zest
2 large eggs
1 cup mashed bananas (3 large)
1 teaspoon mocha-flavored instant coffee powder
1/2 cup butter or margarine, at room temperature
1 cup packed dark brown sugar
1 tablespoon Cocoa Sugar (see page 407)

1 Position a rack in the center of the oven and preheat the oven to 325 degrees. Lightly grease and flour a 10-inch fluted tube pan.

2 Combine the flour, cocoa powder, baking powder, baking soda, salt, diced banana, and orange zest.

3 In a medium bowl, using an electric mixer on low speed, beat the eggs and mashed bananas, mixing until smooth. Beat in the coffee powder.

4 In a large bowl, using an electric mixer on high speed, beat the butter and brown sugar until smooth. In three additions, blend in the dry ingredients alternating with the egg mixture, beginning and ending with the dry ingredients. Blend only until the dry ingredients are incorporated. Scrape the mixture into the pan and spread evenly.

5 Bake for 60 to 65 minutes, or until a cake tester inserted into the center comes out clean. The cake will feel firm to the touch in the center. Cool in the pan on a wire rack. Invert onto the rack and cool completely.

6 Place cake on a serving plate and dust with cocoa sugar.

68 ■ CHOCOLATE BANANA CAKE II

YIELD: *8 to 10 servings*
BAKING TIME: *60 minutes*

1/2 cup chocolate wafer cookie crumbs
2 3/4 cups all-purpose flour
1 1/4 teaspoons baking soda
1/2 teaspoon salt
1 cup butter or margarine, melted
1 cup granulated sugar
1/2 cup packed light brown sugar
2 large eggs
3 tablespoons crème de banana
1 teaspoon banana extract
2 cups (6 large) mashed bananas
1 cup (6 ounces) semisweet chocolate chips
1 cup walnuts, chopped
1 cup flaked coconut

1 Position a rack in the center of the oven and preheat the oven to 350 degrees. Grease two 8 by 3-inch loaf pans. Sprinkle with the cookie crumbs.

2 Combine the flour, baking soda, and salt.

3 In a large bowl, using an electric mixer on medium speed, beat together the melted butter and sugars. Beat in the eggs, one at a time. Beat in the crème de banana and banana extract. Beat on high speed for 3 minutes, or until smooth. Beat in the bananas. Gradually blend in the dry ingredients. Stir in the chocolate chips, walnuts, and coconut. Divide the mixture between the prepared pans and spread evenly.

4 Bake for 55 to 60 minutes, or until a cake tester inserted into the center comes out clean. Cool in the pans on wire racks for 15 minutes. Invert onto wire racks to cool completely.

BAKING NOTES: This cake does not require a frosting or topping. If you wish to have something on the top try Chocolate-Almond Sauce I (see page 395) or Raspberry Sauce (see page 416).

69 ▪ CHOCOLATE BANANA ICEBOX CAKE

YIELD: *12 servings*
CHILL TIME: *2 hours*

PUDDING

2 cups milk
¾ cup granulated sugar
2½ tablespoons cornstarch
1 large egg, lightly beaten
2 ounces unsweetened chocolate, grated or finely chopped
1 teaspoon chocolate syrup

ASSEMBLY

16 graham crackers
4 ripe medium bananas, thinly sliced

1 To make the pudding, in a heavy medium saucepan, mix the milk, sugar, and cornstarch. Heat, stirring constantly, until the mixture boils. Reduce the heat to low.

2 Place the egg in a cup and beat in 2 tablespoons of the hot milk mixture. Mix in the grated chocolate. Add the egg mixture to the hot milk mixture in the pan and blend thoroughly. Remove from the heat and stir in the chocolate syrup. Cool slightly before using.

3 To assemble, place a of layer the graham crackers in the bottom of an 8-inch square pan, place a layer of bananas on top, and spoon a thin layer of the chocolate pudding on top of the bananas. Repeat the layering until all the graham crackers and bananas have been used. Pour the remaining chocolate over the top and chill in the refrigerator for 2 hours before serving.

BAKING NOTES: One box (3.4 ounces) chocolate instant pudding can be substituted for the pudding recipe given here. Garnish the top with crushed graham crackers and sliced bananas before chilling, if desired.

70 ▪ CHOCOLATE BANANA LOAF

YIELD: *10 to 12 servings*
BAKING TIME: *70 minutes*

2 cups cake flour
1½ teaspoons baking powder
½ teaspoon baking soda
Pinch of salt
½ cup butter or margarine, at room temperature
1⅔ cups granulated sugar
2 large eggs, beaten
¼ cup sour cream
1 cup mashed bananas (3 large)
1 teaspoon chocolate extract
2 cups (12 ounces) semisweet chocolate chips
Cocoa Sugar for dusting (see page 407)

1 Position a rack in the center of the oven and preheat the oven to 350 degrees. Lightly grease a 9 by 5-inch loaf pan.

2 Combine the flour, baking powder, baking soda, and salt.

3 In a large bowl, using an electric mixer on high speed, beat the butter and sugar until light and fluffy. Beat in the eggs and sour cream. Stir in the bananas and chocolate extract. Gradually blend in the dry ingredients, mixing just until moistened. Fold in the chocolate chips. Pour the mixture into the prepared pan.

4 Bake for 60 to 70 minutes, or until a cake tester inserted into the center comes out clean. Cool in the pan on a wire rack for 10 minutes. Invert onto the wire rack to cool completely. Dust with the cocoa sugar and serve.

BAKING NOTES: Serve with chocolate whipped cream (see page 406) on the side, if desired.

71 ■ CHOCOLATE BAR CAKE

YIELD: *16 servings*
BAKING TIME: *90 minutes*

8 ounce milk chocolate candy bar, grated or finely chopped
½ cup chocolate syrup
2½ cups all-purpose flour
¾ teaspoon baking soda
Pinch of salt
5 large eggs
1 cup (2 sticks) butter or margarine, at room temperature
2 cups granulated sugar
1 teaspoon hazelnut extract or liqueur
1½ cups chocolate-flavored yogurt
¼ cup honey
¾ cup chopped pecans

1 Position a rack in the lower half of the oven and preheat the oven to 350 degrees. Lightly grease and flour a 10-inch tube pan.

2 In a small saucepan over a low heat, melt the chocolate candy bar with the chocolate syrup, stirring until smooth. Remove from the heat.

3 Combine the flour, baking soda, and salt.

4 In a medium bowl, using an electric mixer on medium-high speed, beat the eggs until thick and light-colored.

5 In a large bowl, using an electric mixer, beat the butter and sugar until fluffy. Beat in the hazelnut extract. Beat in the eggs. In three additions, blend in the dry ingredients, alternating with the yogurt, beginning and ending with the dry ingredients. Stir in the honey and pecans. Add 2 cups of the batter to the candy bar mixture and stir until combined.

6 Pour the chocolate batter into the prepared pan. Pour the remaining light batter on top.

7 Bake for 40 minutes. Reduce the oven temperature to 325 degrees and bake for 45 to 50 minutes, or until a cake tester inserted into the top portion of the cake comes out clean. Cool in the pan on a wire rack. Transfer to a serving plate. Cover with Chocolate Glaze II (see page 401) and garnish with fresh edible flowers.

BAKING NOTES: The flavor of this cake can be varied greatly by using various flavored extracts in the light cake portion. A drop or two of mint or peppermint extract or oil added to the chocolate portion will also enhance the flavor.

72 ■ CHOCOLATE BLACK BEAN CAKE

YIELD: *16 servings*
BAKING TIME: *45 minutes*

CAKE

1 cup butter-flavored vegetable shortening
8 ounces unsweetened chocolate, grated or finely chopped
2 cups cooked black beans
½ cup crème de cacao
5 large eggs
1 cup granulated sugar
1 teaspoon chocolate extract
1 cup all-purpose flour

GLAZE

2 tablespoons butter
2 ounces semisweet chocolate, grated or finely chopped
1 cup powdered sugar
1 tablespoon boiling water

1 Position a rack in the center of the oven and preheat the oven to 325 degrees. Grease and flour a 10-inch Bundt pan.

2 To make the cake, in a saucepan, over low heat, melt the shortening and unsweetened chocolate, stirring until smooth. Remove from the heat.

3 In the container of a blender, combine the black beans and crème de cacao and puree until they form a smooth paste.

4 In a large bowl, using an electric mixer on high speed, beat the eggs until thick and light-colored. On low speed, beat in the sugar. By hand, whisk in the melted chocolate mixture and pureed beans. Mix in the extract. Gradually mix in the flour just until blended. Scrape the batter into the prepared pan and spread evenly.

5 Bake for 40 to 45 minutes, or until a cake tester inserted into the center comes out clean. Cool in the pan on a wire rack for 30 minutes. Invert onto a serving plate.

6 Meanwhile, to make the chocolate glaze, in the top of a double boiler, over simmering water, melt the butter and semisweet chocolate, stirring until smooth. Add the powdered sugar and water and stir until smooth. Cool slightly. Pour the glaze in a thin stream over the top of the cake, allowing the excess glaze to run down the sides.

BAKING NOTES: For a variation, substitute coffee liqueur or any fruit-flavored brandy for the crème de cacao.

73 ■ CHOCOLATE BLISS

YIELD: *12 servings*
BAKING TIME: *30 minutes*

1¼ cups all-purpose flour
½ teaspoon baking soda
¼ teaspoon salt
⅓ cup canola oil
1 cup granulated sugar
2 envelopes pre-melted unsweetened chocolate
1 large egg
½ teaspoon vanilla or chocolate extract
¾ cup water
1 cup (6 ounces) semisweet chocolate chips

1 Position a rack in the center of the oven and preheat the oven to 350 degrees. Lightly grease and flour a 9-inch square pan.

2 Combine the flour, baking soda, and salt.

3 In a large bowl, with a wire whisk, beat the oil, sugar, chocolate, egg, vanilla extract, and water until smooth. Gradually blend in the dry ingredients. Spread the mixture evenly in the prepared pan.

4 Bake for 25 to 30 minutes, or until a cake tester inserted into the center comes out clean.

5 Spread the chocolate chips over the hot cake and when melted use a metal spatula to smooth out.

6 Cool in the pan on a wire rack. Cut into squares.

74 ■ CHOCOLATE BUTTER CAKE

YIELD: *12 servings*
BAKING TIME: *35 minutes*

CAKE

3 ounces unsweetened chocolate, grated or finely chopped
2 cups all-purpose flour
1 teaspoon baking powder
¼ teaspoon cream of tartar
½ teaspoon salt
½ cup butter, at room temperature
1⅓ cups granulated sugar
2 large eggs
¾ cup sour cream
1 teaspoon vanilla extract

74

73

FILLING AND FROSTING

2 cups powdered sugar
1 cup vegetable shortening
1 teaspoon chocolate syrup
1½ cups Chocolate Rum Icing (see page 404)

1 Position a rack in the center of the oven and preheat the oven to 350 degrees. Lightly grease and flour two 9-inch round cake pans.

2 To make the cake, melt the chocolate (see page 13). Remove from the heat.

3 Combine the flour, baking powder, cream of tartar, and salt.

4 In a large bowl, using an electric mixer on high speed, beat the butter and sugar until light and fluffy. Beat in the eggs. Beat in the sour cream and vanilla extract. Beat in the melted chocolate. Gradually stir in the dry ingredients. Divide the mixture evenly between the prepared pans.

5 Bake for 30 to 35 minutes, or until a cake tester inserted into the center comes out clean. Cool in the pans on wire racks for 10 minutes. Invert onto the racks to cool completely.

6 To make the filling, in a medium bowl, using an electric mixer on medium speed, beat the powdered sugar, shortening, and chocolate syrup until smooth and spreadable.

7 Make the icing.

8 To assemble, place one cake layer on a serving plate and spread evenly with the filling. Place the second layer on top and frost the top and sides of the cake with the icing.

75 ■ CHOCOLATE BUTTERMILK CAKE

YIELD: *12 servings*
BAKING TIME: *45 minutes*

4 ounces unsweetened chocolate, grated or finely chopped
2 cups all-purpose flour
1½ teaspoons baking soda
Pinch of salt
1 cup butter or margarine, at room temperature
1¾ cups granulated sugar
4 large eggs
1⅓ cups buttermilk or sour milk
1 teaspoon chocolate extract or crème de cacao
1½ cups Chocolate Buttercream (see page 395)
Grated chocolate or chocolate curls for garnish (see page 422)

1 Preheat the oven 325 degrees. Lightly grease and flour two 9-inch round cake pans.

2 Melt the chocolate (see page 13). Remove from the heat.

3 Combine the flour, baking soda, and salt.

4 In a large bowl, using an electric mixer on high speed, beat the butter and sugar until fluffy. Mix in the eggs, one at a time, beating well after each addition. In three additions, blend in the dry ingredients, alternating with the buttermilk, beginning and ending with the dry ingredients. Stir in the melted chocolate and chocolate extract. Divide the mixture evenly between the prepared pans.

5 Bake for 35 to 45 minutes, or until a cake tester inserted into the center comes out clean. Cool in the pans on wire racks for 5 minutes. Invert onto the racks and cool completely.

6 Make the frosting.

7 To assemble, place one cake layer on a serving plate. Spread with some of the buttercream and top with the second layer. Frost the tops and sides with the buttercream. Garnish with grated chocolate or chocolate curls.

BAKING NOTES: As a variation, use a serrated knife and slice each cake layer horizontally to make four layers. Place one layer on a plate and sread Chocolate Whipped Cream (see page 406) over the top. Sprinkle chopped chocolate or finely diced peaches or pears over the whipped cream. Place the second layer on top of the chocolate or diced fruit, and repeat the process. Build up the layers spreading the frosting over the top of the fourth layer.

76 ■ CHOCOLATE BUTTERMILK CUPCAKES

YIELD: *24 servings*
BAKING TIME: *20 minutes*

2 ounces semisweet chocolate, grated or finely chopped
2 ounces unsweetened chocolate, grated or finely chopped
2 cups all-purpose flour
1½ teaspoons baking soda
Pinch of salt
1 cup butter or margarine, at room temperature
1¾ cups granulated sugar
4 large eggs
1½ cups buttermilk
1½ teaspoons cherry extract or brandy
24 large maraschino cherries, drained and patted dry

1 Position a rack in the center of the oven and preheat the oven to 325 degrees. Lightly grease or line with paper baking cups twenty-four 2¾-inch muffin cups.

2 Melt the chocolates (see page 13). Remove from the heat.

3 Combine the flour, baking soda, and salt.

4 In a large bowl, using an electric mixer on high speed, beat the butter and sugar until fluffy. Beat in the eggs, one at a time, beating well after each addition. In three additions, blend in the dry ingredients, alternating with the buttermilk, beginning and ending with the dry ingredients. Stir in the cherry extract and melted chocolate. Spoon the mixture into the prepared muffin pans, filling each one about two-thirds full. Press a cherry deep into the center of each cupcake.

5 Bake for 15 to 20 minutes, or until a cake tester inserted into the center comes out clean. Cool in the pan on wire racks for 5 minutes. Transfer to the racks to cool completely.

77 ■ CHOCOLATE CAKE

YIELD: *12 to 15 servings*
BAKING TIME: *30 minutes*

2 ounces unsweetened chocolate, grated or finely chopped
2 cups all-purpose flour
1 teaspoon baking soda
1/2 teaspoon salt
1/2 cup butter-flavored shortening, melted
1 3/4 cups granulated sugar
2 large eggs
1 teaspoon coffee liqueur
1 cup buttermilk
1 3/4 cups Chocolate Fudge Frosting I (see page 400)

1 Position a rack in the center of the oven and preheat the oven to 350 degrees. Lightly grease a 13 by 9-inch pan.

2 Melt the chocolate (see page 13). Remove from the heat.

3 Combine the flour, baking soda, and salt.

4 In a large bowl, using an electric mixer on high speed, beat the vegetable shortening and sugar until fluffy and smooth. Beat in the melted chocolate. Beat in the eggs. Beat in the liqueur and buttermilk. Gradually stir in the dry ingredients. Pour the mixture into the prepared pan and spread evenly.

5 Bake for 25 to 30 minutes, or until a cake tester inserted into the center comes out clean. Cool in the pan on a wire rack.

6 Make the frosting.

7 Leave the cake in the pan and spread the frosting over the top or invert the cake onto a serving platter and frost the top and sides of the cake.

BAKING NOTES: Milk soured by adding 1 teaspoon of vinegar to 1 cup of milk can be used in place of the buttermilk.

78 ■ CHOCOLATE CAKE WITH LIQUEUR

YIELD: *12 to 15 servings*
BAKING TIME: *80 minutes*

3 cups all-purpose flour
4 teaspoons Dutch processed cocoa powder
1/2 teaspoon baking powder
1/4 teaspoon salt
1 cup vegetable shortening
3 cups granulated sugar
3 large eggs
2 teaspoons chocolate extract
2 teaspoons coffee liqueur
1 cup milk
2 1/2 cups Creamy Chocolate Frosting (see page 408)
Crushed Heath Bar™ candy for garnish

1 Position a rack in the center of the oven and preheat the oven to 325 degrees. Lightly grease a 13 by 9-inch baking pan.

2 Combine the flour, cocoa powder, baking powder, and salt.

3 In a large bowl, using an electric mixer on high speed, beat the vegetable shortening and sugar until light and fluffy. Mix

in the eggs, one at a time, beating well after each addition. Beat in the chocolate extract and liqueur. Beat in the milk. Gradually blend in the dry ingredients. Pour this mixture into the prepared pan.

4 Bake for 1 hour and 20 minutes, or until a cake tester inserted into the center comes out clean. Do not open the oven door for the first hour of baking. Cool the pan on a wire rack.

5 Make the frosting.

6 Frost the top of the cake with the frosting and garnish with the crushed candies.

79 ■ CHOCOLATE CAKE WITH SOUR CREAM

YIELD: *12 servings*
BAKING TIME: *50 minutes*

3/4 cup plus 2 tablespoons all-purpose flour
1 tablespoon Dutch processed cocoa powder
1 teaspoon baking powder
1/2 teaspoon baking soda
1/2 teaspoon salt
1 1/4 cups granulated sugar
2 large eggs, separated
2 ounces unsweetened chocolate, grated or finely chopped
1/3 cup boiling water
10 tablespoons butter or margarine, at room temperature
1/2 cup sour cream or chocolate-flavored yogurt
1 tablespoon chocolate extract
Chocolate Glaze IV (see page 401)

1 Position a rack in the center of the oven and preheat the oven to 375 degrees. Lightly grease an 8-inch springform pan. Line the bottom with waxed paper and grease the paper.

79

77

80

2 To make the cake, combine the flour, cocoa powder, baking powder, baking soda, and salt.

3 In a medium bowl, using an electric mixer on medium-high speed, beat the egg whites until stiff but not dry. Beat in 1/4 cup of the sugar.

4 In a large bowl, combine the chocolate and boiling water, stirring until smooth. Add the remaining 1 cup sugar and stir until dissolved. Using an electric mixer on medium speed beat in the egg yolks. Add the butter, sour cream, and chocolate extract and beat until well blended. Gradually fold in the dry ingredients, alternating with the egg whites, mixing just until blended. Do not overmix. Scrape the mixture into the prepared pan and smooth the top.

5 Bake for 45 to 50 minutes, or until a cake tester inserted into the center comes out clean. Cool in the pan on a wire rack. Remove the side of the pan and invert onto a plate.

6 Make the chocolate glaze. Spread the glaze evenly over the top and sides of the cake.

80 ■ CHOCOLATE CELEBRATION CAKE

YIELD: *12 servings*
BAKING TIME: *30 minutes*

CAKE

3 ounces unsweetened chocolate, grated or finely chopped
2 cups all-purpose flour
2 teaspoons baking powder
1/4 teaspoon salt
1/4 cup butter or margarine, at room temperature
2 cups granulated sugar
2 large eggs, separated
1 cup milk
1/4 cup heavy cream
2 teaspoons chocolate or vanilla extract

FILLING AND FROSTING

2 cups Coffee Mocha Icing (see page 408)
2 kiwifruits, peeled and thinly sliced, for filling and garnish
Chocolate Leaves (see page 422) for garnish

1 Position a rack in the center of the oven and preheat the oven to 350 degrees. Lightly grease three 9-inch round cake pans. Line the bottoms with waxed paper and grease the paper.

2 Melt the chocolate (see page 13). Remove from the heat.

3 Combine the flour, baking powder, and salt.

4 In a large bowl, using an electric mixer on medium speed, beat the butter and sugar until light and fluffy. Beat in the egg yolks, one at a time, beating well after each addition. Beat in the melted chocolate. In three additions, gradually stir in the dry ingredients, alternating with the milk and cream, beginning and ending with the dry ingredients.

5 In a medium bowl, using an electric mixer with clean beaters on high speed, beat the egg whites until stiff but not dry. Gently fold into the chocolate batter. Stir in the chocolate extract. Scrape the mixture into the prepared pans and spread evenly.

6 Bake for 25 to 30 minutes, or until a cake tester inserted into the center comes out clean. Cool in the pans on the wire racks for 15 minutes. Invert onto the racks to cool completely.

7 Make the icing.

8 To assemble, place one cake layer on a serving plate and spread with a thin layer of the icing. Arrange a ring of sliced kiwifruit on the icing. Top with the second cake layer, spread with icing, and top with more kiwifruit. Top with the remaining cake layer. Frost the top and sides of the cake with the icing. Garnish with kiwifruit and chocolate leaves.

BAKING NOTES: For a festive look, use a variety of thinly sliced fruit.

81 ■ CHOCOLATE CELEBRITY CAKE

YIELD: *12 servings*
BAKING TIME: *25 minutes*

CAKE

2 ounces unsweetened chocolate, grated or finely chopped
2 cups cake flour, sifted
1/2 teaspoon baking powder
1 teaspoon salt
1/2 cup butter or margarine, at room temperature
2 cups granulated sugar
1 teaspoon chocolate or vanilla extract
2 large eggs
3/4 cup water
3/4 cup milk

FILLING

1/2 cup powdered sugar
2 tablespoons cornstarch or arrowroot
1 tablespoon butter or margarine
Pinch of salt
1/2 cup water
2 cups (12 ounces) semisweet chocolate chips
1 ounce semisweet chocolate, grated or finely chopped

FROSTING

2 cups powdered sugar
1/2 cup butter or margarine
1 tablespoon light corn syrup
1 cup (6 ounces) semisweet chocolate chips
1 cup marshmallow creme
2 tablespoons milk
1 cup evaporated milk
Chocolate curls (see page 422) or lemon slices for garnish

1 Position a rack in the center of the oven and preheat the oven to 350 degrees. Lightly grease and flour two 9-inch round cake pans.

2 To make the cake, melt the chocolate (see page 13). Remove from the heat.

3 Combine the flour, baking powder, and salt.

4 In a large bowl, using an electric mixer on high speed, beat the butter and sugar. Beat in the melted chocolate and chocolate extract. Beat in the eggs. Beat in the water and milk. Gradually blend in the dry ingredients. Pour the mixture into the prepared pans.

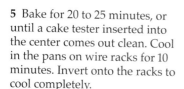

5 Bake for 20 to 25 minutes, or until a cake tester inserted into the center comes out clean. Cool in the pans on wire racks for 10 minutes. Invert onto the racks to cool completely.

6 Meanwhile, to make the filling, in a saucepan over medium heat, combine the powdered sugar, cornstarch, butter, salt, and water, stirring until smooth. Cook until the mixture thickens and starts to bubble. Remove from the heat and add the chocolate chips and grated chocolate, stirring until the mixture is thick and smooth. Chill for 30 to 45 minutes, or until thick.

7 Meanwhile, to make the frosting, in a medium saucepan over low heat, stir the powdered sugar, butter, and corn syrup until combined. Insert a candy thermometer and cook until the mixture reaches 236 degrees. Remove from the heat and add the chocolate chips, marshmallow creme, and milks, and beat until cooled and thick.

8 To assemble, trim the tops off the cake layers, and place one on a large serving plate. Spread the filling over the top and place the second layer on top. Spread the frosting over the top and sides of the cake and garnish with chocolate curls or lemon slices.

82 ∎ CHOCOLATE CELESTIAL CAKE

YIELD: *12 servings*
BAKING TIME: *35 minutes*

1¹/₂ cups all-purpose flour
1 cup granulated sugar
¹/₄ cup Dutch processed cocoa powder
1¹/₂ teaspoons baking powder
1 teaspoon baking soda
¹/₂ teaspoon salt
1 cup water
5 tablespoons canola oil
1 tablespoon white vinegar
1 teaspoon chocolate or vanilla extract

Chocolate Cream Cheese Frosting III (see page 397)
Unsweetened cocoa powder for dusting

1 Position a rack in the center of the oven and preheat the oven to 350 degrees. Lightly grease and flour an 8-inch square pan.

2 In a large bowl, combine the flour, sugar, cocoa powder, baking powder, baking soda, and salt. Make a well in the center and add, all at once, the water, oil, vinegar, and chocolate extract. Beat well until smooth. Pour the mixture into the prepared pan.

3 Bake for 30 to 35 minutes, or until a cake tester inserted into the center comes out clean. Cool in the pan on a wire rack for 5 minutes. Invert onto the rack to cool completely.

4 Meanwhile, make the frosting.

5 Place the cake on a serving plate. Spread the frosting on the top and sides of the cake and sprinkle with cocoa powder. Chill until ready to serve.

83 ∎ CHOCOLATE CRUMB SATISFACTION

YIELD: *16 servings*
BAKING TIME: *40 minutes*

¹/₃ cup all-purpose flour
1³/₄ cups sponge cake crumbs (see Baking notes)
³/₄ cup Dutch processed cocoa powder
8 large eggs, separated
Pinch of salt
²/₃ cup granulated sugar
1 tablespoon fresh lemon juice
Chocolate Whipped Cream (see page 406)
Sliced strawberries or whole raspberries for garnish

1 Position a rack in the center of the oven and preheat the oven to 350 degrees.

2 Combine the flour, cake crumbs, and cocoa powder

3 In a large bowl, using an electric mixer on high speed, beat the egg whites and salt until stiff but not dry.

4 In another large bowl, using an electric mixer on high speed, beat the sugar and egg yolks until thick and light-colored. Beat in the lemon juice. Gradu-

ally blend in the dry ingredients. Fold in the beaten egg whites. Pour the mixture into a 10-inch tube pan.

5 Bake for 35 to 40 minutes, or until a cake tester inserted into the center comes out clean. Cool in the pan on a wire rack for 10 minutes. Invert onto the tube on a cake rack to cool completely.

6 Make the frosting.

7 Place cake on a serving plate and frost with the chocolate whipped cream. Garnish with strawberries or raspberries.

BAKING NOTES: To make sponge cake crumbs: thinly slice sponge cake. Allow the slices to dry at room temperature for 24 to 36 hours. Crush or grind into crumbs. Ladyfinger crumbs or any soft cookie can be used in place of the sponge cake crumbs.

84 ∎ CHOCOLATE DELIGHT CAKE

YIELD: *12 servings*
BAKING TIME: *20 minutes*

1²/₃ cups all-purpose flour
1 cup granulated sugar
³/₄ cup Dutch processed cocoa powder
1¹/₂ teaspoons baking powder
1 teaspoon salt
1 cup buttermilk
¹/₂ cup butter or margarine, at room temperature
2 teaspoons crème de cacao or chocolate extract
1¹/₂ cups Custard Filling (see page 409)
Grand Marnier Sauce (see page 411)

1 Position a rack in the center of the oven and preheat the oven to 375 degrees. Lightly grease and flour two 9-inch round cake pans.

2 Combine the flour, sugar, cocoa powder, baking powder, and salt.

3 In a large bowl, using an electric mixer on medium speed, beat the buttermilk, butter, and crème de cacao until smooth. Gradually blend in the dry ingredients. Divide the mixture between the prepared pans.

4 Bake for 18 to 20 minutes, or until a cake tester inserted into the center comes out clean. Cool in the pans on wire racks for 10 minutes. Invert onto the racks to cool completely.

5 Make the custard filling and Grand Marnier sauce.

6 To assemble, place one of the cake layers on a serving plate and spread with the custard filling. Place the second layer on top and pour the Grand Marnier sauce over the top of the cake, letting it drip down the sides.

85 ■ CHOCOLATE DREAM CAKE

YIELD: *12 to 15 servings*
BAKING TIME: *60 minutes*

CREAM CHEESE BATTER

8 ounces cream cheese, at room temperature
1 large egg
¼ cup granulated sugar
3 tablespoons heavy cream
2 tablespoons butter or margarine, at room temperature
1 tablespoon all-purpose flour
½ teaspoon chocolate extract

CHOCOLATE BATTER

2 ounces unsweetened chocolate, grated or finely chopped
2 ounces semisweet chocolate, grated or finely chopped
2 cups all-purpose flour
1½ teaspoons baking powder
1 teaspoon baking soda
¼ teaspoon salt

½ cup butter or margarine, at room temperature
2 cups granulated sugar
2 large eggs
1⅓ cups buttermilk
1 teaspoon chocolate extract
2 cups Chocolate Fudge Frosting II (see page 401)

1 Position a rack in the center of the oven and preheat the oven to 350 degrees. Lightly grease and flour a 13 by 9-inch pan.

2 To make the cream cheese batter, in a medium bowl, using an electric mixer on medium speed, beat the cream cheese, egg, and sugar until smooth. Beat in the cream, butter, flour, and chocolate extract until thoroughly blended. Set aside.

3 To make the chocolate batter, melt the chocolates (see page 13). Remove from the heat.

4 Combine the flour, baking powder, baking soda, and salt.

5 In a large bowl, using an electric mixer on medium speed, beat the butter and sugar until light and fluffy. Beat in the eggs, one at a time, beating well after each addition. In three additions, stir in the dry ingredients, alternating with the buttermilk, beginning and ending with the dry ingredients. Using a wooden spoon, stir in the melted chocolate and chocolate extract.

6 Spread half of the chocolate batter evenly onto the bottom of the prepared pan. Carefully spread all of the cream cheese batter over the top. Spread the remaining chocolate batter over the top.

7 Bake for 55 to 60 minutes, or until a cake tester inserted into the center comes out clean. Cool in the pan on a wire rack.

8 Make the chocolate fudge frosting. Spread the frosting evenly over the top of the cake. Cut into squares.

86 ■ CHOCOLATE EUPHORIA CAKE

YIELD: *12 servings*
BAKING TIME: *30 minutes*

CAKE

2½ ounces unsweetened chocolate, grated or finely chopped
2 cups all-purpose flour
1 teaspoon baking soda
¼ cup butter or margarine, at room temperature
2 cups granulated sugar
2 large eggs
1 cup buttermilk
1 teaspoon chocolate or vanilla extract
2 tablespoons cider vinegar

83

84

86

FROSTING

5 ounces semisweet chocolate, grated or finely chopped
½ cup butter or margarine, at room temperature
2 cups powdered sugar
⅓ cup evaporated milk
1 teaspoon vanilla or chocolate extract
½ teaspoon salt

1 Position a rack in the center of the oven and preheat the oven to 350 degrees. Lightly grease and flour an 8-inch round cake pan.

2 Melt the chocolate (see page 13). Remove from the heat.

3 Combine the flour and baking soda.

4 In a large bowl, using an electric mixer on high speed, beat the butter and sugar until light and fluffy. Beat in the eggs. Beat in the buttermilk, chocolate extract, and vinegar. Pouring it in a thin stream, beat in the melted chocolate. Gradually blend in the dry ingredients. Pour the mixture into the prepared pan.

5 Bake for 25 to 30 minutes, or until a cake tester inserted into the center comes out clean. Cool in the pan on a wire rack 10 minutes. Invert onto the rack to cool completely. Place the cake on a serving plate.

6 To make the frosting, melt the chocolate (see page 13). Remove from the heat.

7 In a large bowl, using an electric mixer on high speed, beat the butter and powdered sugar until light and fluffy. Beat in the evaporated milk, vanilla extract, and salt. In a steady stream, beat in the melted chocolate. Spread evenly over the top and sides of the cake.

87 ■ CHOCOLATE FRUITCAKE I

YIELD: *10 to 12 servings*
BAKING TIME: *60 minutes*

CAKE

2 cups all-purpose flour
1 tablespoon baking powder
¼ cup Dutch processed cocoa powder
2½ cups candied fruit
½ cup butter or margarine, at room temperature
1 cup packed light brown sugar
3 large eggs
¾ cups milk

ALMOND PASTE

½ cup fresh lemon juice
2 cups blanched almonds
1 cup granulated sugar

TOPPING

6 ounces semisweet chocolate, grated or finely chopped
¼ cup boiling water
1 teaspoon mocha-flavored instant coffee powder
2 tablespoons powdered sugar
4 large egg yolks
½ cup butter or margarine, at room temperature
3 tablespoons amaretto
Glacé cherry halves for garnish

1 Position a rack in the center of the oven and preheat the oven to 350 degrees. Lightly grease and dust with cocoa powder a 9 by 5-inch loaf pan.

2 Combine the flour, baking powder, cocoa powder, and candied fruit.

3 In a large bowl, using an electric mixer on medium speed, beat the butter and brown sugar until fluffy. Add the eggs, one at a time, beating well after each addition. In three additions, blend in the dry ingredients, alternating with the milk, beginning and ending with the dry ingredients. Scrape the batter into the prepared pan and spread evenly.

4 Bake for 55 to 60 minutes, or until a cake tester inserted into the center comes out clean. Cool in the pan on a wire rack for 10 minutes. Invert onto the rack to cool completely.

5 To make the almond paste, place the lemon juice and 1 cup of the almonds in the container of a blender and process on high for a few seconds until the nuts are finely ground. Add the sugar and process until combined. Add the remaining 1 cup nuts and process until the mixture is a smooth paste. Remove from the container and chill until ready to use.

6 Meanwhile, to make the topping, in a small bowl, stir the chocolate and the boiling water, blending until smooth. Place the chocolate mixture, coffee powder, and powdered sugar in the container of a blender. Process for 1 or 2 seconds. Add the egg yolks, one at a time, processing for a second or two after each

89

87

88

addition. Add the butter and amaretto and blend on high speed until the mixture is smooth. If the frosting seems too thin, add a little more powdered sugar, a teaspoonful at a time, until a spreadable consistency.

7 To assemble, place the cake on a serving platter. Spread the almond paste evenly over the top and sides of the cake in a smooth, even layer. Spread the topping over the almond paste. Garnish with the cherries.

88 ■ CHOCOLATE FRUITCAKE II

YIELD: *10 to 12 servings*
BAKING TIME: *120 minutes*
SOAKING TIME: *several weeks*

4 ounces unsweetened chocolate, grated or finely chopped
2 cups all-purpose flour
1 teaspoon baking powder
1 cup chopped pecans or almonds
1/2 cup chopped hazelnuts or walnuts
1 cup candied fruit mix
1 cup golden raisins
1/2 cup chopped maraschino cherries
6 large eggs, separated
3/4 cup butter or margarine, at room temperature
1 cup granulated sugar
1/2 cup packed light brown sugar
1/4 cup amaretto, plus more for soaking cake

1 Position a rack in the center of the oven and preheat the oven to 250 degrees. Grease a 9 by 5-inch loaf pan.

2 Melt the chocolate (see page 13). Remove from the heat.

3 Combine the flour, baking powder, pecans, hazelnuts, candied fruit, raisins, and cherries. Toss until the clumps are separated and the pieces are coated with flour.

4 In a medium bowl, using an electric mixer on high speed, beat the egg whites until stiff peaks form.

5 In a large bowl, using an electric mixer on medium speed, beat the butter and sugars until light and fluffy. Beat in the egg yolks in one addition. By hand,

blend in the melted chocolate. In three additions, gradually stir in the dry ingredients, alternating with the 1/4 cup amaretto. Fold in the beaten egg whites. Scrape the mixture into the prepared pan and spread evenly.

6 Bake for 2 hours, or until a cake tester inserted into the center comes out clean. Cool in the pan for 10 minutes. Invert onto a wire rack to cool completely. Wrap in waxed paper or aluminum foil, place in a plastic bag, and store at room temperature for several weeks before using. About every 3 or 4 days, unwrap and sprinkle 1 or 2 tablespoons of amaretto over the cake and rewrap. The cake may be served anytime after several weeks to 1 1/2 to 2 months.

BAKING NOTES: In place of mixed fruit, this cake can be made with all cherries, apricots, prunes, or any other dried fruit that can be diced into small pieces. Liqueur can be used in place of the amaretto. There are some bakers who like to soak candied fruit and raisins before blending into the cake, but with the long baking time for this cake it isn't necessary.

89 ■ CHOCOLATE FUDGE CAKE I

YIELD: *12 servings*
BAKING TIME: *35 minutes*
FREEZING TIME: *1 hour*

CAKE

10 large eggs, separated
1 tablespoon distilled white vinegar
1 tablespoon water
1 3/4 cups granulated sugar
7 ounces unsweetened chocolate, grated or finely chopped
3 ounces semisweet chocolate, grated or finely chopped
3/4 cup butter or margarine, at room temperature
4 1/2 teaspoons coffee liqueur (see Baking notes)
4 1/2 teaspoons baking powder

FILLING

4 1/2 tablespoons instant coffee powder
6 tablespoons hot water
3 ounces unsweetened chocolate, grated or finely chopped
1 1/2 cups butter or margarine
3 cups powdered sugar, sifted
4 large egg yolks

GLAZE

9 tablespoons water
6 tablespoons butter or margarine
3 tablespoons canola oil
3 tablespoons grated or finely chopped unsweetened chocolate
9 tablespoons granulated sugar
1 cup Dutch processed cocoa powder
2 tablespoons Kahlúa (see Baking notes)
White Chocolate Leaves (see page 422) for garnish
Fresh chrysanthemums for garnish

1 Position a rack in the center of the oven and preheat the oven to 350 degrees. Lightly grease and flour three 9-inch round cake pans. Line the bottoms with waxed paper and butter the paper.

2 To make the cake, in a large bowl, using an electric mixer on high speed, beat the egg whites until foamy. Gradually add the vinegar and water, beating on high speed until the whites hold stiff peaks.

3 In the top of a double boiler over simmering water, combine the sugar and chocolates, stirring constantly until smooth. Remove from the heat. Using a metal spoon, beat in the butter and liqueur until smooth.

4 In another large bowl, using an electric mixer on medium speed, beat the egg yolks until thick and light-colored. Beat in the baking powder. Pouring it in a thin stream, beat in the chocolate mixture. Fold in the egg whites, one-fourth at a time, blending until no white streaks remain. Pour the mixture into the prepared pans.

5 Bake for 30 to 35 minutes, or until a cake tester inserted into the center comes out clean. Cool in the pans on wire racks for 10 minutes. Invert onto the racks to

cool completely. The cakes will sink in the center as they cool.

6 Meanwhile, to make the filling, in the top of a double boiler over simmering water, combine the coffee powder, hot water, and chocolate, stirring constantly until smooth. Remove from the heat.

7 In a medium bowl, using an electric mixer on medium speed, beat the butter and powdered sugar until thick and smooth. Beat in the egg yolks. Add the chocolate mixture and beat until a thick, spreadable consistency.

8 To make the glaze, in a medium saucepan, bring the water, butter, and oil to a boil. Remove from the heat and cool slightly. Stir in the chocolate, sugar, cocoa powder, and Kahlúa. Beat with an eletric mixer on low speed until the mixture is very thick.

9 To assemble, remove the waxed paper, and invert one cake layer onto a serving plate. Spread the layer with half of the filling and top with a second cake layer. Spread with the

remaining filling and invert the last layer on top. Smooth out any filling that has oozed between the layers. Freeze for 1 hour, or until solid.

10 Pour the glaze over the frozen cake and let it drip down the sides. Smooth out the glaze on the sides and let the cake stand at room temperature to defrost. Garnish with white chocolate leaves and fresh white chrysanthemums before serving.

BAKING NOTES: The liqueur and Kahlúa should be used at room temperature so they will blend more easily with the chocolate. Plastic or silk flowers can be used in place of the live chrysanthemums. To use edible flowers other than chrysanthemums, see page 22 for safe substitutes. Many fresh flowers are poisonous.

90 ■ CHOCOLATE FUDGE CAKE II

YIELD: *12 servings*
BAKING TIME: *30 minutes*

1/2 **cup butter or margarine**
3 **ounces unsweetened chocolate, grated or finely chopped**
3 **ounces semisweet chocolate, grated or finely chopped**
3 **tablespoons coffee liqueur**
3/4 **cup chopped pecans**
2 **tablespoons all-purpose flour**
6 **large eggs, separated**
1/2 **cup granulated sugar**
2 **tablespoons all-purpose flour**
1 **teaspoon chocolate extract**

FROSTING

1 1/2 **cups Chocolate Frosting IV (see pages 400)**
Fresh fruit or edible fresh flowers (see page 22) for garnish

1 Position a rack in the center of the oven and preheat the oven to 350 degrees. Lightly grease and flour two 8-inch square pans.

81

91

82

85

72

2 To make the cake, in a saucepan over medium heat, melt the butter. Remove from the heat and mix in the chocolates and liqueur, stirring until smooth. Stir in the pecans.

3 In a large bowl, using an electric mixer on high speed, beat the egg whites until foamy. Add ¼ cup of the sugar and beat until stiff but not dry.

4 In a medium bowl, using an electric mixer on medium speed, beat the egg yolks until thick and light-colored. Beat in the remaining ¼ cup sugar. Pouring it in a thin stream, beat in the chocolate mixture. Beat in the flour. Stir in the chocolate extract. Fold in the egg whites, a little at a time, until just blended. Scrape into the prepared pans and spread evenly.

5 Bake for 25 to 30 minutes, or until a cake tester inserted into the center comes out clean and the cakes start to pull away from the sides of the pan. Cool in the pans on wire racks for 8 to 10 minutes.

6 Make the frosting.

7 To assemble, remove the cakes from the pans and place one on a serving plate. Spread frosting evenly over the top and place the second layer on top. Frost the top and sides of the cake. Garnish with fresh fruit or flowers.

BAKING NOTE: To make the cake appear larger, use a serrated knife and cut each layer in half horizontally to make four layers. Assemble as directed above.

91 ■ CHOCOLATE FUDGE CAKE III

YIELD: 12 servings
BAKING TIME: 30 minutes

CAKE

2¾ cups all-purpose flour
2 teaspoons baking powder
½ teaspoon salt
1 cup Dutch processed cocoa powder
2 cups boiling water
1 cup butter or margarine, at room temperature
2½ cups granulated sugar
4 large eggs
1½ teaspoons chocolate or almond extract

FROSTING

1 cup (6 ounces) semisweet chocolate chips
1 cup butter or margarine
½ cup light cream or evaporated milk
2½ cups powdered sugar

FILLING

1 cup heavy cream
¼ cup powdered sugar
1 teaspoon coffee liqueur

1 Position a rack in the center of the oven and preheat the oven to 350 degrees. Lightly grease and flour three 9-inch round cake pans.

2 To make the cake, combine the flour, baking powder, baking soda, and salt.

3 In a medium bowl, combine the cocoa powder and boiling water, stirring until smooth.

4 In a large bowl, using an electric mixer on high speed, beat the butter and sugar until light and fluffy. Beat in the eggs, one at a time. Beat in the chocolate extract. Beat in the cocoa mixture. Gradually stir in the dry ingredients. Pour the mixture into the prepared pans.

5 Bake for 25 to 30 minutes, or until a cake tester inserted into the center comes out clean. Cool in the pans on wire racks for 10 minutes. Invert the cakes onto the racks to cool completely.

6 To make the frosting, in a medium saucepan, combine the chocolate chips, butter and cream. Cook, over medium heat, stirring until smooth. Remove from the heat. Using an electric mixer on medium speed, mix in the powdered sugar. Beat until the mixture is cool and is a spreadable consistency.

7 To make the filling, using an electric mixer on medium speed, beat the cream, powdered sugar, and liqueur until soft peaks form.

8 To assemble, place one cake layer on a serving plate and spread with half of the filling. Top with the second cake layer and spread with the remaining filling. Top with the third cake layer and spread the frosting on the top and sides of cake.

92 ■ CHOCOLATE FUDGE CAKE WITH ALMONDS

YIELD: *16 servings*
BAKING TIME: *35 minutes*

CAKE

¹/₂ cup ground almonds
6 ounces semisweet chocolate, grated or finely chopped
¹/₂ cup butter or margarine
¹/₄ cup milk
5 large eggs, separated
1¹/₂ cups powdered sugar
¹/₃ cup amaretto
1 tablespoon instant coffee powder
1 tablespoon cornstarch
1 teaspoon chocolate extract

TOPPING

³/₄ cup coffee liqueur
10 tablespoons orange preserves

GLAZE

6 ounces semisweet chocolate, grated or finely chopped
¹/₄ cup heavy cream or milk
1 teaspoon instant coffee powder
3 tablespoons vegetable oil
Edible fresh flowers and leaves (see page 22) for garnish

1 Preheat the oven to 350 degrees. Lightly grease a 10-inch springform pan.

2 To make the cake, in a medium saucepan, over low heat, combine the almonds, chocolate, butter, and milk and cook until the chocolate is melted and smooth. Transfer to a large bowl.

3 In another large bowl, using an electric mixer on medium speed, beat the egg yolks until thick and light-colored. Beat in ³/₄ cup of the powdered sugar.

4 In another bowl, using an electric mixer with clean beaters on high speed, beat the egg whites until foamy. Gradually add the remaining ³/₄ cup powdered sugar and beat until stiff but not dry.

5 Stir the egg yolk mixture into the chocolate mixture. Stir in the amaretto, coffee powder, cornstarch, and chocolate extract. Fold in one-third of the egg whites, stirring until no white streaks remain. Then fold in the remaining egg whites. Scrape the mixture into the prepared pan and spread evenly.

6 Bake for 35 minutes or until a cake tester inserted into the center comes out with moist crumbs clinging to it. Cool completly in the pan on a wire rack. Invert onto a plate with a raised rim.

7 To make the topping, in a small sauce pan over medium heat, warm the coffee liqueur slightly. Gently pour it over the cake. Spread the orange preserves evenly in a circle over the top, leaving the outer ¹/₂ inch ring clean. Then spread preserves in a ¹/₄ inch ring on the outer edges of the top of the cake. You will have created a "groove" between the preserves.

8 To make the glaze, in a small saucepan over low heat, combine the chocolate, cream, and coffee powder and cook, stirring, until smooth. Stir in the oil. Remove from the heat. Carefully spoon into the groove around the edge of the cake, allowing the warm chocolate to drip down the sides and form a pool around the bottom of the cake. Garnish with edible fresh flowers and green leaves.

BAKING NOTES: Pansies work well for decorating this cake.

93 ■ CHOCOLATE FUDGE CHEESECAKE I

YIELD: *12 servings*
BAKING TIME: *70 minutes*
CHILL TIME: *3 hours*

CRUST

1¹/₄ cups chocolate graham cracker crumbs
2 tablespoons granulated sugar
3 tablespoons butter or margarine, melted

FILLING

11 ounces cream cheese, at room temperature
1 cup granulated sugar
¹/₄ cup Dutch processed cocoa powder
2 teaspoons coffee liqueur
3 large eggs

1 Position a rack in the center of the oven and preheat the oven to 350 degrees. Lightly grease a 9-inch springform pan.

2 To make the crust, in a large bowl, combine the crumbs and sugar. Mix in the melted butter. Press the mixture evenly onto the bottom of the prepared pan.

3 Bake for 10 minutes. Cool on a wire rack. Reduce the oven temperature to 300 degrees.

4 To make the filling, in a large bowl, using an electric mixer on medium speed, beat the cream cheese and sugar until smooth. Beat in the cocoa powder until blended. Beat in the coffee liqueur. Beat in the eggs. Pour over the crust and bake for 1 hour, or until firm. Cool slightly. Cover with waxed paper and chill for at least 3 hours. Remove the side of the pan before serving.

BAKING NOTES: This cheesecake can be prepared and refrigerated up to 48 hours in advance of serving.

94 ■ CHOCOLATE FUDGE CHEESECAKE II

YIELD: *12 to 14 servings*
BAKING TIME: *90 minutes*
CHILL TIME: *24 hours*

Chocolate Cookie Crumb Crust (see page 267)
3 ounces semisweet chocolate, grated or finely chopped
1 ounce white chocolate, grated or finely chopped
4 ounces unsweetened chocolate, grated or finely chopped
24 ounces cream cheese, at room temperature
1 cup granulated sugar
3 large eggs
2 tablespoons heavy cream or evaporated milk
1 cup sour cream or chocolate-flavored yogurt
1/2 teaspoon salt
2 teaspoons instant espresso powder
1 tablespoon hot water
1/2 cup coffee liqueur
2 teaspoons chocolate extract
1 cup Chocolate Whipped Cream (see page 406)
Chocolate leaves (see page 422) and chocolate sprinkles for garnish

1 Make the crust and press onto the bottom of a 9 or 10-inch springform pan.

2 Preheat the oven to 350 degrees.

3 Melt the chocolates (see page 13). Remove from the heat.

4 In a large bowl, using an electric mixer on medium speed, beat the cream cheese and sugar until smooth. Beat in the eggs, one at a time, beating well after each addition. Beat in the melted chocolate mixture. Beat in the cream, sour cream, salt, espresso powder, water, liqueur, and chocolate extract. Pour the mixture into the prepared pan.

5 Bake for 40 to 45 minutes, or until the edges are browned and pull away from the sides of the pan. The center will not be set. Turn off the heat and leave undisturbed in the oven for an additional 45 minutes. Remove from the oven, cover with a plate, and chill at least 24 hours.

6 Make the chocolate whipped cream and chill 30 minutes before using.

7 Remove the side of the pan. Spread the whipped cream over the cheesecake and garnish with the chocolate sprinkles and chocolate leaves.

95 ■ CHOCOLATE FUDGE CHEESECAKE PETITS FOURS

YIELD: *40 to 45 servings*
BAKING TIME: *45 minutes*
CHILL TIME: *30 minutes*

2 recipes Chocolate Cookie Crumb Crust (see page 267)
4 ounces semisweet chocolate, grated or finely chopped
1 1/2 teaspoons instant espresso powder
1/2 teaspoon hot water
12 ounces cream cheese, at room temperature
1/2 cup granulated sugar
2 large eggs
1 cup sour cream
2 teaspoons crème de cacao
3/4 teaspoon chocolate or vanilla extract
Grated semisweet and white chocolate for garnish

1 Position a rack in the center of the oven and preheat the oven to 325 degrees.

2 Make the chocolate wafer cookie crumb crust. Press evenly onto the bottoms of three 8-inch square pans.

3 Melt the chocolate (see page 13). Remove from the heat.

4 In a cup, dissolve the espresso powder in the hot water.

5 In a large bowl, using an electric mixer on medium speed, beat the cream cheese and sugar until smooth. Beat in the eggs, one at a time, beating well after each addition. Beat in the sour cream, crème de cacao, chocolate extract, espresso mixture, and melted chocolate. Pour the mixture into the prepared pans.

5 Bake for 30 minutes. Turn off the oven and leave the cheesecake undisturbed for 15 minutes. Cool in the pans on wire racks. Chill for 20 to 30 minutes. Cut each cheesecake into 1 1/2-inch squares. Sprinkle the squares, half with semisweet chocolate and half with white chocolate.

BAKING NOTES: Wipe the knife blade clean after each cut of the cheesecake for best results. Garnish the petit fours with chocolate leaves (see page 422) for a special occasion.

92

93

95

96 ■ CHOCOLATE FUDGE CHERRY CAKE

YIELD: *12 to 15 servings*
BAKING TIME: *35 minutes*

CAKE

1½ cups all-purpose flour
¼ cup Dutch processed cocoa
   powder
1 teaspoon baking powder
½ teaspoon baking soda
¼ teaspoon salt
6 tablespoons canola oil
1 cup granulated sugar
1 tablespoon vinegar
1 teaspoon chocolate extract
1 can (21 ounces) cherry pie filling

FROSTING

1 cup milk
1 package (3.4 ounces) chocolate
   instant pudding mix
1 cup whipped topping

1 Position a rack in the center of the oven and preheat the oven to 350 degrees. Lightly grease and flour a 13 by 9-inch pan.

2 To make the cake, combine the flour, cocoa powder, baking powder, baking soda, and salt.

3 In a large bowl, using an electric mixer on medium speed, beat together the oil and sugar until combined. Beat in the vinegar and chocolate extract. Gradually stir in the dry ingredients. Blend in the pie filling. Scrape the mixture into the prepared pan and spread evenly.

4 Bake for 30 to 35 minutes, or until a cake tester inserted into the center comes out clean. Cool in the pan on a wire rack.

5 To make the frosting, using an electric mixer on medium-high speed, beat together the milk, pudding mix, and whipped topping until a spreadable consistency. Spread the frosting over the top of the cake in the pan.

97 ■ CHOCOLATE FUDGE CHERRY ROLL

YIELD: *12 to 16 servings*
BAKING TIME: *10 minutes*
CHILL TIME: *30 minutes*
FREEZE TIME: *60 minutes*

CAKE

½ cup cake flour
½ cup Dutch processed cocoa
   powder
1 teaspoon baking powder
½ teaspoon salt
4 large eggs
1 teaspoon Cheri-Suisse or cherry
   liqueur
¾ cup granulated sugar

FILLING

1 quart cherry ice cream, softened

TOPPING

1 cup heavy cream
3 tablespoons Dutch processed
   cocoa powder
2 tablespoons powdered sugar
Chocolate leaves and glacé cherry
   halves for garnish

1 Position a rack in the center of the oven and preheat the oven to 400 degrees. Lightly grease a 15½ by 10½-inch jelly-roll pan. Line the bottom of the pan with waxed paper and grease the paper.

2 To make the cake, combine and sift the flour, cocoa powder, baking powder, and salt.

3 In a large bowl, using an electric mixer on medium-high speed, beat the eggs until thick and light-colored. Beating on low speed, add the Cheri-Suisse and sugar. Gradually add the dry ingredients, mixing just until blended. Do not overmix. Scrape the mixture into the prepared pan and spread evenly.

4 Bake for 8 to 10 minutes, or until the top springs back when gently touched. Cool in the pan on a wire rack for 2 minutes. Invert onto a flat surface covered with waxed paper to cool completely.

5 Starting with one of the long sides, roll up the cake jelly roll fashion. Wrap in a towel or waxed paper and refrigerate 30 minutes, or until completely chilled.

6 To assemble, unroll the cake. Spread the ice cream in an even layer over the cake. Roll the cake up, wrap in waxed paper, and freeze for at least 1 hour, or until ready to serve.

7 Meanwhile, to make the topping, in a medium bowl using an electric mixer on medium speed, beat the heavy cream until it starts to thicken. Add the cocoa powder and powdered sugar, and continue beating until the mixture is thick and forms stiff peaks. Spread the topping over the sides and ends of the frozen cake roll and garnish with the chocolate leaves and cherry halves.

BAKING NOTES: One of the secrets of this cake is to make sure that the rolled cake is well chilled before spreading the ice cream over it. It is important to work quickly with the ice cream to prevent it from getting too soft.

98 ■ CHOCOLATE FUDGE CHERRY UPSIDE-DOWN CAKE

YIELD: *12 to 15 servings*
BAKING TIME: *35 minutes*

1 can (14 ounces) cherry pie filling
2¼ cups all-purpose flour
¾ cup Dutch processed cocoa
   powder
1½ teaspoons baking soda
½ teaspoon salt
1½ cups cherry-flavored brandy or
   maraschino liqueur
1½ cups water
1½ cups granulated sugar
½ cup canola oil
¼ cup wine vinegar
Whipped cream for serving

1 Position a rack in the center of the oven and preheat the oven to 350 degrees. Lightly grease a 13 by 9-inch pan. Spread the pie filling evenly over the bottom of the pan.

2 Combine the flour, cocoa powder, baking soda, and salt.

3 In a large bowl, using an electric mixer on medium speed, beat the brandy, water, sugar, oil, and vinegar until combined.

Gradually blend in the dry ingredients, mixing just until blended. Slowly pour the mixture over the cherries in the pan.

4 Bake for 30 to 35 minutes, or until a cake tester inserted into the center comes out clean. Cool in the pan on a wire rack for 15 minutes. Invert onto a serving platter. Serve with the whipped cream on the side.

99 ■ CHOCOLATE FUDGE CHESTNUT CAKE

YIELD: *10 to 12 servings*
BAKING TIME: *30 minutes*

CAKE

4 ounces semisweet chocolate, grated or finely chopped
2 ounces unsweetened chocolate, grated or finely chopped
¼ cup kirsch liqueur
¾ cup (7 ounces) chestnut puree
4 large eggs, separated
6 tablespoons (¾ stick) butter or margarine
1 teaspoon chocolate extract
⅓ cup all-purpose flour
pinch of salt
½ cup granulated sugar

GLAZE

4 ounces unsweetened chocolate, grated or finely chopped
¼ cups heavy cream

TOPPING

1 cup heavy cream
2 tablespoons granulated sugar
1 tablespoon hazelnut liqueur
Chocolate Leaves (see page 422) for garnish
Ground chestnuts or hazelnuts for garnish

1 Position a rack in the center of the oven and preheat to 375 degrees. Lightly grease a 9-inch round layer pan. Line the bottom of the pan with waxed paper and grease the paper.

2 To make the cake, in the top of a double boiler over low heat, melt the two chocolates and liqueur together, stirring until smooth. Remove from the heat and beat in the chestnut puree. Beat in the egg yolks, one at a time, beating vigorously after each addition. Return to the heat and cook, stirring constantly, until smooth and thickened. Remove from the heat and stir in the butter and chocolate extract. Stir until smooth. Gradually stir in the flour a little at a time.

3 In a medium bowl, using an electric mixer, beat the egg whites until foamy. Add the pinch of salt and continue beating until stiff but not dry. Sprinkle the sugar over the top of the whites and fold into the mixture. Fold one-third of the whites at a time into the chocolate mixture, mixing until streaks no longer appear.

4 Pour the mixture into the prepared baking pan and bake for 25 to 30 minutes, or until a cake tester inserted into the edge is removed clean. The center will still be soft. Cool in the pan on a wire rack before inverting onto a serving plate or cake round.

5 To make the glaze, in the top of a double boiler, over a low heat, melt together the chocolate and cream, stirring until smooth. Remove from the heat and cool to lukewarm before spreading evenly over the top and sides of the cake.

6 To prepare the topping, in a medium bowl, using an electric mixer, whip the cream and sugar together until foamy. Add the liqueur and beat until the mixture is stiff. Using a pasty bag fitted with a large star tip, press a mound of mixture into the center of the cake and decorated around the top edge and sides with rosettes. Garnish with chocolate leaves and a sprinkling of ground chestnuts or hazelnuts.

100 ■ CHOCOLATE FUDGE CHIFFON CAKE I

YIELD: *16 servings*
BAKING TIME: *65 minutes*

4 ounces semisweet chocolate, grated or finely chopped
¾ cup boiling water
1⅔ cups all-purpose or cake flour
1½ cups granulated sugar
2 tablespoons instant coffee powder
2 teaspoons baking powder
¾ teaspoon salt
7 large eggs, separated
½ cup canola oil
½ teaspoon cream of tartar
1 cup Chocolate Whipped Cream (see page 406)
1½ tablespoons Cocoa Sugar (see page 407)
Grated white chocolate for garnish

97

100

1 Position a rack in the center of the oven and preheat the oven to 350 degrees.

2 In a small bowl, combine the chocolate with the boiling water, stirring until smooth.

3 In a large bowl, combine the flour, 1¼ cups of the sugar, coffee powder, baking powder, and salt. Add the egg yolks, oil, and chocolate mixture. Using an electric mixer on medium speed, beat until the batter is very smooth.

4 In a large bowl, using an electric mixer with clean beaters on high speed, beat the egg whites and cream of tartar until foamy. Add the remaining ¼ cup sugar and beat until stiff but not dry. Fold the whites into the chocolate mixture, mixing just until blended. Pour into an ungreased 10-inch tube pan.

5 Bake for 60 to 65 minutes, or until a cake tester inserted into the center comes out clean. Cool in the pan upside down on a wire rack. Remove cake from pan.

6 Prepare the chocolate whipped cream.

7 To assemble, using a serrated knife, cut the cake into two layers. Place the bottom layer on a serving plate and spread with chocolate whipped cream. Top with the second cake layer. Spread with whipped cream over the top and sides. Sprinkle the top with cocoa sugar and grated white chocolate.

BAKING NOTES: This cake can also be cut into three layers, if desired.

101 ■ CHOCOLATE FUDGE CHIFFON CAKE II

YIELD: *16 servings*
BAKING TIME: *70 minutes*
CHILLING TIME FOR CRÈME FRAÎCHE: *8 hours*

CAKE

½ cup Dutch processed cocoa powder
3 tablespoons mocha-flavored instant coffee powder
¼ cup boiling water
½ cup coffee liqueur
1¾ cup cake flour
1¾ cups granulated sugar
1½ teaspoons baking soda
7 large eggs, separated, plus 2 large egg whites
½ teaspoon salt
½ teaspoon cream of tartar
½ cup canola oil
2 teaspoons chocolate or vanilla extract

TOPPING

1 cup Apricot Glaze (see page 394)
1¼ cups Crème Fraîche (see page 409) (see Baking notes)

1 Position a rack in the center of the oven and preheat the oven to 325 degrees.

2 To make the cake, in a small bowl, mix the cocoa powder, coffee powder, and boiling water until blended. Add the liqueur.

3 Combine the flour, sugar, and baking soda.

4 In a large bowl, using an electric mixer on medium-high speed, beat the egg whites, salt, and cream of tartar until stiff but not dry.

5 In another large bowl, using an electric mixer on medium speed, beat the egg yolks until thick and light-colored. Beat in the oil and chocolate extract. Stir in the cocoa powder mixture. Gradually blend in the dry ingredients.

6 Fold the yolk mixture into the egg whites, one-third at a time. Do not overmix. Pour the mixture into an ungreased 10-inch tube pan.

7 Bake for 60 to 70 minutes, or until a cake tester inserted into the center comes out clean. Cool in the pan upside down on a wire rack. If the cake has risen above the edge of the pan, invert onto a metal funnel or glass bottle.

8 Meanwhile, make the glaze.

9 To assemble, remove the cake from the pan and place on a serving plate. Brush an even coating of the apricot glaze over the top and sides of the cake. Let set for 15 minutes, or until the surface is just sticky. Spread the crème fraîche over the cake. Chill until ready to serve.

BAKING NOTES: Make the crème fraîche the day before making this recipe because it takes at least 8 hours to culture the cream.

101
102
104

102 ■ CHOCOLATE FUDGE CHIP CAKE I

YIELD: *12 servings*
BAKING TIME: *40 minutes*

2 cups cake flour
1 teaspoon baking powder
1 teaspoon baking soda
1/2 cup butter or margarine, at room temperature
1 cup granulated sugar
2 large eggs
1 cup chocolate-flavored yogurt
1 teaspoon chocolate or vanilla extract
1 cup semisweet chocolate chips
2 teaspoons Cocoa Sugar (see page 407)
Cocoa Cream Topping (see page 406)
Sliced fresh strawberries for garnish

1 Position a rack in the center of the oven and preheat the oven to 350 degrees. Lightly grease and flour a 8-inch square or 8-inch springform pan.

2 Combine the flour, baking powder, and baking soda.

3 In a large bowl, using an electric mixer on medium-high speed, beat the butter and sugar together until light and fluffy. Beat in the eggs, one at a time, beating well after each addition. Beat in the yogurt and chocolate extract. Gradually blend in the dry ingredients. Fold in the chocolate chips. Scrape the batter into the prepared pan and spread evenly.

4 Bake for 35 to 40 minutes, or until a cake tester inserted into the center comes out clean. Cool in the pan on a wire rack for 10 minutes. Invert onto a wire rack to cool completely.

5 Make the cocoa sugar and the cocoa cream topping.

6 Place the cake on a serving plate and dust with the cocoa sugar. Spread the topping over the top and sides of the cake. Garnish with sliced strawberries.

103 ■ CHOCOLATE FUDGE CHIP CAKE II

YIELD: *16 servings*
BAKING TIME: *45 minutes*

2 cups all-purpose flour
2 teaspoons baking soda
Pinch of salt
1 cup butter or margarine, at room temperature
1 1/2 cups granulated sugar
1 cup chocolate-flavored yogurt
2 large eggs
2 tablespoons heavy cream or evaporated milk
1 tablespoon crème de cacao
1 cup semisweet miniature chocolate chips
Cocoa Sugar (see page 407) for dusting

1 Position a rack in the center of the oven and preheat the oven to 350 degrees. Lightly grease a 10-inch tube pan.

2 Combine the flour, baking soda, and salt

3 In a large bowl, using an electric mixer on medium speed, beat the butter and sugar until light and fluffy. Beat in the yogurt. Beat in the eggs, one at a time, beating well after each addition. Beat in the cream and crème de cacao. Gradually blend in the dry ingredients. Fold in the chocolate chips. Scrape the mixture into the prepared pan and spread evenly.

4 Bake for 40 to 45 minutes, or until a cake tester inserted into the center comes out clean. Cool in the pan on a wire rack for 30 minutes. Invert onto a serving plate. Sprinkle with cocoa sugar and serve.

104 ■ CHOCOLATE FUDGE CHIP DATE CAKE

YIELD: *12 servings*
BAKING TIME: *40 minutes*
CHILL TIME: *4 hours*

FROSTING

2 cups heavy cream
12 ounces semisweet chocolate, grated or finely chopped

CAKE

1 3/4 cups all-purpose flour
1 cup (6 ounces) semisweet chocolate chips
3 tablespoons Dutch processed cocoa powder
1 teaspoon baking soda
1 cup dates, pitted and chopped
1 cup boiling water
1 cup butter or margarine, at room temperature
1 cup granulated sugar
2 large eggs
2 teaspoons chocolate or vanilla extract

1 Position a rack in the center of the oven and preheat the oven to 350 degrees. Lightly grease and flour two 8-inch round cake pans.

2 To make the frosting, in a saucepan, over low heat, bring the cream to a simmer. Remove from the heat and add the chocolate, stirring until blended. Cool slightly, cover, and chill for 3 hours.

3 To make the cake, combine the flour, chocolate chips, cocoa powder, and baking soda.

4 Place the dates in a small bowl and cover with the boiling water.

5 In a large bowl, using an electric mixer on medium speed, beat the butter and sugar until light and fluffy. Beat in the eggs, one at a time, beating well after each addition. Beat in the chocolate extract. Beat in the date mixture. Gradually stir in the dry ingredients. Divide the mixture between the prepared pans and spread evenly.

6 Bake for 35 to 40 minutes, or until a cake tester inserted into the center comes out clean. Cool in the pans on wire racks for 10 minutes. Invert onto the racks to cool completely. Chill cakes for 1 hour.

7 To assemble, place one of the cake layers on a serving plate and spread with the frosting. Top with the second layer and spread the frosting on the top and sides of the cake. Chill 1 hour or until serving.

105 ■ CHOCOLATE FUDGE CHIP HOLIDAY CAKE

YIELD: *10 to 12 servings*
BAKING TIME: *75 minutes*

1 cup all-purpose flour
½ cup whole wheat flour
1 cup glacé cherry halves
1½ teaspoons baking powder
¼ teaspoon salt
3 large eggs
1 cup granulated sugar
1 cup chopped pecans or walnuts
1 cup chopped almonds or
  hazelnuts
¾ cup (6 ounces) miniature chocolate chips
¾ cup Dessert Syrup (see page 409)
  for garnish

1 Position a rack in the center of
the oven and preheat the oven
to 325 degrees. Lightly grease a
9 by 5-inch loaf pan. Place a pan
of water on the bottom rack of
the oven.

2 Combine the flours, glacé
cherries, baking powder, and
salt.

3 In a large bowl, using an electric mixer on medium speed,
beat the eggs until thick and
light-colored. Beat in the sugar.
Gradually stir in the dry ingredients just until blended. Do not
overmix. Fold in the pecans,
almonds, and chocolate chips.
Pour the mixture into the prepared pan.

4 Bake for 70 to 75 minutes, or
until the cake pulls away from
the sides of the pan and a cake
tester inserted into the center
comes out clean. Cool in the pan
on a wire rack for 5 minutes.
Invert onto a cake rack to cool
completely.

5 Make the dessert glaze.

6 Place the cake on a serving
platter and brush with the
dessert glaze.

BAKING NOTES: A simple garnish
such as a dessert glaze is all this
cake needs. The pan of water in
the oven creates a moist baking
environment for the cake.

106 ■ CHOCOLATE FUDGE CHIP POUND CAKE

YIELD: *10 to 12 servings*
BAKING TIME: *60 minutes*

1½ cups whole wheat flour
1 cup all-purpose flour
½ teaspoon baking powder
3 large eggs
¾ cup granulated sugar
2 teaspoons chocolate extract
½ cup butter or margarine, melted
¼ cup milk
½ cup semisweet chocolate chips
½ cup white chocolate chips

1 Position a rack in the center of
the oven and preheat the oven
to 325 degrees. Lightly grease
and flour a 9 by 5-inch loaf pan.

2 Combine the flours and baking powder.

3 In a large bowl, using an electric mixer on medium speed,
beat the eggs until thick and
light-colored. Beat in the sugar
and chocolate extract. Beat in
the butter and milk. Gradually
blend in the dry ingredients just
until blended. Fold in the chocolate chips. Scrape the batter into
the prepared pan and spread
evenly.

4 Bake for 55 to 60 minutes, or
until a cake tester inserted into
the center comes out clean. Cool
in the pan on a wire rack for 10
minutes. Invert onto the rack to
cool completely.

BAKING NOTES: Traditionally
pound cakes are served plain,
but Raspberry Sauce (see page
416) goes very well with this
cake.

107 ■ CHOCOLATE FUDGE CHOCOLATE CAKE

YIELD: *12 servings*
BAKING TIME: *75 minutes*
CHILL TIME: *12 hours*

4 ounces unsweetened chocolate,
  grated or finely chopped
4 ounces semisweet chocolate,
  grated or finely chopped
1 cup butter or margarine
1 cup granulated sugar
4 large eggs
2 tablespoons Cocoa Sugar (see
  page 407)
1 cup Chocolate Whipped Cream
  (see page 406)
Chocolate Curls for garnish (see
  page 422)

1 Position a rack in the center of
the oven and preheat the oven
to 325 degrees. Lightly grease a
9-inch springform pan. Line the
bottom of the pan with waxed
paper.

105

107

108

2 In a large saucepan, over low heat, melt the chocolates, stirring until smooth. Add the butter and stir until blended. Blend in the sugar. Remove from the heat. Using an electric mixer on medium speed, add the eggs all at once and beat until the mixture thickens slightly. Pour into the prepared pan. Place the pan in a large roasting pan and place on the oven rack. Pour boiling water into the roasting pan until it comes halfway up the sides of the springform pan.

3 Bake for 70 to 75 minutes, or until the cake pulls away from the sides of the pan. Cool in the pan on a wire rack for 2 to 4 hours.

4 Remove the side of the pan. Place a serving plate on top of the cake and invert. Remove the springform bottom. Do not remove the waxed paper. Chill in the refrigerator for at least 8 hours.

5 Prepare the chocolate whipped cream.

6 Remove the waxed paper from the cake bottom and sprinkle with the cocoa sugar. Spread the whipped cream over the top and sides of the cake. Sprinkle the chocolate curls over the top.

BAKING NOTES: Chocolate cigarettes, chocolate cones, and chocolate leaves (see Garnishes) can be used in place of the chocolate curls to give the cake a more festive look.

108 ■ CHOCOLATE FUDGE CREAM ROLL

YIELD: *12 to 16 servings*
BAKING TIME: *12 minutes*

CAKE

1 cup all-purpose flour
1/4 cup Dutch processed cocoa powder
1 teaspoon baking powder
1/4 teaspoon salt
1 cup granulated sugar
3 large eggs
1/2 cup strong brewed coffee
1/2 cup coffee liqueur
1 teaspoon crème de cacao

FROSTING

8 ounces unsweetened chocolate, grated or finely chopped
1/4 cup strong brewed coffee
1 cup butter or margarine, at room temperature
1/4 cup light corn syrup
4 large egg yolks

FILLING

2 teaspoons instant coffee powder
1 1/2 cups heavy cream
1/2 cup powdered sugar
1/3 cup sliced or slivered almonds for garnish

1 Position a rack in the center of the oven and preheat the oven to 375 degrees. Line a 15 1/2 by 10 1/2-inch jelly-roll pan with waxed paper.

2 To make the cake, combine the flour, cocoa powder, baking powder, and salt.

3 In a large bowl, using an electric mixer on medium-high speed, beat the sugar and eggs until smooth. Beat in the coffee, liqueur, and crème de cacao. Gradually blend in the dry ingredients. Scrape the mixture into the prepared pan and spread evenly.

4 Bake for 10 to 12 minutes, or until the center springs back when touched. Run a knife around the sides of the cake to loosen from the pan and invert onto a clean dish towel dusted with powdered sugar. Remove the waxed paper and trim the edges on all sides. Starting with one of the the short sides, lift the edge of the cake up with the dish towel and loosely roll up the cake. Place seam-side down on a wire rack to cool.

5 Meanwhile, to make the frosting, in a medium saucepan, melt the chocolate with the coffee, stirring until smooth. Remove from the heat and add the butter, stirring until blended and cooled.

6 In a small saucepan, boil the corn syrup for 2 minutes. Meanwhile, in a small bowl, using an electric mixer on medium speed, beat the egg yolks until they are thick and light-colored. Pouring it in a thin stream, beat the corn syrup into the yolks. Beat the

chocolate mixture into the yolk mixture. Chill until thickened to a spreadable consistency.

7 Meanwhile, to make the cream filling, dissolve the coffee powder in 1 1/2 tablespoons of the cream. In a large bowl, using an electric mixer on medium-high speed, beat the remaining cream and the powdered sugar until stiff peaks form. Gently fold in the dissolved coffee mixture. Chill until ready to assemble the cake.

8 To assemble, carefully unroll the cooled cake roll. Spread with the cream filling and roll the cake up jelly-roll fashion. Place on a serving plate and spread the frosting over the top and ends of the roll. Keep chilled until ready to serve. Garnish with the almonds.

109 ■ CHOCOLATE FUDGE DELIGHT CAKE

YIELD: *12 servings*
BAKING TIME: *30 minutes*

2 1/4 cups all-purpose flour
1 teaspoon salt
1 teaspoon baking soda
4 ounces unsweetened chocolate, grated or finely chopped
1/4 cup water
1 cup butter or margarine
11 ounces cream cheese, at room temperature
2 cups powdered sugar
3 large eggs
1 cup buttermilk
1/4 cup vegetable shortening

1 Position a rack in the center of the oven and preheat the oven to 350 degrees. Lightly grease three 8-inch round cake pans.

2 Combine the flour, salt, and baking soda.

3 In a medium saucepan, over low heat, melt the chocolate with the water and butter, stirring until smooth. Remove from the heat and pour into a large bowl and let the chocolate cool slightly. Using an electric mixer on medium speed, beat in the cream cheese and powdered sugar until combined.

4 In a large bowl, using an electric mixer on medium speed, beat the eggs and buttermilk until fluffy and combined. Beat in 3 cups of the chocolate mixture. Beat in the shortening. Gradually blend in the dry ingredients. Pour the mixture into the prepared pans. Reserve and chill the remaining chocolate mixture for frosting the cake.

5 Bake for 25 to 30 minutes, or until a cake tester inserted into the center comes out clean. Cool in the pans on wire racks for 5 to 7 minutes. Invert the cakes onto the racks to cool completely.

6 To assemble, place one of the cake layers on a serving plate and spread with some of the reserved chocolate mixture. Top with another cake layer and spread with more of the chocolate mixture. Top with the remaining cake layer and frost the top and the sides of the cake with the chocolate mixture.

110 ■ CHOCOLATE FUDGE DEVIL'S CAKE

12 SERVINGS
BAKING TIME: *35 to 40 minutes*
CHILL TIME: *50 minutes*

CAKE

1 box (18.5 ounces) chocolate cake mix

FILLING

1 cup pitted dates
1 cup hot water
Pinch of salt
1/4 teaspoon orange or lemon zest
2 teaspoons unsweetened grapefruit juice
2 tablespoons honey or corn syrup

TOPPING

3/4 cup granulated sugar
1 1/2 tablespoons all-purpose flour
1/4 teaspoon salt
1 teaspoon lemon zest
1/3 cup fresh lemon juice
1 large egg
1 tablespoon butter-flavored vegetable shortening
1 cup heavy cream
Chopped pecans for garnish

1 Position a rack in the center of the oven and preheat the oven to 350 degrees. Lightly grease and flour two 9-inch round cake pans.

2 Prepare the cake according to the package directions and spread evenly into the prepared pans. Bake according to the package directions. Remove from the oven and cool in the pans on wire racks.

3 Meanwhile, to prepare the filling, in a saucepan over low heat, simmer the dates and water together for 15 minutes. Remove from the heat and drain.

4 In the container of a blender, combine the dates, salt, zest, grapefruit juice, and honey, blending on high speed until smooth. Chill for 30 minutes.

5 Meanwhile, to make the topping, in the top of a double boiler over simmering water, combine the sugar, flour, salt, lemon zest, lemon juice, and egg, stirring by hand until smooth and thickened. Remove from the heat and stir in the shortening.

6 In a medium bowl, using an electric mixer on high speed, beat the cream until stiff and fold into the cooled mixture.

7 To assemble, place one of the cake rounds on a serving plate and spread the date mixture evenly over the top. Place the second layer on top of the first, and spread the topping evenly over the top and sides of the cake. Sprinkle the top of the cake with the pecans. Chill for 20 minutes before serving.

111 ■ CHOCOLATE FUDGE EGGNOG CAKE

YIELD: *16 servings*
BAKING TIME: *60 minutes*
CHILL TIME: *30 minutes*

CAKE

3/4 cup cake flour
1/4 cup Dutch processed cocoa powder
13 large egg whites
1¼ cups granulated sugar
1 teaspoon cream of tartar
1 teaspoon vanilla extract or Liquore Galliano
1 tablespoon powdered sugar for dusting

EGGNOG

1/4 cup milk
1 tablespoon unflavored gelatin
8 ounces semisweet chocolate, grated or finely chopped
1½ cups heavy cream
2 large eggs yolks
3/4 cup powdered sugar
3 tablespoons coffee liqueur

1 Position a rack in the center of the oven and preheat the oven to 350 degrees.

2 To make the cake, combine the cake flour and cocoa powder. Sift twice.

3 In a large bowl, using an electric mixer on high speed, beat the egg whites until foamy. Blend in the sugar, cream of tartar, and vanilla extract and whip on high speed until stiff but not dry. Gradually fold in the dry ingredients, mixing just until blended. Pour the batter into an ungreased 10-inch tube pan.

4 Bake for 55 to 60 minutes, or until a cake tester inserted into the center comes out clean. Invert the pan onto its tube or

onto the legs on the pan and cool completely. Remove the cake from the pan and place on a serving platter. Dust with the powdered sugar.

5 Chill a 9-inch springform pan.

6 Meanwhile, to prepare the eggnog, place the milk in a small saucepan and sprinkle with the gelatin. Let stand 1 minute to soften. Stir over low heat until completely dissolved. Remove from the heat.

7 Melt the chocolate (see page 13). Remove from the heat.

8 In a small bowl, using an electric mixer on high speed, whip 1 cup of heavy cream until stiff peaks form.

9 In another small bowl, whip the remaining ½ cup cream until stiff peaks forms. In a large bowl, using an electric mixer on medium speed, beat the egg yolks until thick and light-colored. Beat in the powdered sugar and liqueur, beating well. Add the ½ cup whipped cream and fold gently together. Fold in the melted chocolate and the remaining 1 cup of whipped cream. Fold in the cooled gelatin mixture.

10 To assemble, line the bottom of the chilled springform pan with ½-inch thick slices of the cake. Line the sides of the pan with ½-inch thick cake slices that have been cut into 1-inch strips. Pour a thin layer of the eggnog over the slices in the bottom, place another layer of cake slices on top of the eggnog and continue until the eggnog and cake slices are completely used up. Chill for 30 minutes, or until firm.

11 Remove the sides from the pan.

103

111

106

112 ■ CHOCOLATE-FUDGE-FROSTED GENOISE CAKE

YIELD: *12 servings*
BAKING TIME: *30 minutes*

6 large eggs
1 cup granulated sugar
1/2 cup butter, melted, clarified, and cooled (see Baking notes)
1 teaspoon vanilla or almond extract
1 cup all-purpose flour
3/4 cup Lemon Filling (see page 413)
2 cups Chocolate Frosting IV (see page 400)

1 Preheat the oven to 350 degrees. Lightly grease two 9-inch round cake pans.

2 To make the cake, in a large bowl, using an electric mixer on medium speed, beat the eggs until light-colored. Beat in the sugar. Set the bowl over a pan of hot water and let stand, stirring occasionally, until lukewarm. (Do not allow bottom of the bowl to touch the water.) Remove from the water and beat on high speed until the eggs are almost tripled in volume, about 10 to 15 minutes. The mixture should resemble a thick, whipped mayonnaise.

3 In a small bowl, using a fork, beat the butter and vanilla until fluffy.

4 Fold one-third of the flour along with one-third of the butter mixture into the egg mixture. Repeat two more times. Do not overmix. Divide the mixture between the prepared pans and spread evenly.

5 Bake for 25 to 30 minutes, or until golden brown and the cake has pulled away from the sides of the pans. Cool in the pans on a wire rack for 20 minutes. Invert onto wire racks to cool completely.

6 Prepare the lemon filling and the chocolate frosting.

7 To assemble, place one cake layer on a serving plate and spread the lemon filling in an even layer over the top. Top with the second layer and press lightly into place. Spread the chocolate frosting evenly over the top and sides of the cake. Serve at once or chill until ready to serve. Garnish with chocolate curls and a lemon slices.

BAKING NOTES: To clarify butter, in a medium saucepan, melt the butter over very low heat. Skim off the foam that rises to the top using a ladle, taking care to remove as little of the clear, yellow fat as possible. Let the butter cool slightly and settle. Carefully strain the butter through a fine sieve into a bowl or glass container, leaving the milky residue on the bottom of the saucepan. Discard the residue.

113 ■ CHOCOLATE FUDGE UPSIDE-DOWN CAKE

YIELD: *16 servings*
BAKING TIME: *45 minutes*

1 cup all-purpose flour
1 1/4 teaspoons baking powder
1/4 teaspoon salt
2 ounces unsweetened chocolate, grated or finely chopped
3 tablespoons butter, melted
3 tablespoons packed light brown sugar
1 cup walnuts, coarsely chopped
1 large egg, separated
2 tablespoons butter, at room temperature
1 cup granulated sugar
1/4 teaspoon vanilla or almond extract
3/4 cup milk

1 Position a rack in the center of the oven and preheat the oven to 350 degrees. Grease and flour a 10-inch Bundt pan.

2 Combine the flour, baking powder, and salt.

3 Melt the chocolate (see page 13). Remove from the heat.

4 In a small bowl, using an electric mixer on medium speed, beat the 3 tablespoons melted butter and the brown sugar until blended. Mix in the walnuts and spread evenly over the bottom of the prepared pan.

5 In a small bowl, using an electric mixer on high speed, beat the egg white until stiff but not dry.

6 In a large bowl, using an electric mixer on medium speed, beat the 2 tablespoons of butter and the granulated sugar until light and fluffy. Beat in the egg yolk and vanilla. Stir in the melted chocolate. In three additions, blend in the dry ingredients, alternating with the milk, beginning and ending with the dry ingredients. Mix until the batter is smooth and well blended. Fold in the egg white. Pour the batter into the prepared pan.

6 Bake for 25 to 45 minutes, or until a cake tester inserted into the center comes out clean. Let cool for 10 minutes. Invert onto a cake rack to cool completely.

BAKING NOTES: Do not overbake the cake or the frosting in the bottom of the pan will dry out.

114 ■ CHOCOLATE GENOISE

YIELD: *12 servings*
BAKING TIME: *40 minutes*

1/4 cup cake flour, sifted
1/4 cup Dutch processed cocoa powder
3 large eggs, separated and at room temperature
1/2 cup powdered sugar, sifted twice
1/4 cup butter, melted and clarified (see Baking notes, recipe #112)
1 teaspoon amaretto
1 cup Raspberry Sauce (see page 416)

1 Position a rack in the center of the oven and preheat the oven to 350 degrees. Lightly grease the bottom of a 9-inch spring-form pan and line with waxed paper. Lightly grease and flour the paper and side of the pan.

2 Combine the flour and cocoa powder.

3 In a large bowl, using an electric mixer on high speed, beat the egg whites until soft peaks form. Add the powdered sugar and continue to beat until stiff but not dry. Beat in the egg yolks. Fold in the dry ingredi-

ents, a little at a time, blending well after each addition.

4 In a small bowl, stir ¼ cup of the batter and the clarified butter until thoroughly mixed. Fold the butter mixture into the remaining batter. Blend in the amaretto. Pour into the prepared pan.

5 Bake for 35 to 40 minutes, or until the center springs back when touched. Cool in the pan on a wire rack for 20 minutes. Remove the side of the pan and invert onto the rack to cool completely.

6 Make the sauce.

7 To assemble, using a serrated knife, slice the cake in half horizontally. Place one cake layer on a serving plate and spread evenly with frosting. Top with the second layer and spread frosting on the top and sides of the cake.

BAKING NOTES: Traditionally, this cake is frosted with a ganache. For best results, the eggs should be at room temperature and the clarified butter should be lukewarm. There is no substitution for clarified butter.

115 ■ CHOCOLATE GINGERBREAD

YIELD: *10 to 12 servings*
BAKING TIME: *30 minutes*

2 ounces unsweetened chocolate, grated or finely chopped
2 cups all-purpose flour
2 teaspoons baking powder
1½ teaspoons ground cinnamon
1½ teaspoons ground ginger
¼ teaspoon salt
⅓ cup butter or margarine, at room temperature
½ cup granulated sugar
2 large eggs
¼ cup molasses
½ cup milk
Powdered sugar for dusting

1 Position a rack in the center of the oven and preheat the oven to 350 degrees. Lightly grease a 9 by 5-inch loaf pan.

2 Melt the chocolate (see page 13). Remove from the heat.

3 Combine the flour, baking powder, spices, and salt.

4 In a large bowl, using an electric mixer on medium speed, beat the butter and sugar until light and fluffy. Beat in the eggs and molasses. Beat in the melted chocolate. In three additions, stir in the dry ingredients, alternating with the milk, beginning and ending with the dry ingredients. Scrape the mixture into the prepared pan and spread evenly.

5 Bake for 25 to 30 minutes, or until a cake tester inserted into the center comes out clean. Cool in the pan on a wire rack for 10 minutes. Invert onto the rack to cool completely. Dust the top with powdered sugar.

116 ■ CHOCOLATE GRATIFICATION CAKE

YIELD: *12 to 15 servings*
BAKING TIME: *35 minutes*

3 cups all-purpose flour
2 cups granulated sugar
½ cup Dutch processed cocoa powder
2 teaspoons baking soda
½ teaspoon salt
1 cup coffee liqueur
1 cup warm water
⅔ cup canola oil
2 tablespoons cider vinegar
2 teaspoons chocolate extract
1 tablespoon Cocoa Sugar (see page 407)
Whipped cream for serving

1 Position a rack in the center of the oven and preheat the oven to 350 degrees.

2 In a 13 by 9-inch pan, combine the flour, sugar, cocoa powder, baking soda, and salt.

3 In a medium bowl, mix the liqueur, water, oil, vinegar, and chocolate extract until combined. Add to the dry ingredients in the pan. Stir gently until well blended. Spread mixture evenly in the pan.

4 Bake for 30 to 35 minutes, or until a cake tester inserted into the center comes out clean. Cool in the pan on a wire rack.

5 Make the cocoa sugar.

6 Dust the top of the cake with the cocoa sugar. When ready to serve, cut into bars and serve with whipped cream on the side.

113

114

117 ■ CHOCOLATE HAPPINESS CAKE

YIELD: *12 servings*
BAKING TIME: *40 minutes*

2²/₃ cups all-purpose flour
¹/₂ cup almonds, finely ground
1 tablespoon baking powder
¹/₂ teaspoon baking soda
¹/₂ teaspoon salt
4 ounces unsweetened chocolate
²/₃ cup plus 3 tablespoons warm milk
4 large eggs, separated, plus 1 large egg yolk
1¹/₃ cups granulated sugar
¹/₃ cup water
²/₃ cup butter or margarine, at room temperature
³/₄ cup packed light brown sugar
1 tablespoon chocolate or vanilla extract
4 cups Ganache I (see page 410)
Sliced fresh fruit in season for garnish

1 Position a rack in the center of the oven and preheat the oven to 375 degrees. Lightly grease and flour a 9-inch round cake pan.

2 Combine the flour, almonds, baking powder, baking soda, and salt.

3 In the top of a double boiler, set over a simmering water, melt the chocolate, stirring until smooth. Stir in the ²/₃ cup of warm milk.

4 In a small bowl, using an electric mixer on medium speed, beat 1 of the the egg yolks until thick and light-colored. On low speed, beat in 1 cup of granulated sugar. Pouring it in a narrow stream, beat in half of the chocolate mixture. Return the egg yolk mixture to the top of the double boiler, adding it to the remaining chocolate mixture. Cook for 3 minutes. Remove from the pan of simmering water.

5 In a cup, combine the water and the remaining 3 tablespoons of warm milk

6 In a medium bowl, using an electric mixer with clean beaters on high speed, whip the egg whites until stiff but not dry. On low speed, beat in the remaining ¹/₃ cup of granulated sugar and continue to beat until soft peaks form.

7 In a medium bowl, using an electric mixer on medium-high speed, cream the butter and brown sugar until fluffy and smooth. Beat in the chocolate extract. On low speed, beat in the remaining 4 egg yolks, one at a time, blending thoroughly before each addition. On low speed, beat in the chocolate mixture. In three additions, blend in the dry ingredients, alternating with the water mixture, beginning and ending with the dry ingredients. Fold in the beaten egg whites. Pour the mixture into the prepared pan.

8 Bake for 35 to 40 minutes, or until a cake tester inserted into the center comes out clean. Cool in the pan for 10 minutes. Invert onto a plate or wire rack to cool completely.

9 Make the ganache.

10 Place the cake on a serving plate and frost the top and sides with the ganache. Garnish with the sliced fruit.

118 ■ CHOCOLATE HAZELNUT CAKE

YIELD: *16 servings*
BAKING TIME: *20 minutes*
CHILL TIME: *overnight*

HAZELNUT CAKE

1 cup ground hazelnuts
¹/₂ cup cake flour
2 tablespoons cornstarch
¹/₄ teaspoon ground cinnamon
4 large eggs, separated, plus 4 large egg yolks
¹/₂ cup plus ¹/₃ cup granulated sugar
2 teaspoons chocolate or hazelnut extract
Pinch of salt

CHOCOLATE MOUSSE

6 ounces unsweetened chocolate, grated or finely chopped
2 ounces semisweet chocolate, grated or finely chopped
¹/₄ cup strong brewed coffee
4 large eggs, separated
1 tablespoon crème de cacao
2 tablespoons granulated sugar
Chocolate Cigarettes (see page 421) for garnish
Fresh mint sprigs for garnish

1 Position a rack in the center of the oven and preheat the oven to 400 degrees. Lightly grease and flour a 10-inch springform pan.

117

119

118

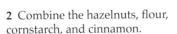

2 Combine the hazelnuts, flour, cornstarch, and cinnamon.

3 In a medium bowl, using an electric mixer on medium speed, beat the egg yolks until thick and light-colored. Add the 1/2 cup sugar and beat until thick. Beat in the chocolate extract.

4 In a large bowl, using an electric mixer with clean beaters on high speed, beat the egg whites and salt until soft peaks form. Add the remaining 1/3 cup sugar, a little at a time, and continue beating until stiff but not dry.

5 Gently fold one-third of the egg whites into the egg yolk mixture, and then fold the egg yolk mixture back into the egg whites. Gradually fold in the dry ingredients. Scrape the mixture into the prepared pan and spread evenly.

6 Bake for 18 to 20 minutes, or until golden brown and a cake tester inserted into the center comes out clean. Cool in the pan on a wire rack.

7 To make the mousse, in the top of a double boiler over simmering water, melt the chocolates with the coffee, stirring until smooth. Remove from the heat.

8 In a medium bowl, using an electric mixer on medium speed, beat the egg yolks until thick and light-colored. Beat in the chocolate mixture. Blend in the crème de cacao.

9 In a medium bowl, using an electric mixer, beat the egg whites until soft peaks form. Add the sugar and continue beating until stiff but not dry. Fold into the chocolate mixture.

10 Spread the mousse evenly over the top of the cake in the pan. Cover and chill overnight, or until the mousse is set.

11 Remove the side of the springform pan. Garnish with chocolate cigarettes and sprigs of mint.

119 ■ CHOCOLATE HONEY CAKE I

YIELD: *12 servings*
BAKING TIME: *30 minutes*

CAKE

4 ounces semisweet chocolate, grated or finely chopped
1 teaspoon baking soda
2 cups all-purpose flour
1/2 teaspoon salt
1 cup milk
3/4 cup honey
1/2 cup butter-flavored vegetable shortening
3/4 cup packed dark brown sugar
2 large eggs
2 teaspoons chocolate extract

FILLING

3/4 pound fresh plums, skinned, pitted, and quartered
1/2 cup port
3 tablespoons powdered sugar

FROSTING

1 1/2 cups granulated sugar
5 tablespoons peppermint schnapps or crème de menthe
1 tablespoon corn syrup
2 large egg whites
1/8 teaspoon peppermint extract
1 ounce semisweet chocolate, melted, for garnish
Chocolate leaves (see page 422) for garnish

1 Position a rack in the center of the oven and preheat the oven to 375 degrees. Lightly grease and flour two 8-inch round cake pans.

2 To make the cake, melt the chocolate (see page 13). Remove from the heat.

3 Combine the flour, baking soda, and salt.

4 Combine the milk and honey.

5 In a large bowl, using an electric mixer on high speed, beat the shortening and brown sugar until fluffy and smooth. On low speed, beat in the melted chocolate. Continue beating and add the eggs, one at a time, beating well after each addition. Stir in the chocolate extract. In three additions, blend in the dry ingredients, alternating with the milk mixture, beginning and ending with the dry ingredients.

Pour the mixture into the prepared pans.

6 Bake for 25 to 30 minutes, or until a ckae tester inserted into the center comes out clean. Cool in the pans on wire racks for ten minutes. Invert onto wire racks to cool completely.

7 Meanwhile, to make the filling, in a medium saucepan, combine the plums and wine, and cook over medium heat until the mixture is reduced to 1 cup. Remove from the heat and stir in the powdered sugar. Return to the heat and cook until the mixture is reduced by one-third. Cool slightly before spreading between the cake layers.

8 Meanwhile, to make the frosting, in the top of a double boiler set over simmering water, combine the sugar, schnapps, corn syrup, and egg whites, stirring constantly, until the mixture is smooth. Increase the temperature to high, and using an electric mixer on medium speed, beat the mixture until it forms stiff peaks. Stir in the peppermint extract.

9 To assemble, place one of the cake layers on a serving plate. Spread the plum filling evenly over the cake and place the second layer on top. Spread the frosting over the top and sides of the cake and drizzle the melted chocolate in straight lines from left to right across the top of the cake. With a spatula or knife, pull the blade over the top of the cake from top to bottom, creating a wavy effect to the chocolate. Decorate with small chocolate leaves around the lines and serve.

120 ■ CHOCOLATE HONEY CAKE II

YIELD: *12 to 15 servings*
BAKING TIME: *40 minutes*

3 cups all-purpose flour
1 cup Dutch processed cocoa
    powder
1 tablespoon baking powder
1/4 teaspoon ground cloves or
    ground nutmeg
1 teaspoon ground cinnamon
1 teaspoon ground allspice
1 teaspoon salt
5 large eggs
2 cups granulated sugar
3 tablespoons honey, warmed
1 cup walnuts or almonds, chopped
1/2 cup White Frosting (see page
    418)

1 Position a rack in the center of
the oven and preheat the oven
to 350 degrees. Lightly grease a
13 by 9-inch pan.

2 Combine the flour, cocoa
powder, baking powder, spices,
and salt.

3 In a large bowl, using an electric mixer on medium speed,
beat the eggs and sugar until
thick and light-colored. Beat in
the honey. Gradually stir in the
dry ingredients. Fold in the walnuts. Scrape the mixture into the
prepared pan and spread
evenly.

4 Bake for 35 to 40 minutes, or
until a cake tester inserted into
the center comes out clean. Cool
in the pan on a wire rack.

5 Make the white sugar icing.
Drizzle the icing over the top of
the cake. Cut into squares.

121 ■ CHOCOLATE ICEBOX CAKE

YIELD: *12 servings*
CHILL TIME: *24 hours*

3/4 cup golden raisins
3/4 cup boiling water
2 tablespoons coffee liqueur
4 ounces unsweetened chocolate,
    grated or finely chopped
1/4 cup heavy cream or evaporated
    milk
3 tablespoons crème de cacao or
    water
1/2 cup butter or margarine, at room
    temperature
10 tablespoons granulated sugar
2 large eggs, separated
1 1/4 cups chocolate wafer cookie
    crumbs
1/2 teaspoon chocolate extract
3/4 cup Chocolate Whipped Cream
    (see page 406)
Grated white chocolate for garnish

1 Lightly grease an 8-inch
square pan. Line the bottom
with waxed paper.

2 In a small bowl, soak the
raisins in the boiling water for 5
minutes. Drain and add the coffee liqueur.

3 In the top of a double boiler
over simmering water, melt the
chocolate with the cream and
crème de cacao, stirring until
smooth.

4 In a large bowl, using an electric mixer on medium speed,
beat the butter and 5 tablespoons of the sugar until light
and fluffy. Beat in the egg yolks
and chocolate mixture. Beat in

the wafer cookie crumbs and
chocolate extract. Fold in the
raisins and liqueur.

5 In a large bowl, using an electric mixer with clean beaters on
high speed, beat the egg whites
until foamy. Sprinkle in the
remaining 5 tablespoons sugar
and beat until stiff but not dry.
Fold 1/2 cup of the egg whites
into the chocolate mixture. Fold
the chocolate mixture into the
egg whites, blending until no
white streaks remain. Scrape the
mixture into the prepared pan
and spread evenly. Cover and
chill for 24 hours.

6 Invert the cake onto a serving
plate and remove the waxed
paper.

7 Make the whipped cream.
Spread the whipped cream over
the top and sides of the cake.
Garnish with grated white
chocolate.

BAKING NOTES: Owing to the
raw eggs used in this recipe, it
should be kept refrigerated at all
times, and for no longer than 3
days.

122 ■ CHOCOLATE JOY CAKE

YIELD: *10 to 12 servings*
BAKING TIME: *35 minutes*

CAKE

2 cups cake flour
1/3 cup Dutch processed cocoa
    powder
1 teaspoon baking powder
1/2 teaspoon baking soda
3 large eggs, separated
1/2 cup butter or margarine, at room
    temperature
1 1/2 cups granulated sugar
1 cup milk or half and half
1 teaspoon chocolate or vanilla
    extract

FILLING

2/3 cup granulated sugar
2/3 cup heavy cream or evaporated
    milk
2 large egg yolks
1 tablespoon arrowroot or
    cornstarch
1 cup pistachios or pecans, finely
    chopped
1 tablespoon butter
1/2 teaspoon crème de cacao

120

123

SAUCE

1 cup granulated sugar
¹/₃ cup Dutch processed cocoa powder
¹/₃ cup heavy cream or evaporated milk
1 large egg
¹/₂ teaspoon Baitz Island Cream liqueur
White chocolate curls and white edible flowers for garnish

1 Position a rack in the center of the oven and preheat the oven to 350 degrees. Lightly grease and flour two 8 by 3-inch loaf pans.

2 To make the cake, combine the flour, cocoa powder, baking powder, and baking soda.

3 In a medium bowl, using an electric mixer on high speed, whip the egg whites until stiff but not dry.

4 In a large bowl, using an electric mixer on high speed, beat the butter and sugar until light and fluffy. Beat in the egg yolks. Beat in the milk and chocolate extract. Gradually blend in the dry ingredients until just incorporated. Fold in the egg whites. Do not overmix. Divide the mixture evenly between the two prepared pans.

5 Bake for 30 to 35 minutes, or until a cake tester inserted into the center comes out clean. Cool in the pan on a wire rack for 5 minutes. Invert onto a the rack to cool completely. Transfer to a serving platter.

6 Meanwhile, to make the cream filling, in the top of a double boiler set over simmering water, whisk the sugar, cream, egg yolks, and arrowroot. Stir constantly until the mixture thickens. Remove from the pan of simmering water and using an electric mixer on low speed, beat in the nuts, butter, and crème de cacao. Beat until the mixture is a spreadable consistency. Cool completely.

7 Meanwhile, to make the sauce, stir the sugar, cocoa powder, and cream until blended. Whisk in the egg. Pour the mixture into the top of a double boiler set over simmering water and cook stirring until thick. Remove from heat and stir in the liqueur. Cool sauce until thickened.

8 To assemble, using a serrated knife, cut the cake in half horizontally. Spread the filling on the bottom half and press the top half into place. Drizzle the chocolate sauce over the top, allowing it to drip down the sides. Garnish with chocolate curls and white edible flowers.

BAKING NOTES: This same recipes can be used to make 24 cupcakes. Grease or paper line 24 muffin cups. Bake for 18 to 20 minutes. Remove the baked cupcakes from the pan and cool on a wire rack. Slice in half and spread a teaspoon of the filling on the bottom half and sandwich with the top half. Set on a serving plate upside down, and drizzle a teaspoonful of the sauce over the top.

123 ■ CHOCOLATE KIRSCH CAKE

YIELD: *12 servings*
BAKING TIME: *30 minutes*

CAKE

2 ounces unsweetened chocolate, grated or finely chopped
1³/₄ cups cake flour, sifted
1 teaspoon baking soda
¹/₂ teaspoon salt
¹/₂ cup vegetable shortening
1¹/₄ cups granulated sugar
2 large eggs
1 teaspoon vanilla extract
1 cup buttermilk
6 tablespoons kirsch

FROSTING AND FILLING BASE

³/₄ cup granulated sugar
¹/₂ cup water
1 teaspoon cornstarch or arrowroot
1¹/₄ cups butter
6 large egg yolks
¹/₈ teaspoon salt
¹/₂ teaspoon vanilla or almond extract
2 ounces unsweetened chocolate, grated or finely chopped

FILLING

¹/₂ cup Almond Paste (see page 394)

1 Position a rack in the center of the oven and preheat the oven to 350 degrees. Lightly grease two 9-inch cake pans.

2 To make the cake, melt the chocolate (see page 13). Remove from the heat.

3 Combine the flour, baking soda, and salt.

4 In a large bowl, using an electric mixer on medium speed, beat the vegetable shortening and sugar until light and fluffy. Beat in the eggs. Beat in the melted chocolate and vanilla. In three additions, blend in the dry ingredients, alternating with the buttermilk, beginning and ending with the dry ingredients. Divide the mixture evenly between the prepared pans.

5 Bake for 25 to 30 minutes, or until a cake tester inserted into the center comes out clean. Do not overbake or the cake will be dry. Cool in the pans for 5 minutes. Remove to wire racks and cool right-side up. As soon as the cakes are cooled, spoon the kirsch over the tops of the layers. Wrap in plastic wrap or place in a plastic bag and seal. Chill until ready to use.

6 Meanwhile, to make the frosting and filling base, in a small saucepan, combine the sugar, water, and cornstarch and bring to a boil. Insert a candy thermometer and cook, stirring constantly, until 238 degrees. Remove from the heat and add the butter without stirring.

7 In a small bowl, using an electric mixer on medium speed, beat the egg yolks until thick and light-colored. Pouring it in a thin stream, add the cooled syrup, beating constantly until light and fluffy. Beat in the salt and vanilla.

8 To make the frosting, melt the chocolate (see page 13). Remove from the heat. Using an electric mixer on medium speed, beat in 1¼ cups of the base mixture. Remove from the heat and beat until the mixture is thickened.

9 To make the filling, spoon the almond paste into a small bowl. Using an electric mixer on medium speed, beat in the remaining base mixture until smooth.

10 To assemble, using a serrated knife, trim the rounded tops off the cake layers. Place one layer on a serving plate and spread evenly with filling. Top with the second layer and spread the frosting on the top and sides of the cake. Chill until ready to serve.

124 ■ CHOCOLATE LOVERS' FUDGE CAKE

YIELD: *16 servings*
BAKING TIME: *80 minutes*

2½ cups all-purpose flour
½ teaspoon baking soda
6 ounces semisweet chocolate, grated or finely chopped
1 cup chocolate syrup
2 teaspoons chocolate or vanilla extract
1 cup butter or margarine, at room temperature
1½ cups granulated sugar
4 large eggs
1 cup buttermilk
2½ cups semisweet chocolate chips
3 ounces white chocolate bark, grated or finely chopped
2 tablespoons plus 2 teaspoons vegetable shortening
Chocolate and White Chocolate Leaves (see page 422) for garnish

1 Position a rack in the center of the oven and preheat the oven to 300 degrees. Generously grease a 10-inch Bundt pan.

2 Combine the flour and baking soda.

3 Melt the chocolate (see page 13). Remove from the heat.

4 Stir in chocolate syrup and and chocolate extract.

5 In a large bowl, using an electric mixer on medium speed, beat the butter and sugar until light and fluffy. Beat in the eggs, one at a time, beating well after each addition. In three additions, mix in the dry ingredients, alternating with the buttermilk, beginning and ending with the dry ingredients. Fold in the chocolate mixture until thoroughly blended. Stir in 1 cup of the chocolate chips. Pour the mixture into the prepared pan.

6 Bake for 1 hour and 20 minutes, or until a cake tester inserted into the center comes out clean. Immediately invert the cake onto a wire rack and cool completely.

7 In the top of a double boiler over simmering water, melt the white chocolate and 2 tablespoons of the shortening, stirring until smooth. Remove from the heat and drizzle over the cake.

8 In a small saucepan, over low heat, melt the remaining 1½ cups chocolate chips and the remaining 2 teaspoons of shortening, stirring until smooth. Drizzle over the white chocolate on the cake. Garnish with white and chocolate leaves.

BAKING NOTES: Edible white flowers (see page 22) can be substituted for the chocolate leaves for garnish.

125 ■ CHOCOLATE MARBLE CAKE

YIELD: *12 servings*
BAKING TIME: *45 minutes*

2 ounces semisweet chocolate, grated or finely chopped
2 cups all-purpose flour
2 teaspoons baking powder
½ teaspoon ground cinnamon
⅛ teaspoon ground cloves
¼ teaspoon salt
3 large eggs, separated
¼ teaspoon baking soda
2 tablespoons boiling water
⅓ cup butter or margarine, at room temperature
1 cup granulated sugar
1 teaspoon almond or chocolate extract

⅔ cup buttermilk
1½ cups Chocolate Frosting III (see page 399)
Chopped nuts or grated chocolate for garnish

1 Position a rack in the center of the oven and preheat the oven to 350 degrees. Lightly grease and flour an 8 or 9-inch square pan. Line the bottom of the pan with waxed paper and grease the paper.

2 Melt the chocolate (see page 13). Remove from the heat.

3 Combine the flour, baking powder, spices, and salt.

4 In a medium bowl, using an electric mixer on high speed, beat the egg whites until stiff but not dry.

5 In a cup, dissolve the baking soda in the boiling water.

6 In a large bowl, using an electric mixer on medium speed, beat the butter and sugar until light and fluffy. Beat in the almond extract. Beat in the egg yolks, one at a time, beating well after each addition. In three additions, blend in the dry ingredients, alternating with the buttermilk, beginning and ending with the dry ingredients. Fold in the egg whites.

7 Pour half of the batter into another bowl. Stir in the melted chocolate and baking soda mixture until blended.

8 Using two large serving spoons, alternately spoon the chocolate and plain batters into the prepared pan. Using a knife, swirl the batters together to create a marbled effect. Do not overmix.

9 Bake for 40 to 45 minutes, or until a cake tester inserted into the center comes out clean. Cool in the pan on a wire rack for 10 minutes. Invert onto the rack to cool completely. Remove the waxed paper and place on a serving plate.

10 Make the chocolate frosting. Spread the frosting evenly over the top and sides of the cake. Garnish with chopped nuts or grated chocolate.

126 ∎ CHOCOLATE MERINGUE CAKE

YIELD: *12 servings*
BAKING TIME: *35 minutes*

CHOCOLATE MERINGUE CAKE

4 ounces semisweet chocolate, grated or finely chopped
1/2 cup all-purpose flour
1/2 teaspoon baking soda
1/4 teaspoon salt
1/4 cup butter or margarine, at room temperature
1 cup granulated sugar
4 large eggs, separated
1 teaspoon chocolate extract
1/4 cup hot water
1/2 cup semisweet chocolate chips
1/2 cup white chocolate chips

WHIPPED CREAM TOPPING

1 cup heavy cream
1/4 cup powdered sugar
Chocolate Curls (see page 422) for garnish

1 Postion a rack in the center of the oven and preheat the oven to 350 degrees. Grease and lightly flour two 8-inch round cake pans.

2 To make the cake, melt the chocolate (see page 13). Remove from the heat.

3 Combine the flour, baking soda, and salt.

4 In a large bowl, using an electric mixer with clean beaters on medium speed, beat the butter and 3/4 cup of the sugar until light and fluffy. Beat in the egg yolks, one at a time, beating well after each addition. Beat in the melted chocolate and chocolate extract. In three additions, blend in the dry ingredients, alternating with the hot water, beginning and ending with the dry ingredients. Divide the mixture evenly between the prepared pans. Sprinkle the chocolate chips over the top.

5 In a large bowl, using an electric mixer with clean beaters on high speed, beat the egg whites until foamy. Add the remaining 1/4 cup sugar, a little at a time, and continue beating until stiff but not dry. Spread the meringue evenly over the tops of the batter in the pans.

6 Bake for 30 to 35 minutes, or until the meringue is golden brown. Cool in the pans on wire racks for 15 minutes. Invert onto wire racks to cool completely.

7 To make the topping, using an electric mixer on medium speed, beat the cream and sugar until soft peaks form.

8 To assemble, place one of the cake layers on a serving plate, meringue side up, and spread with the whipped cream. Top with the second cake layer and spread the remaining whipped cream over the top and sides of the cake. Garnish with chocolate curls and chill until serving.

127 ∎ CHOCOLATE MERINGUE CUPCAKES

YIELD: *12 servings*
BAKING TIME: *60 minutes*

3/4 cup granulated sugar
6 tablespoons Dutch processed cocoa powder
3 large egg whites
1/8 teaspoon cream of tartar
Pinch of salt
1 teaspoon chocolate extract
1 cup semisweet miniature chocolate chips
Chocolate ice cream for filling

1 Place a rack in the center of oven. Do not preheat the oven. Grease twelve 2 1/2-inch muffin cups.

2 Combine the sugar and cocoa powder.

3 In a large bowl, using an electric mixer on high speed, beat the egg whites and cream of tartar until foamy. Add the salt and continue beating until stiff but not dry. Gradually blend in the chocolate extract and dry ingredients. Fold in the chocolate chips. Spoon the mixture into the prepared muffin cups.

126

127

4 Place the pans in the cold oven and turn on the heat to 250 degrees. Bake for 60 minutes. Cool in the pan for 12 minutes. Remove to a wire rack to cool completely. The cupcakes will stick to the pan.

5 To assemble, using a serrated knife, slice the cupcakes in half horizontally. Fill with chocolate ice cream. Serve immediately.

BAKING NOTES: It is normal for the cupcakes to stick to the pan. To remove, loosen by running a thin-bladed knife around the sides.

128 ▪ CHOCOLATE MINI-MARSHMALLOW CAKE

YIELD: *12 servings*
BAKING TIME: *40 minutes*

1 cup all-purpose flour
1½ teaspoons baking powder
Pinch of salt
½ cup butter or margarine, at room temperature
1 cup granulated sugar
4 large eggs
2 cups Chocolate Syrup I (see page 406), plus more for serving
1 teaspoon chocolate or vanilla extract
2½ cups miniature marshmallows
Chocolate Glaze II (see page 401)

1 Position a rack in the center of the oven and preheat the oven to 350 degrees. Lightly grease a 9-inch square pan.

2 Combine the flour, baking powder, and salt.

3 In a large bowl, using an electric mixer on medium speed, beat the butter and sugar until light and fluffy. Beat in the eggs, one at a time, beating well after each addition. Beat in the chocolate syrup. Gradually blend in the dry ingredients. Beat in the chocolate extract. Scrape the batter into the prepared pan and spread evenly.

4 Bake for 35 to 40 minutes, or until a cake tester inserted into the center comes out clean. Sprinkle the marshmallows over the top of the hot cake. Cool in the pan on a wire rack for 30 minutes.

5 Make the glaze. Drizzle the glaze over the top of the cake. Serve with chocolate syrup on the side.

129 ▪ CHOCOLATE MINT CAKE

YIELD: *12 servings*
BAKING TIME: *30 minutes*

CAKE

1 cup all-purpose flour
⅓ cup Dutch processed cocoa powder
1 teaspoon baking powder
¼ teaspoon baking soda
½ teaspoon salt
¾ cup granulated sugar
⅓ cup vegetable shortening
1 large egg
1 teaspoon peppermint extract or peppermint schnapps
⅔ cup milk

FILLING

½ cup Chocolate Filling (see page 398)

121

124

115

112

122

116

TOPPING

2 cups powdered sugar, sifted
2 tablespoons butter or margarine, at room temperature
1/4 teaspoon peppermint extract or peppermint schnapps
2 to 3 tablespoons milk
1 to 2 drops green food coloring
6 chocolate-covered mint candies, diced
Mint sprigs for garnish

1 Position a rack in the center of the oven and preheat the oven to 350 degrees. Lightly grease and flour two 9-inch cake pans.

2 To make the cake, combine the flour, cocoa powder, baking powder, baking soda, and salt.

3 In a large bowl, using an electric mixer on medium speed, beat the sugar and shortening until smooth. Beat in the egg. Beat in the peppermint extract. In three additions, stir in the dry ingredients, alternating with the milk, beginning and ending with the dry ingredients. Divide the batter evenly between the prepared pans.

4 Bake for 25 to 30 minutes, or until a cake tester inserted into the center comes out clean. Cool in the pans on wire racks for 5 minutes. Invert onto the racks to cool completely.

5 Make the chocolate filling.

6 Meanwhile, to make the frosting, in a large bowl, using an electric mixer on medium speed, beat the powdered sugar, butter, and peppermint extract until combined. Mix in enough milk to make a spreadable mixture. Beat in the food coloring.

7 To assemble, place one cake layer on a serving plate and spread with the chocolate filling. Place the second layer on top and spread the frosting over the top and sides of the cake. Decorate with the diced chocolate mints. Garnish with sprigs of mint.

130 ■ CHOCOLATE MOCHA AMARETTO CHEESECAKE

YIELD: *12 servings*
BAKING TIME: *2 hours*
CHILL TIME: *1½ hours*

CRUST

5 tablespoons butter, melted
1¼ cups chocolate wafer cookie crumbs

FILLING

1¼ cups semisweet chocolate chips
1½ tablespoons mocha-flavored instant coffee powder
2 tablespoons amaretto
1 teaspoon coffee liqueur
24 ounces cream cheese, at room temperature
1 cup granulated sugar
3 large eggs
1½ cups sour cream or yogurt

1 Position a rack in the center of the oven and preheat the oven to 350 degrees. Lightly grease a 9-inch springform pan.

2 To make the crust, in a medium bowl, using a pastry blender, combine the butter and the cookie crumbs. Press the mixture onto the bottom and halfway up the sides of the prepared pan. Chill in the freezer 10 minutes, or until ready to use.

3 Melt the chocolate (see page 13). Remove from the heat.

4 In a cup, stir the coffee powder, amaretto, and liqueur until blended.

5 In a large bowl, using an electric mixer on medium speed, beat the cream cheese until smooth. Beat in the sugar and eggs, beating well after each addition. On low speed, in a thin stream, beat in the melted chocolate and amaretto mixture. Fold in the sour cream. Pour the mixture into the prepared pan.

6 Bake for 1 hour. Turn off the oven, partly open the oven door, and leave the cheesecake undisturbed for 1 hour. Cool on a wire rack for 3 hours. Cover loosely with plastic wrap and chill for 1½ hours.

7 Remove the side of the pan and serve.

128

129

130

131 ■ CHOCOLATE MOCHA CAKE

YIELD: *12 to 15 servings*
BAKING TIME: *40 minutes*

6 ounces unsweetened chocolate, grated or finely chopped
2¼ cups all-purpose flour
1 teaspoon baking powder
⅓ cup butter or margarine, at room temperature
3 ounces cream cheese, at room temperature
¾ cup granulated sugar
1½ tablespoons mocha-flavored instant coffee powder
2 large eggs
1 cup plus 1 tablespoon milk
1 teaspoon chocolate or vanilla extract
1½ cups Coffee Mocha Icing (See page 408)

1 Position a rack in the center of the oven and preheat the oven to 350 degrees. Lightly grease and flour a 13 by 9-inch pan.

2 Melt the chocolate (see page 13). Remove from the heat.

3 Combine the flour and baking powder.

4 In a large bowl, using an electric mixer on medium speed, beat the butter, cream cheese, sugar, and coffee powder until smooth. Add the eggs, one at a time, beating well after each addition. Beat in the melted chocolate. Beat in the milk and chocolate extract. Gradually blend in the dry ingredients. Pour the batter into the prepared pan.

5 Bake for 35 to 40 minutes, or until a cake tester inserted into the center comes out clean. Cool in the pan on a wire rack for 10 minutes. Invert onto the rack to cool completely.

6 Make the icing. Frost with the mocha icing.

132 ■ CHOCOLATE MOUSSE CAKE I

YIELD: *16 servings*
BAKING TIME: *20 minutes*
CHILL TIME: *3 hours*

CAKE

½ cup cake flour
1 cup hazelnuts or pecans, finely ground
2 tablespoons cornstarch or arrowroot
¼ teaspoon ground cinnamon
4 large eggs, separated, plus 4 large egg yolks
½ cup plus ⅓ cup granulated sugar
2 tablespoons hazelnut extract
Pinch of salt

MOUSSE AND GARNISHES

8 ounces semisweet chocolate, grated or finely chopped
¼ cup brewed coffee
4 large eggs, separated
2 tablespoons granulated sugar
1 tablespoon coffee liqueur
Strawberries dipped in white chocolate (see page 386, substituting white chocolate) for garnish
White Chocolate Leaves (see page 422) for garnish
Melted white chocolate (see page 13) for piping vine decoration

1 Position a rack in the center of the oven and preheat the oven to 400 degrees. Lightly grease and flour a 10-inch springform pan.

2 To make the cake, combine the flour, hazelnuts, cornstarch, and cinnamon.

3 In a medium bowl, using an electric mixer on medium speed, beat the 8 egg yolks and ½ cup of the sugar until very thick and light-colored. Do not underbeat. Blend in the hazelnut extract.

4 In another medium bowl, using an electric mixer with clean beaters on high speed, beat the 4 egg whites and salt until soft peaks form. Gradually add the remaining ⅓ cup of sugar and beat until stiff but not dry. Gently fold the egg white mixture, one-third at a time, into the egg yolk mixture. Gradually fold in the dry ingredients, mixing just until blended. Do not overmix. Scrape the batter into

the prepared pan and spread evenly.

5 Bake 18 to 20 minutes, or until a cake tester inserted into the center comes out clean. Cool in the pan on a wire rack. The cake will fall as it cools.

6 To make the mousse, in the top of a double boiler, over simmering water, melt the chocolate and coffee, stirring until smooth. Remove from the heat.

7 In a small bowl, using an electric mixer on high speed, beat the egg whites until soft peaks form. Gradually add the sugar and beat until stiff but not dry.

8 By hand, beat the egg yolks into the melted chocolate mixture, one at a time, beating well after each addition. Fold in the liqueur. Gradually fold in the egg whites. Spread the filling over the top of the cake in the pan, cover, and chill until firm to the touch, about 2 to 3 hours.

9 To serve, remove the side of the pan and garnish with the white chocolate-covered strawberries and white chocolate leaves. Using a small pastry bag filled with melted white chocolate, pipe a thin line to represent a vine running between the leaves and strawberries.

BAKING NOTES: Owing to the raw eggs used in this recipe, it should be kept refrigerated at all times, and for no longer than 3 days.

133

131

133 ■ CHOCOLATE MOUSSE CAKE II

YIELD: *16 servings*
CHILL TIME: *8 hours or overnight*

CRUST

3 cups chocolate graham cracker crumbs
½ cup butter, melted

FILLING

2 cups semisweet chocolate chips
2 large eggs, left whole, plus 4 large eggs, separated
2 cups heavy cream
6 tablespoons powdered sugar
2 tablespoons semisweet chocolate, grated or finely chopped, for garnish

1 To make the crust, in a large bowl, combine the graham cracker crumbs and butter. Press onto the bottom of a 10-inch springform pan. Chill in the freezer for 1 hour.

2 Meanwhile, to make the filling, melt the chocolate chips (see page 13). Remove from the heat. Beat in the 2 whole eggs. Beat in the egg yolks. Beat in 1 cup of the cream and the powdered sugar.

3 In a medium bowl, using an electric mixer on high speed, beat the egg whites until stiff but not dry. Stir 2 tablespoons of the chocolate mixture into the beaten egg whites and then fold in the remaining chocolate mixture. Pour onto the chilled crust and chill overnight.

4 When ready to serve, using an electric mixer on high speed, beat the remaining 1 cup of cream until soft peaks form. Spoon over the top of the chilled mousse and sprinkle with the grated chocolate.

BAKING NOTES: Owing to the raw eggs used in this recipe, it should be kept refrigerated at all times, and for no longer than 3 days.

134 ■ CHOCOLATE MOUSSE CAKE III

YIELD: *12 servings*
BAKING TIME: *30 minutes*
CHILL TIME: *30 minutes*

COCOA GENOISE CAKE

½ cup all-purpose flour
½ cup Dutch processed unsweetened cocoa powder
6 large eggs
1 cup granulated sugar
½ cup butter or margarine, melted
1 teaspoon chocolate extract
Apricot Glaze (see page 394)

CHOCOLATE MOUSSE

8 ounces semisweet chocolate, grated or finely chopped
½ cup heavy cream
3 large eggs, separated
¼ cup granulated sugar
2 tablespoons coffee liqueur
1 tablespoon strong brewed coffee
Apricot Roses or leaves (see page 420) for garnish
Grated white chocolate for garnish

1 Position a rack in the center of the oven and preheat the oven to 350 degrees. Lightly grease and flour three 8-inch round cake pans. Line the bottoms of the pans with waxed paper.

2 To make the cake, combine the flour and cocoa powder.

3 In a large bowl, using an electric mixer on medium speed, beat the eggs until thick and light-colored. Beat in the sugar. Set the bowl over a saucepan of hot water. Do not allow the bottom of the bowl to touch the water. Beat until the mixture is warm to the touch. Remove from the saucepan and beat until the mixture is thickened and cooled. Gradually fold in the dry ingredients. Do not overmix. Fold in the butter and chocolate extract, mixing just until blended. Pour the batter into the prepared pans.

4 Bake for 25 to 30 minutes, or until the cakes spring back when gently touched and a cake tester inserted into the center comes out clean. Invert onto wire racks to cool completely. Cover and chill the cakes while preparing the glaze and mousse.

5 Meanwhile, make the apricot glaze. Cover and chill until ready to use.

6 To make the mousse, melt the chocolate (see page 13). Remove from the heat.

7 In a small bowl, using an electric mixer on high speed, beat the heavy cream until soft peaks form.

8 In another small bowl, using an electric mixer with clean beaters on high speed, beat the egg whites until stiff but not dry.

9 In a large bowl, using an electric mixer on medium speed, beat the egg yolks until thick and light-colored. Beat in the sugar. Beat in the liqueur and coffee. Beat in the melted chocolate. Fold in the egg whites. Fold in the whipped cream. Chill the mixture for 20 to 30 minutes, or until a spreadable consistency.

10 To assemble, place one of the cake layers on a serving plate. Using a fork, poke holes all over the top of the cake. Brush 2 tablespoons of the apricot glaze over the cake. Spread one-third of the mousse evenly over the top. Repeat with the remaining cake layers, glaze, and mousse, spreading the remaining third of the mousse over the top and sides of the cake. Garnish with apricot roses and grated white chocolate. Refrigerate until serving.

BAKING NOTES: Owing to the raw eggs used in this recipe, it should be kept refrigerated at all times, and for no longer than 3 days.

132

135 ■ CHOCOLATE NUT CAKE

YIELD: *16 servings*
BAKING TIME: *50 minutes*

CHOCOLATE CAKE

6 ounces unsweetened chocolate, grated or finely chopped
1/2 cup butter or margarine
3 large eggs
3/4 cup granulated sugar
1 teaspoon chocolate or vanilla extract
6 tablespoons all-purpose flour
1 cup miniature marshmallows
1/2 cup chopped walnuts

POWDERED SUGAR TOPPING

1/2 cup powdered sugar
1 tablespoon milk

1 Position a rack in the center of the oven and preheat the oven to 350 degrees. Lightly grease and flour a 9-inch Bundt pan.

2 To make the cake, in the top of a double boiler over simmering water, melt the chocolate and butter, stirring constantly until smooth. Remove from the heat.

3 In a large bowl, using an electric mixer on medium speed, beat the eggs until thick and light-colored. Beat in the sugar. Beat in the chocolate extract. Beat in the chocolate mixture, alternating with the flour, mixing just until blended. Stir in the marshmallows and walnuts. Pour into the prepared pan.

4 Bake for 45 to 50 minutes, or until a cake tester inserted into the center comes out clean. Cool in the pan on a wire rack for 10 minutes. Invert onto the rack to cool completely.

5 To make the topping, in a small bowl, stir the powdered sugar and milk until blended. If the topping is too thin, add more powdered sugar, a teaspoonful at a time. If it is too thick, add water, a drop at a time.

6 Place the cake on a serving plate. Drizzle the topping over the top of the cake.

136 ■ CHOCOLATE NUT LOAF

YIELD: *20 to 24 servings*
BAKING TIME: *60 minutes*

2 1/2 cups all-purpose flour
1 cup pecans, finely ground
1 teaspoon baking soda
1/4 teaspoon salt
3 ounces semisweet chocolate, grated or finely chopped
1 cup vegetable shortening
2 cups granulated sugar
5 large eggs
2 teaspoons crème de cacao or chocolate extract
1 1/3 cups buttermilk
1/2 cup Chocolate Glaze II (see page 401)

1 Position a rack in the center of the oven and preheat the oven to 350 degrees. Lightly grease two 9 by 5-inch loaf pans.

2 Combine the flour, pecans, baking soda, and salt.

3 Melt the chocolate (see page 13). Remove from the heat.

4 In a large bowl, using an electric mixer on medium speed, beat the shortening and sugar until fluffy. Beat in the eggs, beating well until blended. Beat in the melted chocolate and crème de cacao. In three additions, blend in the dry ingredients, alternating with the buttermilk, beginning and ending with the dry ingredients. Divide the mixture evenly between the prepared pans.

5 Bake for 55 to 60 minutes, or until a cake tester inserted into the center comes out clean. Cool in the pans for 10 minutes. Invert onto wire racks to cool completely.

6 Make the chocolate glaze. Spread glaze over the tops of the cooled cakes.

BAKING NOTES: For a more festive garnish, fill a pastry bag with chocolate whipped cream (see page 406) and pipe a fancy design over the glazed cake.

137 ■ CHOCOLATE NUTMEG CAKE

YIELD: *12 to 15 servings*
BAKING TIME: *45 minutes*

1 3/4 cups all-purpose flour
1/2 cup pecans or hazelnuts, chopped
1 teaspoon baking soda
1 teaspoon ground nutmeg
1/4 teaspoon salt
2 ounces unsweetened chocolate, grated or finely chopped
1 cup boiling water
1 1/2 cups butter or margarine, at room temperature
1 cup granulated sugar
2 large eggs
1 teaspoon chocolate or almond extract
1 cup white chocolate chips

1 Position a rack in the center of the oven and preheat the oven to 350 degrees. Lightly grease and flour a 13 by 9-inch pan.

2 Combine the flour, pecans, baking soda, nutmeg, and salt.

3 Place the grated chocolate in a small bowl and pour the boiling water over it. Stir until smooth. Cool.

4 In a large bowl, using an electric mixer on medium speed, beat the butter and sugar until light and fluffy. Beat in the eggs, one at a time, beating well after each addition. Beat in the chocolate extract. In three additions, blend in the dry ingredients, alternating with the chocolate mixture, beginning and ending with the dry ingredients. Pour the mixture into the prepared pan.

5 Bake for 40 to 45 minutes, or until a cake tester inserted into the center comes out clean. Immediately sprinkle the hot cake with the chocolate chips and let stand 30 seconds to melt. Spread the chocolate chips evenly across the top. Cool in the pan on a wire rack.

BAKING NOTES: This cake works well for a casual special occasion such as a picnic or barbecue.

138 ■ CHOCOLATE ORANGE-FLAVORED CAKE WITH HAZELNUTS

YIELD: *12 servings*
BAKING TIME: *30 minutes*

CAKE

¼ cup sourdough bread crumbs
¼ cup orange liqueur
4 large eggs, separated
2 ounces semisweet chocolate, grated or finely chopped
6 tablespoons butter or margarine, at room temperature
⅓ cup granulated sugar
½ cup hazelnuts, finely ground

FILLING

½ cup hazelnuts, finely ground
½ cup powdered sugar
2 tablespoons butter or margarine, at room temperature
2 tablespoons heavy cream
1 tablespoon amaretto
Cocoa powder for garnish
Fresh mint sprigs for garnish
Edible flowers for garnish

1 Position a rack in the center of the oven and preheat the oven to 325 degrees. Lightly grease two 8-inch round cake pans.

2 To make the cake, in a small bowl, combine the bread crumbs and liqueur.

3 In a medium bowl, using an electric mixer on low speed, beat the egg whites until stiff but not dry.

4 Melt the chocolate (see page 13). Remove from the heat.

5 In a medium bowl, using an electric mixer on high speed, beat the butter and sugar until light and fluffy. Beat in the egg yolks one at a time, beating well after each addition. Stir in the melted chocolate and hazelnuts. Stir in the bread crumb mixture. Fold in the beaten egg whites. Pour into the prepared pans.

6 Bake for 25 to 30 minutes, or until a cake tester inserted into the center comes out clean. Cool in the pans on wire racks for 5 minutes. Invert onto the racks to cool completely.

7 Meanwhile to make the filling, in a medium bowl, combine the hazelnuts and powdered sugar. Using a pastry blender or two knives, cut in the butter. Stir in the cream and amaretto. The mixture should be a little thick. If too thin, add more powdered sugar, a teaspoonful at a time.

8 To assemble, place one cake layer on a serving plate. Spread the filling evenly over the top. Place the second layer on top of the filling and press gently so the filling oozes to the edges. Sprinkle with cocoa powder and garnish with mint sprigs and edible flowers.

BAKING NOTES: The layers of this cake tend to be very thin. For a variation, after spreading the filling over the bottom layer, arrange very thinly sliced fruit, such as peaches, apricots, strawberries, or kiwifruit, on top of the filling and then place the second layer on top. Any orange-flavored brandy or liqueur can be used for flavoring.

139 ■ CHOCOLATE PEANUT BUTTER CAKE

YIELD: *12 to 15 servings*
BAKING TIME: *40 minutes*

2½ cups all-purpose flour
2 cups packed light brown sugar
1 cup peanut butter
½ cup vegetable shortening
1 cup milk
3 large eggs
1 teaspoon baking powder
½ teaspoon baking soda
1 teaspoon chocolate or vanilla extract
1 cup semisweet chocolate chips

1 Position a rack in the center of the oven and preheat the oven to 350 degrees. Lightly grease a 13 by 9-inch pan.

2 In a large bowl, using an electric mixer on medium speed, beat the flour, brown sugar, peanut butter, and shortening until crumbly. Measure 1 cup for the topping and reserve.

3 Add the milk, eggs, baking powder, baking soda, and chocolate extract to the remaining flour mixture and beat on medium speed until combined. Pour into the prepared pan and sprinkle the reserved mixture over the top.

135

137

139

4 Bake for 35 to 40 minutes, or until a cake tester inserted into the center comes out clean. Immediately sprinkle the hot cake with the chocolate chips and let stand 30 seconds to melt. Spread the chocolate chips evenly across the top. Cool in the pan on a wire rack. Cut into squares.

BAKING NOTES: This fun cake makes a delicious after-school snack for children.

140 ■ CHOCOLATE PETIT FOURS

YIELD: *96 servings*
BAKING TIME: *30 minutes*

CAKE

2 cups all-purpose flour
1/2 cup almonds, finely ground
12 ounces semisweet chocolate, grated or finely chopped
1/2 teaspoon baking powder
Pinch of salt
1 cup butter or margarine
1 cup packed light brown sugar
2 teaspoons chocolate extract

FROSTING

1 1/2 cups powdered sugar
3 tablespoons light corn syrup
2 tablespoons milk
1/4 teaspoon almond extract
1 1/2 cups Chocolate Glaze IV (see page 401)

1 Position a rack in the center of the oven and preheat the oven to 350 degrees. Lightly grease or line with waxed paper a 13 by 9-inch pan.

2 To make the cake, combine the flour, almonds, chocolate, baking powder, and salt.

3 In a large bowl, using an electric mixer on medium speed, beat the butter, brown sugar, and chocolate extract until fluffy. Gradually stir in the dry ingredients. Scrape into the prepared pan and spread evenly.

4 Bake for 25 to 30 minutes, or until a cake tester inserted into the center comes out clean. Cool in the pan on a wire rack.

5 Meanwhile, to make the frosting, in a small bowl, combine all of the ingredients except the

chocolate glaze, and using an electric mixer on medium speed, beat until a smooth and spreadable consistency. Spread over the cooled cake in the pan.

6 Make the chocolate glaze. Drizzle the glaze, first from left to right and then from top to bottom, over the frosted cake. Cut into 1-inch squares and serve on a decorative plate.

BAKING NOTES: The yield will vary, depending on the size the squares that are cut.

141 ■ CHOCOLATE PIE CAKE

YIELD: *15 servings*
BAKING TIME: *8 minutes*

2 cups all-purpose flour
1/3 cup Dutch processed cocoa powder
2 tablespoons sugar
1/2 teaspoon salt
1 cup butter-flavored vegetable shortening
Water, to soften
Chocolate Cream Filling (see page 397)
Raspberry Sauce (see page 416)

1 Position a rack in the center of the oven and preheat the oven to 450 degrees. Lightly grease three baking sheets.

2 In a large bowl, combine the flour, cocoa powder, sugar, and salt. Using a pastry blender or two knives scissor fashion, cut in the shortening until it looks like a coarse meal. Sprinkle the water, a tablespoon at a time, over the dry mix and blend until a soft dough forms. Divide the dough into balls the size of baseballs.

3 On a floured surface, roll each ball out to a thickness of 1/8 inch and cut into 6 or 8-inch rounds. Place the rounds on the prepared baking sheets and stab all over with a fork.

4 Bake for 6 to 8 minutes, or until dry in appearance. Transfer to wire racks to cool completely.

5 Make the filling and sauce.

6 To assemble, place one round on a large serving plate, spoon a tablespoon of the filling on top and spread almost to the edge. Place a second round on top and continue until all of the rounds and filling are used.

7 Spread an even layer of sauce over the top of the cakes, allowing the excess to drip down the sides.

142 ■ CHOCOLATE POTATO CAKE

YIELD: *12 servings*
BAKING TIME: *40 minutes*

4 ounces unsweetened chocolate, grated or finely chopped
2 cups all-purpose flour
1/4 cup pecans or pistachio nuts, finely chopped

141

142

2 teaspoons baking powder
1 teaspoon ground cinnamon
1 teaspoon ground nutmeg
1/4 teaspoon ground cloves
Pinch of salt
1 cup butter or margarine, at room temperature
2 cups granulated sugar
4 large eggs
1 cup hot mashed potatoes
1/2 cup milk
1 tablespoon vanilla or almond extract
1 1/2 cups Simple Chocolate Frosting (see page 416)

1 Position a rack in the center of the oven and preheat the oven to 350 degrees. Lightly grease and flour two 8-inch cake pans.

2 Melt the chocolate (see page 13). Remove from the heat.

3 Combine the flour, pecans, baking powder, spices, and salt.

4 In a large bowl, using an electric mixer on medium speed, beat the butter and sugar until light and fluffy. Beat in the eggs, one at a time. Beat in the hot mashed potatoes and milk. Beat in the vanilla extract and melted chocolate. Gradually blend in the dry ingredients. Divide the mixture between the prepared pans and spread evenly.

5 Bake for 35 to 40 minutes, or until a cake tester inserted into the center comes out clean. Cool in the pans on wire racks for 10 minutes. Invert onto the racks to cool completely.

6 Make the frosting.

7 To assemble, place one cake layer on a serving plate and spread with the frosting. Top with the second layer and spread the frosting on the top and sides of the cake.

143 ■ CHOCOLATE POUND CAKE I

YIELD: *20 to 24 servings*
BAKING TIME: *90 minutes*

2 cups all-purpose flour
1/4 cup walnuts or pecans, finely chopped
1 tablespoon finely grated orange zest
1 teaspoon baking powder
1/4 teaspoon ground nutmeg
1/2 teaspoon salt
2 ounces unsweetened chocolate, grated or finely chopped
2 ounces semisweet chocolate, grated or finely chopped
1 cup butter or margarine, at room temperature
1 1/2 cups granulated sugar
1 teaspoon chocolate extract
5 large eggs
1/4 cup fresh orange juice, strained
1 1/2 cups Rum Cream Frosting (see page 416)
1/2 cup Raspberry Sauce (see page 416)

1 Position a rack in the center of the oven and preheat the oven to 300 degrees. Lightly grease two 9 by 5-inch loaf pans.

2 Combine the flour, walnuts, orange zest, baking powder, nutmeg, and salt.

3 Melt the chocolate (see page 13). Remove from the heat.

4 In a large bowl, using an electric mixer on medium speed, beat the butter and sugar until fluffy. Beat in the chocolate extract. Beat in the eggs, one at a time, beating well after each addition. Beat in the melted chocolate. In three additions, stir in the dry ingredients, alternating with the orange juice, beginning and ending with the dry ingredients. Divide the batter between the prepared pans.

5 Bake for 85 to 90 minutes, or until a cake tester inserted into the center comes out clean. Cool in the pan on a wire rack for 10 minutes. Invert onto the rack to cool completely.

6 Make the frosting and sauce.

7 To assemble, place the cake on a serving plate and frost the sides with the frosting. Spread the top of the cake with the raspberry sauce.

144 ■ CHOCOLATE POUND CAKE II

YIELD: *20 to 24 servings*
BAKING TIME: *80 minutes*

CAKE

3 cups all-purpose flour
5 tablespoons Dutch processed cocoa powder
1/2 teaspoon baking powder
1/2 teaspoon salt
1 1/2 cups butter-flavored vegetable shortening
3 cups granulated sugar
5 large eggs
1 cup milk
1 teaspoon crème de cacao

TOPPING

1 1/4 cups powdered sugar
1/3 cup milk
2 tablespoons butter or margarine
1 ounce unsweetened chocolate, grated or finely chopped
2 teaspoons coffee liqueur

1 Position a rack in the center of the oven and preheat the oven to 325 degrees. Lightly grease two 9 by 5-inch loaf pans.

2 To make the cake, combine the flour, cocoa powder, baking powder, and salt.

3 In a large bowl, using an electric mixer on medium speed, beat the shortening and sugar until fluffy. Beat in the eggs, one at a time. Beat in the milk and crème de cacao. Gradually stir in the dry ingredients. Divide the mixture between the prepared pans.

4 Bake for 70 to 80 minutes, or until a cake tester inserted into the center comes out clean. Cool in the pan on a wire rack for 3 to 5 minutes. Invert onto the rack to cool completely.

5 To make the topping, in a medium saucepan, combine the powdered sugar, milk, butter, and chocolate. Insert a candy thermometer and cook until 236 degrees. Remove from the heat and stir in the liqueur. Using an electric mixer on low speed, beat until the mixture cools.

6 Place the cake on a serving plate. Spread the topping over the top of the cake, allowing it to run down the sides.

145 ■ CHOCOLATE PRUNE CAKE

YIELD: *16 servings*
BAKING TIME: *60 minutes*
STANDING TIME: *overnight*

CAKE

¾ cup all-purpose flour
1 cup plus 3 tablespoons granulated sugar
1 teaspoon ground cinnamon
¾ teaspoon ground allspice
1¾ cups pitted prunes, diced small
⅓ cup crème de prunelle or brandy
9 ounces unsweetened chocolate, grated or finely chopped
5 tablespoons crème de cacao
2 teaspoons hazelnut-flavored instant coffee powder
14 tablespoons butter or margarine
5 large eggs, separated
Pinch of salt
Pinch of cream of tartar

GLAZE

6 tablespoons heavy cream
4½ ounces unsweetened chocolate, grated or finely chopped
3 tablespoons crème de cacao or coffee liqueur

1 To make the cake, combine the flour, ¾ cup of the sugar, and the spices.

2 In a small saucepan, combine the diced prunes, crème de prunelle, and 3 tablespoons of the sugar. Simmer gently for 2 to 3 minutes. Remove from the heat, cover, and let stand for 2 hours.

3 In the top of a double boiler over simmering water, melt the chocolate with the crème de cacao and coffee powder, stirring until smooth. Using a wire whisk, beat in the butter, one tablespoon at a time, whisking until blended after each addition. Gradually blend in the dry ingredients. Beat in the egg yolks and cool until room temperature.

4 Preheat the oven to 350 degrees. Lightly grease and flour a 10-inch Bundt pan.

5 In a large bowl, using an electric mixer on high speed, beat the egg whites, salt, and cream of tartar until soft peaks form. Gradually beat in the remaining ¼ cup of sugar. Beat until stiff but not dry.

6 Lightly whisk the cooled chocolate mixture. Add the egg whites and gently fold until blended. Fold in the prunes. Scrape the batter into the prepared pan and spread evenly.

7 Bake for 55 to 60 minutes, or until the center feels firm and a cake tester inserted into the center comes out with a few crumbs sticking to it. Cool in the pan on a wire rack for 25 minutes. Invert onto the rack to cool completely. Cover with a kitchen towel and let stand at room temperature on the rack overnight.

8 To make the glaze, in a small saucepan, heat the cream just until simmering. Remove from the heat and add the chocolate, stirring until smooth. Stir in the creme de cacao and cool.

9 Place the cake on a serving plate. Spoon the glaze over the top of the cake, allowing it to drip down the sides. Let stand for at least 30 minutes before serving.

146 ■ CHOCOLATE PUDDING CAKE I

YIELD: *12 servings*
BAKING TIME: *25 minutes*

1½ cups all-purpose flour
2 packages (3.4 ounces each) Jell-O Brand chocolate instant pudding mix
2 teaspoons baking powder
¼ teaspoon salt
1 cup minus 1 tablespoon milk
1 large egg
1 cup granulated sugar
2 tablespoons butter or margarine, at room temperature
1 tablespoon chocolate extract
2 cups White Frosting (see page 418)

1 Position a rack in the center of the oven and preheat the oven to 350 degrees. Lightly grease two 8-inch round cake pans.

2 Combine the flour, pudding mix, baking powder, and salt.

3 In a small bowl, combine the milk and egg.

4 In a large bowl, using an electric mixer on medium speed, beat the sugar and butter until light and fluffy. Beat in the milk

mixture and chocolate extract. In four additions, stir in the dry ingredients, mixing just until incorporated after each addition. Divide the mixture between the prepared pans.

5 Bake for 20 to 25 minutes, or until a cake tester inserted into the center comes out clean. Cool in the pans on wire racks for 5 minutes. Invert onto the wire racks to cool completely.

6 Make the white frosting.

7 To assemble, place one cake layer on a serving plate and spread with some of the buttercream. Top with the second cake layer and spread frosting on the top and sides of the cake.

BAKING NOTES: For an attractive garnish, use chocolate curls, and chocolate leaves (see page 422).

147 ■ CHOCOLATE PUDDING CAKE II

YIELD: *12 servings*
BAKING TIME: *35 minutes*

1 cup all-purpose flour
1⅓ cups granulated sugar
6 tablespoons Dutch processed cocoa powder
2 teaspoons baking powder
¼ teaspoon ground nutmeg
½ teaspoon mocha-flavored instant coffee powder
Pinch of salt
½ cup milk
½ cup canola oil
1 teaspoon chocolate extract
½ cup boiling water
½ cup coffee liqueur
Softened chocolate ice cream for serving

1 Position a rack in the center of the oven and preheat the oven to 350 degrees. Lightly grease a 9-inch square pan.

2 In a large bowl, combine the flour, ⅔ cup of the sugar, 4 tablespoons of the cocoa powder, baking powder, nutmeg, coffee powder, and salt.

3 In a small bowl, combine the milk, oil, and chocolate extract. Add to the dry ingredients and stir until blended. Scrape the mixture into the prepared pan and spread evenly. Combine the remaining ⅔ cup sugar and 2 tablespoons cocoa powder. Sprinkle over the top.

4 Combine the boiling water and liqueur and carefully pour over the top of the mixture in the pan. Do not blend.

5 Bake for 30 to 35 minutes, or until a cake tester inserted into the center comes out clean. Cool in the pan for 3 to 5 minutes. Serve the cake warm out of the pan with the chocolate ice cream on the side.

148 ■ CHOCOLATE PUDDING CAKE III

YIELD: *12 servings*
BAKING TIME: *35 minutes*

PUDDING CAKE

1½ cups granulated sugar
1 cup all-purpose flour
⅓ cup Dutch processed cocoa powder
2 teaspoons baking powder
½ teaspoon instant espresso powder
¼ teaspoon ground cinnamon
Pinch of salt
½ cup heavy cream
¼ cup canola oil

COCOA SUGAR TOPPING

⅔ cup granulated sugar
2 tablespoons Dutch processed cocoa powder
Chocolate Whipped Cream (see page 406)

1 Position a rack in the center of the oven and preheat the oven to 350 degrees. Lightly grease an 8-inch square pan.

2 To make the cake, in a large bowl, combine the sugar, flour, cocoa powder, baking powder, espresso powder, cinnamon, and salt.

3 Combine the cream and oil. Gradually blend into the dry ingredients. Scrape the mixture into the prepared pan and spread evenly.

4 To make the topping, combine the sugar and cocoa powder. Sprinkle over the top of the batter in the pan.

5 Bake for 30 to 35 minutes, or until a cake tester inserted into the center comes out clean. Serve warm from the pan. Serve with chocolate whipped cream.

149 ■ CHOCOLATE PUMPKIN CHEESECAKE

YIELD: *12 servings*
BAKING TIME: *68 minutes*
CHILL TIME: *30 minutes*

CRUST

1 cup chocolate wafer cookie crumbs
¼ cup powered sugar
¼ cup butter or margarine, melted

FILLING

24 ounces cream cheese, at room temperature
1 cup granulated sugar
3 tablespoons all-purpose flour
1 teaspoon pumpkin pie spice
4 large eggs
1 cup solid-pack canned pumpkin
1½ cups semisweet chocolate chips
Chocolate Curls (see page 422) for garnish
Chocolate Leaves (see page 422) for garnish

1 Position a rack in the center of the oven and preheat the oven to 350 degrees. Lightly grease a 9-inch springform pan.

2 To make the crust, in a large bowl, combine the cookie crumbs, powdered sugar, and butter. Press the mixture onto the bottom and 1½ inches up the sides of the prepared pan.

3 Bake for 8 minutes. Cool on a wire rack.

4 Increase the oven temperature to 400 degrees.

5 To make the filling, in a large bowl, using an electric mixer on medium speed, beat the cream cheese and granulated sugar until smooth. Beat in the flour and spice. Beat in the eggs, one at a time, beating well after each addition. Beat in the pumpkin. Fold in the chocolate chips. Pour the mixture into the prepared pan.

6 Bake for 10 minutes. Reduce the oven temperature to 250 degrees and bake for 45 to 50 minutes, or until firm. Cool in the pan on a wire rack. Refrigerate 30 minutes, or until chilled.

7 Remove the side of the pan and garnish with chocolate curls and chocolate leaves before serving.

149

145

146

150 ■ CHOCOLATE REVANIE

YIELD: *12 to 15 servings*
BAKING TIME: *45 minutes*

CAKE

1 cup chocolate cake crumbs (see Baking notes)
1½ cups finely ground walnuts
1 tablespoon grated orange zest
6 large eggs, separated
¾ cup granulated sugar
1 teaspoon vanilla extract

SYRUP

2¼ cups water
¾ cup granulated sugar
1 teaspoon ground cinnamon
1 orange slice
½ cup crème de cacao

1 Position a rack in the center of the oven and preheat the oven to 350 degrees. Lightly grease a 13 by 9-inch pan.

2 To make the cake, combine the cake crumbs, walnuts, and orange zest.

3 In a medium bowl, using an electric mixer on high speed, beat the egg whites until stiff but not dry.

4 In a large bowl, using an electric mixer on medium speed, beat the egg yolks until thick and light-colored. Beat in the sugar and vanilla extract. On low speed, beat in the egg whites just until mixed. Gradually blend in the dry ingredients. Scrape the mixture into the prepared pan and spread evenly.

5 Bake for 45 minutes, or until a cake tester inserted into the center comes out clean.

6 While the cake is baking, make the syrup. In a medium saucepan, over medium heat, combine the water, sugar, cinnamon, and orange slice. Cook until the sugar is completely dissolved. Remove from the heat, remove the orange slice, and add the crème de cacao. Pour the hot syrup over the cake, hot from the oven. Cool the cake in the pan on a wire rack. Cut into squares.

BAKING NOTES: To make chocolate cake crumbs, set one-quarter of a non-frosted, non-filled 8-inch cake out for up to three days. After cake has dried, in a large bowl, break into pieces and beat on medium speed until fine crumbs form.

138

134

140

136

144

151 ■ CHOCOLATE RIPPLE CHEESECAKE

YIELD: *12 servings*
BAKING TIME: *82 minutes*
CHILL TIME: *8 hours*

CRUST

¾ cup all-purpose flour
2 tablespoons granulated sugar
¼ teaspoon salt
¼ cup butter

FILLING

24 ounces cream cheese, at room temperature
1 cup granulated sugar
¼ cup all-purpose flour
2 teaspoons almond or vanilla extract
6 large eggs
1 cup sour cream or yogurt
¼ cup chocolate syrup

1 Position a rack in the center of the oven and preheat the oven to 400 degrees. Lightly grease a 9-inch springform pan.

2 To make the crust, in a medium bowl, combine the flour, sugar, and salt. Using a pastry blender, cut in the butter to make a crumbly mixture. Press the mixture evenly onto the bottom of the prepared pan.

3 Bake for 10 minutes. Remove from the oven and cool on a wire rack.

4 Increase the oven temperature to 500 degrees.

5 Meanwhile, to make the filling, in a large bowl, using an electric mixer on medium speed, beat the cream cheese and sugar until smooth. Continue beating on low speed and add the flour and almond extract. Beat in the eggs, one at a time, beating well after each addition. Beat in the sour cream. Place 1½ cups of the mixture in a small bowl and blend in the chocolate syrup.

6 To assemble, pour half of the cream cheese mixture over the baked crust. Drizzle the chocolate mixture over the top. Carefully pour the remaining cream cheese mixture over the top. Insert a knife and swirl the two mixtures to create a marbled effect.

7 Bake for 12 minutes. Reduce the oven temperature to 200 degrees. Bake for 60 minutes, or until firm. Remove from the oven and cool in the pan on a wire rack. Chill for 8 hours before serving.

BAKING NOTES: A chocolate crumb crust (see page 000) will give this cheesecake a more decorative appearance. Garnish with chocolate cones and chocolate leaves (see pages 421 and 422).

151

150

143

148

147

152 ■ CHOCOLATE ROLL I

YIELD: *12 to 16 servings*
BAKING TIME: *20 minutes*
CHILL TIME: *1 hour*

CAKE

½ cup granulated sugar
¼ cup Dutch processed cocoa powder
1 tablespoon all-purpose flour
5 large eggs, separated
1 teaspoon crème de cacao

FILLING (SEE BAKING NOTES)

3 tablespoons powdered sugar
2 tablespoons Dutch processed cocoa powder
1 cup heavy cream
½ teaspoon crème de cacao

SAUCE (SEE BAKING NOTES)

6 tablespoons Dutch processed cocoa powder
⅓ cup heavy cream
1 cup powdered sugar
1 large egg, beaten until light-colored
½ teaspoon crème de cacao

1 Position a rack in the center of the oven and preheat the oven to 350 degrees. Lightly grease and flour a 15½ by 10½-inch jelly-roll pan.

2 To make the cake, combine the sugar, cocoa powder, and flour.

3 In a large bowl, using an electric mixer on high speed, beat the egg whites until stiff but not dry.

4 In another large bowl, using an electric mixer on medium speed, beat the egg yolks until thick and light-colored. Gradually blend in the dry ingredients. Fold in the beaten egg whites. Stir in the crème de cacao. Pour into the prepared pan.

5 Bake for 18 to 20 minutes, or until a cake tester inserted into the center comes out clean and the cake pulls away from the sides of the pan. Cool in the pan for 5 minutes. Invert onto a damp, not wet, cloth.

6 Meanwhile, to make the filling, in a cup, combine the powdered sugar and cocoa powder.

7 In a medium bowl, using an electric mixer on medium-high speed, beat the cream to soft peaks. Fold in the dry ingredients. Fold in the crème de cacao. Chill 30 minutes before using.

8 Meanwhile, to make the sauce, in the top of a double boiler over simmering water, combine the cocoa powder, cream, powdered sugar, beaten egg, and crème de cacao. Cook and stir until the mixture thickens. Remove from the heat. Chill for 30 minutes.

9 To assemble, spread the whipped cream filling over the cooled cake. Starting with one of the long sides, roll up the cake, jelly-roll fashion. Place seam-side down on a serving plate and drizzle the chocolate sauce over the top. Serve with the remaining chocolate sauce in a small bowl on the side.

BAKING NOTES: You may want to make the filling and sauce before making the cake so that they can chill and be ready for use.

153 ■ CHOCOLATE ROLL II

YIELD: *12 to 16 servings*
BAKING TIME: *25 minutes*

CAKE

1 tablespoon active dry yeast
¼ cup warm water
1¼ cups plus ¼ teaspoon granulated sugar
2½ cups all-purpose flour
½ cup Dutch processed cocoa powder
¼ cup butter or margarine
3 large eggs

FILLING AND FROSTING

2 ounces unsweetened chocolate, grated or finely chopped
½ cup honey, warmed
2 tablespoons coffee liqueur
2 cups hazelnuts or pecans, finely ground
½ cup black currants
½ cup Coffee Mocha Icing (see page 408) or 2 tablespoons Cocoa Sugar (see page 407) for garnish

1 In a small bowl, combine the yeast, water, and ¼ teaspoon of the sugar, stirring gently until dissolved. Set aside to proof for 10 minutes.

2 Meanwhile, in a large bowl, combine the flour, remaining 1¼ cups sugar, and cocoa powder. Using a pastry blender, cut in the butter.

154

155

3 Using an electric mixer on medium speed, beat in the eggs, one at a time, beating well after each addition. On slow speed, beat in the yeast mixture. Cover and let rise in a warm place for 1 to 2 hours, or until the dough has doubled in bulk.

4 Meanwhile, to make the filling, melt the chocolate (see page 13). Remove from the heat and stir in the honey and liqueur. Cool slightly. Add the hazelnuts and currants.

5 Preheat the oven to 375 degrees. Lightly grease a baking sheet.

6 On a floured surface, roll out the dough into an oblong 1/2-inch thick. Spread the filling over the top and roll up jelly-roll fashion. Place on the prepared pan.

7 Bake for 20 to 25 minutes, until lightly browned. Remove to a wire rack to cool.

8 Make the icing or the cocoa sugar. Drizzle coffee mocha icing over the top or dust with cocoa sugar.

BAKING NOTES: Serve with a rich mocha coffee.

154 ■ CHOCOLATE ROLL III

YIELD: *12 to 16 servings*
BAKING TIME: *18 minutes*

CAKE

4 ounces unsweetened chocolate, grated or finely chopped
6 large eggs, separated
2/3 cup plus 2 tablespoons granulated sugar
1/2 cup ground almonds
1/4 teaspoon cream of tartar

FILLING

3 large egg yolks
1/3 cup granulated sugar
1/4 cup light corn syrup
1 cup butter or margarine, at room temperature
1/4 cup raspberry jam
1 tablespoon crème de framboise or raspberry liqueur
8 to 10 drops red food coloring

TOPPING

Dutch processed cocoa powder for dusting
Powdered sugar for dusting
16 to 20 Chocolate Leaves (see page 422)
1 ounce semisweet chocolate, melted
Fresh raspberries for garnish

1 Position a rack in the center of the oven and preheat the oven to 350 degrees. Lightly grease a 15 1/2 by 10 1/2-inch jelly-roll pan. Line the pan with waxed paper. Lightly grease and flour the paper.

2 To make the cake, melt the chocolate (see page 13). Remove from the heat.

3 In a large bowl, using an electric mixer on medium speed, beat the egg yolks until thick and light-colored. Beat in 2/3 cup of the granulated sugar. Beat in the melted chocolate and almonds.

4 In another large bowl, using an electric mixer with clean beaters on high speed, beat the egg whites and cream of tartar until foamy. Sprinkle in the remaining 2 tablespoons sugar and beat until stiff but not dry. Gently fold one-third of the egg whites into the chocolate mixture until no white streaks remain. Fold in the remaining whites. Scrape the mixture into the prepared pan and spread evenly.

5 Bake for 15 to 18 minutes, or until the cake loses its gloss. Cover with a damp, not wet, cloth and cool in the pan on a wire rack.

6 Meanwhile, to make the filling, using an electric mixer on medium speed, beat the egg yolks until thick and light-colored.

7 In a small saucepan, over medium heat, combine the sugar and corn syrup. Insert a candy thermometer and boil until 236 degrees. Remove from the heat. Pouring it in a thin stream, add the hot syrup to the egg yolk mixture, beating constantly. Beat until cool. Beat in the butter. Mix in the raspberry jam. Stir in the crème de framboise and food coloring.

8 To assemble, invert the cake onto a flat surface and remove the waxed paper. Spread the filling evenly over the cake, leaving a 1/2-inch border around the edges. Starting with one of the long sides, roll up the cake jelly-roll fashion. Place on a serving plate, seam-side down. Sift the cocoa powder over the top of the cake and then the powdered sugar. Arrange the chocolate leaves on top of the cake. Garnish with fresh raspberries. The melted chocolate can be used in a decorative manner to attach the chocolate leaves and raspberries to the cake.

BAKING NOTE: For another decorative effect, place a paper doily over the log after dusting with cocoa powder. Dust with the powdered sugar and carefully lift off the doily.

155 ■ CHOCOLATE ROULADE

YIELD: *12 to 16 servings*
BAKING TIME: *20 minutes*
CHILL TIME: *8 to 10 hours*

ROULADE

5 ounces semisweet chocolate, grated or finely chopped
5 ounces unsweetened chocolate, grated or finely chopped
8 large eggs, separated
2 cups granulated sugar

COCOA CREAM FILLING AND FROSTING

1 1/2 cups heavy cream
1/4 cup Dutch processed cocoa powder
Grated semisweet chocolate for garnish

1 Position a rack in the center of the oven and preheat the oven to 350 degrees. Line a 15 1/2 by 10 1/2-inch jelly-roll pan with waxed paper and lightly grease the paper.

2 To make the cake, melt the chocolates (see page 13). Remove from the heat.

3 In a medium bowl, using an electric mixer on high speed, beat the egg whites until stiff but not dry.

4 In a large bowl, using an electric mixer on medium speed, beat the egg yolks until thick and light-colored. Beat in the sugar.

5 Beat in the melted chocolate. Fold in the egg whites. Scrape the mixture into the prepared pan and spread evenly.

6 Bake for 15 to 20 minutes, or until set. Cover with a damp, not wet, towel and chill for 8 to 10 hours.

7 To make the filling, in a small bowl, using an electric mixer on high speed, beat the cream until soft peaks form. Chill the cream for 30 minutes.

8 Invert the cake onto the damp towel and remove the waxed paper. Spread a thin layer of the whipped cream over the cake, leaving a 1/4-inch border on each side. Dust the cocoa powder over the top. Starting with one of the long sides, roll up the cake, jelly-roll fashion. Place on a serving plate, seam-side down. Frost the top and sides with whipped cream and garnish with grated chocolate. Chill 30 minutes, or until serving.

BAKING NOTES: Sprinkle chopped nuts over the cream filling, if desired. Chocolate Whipped Cream (see page 406) can be used in place of the plain whipped cream. Or, brush the rolled cake with Dessert Syrup (see page 409) before frosting.

156 ■ CHOCOLATE RUM CAKE

YIELD: *12 servings*
BAKING TIME: *50 minutes*

2¹/2 cups all-purpose flour
5 tablespoons Dutch processed cocoa powder
2 teaspoons baking powder
Pinch of salt
4 large eggs, separated
1 cup butter or margarine, at room temperature
1¹/4 cups granulated sugar
1/2 cup prepared hot chocolate, cooled to room temperature (see Hot Chocolate II, page 29)

1 tablespoon crème de cacao
2 tablespoons rum
Cocoa powder for dusting
1¹/2 cups Chocolate Whipped Cream (see page 406) for serving

1 Position a rack in the center of the oven and preheat the oven to 375 degrees. Lightly grease and flour a 9-inch Bundt pan.

2 Combine the flour, cocoa powder, baking powder, and salt.

3 In a medium bowl, using an electric mixer on high speed, beat the egg whites until stiff but not dry.

4 In a large bowl, using an electric mixer on medium speed, beat the butter and sugar until light and fluffy. Beat in the egg yolks. Beat in the cooled hot chocolate, crème de cacao, and rum. Gradually stir in the dry ingredients. Fold in the beaten egg whites.

5 Bake for 45 to 50 minutes, or until a cake tester inserted into the center comes out clean. Cool for 10 minutes in the pan on a wire rack. Invert the cake onto the rack to cool completely.

6 Dust the cake with cocoa powder. Serve with a dab of chocolate whipped cream on each slice.

157 ■ CHOCOLATE SHEET CAKE I

YIELD: *60 servings*
BAKING TIME: *35 minutes*

3 ounces unsweetened chocolate, grated or finely chopped
3 cups cake flour, sifted
2 teaspoons baking powder
2 teaspoons baking soda
1/2 teaspoon salt
1/4 cup butter or margarine, at room temperature
2 cups granulated sugar
2 teaspoons vanilla extract
2 large eggs, beaten
2 cups buttermilk
3 cups Chocolate Frosting IV (see page 400)

1 Position a rack in the center of the oven and preheat the oven to 350 degrees. Lightly grease and flour a 26 by 18-inch sheet

cake pan (see Baking notes). Line a piece of cardboard the size of the sheet pan with waxed paper or aluminum foil.

2 Melt the chocolate (see page 13). Remove from the heat.

3 Combine the flour, baking powder, baking soda, and salt.

4 In a large bowl, using an electric mixer on medium speed, beat the butter and sugar until light and fluffy. Beat in the vanilla extract and melted chocolate. Beat in the eggs, one at a time. In three additions, blend in the dry ingredients, alternating with the buttermilk, beginning and ending with the dry ingredients. Immediately pour into the prepared pan.

5 Bake for 30 to 35 minutes, or until a cake tester inserted into the center comes out clean. Cool in the pan on a wire rack.

6 Make the frosting.

7 Carefully place the prepared cardboard on top of the cake, and invert the pan onto the cardboard. Frost the top and sides of the cake with frosting. Or, leave the cake in the pan and frost the top only.

BAKING NOTES: A 26 by 18-inch sheet cake pan may not fit in all home ovens. See following recipe for **CHOCOLATE SHEET CAKE II** for home use.

158 ■ CHOCOLATE SHEET CAKE II

YIELD: *24 to 30 servings*
BAKING TIME: *20 minutes*

CAKE

2 cups all-purpose flour
1/2 teaspoon baking soda
1/2 teaspoon salt
1/2 cup butter or margarine
1/2 cup vegetable shortening
1/4 cup Dutch processed cocoa powder
1 cup warm water
2 cups granulated sugar
2 large eggs, beaten
1/2 cup buttermilk
1 teaspoon vanilla or chocolate extract

ICING

½ cup butter or margarine
¼ cup Dutch processed cocoa powder
6 tablespoons milk
1 box powdered sugar, sifted twice
1 cup pecans or hazelnuts, chopped
1 teaspoon coffee liqueur
Pinch of salt

1 Position a rack in the center of the oven and preheat the oven to 350 degrees. Lightly grease a 18 by 13-inch sheet cake pan.

2 To make the cake, combine the flour, baking soda, and salt.

3 In a large saucepan, over medium heat, melt the butter, shortening, and cocoa. Add the water. Remove from the heat and using a wire whisk, beat in the sugar.

4 In a large bowl, using an electric mixer on medium speed, beat the eggs until thick and light-colored. Beat in the buttermilk and vanilla extract. Beat in the cocoa mixture. Gradually blend in the dry ingredients. Pour the mixture into the prepared pan.

5 Bake for 18 to 20 minutes, or until a cake tester inserted into the center comes out clean. Cool slightly in the pan on a wire rack.

6 Meanwhile, to make the icing, in a large saucepan over medium heat, bring the butter, cocoa powder, and milk to a boil. Remove from the heat. Using an electric mixer on medium speed, beat in the powdered sugar, nuts, liqueur, and salt. Spread the warm icing evenly over the cake.

159 ■ CHOCOLATE SOUR CREAM CAKE WITH COCONUT

YIELD: *12 servings*
BAKING TIME: *55 minutes*

CAKE

2 cups plus 2 tablespoons cake flour
1½ teaspoons baking powder
1 teaspoon baking soda
¼ teaspoon salt
3 ounces semisweet chocolate, grated or finely chopped
¼ cup water
3 large whole eggs plus 1 large egg white
Pinch of salt
1¼ cups granulated sugar
1⅓ cups flaked coconut
1 cup sour cream or chocolate-flavored yogurt
½ cup butter or margarine, at room temperature
2 teaspoons crème de cacao

GLAZE

3 ounces unsweetened chocolate, grated or finely chopped
1 tablespoon butter or margarine, at room temperature
3 tablespoons water
1 cup powdered sugar
½ teaspoon chocolate extract

1 Position a rack in the center of the oven and preheat the oven to 350 degrees. Lightly grease and flour a 9-inch tube pan.

2 To make the cake, combine 2 cups of the flour, baking powder, baking soda, and salt.

3 In the top of a double boiler over simmering water, melt the chocolate and water, stirring until smooth. Remove from the heat and cool to room temperature.

4 In a medium bowl, using an electric mixer on high speed, beat the egg white until foamy. Add the salt and gradually beat in ¼ cup of the sugar, a little at a time, until the whites are stiff but not dry. Fold in the remaining 2 tablespoons of flour and the coconut. Set aside.

5 Add the sour cream to the chocolate mixture and stir until blended.

6 In a large bowl, using an electric mixer on medium speed, beat the remaining 1 cup of sugar and the butter. Beat in the whole eggs, one at a time, beating well after each addition. Beat in the crème de cacao. Gradually add the chocolate mixture, alternating with the dry ingredients. Pour 2 cups of the cake batter into the prepared pan. Spread ½ cup of the coconut mixture over the top, and spread another 2 cups of the cake batter over the top of the coconut mixture. Top with another ½ cup of coconut, and then the remaining batter. Top with the remaining coconut mixture.

156

158

7 Bake for 50 to 55 minutes, or until a cake tester inserted into the center comes out clean. Cool in the pan on a wire rack. Remove from the pan, remove the waxed paper, and place on a serving plate.

8 To make the glaze, in a small saucepan, over low heat, melt the chocolate, stirring until smooth. Stir in the butter and water. Stir in the powdered sugar. Remove from the heat and stir in the chocolate extract. Using a wire whisk, whip the frosting until cool. Spread evenly over the top and sides of the cake.

160 ■ CHOCOLATE SPICE CAKE

YIELD: *12 to 15 servings*
BAKING TIME: *35 minutes*

2 ounces semisweet chocolate, grated or finely chopped
1 cup molasses
2½ cups cake flour
1½ teaspoons baking powder
½ teaspoon baking soda
½ teaspoon ground cinnamon
¼ teaspoon ground cloves
¼ teaspoon salt
½ cup packed dark brown sugar
½ cup butter or margarine, at room temperature
¾ cup milk, at room temperature
2 large eggs
1½ cups Chocolate Glaze IV (see page 401)
Sliced fresh fruit, for garnish

1 Position a rack in the center of the oven and preheat the oven to 350 degrees. Lightly grease and flour a 13 by 9-inch pan.

2 Melt the chocolate (see page 13). Remove from the heat and stir in the molasses.

3 Combine the flour, baking powder, baking soda, cinnamon, cloves, and salt, and sift into a large bowl. Add the brown sugar. Using an electric mixer on low speed, beat in the butter and milk. Beat in the eggs, one at a time. Add the chocolate mixture. Pour the mixture into the prepared pan.

4 Bake for 30 to 35 minutes, or until a cake tester inserted into the center comes out clean. Cool in the pan on a wire rack for 10 minutes. Invert onto the rack to cool completely. Place on a serving plate.

5 Make the chocolate glaze.

6 Spread the glaze over the top of the cake. Garnish with sliced fruit.

BAKING NOTES: To make this a very fancy dessert, spread a thin layer of Ganache I (see page 410) on the plate and place the cake on top. Fill a pastry bag with ganache and pipe a ribbon

of the ganache around the base of the cake. Then, using a large star tip, pipe several large rosettes around the cake. Spread a fruit glaze, such as Apricot Glaze (see page 394), over the top and pipe additional rosettes around the top edge. Garnish with brightly colored, freshly washed pansies. The yield will vary depending on the size of the pieces cut.

161 ■ CHOCOLATE SPICED MOCHA CAKE

YIELD: *12 servings*
BAKING TIME: *35 minutes*
CHILL TIME: *2 hours*

2¼ cups all-purpose flour
¼ cup Dutch processed cocoa powder
1 tablespoons baking powder
1 tablespoon instant coffee powder
1 teaspoon ground allspice
¼ teaspoon salt
3 large eggs, separated
1¼ cups granulated sugar
¾ cup butter or margarine, at room temperture
2 teaspoons chocolate or vanilla extract
½ cup ice water
½ cup coffee liqueur
2 cups Coffee Mocha Icing (see page 408)

1 Position a rack in the center of the oven and preheat the oven to 325 degrees. Grease and flour two 9-inch round cake pans.

2 Combine the flour, cocoa powder, baking powder, coffee powder, allspice, and salt.

3 In a medium bowl, using an electric mixer on high speed, beat the egg whites until foamy. Add ¼ cup of the sugar and continue beating until stiff but not dry.

161

4 In a large bowl, using an electric mixer on high speed, beat the butter and the remaining 1 cup sugar until fluffy. Beat in the egg yolks. Beat in the chocolate extract. In three additions, blend in the dry ingredients, alternating with the water and liqueur, beginning and ending with the dry ingredients. Fold in the egg whites, a little at a time. Divide the mixture between the prepared pans and spread evenly.

5 Bake for 30 to 35 minutes, or until a cake tester inserted into the center comes out clean. Cool in the pans on wire racks for 10 minutes. Invert onto the racks to cool completely. Chill cakes for 2 hours before frosting.

6 Meanwhile, make the coffee mocha icing.

7 To assemble, place one cake layer on a serving plate and spread with frosting. Top with the second cake layer and spread frosting on the top and sides of the cake.

162 ■ CHOCOLATE SPONGE CAKE I

YIELD: *16 servings*
BAKING TIME: *35 minutes*

1 cup cake flour
1/3 cup Dutch processed cocoa powder
6 large eggs, separated
Pinch of salt
3/4 cup granulated sugar
1 tablespoon fresh lemon juice, strained
1 teaspoon grated lemon zest
2 cups Chocolate Rum Icing (see pages 404)

1 Position a rack in the center of the oven and preheat the oven to 350 degrees.

2 Combine the cake flour and cocoa powder and sift twice.

3 In a large bowl, using an electric mixer on high speed, beat the egg whites and salt until stiff but not dry.

4 In another large bowl, using an electric mixer on medium speed, beat the egg yolks and sugar until thick and light-

colored. Beat in the lemon juice and lemon zest. Gradually blend in the dry ingredients. Fold in the beaten egg whites. Pour the mixture into an ungreased 9-inch springform pan.

5 Bake for 30 to 35 minutes, or until a cake tester inserted into the center comes out clean. Cool in the pan for 5 minutes before removing springform. Cool completely.

6 Make the chocolate rum icing.

7 Place the cake on the serving plate. Frost the top and sides with the icing.

163 ■ CHOCOLATE SPONGE CAKE II

YIELD: *16 servings*
BAKING TIME: *55 to 60 minutes*
CHILL TIME: *2 hours*

3/4 cup cake flour
1/4 cup Dutch processed cocoa powder
1/4 teaspoon salt
5 large eggs, separated
1 tablespoon Triple Sec
1 cup granulated sugar
2 cups Chocolate Whipped Cream (see page 406)
Grated semisweet chocolate for garnish

1 Position a rack in the center of the oven and preheat the oven to 350 degrees. Lightly grease and flour a 10-inch tube pan.

2 Combine the flour, cocoa powder, and salt. Sift twice.

3 In a large bowl, using an electric mixer on medium speed, beat the egg yolks until very thick and light-colored. Beat in the Triple Sec.

4 In another large bowl, using an electric mixer with clean beaters on high speed, beat the egg whites until stiff but not dry. Fold in the sugar, a little at a time. Gently fold in the egg yolk mixture. Gradually fold in the dry ingredients. Scrape the mixture into the prepared pan and spread evenly.

5 Bake for 55 to 60 minutes, or until a cake tester inserted into the center comes out clean. Cool

in the pan on a wire rack for 10 minutes. Invert onto the wire rack to cool completely. Chill for at least 2 hours.

6 Make the chocolate whipped cream.

7 To assemble, using a serrated knife, cut the cake horizontally into three layers. Place the bottom layer on a serving plate and spread with a generous layer of the whipped cream. Top with the second layer and spread with whipped cream. Top with the third layer. Spread the remaining whipped cream over the top and sides of the cake. Garnish with grated chocolate.

164 ■ CHOCOLATE SUNDAE CAKE I

YIELD: *12 to 15 servings*
BAKING TIME: *35 minutes*

FILLING

1 cup packed dark brown sugar
1/3 cup Dutch processed cocoa powder
2 cups hot water
1 cup pecans or walnuts, finely chopped
2 cups miniature marshmallows

CAKE

2 cups all-purpose flour
1 teaspoon ground cinnamon or ground allspice
1/2 teaspoon salt
1 cup water
1/4 cup buttermilk
1 teaspoon baking soda
1/2 cup butter or margarine
1/2 cup canola oil
1/4 cup Dutch processed cocoa powder
2 large eggs, lightly beaten
2 cups granulated sugar
1 teaspoon vanilla or chocolate extract

1 Position a rack in the center of the oven and preheat the oven to 350 degrees. Lightly grease and flour a 13 by 9-inch pan.

2 To make the filling, in a medium bowl, combine the brown sugar, cocoa powder, and water, stirring until smooth. Pour the mixture into the prepared pan and evenly sprinkle the pecans over the top. Sprinkle marshmallows over the pecans.

3 To make the cake, combine the flour, cinnamon, and salt.

4 In a cup, combine the water, buttermilk, and baking soda.

5 In a saucepan, over low heat, melt the butter with the oil and cocoa powder, stirring until smooth. Remove from the heat and cool slightly.

6 In a large bowl, using an electric mixer on medium speed, beat the eggs and sugar until thick and light-colored. Beat in the vanilla extract and the cocoa mixture. In three additions, blend in the dry ingredients, alternating with the buttermilk mixture, beginning and ending with the dry ingredients. Pour into the prepared pan.

7 Bake for 30 to 35 minutes, or until a cake tester inserted into the center comes out clean. Cool in the pan on a wire rack for 5 minutes. Invert onto a plate. Cut into bars.

BAKING NOTES: Serve with a dollop of Chocolate Whipped Cream (see page 406) on the top, if desired. For a nicer presentation, fill a pastry bag with chocolate whipped cream and pipe rosettes around the base of the cake.

165 ■ CHOCOLATE SUNDAE CAKE II

YIELD: *16 servings*
BAKING TIME: *75 minutes*

2 ounces semisweet chocolate, grated or finely chopped
3 tablespoons hot water
3 tablespoons heavy cream
4¹/₂ cups cake flour
4¹/₂ teaspoons baking powder
¹/₂ teaspoon salt
1¹/₂ cups butter-flavored vegetable shortening
2¹/₄ cups granulated sugar
6 large eggs
1¹/₂ cups milk
1¹/₂ teaspoons crème de cacao
2 cups Ganache III (see page 410)
¹/₂ cup Chocolate Glaze II (see page 401)

1 Position a rack in the center of the oven and preheat the oven to 350 degrees. Lightly grease and flour the bottom of a 10-inch tube pan.

2 In the top of a double boiler over simmering water, melt the chocolate with the water, stirring until smooth. Remove from the heat. Stir in the cream.

3 Combine and sift the flour, baking powder, and salt.

4 In a large bowl, using an electric mixer on medium speed, beat the shortening and sugar until fluffy. Beat in the eggs, one at a time, beating well after each addition. Combine the milk and crème de cacao. In three additions, blend in the dry ingredients, alternating with the milk mixture, beginning and ending with the dry ingredients. Scrape one-fourth of the batter into the prepared pan and drizzle one-third of the chocolate mixture over the top. Repeat until all the batter and chocolate mixture are used, ending with the batter.

5 Bake for 70 to 75 minutes, or until a cake tester inserted into the center comes out clean. Cool in the pan on a wire rack for 10 minutes. Invert onto the rack to cool completely.

6 Make the ganache and chocolate glaze.

7 Place the cake on a serving plate. Frost the top and sides of the cake with ganache. Pour the chocolate glaze in a narrow stream over the top of the cake.

157

152

153

164

BAKING NOTES: It is normal for this cake to crack on the top as it cools.

166 ■ CHOCOLATE SYRUP CAKE

YIELD: *12 to 15 servings*
BAKING TIME: *35 minutes*

1 cup all-purpose flour
1/2 cup pecans or walnuts, finely chopped
1 teaspoon baking powder
1 teaspoon baking soda
1 tablespoon cornstarch or arrowroot
1/4 teaspoon salt
1/2 cup butter or margarine, at room temperature
1 cup granulated sugar
4 large eggs
2 cups Chocolate Syrup I (see page 406)
1 1/2 cups Chocolate Buttercream (see page 395)

1 Position a rack in the center of the oven and preheat the oven to 350 degrees. Lightly grease and flour a 13 by 9-inch pan.

2 Combine the flour, pecans, baking powder, baking soda, cornstarch, and salt

3 In a large bowl, using an electric mixer on medium speed, beat the butter and sugar light and fluffy. Beat in the eggs, one at a time. Beat in the chocolate syrup. Gradually blend in the dry ingredients. Scrape the mixture into the prepared pan and spread evenly.

4 Bake for 30 to 35 minutes, or until a cake tester inserted into the center comes out clean. Cool in the pan on a wire rack.

5 Make the frosting.

6 Spread the frosting over the top of the cake.

167 ■ CHOCOLATE TRANQUILITY CAKE

YIELD: *12 servings*
BAKING TIME: *35 minutes*

CAKE

2 1/4 cups all-purpose flour
1 tablespoon baking powder
1/2 teaspoon baking soda
1 teaspoon salt
2 large eggs, separated
1 1/2 cups granulated sugar
1/3 cup canola oil
1 cup buttermilk
1 1/2 teaspoons chocolate or vanilla extract
2 ounces unsweetened chocolate, grated or finely chopped

FLUFFY FROSTING

1/4 cup water
1/2 cup light corn syrup
4 large egg whites
1 cup powdered sugar
1 tablespoon vanilla or lemon extract
2 teaspoons butter, at room temperature
1 teaspoon fresh lemon juice
2 tablespoons chocolate syrup for garnish

1 Position a rack in the center of the oven and preheat the oven to 350 degrees. Lightly grease and flour two 9-inch round cake pans.

2 Combine the flour, baking powder, baking soda, and salt.

3 In a medium bowl, using an electric mixer, beat the egg whites until foamy. Add 1/2 cup of the sugar, 1 tablespoon at a time, and beat until stiff but not dry.

4 In a large bowl, using an electric mixer on medium speed, beat the oil, buttermilk, and chocolate extract. Gradually blend in the dry ingredients until smooth. Add the egg yolks and remaining 1 cup of sugar and beat 1 minute, or until combined. Fold in the egg whites,

159

162

166

167

163

blending until no white streaks remain visible. Fold in the grated chocolate. Divide the mixture between the prepared pans and spread evenly.

5 Bake for 30 to 35 minutes, or until a cake tester inserted into the center comes out clean. Cool in the pans on wire racks for 5 minutes. Invert onto the racks to cool completely.

6 To make the frosting, in a small saucepan over medium heat, combine the water and corn syrup. Bring to a boil. Cover and simmer for 3 minutes. Remove the cover and insert a candy thermometer. Cook, without stirring, until 234 degrees is reached.

7 Meanwhile, in a medium bowl, using an electric mixer on high speed, beat the egg whites until stiff but not dry. Pouring it in a thin stream, add the hot syrup, beating constantly. Beat in the powdered sugar, vanilla extract, butter, and lemon juice. Beat until the mixture is thick and of a spreadable consistency.

8 To assemble, place one of the cake layers on a serving plate and spread with ¼ cup of the frosting. Top with the second cake layer and spread the remaining frosting over the top and sides of the cake. Drizzle the chocolate syrup over the top of the frosted cake and swirl the chocolate through the white frosting.

168 ■ CHOCOLATE TRELLIS CAKE

YIELD: *12 servings*
BAKING TIME: *25 minutes*

CHOCOLATE TRELLIS

3 ounces semisweet chocolate, grated or finely chopped

COCOA SPONGE CAKE

½ cup cake flour
⅓ cup Dutch processed cocoa powder
5 large eggs, separated
1 teaspoon cream of tartar
¾ cup granulated sugar
1 teaspoon chocolate or vanilla extract

APRICOT GLAZE

⅓ cup apricot preserves
3 tablespoons Grand Marnier or Triple Sec

WHIPPED CREAM FILLING

2 cups heavy cream
¼ cup granulated sugar
4 teaspoons Grand Marnier or Triple Sec
1 ounce semisweet chocolate, grated or finely chopped for garnish

1 On a piece of parchment paper, draw an 8-inch circle. Then draw a series of evenly spaced lines intersecting at 45

degree angles to form a trellis pattern inside the circle. Place the paper on a baking sheet.

2 Melt the chocolate (see page 13). Remove from the heat. Spoon the chocolate into a small paper cone or a pastry bag fitted with a small plain tip. Pipe the chocolate onto the parchment paper, tracing the circle and trellis. Chill until ready to garnish the cake.

3 Position a rack in the center of the oven and preheat the oven to 325 degrees. Lightly grease two 8-inch round cake pans. Line the bottoms with waxed paper and grease the paper.

4 Combine the flour and cocoa powder.

5 In a large bowl, using an electric mixer on high speed, beat the egg whites and cream of tartar until foamy. Gradually beat in ½ cup of the sugar. Beat until stiff but not dry.

6 In another large bowl, using an electric mixer on medium speed, beat the egg yolks until thick and light-colored. Beat in the remaining ¼ cup sugar and the chocolate extract. Fold in the egg whites. Gradually blend in the dry ingredients just until blended. Do not overmix. Divide the mixture between the prepared pans and spread evenly.

7 Bake for 20 to 25 minutes, or until a cake tester inserted into the center comes out clean. Invert onto wire racks and cool completely.

168   169   170

8 To make the glaze, in a blender, puree the apricot preserves and Grand Marnier. Transfer to a small saucepan. Cook over low heat until thickened. Remove from the heat.

9 To make the filling, using an electric mixer on high speed, whip the cream, sugar, and Grand Marnier until stiff peaks form.

10 To assemble, using a serrated knife, cut each cake layer in half horizontally. Place one cake layer on a serving plate and brush with some of the glaze. Spread a thin layer of whipped cream on top. Repeat with the remaining cake layers and glaze. Spread whipped cream over the top and sides of the cake. Press the grated chocolate into the sides of the cake. Fill a pastry bag fitted with a star tip with the remaining whipped cream. Pipe out ten to twelve rosettes around the top edge of the cake and one rosette in the center.

11 Carefully remove the chilled chocolate trellis from the parchment paper and place on top of the cake, resting it on the rosettes.

169 ■ CHOCOLATE TURTLE CAKE

YIELD: *12 to 15 servings*
BAKING TIME: *45 minutes*

CAKE

2 ounces unsweetened chocolate, grated or finely chopped
2¹/₂ cups all-purpose flour
3 tablespoons Dutch processed cocoa powder
2 tablespoons baking soda
¹/₂ teaspoon salt
¹/₂ cup vegetable shortening
2 cups granulated sugar
2 large eggs
1 cup milk
1 tablespoon cider vinegar
³/₄ cup warm water
1 teaspoon vanilla or chocolate extract

FILLING

1 pound caramel candies
²/₃ cup evaporated milk
¹/₂ cup butter or margarine

FROSTING

1¹/₄ cups powdered sugar
5 tablespoons butter or margarine
¹/₃ cup evaporated milk
1 cup semisweet chocolate chips

1 Position a rack in the center of the oven and preheat the oven to 350 degrees. Lightly grease and flour a 13 by 9-inch pan.

2 Melt the chocolate (see page 13). Remove from the heat.

3 Combine the flour, cocoa powder, baking soda, and salt.

4 To make the cake, in a large bowl, using an electric mixer on medium speed, beat the shortening and sugar until fluffy. Beat in the melted chocolate. Beat in the eggs. Combine the milk and vinegar and beat into the mixture. Gradually blend in the dry ingredients. Combine the water and vanilla extract and fold into the mixture. Pour half of the mixture into the prepared pan.

5 Bake for 15 minutes.

6 Meanwhile, to make the filling, in the top of a double boiler over simmering water, melt the caramels with the milk and butter, stirring until smooth. Pour evenly over the top of the partially baked cake. Pour the remaining cake batter over the caramel mixture.

7 Bake for 20 to 30 minutes, or until a cake tester inserted into the top layer only comes out clean. Do not overbake, or the cake will be dry. Cool in the pan on a wire rack.

8 Meanwhile, to make the frosting, in a saucepan, boil the powdered sugar, butter, and milk for one minute. Remove from the heat and stir in the chocolate chips. Immediately spread the frosting over the top of the cake.

BAKING NOTES: If the frosting mixture hardens before you can spread it over the cake, reheat it to a spreadable consistency.

170 ■ CHOCOLATE UPSIDE-DOWN CAKE WITH APRICOTS

YIELD: *12 servings*
BAKING TIME: *50 minutes*

TOPPING

¹/₂ cup packed light brown sugar
¹/₄ cup butter-flavored vegetable shortening
16 ounces canned or skinned fresh apricot halves
2 tablespoons light corn syrup
²/₃ cup flaked coconut

CAKE

4 ounces semisweet chocolate, grated or finely chopped
1¹/₂ cups all-purpose flour
1 cup granulated sugar
¹/₂ teaspoon baking powder
¹/₂ teaspoon baking soda
¹/₄ teaspoon salt
6 tablespoons butter-flavored vegetable shortening
³/₄ cup buttermilk
2 large eggs
1 teaspoon almond extract
1¹/₂ cups Cocoa Cream Topping (see page 406) for serving

1 Position a rack in the center of the oven and preheat the oven to 350 degrees. Lightly grease a 9-inch square pan.

2 To make the topping, in a small saucepan, over low heat, melt the brown sugar and shortening. Spread the mixture evenly in the prepared pan. Layer the apricots on top of the sugar mixture. (If canned apricots are used, be sure they are drained and patted dried with a paper towel.) Drizzle the corn syrup evenly over the top of the apricots and sprinkle the coconut over the corn syrup.

3 To make the cake, melt the chocolate (see page 13). Remove from the heat.

4 In a large bowl, combine the flour, sugar, baking powder, baking soda, and salt. Using a pastry blender, cut in the shortening. Beat in the buttermilk, eggs, and almond extract. Stir in the melted chocolate. Beat well. Carefully spread the mixture over the top of the apricots.

5 Bake for 45 to 50 minutes, or until a cake tester inserted into the center comes out clean. Cool in the pan on a wire rack for 5 minutes. Invert onto a serving plate. Do not remove the pan for 5 minutes. Serve warm with cocoa cream topping.

BAKING NOTES: Peaches, apples, tangerines, or orange slices can be substituted for the apricots in the topping.

171 ■ CHOCOLATE YULE LOG

YIELD: *12 to 16 servings*
BAKING TIME: *15 minutes*

CAKE

1/4 cup granulated sugar
2 tablespoons all-purpose flour
2 tablespoons cornstarch or arrowroot
1/4 cup Dutch processed cocoa powder
5 large eggs, separated
1 teaspoon crème de cacao

FILLING

1/2 cup powdered sugar
5 tablespoons Dutch processed cocoa powder
2 cups heavy cream
2 teaspoons crème de cacao
Chocolate Leaves (see page 422) for garnish
Sliced fresh strawberries for garnish

1 Position a rack in the center of the oven and preheat the oven to 350 degrees. Lightly grease and flour a 15½ by 10½-inch jelly-roll pan. Line the bottom of the pan with waxed paper. Lightly grease and flour the paper.

2 To make the cake, combine and sift the sugar, flour, cornstarch, and cocoa powder.

3 In a medium bowl, using an electric mixer on high speed, beat the egg whites until stiff but not dry.

4 In a large bowl, using an electric mixer on medium speed, beat the egg yolks until thick and light-colored. Fold the egg whites into the egg yolks. Gradually fold in the dry ingredients, a little at a time. Fold in the crème de cacao. Scrape the mix-

ture into the prepared pan and spread evenly.

5 Bake for 12 to 15 minutes, or until a cake tester inserted into the center comes out clean. Cool in the pan on a wire rack for 5 minutes. Invert onto a flat surface covered with waxed paper.

6 To make the filling, sift the powdered sugar and cocoa powder.

7 In a medium bowl, using an electric mixer on high speed, whip the cream until it starts to thicken. Fold in the dry ingredients and the crème de cacao. Whip until soft peaks form.

8 To assemble the log, spread some of the filling evenly across the top of the cake, leaving a 1/4-inch border around the edges. Starting with one of the long sides, roll the cake up jelly-roll fashion. Place seam-side down on a serving plate. Spread the remaining filling over the top and ends. Using a fork, score the sides of the roll to resemble the bark of a tree. Garnish with chocolate leaves and sliced strawberries.

172 ■ CHOCOLATE ZUCCHINI CAKE

YIELD: *16 servings*
BAKING TIME: *40 minutes*

2½ cups all-purpose flour
1¾ cups granulated sugar
1/2 teaspoon baking powder
1/4 cup Dutch processed cocoa powder
1/2 teaspoon ground cinnamon or ground nutmeg
1 teaspoon baking soda
1/2 cup buttermilk
1/2 cup butter or margarine, at room temperature
1/2 cup canola oil
2 large eggs
1 teaspoon chocolate extract
2 cups unpeeled zucchini, grated
3/4 cup Dessert Syrup (see page 409)
Whipped cream for garnish
Fresh fruit for garnish

1 Position a rack in the center of the oven and preheat the oven to 325 degrees. Lightly grease a 10-inch tube pan.

2 Combine the flour, sugar, baking powder, cocoa powder, and cinnamon.

3 In a cup, dissolve the baking soda in the buttermilk

4 In a large bowl, using an electric mixer on medium speed, beat the butter and canola oil until smooth. Beat in the eggs, one at a time. Beat in the chocolate extract. Stir in the zucchini. In three additions, blend in the dry ingredients, alternating with the buttermilk, beginning and ending with the dry ingredients. Pour the mixture into the prepared pan.

5 Bake for 35 to 40 minutes, or until a cake tester inserted into the center comes out clean. Cool in the pan on a wire rack for 8 to 10 minutes. Invert onto the rack to cool completely.

6 Make the dessert syrup.

7 Place the cake on a serving plate. Drizzle the syrup over the top of the cake and let it run down the sides. Garnish with dollops of whipped cream and fresh fruit.

173 ■ CHUNK CHOCOLATE CAKE

YIELD: *12 servings*
BAKING TIME: *60 minutes*

CAKE

3/4 cup golden raisins
3 tablespoons Abricotine or apricot liqueur for soaking
1½ cups plus 2 tablespoons all-purpose flour
1½ teaspoons baking powder
1/2 teaspoon ground cinnamon
1/4 teaspoon ground nutmeg
1/4 teaspoon salt
6 tablespoons heavy cream or evaporated milk
1 teaspoon Abricotine or apricot liqueur
6 ounces semisweet chocolate, chopped into chunks
3/4 cup butter-flavored vegetable shortening
1/2 cup granulated sugar
3 large eggs

GLAZE AND GARNISHES

1/2 cup powdered sugar
1½ tablespoons butter, at room temperature

1 tablespoon Abricotine or apricot liqueur

1 teaspoon heavy cream

1 tablespoon Cocoa Sugar for sprinkling (see page 407)

Chocolate Curls (see page 422) for garnish

Chocolate Leaves (see page 422) for garnish

Apricot Roses (see page 420) for garnish

1 Position a rack in the center of the oven and preheat the oven to 350 degrees. Lightly grease and flour a 9-inch tube pan.

2 To make the cake, in a small saucepan over low heat, combine the raisins and just enough Abricotine to cover. Heat just until warm. Remove from the heat to cool.

3 Combine 1½ cups of the flour, the baking powder, spices, and salt.

4 Drain the raisins, reserving the liquid in a small bowl. Add the cream and liqueur to the reserved liquid.

5 Pat the raisins dry on a paper towel. In another small bowl, combine with the chocolate chunks. Fold in the remaining 2 tablespoons of flour.

6 In a large bowl, using an electric mixer on medium speed, beat the shortening and sugar until fluffy. Beat in the eggs, one at a time, beating well after each addition. In three additions, blend in the dry ingredients, alternating with the liquid ingredients, mixing after each addition just until blended. Fold in the chocolate and raisins.

Scrape the mixture into the prepared pan and spread evenly.

7 Bake for 55 to 60 minutes, or until the center springs back when touched. Cool the cake on a wire rack for 15 minutes. Invert onto the rack to cool completely.

8 To make the glaze, in a large bowl, using an electric mixer on medium speed, beat the powdered sugar, butter, Abricotine, and heavy cream until the mixture thickens a little. Chill until ready to use.

9 To assemble, place the cake on a serving plate and sprinkle with cocoa sugar. Spread the glaze over the top, allowing some to drip down the sides. Garnish with chocolate curls, chocolate leaves, and apricot roses.

174 ■ CHUNKY CHOCOLATE CUPCAKES

YIELD: *12 servings*
BAKING TIME: *25 minutes*

CUPCAKES

1 cup all-purpose flour

1 cup granulated sugar

1½ teaspoons baking powder

¼ teaspoon salt

2 large eggs

¼ cup canola oil

1 teaspoon chocolate or vanilla extract

¼ cup evaporated milk

3 ounces semisweet chocolate, chopped into chunks

FROSTING

2½ cups powdered sugar

3 tablespoons butter or margarine, at room temperature

1 teaspoon grated orange zest

2 tablespoons fresh orange juice, strained

1 drop each red and yellow food coloring

1 ounce semisweet chocolate, grated or finely chopped

1 Position a rack in the center of the oven and preheat the oven to 400 degrees. Line twelve 2½-inch muffin cups with paper baking cups.

2 Combine the flour, sugar, baking powder, and salt.

3 In a large bowl, using an electric mixer on medium speed, beat the eggs, oil, chocolate extract, and milk until smooth. Gradually blend in the dry ingredients, a little at a time. Fold in the chocolate chunks. Spoon the mixture into the prepared muffin cups, filling them half full.

4 Bake for 20 to 25 minutes, or until a cake tester inserted into the center comes out clean. Remove from the pan and cool on wire racks.

5 Meanwhile, to make the frosting, in a large bowl, using an electric mixer on medium speed, beat all of the ingredients except the grated chocolate until smooth. If the frosting is too thin, add more powdered sugar, a teaspoonful at a time. If too thick, add more juice, a few drops at a time.

172

6 Frost the tops of the cupcakes. Sprinkle with the grated chocolate.

175 ■ CIOCCOLATO FOCACCIA

YIELD: *12 servings*
BAKING TIME: *25 minutes*

1½ cups all-purpose flour
1 teaspoon baking powder
1 teaspoon salt
1 cup plus 1 tablespoon water
½ cup quick-cooking oats
½ cup granulated sugar
4 large eggs
2 tablespoons butter or margarine, at room temperature
1 tablespoon amaretto
⅓ cup Dutch processed cocoa powder
1½ cups Strawberry Glaze (see page 416)

1 Position a rack in the center of the oven and preheat the oven to 350 degrees. Lightly grease two 8-inch cake pans.

2 Combine the flour and baking powder.

3 In a medium saucepan, dissolve the salt in the water and bring to a boil. Add the oatmeal, stirring until the liquid returns to a boil. Cover and remove from the heat. Let stand until the liquid is absorbed, about 5 minutes.

4 In the container of a blender, combine the sugar, eggs, butter, and amaretto. Blend on high speed for 30 seconds, or until smooth. On low speed, blend in the cocoa powder. Pour in the hot cooked oatmeal and blend on high speed for 2 minutes Scrape down the sides of the container. Blend on high for 30 seconds, or until the mixture is liquified.

5 In a large bowl, combine the chocolate mixture and the dry ingredients. Divide the batter between the prepared pans.

6 Bake for 20 to 25 minutes, or until a cake tester inserted into the center comes out clean. Cool in the pan on a wire rack.

7 Make the glaze.

8 To assemble, using a sharp knife, remove the rounded tops from the cake layers. Place one of the layers on a serving plate and spread with glaze. Top with the second layer and spread the top and sides of the cake with glaze.

176 ■ COCOA CAKE

YIELD: *12 servings*
BAKING TIME: *25 minutes*

CAKE

2 cups all-purpose flour
6 tablespoons Dutch processed cocoa powder
2 teaspoons baking powder
½ cup butter or margarine, at room temperature
1¼ cups packed light brown sugar
2 large eggs, beaten
1 cup milk
1 teaspoon chocolate or vanilla extract

FROSTING

1 cup powdered sugar
2 tablespoons Dutch processed cocoa powder
2 tablespoons butter, melted
2 to 3 tablespoons hot strong brewed coffee
½ teaspoon coffee liqueur
Thinly sliced oranges or crushed chocolate-covered coffee bean candies for garnish

1 Preheat the oven to 350 degrees. Lightly grease two 9-inch round cake pans.

2 To make the cake, combine the flour, cocoa powder, and baking powder.

3 In a large bowl, using an electric mixer on medium speed, beat the butter and brown sugar until fluffy. Beat in the eggs, one at a time, beating well after each addition. In three additions, blend in the dry ingredients, alternating with the milk, beginning and ending with the dry ingredients. Mix each addition just until blended. Stir in the chocolate extract. Divide the mixture between the prepared pans and spread evenly.

4 Bake for 20 to 25 minutes, or until a cake tester inserted into the center comes out clean. Cool in the pans on wire racks for 10

minutes. Invert onto the racks to cool completely.

5 Meanwhile, to make the frosting, in a medium bowl, using an electric mixer on low speed, blend the powdered sugar, cocoa powder, and butter. Add enough of the hot coffee to make a very smooth, spreadable consistency. If the frosting is too thin, add a little more powdered sugar, a teaspoonful at a time. Stir in the liqueur.

6 To assemble, place one of the cake layers on a serving plate. Spread with a layer of the frosting. Place the second cake layer on top, press down lightly, and spread the remaining frosting over the top and sides of the cake. Garnish with fresh fruit or crushed candies.

BAKING NOTES: For extra flavor, try a technique found in a very old recipe: Dip the knife in the strong coffee several times as you spread the frosting.

177 ■ COCOA CAKE II

YIELD: *12 servings*
BAKING TIME: *30 minutes*

1¾ cups all-purpose flour
1 cup granulated sugar
¾ cup Dutch processed cocoa powder
1 teaspoon baking soda
¼ teaspoon salt
1 cup buttermilk
½ cup canola oil
2½ teaspoons chocolate extract
1¼ cups Chocolate Rum Sauce (see page 404)

1 Position a rack in the center of the oven and preheat the oven to 350 degrees. Lightly grease and flour a 9-inch square pan.

2 Combine the flour, sugar, cocoa powder, baking soda, and salt.

3 In a large bowl, using an electric mixer on medium speed, beat the buttermilk, oil, and chocolate extract. Using a wooden spoon, gradually stir in the dry ingredients until well mixed. Scrape the mixture into the prepared pan and spread evenly.

4 Bake for 25 to 30 minutes, or until a cake tester inserted into the center comes out clean. Cool in the pan on a wire rack for 10 minutes. Invert onto the rack to cool completely.

5 Make the chocolate rum sauce.

6 Place the cake on a serving plate. Spoon the sauce over the top of the cake. Cut into squares.

178 ■ COCOA CHERRY CUPCAKES

YIELD: *24 servings*
BAKING TIME: *20 minutes*

24 maraschino cherries, stems removed
2½ cups all-purpose flour
1⅔ cups granulated sugar
½ cup Dutch processed cocoa powder
1 tablespoon baking soda
½ teaspoon salt
⅔ cup butter-flavored vegetable shortening
¾ cup milk
3 large eggs
⅔ cup light cream
2 teaspoons chocolate extract
1½ cups White Frosting (see page 418)

1 Position a rack in the center of the oven and preheat the oven to 350 degrees. Lightly grease or line with paper baking cups 24 2¾-inch muffin cups.

2 Drain the cherries and pat dry with a paper towel.

3 In a large bowl, combine the flour, sugar, cocoa powder, baking soda, and salt. Using a pastry blender or two knives scissor fashion, cut in the shortening to make a crumbly mixture. Add the milk. Using an electric mixer on low speed, blend thoroughly. Add the eggs, cream, and chocolate extract and beat for at least 2 minutes. Spoon the mixture into the prepared pans. Press a cherry into the batter in each muffin cup, being sure the cherry is completely covered with batter.

4 Bake for 15 to 20 minutes, or until a cake tester inserted at the edge of the cupcakes comes out clean. Cool in the pan on wire racks for 5 minutes. Transfer to the racks to cool completely.

5 Make the cream cheese frosting.

6 Spread the frosting over the tops of the cupcakes.

179 ■ COCOA GINGERBREAD CAKE

YIELD: *12 to 15 servings*
BAKING TIME: *45 minutes*

2 cups all-purpose flour
¼ cup Dutch processed cocoa powder
½ teaspoon ground ginger
½ teaspoon ground cinnamon
¼ teaspoon ground nutmeg
¼ teaspoon ground cloves
¼ teaspoon salt

1 teaspoon baking soda
1 cup warm water
½ cup butter-flavored vegetable shortening
1 cup granulated sugar
1 cup dark molasses
2 large eggs
1 cup Chocolate Glaze I (see page 401)
2 tablespoons powdered sugar for dusting

1 Position a rack in the center of the oven and preheat the oven to 350 degrees. Lightly grease and flour a 13 by 9-inch pan.

2 Combine the flour, cocoa powder, spices, and salt.

3 Dissolve the baking soda in the water.

4 In a large bowl, using an electric mixer on medium speed, beat the shortening and sugar until fluffy. Beat in the molasses. Beat in the eggs. In three additions, blend in the dry ingredients, alternating with the water, beginning and ending with the dry ingredients. Mix only until just blended. Scrape the mixture into the prepared pan and spread evenly.

5 Bake for 40 to 45 minutes, or until a cake tester inserted into the center comes out clean. Cool the cake in the pan for 5 minutes. Invert onto a serving plate to cool completely.

6 Make the chocolate glaze.

7 Place a doily the same dimensions as the cake on top of the cake. Dust with powdered sugar and carefully lift off the doily.

178

179

Using a pastry bag fitted with the smallest round tip, press the chocolate glaze over the top, tracing the outlines the powdered sugar left through the doily on the cake.

BAKING NOTES: Substitute ½ teaspoon of allspice for the nutmeg and cloves if desired.

180 ■ COCOA OATMEAL CAKE

YIELD: *12 to 15 servings*
BAKING TIME: *40 minutes*

1¾ cups all-purpose flour
3 tablespoons Dutch processed cocoa powder
1 teaspoon baking soda
¼ teaspoon salt
1¾ cups boiling water
1 cup quick-cooking oats
½ cup butter or margarine, at room temperature
1 cup packed light brown sugar
2 large eggs
1 cup chopped walnuts
1 cup semisweet chocolate chips

1 Position a rack in the center of the oven and preheat the oven to 350 degrees. Lightly grease a 13 by 9-inch pan.

2 Combine the flour, cocoa powder, baking soda, and salt.

3 In a large bowl, pour the boiling water over the oats and let stand for at least 10 minutes.

4 In a small bowl, using an electric mixer on medium speed, beat the butter and brown sugar until fluffy. Beat in the eggs, one at a time, beating well after each addition. Add to the oatmeal. Using a wooden spoon, blend until smooth. Gradually stir in the dry ingredients. Scrape the mixture into the prepared pan. Sprinkle the walnuts and chocolate chips evenly over the top.

5 Bake for 35 to 40 minutes, or until a cake tester inserted into the center comes out clean. Spread the chocolate chips over the top. Cool in the pan on a wire rack. Cut into squares.

181 ■ COCONUT FUDGE CAKE I

YIELD: *16 servings*
BAKING TIME: *75 minutes*

FILLING

8 ounces cream cheese, at room temperature
¼ cup granulated sugar
1 teaspoon crème de cacao
1 large egg
1 cup semisweet chocolate chips
½ cup flaked coconut

CAKE

3 cups all-purpose flour
¾ cup Dutch processed cocoa powder
½ cup pecans or walnuts, chopped
2 teaspoons baking powder
2 teaspoons baking soda
¼ teaspoon salt
1 cup strong brewed coffee
1 cup buttermilk
2 teaspoons chocolate or vanilla extract
2 cups granulated sugar
1 cup canola oil
2 large eggs

GLAZE

1 cup powdered sugar
3 tablespoons Dutch processed cocoa powder
2 tablespoons butter or margarine, at room temperature
2 tablespoons coffee liqueur
1 tablespoon hot water
Apricot Roses (see page 420)
Fresh mint leaves for garnish

1 Position a rack in the center of the oven and preheat the oven to 350 degrees. Lightly grease and flour a 10-inch Bundt pan.

2 To make the filling, in a medium bowl, using an electric mixer on medium speed, beat the cream cheese, sugar, and crème de cacao until smooth. Beat in the egg. Stir in the chocolate chips and coconut.

3 To make the cake, combine the flour, cocoa powder, pecans, baking powder, baking soda, and salt.

4 In a small bowl, combine the coffee, buttermilk, and chocolate extract.

5 In a large bowl, using an electric mixer on medium speed, beat the sugar, oil, and eggs for 2 minutes, or until thick and smooth. In three additions, blend in the dry ingredients, alternating with the coffee mixture, beginning and ending with the dry ingredients. Pour half of the batter into the prepared pan. Spoon the filling mixture onto the top of the batter in the pan, leaving a border around the sides of the pan. Carefully spoon the remaining batter over the top of the filling.

6 Bake for 70 to 75 minutes, or until a cake tester inserted into the center comes out clean. Cool in the pan on a wire rack for 15 minutes. Invert the cake onto the rack to cool completely.

7 To make the glaze, in a small bowl, combine the powdered sugar, cocoa powder, butter, liqueur, and water. Using an electric mixer on medium speed, whip until thick and smooth.

8 Place the cake on a serving plate. Drizzle the glaze over the top of the cake, allowing it to drip down the sides. Garnish with apricot roses and mint leaves.

182 ▪ COCONUT FUDGE CAKE II

YIELD: *16 servings*
BAKING TIME: *75 minutes*

COCONUT CREAM CHEESE FILLING

8 ounces cream cheese, at room temperature

¼ cup granulated sugar

1 teaspoon vanilla or chocolate extract

1 large egg

1 cup semisweet chocolate chips

½ cup flaked coconut

FUDGE CAKE

3 cups all-purpose flour

¾ cup Dutch processed cocoa powder

2 teaspoons baking powder

2 teaspoons baking soda

½ teaspoon salt

1 cup canola oil

2 cups granulated sugar

2 large eggs

1 cup buttermilk

1 cup strong brewed coffee

1 teaspoon vanilla or chocolate extract

½ cup walnuts or pecans, chopped

2 cups Chocolate Glaze III (see page 401)

1 Position a rack in the center of the oven and preheat the oven to 350 degrees. Lightly grease and flour a 10-inch Bundt pan.

2 To make the filling, in a medium bowl, using an electric mixer on medium speed, beat the cream cheese, sugar, and vanilla until smooth. Beat in the egg. Stir in the coconut and chocolate chips.

3 To make the cake, combine the flour, cocoa powder, baking powder, baking soda, and salt.

4 In a large bowl, using an electric mixer on medium speed, beat the oil, sugar, and eggs until thick and light-colored. Add the dry ingredients, buttermilk, coffee, and vanilla extract. Beat for 2 to 3 minutes. Fold in the nuts. Spread half of the cake batter onto the bottom of the prepared pan. Spoon the filling mixture over the top and carefully spread with the remaining mixture.

5 Bake for 70 to 75 minutes, or until a cake tester inserted into the center comes out clean. The cream cheese filling will still be moist. Cool in the pan on a wire rack for 15 minutes. Invert onto a serving plate to cool completely.

6 Make the chocolate glaze. Drizzle the glaze over the top of the cake.

180

181

175

177

182

176

183 ■ COFFEE-FLAVORED CHEESECAKE

YIELD: *12 servings*
BAKING TIME: *2 hours 15 minutes*
CHILL TIME: *overnight*

1 recipe Chocolate Cookie Crumb
  Crust (see page 267)
2 teaspoons mocha-flavored instant
  coffee powder
1 teaspoon boiling water
7 tablespoons all-purpose flour
1 tablespoon Dutch processed
  cocoa powder
1 teaspoon instant espresso powder
1/4 teaspoon baking powder
Pinch of salt
16 ounces cream cheese, at room
  temperature
1 cup granulated sugar
3 large eggs
2 tablespoons coffee liqueur
1 cup chocolate-flavored yogurt or
  sour cream
Seasonal fresh fruit for garnish

1 Position a rack in the center of
the oven and preheat the oven
to 350 degrees.

2 Make the crust as directed
and press into a 9-inch springform pan. Do not bake the crust.

3 In a cup, dissolve the mocha
coffee powder in the boiling
water.

4 Combine the flour, cocoa
powder, espresso powder, baking powder, and salt.

5 In a large bowl, using an electric mixer on medium speed,
beat the cream cheese and sugar
until smooth. Beat in the eggs,
one at a time, beating well after
each addition. Beat in the
liqueur and mocha coffee mixture. In three additions, blend in
the dry ingredients, alternating
with the yogurt, beginning and
ending with the dry ingredients.
Spread the mixture evenly over
the prepared crust.

6 Bake for 45 minutes. Turn the
oven off and leave the cheesecake undisturbed for 30 minutes. Open the oven door
slightly and leave the cheesecake in the oven for 1 hour. Chill
overnight.

7 Remove the side of the pan.
Garnish the cheesecake with
fresh fruit.

184 ■ COFFEE-FLAVORED CHOCOLATE CAKE I

YIELD: *12 servings*
BAKING TIME: *30 minutes*

CHOCOLATE CAKE

4 ounces unsweetened chocolate,
  grated or finely chopped
1/2 cup butter or margarine
2 cups buttermilk
1 teaspoon instant coffee powder
2 1/2 cups all-purpose flour
2 teaspoons baking soda

2 large eggs
2 cups granulated sugar
1 tablespoon coffee liqueur

CHOCOLATE COFFEE ICING

4 ounces unsweetened chocolate,
  grated or finely chopped
1/2 cup butter or margarine
2 teaspoons instant coffee powder
2 teaspoons coffee liqueur
2 cups powdered sugar
1/2 cup heavy cream

1 Position a rack in the center of
the oven and preheat the oven
to 350 degrees. Lightly grease
and flour two 8-inch round cake
pans.

2 In the top of a double boiler
over simmering water, melt the
chocolate and butter, stirring
until smooth. Remove from the
heat. Stir in the buttermilk and
coffee powder.

3 Combine the flour and baking
soda.

4 In a large bowl, using an electric mixer on medium speed,
beat the eggs and sugar until
thick and light-colored. Fold in
the coffee liqueur. In three additions, blend in the dry ingredients, alternating with the
chocolate mixture, beginning
and ending with the dry ingredients. Divide the mixture
between the prepared pans.

5 Bake for 25 to 30 minutes, or
until a cake tester inserted into
the center comes out clean. Cool
in the pans on wire racks. Invert
onto the racks to cool
completely.

6 To make the icing, in the top
of a double boiler over simmering water, melt the chocolate
and butter, stirring until
smooth. Remove from the heat.

Stir in the coffee powder and coffee liqueur.

7 In a medium bowl, using an electric mixer on medium speed, beat the powdered sugar and cream until blended. Pouring it in a thin stream, beat in the chocolate mixture. Whip on high speed until the mixture thickens to a spreadable consistency. If the icing is too thin, add more powdered sugar, a teaspoonful at a time.

8 To assemble, place one of the cake layers on a serving plate and spread with icing. Top with the second cake layer. Spread the remaining icing over the top and sides of the cake.

BAKING NOTES: For a variation, use the icing only for the filling and on the sides of the cake. Spread a fruit glaze (like Apricot Glaze, page 394) or fruit preserves on the top and garnish with rosettes of whipped cream.

185 ■ COFFEE-FLAVORED CHOCOLATE CAKE II

YIELD: *12 to 15 servings*
BAKING TIME: *35 minutes*

CAKE

2 cups all-purpose flour
3/4 cup Dutch processed cocoa powder
2 teaspoons baking powder
1 teaspoon baking soda
1/4 teaspoon salt
1/2 cup canola oil
2 teaspoons cider vinegar
1 cup milk
1 cup strong brewed coffee
2 cups granulated sugar
2 large eggs

FROSTING

3 ounces semisweet chocolate, grated or finely chopped
5 cups powdered sugar
6 tablespoons dark rum
2 tablespoons crème de cacao
Dark sprinkles for garnish

1 Position a rack in the center of the oven and preheat the oven to 350 degrees. Lightly grease a 13 by 9-inch pan.

2 To make the cake, combine the flour, cocoa powder, baking powder, baking soda, and salt.

3 In a large bowl, using an electric mixer on medium-high speed, beat the oil, vinegar, milk, coffee, and sugar until smooth. Beat in the eggs. Gradually blend in the dry ingredients, just until incorporated. Pour the mixture into the prepared pan.

4 Bake for 30 to 35 minutes, or until a cake tester inserted into the center comes out clean. Cool in the pan on a wire rack. Invert onto a serving platter.

5 To make the frosting, melt the chocolate (see page 13). Remove from the heat.

6 In a medium bowl, using an electric mixer on medium speed, beat together the melted chocolate, powdered sugar, and rum until combined. Beat in the crème de cacao and mix until a spreadable consistency. If frosting is too thin, add a little more powdered sugar. If too thick, add a few more drops of crème de cacao.

7 To frost the cake, spread the frosting in a even layer on the top and sides of the cake. Pipe any remaining frosting through a pastry bag fitted with a star tip to make rosettes around the top edge of the cake. Lightly sprinkle the top of the cake with dark sprinkles.

186 ■ CORA'S CHEESECAKE WITH CHOCOLATE TOPPING

YIELD: *12 to 16 servings*
BAKING TIME: *90 minutes*
CHILL TIME: *3 hours*

4 cups large-curd cottage cheese
1/4 cup chocolate wafer cookie crumbs
1/4 cup finely chopped almonds
8 ounces cream cheese, at room temperature
2/3 cup granulated sugar

1/4 cup milk
2 tablespoons all-purpose flour
2 teaspoons Lemonier liqueur or fresh lemon juice
3 large egg whites
1 cup Chocolate Glaze I (see page 401)

1 The day before you plan to bake the cheesecake, line a strainer with a double thickness of cheesecloth and place over a medium bowl. Place the cottage cheese in the strainer, cover with a piece of waxed paper, and place a weight on the top, such as a can of tuna fish. Cover and chill for at least 12 hours.

2 Position a rack in the center of the oven and preheat the oven to 300 degrees. Lightly grease a 9-inch springform pan.

3 Sprinkle the cookie crumbs and almonds evenly over the bottom of the prepared pan.

4 Place the cottage cheese in a large bowl and discard the drained liquid. Add the cream cheese. Using an electric mixer on medium speed, beat until smooth. Beat in the sugar, milk, flour, liqueur and egg whites. Continue beating on medium speed for about 2 minutes, or until combined. Carefully spoon the mixture into the pan to avoid disturbing the crumb mixture on the bottom.

5 Bake for 60 minutes. Turn off the oven and leave the cheesecake undisturbed for 30 minutes. Cool in the pan on a wire rack for 15 minutes.

6 Make the chocolate glaze. Spread the glaze evenly over the top of the cheesecake. Cover and chill for at least 3 hours.

7 To serve, carefully run a thin-bladed knife around the sides of the cheesecake to loosen it and remove the side of the pan.

187 ■ CRACKER CRUMB AND NUT CAKE

YIELD: *8 to 12 servings*
BAKING TIME: *35 minutes*

3 cups chocolate graham cracker crumbs
1 cup finely chopped pecans
3 tablespoons baking powder
1 cup butter-flavored vegetable shortening
1 cup granulated sugar
4 large eggs
2 teaspoons vanilla extract
1 cup milk
2 cups Cocoa Frosting (see page 406)

1 Position a rack in the center of the oven and preheat the oven to 350 degrees. Lightly grease and flour three 8-inch round cake pans.

2 Combine the crumbs, pecans, and baking powder

3 In a large bowl, using an electric mixer on high speed, beat the shortening and sugar until fluffy. Beat in the eggs, one at a time, beating well after each addition. Stir in the vanilla extract. In three additions, blend in the dry ingredients, alternating with the milk, until just moistened. Divide the mixture evenly between the prepared pans and spread evenly.

4 Bake for 30 to 35 minutes, or until a cake tester inserted into the center comes out clean. Cool in the pans on wire racks for 5 minutes. Invert onto the racks to cool completely.

5 Make the frosting.

6 Place one of the cake layers on a serving plate and spread with some of the frosting. Top with the second cake layer and spread the frosting over the top. Place the third layer on top and frost the top and sides of the cake.

188 ■ CREAM CHEESE MOCHA CAKE

YIELD: *12 servings*
BAKING TIME: *40 minutes*
CHILL TIME: *2 hours*

CRUST

2 cups chocolate wafer cookie crumbs
1/4 cup butter, at room temperature

FILLING

4 ounces semisweet chocolate, grated or finely chopped
16 ounces cream cheese, at room temperature
1/2 cup granulated sugar
1/2 teaspoon chocolate extract
3 tablespoons strong brewed coffee or coffee liqueur
2 large eggs
Sliced papaya and mango for garnish

1 Position a rack in the center of the oven and preheat the oven to 350 degrees. Lightly grease a 9-inch springform pan.

2 To make the crust, in a large bowl, using a pastry blender, cut the butter into the crumbs to make a crumbly mixture. Press firmly onto the bottom and 1/2 inch up the sides of the prepared pan.

3 To make the filling, melt the chocolate (see page 13). Remove from the heat.

4 In a large bowl, using an electric mixer on medium speed, beat the cream cheese and sugar until smooth. Beat in the chocolate extract, melted chocolate, and coffee. Beat in the eggs. Pour the mixture into the prepared crust. Sprinkle a few chocolate wafer cookie crumbs over the top, if desired.

5 Bake for 35 to 40 minutes, or until firm. Cool in the pan on a wire rack for 30 minutes. Chill for 2 hours or until completely chilled.

6 When ready to serve, remove the side of the springform pan. Place the cake on a serving plate. Garnish with sliced papaya and mango.

189 ■ CREAMY COCOA CAKE

YIELD: *12 servings*
BAKING TIME: *30 minutes*

CAKE

2 cups cake flour
1 1/2 teaspoons baking powder
1/2 teaspoon baking soda
1/4 teaspoon salt
1/2 cup Dutch processed cocoa powder
1/3 cup boiling water
1 1/2 cups granulated sugar
2/3 cup sour cream or yogurt
2/3 cup butter, at room temperature
3 large eggs
1 1/2 teaspoons chocolate or vanilla extract

FROSTING

1 cup chocolate-flavored yogurt
1 tablespoon powdered sugar
2 teaspoons Dutch processed cocoa powder
1 teaspoon crème de cacao
1/2 teaspoon chocolate extract

GARNISH

Chocolate sprinkles
Chocolate Leaves (see page 422) or Chocolate Cones (see page 421)

1 Position a rack in the center of the oven and preheat the oven to 350 degrees. Lightly grease and flour a 9-inch springform pan. Line the bottom of the pan with waxed paper and grease the paper.

2 To make the cake, combine the flour, baking powder, baking soda, and salt.

3 In a medium bowl, combine the cocoa powder and boiling water. Stir in the sugar. Cool slightly. Stir in the sour cream.

4 In a large bowl, using an electric mixer on medium speed, beat the butter until creamy. Blend in the dry ingredients, mixing just until incorporated. Beat in the eggs, chocolate extract, and half of the cocoa mixture, beating on low speed for 1 minute, or until smooth. Beat in the remaining cocoa mixture, beating on high speed for 2 minutes, or until fluffy. Pour the batter into the prepared pan.

5 Bake for 25 to 30 minutes, or until a cake tester inserted into the center comes out clean, or the cake pulls away from the sides of the pan. Cool on a wire rack for 5 minutes. Remove the side of the pan and invert the cake onto the rack to cool completely.

6 Meanwhile, to make the frosting, in a medium bowl, combine the yogurt, powdered sugar, cocoa powder, crème de cacao, and chocolate extract, stirring until smooth. Cover and chill until ready to use.

7 To assemble, remove the waxed paper and place the cake on a platter. Spread some of the frosting evenly around the sides of the cake. Spread the remaining frosting on the top. Sprinkle chocolate sprinkles over the top and garnish with chocolate leaves or cones.

190 ■ DARK CHOCOLATE CHEESECAKE

YIELD: *12 servings*
BAKING TIME: *2½ hours*
CHILL TIME: *1 hour*

CRUST

1½ cups vanilla wafer cookie crumbs
¼ cup powdered sugar
6 tablespoons butter or margarine, at room temperature

FILLING

5 ounces semisweet chocolate, grated or finely chopped
24 ounces cream cheese, at room temperature
¾ cup granulated sugar
3 large eggs
1 cup chocolate-flavored yogurt
1 teaspoon crème de cacao

GARNISH

½ cup Chocolate Whipped Cream (see page 406)
Chocolate Curls (see page 422)
Peeled and thinly sliced kiwifruit

1 Position a rack in the center of the oven and preheat the oven to 275 degrees. Lightly grease a 9-inch springform pan.

2 To make the crust, in a large bowl, combine the cookie crumbs and sugar. Using a pastry blender, cut in the butter to form a crumbly mixture. Press evenly onto the bottom and about 1½ inches up the sides of the prepared pan.

3 To make the filling, melt the chocolate (see page 13). Remove from the heat.

4 In a large bowl, using an electric mixer on medium speed, beat the melted chocolate, cream cheese, sugar, and eggs until smooth. Beat in the yogurt and crème de cacao. Pour the mixture over the top of the crust.

5 Bake for 1 hour and 45 minutes. Turn off the oven. Cool the cheesecake in the oven with the door slightly open for 45 minutes. Refrigerate for 1 hour, or until firm.

6 Remove the side of the pan and place the cake on a serving plate. Garnish with small dollops or rosettes of chocolate whipped cream, chocolate curls, and thinly sliced kiwifruit.

191 ■ DARK MYSTERY CHOCOLATE CAKE

YIELD: *12 servings*
BAKING TIME: *30 minutes*

CAKE

5 ounces unsweetened chocolate, grated or finely chopped
½ cup boiling water
1 cup chocolate-flavored yogurt
2 cups cake flour
1½ teaspoons baking powder
1 teaspoon baking soda
1 cup granulated sugar
⅔ cup packed dark brown sugar
⅔ cup butter, melted
3 large eggs
2 teaspoons bittersweet chocolate liqueur

SAUCE

½ cup water
½ cup Dutch processed cocoa powder
½ cup granulated sugar
¼ cup light corn syrup
2 tablespoons Kahlúa
1 teaspoon coffee liqueur

187

190

189

1 Position a rack in the center of the oven and preheat the oven to 350 degrees. Lightly grease and flour a 9-inch springform pan. Line with waxed paper and grease the paper.

2 In a small bowl, combine the chocolate and boiling water, stirring until smooth. Cool slightly and stir in the yogurt.

3 Combine and sift the flour, baking powder, baking soda, and the sugars.

4 In a large bowl, combine the butter and dry ingredients, stirring until the flour is barely moistened. Using an electric mixer on medium speed, beat in the eggs until smooth. Beat in the chocolate mixture and liqueur, beating on medium speed, until streaks disappear. Pour the mixture into the prepared pan.

5 Bake for 25 to 30 minutes, or until a cake tester inserted into the center comes out clean. Cool in the pan on a wire rack for 5 minutes. Remove the side of the pan and invert onto the rack to cool completely.

6 Meanwhile, to make the sauce, in a medium saucepan, combine the water, cocoa powder, sugar, and corn syrup. Stirring constantly, over medium heat, bring to a boil. Stir in the Kahlùa and cook for 1 to 2 minutes. Remove from the heat, cool slightly, and stir in the liqueur.

7 Slice the cake and place on individual serving plates. Spoon the sauce over each slice of cake.

192 ■ DECADENT CHOCOLATE CAKE

YIELD: *16 servings*
BAKING TIME: *50 minutes*

2 cups all-purpose flour
1 teaspoon baking powder
1 teaspoon baking soda
¼ teaspoon salt
1 cup boiling water
3 ounces unsweetened chocolate, grated or finely chopped
½ cup butter or margarine
1 teaspoon crème de cacao
2 large eggs, separated
2 cups granulated sugar
½ cup chocolate-flavored yogurt
1 cup Chocolate Frosting III (see page 399)

1 Position a rack in the center of the oven and preheat the oven to 350 degrees. Lightly grease and flour a 10-inch tube pan.

2 Combine the flour, baking powder, baking soda, and salt.

3 In a small bowl, combine the boiling water, chocolate, and butter, stirring until the chocolate is melted and smooth. Mix in the crème de cacao

4 In a small bowl, using an electric mixer on high speed, beat the egg whites until stiff but not dry.

5 In a large bowl, using an electric mixer on medium speed, beat the sugar and egg yolks until thick and light-colored. Beat in the yogurt. Slowly beat in the chocolate mixture. Gradually blend in the dry ingredients. Gently fold in the egg whites. Pour into the prepared pan.

6 Bake for 45 to 50 minutes, or until a cake tester inserted into the center comes out clean. Cool in the pan on a wire rack for 10 minutes. Invert onto the rack to cool completely.

7 Make the frosting.

8 Place the cake on a serving plate. Frost the top and sides of the cake with the frosting.

193 ■ DEEP DARK CHOCOLATE CAKE

YIELD: *12 servings*
BAKING TIME: *30 minutes*
CHILL TIME: *30 minutes*

6 ounces unsweetened chocolate, grated or finely chopped
½ cup butter or margarine
3 large eggs
¾ cup granulated sugar
1 teaspoon chocolate or vanilla extract
6 tablespoons all-purpose flour
1 cup White Chocolate Sauce (see page 418) for serving
1 cup Kahlúa Cocoa Sauce (see page 413) for serving
1½ cups Chocolate Glaze IV (see page 401)

192

194

1 Position a rack in the center of the oven and preheat the oven to 350 degrees. Lightly grease an 8-inch springform pan and line the bottom with waxed paper.

2 In the top of a double boiler over simmering water, melt the chocolate and butter, stirring constantly until smooth. Remove from the heat.

3 In a large bowl, using an electric mixer on medium speed, beat the eggs until thick and light-colored. Beat in the sugar. Beat in the chocolate extract. Beat in the chocolate mixture, alternating with the flour, until just blended. Pour into the prepared pan.

4 Bake for 28 to 30 minutes, or until a cake tester inserted into the center comes out clean. Cool in the pan on a wire rack for 30 minutes Remove the side of the pan and invert the cake onto a plate. Remove the waxed paper.

5 Make the white chocolate sauce and the Kahlúa cocoa sauce.

6 Make the chocolate glaze. Pour the glaze over the top of the cake, and use a knife to smooth it over the top and sides. Allow the glaze to refrigerate and set for 30 minutes.

7 To serve, pour spoonfuls of the warm Kahlúa sauce around the edges of individual dessert plates, allowing it to run towards the plate centers. Place a slice of the cake in the center of each plate. Drizzle the warm white chocolate sauce in a thin stream from the end of a spoon in a decorative pattern over the Kahlúa sauce. Serve at once with the two warm sauces on the side.

194 ■ DESERT DATE CAKE

YIELD: *12 servings*
BAKING TIME: *45 minutes*

1/2 cup dates, pitted and chopped
1/2 teaspoon baking soda
1/4 cup boiling water
2 ounces unsweetened chocolate, grated or finely chopped
3/4 cup all-purpose flour
1/4 teaspoon salt
1/2 cup butter or margarine
2/3 cup granulated sugar
1 large egg
1/2 teaspoon vanilla or chocolate extract
1/3 cup sour cream or yogurt
2 cups Ganache III (see page 410)

1 Position a rack in the center of the oven and preheat the oven to 350 degrees. Lightly grease and flour a 9-inch square pan.

2 In a small saucepan, over low heat, combine the dates, baking soda, and boiling water. Simmer for 5 minutes. Pour the mixture into the container of a blender and blend on high speed for 10 seconds, or until the mixture forms a paste.

3 Melt the chocolate (see page 13). Remove from the heat.

4 Combine the flour and salt.

5 In a large bowl, using an electric mixer on medium speed, beat the butter and sugar until light and fluffy. Beat in the egg. Beat in the vanilla extract. Pouring it in a thin stream, beat in the melted chocolate. In three additions, blend in the dry ingredients, alternating with the sour cream, beginning and ending with the dry ingredients. Pour into the prepared pan and spread evenly.

6 Bake for 40 to 45 minutes, or until a cake tester inserted into the center comes out clean. Cool on a wire rack for 10 minutes. Invert onto the rack to cool completely.

7 Make the ganache.

8 Place the cake on a serving plate. Pour the ganache over the top of the cake, letting it drip down the sides. Chill until ready to serve.

195 ■ DEVIL'S FOOD CAKE I

YIELD: *12 to 15 servings*
BAKING TIME: *35 minutes*

2 cups all-purpose flour
1/2 teaspoon salt
1 teaspoon ground cinnamon
1 cup water
1/4 cup buttermilk
1 teaspoon baking soda
1/2 cup butter or margarine, at room temperature
1/2 cup canola oil
1/4 cup Dutch processed cocoa powder
2 large eggs, slightly beaten
2 cups granulated sugar
1 teaspoon vanilla or almond extract
1 cup Chocolate Frosting (see page 399)

1 Position a rack in the center of the oven and preheat the oven to 350 degrees. Lightly grease and flour a 13 by 9-inch pan.

2 Combine the flour, salt, and cinnamon.

3 In a small bowl, combine the water, buttermilk, and baking soda.

4 In a saucepan, over low heat, melt the butter, oil, and cocoa powder, stirring until smooth. Remove from the heat and cool slightly.

5 In a large bowl, using an electric mixer on medium speed, beat the eggs and sugar until thick and light-colored. Beat in the vanilla extract and the cocoa mixture. In three additions, blend in the dry ingredients, alternating with the buttermilk mixture, beginning and ending with the dry ingredients. Pour into the prepared pan.

6 Bake for 30 to 35 minutes, or until a cake tester inserted into the center comes out clean. Cool slightly in the pan on a wire rack.

7 While baking, prepare the chocolate frosting. Frost the top of the warm cake with the chocolate frosting.

196 ■ DEVIL'S FOOD CAKE II

YIELD: *12 servings*
BAKING TIME: *35 minutes*
CHILL TIME: *30 minutes*

DEVIL'S FOOD CAKE

3 ounces unsweetened chocolate, grated or finely chopped
2¼ cups all-purpose flour
2 teaspoons baking soda
½ teaspoon salt
½ cup butter or margarine, at room temperature
2 cups granulated sugar
1 teaspoon chocolate or vanilla extract
3 large eggs
½ teaspoon red food coloring (optional)
½ cup buttermilk
1 cup boiling water

PLUM FILLING

¾ pound fresh plums, skinned, pitted, and quartered
½ cup crème de prunelle or port
3 tablespoons powdered sugar

COCOA TOPPING

½ cup Dutch processed cocoa powder
½ cup granulated sugar
½ cup heavy cream
¼ cup butter or margarine

1 Position a rack in the center of the oven and preheat the oven to 350 degrees. Lightly grease and flour two 9-inch round cake pans.

2 Melt the chocolate (see page 13). Remove from the heat.

3 Combine the flour, baking soda, and salt.

4 In a large bowl, using an electric mixer on medium speed, beat the butter and sugar until light and fluffy. Beat in the chocolate extract. Beat in the eggs, one at a time, beating well after each addition. On low speed, beat in the melted chocolate and food coloring. In three additions, blend in the dry ingredients, alternating with the buttermilk, beginning and ending with the dry ingredients. Beat in the boiling water, mixing until just blended. Divide the mixture between the pans.

5 Bake for 30 to 35 minutes, or until a cake tester inserted into the center comes out clean. Cool in the pans on wire racks for 5 minutes. Invert onto the racks to cool completely.

6 To make the filling, in a saucepan, over low heat, combine the plums and crème de prunelle and cook until the mixture is reduced to 1 cup. Remove from the heat and stir in the powdered sugar. Return to the heat and cook until the mixture is reduced by one-third. Remove from the heat.

7 To make the topping, in a saucepan over low heat, combine the cocoa powder, sugar, cream, and butter, and stir until smooth. Cook for 5 minutes, or until thickened.   Remove from the heat and cool for 10 to 15 minutes.

8 To assemble, place one cake layer on a serving plate, and spread the plum filling evenly over the top. Top with the second cake layer and pour the topping over the cake, allowing it to run down the sides. Chill for 30 minutes until the topping is hard before serving.

197 ■ DOUBLE CHOCOLATE CAKE

YIELD: *12 servings*
BAKING TIME: *35 minutes*

CHOCOLATE LAYER FILLING

2 ounces unsweetened chocolate, grated or finely chopped
2 ounces semisweet chocolate, grated or finely chopped
1 can (14 ounces) sweetened condensed milk
2 tablespoons butter or margarine

CAKE BATTER

2 cups all-purpose flour
1 teaspoon ground cinnamon
½ teaspoon salt
½ cup butter or margarine
½ cup canola oil
¼ cup Dutch processed cocoa powder
1 cup water
¼ cup buttermilk
1 teaspoon baking soda
2 large eggs, slightly beaten
2 cups granulated sugar
1 teaspoon vanilla or almond extract

SAUCE

4 ounces semisweet chocolate, grated or finely chopped
1 cup granulated sugar
1 cup heavy cream
2 tablespoons slivered almonds, toasted
1 tablespoon amaretto
½ teaspoon chocolate extract
Fresh mint sprigs for garnish

1 Position a rack in the center of the oven and preheat the oven to 350 degrees. Lightly grease two 9-inch round cake pans. Line the bottoms with waxed paper and grease the paper.

2 To make the filling, in the top of a double boiler over simmering water, melt the chocolates, stirring until smooth. Slowly stir in the condensed milk and butter until smooth. Remove from the heat. Pour half of the mixture into each of the prepared pans.

3 To make the cake, combine the flour, cinnamon, and salt.

4 In a saucepan, over low heat, melt the butter with the oil and cocoa powder, stirring until smooth. Remove from the heat and cool slightly.

196

197

5 In a cup, combine the water, buttermilk, and baking soda.

6 In a large bowl, using an electric mixer on medium speed, beat the eggs and sugar until thick and light-colored. Beat in the vanilla extract and the cocoa mixture. In three additions, blend in the dry ingredients, alternating with the buttermilk mixture, beginning and ending with the dry ingredients. Pour into the prepared pans.

7 Bake for 30 to 35 minutes, or until a cake tester inserted into the center comes out clean. Cool in the pans on wire racks for 10 minutes. Invert one cake layer onto a serving plate and remove the waxed paper. Top with the second cake layer, and remove the waxed paper.

8 To make the sauce, in the top of a double boiler over simmering water, melt the chocolate, stirring until smooth. Add the sugar and cream, reduce the heat to low, and cook, stirring constantly, for 5 to 7 minutes, or until smooth and thick like a custard. Do not allow the mixture to boil. Remove from the heat. Mix in the almonds, amaretto, and chocolate extract.

9 To serve, garnish the cake with mint sprigs and serve with warm chocolate sauce on the side.

198 ■ DOUBLE CHOCOLATE POUND CAKE I

YIELD: *10 to 12 servings*
BAKING TIME: *60 minutes*

2 cups all-purpose flour
¼ cup rolled oats
¼ cup Dutch processed cocoa powder
1¼ teaspoons baking powder
1 teaspoon baking soda
1 teaspoon ground allspice
¾ cup semisweet chocolate chips
Pinch of salt
1¼ cups unsweetened applesauce
¾ cup packed light brown sugar
½ cup canola oil

1 Position a rack in the center of the oven and preheat the oven to 350 degrees. Lightly grease a 9 by 5-inch pan.

2 Combine the flour, oats, cocoa powder, baking powder, baking soda, allspice, chocolate chips, and salt.

3 In a large bowl, using an electric mixer on low speed, beat the applesauce, brown sugar, and oil. Stirring by hand, gradually blend in the dry ingredients. Spread evenly into the prepared pan.

4 Bake for 55 to 60 minutes, or until a cake tester inserted into the center comes out clean. Cool in the pan on a wire rack for 10 minutes. Invert onto the wire rack to cool completely.

BAKING NOTES: Although no icing, glaze, or frosting is needed, if this is to be used for a festive occasion, place a doily over the top of the loaf and sprinkle a powdered sugar over the top.

199 ■ DOUBLE CHOCOLATE POUND CAKE II

YIELD: *10 to 12 servings*
BAKING TIME: *40 minutes*

3 ounces semisweet chocolate, grated or finely chopped
2 cups cake flour
1 teaspoon baking soda
1 cup (6 ounces) semisweet chocolate chips
3 large eggs, separated
½ cup butter or margarine, at room temperature
2 cups packed light brown sugar
½ cup sour cream or yogurt
½ cup ice water
2 cups Chocolate Whipped Cream (see page 406) for garnish
2 cups fresh strawberries for garnish

1 Position a rack in the center of the oven and preheat the oven to 375 degrees. Lightly grease a 9 by 5-inch loaf pan.

2 Melt the chocolate (see page 13). Remove from the heat.

3 Combine the flour, baking soda, and chocolate chips.

4 In a medium bowl, using an electric mixer on high speed, beat the egg whites until stiff peaks form.

5 In a large bowl, using an electric mixer on medium speed, beat the butter and brown sugar until fluffy. Add the egg yolks and beat until light-colored and smooth. Beat in the sour cream. Pouring it in a thin stream, beat in the melted chocolate. In three additions, blend in the dry ingredients, alternating with the ice water, beating well after each addition. Gently fold in the egg whites. Pour into the prepared pan.

198

6 Bake for 40 minutes, or until a cake tester inserted into the center comes out clean. Cool completely in the pan on a wire rack. Remove the cake from the pan and place on a serving plate.

7 Fill a pastry bag fitted with a fluted tip with the chocolate whipped cream. Pipe a decoration on the top of the cake. Garnish with sliced, halved, and whole strawberries.

200 ■ DOUBLE CHOCOLATE ZUCCHINI CAKE

YIELD: *12 to 15 servings*
BAKING TIME: *45 minutes*

2½ cups all-purpose flour
¼ cup Dutch processed cocoa powder
1 teaspoon baking powder
¼ teaspoon baking soda
½ teaspoon salt
2 cups grated zucchini
6 ounces semisweet chocolate, grated or finely chopped
1 cup hazelnuts or pecans, chopped
1 cup vegetable shortening
1½ cups granulated sugar
1 teaspoon chocolate or vanilla extract
2 large eggs
½ cup chocolate-flavored yogurt
Powdered sugar for dusting

1 Position a rack in the center of the oven and preheat the oven to 350 degrees. Lightly grease a 13 by 9-inch pan.

2 Combine the flour, cocoa powder, baking powder, baking soda, salt, zucchini, chocolate, and hazelnuts.

3 In a large bowl, using an electric mixer on medium speed, beat the shortening and sugar until smooth. Beat in the chocolate extract. Beat in the eggs. Beat in the yogurt. Gradually blend in the dry ingredients. Pour the mixture into the prepared pan and spread evenly.

4 Bake for 40 to 45 minutes, or until a cake tester inserted into the center comes out clean. Cool in the pan on a wire rack. Dust the top of the cake with powdered sugar.

201 ■ ESPRESSO CHOCOLATE CHEESECAKE

YIELD: *16 servings*
BAKING TIME: *2 hours*
CHILL TIME: *overnight*

CRUST

¾ cup graham cracker crumbs
½ cup toasted hazelnuts
2 tablespoons granulated sugar
¼ cup butter or margarine, at room temperature
4 ounces semisweet chocolate, grated or finely chopped

FILLING

1 pound unsweetened chocolate, grated or finely chopped
3 tablespoons Dutch processed cocoa powder
3 tablespoons mocha-flavored instant espresso powder
Pinch of salt

188

193

191

185

1½ cups heavy cream
½ cup coffee liqueur
2 pounds cream cheese, at room temperature
1¼ cups granulated sugar
4 large eggs

TOPPING

Raspberry Sauce (see page 416)

1 Position a rack in the center of the oven and preheat the oven to 375 degrees. Lightly grease a 10-inch springform pan.

2 To make the crust, in a large bowl, combine the crumbs, nuts, and sugar. Using a pastry blender, cut in the butter to make a crumbly mixture. Press the mixture evenly onto the bottom of the prepared pan.

3 Bake for 8 minutes. Cool in the pan on a wire rack. Place the pan in the freezer until ready to use.

4 Melt the semisweet chocolate (see page 13). Remove from the heat. Spread evenly over the chilled crust.

5 Reduce the oven temperature to 350 degrees. Lightly regrease the sides of the springform pan.

6 To make the filling, melt the chocolate (see page 13). Remove from the heat.

7 Combine the cocoa powder, espresso powder, and salt. Sift.

8 In a large saucepan, over medium heat, heat ½ cup of the heavy cream just until simmering. Stir in the dry ingredients. Remove from the heat and stir in the liqueur and the remaining 1 cup cream.

9 In a large bowl, using an electric mixer on medium speed, beat the cream cheese and sugar until smooth. Beat in the melted chocolate. Beat in the cream mixture. Beat in the eggs, one at a time, beating well after each addition. Pour the mixture into the prepared pan. Place the springform pan in a large roasting pan. Place the roasting pan on the oven rack. Pour boiling water into the roasting pan until it comes halfway up the side of the springform pan.

10 Bake for 1 hour. Turn off the oven and leave the cheesecake undisturbed for 1 hour. Remove from the oven and cool on a wire rack. Remove the side of the pan and transfer the cheesecake to a serving plate. Chill overnight.

11 To serve, cut into wedges and place on individual serving plates. Spoon a little of the raspberry sauce over the top of each slice. Serve with the remaining sauce in a bowl on the side.

BAKING NOTES: The raspberry sauce can also be spooned over the top of the unsliced cheesecake and chilled up to 1 hour before serving. A sprig of mint makes a colorful garnish. As an alternative, omit the raspberry sauce and spread a thin layer of Chocolate Glaze II (see page 401) over the top. Drizzle melted white chocolate bark over the glaze.

199

195

200

201

202 ∎ EVERYDAY CHOCOLATE CAKE

YIELD: *12 servings*
BAKING TIME: *45 minutes*

3 ounces unsweetened chocolate, grated or finely chopped
3/4 cup ground walnuts
1/2 cup all-purpose flour
3 large eggs, separated
1/4 teaspoon cream of tartar
Pinch of salt
3/4 cup butter or margarine, at room temperature
1 1/2 cups granulated sugar
2 teaspoons chocolate or vanilla extract
3 tablespoons hot water
1 1/2 cups Green Crème de Menthe Icing (see page 411)
Dark or white chocolate leaves for garnish (see page 422)

1 Position a rack in the center of the oven and preheat the oven to 350 degrees. Grease a 9-inch round cake pan. Line the bottom with waxed paper and grease the paper.

2 Melt the chocolate (see page 13). Remove from the heat.

3 Combine the walnuts and flour.

4 In a medium bowl, using an electric mixer on high speed, beat the egg whites, cream of tartar, and salt until stiff but not dry.

5 In a large bowl, using an electric mixer on medium speed, beat the butter, sugar, and chocolate extract until fluffy. Beat in the egg yolks, one at a time, beating well after each addition. Beat in the melted chocolate and hot water. Blend in the dry ingredients. Gently fold in the egg whites. Scrape the mixture into the prepared pan and spread evenly.

6 Bake for 40 to 45 minutes, or until a cake tester inserted into the center comes out clean. The top of the cake will crack. Cool in the pan on a wire rack. Invert onto a serving plate. Remove the waxed paper.

7 Make the frosting. Spread the top and sides of the cake with the frosting. Garnish with the chocolate leaves.

203 ∎ FAMILY SECRET CHOCOLATE CAKE

YIELD: *16 servings*
BAKING TIME: *45 minutes*

2 1/4 cups all-purpose flour
1 teaspoon baking soda
1/2 teaspoon salt
1 cup boiling water
3 ounces unsweetened chocolate, grated or finely chopped
1/2 cup butter or margarine, at room temperature
1 cup granulated sugar
1 cup packed light brown sugar
2 large eggs
1 tablespoon crème de cacao
1/2 cup buttermilk
1 1/2 cups Ganache III (see page 410)
Seasonal fresh fruit or edible flowers (see page 22) for garnish

1 Position a rack in the center of the oven and preheat the oven to 350 degrees. Lightly grease a 10-inch tube pan.

2 Combine the flour, baking soda, and salt.

3 In a small bowl, pour the boiling water over the chocolate and stir until smooth.

4 In a large bowl, using an electric mixer on medium speed, beat the butter and the sugars until fluffy. Beat in the eggs, one at a time, beating well after each addition. Beat in the crème de cacao. In three additions, blend in the dry ingredients, alternating with the buttermilk, beginning and ending with the dry ingredients. Pour the batter into the prepared pan.

5 Bake 40 to 45 minutes, or until a cake tester inserted into the center comes out clean. Cool in the pan on a wire rack for 8 to 10 minutes. Invert onto a wire rack to cool completely.

6 Make the ganache.

7 To assemble, using a serrated knife, slice the cake in half horizontally. Spread a layer of the ganache the diameter of the cake on a serving plate. Place the bottom half of the cake on top of the ganache. Spread a layer of the ganache over the cake layer and place the second cake layer on top. Do not press down. Spread the remaining ganache over the top and sides of the cake. Garnish with fresh fruit or edible flowers.

204 ∎ FANTASTIC PUDDING CAKE

YIELD: *12 to 15 servings*
BAKING TIME: *14 minutes*
CHILL TIME: *4 hours*

CRUST

1 cup all-purpose flour
1/2 cup chocolate graham cracker crumbs
1 cup pecans or hazelnuts, finely ground
1/2 cup butter or margarine, at room temperature

FIRST LAYER

8 ounces cream cheese, at room temperature
1 cup whipped topping
1 cup powdered sugar
1 teaspoon raspberry liqueur

SECOND LAYER

4 cups milk, warmed slightly
3 packages (3.4 ounces each) Jell-O Brand instant chocolate pudding mix

THIRD LAYER

1 cup whipped topping
1 cup pecans or almonds, coarsely chopped

1 Position a rack in the center of the oven and preheat the oven to 375 degrees. Lightly grease a 13 by 9-inch pan.

2 To make the crust, in a large bowl, combine the flour, graham cracker crumbs, and pecans. Using a pastry blender, cut in the butter to form a crumbly mixture. Press onto the bottom of the prepared pan.

3 Bake for 14 minutes. Cool in the pan on a wire rack. Chill for 1 hour.

4 Meanwhile, to make the first layer, in a medium bowl, using an electric mixer on medium speed, beat the cream cheese until smooth. Beat in the whipped topping. Beat in the powdered sugar and liqueur. Spread this mixture evenly over the chilled crust. Chill for 1 hour.

5 Meanwhile, to make the second layer, whisk the milk and pudding mix until combined. Chill until it just starts to thicken. Do not let the pudding set. Whisk the pudding until smooth. Pour it over the first layer. Chill for 1 hour.

6 Meanwhile, to make the third layer, in a small bowl, whisk the whipped topping until very smooth. Spread this over the second layer and sprinkle with the chopped pecans. Chill for 2 hours. Cut into bars just before serving.

205 ■ FAST 'N EASY CHOCOLATE SHEET CAKE

YIELD: *24 servings*
BAKING TIME: *35 minutes*

1 package (3.4 ounces) cook-and-serve chocolate pudding mix
1 box (18.5 ounces) chocolate cake mix
2 cups semisweet chocolate chips
1 cup chopped walnuts

1 Position a rack in the center of the oven and preheat the oven to 350 degrees. Lightly grease an 11½ by 17½-inch sheet pan. Line the pan with waxed paper and grease the paper.

2 Make the pudding mix according to the package directions and pour into a large mixing bowl. Gradually blend in the cake mix. Spread evenly onto the bottom of the prepared pan. Sprinkle the chocolate chips over the top.

3 Bake for 30 to 35 minutes, or until a cake tester inserted into the center comes out clean. Spread the melted chocolate chips evenly over the top of the cake and sprinkle the walnuts on top. Cool in the pan on a wire rack. Cut into squares.

206 ■ FEATHERY FUDGE CAKE

YIELD: *12 servings*
BAKING TIME: *35 minutes*

3 ounces unsweetened chocolate, grated or finely chopped
2 cups all-purpose flour
1¼ teaspoons baking soda
¼ teaspoon salt
⅔ cup butter-flavored vegetable shortening
1¾ cups granulated sugar
2 large eggs
1 teaspoon crème de cacao
1¼ cups water
2 cups Chocolate Frosting VI (see page 400)
Fresh fruit or Chocolate Leaves (see page 422) for garnish

1 Position a rack in the center of the oven and preheat the oven to 350 degrees. Lightly grease and flour two 9-inch round cake pans.

2 Melt the chocolate (see page 13). Remove from the heat.

3 Combine the flour, baking soda, and salt.

4 In a large bowl, using an electric mixer on medium speed, beat the shortening and sugar until fluffy. Beat in the eggs, one at a time, beating well after each addition. Beat in the crème de cacao and melted chocolate. In three additions, blend in the dry ingredients, alternating with the water, beginning and ending with the dry ingredients. Pour the mixture into the prepared pans.

5 Bake for 30 to 35 minutes, or until a cake tester inserted into the center comes out clean. Cool in pans on wire racks for 5 minutes. Invert onto the racks.

6 Make the frosting.

7 To assemble, place one of the cake layers on a serving plate

202

203

206

and spread with some of the frosting. Top with the second cake layer and spread the remaining frosting on the top and sides of the cake. Use a fork to inscribe a feathery effect in the top of the frosting. Garnish with fresh fruit or chocolate leaves.

207 ■ FIREFIGHTERS' CHOCOLATE BARS

YIELD: *12 servings*
BAKING TIME: *30 minutes*

CHOCOLATE CAKE

4 ounces semisweet chocolate, grated or finely chopped
¾ cup all-purpose flour
½ cup chopped almonds or pecans
1 teaspoon baking powder
3 large eggs, separated
6 tablespoons butter or margarine at room temperature
2 tablespoons granulated sugar
1 teaspoon chocolate extract
¼ cup milk

POWDERED SUGAR ICING

2 tablespoons butter or margarine,
2 cups powdered sugar
2 tablespoons water
1 teaspoon crème de cacao
2 ounces semisweet chocolate, grated or finely chopped for garnish

1 Position a rack in the center of the oven and preheat the oven to 350 degrees. Lightly grease an 8 or 9-inch square pan.

2 Melt the chocolate (see page 13). Remove from the heat.

3 Combine the flour, almonds, and baking powder.

4 In a small bowl, using an electric mixer on high speed, beat the egg whites until stiff but not dry.

5 In a large bowl, using an electric mixer on medium speed, beat the butter and sugar until light and fluffy. Beat in the egg yolks. Beat in the melted chocolate and chocolate extract. In three additions, blend in the dry ingredients, alternating with the milk, beginning and ending with the dry ingredients. Gently fold the egg whites into the batter. Scrape the mixture into the prepared pan and spread evenly.

6 Bake for 28 to 30 minutes, or until a cake tester inserted into the center comes out clean. Cool in the pan on a wire rack for 10 minutes. Invert onto the rack to cool completely. Place on a serving plate.

7 To make the icing, in a medium saucepan, over low heat, melt the butter. Add the

powdered sugar, stirring constantly until blended. Remove from the heat and add the water and crème de cacao, stirring until smooth. Spread over the top of the cake.

8 To make the garnish, melt the chocolate (see page 13). Immediately drizzle over the top of the icing and spread evenly. Cut into squares.

208 ■ FIT FOR AN ANGEL

YIELD: *16 servings*
BAKING TIME: *60 minutes*
CHILL TIME: *30 minutes*

CAKE

1¼ cups powdered sugar
¾ cup cake flour
¼ cup Dutch processed cocoa powder
¼ teaspoon salt
10 large egg whites
1 teaspoon cream of tartar
1 teaspoon vanilla or almond extract

FILLING

1 quart chocolate ice cream, softened slightly
1 quart strawberry ice cream, softened slightly

TOPPING

2 cups Chocolate Whipped Cream (see page 406)
Fresh whole or sliced strawberries for garnish

1 Position a rack in the center of the oven and preheat the oven to 300 degrees.

2 Combine 1 cup of the powdered sugar, the flour, cocoa powder, and salt. Sift twice.

3 In a very large bowl, using an electric mixer on high speed, beat the egg whites until foamy. Add the cream of tartar and beat for 2 minutes. Add the remaining ¼ cup powdered sugar and beat until stiff but not dry. Grad-

208

207

ually fold in the dry ingredients, 2 tablespoons at a time. Add the vanilla extract. Pour into an ungreased 10-inch tube pan.

4 Bake for 50 minutes. Turn off the oven and leave the cake in the oven for 10 minutes. Invert the pan onto its tube or onto a wire rack. Do not disturb until completely cool. Remove the cake from the pan.

5 To assemble, using a serrated knife, cut the cake horizontally into three layers. Place the first cake layer on a serving plate and spread with the chocolate ice cream. Place the second cake layer on top of the ice cream and spread with the strawberry ice cream. Place the third cake layer on top. Freeze for 30 minutes, or until ready to serve.

6 When ready to serve, spread the chocolate whipped cream over the top and sides of the cake. Garnish each slice with whole or sliced strawberries.

209 ■ FOUR-LAYER CHOCOLATE CAKE

YIELD: *12 servings*
BAKING TIME: *25 minutes*

CAKE

½ cup Dutch processed cocoa powder
⅓ cup all-purpose flour
3 large eggs, separated, plus 1 large egg white
⅛ teaspoon cream of tartar
½ cup plus 2 tablespoons granulated sugar
¼ cup butter or margarine, melted and clarified (see page 000)

SYRUP

⅓ cup granulated sugar
⅓ cup water
3 tablespoons grated orange zest
2 tablespoons Grand Marnier

FILLING

1⅓ cups heavy cream
1 pound semisweet chocolate, grated or finely chopped
⅓ cup orange marmalade

GARNISH

Chocolate Curls (see page 422)
Chocolate-covered strawberries or cherries (see pages 171–172), optional

1 Position a rack in the center of the oven and preheat the oven to 375 degrees. Lightly butter and flour an 8-inch square pan.

2 To make the cake, combine the cocoa powder and flour.

3 In a medium bowl, using an electric mixer on high speed, beat the 4 egg whites with the cream of tartar until soft peaks form. Continue beating and add 2 tablespoons of the sugar. Beat until the mixture forms stiff peaks.

4 In a large bowl, using an electric mixer on medium speed, beat the egg yolks until thick and light-colored. Continue beating on low speed and add the remaining ½ cup sugar. Gradually fold in the dry ingredients, alternating with the clarified butter, mixing after each addition just until blended. Fold in the whites until no streaks remain. Pour the batter into the prepared pan and spread evenly.

5 Bake for 20 to 25 minutes, or until a cake tester inserted into the center comes out clean. Cool for 5 minutes on a wire rack. Invert onto the rack to cool completely.

6 Meanwhile, to make the syrup, in a small saucepan, combine the sugar, water, and orange zest. Bring to a boil and simmer for 5 minutes, stirring occasionally. Remove from the heat, strain, and cool slightly. Stir in the Grand Marnier.

7 Meanwhile, to make the filling, in a medium saucepan over medium-high heat, heat the cream just until simmering. Pour the cream over the chocolate, in a medium bowl, and stir until smooth. Cool. Chill for 1 hour, stirring occasionally. Just before assembling the cake, using an electric mixer on low speed, beat the filling until soft peaks form.

8 To assemble, using a serrated knife, cut the cake horizontally into four layers. Brush each layer with the syrup. Place the first cake layer on a serving plate and spread with one-third of the orange marmalade.

Spread some of the cream filling over the top. Continue until all the cake layers and marmalade are used, ending with a cake layer. Spread the remaining filling over the top and sides of the cake. Garnish with chocolate curls. Place chocolate-covered strawberries or cherries around the base of the cake as a final decoration. Chill for 30 minutes before serving.

BAKING NOTES: This same cake can be prepared using any variety of preserves, liqueur, and cream filling.

210 ■ FRENCH CHOCOLATE CAKE

YIELD: *12 servings*
BAKING TIME: *20 minutes*

CAKE

½ cup Dutch processed cocoa powder
¾ cup boiling water
3 large egg whites
½ cup butter or margarine, at room temperature
2 cups granulated sugar
¼ teaspoon chocolate extract
½ teaspoon baking soda
½ cup sour cream or chocolate-flavored yogurt
2 cups all-purpose flour
Pinch of salt

ICING

2 cups Chocolate Icing (see page 402)

1 Preheat the oven to 350 degrees. Lightly grease and flour two 8-inch round cake pans.

2 To make the cake, in a small bowl, combine the cocoa powder and boiling water

3 In a medium bowl, using an electric mixer, beat the egg whites until stiff but not dry.

4 In a large bowl, using an electric mixer on medium speed, beat the butter and sugar until light and fluffy. Beat in the cocoa mixture. Beat in the chocolate extract, baking soda, and sour cream. Combine and fold in the flour and salt. Fold in the egg whites. Divide the mixture evenly between the two prepared pans and smooth the tops.

5 Bake for 15 to 20 minutes, or until a cake tester inserted into the center comes out clean. Cool in the pan for 10 minutes. Invert onto the wire rack to cool completely.

6 Meanwhile, make the icing according to the recipe directions.

7 To assemble, place one layer on a serving plate, spread the icing over the top and place the second layer on top. Spread the remaining icing evenly over the sides and top. The top may be garnished with chopped nuts, chocolate curls, or thinly sliced fruit.

211 ■ FUDGE CAKE

YIELD: *12 servings*
BAKING TIME: *30 minutes*

CAKE

2 cups cake flour
1 teaspoon baking soda
¼ teaspoon salt
4 ounces unsweetened chocolate, grated or finely chopped
½ cup hot water
1¾ cups granulated sugar
½ cup butter or margarine, at room temperature
3 large eggs
⅔ cup milk
1 teaspoon chocolate or vanilla extract

FILLING

1 large egg white
2 tablespoons light corn syrup
¾ cup granulated sugar
1 tablespoon water
Pinch of salt
1 tablespoon coffee liqueur

GLAZE

2 tablespoons butter or margarine
1 ounce semisweet chocolate, grated or finely chopped
1 cup powdered sugar
1 tablespoon boiling water
Fruit preserves for garnish

1 Position a rack in the center of the oven and preheat the oven to 350 degrees. Lightly grease two 9-inch round cake pans. Line the bottoms with waxed paper and grease the paper. Flour the pans.

2 Combine and sift the flour, baking soda, and salt.

3 In the top of a double boiler over simmering water, combine the chocolate and hot water, stirring until smooth. Add ½ cup of the sugar and cook for 2 to 3 minutes, stirring constantly until thickened. Remove from the heat.

4 In a large bowl, using an electric mixer on medium speed, beat the butter and remaining 1¼ cup sugar until light and fluffy. Add the eggs, one at a time, beating well after each addition. In three additions, beat in the dry ingredients, alternating with the milk, beginning and ending with the dry ingredients. Do not overmix. On low speed, beat in the chocolate mixture, pouring it in a thin stream. Beat in the chocolate extract. Divide the mixture evenly between the prepared pans.

5 Bake for 25 to 30 minutes, or until a cake tester inserted into the center comes out clean. Cool in the pans on wire racks. Invert onto the racks to cool completely.

6 Meanwhile, to make the filling, in the top of a double boiler, combine the egg white, corn syrup, sugar, water, and salt. Set over a pan of simmering water. Using an electric mixer on medium speed, beat until the mixture forms stiff peaks. Remove from the pan of water and continue to beat for 1 minute longer until smooth. Stir in the liqueur.

7 Meanwhile, to make the glaze, in the top of a double boiler over simmering water, melt the butter and chocolate, stirring until smooth. Add the powdered sugar and water and stir until smooth. Remove from the heat.

8 To assemble, place one cake layer on a serving plate and spread the filling evenly over the top. Place the second cake layer on top and press down lightly. Spread the glaze over the top of the cake, allowing a little to drip down the sides. Garnish each serving with dabs of fruit preserves and serve.

211

212

212 ■ FUDGE CUPCAKES

YIELD: *12 servings*
BAKING TIME: *35 minutes*

2/3 cup (4 ounces) semisweet chocolate chips
1 cup butter or margarine
1 1/2 cups pecans or almonds, finely ground
1 3/4 cups granulated sugar
1 cup all-purpose flour
4 large eggs
1 teaspoon chocolate extract

1 Position a rack in the center of the oven and preheat the oven to 350 degrees. Line twelve 2 1/2-inch muffin cups with paper baking cups.

2 In the top of a double boiler over simmering water, melt the chocolate chips and butter, stirring until smooth. Remove from the heat and stir in the pecans.

3 In a large bowl, using an electric mixer on medium speed, beat the sugar, flour, eggs, and chocolate extract until combined. Stir in the chocolate mixture. Spoon into the prepared pan, filling each cup two-thirds full.

4 Bake for 30 to 35 minutes, or until a cake tester inserted into the center comes out clean. Remove from the pan to wire racks and cool for 10 minutes. Serve the cupcakes warm.

214

213

213 ■ FUDGE TRUFFLE CHEESECAKE

YIELD: *12 servings*
BAKING TIME: *65 minutes*
CHILL TIME: *30 minutes*

CRUST

1 1/2 cups vanilla or chocolate wafer cookie crumbs
1/3 cup Dutch processed cocoa powder
6 tablespoons powdered sugar
1/3 cup butter, melted

FILLING

12 ounces cream cheese, at room temperature
1 can (14 ounces) sweetened condensed milk
1 cup semisweet chocolate chips
4 large eggs
1/2 cup coffee liqueur
2 teaspoons almond or hazelnut extract
Chocolate Sauce VI (see page 405), for serving

1 Position a rack in the center of the oven and preheat the oven to 300 degrees. Lightly grease a 9-inch springform pan.

2 To make the crust, in a large bowl, combine the cookie crumbs, cocoa powder, powdered sugar, and butter and mix thoroughly. Press the mixture onto the bottom of the prepared pan. Chill while preparing the filling.

3 Meanwhile, to make the filling, in a large bowl, using an electric mixer on medium speed, beat the cream cheese until smooth. Beating on low speed, beat in the condensed milk. Beat in the eggs, one at a time, beating well after each addition. Stir in the liqueur and almond extract. Pour the batter into the prepared pan.

4 Bake for 65 minutes, or until the center is set firm. Turn off the oven and open the door slightly. Leave the cheesecake in the oven to cool completely. Chill 30 minutes, or until ready to serve.

5 Make the chocolate sauce.

6 When ready to serve, remove the side of the pan and slice into wedges. Spoon sauce on top.

214 ■ GÂTEAU AUX MARRONS

YIELD: *12 servings*
BAKING TIME: *45 minutes*

CAKE

1 1/4 cups butter or margarine, at room temperature
1 cup granulated sugar
6 tablespoons Dutch processed cocoa powder
5 large eggs, separated
3/4 cup sweetened chestnut puree
1/2 cup almonds, finely ground

FILLING AND TOPPING

1 cup raspberry preserves
2 tablespoons Grand Marnier
1 cup sweetened chestnut puree (see Baking notes)
1 1/2 cups Chocolate Glaze I (see page 401)
Whole fresh strawberries for garnish
Thinly sliced oranges for garnish

1 Position a rack in the center of the oven and preheat the oven to 350 degrees. Grease a 9-inch springform pan.

2 To make the cake, in a large bowl, using an electric mixer on medium speed, beat the butter, sugar, and cocoa powder until fluffy. Beat in the egg yolks, one at a time, beating well after each addition.

3 In a small bowl, using an electric mixer on high speed, beat the egg whites until stiff.

4 Fold the egg whites into the yolk mixture. Fold in the chestnut puree and almonds. Pour the mixture into the prepared pan.

5 Bake for 45 minutes, or until the cake pulls away from the side of the pan and a cake tester inserted into the center comes out clean. Cool in the pan on a wire rack for 10 minutes. Invert onto the rack to cool completely.

6 To make the filling, combine the raspberry preserves and Grand Marnier.

7 To assemble, using a serrated knife, slice the cake horizontally into three layers. Place the bottom layer on a serving plate and spread with half of the raspberry preserves. Place the sec-

ond cake layer on top, and spread with the remaining raspberry preserves. Place the third cake layer on top and frost the sides of the cake with the chestnut puree. Top with the chocolate glaze. Garnish with strawberries and orange slices.

BAKING NOTES: Chestnut puree can be found in many supermarkets or in gourmet food stores.

215 ■ GERMAN CHOCOLATE CAKE

YIELD: *12 servings*
BAKING TIME: *35 minutes*

CAKE

2½ cups all-purpose flour
1 teaspoon baking soda
Pinch of salt
4 ounces Baker's German's bittersweet chocolate, grated or finely chopped
½ cup water
1 cup vegetable shortening
2 cups granulated sugar
4 large eggs
1 cup buttermilk or sour cream
1 teaspoon vanilla extract or coffee liqueur

FILLING

½ cup butter or margarine
1 can (14 ounces) evaporated milk
3 large egg yolks, beaten until thickened
1 cup powdered sugar

FROSTING

1 cup heavy cream
1 cup powdered sugar
3 large egg yolks
2 tablespoons all-purpose flour
2 tablespoons butter or margarine, at room temperature
1 teaspoon chocolate or vanilla extract
1½ teaspoon crème de cacao
1 cup flaked coconut
1 cup pecans or walnuts, chopped
½ cup maraschino cherries, drained and diced, for assembly
10 maraschino cherry halves for garnish

1 Position a rack in the center of the oven and preheat the oven to 350 degrees. Lightly grease and flour three 8-inch round cake pans.

2 To make the cake, combine the flour, baking soda, and salt.

3 In the top of a double boiler over simmering water, melt the chocolate with the water, stirring until smooth. Remove from the heat.

4 In a large bowl, using an electric mixer on medium speed, beat the shortening and sugar until fluffy. Beat in the eggs, one at a time. Beat in the buttermilk and vanilla extract. On low speed, beat in the chocolate, pouring it in a thin stream. Gradually blend in the dry ingredients. Pour the mixture into the prepared pans.

5 Bake for 30 to 35 minutes, or until a cake tester inserted into the center comes out clean. Cool in the pans on wire racks for 10 minutes. Invert onto the racks to cool completely.

6 To make the filling, in a medium saucepan, over low heat, combine the butter, milk, egg yolks, and powdered sugar, stirring constantly until the mixture thickens. Remove from the heat and, using an electric mixer on medium speed, beat to a spreadable consistency.

7 To make the frosting, combine the cream, powdered sugar, egg yolks, flour, butter, and chocolate extract in the top of a double boiler. Set over a pan of simmering water and stir constantly until smooth and thick. Remove from the heat and stir in crème de cacao. Fold in the coconut and pecans.

8 To assemble the cake, using a serrated knife, slice the rounded tops off the cake layers. Place one cake layer on a serving plate and spread half of the filling over the top. Sprinkle with half of the chopped cherries. Place the second cake layer on top of the first and lightly press it into place. Repeat with the remaining filling and cherries, and place the third cake layer on top. Spread the frosting over the sides and the top of the cake. Decorate with the cherry halves.

216 ■ GERMAN CHOCOLATE SUPREME

YIELD: *12 to 15 servings*
BAKING TIME: *45 minutes*

CAKE

1 cup flaked coconut
1 cup pecans or walnuts, chopped
1¾ cups all-purpose flour
1¼ teaspoons baking soda
½ teaspoon baking powder
½ cup butter or margarine
¾ cups German's nonalkalized unsweetened cocoa powder
2 cups powdered sugar
2 large eggs
1 cup buttermilk
2 teaspoons chocolate or vanilla extract

TOPPING

8 ounces cream cheese, at room temperature
½ cup butter, margarine, or vegetable shortening, at room temperature
2 cups powdered sugar
1 tablespoon raspberry liqueur

1 Position a rack in the center of the oven and preheat the oven to 350 degrees. Lightly grease a 13 by 9-inch pan. Sprinkle the coconut and pecans evenly over the bottom of the pan.

2 To make the cake, combine the flour, baking soda, and baking powder.

3 In a small saucepan over medium heat, melt the butter. Gradually blend in the cocoa powder. Remove from the heat.

4 In a large bowl, using an electric mixer on medium speed, beat the powdered sugar and eggs until thick and light-colored. Beat in the buttermilk and chocolate extract. Pouring it in a steady stream, beat in the cocoa mixture. Gradually blend in the dry ingredients. Scrape the mixture over the top of the coconut and pecans in the prepared pan and spread evenly.

5 To make the topping, in a medium bowl, using an electric mixer on medium speed, beat the cream cheese and butter until smooth. Beat in the powdered sugar and liqueur. Spoon this mixture evenly over the top of the batter in the pan.

6 Bake for 40 to 45 minutes, or until a cake tester inserted into the center comes out clean. Cool in the pan on a wire rack.

217 ■ GOOD GUYS' CHOCOLATE CAKE

YIELD: *12 to 15 servings*
BAKING TIME: *35 minutes*
CHILL TIME: *30 minutes*

2¹/₂ cups all-purpose flour
1 teaspoon baking soda
Pinch of salt
4 ounces unsweetened chocolate, grated or finely chopped
¹/₂ cup water
2 cups granulated sugar
1 cup vegetable shortening
4 large eggs
1 cup buttermilk
1 teaspoon vanilla or chocolate extract
1¹/₄ cups warm Chocolate Syrup II (see page 406) for topping
2 cups whipped topping for garnish
3 candy bars (8 ounces each), crushed, for garnish

1 Position a rack in the center of the oven and preheat the oven to 350 degrees. Lightly grease and flour a 13 by 9-inch pan.

2 Combine the flour, baking soda, and salt.

3 In the top of a double boiler over simmering water, melt the chocolate with the water, stirring until smooth.

4 In a large bowl, using an electric mixer on medium speed, beat the shortening and sugar until fluffy. Beat in the eggs, one at a time. Beat in the buttermilk and vanilla extract. Pouring it in thin stream, beat in the chocolate mixture. Gradually blend in the dry ingredients. Pour the mixture into the prepared pan.

5 Bake for 30 to 35 minutes, or until a cake tester inserted into the center comes out clean. Cool in the pan on a wire rack for 10 minutes. Using a large fork, poke holes 1¹/₂ inches apart all over the top of the cake. Pour the chocolate syrup over the warm cake and cool completely. Chill for 30 minutes before serving.

6 To serve, spread the whipped topping over the top of the cake and sprinkle with the crushed candy bars.

218 ■ GRASSHOPPER CAKE

YIELD: *16 servings*
BAKING TIME: *60 minutes*
CHILL TIME: *60 minutes*

CAKE

2¹/₂ cups cake flour
1 tablespoon baking powder
¹/₂ teaspoon salt
7 large eggs, separated
¹/₂ teaspoon cream of tartar
1¹/₂ cups granulated sugar
²/₃ cup chocolate syrup
¹/₂ cup canola oil
1 teaspoon coffee liqueur

FILLING

1 envelope unflavored gelatin
¹/₄ cup cold water
¹/₂ cup green crème de menthe
¹/₃ cup crème de cacao
¹/₃ cup cream cheese, at room temperature
¹/₃ cup whipped topping mix
Kiwifruit and lime slices for garnish

1 Position a rack in the center of the oven and preheat the oven to 350 degrees. Lightly grease a 10-inch Bundt or tube pan.

2 To make the cake, combine and sift the flour, baking powder, and salt.

3 In a medium bowl, using an electric mixer on high speed, beat the egg whites and cream of tartar until they form stiff peaks.

4 In a large bowl, using an electric mixer on medium speed, beat the sugar, chocolate syrup, and oil until smooth. Beat in the egg yolks. Beat in the liqueur. Gradually blend in the dry ingredients. Fold in the beaten egg whites. Scrape the mixture into the prepared pan and spread evenly.

5 Bake for 55 to 60 minutes, or until a cake tester inserted into the center comes out clean. Cool in the pan on a wire rack for 10 minutes. Invert onto the rack. Chill for 1 hour.

6 Meanwhile, to make the filling, in a small saucepan, soften the unflavored gelatin in the cold water for 1 minute. Stir over low heat until completely dissolved. Remove from the heat. Stir in the creme de menthe and crème de cacao.

215

217

7 In a small bowl, using an electric mixer on medium speed, beat the cream cheese and whipped topping mix until smooth. Stir in the gelatin mixture and chill until a spreadable consistency.

8 To assemble the cake, using a serrated knife, cut the cake horizontally into three layers. Place the bottom cake layer on a serving plate and spread with one third of the filling. Top with the second cake layer and spread with one third of the filling. Top with the third cake layer. Spread the remaining filling on top. Garnish with sliced kiwifruit and lime slices around the base of the cake.

219 ■ GRASSHOPPER CHEESECAKE

YIELD: *12 servings*
BAKING TIME: *40 minutes*
CHILL TIME: *30 minutes*

CRUST

1½ cups chocolate wafer cookie crumbs
1 tablespoon granulated sugar
2 tablespoons butter or margarine, melted

FILLING

16 ounces cream cheese, at room temperature
1 cup granulated sugar
3 large eggs
¼ cup green crème de menthe
2 tablespoons crème de cacao

TOPPING

3 ounces semisweet chocolate, grated or finely chopped
½ cup sour cream or yogurt

1 Position a rack in the center of the oven and preheat the oven to 350 degrees. Lightly grease an 8-inch springform pan.

2 To make the crust, in a small bowl, combine the cookie crumbs, sugar, and the melted butter. Press firmly onto the bottom and 1-inch up the sides of the prepared pan. Chill.

3 To make the filling, in a large bowl, using an electric mixer on medium speed, beat the cream cheese and sugar until smooth. Beat in the eggs. Continue beating until the mixture is very smooth. Stir in the crème de menthe and crème de cacao. Pour into the chilled crust.

4 Bake for 35 to 40 minutes, or until firm. Cool in the pan on a wire rack.

5 Meanwhile, to make the topping, melt the chocolate (see page 13). Remove from the heat and cool slightly. Stir in the sour cream. Spread over the top of the cooled cheesecake. Chill 30 minutes, or until serving.

6 Remove the side of the pan and place the cheesecake on a serving plate.

220 ■ HOLIDAY CHOCOLATE CAKE

YIELD: *12 servings*
BAKING TIME: *35 minutes*

CAKE

1¾ cups all-purpose flour
¾ cup Dutch processed cocoa powder
2 teaspoons baking powder
1 teaspoon baking soda
½ teaspoon salt
1 cup granulated sugar
1 cup powdered sugar

204

205

209

220

½ cup canola oil
2 large eggs
1 cup buttermilk
2 tablespoons coffee liqueur
1 cup minus 2 tablespoons strong
  brewed coffee

FILLING

1 tablespoon crème de fraises
15 ounces ricotta cheese
2 tablespoons heavy cream
2 cups fresh strawberries, sliced
½ cup pecans or pistachio nuts,
  chopped

TOPPING

1 cup powdered sugar
½ cup Dutch processed cocoa
  powder
2 cups heavy cream
1 teaspoon crème de cacao
Strawberries and pecan halves for
  garnish
Fresh mint sprig for garnish

1 Position a rack in the center of the oven and preheat the oven to 350 degrees. Lightly grease two 9-inch round cake pans. Place a large mixing bowl in the freezer to chill.

2 To make the cake, combine the flour, cocoa powder, baking powder, baking soda, and salt.

3 In a large bowl, using an electric mixer on medium speed, beat the sugars and oil until smooth. Beat in the eggs, buttermilk, and liqueur. Beat in the coffee. Gradually blend in the dry ingredients. Pour the batter into the prepared pans.

4 Bake for 30 to 35 minutes, or until a cake tester inserted into the center comes out clean. Cool in the pans on wire racks for 10 minutes. Invert onto the racks to cool completely.

5 To make the filling, in a small bowl, using an electric mixer on medium speed, beat the liqueur, ricotta cheese, and heavy cream until smooth.

6 To assemble, using a serrated knife, slice each cake layer in half horizontally. Place one of the layers on a serving plate.

Spread one-third of the filling over the bottom layer and sprinkle with one-third of the pecans and sliced strawberries. Repeat with the remaining cake layers, filling, pecans, and strawberries, ending with the fourth cake layer.

7 Thirty minutes before you are ready to serve the cake, make the topping. Sift the powdered sugar and cocoa powder. In the chilled bowl, using an electric mixer on high speed, beat the cream until frothy. Gradually beat in the cocoa mixture. Blend in the crème de cacao. Beat until the mixture is thick enough to spread on the cake.

8 Frost the top and the sides of the cake with the chocolate whipped cream. Decorate the top with pecan halves, sliced strawberries, and mint sprig. Serve at once.

210

219

216

218

221 ■ HONEY CHOCOLATE CAKE

YIELD: *16 servings*
BAKING TIME: *85 minutes*

2¹/₂ cups all-purpose flour
³/₄ teaspoon baking soda
¹/₄ teaspoon salt
8 ounces milk chocolate, grated or finely chopped
¹/₂ cup chocolate syrup
1 cup butter or margarine, at room temperature
2 cups granulated sugar
1 teaspoon chocolate or vanilla extract
5 large eggs
1¹/₂ cups sour cream or yogurt
1 cup pecans, finely chopped
¹/₄ cup honey, warmed

1 Position a rack in the center of the oven and preheat the oven to 350 degrees. Lightly grease and flour a 10-inch tube pan.

2 Combine the flour, baking soda, and salt.

3 In a small bowl, set over a bowl of hot water, melt the chocolate with the chocolate syrup, stirring until smooth.

4 In a large bowl, using an electric mixer on medium speed, beat the butter and sugar until light and fluffy. Beat in the chocolate extract. Beat in the eggs, one at a time, beating well after each addition. In three additions, blend in the dry ingredients, alternating with the sour cream, beginning and ending with the dry ingredients. Remove 2 cups of the batter and set aside. Slowly beat the melted chocolate into the remaining batter. Scrape the mixture into the prepared pan and spread evenly.

5 Add the pecans and honey to the reserved 2 cups of batter. Spoon this mixture evenly over the top of the batter in the pan.

6 Bake for 40 minutes. Reduce the oven temperature to 325 degrees. Continue to bake for 40 to 45 minutes or until a cake tester inserted into the center comes out clean. Cool the cake in the pan on a wire rack for 1 hour. Invert onto a serving plate.

BAKING NOTES: The milk chocolate will be easier to grate if it is chilled first. The pecan-honey mixture forms a topping on this cake, so no frosting or icing is required. For a fancy occasion, garnish with white chocolate leaves (see page 422) or fresh white chrysanthemums or petals.

222 ■ HOT FUDGE SUNDAE CAKE

YIELD: *12 servings*
BAKING TIME: *40 minutes*

1 cup all-purpose flour
³/₄ cup granulated sugar
2 teaspoons baking powder
¹/₄ teaspoon salt
¹/₂ cup milk
2 tablespoons canola oil
1 teaspoon chocolate or vanilla extract
1 cup chopped walnuts
1 cup packed light brown sugar
¹/₄ cup Dutch processed cocoa powder
1³/₄ cup very hot water
Chocolate ice cream for serving
Chocolate Sauce III (see page 404) for serving

1 Position a rack in the center of the oven and preheat the oven to 350 degrees.

2 In a large bowl, combine the flour, granulated sugar, baking powder, and salt. Using a fork, stir in the milk, oil, and chocolate extract until smooth.

3 Spread the walnuts evenly on the bottom of a 9-inch square pan. Pour the batter over the walnuts and spread evenly, being careful not to disturb the nuts. Sprinkle the brown sugar over the top of the batter. Dust the cocoa powder over the brown sugar. Gently pour the hot water over the top.

4 Bake for 40 minutes. While still warm, spoon into dessert dishes and top with a scoop of chocolate ice cream. Spoon hot chocolate sauce over the top. Serve immediately.

223 ■ ICE WATER CHOCOLATE CAKE

YIELD: *12 to 15 servings*
BAKING TIME: *40 minutes*

2 ounces unsweetened chocolate, grated or finely chopped
2 cups all-purpose flour
1 teaspoon baking soda
1 teaspoon salt
2 large eggs, separated
1 teaspoon cream of tartar
¹/₂ cup butter-flavored vegetable shortening
1¹/₂ cups granulated sugar
1 cup ice water
1 teaspoon chocolate or almond extract
1 cup Almond Sauce (see page 395)
Seasonal fresh fruit for garnish

1 Position a rack in the center of the oven and preheat the oven to 350 degrees. Lightly grease a 13 by 9-inch pan.

2 Melt the chocolate (see page 13). Remove from the heat.

3 Combine the flour, baking soda, and salt.

4 In a small bowl, using an electric mixer on high speed, beat the egg whites until foamy. Add the cream of tartar and beat until stiff peaks form.

5 In a large bowl, using an electric mixer on medium speed, beat the shortening and sugar until fluffy. Beat in the egg yolks. Beat in the melted chocolate. Beat in the ice water and chocolate extract. Gradually beat in the dry ingredients. Fold in the egg whites. Scrape the mixture into the prepared pan and spread evenly.

6 Bake for 35 to 40 minutes, or until a cake tester inserted into the center comes out clean. Cool in the pan on a wire rack. Invert onto a serving plate.

7 Make the glaze.

8 Spread the sauce on the top and sides of the cake. Garnish with fruit.

224 ■ IRISH COFFEE CAKE

YIELD: *12 servings*
BAKING TIME: *30 minutes*
FREEZE TIME: *1 HOUR*

3 tablespoons Dutch processed cocoa powder, plus extra for dusting the cake pan
1 cup minus 2 tablespoons all-purpose flour
2 ounces unsweetened chocolate, grated or finely chopped
2 ounces semisweet chocolate, grated or finely chopped
1/2 cup butter or margarine
1/2 cup Irish whisky
3 large eggs, separated
1 cup granulated sugar
2 cups Cocoa Cream Topping (see page 406)
Watercress or celery leaves for garnish

1 Position a rack in the center of the oven and preheat the oven to 350 degrees. Grease a 9-inch round cake pan. Line the bottom with waxed paper and grease the paper. Dust with cocoa powder, shaking out the excess.

2 Combine the 3 tablespoons of cocoa powder and the flour.

3 In the top of a double boiler over simmering water, melt the chocolates and the butter, stirring until smooth. Remove from the heat and blend in the whisky.

4 In a medium bowl, using an electric mixer on high speed, beat the egg whites until stiff but not dry.

5 In a large bowl, using an electric mixer on medium speed, beat the egg yolks until thick and light-colored. Beat in the sugar. Beat in the chocolate mixture. Gradually blend in the dry ingredients, mixing until just blended. Stir in the egg whites in one addition. Scrape the mixture into the prepared pan and spread evenly.

6 Bake for 25 to 30 minutes, or until a cake tester inserted into the center comes out clean. Cool in the pan on a wire rack for 15 minutes. Invert onto the rack to cool completely. Freeze for 1 hour.

7 Transfer the cake to a serving plate. Spread the cocoa cream topping over the top and sides of the cake. Garnish with several sprigs of fresh watercress or with celery leaves.

225 ■ IRISH POTATO CAKE

YIELD: *12 to 15 servings*
BAKING TIME: *45 minutes*

4 ounces semisweet chocolate, grated or finely chopped
3 cups all-purpose flour
1 cup walnuts, finely chopped
2 teaspoons baking powder
1 teaspoon ground cinnamon
1 teaspoon ground cloves
1/4 teaspoon ground nutmeg
4 large eggs, separated
1 cup butter-flavored vegetable shortening
2 cups granulated sugar
1 cup cold mashed potatoes
1/2 cup milk

1 Position a rack in the center of the oven and preheat the oven to 350 degrees. Lightly grease and flour a 13 by 9-inch pan.

2 Melt the chocolate (see page 13). Remove from the heat.

3 Combine the flour, walnuts, baking powder, and spices.

4 In a medium bowl, using an electric mixer on high speed, beat the egg whites until stiff but not dry.

5 In a small bowl, using an electric mixer on medium speed, beat the egg yolks until thick and light-colored.

6 In a large bowl, using an electric mixer on medium speed, beat the shortening and sugar until fluffy. Beat in the beaten egg yolks. Beat in the mashed potatoes and melted chocolate. In three additions, blend in the dry ingredients, alternating with the milk, beginning and ending with the dry ingredients. Fold in the beaten egg whites. Scrape the mixture into the prepared pan and spread evenly.

7 Bake for 40 to 45 minutes, or until a cake tester inserted into the center comes out clean. Cool in the pan on a wire rack. Invert the cake onto a serving plate. Cut into small or large bars.

221

224

226 ■ ITALIAN-STYLE FRUIT CAKE

YIELD: *12 servings*
BAKING TIME: *40 minutes*

½ cup raisins
¼ cup golden raisins
½ cup chopped candied orange peel
¼ cup chopped candied lemon peel
1¼ cup chopped almonds
1½ cups chopped pine nuts
1½ cups all-purpose flour
½ teaspoon ground cinnamon
½ teaspoon ground nutmeg
6 ounces semisweet chocolate, grated or finely chopped
¾ cup honey or light corn syrup
¾ cup sugar
1½ teaspoons baking soda

1 Position a rack in the center of the oven and preheat the oven to 350 degrees. Lightly grease a 9-inch square pan. Line with waxed paper and grease the paper.

2 Combine the raisins, peel, nuts, flour, and spices.

3 In a large saucepan, over low heat, combine the chocolate, honey, sugar, and baking soda and stir constantly until the mixture comes to a boil. Remove from the heat and immediately stir in the dry ingredients until well blended. Scrape into the prepared pan and spread evenly.

4 Bake for 35 to 40 minutes, or until a cake tester inserted into the center comes out clean. Cool in the pan on a wire rack for 5 minutes. Invert onto the rack to cool completely. Remove the paper and place on the serving plate.

227 ■ ITALIANO CIOCCOLATO TORTE

YIELD: *10 to 12 servings*
BAKING TIME: *60 minutes*
CHILL TIME: *24 hours*

CAKE

⅔ cup all-purpose flour
Pinch of salt
½ cup butter or margarine, at room temperature
¾ cup granulated sugar
⅛ teaspoon fresh lemon juice
2 large eggs

FROSTING AND FILLING

4 ounces semisweet chocolate, grated or finely chopped
¼ cup strong brewed coffee
5 tablespoons butter, at room temperature
1 cup Chocolate Ricotta Filling (see page 403)
½ cup toasted chocolate cake crumbs
Chocolate Curls (see page 422)

1 Position a rack in the center of the oven and preheat the oven to 325 degrees. Lightly grease and flour a 6 by 3-inch loaf pan.

2 To make the cake, combine the flour and salt.

3 In a medium bowl, using an electric mixer on medium speed, beat the butter and sugar until light and fluffy. Beat in the lemon juice. Beat in the eggs, one at a time, beating well after each addition. Gradually blend in the dry ingredients. Scrape the mixture into the prepared pan and spread evenly.

4 Bake for 55 to 60 minutes, or until a cake tester inserted into the center comes out clean. Cool in the pan on a wire rack for 10 minutes. Invert onto the wire rack to cool completely.

5 To make the frosting, melt the chocolate (see page 13). Stir in the coffee. Remove from the heat and add the butter, beating until smooth. Chill for 15 to 20 minutes until a spreadable consistency.

6 Meanwhile, make the chocolate ricotta filling.

7 To assemble, carefully trim the cake to make a perfectly square log. Then, using a ser-

228

226

229

rated knife, slice the cake horizontally into six $1/2$ inch layers. Place the bottom layer on a serving plate and spread one-fifth of the ricotta filling over the top. Continue until all the layers and filling are used. Do not spread filling on the top layer. Spread the frosting evenly over the top and sides of the cake. Sprinkle with chocolate cake crumbs and decorate with chocolate curls. Chill for 24 hours before serving.

228 ■ MACADAMIA FUDGE CAKE

YIELD: *12 servings*
BAKING TIME: *35 minutes*
CHILL TIME: *1 hour*

CAKE

1 cup all-purpose flour
$1/4$ cup Dutch processed cocoa powder
$1/2$ teaspoon baking powder
$1/4$ teaspoon baking soda
$1/4$ teaspoon salt
$1/2$ cup butter or margarine, at room temperature
$3/4$ cup granulated sugar
$3/4$ cup sour cream or yogurt
$1^1/2$ teaspoons instant coffee powder
$1/2$ teaspoon coffee liqueur
1 large egg

TOPPING

1 cup heavy cream
$1/2$ cup powdered sugar
2 tablespoons butter or margarine
1 tablespoon dark corn syrup
4 ounces semisweet chocolate, grated or finely chopped
1 cup macadamia nuts, chopped

1 Position a rack in the center of the oven and preheat the oven to 350 degrees. Lightly grease a 9-inch square pan and line the bottom with waxed paper.

2 To make the cake, combine the flour, cocoa powder, baking powder, baking soda, and salt.

3 In a large bowl, using an electric mixer on medium speed, beat the butter and sugar until light and fluffy. Beat in the sour cream. Beat in the coffee powder and liqueur. Beat in the egg. Gradually blend in the dry

ingredients. Pour the batter into the prepared pan.

4 Bake for 30 to 35 minutes, or until a cake tester inserted into the center comes out clean. Cool in the pan on a wire rack for 10 minutes. Invert the cake onto the rack to cool completely. Discard the waxed paper.

5 Meanwhile, to make the topping, in a medium saucepan, over medium heat, combine the cream, powdered sugar, butter, and corn syrup. Bring to a boil, stirring constantly. Reduce the heat to medium, add the chocolate, and cook for 5 minutes, stirring constantly until smooth. Remove from the heat. Cool slightly. Stir in the macadamia nuts.

6 To assemble, place the cake on a serving plate. Pour the topping over the cake, allowing it to run down the sides. Chill for 1 hour, or until serving.

229 ■ MAHOGANY CAKE I

YIELD: *12 servings*
BAKING TIME: *35 minutes*
CHILL TIME: *30 minutes*

CAKE

$2^1/2$ ounces unsweetened chocolate, grated or finely chopped
$1^3/4$ cups all-purpose flour
1 teaspoon baking soda
Pinch of salt
$1/2$ cup butter or margarine, at room temperature
$1^1/2$ cups granulated sugar
4 large eggs
$1/2$ cup buttermilk
1 teaspoon vanilla extract

ICING

1 large egg white
Pinch of salt
1 cup light corn syrup
1 teaspoon vanilla or chocolate extract
Seasonal fresh fruit for garnish

1 Position a rack in the center of the oven and preheat the oven to 350 degrees. Lightly grease and flour three 8-inch round cake pans.

2 To make the cake, melt the chocolate (see page 13). Remove from the heat.

3 Combine the flour, baking soda, and salt.

4 In a large bowl, using an electric mixer on medium speed, beat the butter and sugar until light and fluffy. Beat in the melted chocolate. Beat in the eggs, one at a time, beating well after each addition. Beat in the buttermilk and vanilla extract. Gradually blend in the dry ingredients. Pour the mixture into the prepared pans.

5 Bake for 30 to 35 minutes, or until a cake tester inserted into the center comes out clean. Cool in the pans on wire racks for 10 minutes. Invert onto the racks to cool completely.

6 To make the icing, in a small bowl, using an electric mixer on high speed, beat the egg white and salt until stiff but not dry. Add the corn syrup, beating until the mixture forms very stiff peaks. Fold in the vanilla.

7 To assemble, using a serrated knife, slice the rounded tops off the cakes. Place one cake layer on a serving plate and spread with an even layer of the icing. Place the second cake layer on top and spread with icing. Top with the third cake layer and spread the remaining icing over the top and the sides. Garnish with fruit. Chill for 30 minutes before serving.

230 ■ MAHOGANY CAKE II

YIELD: *12 servings*
BAKING TIME: *30 minutes*

CAKE

2 cups cake flour, sifted
$2^1/2$ teaspoons baking powder
$1/4$ teaspoon baking soda
$1/2$ cup plus $2/3$ cup milk
$1/2$ cup Dutch processed cocoa powder
$1/2$ cup vegetable shortening
3 large eggs
1 teaspoon vanilla or chocolate extract

FROSTING

1½ cups powdered sugar
4 teaspoons Dutch processed cocoa
    powder
1 large egg yolk
2 tablespoons butter or margarine,
    at room temperature
1 teaspoon coffee liqueur
1 tablespoon heavy cream

1 Position a rack in the center of the oven and preheat the oven to 350 degrees. Lightly grease and flour three 8-inch round cake pans.

2 To make the cake, combine the flour, baking powder, and baking soda.

3 In a small saucepan, over medium heat, combine ½ cup of the milk and the cocoa powder, stirring until the mixture thickens. Remove from the heat.

4 In a large bowl, using an electric mixer on medium speed, beat the shortening until fluffy. Beat in the eggs, one at a time, beating well after each addition. Beat in the vanilla extract and remaining ⅔ cup milk. Beat in the cocoa mixture. Gradually blend in the dry ingredients. Pour the mixture into the pans.

5 Bake for 25 to 30 minutes, or until a cake tester inserted into the center comes out clean. Cool in the pans on wire racks for 10 minutes. Invert onto the racks to cool completely.

6 Meanwhile, to make the frosting, in a large bowl, combine the powdered sugar and cocoa powder. Using an electric mixer on medium speed, beat in the egg yolk and butter until blended. Beat in the liqueur. Blend in enough cream to make the mixture a spreadable consistency.

7 To assemble, place one of the cake layers on a serving plate and spread with some of the frosting. Top with the second cake layer and spread with frosting. Top with the third cake layer and spread frosting over the top and sides of the cake.

BAKING NOTES: Owing to the raw egg yolk in this recipe, it should be kept refrigerated at all times, and for no longer than 3 days.

231 ■ MANDARIN ORANGE CAKE WITH GANACHE

YIELD: *12 servings*
BAKING TIME: *30 minutes*
CHILL TIME: *30 minutes*

2 cups cake flour
½ cup Dutch processed cocoa
    powder
1½ teaspoons baking powder
½ teaspoon baking soda
½ teaspoon salt
1 cup granulated sugar
1 cup buttermilk
⅔ cup canola oil
2 large eggs
2 teaspoons apricot liqueur
3½ cups Ganache II (see page 410)
26 mandarin orange wedges for
    assembly

1 Position a rack in the center of the oven and preheat the oven to 350 degrees. Lightly grease and flour the bottoms of two 9-inch round cake pans.

2 Combine and sift the flour, cocoa powder, baking powder, baking soda, and salt.

3 In a large bowl, using an electric mixer on medium speed, beat the sugar, buttermilk, and oil until smooth. Beat in the eggs. Gradually mix in the dry ingredients until just blended. Stir in the liqueur. Divide the mixture between the prepared pans.

4 Bake for 25 to 30 minutes, or until a cake tester inserted into the center comes out clean. Cool in the pans on wire racks for 5 minutes. Invert onto wire racks to cool completely.

5 Meanwhile, make and chill the ganache. Whip the ganache just before assembling and serving the cake.

6 To assemble the cake, place one cake layer on a serving plate and spread generously with the whipped ganache. Place 14 or more orange wedges on top of the ganache. Place the second cake layer on top of the first and press down lightly. Frost the sides and top of the cake

with the remaining ganache. Garnish the top of the cake with the remaining orange wedges. Serve at once.

BAKING NOTES: It is very easy and it does not take much time to whip and spread the ganache just before serving.

232 ■ MARBLE CHOCOLATE CAKE

YIELD: *16 servings*
BAKING TIME: *65 minutes*

3 cups cake flour, sifted twice
¼ teaspoon baking soda
½ teaspoon salt
1 cup butter or margarine, at room
    temperature
3 cups granulated sugar
1 teaspoon coffee liqueur
6 large eggs
1 cup buttermilk
¾ cup chocolate syrup
1½ cups Cocoa Glaze (see page
    407)

1 Position a rack in the center of the oven and preheat the oven to 350 degrees. Lightly grease and flour a 10-inch tube pan.

2 Combine the cake flour, baking soda, and salt.

3 In a large bowl, using an electric mixer on medium speed, beat the butter and sugar until light and fluffy. Beat in the liqueur. Beat in the eggs, one at a time. Beat in the buttermilk. Gradually blend in the dry ingredients. Pour the mixture into the prepared pan. Pour the chocolate syrup over the top of the batter and swirl it around with a metal cake spatula or knife.

4 Bake for 60 to 65 minutes, or until a cake tester inserted into the center comes out clean. Cool in the pan on a wire rack for 10 minutes. Invert onto the rack to cool completely.

5 Make the glaze.

6 Pour the glaze over the top of the cake and let it run down the sides.

233 ■ MARSH-MALLOW CHOCOLATE ROLL CAKE

YIELD: *12 to 16 servings*
BAKING TIME: *20 minutes*
CHILL TIME: *30 minutes*

GENOISE CAKE

½ cup all-purpose flour
¼ teaspoon salt
3 tablespoons butter or margarine
5 large eggs
⅔ cup granulated sugar
1 teaspoon chocolate extract

FILLING

Apricot Glaze (see page 394)
Hazelnut Filling (see page 411)

MARSHMALLOW TOPPING

2 ounces semisweet chocolate, grated or finely chopped
¼ cup granulated sugar
¼ cup milk
1 jar (7 ounces) marshmallow crème
2 tablespoons hot water
½ teaspoon chocolate extract
1½ tablespoons grated semisweet chocolate for garnish

1 Position a rack in the center of the oven and preheat the oven to 350 degrees. Lightly grease a 15½ by 10½-inch jelly-roll pan. Line the pan with waxed paper and grease the paper.

2 To make the cake, combine the flour and salt.

3 In a small saucepan, over low heat, melt the butter. Remove from the heat.

4 In the top of a double boiler, combine the eggs and sugar. Using a wire whisk, beat just until blended. Place over a pot of hot water. Do not let the bottom of the bowl touch the water. Whisk slowly until the mixture is lukewarm to the touch. Remove from the heat. Using an electric mixer on medium speed, beat until the batter falls in a ribbon back on itself. Gradually fold in the dry ingredients. Fold in the butter and chocolate extract. Scrape the mixture into the prepared pan and spread evenly.

5 Bake for 15 to 20 minutes, or until a cake tester inserted into the center comes out clean. Invert onto a damp, not wet, towel, or a sheet of waxed paper dusted with powdered sugar. Remove the waxed paper from the cake and trim the sides evenly.

6 Make the apricot glaze and the hazelnut filling.

7 To make the topping, melt the chocolate (see page 13). Remove from the heat.

8 In a small saucepan, over low heat, combine the sugar and milk and stir until the sugar is dissolved. Increase the temperature to medium and bring to boil. Simmer for 5 minutes.

9 In the top of a double boiler over simmering water, combine the marshmallow crème, hot water, and chocolate extract. Stir in the melted chocolate. Slowly stir in the milk mixture. Remove from the heat. Using an electric mixer on medium speed, beat until cool and a spreadable consistency.

10 To assemble, spread the apricot glaze over the cake, leaving a ½-inch border on each side. Spread the hazelnut filling evenly over the top of the glaze. Starting on one of the long sides, roll up the cake jelly-roll fashion. Place on a serving plate, seam-side down, cover with a damp towel, and chill for 30 minutes. Spread the marshmallow topping over the top and sides of the cake. Sprinkle with the grated chocolate.

234 ■ MARSH-MALLOW FUDGE CAKE

YIELD: *12 to 15 servings*
BAKING TIME: *35 minutes*

CAKE

1½ cups butter or margarine
3 ounces semisweet chocolate, grated or finely chopped
1½ cups all-purpose flour
1 teaspoon baking powder
4 large eggs
1 cup granulated sugar
2 teaspoons chocolate or vanilla extract
2 cups miniature marshmallows

232

233

TOPPING

1/2 cup butter or margarine
2 ounces unsweetened chocolate, grated or finely chopped
1/2 cup evaporated milk or heavy cream
1 teaspoon coffee liqueur
2 cups powdered sugar

1 To make the cake, preheat the oven to 350 degrees. Lightly grease a 13 by 9-inch pan.

2 In the top of a double boiler over simmering water, melt the butter and chocolate, stirring occasionally until smooth. Remove from the heat.

3 Combine the flour and baking powder.

4 In a large bowl, using an electric mixer on medium speed, beat the eggs and sugar until thick and light-colored. Gradually blend in the dry ingredients. Stir in the chocolate extract. Fold in the melted chocolate. Scrape the mixture into the prepared pan and spread evenly.

5 Bake for 30 to 35 minutes, or until a cake tester inserted into the center comes out clean. Spread the marshmallows over the top and cool in the pan on a wire rack.

6 Meanwhile, to make the topping, in the top of the double boiler over simmering water, melt the butter and chocolate, stirring until smooth. Stir in the milk and coffee liqueur. Simmer for 2 minutes, remove from the heat, and stir in the powdered sugar. Immediately pour the hot topping over the marshmallows on the cake. Cool completely. Cut into squares.

235 ■ MAYONNAISE CHOCOLATE CAKE

YIELD: *12 servings*
BAKING TIME: *35 minutes*

1 1/2 cups all-purpose flour
3/4 cup granulated sugar
1 teaspoon baking soda
Pinch of salt
2/3 cup coffee liqueur
1/2 cup mayonnaise
1/3 cup chocolate syrup
1 tablespoon cider vinegar
1 teaspoon chocolate extract
1 1/3 cups Kahlúa Cocoa Sauce (see page 413)

1 Position a rack in the center of the oven and preheat the oven to 350 degrees.

2 Combine the flour, sugar, baking soda, and salt.

3 In a large bowl, using an electric mixer on medium speed, beat the liqueur, mayonnaise, chocolate syrup, vinegar, and chocolate extract. Gradually stir in the dry ingredients, blending well after each addition. Scrape the mixture into an ungreased 8-inch square pan and spread evenly.

4 Bake for 30 to 35 minutes, or until a cake tester inserted into the center comes out clean. Cool in the pan on a wire rack for 10 minutes. Invert onto the rack to cool completely.

5 Make the Kahlúa sauce. Serve the cake with the sauce on the side. Or, drizzle over the top of the cake and serve with additional sauce on the side.

222

223

234

225

235

236 ■ MERINGUE CAKE WITH CHOCOLATE MINT FILLING

YIELD: *12 servings*
BAKING TIME: *65 minutes*

CAKE

3 large egg whites
Pinch of salt
6 ounces granulated sugar, plus additional for dusting
1 teaspoon white vinegar

FILLING

6 ounces unsweetened chocolate, grated or finely chopped
1/2 cup water
3 large egg yolks
2 drops peppermint extract
3/4 cup Chocolate Whipped Cream (see page 406)
Peeled, sliced kiwifruit and sliced peaches for garnish

1 Position a rack in the center of the oven and preheat the oven to 325 degrees. Line two baking sheets with parchment paper and draw two 7-inch circles on each pan.

2 To make the cake, in a large bowl, using an electric mixer on high speed, beat the egg whites and salt until stiff but not dry. Stir in the sugar, a little at a time. Sprinkle the vinegar over the top and fold to incorporate. Divide the mixture evenly between the circles. Fill in the circles with the mixture, spreading no thicker than 1½ inches. Dust the tops with granulated sugar.

3 Bake for 45 minutes. Turn off the oven and leave undisturbed for an additional 20 minutes without opening the door. Remove the meringue circles from the paper and transfer to wire racks, turning the layers over to cool completely.

4 Meanwhile, to make the filling, melt the chocolate (see page 13). Remove from the heat and beat in the water and egg yolks. Return to the heat and continue cooking, stirring until the mixture is very thick. Remove from the heat and cool to room temperature.

5 Make the chocolate whipped cream.

6 To assemble, place one of the meringues on a serving plate and spread with one-third of the chocolate filling. Top with the second meringue. Repeat until all the meringues and filling have been used, ending with a meringue layer. Spread the chocolate whipped cream on top of the cake. Garnish with sliced kiwifruit and peaches.

237 ■ MEXICALI CHOCOLATE CHEESECAKE

YIELD: *12 servings*
BAKING TIME: *60 minutes*
CHILL TIME: *30 minutes*

CRUST

1 cup graham cracker crumbs
1/2 cup almonds, finely ground
3 tablespoons butter or margarine, melted

FILLING

6 ounces unsweetened chocolate, grated or finely chopped
2 tablespoons Tía Maria
1 teaspoon chocolate extract
1 teaspoon almond extract
24 ounces cream cheese, at room temperature
1½ cups granulated sugar
6 large eggs
1 cup heavy cream
2 teaspoons ground cinnamon
Thinly sliced peaches and peeled, thinly sliced kiwifruit for garnish

236

237

230

231

7

1 Position a rack in the center of the oven and preheat the oven to 350 degrees. Lightly grease a 9-inch springform pan.

2 To make the crust, in a large bowl, combine the graham cracker crumbs, almonds, and melted butter. Press the mixture onto the the bottom of the prepared pan.

3 Bake for 5 minutes. Cool on a wire rack.

4 To make the filling, melt the chocolate (see page 13). Remove from the heat and stir in the Tía Maria and two extracts.

5 In a large bowl, using an electric mixer on medium speed, beat the cream cheese, sugar, eggs, and cream until smooth. Beat in the cinnamon. On low speed, beat in the chocolate mixture. Pour over the crust.

6 Bake for 60 minutes, or until the cake is set firm. Cool in the pan on a wire rack for 1 hour. Refrigerate for 30 minutes or until completely chilled.

7 One hour before serving, remove the side of the pan and transfer the cake to a serving plate. Garnish with sliced peaches and kiwifruit.

238 ▪ MISSISSIPPI MUD CAKE I

YIELD: *16 servings*
BAKING TIME: *90 minutes*

2 cups all-purpose flour
1 teaspoon baking soda
Pinch of salt
5 ounces unsweetened chocolate, grated or finely chopped
1³/₄ cups strong brewed coffee
¹/₄ cup bourbon
1 cups butter or margarine, at room temperature
2 cups powdered sugar
2 large eggs, beaten
1 teaspoon vanilla extract
2 cups Chocolate Coconut Frosting (see page 396)

1 Position a rack in the center of the oven and preheat the oven to 275 degrees. Lightly grease and flour a 10-inch tube pan.

2 Combine the flour, baking soda, and salt.

3 In the top of a double boiler over simmering water, melt the chocolate with the coffee, stirring until smooth. Remove from the heat and stir in the bourbon.

4 In a large bowl, using an electric mixer on medium speed, beat the butter and powdered sugar until light and fluffy. Slowly beat in the chocolate mixture. Beat in the eggs and vanilla extract. Gradually blend in the dry ingredients. Scrape the mixture into the prepared pan and spread evenly.

5 Bake for 1 hour and 30 minutes, or until a cake tester inserted into the center comes out clean. Cool in the pan on a wire rack. Invert onto a serving plate.

6 Make the frosting.

7 Spread the frosting evenly over the top and sides of the cake.

239 ▪ MISSISSIPPI MUD CAKE II

YIELD: *12 to 15 servings*
BAKING TIME: *40 minutes*

1¹/₂ cups all-purpose flour
3 tablespoons Dutch processed cocoa powder
1¹/₂ cups flaked coconut
1¹/₂ cups walnuts, chopped
1 cup margarine, softened
2 cups granulated sugar
4 large eggs
1 teaspoon vanilla extract
1¹/₂ cups Chocolate Buttercream (see page 395)

1 Position a rack in the center of the oven and preheat the oven to 350 degrees. Lightly grease and flour a 13 by 9-inch pan.

2 Combine the flour, cocoa powder, coconut, and walnuts.

3 In a large bowl, using an electric mixer on medium speed, beat the margarine and sugar until fluffy. Beat in the eggs, one at a time, beating well after each addition. Beat in the vanilla extract. Gradually blend in the dry ingredients just until mixed.

Pour the mixture into the prepared pan.

4 Bake for 35 to 40 minutes, or until a cake tester inserted into the center comes out clean. Cool in the pan on a wire rack.

5 Make the frosting.

6 Spread the frosting over the top of the cake.

240 ▪ MISSISSIPPI MUD CAKE III

YIELD: *16 servings*
BAKING TIME: *70 minutes*

2 cups all-purpose flour
1 teaspoon baking soda
¹/₄ teaspoon salt
2 ounces unsweetened chocolate, grated or finely chopped
2 ounces semisweet chocolate, grated or finely chopped
1 ounce white chocolate, grated or finely chopped
¹/₄ cup mocha-flavored instant coffee powder
2 tablespoons boiling water
1 cup cold water
2 tablespoons coffee liqueur
¹/₂ cup amaretto
1 cup butter or margarine, at room temperature
2 cups granulated sugar
1 teaspoon almond extract
3 large eggs plus 1 large egg yolk
¹/₄ cup sour cream or chocolate-flavored yogurt
1 cup Chocolate Glaze I (see page 401)
Chocolate Cigarettes for garnish (see page 421)

1 Position a rack in the center of the oven and preheat the oven to 325 degrees. Lightly grease and flour a 10-inch tube pan.

2 Combine the flour, baking soda, and salt.

3 Melt the chocolates (see page 13). Remove from the heat.

4 In a small bowl, combine the coffee powder and boiling water. Stir in the cold water, coffee liqueur, and amaretto.

5 In a large bowl, using an electric mixer on medium speed, beat the butter and sugar until light and fluffy. Beat in the almond extract. Beat in the eggs, one at a time, beating well after each addition. Beat in the egg

yolk. Beat in the sour cream. Beat in the melted chocolates. In three additions, blend in the dry ingredients, alternating with the coffee mixture, beginning and ending with the dry ingredients. Pour the mixture into the prepared pan.

6 Bake for 65 to 70 minutes, or until a cake tester inserted into the center comes out clean. Cool in the pan on a wire rack for 10 to 15 minutes. Invert onto a serving plate.

7 Make the chocolate glaze.

8 Pour the glaze over the top of the cake, spread to the edges, and let the glaze drip down the sides of the cake.

241 ■ MOCHA CHOCOLATE CHEESECAKE

YIELD: *12 servings*
BAKING TIME: *2 hours 20 minutes*
CHILL TIME: *2 hours*

CRUST

1½ cups shortbread cookie crumbs
1½ tablespoons powdered sugar
¼ cup butter or margarine, at room temperature

FILLING

1 cup semisweet chocolate chips
2 pounds cream cheese, at room temperature
1½ cups granulated sugar
3 large eggs
2 tablespoons heavy cream
½ cup sour cream or chocolate-flavored yogurt

½ cup strong brewed coffee
1 teaspoon chocolate or vanilla extract
Chocolate Curls (see page 422) for garnish

1 Position a rack in the center of the oven and preheat the oven to 350 degrees.

2 To make the crust, in a medium bowl, combine the cookie crumbs and sugar. Using a pastry blender, cut the butter into the crumb mixture. Press onto the bottom of a 9-inch springform pan.

3 To make the filling, melt the chocolate chips (see page 13). Remove from the heat.

4 In a large bowl, using an electric mixer on medium speed, beat the cream cheese and sugar until smooth. Beat in the eggs, one at a time. On low speed, beat in the melted chocolate, mixing only until blended. On medium speed, blend in the cream and sour cream. Blend in the coffee and chocolate extract. Pour the batter into the prepared pan over the top of the crust.

5 Bake for 1 hour and 50 minutes, or until the sides firm up. The center will be soft, but become firm after cooling. Turn off the oven, open the door slightly and cool for 30 minutes

in the oven. Remove to a wire rack to cool completely. Chill for 2 hours.

6 Remove the side of the pan. Garnish with chocolate curls.

242 ■ MOCHA NUT CAKE

YIELD: *12 to 16 servings*
BAKING TIME: *10 minutes*

1½ cups all-purpose flour
1 cup ground pecans or hazelnuts
8 large eggs
1½ cups granulated sugar
1½ teaspoons almond extract
1½ cups Chocolate Buttercream (see page 395)
½ cup Dessert Syrup (see page 409) made with coffee liqueur
1½ cups Ganache III (see page 410)
Chocolate sprinkles
Chocolate Leaves (see page 422)

1 Position a rack in the center of the oven and preheat the oven to 350 degrees. Line a 17½ by 11½-inch jelly-roll pan with waxed paper. Grease and flour the paper.

2 Combine the flour and pecans.

3 In a large bowl, using an electric mixer on medium speed, beat the eggs until thick and light-colored. Beat in the sugar and almond extract. Gradually blend in the dry ingredients until just mixed. Scrape the batter into the prepared pan and spread evenly.

238

242

239

4 Bake for 8 to 10 minutes, or until a cake tester inserted into the center comes out clean. Invert onto a wire rack, remove the paper, and cool completely.

5 Meanwhile, make the buttercream, the dessert syrup using coffee liqueur, and the ganache.

6 To assemble, cut the cake widthwise into two rectangles, each measuring approximately 8½ by 5½ inches. Using a serrated knife, cut each rectangle in half horizontally. Brush each cake layer with the dessert syrup. Set one cake layer on a serving plate and spread with half of the ganache. Top with a second cake layer and spread with half of the buttercream. Top with the third cake layer and spread the remaining ganache. Top with the fourth cake layer. Frost the top and sides of the cake with the remaining buttercream. Sprinkle the cake with chocolate sprinkles and garnish with chocolate leaves.

243 ■ MOCHA SWIRL CAKE

YIELD: *10 to 12 servings*
BAKING TIME: *60 minutes*

3 cups all-purpose flour
3 tablespoons baking powder
¼ teaspoon salt
1 ounce unsweetened chocolate, grated or finely chopped
4 large egg whites
½ cup butter or margarine, at room temperature
1½ cups plus 1 tablespoon granulated sugar
1 cup milk
1 teaspoon almond extract
2 tablespoons instant coffee powder
½ teaspoon baking soda
1 cup Coffee Mocha Icing (see page 408)

1 Position a rack in the center of the oven and preheat the oven to 350 degrees. Lightly grease and flour an 9 by 5-inch loaf pan. Line the pan with waxed paper and grease and flour the paper.

2 Combine the flour, baking powder, and salt

3 Melt the chocolate (see page 13). Remove from the heat.

4 In a medium bowl, using an electric mixer on high speed, beat the egg whites until stiff but not dry.

5 In a large bowl, using an electric mixer, beat the butter and 1½ cups of the sugar until light and fluffy. In three additions, blend in the dry ingredients, alternating with the milk, beginning and ending with the dry ingredients. Beat in the almond extract. Fold in the egg whites.

6 Remove one-quarter of the batter to another bowl. Add the melted chocolate, remaining 1 tablespoon sugar, coffee powder, and baking soda.

7 Spread the plain batter evenly into the prepared pan. Spoon the chocolate batter over the top. Using a knife, swirl the batters in a zigzag pattern. Do not overmix.

8 Bake for 60 minutes, or until a cake tester inserted into the center comes out clean. Cool in the pan on a wire rack for 5 minutes. Invert onto the rack to cool completely. Remove the paper.

9 Make the coffee mocha icing.

10 Place the cake on a serving plate and frost with the icing.

244 ■ MOIST CHOCOLATE CAKE WITH PLUM SAUCE

YIELD: *12 to 15 servings*
BAKING TIME: *30 minutes*

CAKE

2 cups all-purpose flour
1 cup granulated sugar
½ cup Dutch processed cocoa powder
1½ teaspoons baking soda
1¼ cups cold water
¾ cup mayonnaise
1 teaspoon chocolate extract or crème de prunelle

SAUCE

¾ **pound fresh plums, skinned, pitted, and quartered**
½ **cup crème de prunelle or marsala**
3 **tablespoons powdered sugar**
Cocoa Sugar (see page 407) for dusting
White Chocolate Leaves (see page 422) for garnish

1 Position a rack in the center of the oven and preheat the oven to 350 degrees. Lightly grease and flour a 13 by 9-inch pan.

2 To make the cake, combine the flour, sugar, cocoa powder, and baking soda.

3 In a large bowl, using an electric mixer on low speed, beat the cold water, mayonnaise, and chocolate extract until smooth. Gradually blend in the dry ingredients, a little at a time. Pour the mixture into the prepared pan.

4 Bake for 25 to 30 minutes, or until a cake tester inserted into the center comes out clean. Cool completely in the pan on a wire rack. Invert onto a serving plate.

5 Meanwhile, to make the plum sauce, in a large saucepan over medium heat, combine the plums and crème de prunelle. Cook until the mixture is reduced to 1 cup. Remove from the heat

and stir in the powdered sugar. Return to the heat and cook until the mixture is reduced by one-third. Cool slightly.

6 When ready to serve, dust the cake with cocoa sugar and spread the plum sauce evenly over the top, allowing some to drip down the sides. Garnish with white chocolate leaves.

245 ■ MRS. G'S CHOCOLATE LOAF CAKE

YIELD: *24 servings*
BAKING TIME: *30 minutes*

1/2 cup heavy cream
3 ounces semisweet chocolate, grated or finely chopped
2 cups all-purpose flour
1 tablespoon baking powder
2 teaspoons grated orange zest
1/4 teaspoon salt
4 large eggs, separated
1 cup plus 1/4 teaspoon granulated sugar
3/4 cup butter-flavored vegetable shortening
2 1/2 cups Coffee Mocha Icing (see page 408)
Chocolate Curls (see page 422) for garnish

1 Position a rack in the center of the oven and preheat the oven to 350 degrees. Lightly grease and flour two 8 by 5-inch loaf pans.

2 In a small saucepan over low heat, combine the cream and chocolate and stir until the chocolate is melted and the mixture is smooth. Remove from the heat

3 Combine the flour, baking powder, orange zest, and salt.

4 In a medium bowl, using an electric mixer on high speed, beat the egg whites and 1/4 teaspoon of sugar until stiff but not dry.

5 In a medium bowl, using an electric mixer on high speed, beat the egg yolks until thick and light-colored.

6 In a large bowl, using an electric mixer on high speed, beat the shortening and remaining 1 cup sugar until fluffy. Slowly beat in the chocolate mixture. Beat in the egg yolks. Gradually blend in the dry ingredients. Gradually fold in the egg whites. Divide the mixture evenly between the prepared pans and spread evenly.

7 Bake 25 to 30 minutes, or until a cake tester inserted into the center comes out clean. Cool in the pans on wire racks for 5 minutes. Invert onto the wire racks to cool completely

8 Meanwhile, make the mocha frosting.

9 Place the cakes on serving plates and spread the frosting evenly over the top, sides, and ends of the baked loaves. Garnish with chocolate curls.

246 ■ NEVADA GOLD NUGGET CAKE

YIELD: *12 to 15 servings*
BAKING TIME: *60 minutes*
CHILL TIME: *1 hour*

2 cups cake flour, sifted
1/2 cup Dutch processed cocoa powder
1/2 teaspoon salt
1 1/2 cups granulated sugar
1 tablespoon crème de cacao
8 large eggs
1/4 cup butter, clarified and cooled
1 cup Ganache I (see page 410)
1/2 cup Dessert Syrup (see page 409)
1 cup gold sprinkles for garnish

1 Position a rack in the center of the oven and preheat the oven to 350 degrees. Lightly grease and flour a 13 by 9-inch pan.

2 Combine the flour, cocoa powder, and salt.

3 Spread the sugar evenly on a sheet pan and heat in the oven with the temperature reduced to 100 degrees.

4 In a large bowl, using an electric mixer on medium speed, beat the eggs and hot sugar until very light and thick, at least 12 minutes. Stir in the crème de cacao. Gently fold in the dry ingredients, a little at a time, being very careful not to deflate the mixture. Gently fold in the clarified butter. Do not overmix or the cake will be tough. Immediately scrape the mixture into the prepared pan and spread evenly.

5 Bake for 55 to 60 minutes, or until a cake tester inserted into the center comes out clean. Cool in the pan on a wire rack. Invert onto the bottom of a baking sheet to cool.

6 Make the ganache and dessert syrup.

7 To assemble, using a serrated knife, cut the cake in half horizontally. Spread a layer of ganache the dimensions of the cake on a serving plate, and place the bottom cake layer on top of the ganache. Moisten the cake layer with syrup and spread a layer of ganache on the cake layer. Place the top cake layer on top of the ganache and

244

245

moisten it with syrup. Spread the remaining ganache on the top and sides of the cake.

8 To decorate, fill a pastry bag with mocha buttercream, and pipe three evenly spaced lines horizontally and four vertically to create a checkerboard with sixteen squares. In the center of each square, pipe a large rosette. Chill the cake for at least 1 hour.

9 Just before cutting, carefully brush a thin coating of syrup on each rosette and sprinkle with gold sprinkles. Cut and serve at once.

BAKING NOTES: Both gold and silver sprinkles are available commercially. This recipe originally called for genuine gold leaf to cover the rosettes, but the sprinkles are easier to obtain. Do not delay in getting the cake into the oven. A delay will cause a loss of volume.

247 ■ OATMEAL CHOCOLATE CHIP CAKE

YIELD: *12 to 15 servings*
BAKING TIME: *40 minutes*

1¾ cups all-purpose flour
1 cup almonds, finely ground
2 tablespoons Dutch processed cocoa powder
1 teaspoon baking soda
½ teaspoon salt
1¾ cups boiling water

1 cup quick-cooking oats
½ cup butter or margarine, at room temperature
1 cup packed light brown sugar
2 large eggs
½ cup (3 ounces) semisweet chocolate chips
1 cup Chocolate Buttercream (see page 395)

1 Position a rack in the center of the oven and preheat the oven to 350 degrees. Lightly grease a 13 by 9-inch pan.

2 Combine the flour, almonds, cocoa powder, baking soda, and salt.

3 In a small bowl, stir the boiling water and oats. Let stand for 10 minutes without stirring.

4 In a large bowl, using an electric mixer on medium speed, beat the butter and brown sugar until fluffy. Beat in the eggs. Beat in the oatmeal. Gradually blend in the dry ingredients. Pour into the prepared pan. Sprinkle the chocolate chips over the top.

5 Bake for 35 to 40 minutes, or until a cake tester inserted into the center comes out clean. Cool in the pan on a wire rack.

6 Make the frosting.

7 Spread the frosting over the top of the cake.

248 ■ OLD ENGLISH CHOCOLATE CAKE

YIELD: *12 servings*
BAKING TIME: *75 minutes*

1 ounce unsweetened chocolate, grated or finely chopped
2 tablespoons cornstarch or arrowroot
1½ teaspoons water
½ teaspoon all-purpose flour
½ teaspoon baking powder
6 large eggs, separated
1½ cups granulated sugar
3 cups chopped walnuts
2 cups Chocolate Glaze IV (see page 401)
3 tablespoons chopped pecans for garnish

1 Position a rack in the center of the oven and preheat the oven to 375 degrees. Lightly grease a 9-inch round pan. Line the bottom with waxed paper and grease the paper.

2 Melt the chocolate (see page 13). Remove from the heat.

3 In a cup, dissolve the cornstarch in the water.

4 Combine the flour and baking powder.

5 In a large bowl, using an electric mixer on high speed, beat the egg whites until stiff but not dry.

6 In a large bowl, using an electric mixer on medium speed, beat the egg yolks until thick and light-colored. Beat in the sugar. Beat in the walnuts, melted chocolate, and cornstarch mixture. Gradually stir in the dry ingredients. Fold in the egg whites. Scrape into the prepared pan and spread evenly.

7 Bake for 60 to 75 minutes, or until a cake tester inserted into the center comes out clean. The cake will split on top. Cool in

247

248

the pan on a wire rack for 5 minutes. Invert onto the rack to cool completely. Remove the waxed paper and place on a serving plate.

8 Make the chocolate glaze.

9 Spread the chocolate glaze over the top and sprinkle with the pecans.

249 ■ OLD-FASHIONED CHOCOLATE CAKE I

YIELD: *12 servings*
BAKING TIME: *35 minutes*

CAKE

1³/₄ cups all-purpose flour
1 teaspoon baking soda
¹/₄ teaspoon salt
1 cup (6 ounces) semisweet chocolate chips
¹/₂ cup water
6 tablespoons butter-flavored vegetable shortening
¹/₂ cup granulated sugar
¹/₂ cup packed light brown sugar
2 large eggs
1 teaspoon chocolate or vanilla extract
²/₃ cup buttermilk

FROSTING

1 cup granulated sugar
1 cup boiling water
3 tablespoons cornstarch or arrowroot
¹/₈ teaspoon salt
1 cup (6 ounces) semisweet chocolate chips
2 tablespoons butter or margarine
1 teaspoon vanilla or chocolate extract

1 Position a rack in the center of the oven and preheat the oven to 350 degrees. Lightly grease two 9-inch round cake pans.

2 To make the cake, combine the flour, baking soda, and salt.

3 In the top of a double boiler over simmering water, melt the chocolate chips with the water, stirring until smooth. Remove from the heat.

4 In a large bowl, using an electric mixer on medium speed, beat the shortening and sugars until fluffy. Beat in the eggs, one at a time, beating well after each addition. Beat in the chocolate

extract. Beat in the chocolate mixture. In three additions, add the dry ingredients, alternating with the buttermilk, beginning and ending with the dry ingredients. Divide the mixture between the prepared pans.

5 Bake for 30 to 35 minutes, or until a cake tester inserted into the center comes out clean. Cool in the pans on wire racks for 5 to 10 minutes. Invert onto the racks to cool completely.

6 Meanwhile, to make the frosting, in a saucepan over medium heat, combine the sugar, boiling water, cornstarch, and salt. Bring to a boil and cook for 1 to 1¹/₂ minutes, until thickened. Remove from the heat. Add the chocolate and stir until smooth. Mix in the butter and vanilla.

7 To assemble, place one of the cake layers on a serving plate and spread with some of the warm frosting. Place the second layer on top and spread frosting over the top and sides of the cake.

250 ■ OLD-FASHIONED CHOCOLATE CAKE II

YIELD: *12 servings*
BAKING TIME: *30 minutes*
FREEZE TIME: *15 minutes*

CAKE

2 cups all-purpose flour
²/₃ cup Dutch processed cocoa powder
1 teaspoon baking powder
¹/₄ teaspoon cream of tartar
1 teaspoon salt
²/₃ cup butter or margarine, at room temperature
1²/₃ cups granulated sugar
3 large eggs, at room temperature
¹/₂ teaspoon vanilla or chocolate extract
1¹/₃ cups water, at room temperature

ICING

1¹/₂ cups powdered sugar
3 tablespoons Dutch processed cocoa powder
¹/₂ cup milk
¹/₄ cup plus 2 tablespoons butter or margarine
¹/₂ teaspoon chocolate syrup

1 Position a rack in the center of the oven and preheat the oven to 350 degrees. Lightly grease and flour a 9-inch round cake pan.

2 To make the cake, combine the flour, cocoa powder, baking powder, cream of tartar, and salt.

3 In a large bowl, using an electric mixer on medium speed, beat the butter and sugar until light and fluffy. Beat in the eggs, one at a time, beating well after each addition. Beat in the vanilla extract and water. Gradually blend in the dry ingredients. Pour into the prepared pan.

4 Bake for 25 to 30 minutes, or until a cake tester inserted into the center comes out clean. Cool in the pan on a wire rack. Freeze the cake for 15 minutes before icing.

5 Meanwhile, to make the icing, combine the powdered sugar and cocoa powder.

6 In a medium saucepan over low heat, warm the milk, butter, and chocolate syrup, stirring until smooth. Mix in the dry ingredients and bring to a boil, stirring constantly. Boil for 2 minutes, or until a spreadable consistency. Remove from the heat and cool slightly.

7 Spread the icing over the top of the chilled cake.

251 ■ OLD-FASHIONED CHOCOLATE CAKE III

YIELD: *16 servings*
BAKING TIME: *70 minutes*

CAKE

2¹/₂ cups all-purpose flour
³/₄ cup Dutch processed cocoa powder
1 tablespoon baking soda
¹/₄ teaspoon salt
1 cup butter or margarine, at room temperature
2 cups granulated sugar
4 large eggs
1 cup buttermilk
²/₃ cup water
1 teaspoon chocolate or vanilla extract

COCOA FROSTING

½ cup butter or margarine, at room temperature
½ cup Dutch processed cocoa powder
¼ teaspoon salt
1 teaspoon chocolate extract or amaretto liqueur
4 cups powdered sugar
4 to 6 tablespoons hot milk

1 Position a rack in the center of the oven and preheat the oven to 350 degrees. Lightly grease and flour a 10-inch tube pan.

2 To make the cake, combine the flour, cocoa powder, baking soda, and salt

3 In a large bowl, using an electric mixer on medium speed, blend the butter and sugar until light and fluffy. Beat in the eggs, one at a time, beating well after each addition. Combine the buttermilk and water. In three additions, blend in the dry ingredients, alternating with the liquids, beginning and ending with the dry ingredients. Stir in the chocolate extract. Scrape the mixture into the prepared pan and spread evenly.

4 Bake for 70 minutes, or until a cake tester inserted into the center comes out clean. Cool in the pan on a wire rack for 10 minutes. Invert onto the rack to cool completely.

5 Meanwhile, to make the frosting, using an electric mixer on medium speed, beat the butter, cocoa powder, salt, and chocolate extract. Gradually blend in the powdered sugar, alternating with the hot milk, and continue beating until spreadable consistency.

6 Place the cake on a serving plate. Spread the frosting over the top and sides of the cake.

BAKING NOTES: This recipe can also be made as a layer cake. The baking time is 35 to 40 minutes for two 8- or 9-inch cake layers.

---

252 ■ ONE-EGG CHOCOLATE CAKE

YIELD: *12 servings*
BAKING TIME: *40 minutes*

2 cups cake flour
1¼ cups granulated sugar
1 teaspoon baking soda
½ teaspoon salt
½ cup butter-flavored vegetable shortening
3 ounces semisweet chocolate, grated or finely chopped
1 teaspoon chocolate or vanilla extract
1 large egg
1 cup buttermilk
1½ cups Fudge Frosting (see page 410)

1 Position a rack in the center of the oven and preheat the oven to 350 degrees. Lightly grease and flour two 8-inch round cake pans.

2 Combine the flour, sugar, baking soda, and salt.

3 In the top of a double boiler over simmering water, melt the shortening and chocolate, stirring until smooth. Remove from the heat, and using an electric mixer on medium speed, beat in the chocolate extract and egg. In three additions, beat in the dry ingredients, alternating with the buttermilk, beginning and ending with the dry ingredients. Pour the mixture into the prepared pans.

4 Bake for 35 to 40 minutes, or until a cake tester inserted into the center comes out clean. Cool in the pans on wire racks for 5 minutes. Invert the layers onto the racks to cool completely.

5 Make the fudge frosting.

6 To assemble, place the first layer on a serving platter. Spread the top and sides of the layer with frosting. Place the second layer on the top of the frosting. Spread the frosting evenly over the top and sides of the cake.

---

253 ■ ONE, TWO, THREE, FOUR CHOCOLATE CAKE

YIELD: *12 servings*
BAKING TIME: *18 minutes*
CHILL TIME: *overnight*

CAKE

4 large eggs, separated
1¼ cups butter or margarine
1 cup granulated sugar
¾ cup Dutch processed cocoa powder
1 teaspoon cornstarch or arrowroot
2 teaspoons chocolate extract

TOPPING

1 cup heavy cream
2 tablespoons granulated sugar
¼ cup hazelnuts or pistachio nuts, chopped

1 Position a rack in the center of the oven and preheat the oven to 425 degrees. Lightly grease and flour an 8-inch springform pan.

2 To make the cake, in a small bowl, using an electric mixer on high speed, beat the egg whites until stiff but not dry.

3 In a large saucepan, over low heat, melt the butter, sugar, and cocoa powder, stirring constantly until smooth. Remove from the heat. Stir in the cornstarch until smooth. Using an electric mixer on medium speed, beat in the chocolate extract. On low speed, beat in the egg yolks, one at a time, blending well after each addition. Fold in the egg whites. Scrape the mixture into the prepared pan and spread evenly.

4 Bake for 15 to 18 minutes, or until firm around the edges. Cool in the pan on a wire rack for 5 minutes. Remove the side of the pan. Chill overnight.

5 When ready to serve, make the topping. In a small bowl, using an electric mixer on medium speed, whip the cream and sugar until soft peaks form. Spread over the top of the chilled cake and sprinkle with the nuts.

254 ■ PANFORTE CIOCCOLATO

YIELD: *12 servings*
BAKING TIME: *40 minutes*

½ cup all-purpose flour
⅓ cup Dutch processed cocoa
powder
1 teaspoon ground cinnamon
½ teaspoon ground allspice
¼ teaspoon white pepper
1½ teaspoons instant coffee
powder
½ cup candied orange peel, diced
½ cup candied lemon peel, diced
½ cup candied citron, diced
1 cup toasted almonds
1 cup toasted hazelnuts
½ cup honey
½ cup granulated sugar
Cocoa Sugar for dusting (see page
407)

1 Position a rack in the center of
the oven and preheat the oven
to 325 degrees. Lightly grease
and flour a 9-inch springform
pan.

2 In a large bowl, combine the
flour, cocoa powder, spices, and
coffee powder. Add the candied
orange and lemon peels and citron and toss until coated. Mix in
the nuts.

3 In a small saucepan, over
medium heat, warm the honey
and sugar, stirring until the
sugar is dissolved. Insert a
candy thermometer and cook,
without stirring, until 248
degrees. Using a wooden spoon,
immediately stir into the dry
ingredients until thoroughly
mixed. Immediately pour into
the prepared pan. The mixture
will be very dry. Using a piece
of waxed paper or plastic wrap
to protect your fingers, press
down on the mixture in the pan
as hard as you can.

4 Bake for 40 minutes and do
not overbake. There is no doneness test for this cake. Cool in
the pan on a wire rack until
completely cool and firm.
Remove the side of the pan and
transfer the cake to a serving
plate. Dust the top with the
cocoa sugar.

BAKING NOTES: There are many
variations on this recipe. It is not
difficult to make and the secret
is that you must work very
quickly once the sugar and
honey have reached the proper
temperature.

255 ■ PERFECT CHOCOLATE CAKE

YIELD: *12 servings*
BAKING TIME: *30 minutes*
CHILL TIME: *2 hours*

CAKE

2¾ cups all-purpose flour
1 teaspoon baking powder
½ teaspoon salt
½ cup Dutch processed cocoa
powder
2 cups boiling water
1 cup butter or margarine, at room
temperature
2½ cups granulated sugar
1 tablespoon crème de cacao
4 large eggs

FILLING

1 cup heavy cream
¼ cup powdered sugar
1 teaspoon coffee liqueur

FROSTING

6 ounces unsweetened chocolate,
grated or finely chopped
1 cup butter or margarine, at room
temperature
½ cup light cream
2½ cups powdered sugar
Chocolate chips or grated chocolate
for garnish

1 Position a rack in the center of
the oven and preheat the oven
to 350 degrees. Lightly grease
and flour three 9-inch round
cake pans.

2 To make the cake, combine
the flour, baking powder, and
salt.

3 In a small bowl, blend the
cocoa and boiling water, stirring
constantly until smooth.

4 In a large bowl, using an electric mixer on medium speed,
beat the butter and sugar until
light and fluffy. Beat in the
crème de cacao and eggs. Pouring in a thin stream, beat in the
cocoa mixture. Gradually blend
in the dry ingredients. Pour the
mixture into the prepared pans.

5 Bake for 25 to 30 minutes, or
until a cake tester inserted into
the center comes out clean. Cool
in the pans on wire racks for 5
minutes. Remove the cakes to
the racks to cool completely.
Chill for 1 hour before
assembling.

254

6 Meanwhile, to make the filling, using an electric mixer on medium speed, whip the cream until soft peaks form. Slowly beat in the powdered sugar and liqueur. Place one of the chilled cake layers on a serving plate and spread with half of the whipped cream filling. Place the second cake layer on top and spread with the remaining filling. Top with the third cake layer. Chill for 1 hour before frosting.

7 Meanwhile, to make the frosting, melt the chocolate (see page 13). Remove from the heat. Cool slightly.

8 Transfer the chocolate to a medium bowl. Add the butter and cream. Using an electric mixer on medium speed, beat until smooth. Add the powdered sugar and beat until a spreadable consistency. Spread this frosting around the sides and top of the assembled cake. Garnish the top of the cake with chocolate chips or grated chocolate.

256 ■ PISTACHIO NUT CAKE

YIELD: *12 to 14 servings*
BAKING TIME: *90 minutes*
CHILL TIME: *overnight*

½ cup Chocolate Glaze II (see page 401)
3 cups ground pistachio nuts
2½ cups all-purpose flour
1 tablespoon grated lemon zest
6 large eggs, separated
1 teaspoon cream of tartar
1½ cups butter or margarine, at room temperature
2 cups granulated sugar
1 cup milk
¼ cup Triple Sec or Mandarino liqueur
1 tablespoon almond extract
3 ounces white chocolate, grated or finely chopped
12 White Chocolate Leaves (see page 422)

1 Make the glaze and chill overnight.

2 Position a rack in the center of the oven and preheat the oven to 300 degrees. Lightly grease and flour a 9-inch tube pan.

3 To make the cake, combine the pistachio nuts, flour, and lemon zest.

4 In a medium bowl, using an electric mixer on high speed, beat the egg whites and cream of tartar until stiff but not dry.

5 In a large bowl, using an electric mixer on medium speed, beat the butter and sugar until light and fluffy. Beat in the egg

246

241

250

240

249

yolks, milk, liqueur, and almond extract. Gradually blend in the dry ingredients. Fold in the egg whites. Spread the batter into the prepared pan and spread evenly. Do not disturb the batter once it has been poured into the pan.

6 Bake for 85 to 90 minutes, or until a cake tester inserted into the center comes out clean. Cool in the pan on a wire rack for 30 minutes. Invert onto the wire rack to cool completely.

7 To assemble, place the cake on a serving plate. In the top of a double boiler over simmering water, warm the glaze, stirring until smooth. Gently spread over the top, sides, and center cavity of the cake. Be sure all areas of the cake are covered with the glaze. Chill in the refrigerator until the glaze is set.

8 Meanwhile, melt the white chocolate (see page 13). Remove from the heat. Using a small paper cone, drizzle a lattice pattern over the top and sides of the cake. To do the sides simply tilt the cake plate just enough to allow the white chocolate to be applied. Garnish with the white chocolate leaves.

257 ■ PISTACHIO PUDDING CHOCOLATE CAKE

YIELD: *12 to 14 servings*
BAKING TIME: *45 minutes*

½ **cup chopped pistachios**
1 **box (18.5 ounces) yellow cake mix**
1 **package (3.4 ounces) Jell-O Brand pistachio instant pudding mix**
1 **cup canola oil**
½ **cup orange juice**
3 **large eggs**
½ **cup club soda**
¾ **cup chocolate syrup**
Powdered sugar for garnish

1 Position a rack in the center of the oven and preheat the oven to 350 degrees. Lightly grease and flour a 10-inch Bundt pan. Sprinkle the pistachio nuts evenly over the bottom of the prepared pan.

2 In a large bowl, using an electric mixer on medium speed, beat the cake mix, pudding mix, oil, orange juice, eggs, and club soda until blended. Spoon half of the mixture into the prepared pan, being careful not to disturb the pistachio nuts.

3 Add the chocolate syrup to the remaining batter and stir until well blended. Pour over the top of the mixture in the pan. Using a knife, swirl the batters two or three times. Do not overmix or touch the bottom or sides of the pan.

4 Bake for 40 to 45 minutes, or until a cake tester inserted into a light section of the cake comes out clean. Cool in the pan on a wire rack for 15 minutes. Invert onto the rack to cool completely. Place on a serving plate. Dust with powdered sugar.

255

256

251

253

257

258 ■ PLAIN CHOCOLATE CAKE I

YIELD: *12 servings*
BAKING TIME: *25 minutes*

4 ounces semisweet chocolate, grated or finely chopped
1 cup all-purpose flour
1 tablespoon baking powder
1 teaspoon salt
1/2 cup butter or margarine, at room temperature
1 cup granulated sugar
2 large eggs
3/4 cup milk
1 teaspoon vanilla or chocolate extract
1 1/2 cups Never Fail Chocolate Frosting I (see page 414)
Chocolate Curls (see page 422) or chopped nuts for garnish

1 Position a rack in the center of the oven and preheat the oven to 350 degrees. Lightly grease and flour two 9-inch round cake pans.

2 Melt the chocolate (see page 13). Remove from the heat.

3 Combine the flour, baking powder, and salt.

4 In a large bowl, using an electric mixer on medium speed, beat the butter and sugar until light and fluffy. Beat in the melted chocolate. Beat in the eggs. Beat in the milk and vanilla extract. Gradually blend in the dry ingredients. Divide the mixture between the prepared pans.

5 Bake for 20 to 25 minutes, or until a cake tester inserted into the center comes out clean. Cool in the pans on wire racks.

6 Make the frosting.

7 To assemble, place one cake layer on a serving platter and spread the frosting over the top and sides of the cake. Place the second cake on top of the first cake and spread the frosting evenly over the top and sides of the cake. Garnish with the grated chocolate or nuts.

259 ■ PLAIN CHOCOLATE CAKE II

YIELD: *12 to 16 servings*
BAKING TIME: *35 minutes*

CHOCOLATE CAKE

3 ounces unsweetened chocolate, grated or finely chopped
2 cups all-purpose flour
1 teaspoon baking soda
1/4 teaspoon salt
1/2 cup butter or margarine, at room temperature
1 1/4 cups granulated sugar
1 large egg
1 teaspoon chocolate extract
1 cup buttermilk

COCOA TOPPING

1 cup powdered sugar
1/4 cup heavy cream or milk
1/4 cup butter or margarine, at room temperature
1/4 cup Dutch processed cocoa powder
2 teaspoons chocolate extract
1/4 cup chopped nuts for garnish

1 Position a rack in the center of the oven and preheat the oven to 350 degrees. Lightly grease a 9-inch square pan.

2 Melt the chocolate (see page 13). Remove from the heat.

3 To make the cake, combine the flour, baking soda, and salt.

4 In a large bowl, using an electric mixer on medium speed, beat the butter and sugar until light and fluffy. Beat in melted chocolate, egg, and chocolate extract. In three additions, stir in the dry ingredients, alternating with the buttermilk, beginning and ending with the dry ingredients. Mix well after each addition. Scrape into the prepared pan and spread evenly.

5 Bake for 30 to 35 minutes, or until a cake tester inserted into the center comes out clean. Cool in the pan on a wire rack.

6 To make the topping, in a small bowl, using an electric mixer on medium speed, beat the powdered sugar, cream, butter, cocoa powder, and chocolate extract until a spreadable consistency. If the topping is too thin, add more powdered sugar, a tablespoon at a time. If too thick, add milk, a half-teaspoon at a time. Spread the topping evenly over the top of the cake. Sprinkle with the chopped nuts. Cut into squares.

260 ■ QUICKIE CHEESECAKE

YIELD: *12 servings*
BAKING TIME: *55 minutes*
CHILL TIME: *30 minutes*

CRUST

1 cup chocolate sandwich cookies, crushed
3 tablespoons butter, margarine, or vegetable shortening, at room temperature

262

FILLING

9 ounces cream cheese
3/4 cup granulated sugar
3 large eggs
1 teaspoon lemon extract
1 cup miniature semisweet chocolate chips

1 Position a rack in the center of the oven and preheat the oven to 350 degrees.

2 To make the crust, in a medium bowl, using a fork, mix the butter into the cookie crumbs. Press evenly onto the bottom of a 9-inch springform pan.

4 Bake for 10 minutes. Cool on a wire rack.

5 To make the filling, in a medium bowl, using an electric mixer on medium speed, beat the cream cheese and sugar until smooth. Beat in the eggs, one at a time, beating well after each addition. Stir in the lemon extract and chocolate chips. Pour the mixture over the baked crust.

6 Bake for 40 to 45 minutes, or until firm. Cool in the pan on a wire rack. Chill for 30 minutes or until ready to serve. Remove the side of the pan and cut into wedges.

260

261 ■ RED DEVIL'S FOOD CAKE

YIELD: *12 servings*
BAKING TIME: *30 minutes*

2 cups cake flour
1 teaspoon baking soda
1/4 teaspoon salt
2 ounces semisweet chocolate, grated or finely chopped
1/2 cup butter or margarine
1 1/2 cups granulated sugar
2 large eggs
1 teaspoon chocolate or vanilla extract
1/2 cup buttermilk
1/2 cup boiling water
1 tablespoon Cocoa Sugar (see page 407) for dusting

1 Position a rack in the center of the oven and preheat the oven to 350 degrees. Lightly grease two 8-inch round cake pans. Line the bottoms with waxed paper. Butter the paper and flour the pans.

2 Combine and sift the flour, baking soda, and salt.

3 In the top of a double boiler over simmering water, melt the chocolate and butter, stirring until smooth. Remove from the heat and stir in the sugar.

4 In a large bowl, using an electric mixer on medium speed, beat the eggs until thick and light-colored. Pouring it in a thin stream, beat in the chocolate mixture. Beat in the chocolate extract. Combine the buttermilk and boiling water. In three additions, blend in the dry ingredients, alternating with the buttermilk mixture, beginning and ending with the dry ingredients. Beat until well blended. The batter will be thin. Divide evenly between the prepared pans.

5 Bake for 25 to 30 minutes, or until a cake tester inserted into the center comes out clean. Cool for 5 minutes in the pans on wire racks. Invert onto the racks to cool completely.

6 Dust with cocoa sugar.

262 ■ RICH COFFEE CHOCOLATE CAKE

YIELD: *12 servings*
BAKING TIME: *35 minutes*

1 3/4 cups all-purpose flour
1 teaspoon baking soda
1/4 teaspoon salt
2 ounces unsweetened chocolate, grated or finely chopped
1 cup strong brewed coffee
1/2 cup Dutch processed cocoa powder
1/2 cup vegetable shortening
1 1/4 cups granulated sugar
1 teaspoon chocolate or vanilla extract
2 large eggs
1 1/2 cup Coffee Mocha Icing (see page 408)

1 Position a rack in the center of the oven and preheat the oven to 350 degrees. Lightly grease and flour two 8-inch round cake pans.

2 Combine the flour, baking soda, and salt.

3 Melt the chocolate (see page 13). Remove from the heat.

4 In a small bowl, blend the coffee and cocoa until smooth. Stir it into the melted chocolate. Reheat the chocolate if necessary.

4 In a large bowl, using an electric mixer on medium speed, beat the shortening and sugar until fluffy. Beat in the chocolate extract. Gradually add the dry ingredients, alternating with the chocolate mixture. Divide evenly between the prepared pans.

5 Bake for 30 to 35 minutes, or until a cake tester inserted into the center comes out clean. Cool in the pans on a wire rack for 5 minutes. Invert onto the rack to cool completely.

6 Make the frosting.

7 To assemble, place one layer on a serving plate. Spread the frosting over the top of the first layer. Place the second layer on top of the first and frost the top and sides of the cake.

263 ■ RICOTTA CAKE

YIELD: *12 servings*
CHILL TIME: *8 hours*

3 packages (6 ounces each) ladyfinger cookies
1 cup heavy cream
3 pounds ricotta cheese
3/4 cup granulated sugar
1/4 cup crème de cacao
5 ounces semisweet chocolate,
grated or finely chopped
1/4 teaspoon grated lemon zest
1/4 teaspoon grated orange zest
1/4 teaspoon ground cinnamon
1 cup pistachio nuts, chopped

1 Lightly grease the bottom and
sides of a 9-inch springform
pan.

2 Line the bottom and side of
the prepared baking pan with
ladyfingers, separating them
into halves and trimming them
to fit, if necessary.

3 In a medium bowl, using an
electric mixer on medium-high
speed, beat the cream until stiff
peaks form.

4 In a medium bowl, using an
electric mixer on medium speed,
beat the ricotta cheese until a
smooth paste. Beat in the sugar
and crème de cacao. Stir in the
chocolate, lemon zest, orange

zest, and cinnamon. Fold in the
whipped cream.

5 Spread half of the ricotta mixture into the prepared pan. Place
a layer of ladyfingers on top of
the ricotta mixture. Spread
remaining ricotta mixture on top
of the ladyfingers. Chill for at
least 8 hours.

6 To serve, remove the side of
the pan and sprinkle the
chopped pistachio nuts on top.

264 ■ SAUCEPAN CHOCOLATE CAKE

YIELD: *12 servings*
BAKING TIME: *35 minutes*

1 cup all-purpose flour
1 teaspoon baking soda
1/2 teaspoon baking powder
1/2 teaspoon salt
2 ounces unsweetened chocolate,
grated or finely chopped
2 tablespoons butter or margarine
1/2 cup granulated sugar
1/3 cup water
1/2 cup dark corn syrup
1 large egg
1/4 cup buttermilk
1 teaspoon chocolate extract
1 1/2 cups Caramel Glaze (see page
395)

1 Position a rack in the center of
the oven and preheat the oven
to 350 degrees. Lightly grease
and flour an 8-inch square pan.

2 Combine the flour, baking
soda, baking powder, and salt.

3 In the top of a double boiler
over simmering water, melt the
chocolate and butter, stirring
until smooth. Stir in the sugar
and water. Remove from the
heat. Stir in the corn syrup and
let cool. Add the egg and beat
slightly. Add the dry ingredients, in one addition, stirring
until smooth. Add the buttermilk and chocolate extract. Pour
the mixture into the prepared
pan.

4 Bake for 30 to 35 minutes, or
until a cake tester inserted into
the center comes out clean. Cool
in the pan on a wire rack for 5
minutes.

5 Make the caramel glaze.

6 Invert the cake onto a serving
plate. Spread the caramel glaze
over the top of the warm cake
and let it drip down the sides.
Cool completely before serving.

265 ■ SAUERKRAUT FUDGE CAKE

YIELD: *12 servings*
BAKING TIME: *60 minutes*

COCOA SAUERKRAUT CAKE

1 cup sauerkraut
2 1/4 cups all-purpose flour
3 cups granulated sugar
1/2 cup Dutch processed cocoa
powder
1 teaspoon baking powder
1 teaspoon baking soda

263

264

265

¼ teaspoon salt
⅔ cup butter or margarine, at room
   temperature
3 large eggs
1 teaspoon vanilla extract
1 cup water

COCOA WHIPPED TOPPING

1½ cups heavy cream
3 tablespoons granulated sugar
1 tablespoon instant coffee powder
2 teaspoon Dutch processed cocoa
   powder
2 tablespoons coffee liqueur

1 Position a rack in the center of
the oven and preheat the oven
to 350 degrees. Lightly grease
two 8-inch round cake pans.
Line the bottom of the pan with
waxed paper and grease the
paper.

2 Drain, rinse, and finely chop
the sauerkraut. Pat dry between
paper towels.

3 Combine the flour, 1½ cups of
the sugar, the cocoa powder,
baking powder, baking soda,
and salt.

4 In a medium bowl, using an
electric mixer on medium speed,
beat the butter and the remaining 1½ cups of sugar until light
and fluffy.

5 In a large bowl, using an electric mixer on medium speed,
beat the eggs until thick and
light-colored. Beat in the vanilla
extract and the water. Gradually
beat in the butter mixture, alternating with the dry ingredients.
Fold in the sauerkraut. Divide
the mixture between the prepared pans and spread evenly.

6 Bake for 60 minutes, or until a
cake tester inserted into the center comes out clean. Cool in the
pans on wire racks for 10 minutes. Invert onto the racks to
cool completely.

7 To make the topping, in a
large bowl, using an electric
mixer on medium-high speed,
beat the cream and sugar until
slightly thickened. Add the coffee powder and cocoa powder
and beat until soft peaks form.

8 To assemble, place one of the
cake layers on a serving plate
and spread with an even layer
of the topping. Top with the sec-

ond cake layer and press gently
in place. Spread the topping
over the top and sides of the
cake. Chill until serving.

BAKING NOTES: For a special
occasion, fill a pastry bag fitted
with a star tip with some of the
topping and pipe rosettes on the
top of the frosted cake. Garnish
each rosettes with chocolate
leaves (see page 422).

266 ■ SCHWEIZER SCHOKOLADE KUCHEN

YIELD: *12 servings*
BAKING TIME: *30 minutes*
CHILL TIME: *30 minutes*

CAKE

1¾ cups all-purpose flour
2 teaspoons baking powder
¼ teaspoon baking soda
½ teaspoon salt
3 ounces unsweetened chocolate,
   grated or finely chopped
1½ cups granulated sugar
½ cup vegetable shortening
1½ cups heavy cream
2 large eggs, at room temperature
1 teaspoon chocolate or vanilla
   extract

CHOCOLATE FROSTING

5 ounces unsweetened chocolate,
   grated or finely chopped
2¼ cups powdered sugar
¼ cup hot water
2 large egg yolks
6 tablespoons butter or margarine,
   at room temperature

FILLING

¾ pound fresh plums, skinned, pitted, and quartered
½ cup crème de prunelle or
   marsala
3 tablespoons powdered sugar

1 Position a rack in the center of
the oven and preheat the oven
to 350 degrees. Lightly grease
two 9-inch round cake pans.

2 To make the cake, combine
the flour, baking powder, baking
soda, and salt.

3 Melt the chocolate (see page
13). Remove from the heat.

4 In a large bowl, using an electric mixer on medium speed,
beat the sugar and shortening
until fluffy. In three additions,
blend in the dry ingredients,
alternating with cream, beginning and ending with the dry
ingredients, mixing just until
blended. Add the eggs, chocolate extract, and melted chocolate. Beat on medium speed
until well blended. Divide the
mixture between the prepared
pans.

5 Bake for 25 to 30 minutes, or
until a cake tester inserted into
the center comes out clean. Cool
in the pans on wire racks for 5
minutes. Invert onto racks to
cool completely.

6 To make the frosting, melt the
chocolate (see page 13). Add the
powdered sugar and water, and
stir until blended. Beat in the
egg yolks, one at a time, beating
well after each addition.
Remove from the heat and beat
in the butter until thick and
smooth.

7 To make the filling, in a large
saucepan over low heat, combine the plums and crème de
prunelle. Cook until the mixture
is reduced to 1 cup. Remove
from the heat and stir in the
powdered sugar. Return to the
heat and continue cooking until
the mixture is reduced by one-
third. Cool slightly before
assembling the cake.

8 To assemble the cake, place
one of the cake layers on a serving plate. Spread the plum filling evenly over the top and
place the second cake layer on
the top. Spread the frosting over
the top and sides of the cake.
Chill for 30 minutes before
serving.

267 ■ SELF-FROSTING CHOCOLATE CAKE

YIELD: *12 to 15 servings*
BAKING TIME: *45 minutes*

1 cup pecans, finely chopped
1 cup flaked coconut
2 cups cake flour
3/4 teaspoon baking soda
1/2 teaspoon salt
3 ounces unsweetened chocolate, grated or finely chopped
1 1/2 cups butter or margarine, at room temperature
8 ounces cream cheese, at room temperature
1 cup powdered sugar
1 1/3 cups granulated sugar
3/4 cup sour cream or yogurt
3 large eggs
1 teaspoon chocolate or vanilla extract

1 Position a rack in the center of the oven and preheat the oven to 300 degrees. Lightly grease a 13 by 9-inch pan. Spread the pecans and coconut evenly over the bottom.

2 Combine the flour, baking soda, and salt.

3 Melt the chocolate (see page 13). Remove from the heat.

4 In a small bowl, using an electric mixer on medium speed, beat 1 cup of the butter, the cream cheese, and powdered sugar until light and smooth.

5 In a large bowl, using an electric mixer on medium speed, beat the remaining 1/2 cup butter, the granulated sugar, and sour cream until smooth. Beat in the eggs. Beat in the chocolate extract and melted chocolate. Spoon this mixture over the pecans and coconut in the prepared pan. Spoon the cream cheese mixture over the top of the chocolate mixture.

6 Bake for 40 to 45 minutes, or until a cake tester inserted into the center comes out clean. Cool for 1 minute in the pan on a wire rack. Invert the cake onto the rack. Do not remove the pan from the top of the cake for another 5 to 10 minutes. Invert cake onto a serving plate and serve.

268 ■ SICILIAN CHEESECAKE

YIELD: *16 servings*
BAKING TIME: *60 minutes*
CHILL TIME: *60 minutes*

CAKE

3 1/2 cups all-purpose flour
1 1/2 teaspoons baking powder
1/4 teaspoon salt
1 cup butter or margarine, at room temperature
2 cups granulated sugar
6 large egg yolks
1 cup milk
2 teaspoons Campari

ASSEMBLY AND FILLING

6 tablespoons Campari
15 ounces ricotta cheese
2 tablespoons heavy cream

TOPPING

6 ounces semisweet chocolate, grated or finely chopped
6 ounces unsweetened chocolate, grated or finely chopped
1/4 cup butter
3 cups powdered sugar
1/2 cup hot strong brewed coffee
1 1/2 teaspoons crème de cacao
Fresh mint sprigs for garnish
Peeled, sliced kiwifruit for garnish

1 Position a rack in the center of the oven and preheat the oven to 350 degrees. Lightly grease and flour a 10-inch Bundt pan.

2 To make the cake, combine the flour, baking powder, and salt.

3 In a large bowl, using an electric mixer on medium speed, beat the butter and sugar until light and fluffy. Beat in the egg yolks, milk, and Campari. Gradually blend in the dry ingredients. Beat on medium speed for 3 minutes, or until smooth. Pour the mixture into the prepared pan.

4 Bake for 1 hour, or until a cake tester inserted into the center comes out clean. Cool in the pan on a wire rack for 15 minutes. Invert onto the rack to cool completely.

5 To assemble, using a serrated knife, cut the cake horizontally into four layers. Brush each cake layer with 1 tablespoon of the

267

269

Campari. Place the bottom layer on a serving plate. **6** In a medium bowl, using an electric mixer on medium speed, beat the ricotta cheese, remaining Campari, and heavy cream until smooth. Spread one-third of the filling on the bottom cake layer and sprinkle with one-third of the chocolate. Top with the second cake layer and spread one-third of the filling evenly over it and sprinkle with one-third of the chocolate. Place the third cake layer on top and spread with the remaining filling and sprinkle with remaining chocolate. Top with the fourth cake layer and press gently into place. Refrigerate the cake for 1 hour.

7 Meanwhile, to make the topping, in the top of a double boiler over simmering water, melt the chocolates and butter, stirring until smooth. Remove from the heat and stir in the powdered sugar, coffee, and crème de cacao. Beat until smooth. Spread the topping over the top of the cake, allowing it to run down the sides. Refrigerate until ready to serve. Decorate the top with sprigs of mint and thinly sliced kiwifruit.

BAKING NOTES: The chocolate frosting shouldn't be too thick; it should run down the sides and will thicken when chilled.

269 ■ SICILIAN CHEESECAKE WITH CHOCOLATE FROSTING

YIELD: *10 to 12 servings*
BAKING TIME: *40 minutes*
CHILL TIME: *8 hours*

CAKE

6 large eggs, separated
1/2 cup granulated sugar
2 tablespoons Frangelico
2 tablespoons grated orange zest
1 tablespoon fresh lemon juice, strained
1 cup all-purpose flour
1/2 teaspoon cream of tartar
1/4 cup powdered sugar

FILLING

1 pound ricotta cheese
1/4 cup powdered sugar
2 tablespoons sour cream or yogurt
2 tablespoons Mandarino liqueur
1/4 cup chopped candied orange peel
1/4 cup chopped pistachio nuts
2 tablespoons semisweet chocolate, grated or finely chopped
1 1/2 cups Coffee Mocha Icing (see page 408)

1 Position a rack in the center of the oven and preheat the oven to 350 degrees. Lightly grease and flour an 11 by 5-inch loaf pan.

2 To make the cake, in a large bowl, using an electric mixer on medium speed, beat the egg yolks until thick and light-colored. Continue beating and add the granulated sugar, Frangelico, orange zest, and lemon juice. Gradually blend in the flour, a little at a time.

3 In medium bowl, using an electric mixer with clean beaters on high speed, beat the egg whites and cream of tartar until foamy. Add the powdered sugar, a little at a time, and continue beating until stiff but not dry. Gently fold one-third of the egg white mixture into the egg yolk mixture. Fold in the remaining whites until completely blended and no white streaks remain. Pour the mixture into the prepared pan and spread evenly.

4 Bake for 35 to 40 minutes, or until a cake tester inserted into the center comes out clean. Cool in the pan on a wire rack for 5 minutes. Invert onto the rack to cool completely.

5 Meanwhile, to make the filling, press the ricotta cheese through a sieve into a large bowl. Beat in the powdered sugar, sour cream, and Mandarino. Mix in the candied peel and pistachio nuts. Fold in the grated chocolate and chill the filling for at least 1 hour.

6 Meanwhile, make the mocha frosting.

7 To assemble, using a serrated knife, cut the cake horizontally

into four equal layers. Place the bottom cake layer on a serving plate. Spread a little of the filling over the bottom layer, top with the second, and continue until the last cake layer is placed on top. Chill for 4 to 6 hours before frosting the cake.

8 To frost, spread an even layer of the frosting over the top and sides of the cake. Fill a pastry bag fitted with a medium star tip with the remaining frosting and press out small rosettes along the top and sides of the cake. Chill 30 minutes or unitl ready to serving.

BAKING NOTES: The frosted cake can also be garnished with shaved chocolate or chocolate curls.

270 ■ SOCIABLE CHOCOLATE CAKE

YIELD: *12 servings*
BAKING TIME: *25 minutes*

2 cups all-purpose flour
1/2 cup Dutch processed cocoa powder
2 1/2 teaspoons baking powder
1 teaspoon salt
3/4 cup butter or margarine, at room temperature
1 1/3 cups violet sugar or granulated sugar (see Baking notes)
3 large eggs
1 teaspoon chocolate or vanilla extract
1/2 cup heavy cream
1/2 cup Cocoa Frosting (see page 406)
Real or candied violets for garnish

1 Position a rack in the center of the oven and preheat the oven to 350 degrees. Lightly grease and flour two 9-inch round cake pans.

2 Combine the flour, cocoa powder, baking powder, and salt.

3 In a large bowl, using an electric mixer on medium speed, beat the butter and sugar until light and fluffy. Beat in the eggs, one at a time, beating well after each addition. Beat in the chocolate extract. In three additions, stir in the dry ingredients, alternating with the heavy cream, beginning and ending with the dry ingredients. Divide the mixture evenly between the prepared pans.

4 Bake for 20 to 25 minutes, or until a cake tester inserted into the center comes out clean. Cool in the pans on wire racks for 10 minutes. Invert onto the racks to cool completely.

5 Make the frosting.

6 To assemble, place one of the cakes on a serving plate and spread with the frosting. Top with the second cake layer and spread the frosting on the top and sides of the cake. Garnish with real or candied violets.

BAKING NOTE: Violet sugar is made by cutting or chopping up the petals of 15 violets. Mix these with 1⅓ cups granulated sugar. Place in an airtight container and let stand for 48 hours before using.

271 ■ SOUR CREAM CHOCOLATE CHIP CAKE

YIELD: *16 servings*
BAKING TIME: *90 minutes*

2 cups semisweet chocolate chips
4 cups all-purpose flour
2 teaspoons baking soda
1 cup butter or margarine, at room temperature
2 cups granulated sugar
4 large eggs, at room temperature
2 cups sour cream
1 tablespoon crème de cacao
1 cup chopped walnuts
1 cup Chocolate Glaze III (see page 401)

1 Position a rack in the center of the oven and preheat the oven to 350 degrees. Lightly grease and flour a 10-inch Bundt pan. Sprinkle 1 cup of the chocolate chips evenly over the bottom of the prepared pan.

2 Combine the flour and baking soda.

3 In a large bowl, using an electric mixer on medium speed, beat the butter and sugar until light and fluffy. Beat in the eggs, one at a time, being well after

each addition. Beat in the sour cream and crème de cacao. Using a wooden spoon, gradually blend in the dry ingredients. Fold in the walnuts and remaining 1 cup of chocolate chips. Spoon the mixture over the chocolate chips in the prepared pan.

4 Bake for 85 to 90 minutes, or until a cake tester inserted into the center comes out clean. Cool in the pan on a wire rack for 10 minutes. Invert onto the rack to cool completely. Place on a serving plate.

5 Make the chocolate glaze. Drizzle the glaze over the top of the cake, allowing it to run down the sides.

272 ■ SOUR CREAM AND CRANBERRY CHOCOLATE PUDDING CAKE

YIELD: *12 to 16 servings*
BAKING TIME: *60 minutes*

1 cup all-purpose flour
⅔ cup sugar
½ cup Dutch processed cocoa powder
2 teaspoons baking powder
¼ teaspoon salt
1¼ cups sour cream
¼ cup canola oil
1 cup dried cranberries
½ cup chopped walnuts
¾ cup packed brown sugar
1½ cups hot water
½ cup heavy cream

1 Position a rack in the center of the oven and preheat the oven to 350 degrees.

2 In a large bowl, combine the flour, sugar, cocoa powder, baking powder, and salt. Using an electric mixer on low speed, beat in ¾ cup of the sour cream and the oil. Stir in the walnuts and cranberries. Scrape the mixture into an ungreased 9-inch square pan and spread evenly.

3 In a small bowl, combine the brown sugar and hot water. Gently spoon over the top of the batter in the pan.

4 Bake for 50 to 60 minutes, or until the top of the cake is a golden brown. Cool in the pan on a wire rack.

5 In a medium bowl, using an electric mixer on high speed, whip the cream until soft peaks form. Blend in the remaining ½ cup of sour cream. Spread some of the cream topping evenly over the cooled cake. Cut into squares. Serve with remaining cream topping on the side.

BAKING NOTES: An alternate garnish is to drizzle chocolate syrup over the whipped cream topping on the cake.

273 ■ SOURDOUGH CHOCOLATE CAKE

YIELD: *12 to 15 servings*
BAKING TIME: *45 minutes*
STARTER TIME: 24 HOURS

STARTER

⅔ cup all-purpose flour
1 teaspoon active dry yeast
⅔ cup lukewarm water

CAKE

1½ cups all-purpose flour
½ cup sourdough starter
1 cup lukewarm water
¼ cup nonfat dry milk powder
3 ounces unsweetened chocolate, grated or finely chopped
½ cup butter or margarine, at room temperature
1 cup granulated sugar
2 tablespoons Dutch processed cocoa powder
1½ teaspoons baking soda
1 teaspoon chocolate or vanilla extract
¼ teaspoon salt
2 large eggs

1 To make the starter, in a small bowl, combine the flour, yeast, and water, stirring until just mixed. Cover and let stand at room temperature for 24 hours. Use ½ cup of the starter to make the cake.

2 To make the cake, in a medium bowl, combine the flour, starter, water, and milk powder, blending with a spoon until smooth. Cover and let

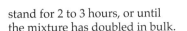

stand for 2 to 3 hours, or until the mixture has doubled in bulk.

3 Preheat the oven to 350 degrees. Lightly grease and flour a 13 by 9-inch pan.

4 Melt the chocolate (see page 13). Remove from the heat.

5 In a large bowl, using an electric mixer on medium speed, beat the butter, sugar, cocoa powder, baking soda, vanilla extract, and salt. Beat in the eggs, one at a time, beating well after each addition. Beat in the melted chocolate. Beat in the starter mixture. Scrape into the prepared pan and spread evenly.

6 Bake for 40 to 45 minutes, or until a cake tester inserted into the center comes out clean. The top may crack but be very careful not to overbake. Cool in the pan on a wire rack for 10 minutes. Invert onto the rack to cool completely.

BAKING NOTES: This cake is considered difficult to make because of the long preparation time. Any starter that may be left over can be used in the preparation of sour dough bread. Any pan other than that recommended may cause an excessive amount of rising.

274 ■ SOUR MILK CHOCOLATE CAKE

YIELD: *12 servings*
BAKING TIME: *35 minutes*

1¾ cups all-purpose flour
1 teaspoon baking soda
¼ teaspoon salt
2 ounces unsweetened chocolate, grated or finely chopped
1½ cup vegetable shortening
1¼ cups granulated sugar
1 teaspoon chocolate or vanilla extract
2 large eggs
1 cup sour milk or buttermilk (see Baking notes)
1½ cups Creamy Chocolate Cherry Frosting (see page 408)

1 Position a rack in the center of the oven and preheat the oven to 350 degrees. Lightly grease and flour two 8-inch round cake pans.

2 Combine the flour, baking soda, and salt.

3 Melt the chocolate (see page 13). Remove from the heat.

4 In a large bowl, using an electric mixer on medium speed, beat the shortening and sugar until fluffy. Beat in the melted chocolate and chocolate extract. Beat in the eggs. In three additions, blend in the dry ingredients, alternating with the sour milk, beginning and ending with the dry ingredients. Divide evenly between the prepared pans.

5 Bake for 30 to 35 minutes, or until a cake tester inserted into the center comes out clean. Cool in the pans on wire racks for 5 minutes. Invert onto the racks to cool completely.

6 Make the creamy chocolate cherry frosting.

7 Place one of the cake layers on a serving plate and spread with some of the frosting. Top with the second cake layer and spread frosting over the top and sides of the cake.

BAKING NOTES: To make the sour milk, add 1 tablespoon lemon juice to 1 cup milk.

275 ■ SOUTH OF THE BORDER CAKE

YIELD: *12 servings*
BAKING TIME: *35 minutes*

1 cup nonalkalized cocoa powder
1¾ cups granulated sugar
1½ cups buttermilk
2¼ cups all-purpose flour
1 teaspoon baking soda
½ teaspoon salt
½ cup butter or margarine, at room temperature
2 large eggs
1½ teaspoons crème de cacao or chocolate extract
1 cup Lemon Filling (see page 413)
1 cup Lemon Glaze (see page 413)

1 Position a rack in the center of the oven and preheat the oven to 350 degrees. Lightly grease and flour two 9-inch round cake pans.

2 In a medium bowl, combine the cocoa powder, ½ cup of the sugar, and ½ cup of the butter-

271

272

milk, stirring until the sugar is dissolved.

3 Combine the flour, baking soda, and salt.

4 In a large bowl, using an electric mixer on medium speed, beat the butter and remaining 1¼ cups sugar until light and fluffy. Beat in the eggs, one at a time, beating well after each addition. In three additions, blend in the dry ingredients, alternating with the remaining 1 cup buttermilk, beginning and ending with the dry ingredients. Mix in the crème de cacao and cocoa mixture. Divide the mixture between the prepared pans.

5 Bake for 30 to 35 minutes, or until a cake tester inserted into the center comes out clean. Cool in the pans on wire racks for 5 to 10 minutes. Invert onto the racks to cool completely.

6 Make the lemon filling and lemon glaze.

7 To assemble, place one of the cake layers on a serving plate and spread with the filling. Place the second cake layer on top. Pour the glaze over the top of the cake, allowing it to drip down the sides.

276 ■ SOUTHERN LADY

YIELD: *16 servings*
BAKING TIME: *45 minutes*

1 cup dates, pitted and chopped (½ pound whole dates)
1 cup boiling water
1 teaspoon baking soda
1⅓ cups all-purpose flour
1 cup semisweet chocolate chips
½ cup pecans, toasted and chopped
2 tablespoons Dutch processed cocoa powder
½ teaspoon ground cinnamon
½ cup butter or margarine, at room temperature
1 cup granulated sugar
2 large eggs
1 teaspoon almond or rum extract
Cocoa Sugar (see page 407) for dusting
Apricot Roses (see page 420) for garnish
Chocolate Leaves (see page 422) for garnish

1 Position a rack in the center of the oven and preheat the oven to 350 degrees. Lightly grease and flour a 10-inch tube pan.

2 In a medium bowl, combine the dates, water, and baking soda.

3 Combine the flour, chocolate chips, pecans, cocoa powder, and cinnamon.

4 In a large bowl, using an electric mixer on medium speed, beat the butter and sugar until light and fluffy. Beat in the eggs, one at a time, beating well after each addition. Beat in the almond extract. Gradually blend in the dry ingredients, a little at a time. Fold in the date mixture just until blended. Scrape the mixture into the prepared pan and spread evenly.

5 Bake for 40 to 45 minutes, or until a cake tester inserted into the center comes out clean. Cool in the pan on a wire rack for 10 to 15 minutes. Invert onto the rack to cool completely. Dust with cocoa sugar and garnish with apricot roses and chocolate leaves.

266

270

268

259

261

277

277 ■ SOUTHERN-STYLE CHOCOLATE CAKE

YIELD: *12 servings*
BAKING TIME: *45 minutes*
CHILL TIME: *1 hour*

2 cups all-purpose flour
1 teaspoon baking soda
¼ teaspoon salt
4 ounces unsweetened chocolate, grated or finely chopped
2 tablespoons butter or margarine
4 large eggs, separated
2 cups granulated sugar
1 teaspoon chocolate extract
3 tablespoons instant coffee powder
1¾ cups buttermilk
¾ cup Chocolate Custard Filling (see page 397)
2 cups Chocolate Custard Sauce (see page 398)

1 Position a rack in the center of the oven and preheat the oven to 350 degrees. Lightly grease and flour two 9-inch round cake pans.

2 Combine the flour, baking soda, and salt.

3 Melt the chocolate (see page 13). Stir in the butter. Remove from the heat.

4 In a medium bowl, using an electric mixer on high speed, beat the egg yolks until thick and light-colored. Beat in the sugar, chocolate extract, and coffee powder. Reduce speed to medium and add the chocolate mixture. In three additions, blend in the dry ingredients, alternating with the buttermilk, beginning and ending with the dry ingredients. Divide the mixture between the prepared pans and spread evenly.

5 Bake for 40 to 45 minutes, or until a cake tester inserted into the center comes out clean. Invert the cakes onto wire racks but do not remove the pan for 10 minutes. Remove the pans, and place the cakes right side up on the racks to cool completely.

6 Make the filling and sauce.

7 To assemble, place one of the cake layers on a serving plate and spread with the filling. Top with the second cake layer. Pour the chocolate custard sauce over the top of the cake and let it drip down the sids. Chill for at least 1 hour before serving.

274

276

273

275

278 ■ SPRING'S LOVE CAKE

YIELD: *12 servings*
BAKING TIME: *40 minutes*
CHILL TIME: *30 minutes*

2½ cups all-purpose flour
1 teaspoon baking soda
½ teaspoon salt
2 ounces unsweetened chocolate, grated or finely chopped
2 ounces semisweet chocolate, grated or finely chopped
⅓ cup mint-flavored chocolate chips
½ cup boiling water
4 large eggs, separated
1 cup butter or margarine, at room temperature
2 cups granulated sugar
1 teaspoon white crème de menthe
1 cup buttermilk
1 cup Chocolate Quark Cream Filling (see page 403)
2 cups Crème Chantilly (see page 409)
½ cup Raspberry Sauce (see page 416)

1 Position a rack in the center of the oven and preheat the oven to 350 degrees. Lightly grease three 9-inch round cake pans.

2 Combine the flour, baking soda, and salt.

3 In the top of a double boiler over simmering water, melt the chocolates, chocolate chips, and boiling water, stirring until smooth. Remove from the heat.

4 In a medium bowl, using an electric mixer on high speed, beat the egg whites until stiff but not dry.

5 In a large bowl, using an electric mixer on medium speed, beat the butter and sugar until light and fluffy. Add the egg yolks and beat until the mixture is smooth and light-colored. Beat in the chocolate mixture and crème de menthe. Gradually blend in the dry ingredients, alternating with the buttermilk, beginning and ending with the dry ingredients. Fold in the egg whites. Pour into the prepared pans.

6 Bake for 30 to 40 minutes, or until a cake tester inserted into the center comes out clean. Cool

in the pans on wire racks for 5 minutes. Invert onto the racks to cool completely.

7 Meanwhile, make the chocolate quark cream filling, crème chantilly, and raspberry sauce.

8 To assemble, place one of the cake layers on a serving plate. Spread half of the quark cream evenly over the top, leaving ¼-inch border around the edge. Repeat with the second cake layer and the remaining quark cream. Top with the third cake layer and spread the raspberry sauce over the top, leaving a ½-inch border around the edge. Spread some of the chocolate cream de chantilly around the sides of the cake. Place the remaining chantilly in a pastry bag fitted with a large star tip and pipe a fancy design around the top edge of the cake, around the base, and several large rosettes at evenly spaced intervals around the top. Chill for 1 hour before serving.

279 ■ SURE FIRE DEVIL'S FOOD CAKE

YIELD: *12 servings*
BAKING TIME: *35 minutes*

2 ounces semisweet chocolate, grated or finely chopped
2 cups all-purpose flour
1 teaspoon baking soda
¼ teaspoon salt
½ cup vegetable shortening
2 cups packed dark brown sugar
2 large eggs
1 cup cold water
1 teaspoon chocolate or vanilla extract
½ cup Chocolate Cream Filling (see page 397)
Powdered sugar for dusting

1 Position a rack in the center of the oven and preheat the oven to 350 degrees. Lightly grease and flour two 9-inch round cake pans.

2 Melt the chocolate (see page 13). Remove from the heat.

3 Combine the flour, baking soda, and salt.

4 In a large bowl, using an electric mixer on medium speed,

beat the shortening and brown sugar until fluffy. Beat in the eggs. Beat in the cold water and chocolate extract. Pouring it in a thin stream, beat in the melted chocolate. Gradually blend in the dry ingredients. Divide the batter between the prepared pans.

5 Bake for 30 to 35 minutes, or until a cake tester inserted into the center comes out clean. Cool in the pans on wire racks.

6 Make the filling.

7 Place one cake layer on a serving plate. Spread all the filling evenly over the top of the cake. Gently place the second layer on top of the first layer. Dust with powdered sugar.

280 ■ SWEET CHOCOLATE CAKE

YIELD: *12 servings*
BAKING TIME: *35 minutes*

CAKE

1¾ cups cake flour, sifted
1 teaspoon baking powder
½ teaspoon baking soda
½ teaspoon salt
3 ounces milk chocolate, grated or finely chopped
⅓ cup boiling water
3 large eggs, separated
½ cup butter or margarine, at room temperature
1 cup granulated sugar
1 teaspoon chocolate extract
⅔ cup buttermilk

FROSTING

1½ cups granulated sugar
2 large egg whites
⅓ cup ice water
¼ teaspoon cream of tartar
Pinch of salt
1 teaspoon vanilla or chocolate extract
Chocolate Curls (see page 422)

1 Position a rack in the center of the oven and preheat the oven to 350 degrees. Lightly grease and flour two 9-inch cake pans.

2 To make the cake, combine the flour, baking powder, baking soda, and salt.

3 In a small bowl, combine the chocolate and boiling water, stirring until smooth.

4 In another small bowl, using an electric mixer on high speed, beat the egg whites until stiff peaks form.

5 In a large bowl, using an electric mixer on medium speed, beat the butter and sugar until light and fluffy. Beat in the egg yolks, one at a time, beating well after each addition. Beat in the chocolate mixture. Beat in the chocolate extract and buttermilk. Buy hand, gradually stir in the dry ingredients. Fold in the egg whites. Divide the batter between the prepared pans.

6 Bake for 30 to 35 minutes, or until a cake tester inserted into the center comes out clean. Cool in the pans on wire racks for 10 minutes. Remove to the racks to cool completely.

7 Meanwhile, to make the frosting, in the top of a double boiler, combine the sugar, egg whites, water, cream of tartar, and salt. Set over a pan of simmering water. Using an electric mixer on medium speed, beat constantly until the mixture forms stiff peaks. (This takes about 7 minutes. Do not overcook.) Remove from the pan of simmering water. Add the vanilla extract and beat until the mixture is a spreadable consistency.

8 To assemble, place one of the cake layers on a serving plate and spread with the frosting. Top with the second cake layer and spread the frosting on the top and sides of the cake. Garnish with shaved chocolate.

281 ■ THREE CHOCOLATE CAKE

YIELD: *16 servings*
BAKING TIME: *50 minutes*

CAKE

5 ounces unsweetened chocolate, grated or finely chopped
3 ounces semisweet chocolate, grated or finely chopped
2 ounces white chocolate, grated or finely chopped
1 cup butter or margarine
5 tablespoons all-purpose flour
1½ teaspoons baking powder
5 large eggs
1¼ cups granulated sugar

TOPPING

White Chocolate Sauce (see page 418)

1 Position a rack in the center of the oven and preheat the oven to 325 degrees. Lightly grease and flour a 10-inch springform pan.

2 In a saucepan over low heat, melt the three chocolates and butter, stirring until smooth. Remove from the heat.

3 Combine the flour and baking powder.

4 In a large bowl, using an electric mixer on high speed, beat the eggs until thick and light-colored. Add the sugar and beat until the mixture thickens. Gradually blend in the dry ingredients. Pouring it in a narrow stream, fold in the chocolate mixture. Scrape into the prepared pan and spread evenly.

5 Bake for 20 minutes, cover with aluminum foil, and bake for an additional 30 minutes. Remove the foil and cool in the pan on a wire rack for 1 hour. Invert onto a serving plate.

6 Meanwhile, make the white chocolate sauce. Cut the cake into wedges and serve with a spoonful of the sauce over the top.

281

280

278

279

282 ■ TRIPLE CHOCOLATE BUNDT CAKE

YIELD: *16 servings*
BAKING TIME: *55 minutes*

1¼ cups all-purpose flour
1½ cups semisweet chocolate chips
1 package (3.4 ounces) Jell-O Brand chocolate instant pudding mix
1 teaspoon baking powder
1 teaspoon baking soda
½ teaspoon salt
2 ounces unsweetened chocolate, grated or finely chopped
2 tablespoons butter or margarine
1 cup granulated sugar
1 large egg
¾ cup milk
1 teaspoon chocolate or vanilla extract

1 Position a rack in the center of the oven and preheat the oven to 350 degrees. Grease and flour a 10-inch Bundt cake or tube pan.

2 Combine the flour, chocolate chips, pudding mix, baking powder, baking soda, and salt.

3 In the top of a double boiler over simmering water, melt the chocolate and butter, stirring until smooth. Remove from the heat and cool slightly.

4 In a large bowl, using an electric mixer on medium speed, beat the sugar and egg until thick and light-colored. Pouring it in a slow steady stream, beat in the chocolate mixture. Beat in the milk. Beat in the chocolate extract. Gradually blend in the dry ingredients. Pour the mixture into the prepared pan.

5 Bake for 50 to 55 minutes, or until a cake tester inserted into the center comes out clean. Cool in the pan on a wire rack for 10 to 15 minutes. Invert the cake onto the rack to cool completely.

283 ■ TRIPLE CHOCOLATE CAKE I

YIELD: *16 servings*
BAKING TIME: *45 minutes*
CHILL TIME: *90 minutes*

1⅓ cups cake flour
1 cup semisweet chocolate chips
½ cup Dutch processed cocoa powder
1 package (3.4 ounces) Jell-O Brand chocolate instant pudding mix
1 teaspoon baking powder
½ teaspoon baking soda
¼ teaspoon salt
6 tablespoons vegetable shortening
1 cup granulated sugar
3 large eggs
1½ teaspoons crème de cacao
½ cup Coffee Mocha Icing (see page 408)
¾ pint chocolate ice cream

1 Position a rack in the center of the oven and preheat the oven to 350 degrees. Lightly grease and flour a 10-inch Bundt or tube pan.

2 Combine the flour, chocolate chips, cocoa powder, pudding mix, baking powder, baking soda, and salt.

3 In a large bowl, using an electric mixer on medium speed,

beat the shortening and sugar until fluffy. Beat in the eggs. Beat in the crème de cacao. Gradually blend in the dry ingredients. Scrape the mixture into the prepared pan and spread evenly.

4 Bake for 40 to 45 minutes, or until a cake tester inserted into the center comes out clean. Cool in the pan on a wire rack for 10 minutes. Invert onto the rack to cool completely.   Chill the cake for 1 hour.

5 Make the mocha frosting.

6 To assemble, place the cake on a serving plate. Spread the frosting on the top and sides of the cake. Fill the hole in the center of the cake with ice cream. Freeze for 30 minutes or until ready to serve.

284 ■ TRIPLE CHOCOLATE CAKE II

YIELD: *16 servings*
BAKING TIME: *55 minutes*

1¼ cups all-purpose flour
2 cups semisweet chocolate chips
1 package (3.4 ounces) Jell-O Brand chocolate instant pudding mix
½ cups walnuts or pecans, finely chopped (optional)
2 teaspoons baking powder
2½ ounces unsweetened chocolate, grated or finely chopped
¼ cup vegetable shortening
1 cup granulated sugar
½ cup cold mashed potatoes
1 large egg
⅓ cup milk
1 teaspoon chocolate or vanilla extract
Powdered sugar or Chocolate Glaze IV (see page 401) for garnish

1 Position a rack in the center of the oven and preheat the oven

284

282

286

to 350 degrees. Lightly grease a 10-inch Bundt pan.

2 Combine the flour, chocolate chips, pudding mix, walnuts, and baking powder.

3 Melt the chocolate (see page 13). Blend in the shortening and sugar. Remove from the heat.

4 In a large bowl, using an electric mixer on medium speed, beat the mashed potatoes and egg until blended. Beat in the milk and chocolate extract. Pouring it in a steady stream, beat in the chocolate mixture. Gradually blend in the dry ingredients. Pour the mixture into the prepared pan.

5 Bake for 50 to 55 minutes, or until a cake tester inserted into the center comes out clean. Cool in the pan on a wire rack for 15 minutes. Remove to the rack to cool completely.

6 Place the cake on a serving plate. Dust the cake with powdered sugar or pour chocolate glaze over the top, allowing it to drip down the sides.

285 ■ TRIPLE FUDGE CAKE

YIELD: *12 to 15 servings*
BAKING TIME: *35 minutes*

2 cup all-purpose flour
1/2 teaspoon salt
1 teaspoon ground cinnamon
1/2 cup butter or margarine, at room temperature
1/2 cup canola oil
4 tablespoon Dutch processed cocoa powder
2 large eggs, slightly beaten
2 cups granulated sugar
1 cup water
1/4 cup buttermilk
1 teaspoon baking soda
1 teaspoon vanilla or almond extract

TOPPING

1/2 cup chopped walnuts
4 ounces semisweet chocolate
1 jar (12 ounces) fudge ice cream topping

GARNISH

Chocolate ice cream
Chocolate wafers

1 Position a rack in the center of the oven and preheat the oven to 350 degrees. Lightly grease and flour a 13 by 9-inch pan.

2 Combine the flour, salt, and cinnamon.

3 In a saucepan, over low heat, melt the butter, oil, and cocoa powder. Remove from the heat and cool slightly.

4 In a cup combine the water, buttermilk, and baking soda.

5 In a large bowl, using an electric mixer, beat the eggs and sugar. Beat in the vanilla extract and the cocoa mixture. Gradually blend in the dry ingredients, alternating with the buttermilk mixture. Pour into the prepared pan. Sprinkle the nuts and chocolate over the top.

6 Bake for 30 to 35 minutes, or until a cake tester inserted into the center comes out clean. While still hot from the oven, using the handle of a wooden spoon, poke holes into the cake spacing the holes about 1 to 1 1/2 inches apart. Spoon the fudge ice cream topping over the top and cool in the pan on a wire rack. When ready to serve, cut into large or small squares and top with a scoop of chocolate ice cream with chocolate wafers on the side.

286 ■ TUNNEL OF FUDGE CAKE

YIELD: *16 servings*
BAKING TIME: *60 minutes*

2 1/2 cups chocolate frosting mix
2 cups all-purpose flour
2 cups walnuts, finely chopped
1 1/2 cups butter or margarine, at room temperature
1 1/2 cups granulated sugar
6 large eggs
Powdered sugar for dusting

1 Position a rack in the center of the oven and preheat the oven to 350 degrees. Grease and flour a 10-inch Bundt pan.

2 Combine the frosting mix, flour, and walnuts.

3 In a large bowl, using an electric mixer on medium speed,

beat the butter and sugar until light and fluffy. Beat in the eggs, one at a time, beating until smooth and light-colored. Gradually blend in the dry ingredients. Pour the batter into the prepared pan.

4 Bake for 55 to 60 minutes, or until the cake pulls from the sides of the pan. The cake will appear soft in the center. Cool in the pan on a wire rack for at least 1 hour.

5 Invert the cake onto a serving plate. Dust the top of the cake with powdered sugar.

287 ■ UNBELIEVABLY EASY CHOCOLATE CAKE

YIELD: *12 servings*
BAKING TIME: *35 minutes*

CAKE

1 1/2 cups all-purpose flour
1 cup granulated sugar
1 cup water
1/3 cup canola oil
3 tablespoons Dutch processed cocoa powder
1 teaspoon chocolate extract
1 tablespoon cider vinegar
1/2 teaspoon baking soda

FROSTING

1/2 cup granulated sugar
1/2 cup flaked coconut
1/2 cup crushed canned pineapple, drained
1/2 cup milk
2 tablespoons vegetable shortening
1 1/2 tablespoons cornstarch or arrowroot

1 Position a rack in the center of the oven and preheat the oven to 350 degrees.

2 To make the cake, in a very large bowl, combine all of the ingredients for the cake and stir by hand until thoroughly mixed. Pour the mixture into an ungreased 8-inch square pan.

3 Bake for 30 to 35 minutes, or until a cake tester inserted into the center comes out clean. Make the frosting while the cake is baking and spread on top of the cake as soon as it comes out of the oven.

4 To make the frosting, in a large saucepan over low heat, combine all of the ingredients for the frosting and bring to a boil. Simmer, stirring, until thickened. Spread over the top of the hot cake. Cool completely before serving.

288 ■ WEST HAVEN CAKE

YIELD: *12 to 15 servings*
BAKING TIME: *40 minutes*

1 cup dates, pitted and finely chopped
1/2 cup hot water
1 3/4 cups all-purpose flour
2 tablespoons Dutch processed cocoa powder
1 teaspoon baking powder
1 cup granulated sugar
1/2 cup canola oil
3 large eggs
1 teaspoon chocolate or vanilla extract
1 cup walnuts, finely chopped
1/2 cup semisweet chocolate chips

1 Position a rack in the center of the oven and preheat the oven to 350 degrees. Lightly grease and flour a 13 by 9-inch pan.

2 In a small bowl, combine the dates and hot water.

3 Combine the flour, cocoa powder, and baking powder.

4 In a large bowl, using an electric mixer on medium speed, beat the sugar, oil, eggs, and chocolate extract until smooth and slightly thickened. Beat in the dry ingredients. Drain the dates and blend into the mixture. Scrape the mixture into the prepared pan and spread evenly. Sprinkle the walnuts and chocolate chips over the top.

5 Bake for 35 to 40 minutes, or until a cake tester inserted into the center comes out clean. Cool in the pan on a wire rack.

289 ■ WESTMINSTER CAKE

YIELD: *12 to 15 servings*
BAKING TIME: *40 minutes*

1 3/4 cups all-purpose flour
1 1/2 cups semisweet chocolate chips
2 teaspoons Dutch processed cocoa powder
1/8 teaspoon salt
1/2 cup walnuts, chopped
1 cup dates, pitted and chopped
1 teaspoon baking soda
1 cup hot water
1 cup butter or margarine, at room temperature
1 cup granulated sugar
2 large eggs
1 teaspoon chocolate or vanilla extract
Whipped cream for serving

1 Position a rack in the center of the oven and preheat the oven to 350 degrees. Lightly grease and flour a 13 by 9-inch pan.

2 Combine the flour, 1 cup of the chocolate chips, cocoa powder, salt, and walnuts.

3 Place the dates in a small bowl and sprinkle the baking soda over them. Add the hot water and soak for 10 minutes.

4 In a large bowl, using an electric mixer on medium speed, beat the butter and sugar until light and fluffy.   Beat in the eggs. Beat in the chocolate extract. Beat in the dates with the water. Gradually blend in the dry ingredients. Pour the mixture into the prepared pan and spread evenly.

5 Bake for 35 to 40 minutes, or until a cake tester inserted into the center comes out clean. Sprinkle the remaining 1/2 cups chocolate chips over top of the cake as soon as it comes out of the oven. Cool the cake slightly. Using a spatula, spread the melted chocolate chips over the top of the cake. Cool in the pan on a wire rack. Serve the cake with whipped cream on top.

290 ■ WET CHOCOLATE CAKE

YIELD: *16 servings*
BAKING TIME: *60 minutes*

2 cups all-purpose flour
1 1/2 teaspoons baking powder
1/2 teaspoon salt
1/2 cup vegetable shortening
2 ounces unsweetened chocolate, grated or finely chopped
1 cup boiling water
1/2 cup milk
1 teaspoon lemon juice
2 cups granulated sugar
2 large eggs
1/4 cup powdered sugar for dusting

1 Position a rack in the center of the oven and preheat the oven to 350 degrees. Lightly grease a 10-inch Bundt pan.

2 Combine the flour, baking powder, and salt.

3 In a small bowl, combine the shortening, chocolate, and boiling water, stirring until smooth.

4 Combine the milk and lemon juice.

5 In a large bowl, using an electric mixer on medium speed, beat the sugar and eggs until thick and light-colored. Beat in the chocolate mixture. Beat in the milk mixture. Gradually blend in the dry ingredients. Pour the mixture into the prepared pan.

289

6 Bake for 55 to 60 minutes, or until a cake tester inserted into the center comes out clean. Cool in the pan on a wire rack for 5 minutes. Invert onto a the rack to cool completely.

7 Place the cake on a serving plate and dust with powdered sugar.

291 ■ WHITE CHOCOLATE CAKE I

YIELD: *12 servings*
BAKING TIME: *35 minutes*

2¹/₂ cups all-purpose flour
1 cup pecans or walnuts, coarsely chopped
1 cup flaked coconut
1 teaspoon baking soda
5 ounces white chocolate, grated or finely chopped
¹/₂ cup boiling water
4 large eggs, separated
1 cup butter or margarine, at room temperature
2 cups granulated sugar
2 teaspoons vanilla extract
1 cup buttermilk
2 cups Coffee Mocha Icing (see page 408)
Thinly sliced limes for garnish
Fresh mint sprigs for garnish

1 Position a rack in the center of the oven and preheat the oven to 350 degrees. Lightly grease and flour three 9-inch round cake pans.

2 Combine the flour, pecans, coconut, and baking soda.

3 In a small bowl, combine the white chocolate and boiling water, stirring until smooth.

4 In a small bowl, using an electric mixer on high speed, beat the egg whites until stiff but not dry.

5 In a large bowl, using an electric mixer on medium speed, beat the butter and sugar until light and fluffy. Beat in the egg yolks. Beat in the vanilla extract and buttermilk. Gradually blend in the dry ingredients. Fold in the beaten egg whites. Scrape the mixture into the prepared pans and spread evenly.

6 Bake for 30 to 35 minutes, or until a cake tester inserted into the center comes out clean. Cool in the pans on wire racks for 5 minutes. Invert onto the racks to cool completely.

7 Make the mocha frosting.

8 To assemble, place one cake layer on a serving plate and spread with some of the frosting. Place the second cake layer on top and spread with frosting. Top with the third cake layer and spread frosting on the top and sides of the cake. Garnish with mint sprigs and lime slices.

292 ■ WHITE CHOCOLATE CAKE II

YIELD: *12 servings*
BAKING TIME: *20 minutes*

CAKE

2¹/₂ cups cake flour, sifted
1 teaspoon baking soda
4 ounces white chocolate, grated or finely chopped
¹/₂ cup boiling water
4 large eggs, separated
1 cup butter or margarine, at room temperature
2 cups granulated sugar
1 teaspoon almond extract
1 cup buttermilk
1 cup almonds, finely chopped
1 cup flaked coconut

TOPPING

1 cup vegetable shortening
1 cup powdered sugar
2 large egg whites, slightly beaten
¹/₂ cup sliced almonds for sprinkling

1 Position a rack in the center of the oven and preheat the oven to 350 degrees. Lightly grease and flour three 9-inch round cake pans.

2 To make the cake, combine the flour and baking soda.

3 In the top of a double boiler over simmering water, melt the white chocolate with the boiling water, stirring until smooth.

4 In a small bowl, using an electric mixer on high speed, beat the egg whites until stiff but not dry.

5 In a large bowl, using an electric mixer on medium speed, beat the butter and sugar until light and fluffy. Beat in the egg yolks. Beat in the white chocolate mixture. Beat in the almond extract and buttermilk. By hand, with as few strokes as possible, gradually blend in the dry ingredients. Stir in the almonds and coconut. Fold in the egg whites. Pour the mixture into the prepared pans.

6 Bake for 18 to 20 minutes, or until a cake tester inserted into the center comes out clean. Cool in the pans on wire racks for 10 minutes. Remove to the racks to cool completely.

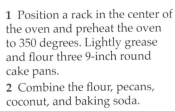

288

291

290

7 Meanwhile, to make the topping, in a medium bowl, using an electric mixer on medium speed, beat the shortening and powdered sugar until fluffy. Beat in the egg whites and continue beating until a spreadable consistency.

8 To assemble, using a serrated knife, slice the rounded tops off the cakes. Place one of the cake layers on a serving plate and spread with some of the topping. Place the second cake layer on top and spread with the topping. Top with the third cake layer and spread the topping over the top and sides of the cake. Sprinkle the sliced almonds over the top.

293 ■ WHITE CHOCOLATE CAKE WITH STRAWBERRIES

YIELD: *10 to 12 servings*
BAKING TIME: *25 minutes*
COOLING AND CHILLING TIME: *90 minutes*

CAKE

¾ cup heavy cream
3 ounces white chocolate, grated or finely chopped
2 teaspoons almond extract
1½ cups all-purpose flour
½ cup ground pecans
1 teaspoon baking powder
6 tablespoons butter or margarine, at room temperature
1 cup granulated sugar
3 large eggs, separated, plus 2 large egg whites, at room temperature

BUTTERCREAM FROSTING

1¼ cups heavy cream
¾ cup chopped pecans
½ cup granulated sugar
4 large egg yolks, at room temperature
2 tablespoons cornstarch or arrowroot
1 teaspoon vanilla extract
1 cup butter or margarine, at room temperature

FILLING

1 pint fresh strawberries
Sliced fresh strawberries for garnish

1 Position a rack in the center of the oven and preheat the oven to 325 degrees. Grease and flour two 9-inch round cake pans.

2 In a medium saucepan, over low heat, warm the heavy cream until bubbles form around the edge of the pan. Remove from the heat and add the white chocolate and almond extract, stirring until smooth.

3 Combine the flour, nuts, and baking powder.

4 In a large bowl, using an electric mixer on medium speed, beat the butter and ¾ cup of the sugar until light and fluffy. Add the egg yolks and beat until thick and light-colored. In three additions, blend in the dry ingredients, alternating with the chocolate mixture, beginning and ending with the dry ingredients.

5 In a medium bowl, using an electric mixer with clean beaters on high speed, beat the egg whites until foamy. Add the remaining ¼ cup sugar, a little at a time, and beat until stiff but not dry. Fold into the chocolate mixture one-half at a time. Scrape the mixture into the prepared pans and spread evenly.

6 Bake for 20 to 25 minutes, or until a cake tester inserted into the center comes out clean. Cool in the pans on wire racks for 10 minutes. Invert onto the racks to cool completely.

7 Meanwhile, to make the frosting, in a large saucepan, bring the cream and pecans to a boil. Remove from the heat and let cool for 1 hour.

8 In a medium bowl, using an electric mixer on medium speed, beat the sugar, egg yolks, and cornstarch until thick and light-colored.

287

283

285

292

9 Return the cream mixture to a simmer and beat into the egg yolk mixture. Return the mixture to the saucepan and continue cooking, stirring constantly, for 5 minutes, or until the mixture thickens. Remove from the heat and add the vanilla extract. Transfer to a bowl, and let cool 1 to 2 hours or until thickened.

10 Meanwhile, for the filling, clean and hull the strawberries. Chill until ready to use.

11 In a large bowl, using an electric mixer on medium speed, beat the butter until light and fluffy. Beat in the cool cream mixture, a little at a time, beating well after each addition.

12 To assemble the cake, place one cake layer on a serving plate and spread 1 cup of the buttercream over the top. Arrange the strawberries in a circular pattern over the top. Spread a very thin layer of the buttercream on the

294

293

bottom of the second cake layer. Place it, buttercream side down, on top of the strawberries. Press down gently. Spread the remaining buttercream over the top and sides of the cake. Chill for at least 1 hour before serving. Garnish with additional sliced strawberries.

BAKING NOTES: Almost any type of buttercream or whipped cream frosting can be used with this cake.

294 ■ WHITE CHOCOLATE CHEESECAKE I

YIELD: *12 servings*
BAKING TIME: *40 minutes*
CHILL TIME: *overnight*

FRUIT

1½ cups fresh raspberries
¾ cup fresh orange juice, strained
¼ cup granulated sugar
3 tablespoons currants
2 tablespoons raspberry liqueur
1 tablespoon grated orange zest
½ teaspoon ground cinnamon

CRUST

Graham Cracker Crust (see page 284)

FILLING

6 ounces white chocolate, grated or finely chopped
16 ounces cream cheese, at room temperature
1 container (8 ounces) cottage cheese, strained to remove liquid
¾ cup granulated sugar
4 large eggs

White Chocolate Curls (see page 422) for garnish
Fresh berries for garnish

1 To make the fruit, in a saucepan over medium heat, combine all of the ingredients. Simmer for 8 to 10 minutes, or until the mixture thickens. Pour into a blender container and blend on high speed for 3 to 5 seconds until pureed. Strain into a bowl and cool.

2 Preheat the oven to 350 degrees. Lightly grease an 8 or 9-inch springform pan.

3 Make the graham cracker crust and press it onto the bottom of the prepared pan.

4 To make the filling, melt the white chocolate (see page 13). Remove from the heat.

5 In a medium bowl, using an electric mixer on medium speed, beat the cream cheese and cottage cheese until smooth. Beat in the sugar. Beat in the eggs, one at a time, beating well after each addition. Beat in the melted white chocolate. Pour half of the filling mixture into the prepared pan and spread evenly. Spread half of the raspberry mixture evenly over the top of the filling mixture. Repeat with the remaining filling and fruit mixture. With a small knife, swirl through the batter. Once or twice will do it. Do not overmix.

6 Bake for 35 to 40 minutes, until the edges are set and golden in color. Cool in the pan on a wire rack. Chill overnight.

7 To serve, remove the side of the pan and garnish with the white chocolate curls and fresh berries.

295 ■ WHITE CHOCOLATE CHEESECAKE II

YIELD: *16 servings*
BAKING TIME: *105 minutes*
CHILL TIME: *8 hours*

CHEESECAKE

Chocolate Cookie Crumb Crust (see page 267)
16 ounces cream cheese, at room temperature
1 cup granulated sugar
1 tablespoon cornstarch
3 large eggs
2 tablespoons fresh lemon juice
1½ teaspoons chocolate or vanilla extract
¼ teaspoon salt
3 cups sour cream

WHITE CHOCOLATE FROSTING

9 ounces white chocolate, grated or finely chopped
12 ounces cream cheese, at room temperature
¾ cup butter or margarine, at room temperature
1½ tablespoons lemon juice

CHERRY TOPPING

½ cup granulated sugar

1½ tablespoons cornstarch or
    arrowroot
1 can (16 ounces) tart pitted red
    cherries
1 teaspoon almond extract

1 Make the crumb crust. Press evenly onto the bottom of a 10-inch springform pan lined with waxed paper. Chill for 1 hour.

2 Position a rack in the center of the oven and preheat the oven to 350 degrees.

3 In a large bowl, using an electric mixer on medium speed, beat the cream cheese and sugar until smooth. Beat in the cornstarch. Beat in the eggs, one at a time, beating well after each addition. Beat in the lemon juice, chocolate extract, and salt. Fold in the sour cream. Pour the mixture into the prepared pan.

Set the pan in a large roasting pan and place on the oven rack. Pour boiling water into the roasting pan until it comes halfway up the sides of the springform pan.

4 Bake for 45 minutes, or until firm. Turn off the oven and leave the cheesecake undisturbed for 1 hour. Cool in the pan on a wire rack. Cover and chill for at least 8 hours.

5 Carefully remove the side of the pan. Transfer to a servng plate leaving the waxed paper in place.

6 To make the frosting, melt the chocolate (see page 13). Remove from the heat.

7 In a large bowl, using an electric mixer on medium speed, beat the cream cheese until smooth. On high speed, beat in the butter and lemon juice. Beat in the melted chocolate. Reserve 1 cup of the frosting. Spread the remaining frosting evenly over the top and sides of the cheesecake.

8 Spoon the reserved frosting

into a pastry bag fitted with a star tip. Pipe the frosting in a decorative pattern around the top and base of the cake.

9 To make the cherry topping, in a medium saucepan, over medium heat, stir the sugar, cornstarch, and ⅓ cup of juice from the can of cherries until thoroughly blended. Stir in the cherries. Bring to a simmer, stirring constantly, until very thick. Remove from the heat and stir in the almond extract. Cool to room temperature. Spoon the filling over the top of the cake and inside the design created by the piped frosting.

BAKING NOTES: Blackberries, raspberries, or strawberries can be used in place of the cherries. Add a few drops of red food coloring to the topping if desired.

296 ■ YUM YUM CUPCAKES

YIELD: *12 cupcakes*
BAKING TIME: *25 minutes*

FILLING

8 ounces cream cheese, at room
    temperature
⅓ cup powdered sugar
1 large egg
6 ounces semisweet chocolate,
    grated or finely chopped
Pinch of salt

CUPCAKES

4 ounces unsweetened chocolate,
    grated or finely chopped
1½ cups all-purpose flour
¼ cup Dutch processed cocoa
    powder
1 teaspoon baking powder

½ teaspoon salt
1 cup granulated sugar
½ cup canola oil
1 tablespoon cider vinegar
1 cup skim milk
1 teaspoon crème de cacao

1 Position a rack in the center of the oven and preheat the oven to 375 degrees. Line twelve 2½-inch muffin cups with paper baking cups.

2 To make the filling, in a large bowl, using an electric mixer on medium speed, beat the cream cheese and powdered sugar until smooth. Beat in the egg. Beat in the chocolate and salt.

3 To make the cupcakes, combine the chocolate, flour, cocoa powder, baking powder, and salt.

4 In a large bowl, using an electric mixer on medium speed, beat the sugar, oil, and vinegar until thick and smooth. Beat in the milk and crème de cacao. By hand, gradually blend in the dry ingredients, mixing until smooth. Fill each of the prepared muffin pan cups half full. Drop a rounded teaspoon of the filling into the center of each cup.

5 Bake for 20 to 25 minutes, or until the top springs back when lightly pressed. Remove the cupcakes from the pan and cool on wire racks.

BAKING NOTES: These cupcakes do not need frosting.

296

Candy

297 ■ ALMOND BRITTLE

MAKES 1½ TO 2 POUNDS

2 cups granulated sugar
⅔ cup water
⅓ cup light corn syrup
¼ cup butter
½ cup unsweetened chocolate, grated or finely chopped
1 teaspoon chocolate extract
½ teaspoon baking soda
1½ cups almonds, coarsely chopped

1 Grease a 15½ by 10½-inch jelly-roll pan.

2 In a saucepan, over medium heat, combine the sugar, water, corn syrup, and butter. Insert a candy thermometer and cook, without stirring, until 300 degrees. Remove from the heat. Quickly stir in the chocolate, chocolate extract, baking soda, and almonds. Pour the mixture onto the prepared pan and spread it out to the sides of the pan. Cool in the pan until hard. Break into pieces.

BAKING NOTES: The secret of this recipe is to spread the brittle very thinly.

298 ■ BAÑO

MAKES 1½ TO 2 POUNDS
CHILL TIME: *1 hour*

1¼ cups milk
3 ounces unsweetened chocolate, grated or finely chopped
3 cups granulated sugar
3 tablespoons butter
1 tablespoon white cornmeal
¼ teaspoon salt

1 Grease an 8-inch square pan.

2 In a saucepan over medium heat, combine the milk and chocolate, stirring until smooth and well blended. Add the sugar, butter, cornmeal, and salt. Insert a candy thermometer and cook until 238 degrees. Immediately pour the mixture into the prepared pan. When cool enough to handle, cut into small rectangles. Remove from the pan and roll into little pencil-shaped rolls. Place on a baking sheet, cover and chill for 1 hour, or until firm. Wrap each candy in waxed paper or plastic wrap.

299 ■ BAVARIAN MINTS

MAKES 1½ TO 2 POUNDS
CHILL TIME: *1 hour*

12 ounces semisweet chocolate, grated or finely chopped
12 ounces unsweetened chocolate, grated or finely chopped
4½ cups dry fondant (see Baking notes)
1 cup heavy cream
2½ tablespoons light corn syrup
3 drops peppermint oil

1 Lightly grease a 13 by 9-inch pan.

2 In the top of a double boiler over simmering water, melt the chocolates, stirring until smooth. Remove from the heat.

3 In a large bowl, combine the fondant, cream, corn syrup, and peppermint oil. Using an electric mixer on medium speed, beat the fondant mixture for 12 to 15 minutes, or until smooth. On low speed, beat in the chocolate, pouring it in a thin stream. Scrape the mixture into the prepared pan and spread evenly. Cover and and chill for 1 hour, or until firm. Cut into squares.

BAKING NOTES: This same mixture can also be made into small rounds by dropping them by the teaspoonful onto a waxed paper-lined baking sheet. Dry fondant is a commercial baking product that should be available at most stores that sell candy-making supplies. Caution: use peppermint oil sparingly.

300 ■ BITTERSWEET CHOCOLATE TRUFFLES

MAKES 4 TO 5 DOZEN
CHILL TIME: *14 hours*

1 pound unsweetened chocolate, grated or finely chopped
1¼ cups heavy cream
2 tablespoons butter or margarine, at room temperature
2 tablespoons crème de cacao
4 tablespoons Dutch processed cocoa powder for dusting hands
1 recipe Dipping Chocolate (see page 186)

1 Melt the chocolate (see page 13). Remove from the heat. Transfer to a large bowl.

2 In a saucepan over low heat, heat the cream until bubbles start to form around the sides of the pan. Add the cream to the chocolate and stir until smooth. Add the butter and stir until blended. Stir in the crème de

298

297

299

cacao. Cover and let stand at room temperature for 1 hour. Chill for 4 hours, or until thickened but not completely set.

3 Line two baking sheets with waxed paper.

4 Fill a pastry bag fitted with a large, plain tip with the chocolate mixture. Pipe out mounds 1 inch in diameter onto the prepared pans. Cover and chill for 6 to 8 hours.

5 Dust your hands with cocoa powder and roll the chilled mounds into balls. Place on the pans and chill for 2 hours.

6 Make a half recipe of the dipping chocolate. Line two more baking sheets with waxed paper.

7 To dip, using a bamboo skewer or a fondue fork, dip half the chilled truffles into the chocolate, coating them completely. Place on the prepared pan. Chill for 1 hour, or until set.

8 Make another half recipe of dipping chocolate and coat and chill the remaining truffles as directed.

9 Place the truffles in an airtight container and refrigerate until serving. To serve, let come to room temperature and place in miniature paper candy cups.

BAKING NOTES: Truffles will keep in an airtight container in the refrigerator for up to 1 month.

301 ■ BLACK AND WHITE SQUARES

MAKES 2 TO 2½ POUNDS
CHILL TIME: *1 hour*

½ cup butter or margarine
2 ounces unsweetened chocolate, grated or finely chopped
2 large egg whites
3 cups powdered sugar
2½ cups flaked coconut
1 teaspoon almond extract
1 cup All-Bran™ cereal

1 Line a 9 by 5-inch loaf pan with waxed paper.

2 In the top of a double boiler over simmering water, melt the butter and chocolate, stirring until smooth. Remove from the heat.

3 In a small bowl, whisk the egg whites until foamy.

4 In a large bowl, combine the powdered sugar, coconut, beaten egg whites, almond extract, and chocolate mixture, blending until thoroughly mixed. Press half of the mixture onto the bottom of the prepared pan.

5 To the mixture in the bowl, add the cereal and press onto the top of the mixture in the pan. Place a piece of waxed paper on top and weight with dried beans or uncooked rice. Chill for 1 hour, or until firm. Remove the waxed paper and beans. Cut into squares.

302 ■ BROWN AND WHITE TRUFFLES

MAKES 2 TO 2½ POUNDS
CHILL TIME: *2 hours*

BROWN TRUFFLES

8 ounces unsweetened chocolate, grated or finely chopped
8 ounces semisweet chocolate, grated or finely chopped
1 can (14 ounces) sweetened condensed milk
½ cup white chocolate sprinkles for rolling

WHITE TRUFFLES

1 large egg white
2 tablespoons heavy cream
1 tablespoon crème de cacao
1 teaspoon chocolate extract
5 cups powdered sugar
½ cup chocolate sprinkles for rolling

1 To make the brown truffles, in the top of a double boiler over simmering water, melt the chocolates, stirring until smooth. Stir in the condensed milk. Remove from the heat and cool until thickened.

2 Using a teaspoon or melon baller, scoop up the cooled chocolate mixture and roll it into 2-inch balls. Roll each ball in the white chocolate sprinkles. Place on a baking sheet, cover, and chill for 1 hour, or until ready to assemble the truffles.

300

301

302

3 To make the white truffles, in a small bowl, using an electric mixer on high speed, beat the egg white until foamy. On low speed, beat in the cream, crème de cacao, and chocolate extract. Gradually blend in the powdered sugar to make a thick dough. Knead until smooth. Cover and let stand at room temperature for 1 hour, or until cooled.

4 When the white mixture is cool, use a tablespoon to scoop up the mixture and roll into 2-inch balls. Roll each ball in the chocolate sprinkles until well coated. Place on a baking sheet, cover and chill for 1 hour, or until ready to assemble the truffles.

5 To assemble, cut each ball in half, and reassemble, pressing together half of a white ball and half of a brown ball. Cover and chill for 1 hour, or until serving.

BAKING NOTES: The use of a melon baller or a very small size ice cream scoop could be helpful in making the balls. Owing to the raw egg white used in this recipe, keep refrigerated at all times, and for no longer than 1 week.

303 ▪ BUTTERMILK HAZELNUT FUDGE

MAKES 2 TO 2½ POUNDS

2 cups granulated sugar
1 cup buttermilk
3 ounces unsweetened chocolate, grated or finely chopped
2 tablespoons butter or margarine
1½ teaspoons crème de cacao or hazelnut liqueur
Pinch of salt
¾ cup hazelnuts, chopped

1 Lightly grease a 9-inch square pan.

2 In a saucepan over low heat, combine the sugar, buttermilk, and chocolate, stirring until smooth and the sugar is dissolved. Insert a candy thermometer and cook until 238 degrees. Remove from the heat and add the butter. Let cool until 110 degrees, and add the

crème de cacao, salt, and hazelnuts. Using a wooden spoon, beat until the mixture loses its gloss. Pour into the prepared pan and spread evenly. Cool until set. Cut into squares.

304 ▪ CHOCOLATE ALMOND BARK

MAKES ¾ POUND

1 cup granulated sugar
3 ounces unsweetened chocolate, grated or finely chopped
1 teaspoon chocolate or vanilla extract
1 cup slivered almonds

1 Line a baking sheet with waxed paper.

2 In the top of a double boiler over simmering water, stir the sugar until melted. Add the chocolate and chocolate extract, stirring until smooth and blended. Remove from heat and stir in the almonds. Immediately scrape onto the prepared pan. Spread evenly. Cool in the pan until set. Break into pieces.

305 ▪ CHOCOLATE ALMOND TRUFFLES

MAKES ALMOST 1 POUND
CHILL TIME: 1 hour

1 ounce unsweetened chocolate, grated or finely chopped
8 ounces semisweet chocolate, grated or finely chopped
¾ cup heavy cream
Pinch of salt
1 teaspoon crème de cacao
¼ cup ground almonds for coating

1 In the top of a double boiler over simmering water, melt the chocolates, stirring until smooth. Stir in the cream and salt and cook for 15 minutes. Remove from the heat and stir in the crème de cacao. Beat with a spoon until the mixture thickens. Chill for 1 hour, or until the mixture is firm but not completely hardened.

2 Using a teaspoon or melon baller, scoop up the mixture and roll it into 1-inch balls. Roll each truffle in the ground almonds until well coated. Place the balls in miniature paper candy cups. Store in an airtight container until serving.

306 ▪ CHOCOLATE APRICOT NUT CLUSTERS

MAKES 1½ TO 2 POUNDS
CHILL TIME: 30 minutes

6 ounces semisweet chocolate, grated or finely chopped
6 ounces unsweetened chocolate, grated or finely chopped
1 cup dried apricots, finely diced
1 cup chopped almonds or hazelnuts

1 Line two baking sheets with waxed paper.

2 In the top of a double boiler over simmering water, melt the chocolates, stirring until smooth. Remove from the heat and stir in the apricots and almonds until blended and coated with chocolate.

3 Drop the mixture, by teaspoonfuls, 1 inch apart onto the prepared pan. Chill for 30 minutes or until hardened. Store in airtight container for one week before using.

BAKING NOTES: Spoon the candy into miniature paper candy cups instead of onto a baking sheet if desired.

309

307

306

307 ■ CHOCOLATE BALLS

MAKES 2 TO 2½ POUNDS
CHILL TIME: *1 hour*

2 ounces unsweetened chocolate, grated or finely chopped
2 ounces semisweet chocolate, grated or finely chopped
1 teaspoon butter or margarine
⅓ cup powdered sugar
⅓ cup Almond Paste (see page 394)
1 tablespoons coffee liqueur
¼ cup Cocoa Sugar (see page 407) for coating

1 In the top of a double boiler over simmering water, melt the chocolates, stirring until smooth. Stir in the butter until blended. Remove from the heat and stir in the powdered sugar and almond paste. Stir in the liqueur until blended.

2 Using a teaspoon or a melon baller, scoop up pieces of the mixture and roll into small balls. Roll each ball in the cocoa sugar. Place the balls on a baking sheet lined with waxed paper, cover, and chill for 1 hour, or until hard.

308 ■ CHOCOLATE BONBONS

MAKES 1½ TO 2 POUNDS
CHILL TIME: *2 hours*

BONBONS

1 ounce unsweetened chocolate, grated or finely chopped
2 ounces semisweet chocolate, grated or finely chopped
⅓ cup butter or margarine
¼ cup heavy cream
1½ teaspoons crème de cacao
3 cups powdered sugar

DIPPING CHOCOLATE

2 ounces unsweetened chocolate, grated or finely chopped
2 ounces semisweet chocolate, grated or finely chopped

1 To make the bonbons, in the top of a double boiler over simmering water, melt the chocolates, stirring until smooth. Add the butter and stir until blended. Remove from the heat. Add the cream and crème de cacao and

stir constantly until smooth. Gradually blend in the powdered sugar. Using a teaspoon or melon baller, scoop up the mixture and roll into balls 1½ to 2 inches in diameter. Place the bonbons on a baking sheet lined with waxed paper. Cover and chill for 1 hour, or until firm.

2 Meanwhile, to make the dipping chocolate, in the top of a double boiler over simmering water, melt the chocolates, stirring until smooth. Remove from the heat.

3 Using a bamboo skewer or a fondue fork, dip the bonbons in the melted chocolate, coating them completely. Place on a waxed paper-lined baking sheet and remove the skewer. Using a spoon, place a drop of chocolate on the tiny hole left by the skewer. Chill about 1 hour, or until hard. Store the bonbons in the refrigerator.

309 ■ CHOCOLATE BONBON CUPS

MAKES 1½ POUNDS
CHILL TIME: *30 minutes*

8 ounces semisweet chocolate, grated or finely chopped
1 cup powdered sugar, sifted twice
1 tablespoon milk
1 tablespoon light corn syrup
½ cup candied fruit, finely chopped
1 teaspoon raspberry or banana extract
2 tablespoons butter or margarine

1 Place 36 miniature paper or aluminum foil candy cups on a baking sheet.

2 In the top of a double boiler over simmering water, melt 4 ounces of the chocolate, stirring constantly until smooth. Remove from the heat. Stir in the powdered sugar, milk, and corn syrup. Stir in the candied fruit and raspberry extract. Spoon this mixture into the prepared cups and chill for 30 minutes, or until firm.

3 Meanwhile, in the top of a double boiler over simmering water, melt the remaining 4

ounces of chocolate and the butter, stirring until smooth. Remove from the heat and cool slightly. Spoon into the chilled candy cups. Chill until firm. Store in a cool place until serving.

BAKING NOTES: For a dark and white chocolate combination, use 4 ounces of semisweet chocolate for the bottom layer, substitute 4 ounces of white chocolate for the top layer of chocolate and omit the butter.

310 ■ CHOCOLATE BRITTLE

MAKES 2 TO 2½ POUNDS

2 ounces semisweet chocolate, grated or finely chopped
2 cups granulated sugar
2/3 cup light corn syrup
1/2 cup water
1/4 teaspoon salt
1 cup peanuts
1 teaspoon crème de cacao

1 Grease two baking sheets or a large marble slab.

2 Melt the chocolate (see page 13). Remove from the heat.

3 In a saucepan, over low heat, combine the sugar, corn syrup, water, and salt, stirring until the sugar is dissolved. Insert a candy thermometer and cook until 275 degrees. Remove from the heat and cool slightly. Stir in the melted chocolate, peanuts, and crème de cacao just until mixed.

4 Pour onto the prepared baking sheet and spread evenly with an oiled metal spatula. Do not scrape out the saucepan. When the candy is cool enough to handle, use the spatula to lift up the candy. Using your fingers, pull the candy as thin as you can. Cool in the pan until hard. Break into pieces.

BAKING NOTES: Any type of nut can be used for this recipe. For a coffee pecan-flavored brittle, use pecans and substitute coffee liqueur for the crème de cacao.

311 ■ CHOCOLATE BUTTERSCOTCH CLUSTERS

MAKES 1¼ POUNDS

1 cup semisweet chocolate chips
1 cup butterscotch-flavored chips
2 tablespoons creamy peanut butter
4 cups Rice Crispies™

1 Line a baking sheet with waxed paper and lightly grease the paper.

2 In the top of a double boiler over simmering water, melt the chocolate chips, butterscotch chips, and peanut butter, stirring until smooth and well blended. Remove from the heat and add the cereal, stirring until all of the cereal is well coated.

3 Drop by teaspoonfuls onto the prepared pan. Cool at room temperature until firm.

312 ■ CHOCOLATE BUTTERSCOTCH DROPS

MAKES 1½ POUNDS

1 cup semisweet chocolate chips
1 cup butterscotch chips
1 can (7 ounces) unsalted peanuts, finely chopped
1 cup puffed rice cereal

1 Line two baking sheets with waxed paper.

2 In the top of a double boiler over simmering water, combine the chocolate and butterscotch chips, stirring until melted and smooth. Stir in the peanuts and cereal.

3 Drop the mixture by rounded teaspoonfuls onto the prepared pans. Chill until firm. Store in airtight container.

313 ■ CHOCOLATE CARAMELS

MAKES 5 TO 6 POUNDS

3 cups granulated sugar
2 cups sweetened condensed milk
1 cup water
1/2 cup corn syrup
3 ounces unsweetened chocolate, grated or finely chopped
3 ounces semisweet chocolate, grated or finely chopped
6 tablespoons butter or margarine

1 Lightly grease a 15½ by 10½-inch jelly-roll pan.

2 In a saucepan over low heat, combine the sugar, condensed milk, water, corn syrup, chocolates, and butter, stirring constantly until smooth. Bring to a boil. Reduce the heat to

310

311

312

315

medium-low. Insert a candy thermometer and cook until 235 degrees. Remove from the heat. Pour into the prepared pan and spread evenly.   Cool until firm. Cut into squares with a sharp knife.

314 ■ CHOCOLATE CARAMELS WITH HONEY

MAKES 4 TO 5 POUNDS

4 ounces semisweet chocolate, grated or finely chopped
3 cups granulated sugar
2 cups heavy cream
1/2 cup light corn syrup
1/2 pound honey comb
3 tablespoons butter or margarine
1/2 cup walnuts, chopped (optional)
2 teaspoon Caramella liqueur

1 Lightly grease a 13 by 9-inch pan.
2 Melt the chocolate (see page 13). Remove from the heat.
3 In a medium saucepan, over medium heat, combine the

sugar, 1 cup of the cream, corn syrup, honey comb, and butter. Bring to a boil. Reduce the heat to medium-low. Insert a candy thermometer and cook until 230 degrees. Add the remaining 1 cup cream and melted chocolate and cook until 248 degrees. Remove from the heat and stir in the walnuts and liqueur. Immediately pour into the prepared pan and cool until firm. Cut into squares.

315 ■ CHOCOLATE COCONUT DROPS

MAKES 2 TO 2 1/4 POUNDS

2 ounces semisweet chocolate, grated or finely chopped
1 can (14 ounces) sweetened condensed milk
2 cups flaked coconut
1/2 cup almonds, chopped

1 Position a rack in the center of the oven and preheat the oven to 350 degrees.
2 Melt the chocolate (see page 13). Remove from the heat and stir in the condensed milk. Fold in the coconut and almonds and stir until well coated. Drop by teaspoonfuls onto an ungreased baking sheet.

3 Place the baking sheet in the oven, turn off the oven, and let the candies set for 15 minutes, or until they have a glazed appearance. Remove from oven and cool completely.

316 ■ CHOCOLATE CORN FLAKE DROPS

MAKES 1 POUND
CHILL TIME: 1 hour

6 ounces semisweet chocolate, grated or finely chopped
1 cup corn flake cereal
1 cup salted peanuts
1/2 cup flaked coconut
1 teaspoon chocolate or vanilla extract

1 Line a baking sheet with waxed paper.
2 Melt the chocolate (see page 13). Remove from the heat. Stir in the cereal, peanuts, coconut, and chocolate extract. Drop by teaspoonfuls onto the prepared baking sheet. Chill for 1 hour, or until firm.

317 ■ CHOCOLATE-COVERED CHERRIES I

MAKES 25 CHERRIES
RESTING TIME: 6 months

25 fresh pitted cherries with stems
2 cups cherry liqueur
3 cups granulated sugar
1 cup water
1/2 teaspoon almond extract
1 recipe Dipping Chocolate (see page 186)

1 Carefully wipe the cherries with a damp cloth, being careful not to break off the stems. In a small bowl, pour 1/2 cup of the liqueur and dip each cherry to coat. Place in a container with an airtight cover.
2 Combine the sugar, water, and almond extract in a saucepan and heat until the sugar has completely dissolved. Remove from the heat and add the remaining 1 1/2 cups of liqueur. Pour the syrup over the cherries in an air tight container, seal, and put aside at room temperature for 6 months.

313

316

317

314

3 Make the dipping chocolate.

4 Remove the cherries from the liqueur and reserve the liqueur for another use. Dry each cherry with a paper towel and place on a baking sheet lined with waxed paper.

5 Dip each cherry in the chocolate, being sure the cherry is completely coated, including the stem joint. Place on the baking sheet and let stand at room temperature until hard. Store between layers of waxed paper in an airtight container.

BAKING NOTES: Leftover dipping chocolate can be reused for other recipes. Some candy makers remove the cherry stems after dipping. If this is done, spoon a small amount of dipping chocolate to seal the tiny hole where the stem pierced the chocolate.

318 ■ CHOCOLATE-COVERED CHERRIES II

MAKES 10 TO 15 CHERRIES
FREEZE TIME: *1 hour*

1 jar (8 ounces) maraschino cherries with stems, drained
½ cup fresh orange juice, strained
1 teaspoon maraschino liqueur
3 ounces semisweet chocolate, grated or finely chopped

1 Place the cherries in a small bowl. Add the orange juice and liqueur. Let stand for 30 minutes. Cover and freeze for 1 hour.

2 Meanwhile, melt the chocolate (see page 13). Remove from the heat.

3 Drain the frozen cherries and wipe dry with paper towels. Dip the frozen cherries in the chocolate. Place each cherry on a waxed paper-lined baking sheet. Let stand at room temperature until firm. Place in the refrigerator until hard.

BAKING NOTES: Any kind of liqueur can be used in place of the maraschino liqueur. Coating chocolate (see page 14) may also be used in place of the semisweet chocolate listed above.

319 ■ CHOCOLATE-COVERED STRAWBERRIES

MAKES 36 STRAWBERRIES

4 ounces semisweet chocolate, grated or finely chopped
5 tablespoons butter or margarine
1 tablespoon light corn syrup
36 fresh strawberries

1 Line a baking sheet with waxed paper.

2 Thoroughly wash, dry, and remove all the green leaves from the strawberries.

3 In the top of a double boiler over simmering water, melt the chocolate and butter with the corn syrup, stirring constantly until smooth. Remove from the heat and place the saucepan in a larger pan of warm water.

4 Holding the strawberries by the tops, dip each one into the chocolate mixture and place on the prepared pan. Let stand at room temperature until hard.

BAKING NOTES: A bamboo skewer can be used to dip the strawberries. Do not dip the strawberries straight down into the chocolate, but at an angle. For a very special occasion, dark chocolate or white chocolate leaves (see page 422) can be used to decorate the top of each strawberry.

320 ■ CHOCOLATE CREAMS

MAKES 2½ TO 3 POUNDS
CHILL TIME: *1 hour*

2 pounds milk chocolate, grated or finely chopped
1 cup heavy cream
1 recipe Dipping Chocolate (see page 186)

1 Lightly grease a 13 by 9-inch pan.

2 To make the cream centers, melt the chocolate (see page 13). Transfer the melted chocolate to a large bowl.

3 In a small saucepan, over low heat, using a candy thermometer, heat the cream to 130

318

319

320

321

degrees. Add the hot cream to the chocolate. Using an electric mixer on medium speed, whip for 3 to 5 minutes, or until thickened. Cover with a damp cloth and freeze for 5 to 8 minutes, or until thickened. Whip on medium speed for 3 to 5 minutes, or until thicker. Pour into the prepared pan and chill 1 hour, or until just set.

4 Using a teaspoon or melon baller, scoop up the chocolate mixture and roll into ¾-inch balls. Place on a waxed paper-lined baking sheet and refrigerate until ready to use.

5 Make the dipping chocolate.

6 To dip, using a bamboo skewer or a fondue fork, dip the centers into the dipping chocolate, coating them completely. Place the coated centers on a waxed paper-lined baking sheet. Keep in the refrigerator.

321 ■ CHOCOLATE CREAM CHEESE FUDGE

MAKES 1 POUND
CHILL TIME: *1 hour*

2 ounces semisweet chocolate, grated or finely chopped
3 ounces cream cheese, at room temperature
1 teaspoon evaporated milk
2 cups powdered sugar
1 teaspoon chocolate extract
1 cup chopped almonds

1 Lightly grease an 8-inch square pan.

2 Melt the chocolate (see page 13). Remove from the heat and, using an electric mixer, beat in the cream cheese and evaporated milk. Beat in the powdered sugar until dissolved. Beat in the chocolate extract. Fold in the almonds. Scrape the mixture into the prepared pan and spread evenly. Chill for 1 hour, or until set. Cut into squares.

322 ■ CHOCOLATE-DIPPED ALMONDS

MAKES 36 ALMONDS

2 ounces semisweet chocolate, grated or finely chopped
1 tablespoon plus 1 teaspoon butter or margarine
3 dozen raw whole almonds

1 Line a baking sheet with waxed paper.

2 In the top of a double boiler over simmering water, melt the chocolate and butter, stirring until smooth. Remove from the heat.

3 Dip only half of each almond in the chocolate and place on the prepared pan. Chill until set. Dip the other half of each almond in the chocolate if desired and chill until set.

323 ■ CHOCOLATE-DIPPED FUDGE CENTERS

MAKES 2½ TO 3 POUNDS
CHILL TIME: *1 hour*

4 cups granulated sugar
2 cups heavy cream
6 ounces semisweet chocolate, grated or finely chopped
¼ cup light corn syrup
Pinch of salt
1 recipe Dipping Chocolate (see page 186)

1 Lightly grease a 15½ by 10½-inch jelly-roll pan.

2 In a saucepan over low heat, combine the sugar, cream, chocolate, corn syrup, and salt, stirring until smooth. Insert a candy thermometer and cook until 235 degrees. Pour the mixture into the prepared pan and cool to lukewarm.

3 Using a metal spatula, work the candy in an under-and-over folding motion until it holds its shape. Form into ¾-inch balls and place on the prepared pan.

4 Make the dipping chocolate.

5 Using a bamboo skewer or a fondue fork, dip the centers into the chocolate, coating completely. Place the coated centers on a waxed paper-lined baking sheet. Cool for 1 hour or until set.

324 ■ CHOCOLATE DIVINITY

MAKES 5 POUNDS
CHILL TIME: *1 hour*

2 large egg whites
Pinch of salt
2½ cups granulated sugar
⅔ cup light corn syrup
½ cup water
⅓ cup Dutch processed cocoa powder
1 cup pecans, finely chopped
½ teaspoon Caramella liqueur

322

323

324

1 Lightly grease a 9-inch square pan.

2 In a medium bowl, using an electric mixer on high speed, beat the egg whites and salt until stiff peaks form.

3 In a saucepan, over medium-low heat, combine the sugar, corn syrup, and water, stirring constantly until the sugar is dissolved. Insert a candy thermometer and cook, without stirring, until 245 degrees. Remove from the heat.

4 Pouring it in a thin stream, beat the hot syrup into the beaten egg whites. Add the cocoa powder and beat until the mixture is very thick and it holds its shape when dropped from a spoon onto waxed paper. Stir in the pecans and Caramella. Scrape the mixture into the prepared pan and spread evenly. Chill for 1 hour, or until firm. Cut into squares.

BAKING NOTES: For thinner pieces of candy, use a 13 by 9-inch pan.

325 ■ CHOCOLATE FONDANT

MAKES 2 TO 2½ POUNDS

3 ounces unsweetened chocolate, grated or finely chopped
¾ cup water
2 cups granulated sugar
2 tablespoons light corn syrup
⅛ teaspoon salt
½ teaspoon chocolate extract

1 In a saucepan over low heat, melt the chocolate with the water, stirring until smooth. Add the sugar, corn syrup, and salt, stirring until the sugar is dissolved. Insert a candy thermometer and bring the mixture to a boil. Cook, stirring, until 236 degrees. Immediately pour onto a cold marble slab and cool to 110 degrees, without touching. Alternatively, pour into a 13 by 9-inch pan and place the pan in water at room temperature.

2 Using a metal spatula, work the fondant in an over-and-under folding motion until cool.

When cool enough to handle, knead until smooth. Knead in the chocolate extract and let stand, uncovered, until cool. Wrap in waxed paper or plastic wrap until ready to use.

BAKING NOTES: The fondant can be rolled into balls, or molded and dipped in chocolate as desired.

326 ■ CHOCOLATE FRUITCUPS

MAKES 2 TO 2½ POUNDS
CHILL TIME: *1 hour*

4 ounces unsweetened chocolate, grated or finely chopped
6 ounces semisweet chocolate, grated or finely chopped
1 cup powdered sugar
1 tablespoon heavy cream
1 tablespoon light corn syrup
½ cup dried apricots, finely chopped
1 teaspoon crème de cacao
2 tablespoons butter or margarine

1 Place 36 miniature paper candy cups on a baking sheet.

2 In the top of a double boiler over simmering water, melt the unsweetened and 4 ounces semisweet chocolate, stirring until smooth. Remove from the heat and mix in the powdered sugar, cream, and corn syrup. Stir in the apricots and crème de cacao. Spoon the mixture into the candy cups. Chill for 1 hour, or until set.

3 In the top of a double boiler over simmering water, melt the remaining 2 ounces semisweet chocolate and butter, stirring until smooth. Remove from the heat and cool slightly. Spoon into the cups over the apricot mixture. Chill for 1 hour, or until firm.

BAKING NOTES: Almost any kind of dried fruit can be used in place of the apricots, such as peaches, mixed fruit, raisins, a mix of raisins and nuts, etc.

327 ■ CHOCOLATE FUDGE

MAKES 5 POUNDS
CHILL TIME: *1 hour*

4½ cups granulated sugar
1½ cups evaporated milk
⅓ cup butter or margarine
½ teaspoon salt
4 cups miniature marshmallows
2 packages (12 ounces each) semisweet chocolate chips
1½ cups walnuts, chopped
1 teaspoon vanilla extract

1 Lightly grease a 13 by 9-inch pan.

2 In a heavy large saucepan, combine the sugar, evaporated milk, butter, and salt. Cook over medium heat, stirring, until smooth. Bring the mixture to a boil. Remove from the heat and add the marshmallows, chocolate chips, walnuts, and vanilla extract. Stir constantly until the marshmallows are melted. Pour into the prepared pan and chill for about 1 hour, or until set. Cut into squares.

BAKING NOTES: To speed up the cooling process, place the prepared pan with the mixture in a larger pan filled with ice cubes or cold water.

328

325

328 ■ CHOCOLATE FUDGE SUPREME

MAKES 1½ POUNDS

2 cups granulated sugar
2 ounces unsweetened chocolate, grated or finely chopped
2 ounces semisweet chocolate, grated or finely chopped
⅔ cup evaporated milk or heavy cream
2 tablespoons corn syrup
2 tablespoon butter or margarine
1 teaspoon chocolate or vanilla extract

1 Lightly grease 9-inch square pan.

2 In a saucepan over low heat, combine the sugar, chocolates, evaporated milk, corn syrup, and butter. Bring the mixture to a boil. Insert a candy thermometer and cook, stirring occasionally, until 234 degrees. Remove from the heat and cool. Using a wooden spoon, beat until the fudge loses its glossy sheen. Blend in the chocolate extract. Pour into the prepared pan and cool until set. Cut into squares.

329 ■ CHOCOLATE FUDGE WITH CHERRIES

MAKES 1½ POUNDS

2 cups granulated sugar
1 cup milk
½ teaspoon salt
2 ounces unsweetened chocolate, grated or finely chopped
2 tablespoons butter or margarine
1 teaspoon crème de cacao
½ cup walnuts, chopped
¼ cup candied cherries, finely chopped

1 Lightly grease a 13 by 9-inch pan.

2 In a saucepan over low heat, combine the sugar, milk, and salt, stirring until blended. Stir in the chocolate. Bring to a boil, stirring occasionally. Insert a candy thermometer and cook until 234 degrees. Remove from the heat and stir in the butter. Cool to 130 degrees.

3 Stir in the crème de cacao. Return to the heat and cook over medium heat until the mixture starts to thicken. Remove from the heat and cool. Fold in the walnuts and cherries. Immediately pour into the prepared pan and cool until set. Cut into squares.

330 ■ CHOCOLATE FUDGE WITH HONEY

MAKES 2 TO 2½ POUNDS

2 cups granulated sugar
⅔ cup heavy cream
½ cup plus 2 tablespoons butter or margarine
4 ounces semisweet chocolate, grated or finely chopped
3 tablespoons honey
¼ teaspoon vanilla extract

1 Lightly grease an 8 or 9-inch square pan.

2 In a saucepan over low heat, combine the sugar and cream, stirring until the sugar is dissolved. Add the butter, chocolate, and honey. Insert a candy thermometer, bring the mixture to a boil, and cook until 235 degrees. Immediately remove from the heat and place the pan in a larger pan of cold water. Cool until 110 degrees, without stirring.

3 Add the vanilla extract. Using a wooden spoon, beat the mixture until very thick. Pour into the prepared pan and cool until set. Cut into squares.

331 ■ CHOCOLATE FUDGE WITH MARSHMALLOWS AND NUTS

MAKES 4 TO 4½ POUNDS

4 cups granulated sugar
1 can (14 ounces) evaporated milk
1 cup butter, at room temperature
1½ cups semisweet chocolate chips
2 jars (7 ounces each) marshmallow creme
1 teaspoon chocolate or vanilla extract
1 cup walnuts, chopped

1 Lightly grease a 13 by 9-inch pan.

2 In a saucepan, combine the sugar, milk, and butter. Insert a candy thermometer and cook, stirring frequently, until 236 degrees. Remove from the heat and mix in the chocolate chips, marshmallow creme, and chocolate extract. Fold in the walnuts.

329

330

327

331

326

Pour into the prepared pan and cool until slightly set. Score the top into squares and cool completely. Cut into squares.

332 ■ CHOCOLATE FUDGE WITH WALNUTS

MAKES 1¼ TO 1½ POUNDS

2 cups granulated sugar
1 cup water
1 cup sweetened condensed milk
3 ounces unsweetened chocolate, grated or finely chopped
1 cup chopped walnuts

1 Lightly grease a 9-inch square pan.

2 In a heavy large saucepan, over medium heat, combine the sugar and water. Bring to a boil and simmer for 1 minute. Stir in the condensed milk. Insert a candy thermometer and cook until 235 degrees, stirring occasionally. Remove from the heat and cool for 10 to 15 minutes. Add the chocolate and walnuts. Using a wooden spoon, beat until thick. Pour into the prepared pan and cool until set. Cut into squares.

BAKING NOTES: For thinner pieces of fudge, use a 13 by 9-inch pan.

333 ■ CHOCOLATE HAZELNUT CLUSTERS

MAKES 2 POUNDS

9 ounces semisweet chocolate, grated or finely chopped
1½ cups hazelnuts
1 teaspoon instant espresso powder
1 teaspoon canola oil

1 Line a baking sheet with waxed paper.

2 Melt the chocolate (see page 13). Remove from the heat. Add the hazelnuts, espresso powder, and oil and stir until the nuts are well coated.

3 Drop the mixture by teaspoonfuls onto the prepared baking sheet. Let cool at room temperature until set. Store in an airtight container.

334 ■ CHOCOLATE HAZELNUT TRUFFLES

MAKES 36 TO 40 TRUFFLES
STANDING TIME: 14 hours
CHILL TIME: 1 hour

9 ounces semisweet chocolate, grated or finely chopped
¾ cup butter or margarine, diced
1 cup powdered sugar
¼ cup heavy cream
½ cup hazelnuts, finely chopped
¼ cup chocolate sprinkles for coating
¼ cup Cocoa Sugar (see page 407) for coating

1 In the top of a double boiler over simmering water, melt the chocolate and butter, stirring until smooth. Remove from the heat and stir in the powdered sugar, cream, and hazelnuts. Blend thoroughly but gently. Cover and let stand at room temperature for 12 to 14 hours, without stirring.

2 Using a teaspoon or melon baller, scoop up the mixture and roll it into 1-inch balls. Roll half of the balls in the chocolate sprinkles and half of the balls in the cocoa sugar until well coated. Place on a waxed paper-lined baking sheet and chill for 1 hour or until firm.

335 ■ CHOCOLATE LOGS

MAKES 1½ TO 1¾ POUNDS
CHILL TIME: 1 hour

2 ounces unsweetened chocolate, grated or finely chopped
½ cup light corn syrup
2 tablespoons butter or margarine
¾ cup powdered milk
1 teaspoon chocolate or vanilla extract
3 cups powdered sugar

1 In the top of a double boiler over simmering water, melt the chocolate, stirring until smooth. Stir in the corn syrup and butter. Stir in the powdered milk. Remove from the heat and stir in the chocolate extract. Gradually blend in the powdered sugar.

2 On a flat surface, knead the mixture until thoroughly blended. Form into a log ¾ inches in diameter. Cut into 2½-inch-long pieces. Place on a wax paper-lined baking sheet and chill for at least one hour. Wrap each log in waxed paper or plastic wrap.

BAKING NOTES: The logs can be rolled in chopped nuts or coconut before chilling and wrapping.

334
335
332
333

336 ■ CHOCOLATE MARZIPAN LOGS

MAKES 1¾ TO 2 POUNDS
CHILL TIME: *6 hours*

12 ounces sweetened chocolate, grated or finely chopped
½ cup heavy cream
¼ cup powdered sugar
7 ounces marzipan

1 Melt 6 ounces of the chocolate (see page 13). Remove from the heat.

2 In a small saucepan, over medium heat, bring the cream to a rolling boil. Whisk the cream into the melted chocolate. Pour the mixture into a large bowl, cover, and let stand at room temperature until thickened, about 3 hours.

3 On a flat surface dusted with powdered sugar, roll the marzipan out into a 12 by 6-inch rectangle. With a sharp knife, trim the rough edges, and cut in half to make two 12 by 3-inch rectangles. Place each rectangle on a waxed paper-lined baking sheet.

4 Fill a pastry bag fitted with a large plain tip with the cooled chocolate mixture. Pipe a straight line of the mixture lengthwise down each of the marzipan rectangles, leaving a ¼-inch border on the top and bottom. Moisten one long edge of each rectangle and roll the marzipan up and over the chocolate, sealing to enclose the cream. Cover the logs with waxed paper or plastic wrap and chill for at least 3 hours.

5 Melt the remaining 6 ounces of chocolate (see page 13). Remove from the heat. Using a dry pastry brush, paint the chocolate over the length of the logs. Let stand at room temperature until the chocolate is firm. Cut into ½ to ¾-inch slices. Chill until serving.

337 ■ CHOCOLATE MARZIPAN TRUFFLES

MAKES 1 TO 1½ POUNDS
CHILL TIME: *1 hour 30 minutes*

12 ounces semisweet chocolate, grated or finely chopped
1 pound marzipan
½ cup hazelnuts, finely ground
1 tablespoon amaretto
¼ cup Dutch processed cocoa powder for coating

1 Melt the chocolate (see page 13). Remove from the heat.

2 In a large bowl, crumble the marzipan. Beat in the melted chocolate to form a smooth paste. Blend in the hazelnuts and amaretto. Cover and refrigerate for 30 minutes, or until thick but not firm.

3 Using a teaspoon or melon baller, scoop up the mixture and roll it into 1-inch balls. Roll each truffle in the cocoa powder until well coated. Chill for 1 hour or until firm before serving.

338 ■ CHOCOLATE MINT FUDGE

MAKES 1½ TO 2 POUNDS

2 cups granulated sugar
1 cup light cream
4 ounces unsweetened chocolate, grated or finely chopped
1 tablespoon water
¼ cup honey
¼ cup green crème de menthe
2 tablespoons butter, at room temperature

1 Lightly grease an 8-inch square pan.

2 In a heavy large saucepan, over medium heat, combine the sugar and cream and bring to a boil. Remove from the heat and cool slightly. Stir in the chocolate. Stir in the water, honey, and crème de menthe. Return to the heat, insert a candy thermometer, and cook until 238 degrees. Add the butter and remove from the heat. Let cool to 110 degrees without stirring.

3 Using a wooden spoon, beat until creamy. Pour into the prepared pan and cool until set. Cut into bars.

339 ■ CHOCOLATE MOCHA FUDGE

MAKES 1½ TO 2 POUNDS

2 cups granulated sugar
1 cup heavy cream
2 ounces unsweetened chocolate, grated or finely chopped
1 teaspoon light corn syrup
Pinch of salt
2 tablespoons butter or margarine
1 cup pecans, finely chopped
1 teaspoon coffee liqueur

338

339

336

337

1 Lightly grease a 9-inch square pan.

2 In a saucepan over low heat, combine the sugar, cream, chocolate, corn syrup, salt, and butter. Insert a candy thermometer and cook until 235 degrees. Remove from the heat and place the pan in a larger pan of cold water. Cool to 130 degrees without stirring.

3 Add the pecans and liqueur. Using a wooden spoon, beat until the mixture begins to thicken. Pour into the prepared pan and cool until set. Cut into squares.

BAKING NOTES: For thinner pieces of fudge, used a 13 by 9-inch pan.

340 ■ CHOCOLATE NOUGAT WITH PISTACHIO NUTS

MAKES 1½ TO 2 POUNDS
STANDING TIME: *8 hours*

2 cups granulated sugar
¼ cup butter or margarine
1 cup light corn syrup
2 large egg whites
2 ounces unsweetened chocolate, grated or finely chopped
¾ cup pistachio nuts, chopped

1 Lightly grease an 8-inch square pan. Line the bottom of the pan with parchment paper.

2 In a medium saucepan, over low heat, melt the sugar and butter, stirring constantly. Add the corn syrup and bring to a boil. Cover and boil for 3 minutes, occasionally scraping down the sides of the pan. Remove the cover and insert a candy thermometer. Boil, uncovered, until 270 degrees.

3 Meanwhile, in a medium bowl, using an electric mixer on high speed, beat the egg whites until stiff peaks form. Pouring it in a thin stream, beat in the hot syrup. Return the mixture to the saucepan and cook, stirring occasionally, until 250 degrees. Remove from the heat.

4 Melt the chocolate (see page 13).

5 Mix the melted chocolate into the syrup mixture. Fold in the pistachio nuts and pour into the prepared pan. Cover with parchment paper, weight the top with dried beans or uncooked rice, and leave undisturbed for at least 8 hours, or until set.

6 Invert the nougat onto a flat surface, remove the parchment paper, and cut into squares. Wrap each piece in waxed paper or plastic wrap.

BAKING NOTES: The squares of nougat can be coated with dipping chocolate (see page 186).

341 ■ CHOCOLATE NUT CRUNCH

MAKES 1½ POUNDS

1¼ cups granulated sugar
1 cup whole almonds
¾ cup butter or margarine
¼ cup water
1½ teaspoons salt
½ teaspoon baking soda
½ cup chopped walnuts
⅓ cup semisweet chocolate chips
½ cup ground almonds

1 Grease a 15½ by 10½-inch jelly-roll pan.

2 In a saucepan, over medium heat, combine the sugar, whole almonds, butter, water, and salt. Bring to a boil. Insert a candy thermometer and simmer, stirring frequently, until 290 degrees.

3 Remove from the heat. Stir in the baking soda and walnuts. Immediately pour into the prepared pan. Sprinkle the chocolate chips over the top. Let stand for 3 minutes. Spread the melted chocolate chips over the top. Sprinkle with the ground almonds. Cool in the pan until set. Break into pieces.

342 ■ CHOCOLATE NUT TOFFEE

MAKES ¾ POUND

¾ cup packed light brown sugar
½ cup butter or margarine, at room temperature
½ cup ground pecans
1 teaspoon chocolate or vanilla extract
½ cup semisweet chocolate, grated or finely chopped

1 Lightly grease an 8 or 9-inch square pan.

2 In a saucepan, over low heat, combine the brown sugar and butter, stirring constantly until smooth. Insert a candy thermometer and cook, stirring constantly, until 270 degrees. Remove from the heat. Stir in the nuts and chocolate extract. Scrape into the prepared pan and spread evenly. Sprinkle the chocolate over the top. Let stand for 3 minutes. Spread the melted chocolate over the top. Cool completely in the pan until set. Break into pieces.

343 ■ CHOCOLATE ORANGE TRUFFLES

MAKES 12 TO 16
CHILL TIME: *1 hour*

12 ounces semisweet chocolate, grated or finely chopped
4 tablespoons butter or margarine, at room temperature
½ cup fresh orange juice, strained
1 tablespoon grated orange zest
1 cup walnuts, chopped for coating

1 Melt the chocolate (see page 13). Remove from the heat and place in a medium bowl. Using an electric mixer on medium speed, beat in the butter until fluffy. Beat in the orange juice and zest. Cover and chill until firm.

2 Using a tablespoon or melon baller, scoop up the truffle mixture and roll it into 1-inch balls. Roll each truffle in the chopped nuts until well coated. Place in self-sealing plastic bags and freeze until serving.

344 ■ CHOCOLATE PEANUT BRITTLE

MAKES 2 TO 2½ POUNDS

1½ cups shelled raw peanuts
1 cup packed light brown sugar
1 cup light corn syrup
2 tablespoons Dutch processed
    cocoa powder
1 teaspoon salt
1 tablespoon butter or margarine,
    at room temperature
1 teaspoon baking soda
1½ teaspoons crème de cacao

1 Grease a 15½ by 10½-inch jelly-roll pan.

2 In a large saucepan, over low heat, combine the peanuts, brown sugar, corn syrup, cocoa powder, and salt, stirring until the sugar is dissolved. Cover and cook for 3 minutes. Wash down the sugar crystals from the side of the pan with a pastry brush dipped in water. Insert a candy thermometer and cook until 280 degrees. Remove from the heat and immediately stir in the butter, baking soda, and crème de cacao.

3 Pour the mixture onto the prepared pan, and using an offset metal spatula or large serving spoon, spread out evenly into a thin layer. Cool in the pan until hard. Break into pieces.

345 ■ CHOCOLATE PEANUT SQUARES

MAKES 1 TO 1½ POUNDS
CHILL TIME: *1 hour*

2 cups old-fashioned oats
1 cup salted peanuts
1 jar (7 ounces) marshmallow
    creme
¼ cup plus 3 tablespoons peanut
    butter
2 tablespoons butter
4 ounces semisweet chocolate,
    grated or finely chopped

1 Lightly grease a 9-inch square pan.

2 In a large bowl, combine the oats and peanuts.

3 In the top of a double boiler over simmering water, combine the marshmallow creme, ¼ cup of the peanut butter, and butter. Cook, stirring occasionally, until smooth. Working quickly, add to the dry ingredients and blend to coat. Scrape the mixture into the prepared pan and spread evenly.

4 In the top of a double boiler over simmering water, combine the chocolate and remaining 3 tablespoons of peanut butter, stirring until smooth. Spread

this mixture evenly over the top of the cereal mixture in the pan. Chill for 1 hour, or until hard. Cut into squares.

346 ■ CHOCOLATE PECAN SLICES

MAKES 24 SLICES
CHILL TIME: *6½ hours*

2 ounces unsweetened chocolate,
    grated or finely chopped
1⅓ cups sweetened condensed
    milk
½ chopped pecans

1 In the top of a double boiler over simmering water, melt the chocolate, stirring until smooth. Stir in the condensed milk and cook for 5 minutes, or until slightly thickened. Remove from the heat and stir in ¼ cup of the pecans. Let cool 30 minutes, or until thick enough to hold its shape.

2 Scrape the mixture onto a piece of waxed paper. Use the waxed paper to form the mixture into a log. Roll the log in the remaining ¼ cup of the pecans. Wrap and chill for 4 to 6 hours, or until set. Cut into 24 slices.

340 341 342 343 344 346 347

BAKING NOTES: For best results, have the mixture cool and thickened enough to form into a log when it is poured onto the waxed paper.

347 ■ CHOCOLATE PEPPERMINT CANDY

MAKES ¾ TO 1 POUND
CHILL TIME: *1 hour*

4 ounces semisweet chocolate, grated or finely chopped
1½ cups crushed peppermint candies (½ pound)

1 Line a baking sheet with waxed paper.

2 Melt the chocolate (see page 13). Remove from the heat and stir in the candy.

3 Drop the mixture by teaspoonfuls onto the prepared pan. Chill until firm.

BAKING NOTES: Almost any hard candy that can be crushed can be substituted for the peppermint candy. Do not use a food processor to crush the candy, as this will make a powder out of the candy. Place the candy between two sheets of waxed paper and pound it with a food mallet or the bottom of a heavy pan.

348 ■ CHOCOLATE PINEAPPLE FUDGE

MAKES 1¼ POUNDS
CHILL TIME: *1 hour*

3 ounces semisweet chocolate, grated or finely chopped
¾ cup heavy cream
2 cups granulated sugar
¼ cup butter or margarine
Pinch of salt
1 teaspoon chocolate or vanilla extract
¼ cup diced candied pineapple
¼ cup diced candied papaya
⅔ cup chopped macadamia nuts

1 Lightly grease an 8 or 9-inch square pan.

2 In a saucepan over low heat, combine the chocolate and cream, stirring until smooth. Add the sugar, butter, and salt and stir until the sugar is dissolved. Bring to a boil. Insert a candy thermometer and simmer, without stirring, until 234 degrees.

3 Remove from the heat, beat until thickened, and stir in the extract, fruit, and nuts. Immediately pour into the prepared pan and spread evenly. Score into squares. Chill until firm. Cut into squares.

349 ■ CHOCOLATE POPCORN

MAKES 1½ POUNDS

3 ounces semisweet chocolate, grated or finely chopped
1½ cups granulated sugar
½ cup light corn syrup
¾ cup water
3 tablespoons butter or margarine
3 quarts air-popped popcorn
2 tablespoons powdered sugar

1 Melt the chocolate (see page 13). Remove from the heat.

2 In a medium saucepan, over medium heat, combine the sugar, corn syrup, and water, stirring until the sugar is dissolved. Insert a candy thermometer and cook until 270 degrees. Remove from the heat and add the butter and melted chocolate. Beat with a wooden spoon until well blended and thickened slightly.

350

351

352

353

347

348

349

3 Place the popcorn in a very large bowl. Mixing constantly with a wooden spoon, add the chocolate syrup mixture, pouring it in a thin stream over the popcorn. Continue mixing and sprinkle with the powdered sugar. Turn out onto a piece of waxed paper and separate into individual pieces.

BAKING NOTES: Hand pick the popcorn so there are no unpopped kernels.

350 ■ CHOCOLATE POTATO KISSES

MAKES 1 POUND
CHILL TIME: *4 hours*

2/3 cup hot mashed potatoes
2 tablespoons butter or margarine, melted
2 cups powdered sugar, sifted
2 1/2 tablespoons Dutch processed cocoa powder
1 teaspoon chocolate extract
Pinch of salt.
1/2 cup flaked coconut

1 Line a baking sheet with waxed paper.

2 Press the mashed potatoes through a ricer into a large bowl. Add the butter and powdered sugar and blend thoroughly. Blend in the cocoa powder. Add the chocolate extract, salt, and coconut.

3 Drop the mixture by teaspoonfuls onto the prepared pan. Chill for 2 to 4 hours or until set. Store in a airtight container.

351 ■ CHOCOLATE RAISIN KISSES

MAKES 2 POUNDS
CHILL TIME: *4 hours*

2 ounces unsweetened chocolate, grated or finely chopped
1 can (14 ounces) sweetened condensed milk
1 1/2 cups seedless raisins

1 Line a baking sheet with waxed paper.

2 In the top of a double boiler over simmering water, melt the chocolate, stirring until smooth. Add the condensed milk and cook until thickened, about 5 minutes. Remove from the heat and add the raisins.

3 Drop the mixture by spoonfuls onto the prepared pan. Chill for 2 to 4 hours, or until set. Wrap the kisses individually in waxed paper or plastic wrap. Store in an airtight container.

352 ■ CHOCOLATE RASPBERRY TRUFFLES

MAKES 4 TO 5 DOZEN TRUFFLES
CHILL TIME: *5 hours*

1 package (10 ounces) frozen raspberries, thawed
1/4 cup powdered sugar, sifted
1 pound semisweet chocolate, grated or finely chopped
3/4 cup heavy cream
2 tablespoons light corn syrup
2 tablespoon crème de framboise
1/2 recipe Dipping Chocolate (see page 186)
3/4 cup Dutch processed cocoa powder for dusting

1 In a medium bowl, mash the raspberries and strain to remove the seeds.

2 In a small saucepan, over medium heat, combine the raspberry puree and powdered sugar. Reduce by half, stirring constantly. Remove from the heat.

3 Melt the chocolate (see page 13). Transfer to a large bowl.

4 In a small saucepan, over medium heat, heat the cream until bubbles start to form around the sides of the pan. Remove from the heat and immediately pour into the chocolate, stirring until smooth. Stir in the corn syrup, raspberry puree, and crème de framboise. Chill for 2 to 3 hours, or until thick but not completely set.

5 Line two baking sheets with waxed paper.

6 Fill a pastry bag fitted with a large plain tip with the chocolate mixture. Pipe out mounds about 1 inch in diameter onto the prepared pans. Cover and freeze for at least 2 hours.

7 Line two more baking sheets with waxed paper.

8 Make the dipping chocolate.

9 Roll the truffles into balls. Using a bamboo skewer or a fondue fork, dip each of the chilled truffles into the chocolate, coating them completely. Place on the prepared pans and dust with cocoa powder. Chill for 1 hour, or until set. Store the truffles in an airtight container and chill until serving. To serve, let come to room temperature and place in miniature candy cups.

BAKING NOTES: The truffles will keep in an airtight container in the refrigerator for up to 1 month.

353 ■ CHOCOLATE RUM TRUFFLES

MAKES 12 TO 16 TRUFFLES
CHILL TIME: *2 hours*

1 1/3 cups graham cracker crumbs
1/3 cup Dutch processed cocoa powder
3 large eggs
1/4 cup water
2 tablespoons light rum
1 tablespoon thawed frozen orange juice concentrate
1 1/4 cups granulated sugar
Cocoa powder for coating

1 Line a baking sheet with waxed paper.

2 Combine the graham cracker crumbs and cocoa powder.

3 Using an electric mixer on medium speed, beat the eggs, water, rum, and orange juice until thick and light-colored. Stir in the sugar. Fold in the dry ingredients.

4 Using a tablespoon or melon baller, scoop up the mixture and roll it into 1-inch balls. Roll each truffle in cocoa powder until well coated and place on the prepared pan. Chill for 1 hour, or until firm. Store in an airtight container in the refrigerator for no more than 1 week.

BAKING NOTES: Any kind of cookie crumbs can be substituted for the graham cracker crumbs. The truffles can also be coated in dipping chocolate (see page 186) instead of rolling in cocoa powder. Owing to the raw eggs used in this recipe, keep refrigerated at all times, and for no longer than 1 week.

354 ■ CHOCOLATE SPIDERS

MAKES 30 TO 36 SPIDERS
CHILL TIME: *8 hours*

12 ounces semisweet chocolate, grated or finely chopped
1 can (5 ounces) chow mein noodles
1 cup salted peanuts

1 Line a baking sheet with waxed paper.

2 Melt the chocolate (see page 13). Remove from the heat. Add the noodles and peanuts and stir and fold until the noodles are well coated.

3 Drop by teaspoonfuls onto the prepared pan. Chill for at least 8 hours, or until ready to serve.

355 ■ CHOCOLATE TAFFY ROLLS

MAKES 3 TO 4 DOZEN
CHILL TIME: *1 hour and 30 minutes*

6 to 8 ounces unsweetened chocolate, grated or finely chopped
1 cup butterscotch chips
2/3 cup heavy cream
1 tablespoon crème de cacao
Pinch of salt
4 cups powdered sugar
1 cup walnuts or pecans, chopped for coating

1 In the top of a double boiler over simmering water, melt the chocolate and butterscotch chips with the cream, stirring constantly until smooth. Remove from the heat and stir in the crème de cacao and salt. Beat in the powdered sugar, 1 cup at a time, beating well after each

addition. Chill for 30 minutes, or until the mixture is thick enough to hold its shape.

2 Working with half of the mixture at a time, pour onto a sheet of waxed paper. Using the waxed paper, form into a 10 to 12-inch log. Roll each log in the walnuts. Chill for 1 hour, or until firm. Cut the logs into 1/2-inch slices.

356 ■ CHOCOLATE TRUFFLES

MAKES 30 TO 36 TRUFFLES
CHILL TIME: *9 hours*

6 ounces milk chocolate, grated or finely chopped
6 ounces semisweet chocolate, grated or finely chopped
3/4 cup heavy cream
1/4 cup butter
1 1/2 tablespoons crème de cacao
1 recipe Dipping Chocolate (see page 186)
Cocoa powder or chopped nuts for coating

1 In a small bowl, combine the chocolates. Chill until cold.

2 In a small saucepan, over medium heat, warm the cream until bubbles start to form around the sides of the pan. Remove from the heat.

3 In another small saucepan, over low heat, melt the butter and cook until hot to the touch. Remove from the heat.

4 Place the the hot butter and cream in the container of a blender and blend on high speed for a few seconds, until smooth. Add the chilled chocolates. Blend on high speed until smooth and incorporated. Pour into a medium bowl and stir in the crème de cacao. Cover and chill for 8 hours.

5 Using a tablespoon or melon baller, scoop up the mixture and roll it into 1-inch balls. Place on a waxed paper-lined baking sheet and freeze until firm.

6 Make the dipping chocolate. Dip each truffle into the chocolate, coating completely. Roll in cocoa powder or chopped nuts.

Place on the baking sheet and chill about 1 hour until set.

357 ■ CHOCOLATE VANILLA WAFER COOKIE CANDY

MAKES 1 1/2 TO 1 3/4 POUNDS
CHILL TIME: *1 hour*

4 ounces semisweet chocolate, grated or finely chopped
1 can (14 ounces) sweetened condensed milk
2 cups vanilla wafer cookie crumbs
1 teaspoon chocolate extract
1 cup pecans, finely chopped
Powdered sugar for coating

1 Lightly grease a 13 by 9-inch pan.

2 In the top of a double boiler over simmering water, melt the chocolate, stirring constantly. Stir in the condensed milk and cook until thickened. Remove from the heat. Stir in the cookie crumbs, chocolate extract, and nuts.

3 Scrape the mixture into the prepared pan and spread evenly. Chill for 1 hour, or until set. Cut into squares. Roll each square in powdered sugar. Wrap individually in waxed paper or plastic wrap and chill until serving.

BAKING NOTES: For a variation, chocolate wafer cookie crumbs can be used.

358 ■ CHOCOLATE WITH CHERRIES

MAKES 2¾ TO 3 POUNDS
CHILL TIME: *2 hours*

1 cup Dutch processed cocoa powder
2 tablespoons water
2 cups granulated sugar
1 cup honey
6 tablespoons light corn syrup
3 large egg whites
1 cup almonds, finely ground
½ cup candied cherry halves
1 teaspoon almond extract

1 Lightly grease or line with waxed paper an 8-inch or 9-inch square pan.

2 In a small bowl, blend the cocoa powder and water, stirring until well blended.

3 In a saucepan, over medium heat, combine the sugar, honey, and corn syrup, stirring until the sugar is dissolved. Insert a candy thermometer and cook until 265 degrees. Remove from the heat.

4 Meanwhile, in a medium bowl, using an electric mixer on high speed, beat the egg whites until stiff peaks form. Pouring it in a thin stream, beat in the hot syrup on low speed. Add the cocoa powder mixture and beat until slightly thickened. Add the almonds, cherries, and almond extract. Pour into the prepared pan. Cool until thickened. Cut into squares. Chill for 2 hours before serving.

BAKING NOTES: For thinner pieces of candy, use a 13 by 9-inch pan.

359 ■ CHOW MEIN CANDY

MAKES ¾ POUND

3½ ounces milk chocolate, grated or finely chopped
3 ounces chow mein noodles
¼ cup slivered almonds

1 Line a baking sheet with waxed paper.

2 Melt the chocolate (see page 13). Remove from the heat. Stir in the noodles and almonds.

3 Drop by spoonfuls onto the prepared pan. Chill until firm.

360 ■ COCOA FUDGE

MAKES 1½ TO 2 POUNDS
CHILL TIME: *1 hour*

¼ cup butter or margarine
3 cups granulated sugar
1½ cups boiling water
⅔ cup Dutch processed cocoa powder
⅛ teaspoon cream of tartar
6 tablespoons powdered milk
1 teaspoon crème de cacao

1 Lightly grease a 9-inch square pan.

2 In a large saucepan, over medium heat, melt the butter. Stir in the sugar, boiling water, cocoa powder, and cream of tartar. Bring to a boil over medium heat. Insert a candy thermometer and cook until 236 degrees. Remove from the heat. Cool until 110 degrees.

3 Stir in the powdered milk and crème de cacao. Pour into the prepared pan and chill 1 hour, or until firm. Cut into squares.

354

360

359

358

356

357

361 ■ COCOA FUDGE TREATS

MAKES 2 POUNDS

3 cups granulated sugar
1½ cups evaporated milk
⅔ cup Dutch processed cocoa
   powder
⅛ teaspoon salt
¼ cup butter or margarine
1 teaspoon chocolate extract

1 Grease a 9-inch square pan.

2 In a large saucepan, over medium heat, combine the sugar, evaporated milk, cocoa powder, and salt. Insert a candy thermometer and cook, stirring constantly, until 234 degrees. Remove from the heat and add the butter and chocolate extract. Cool for 5 minutes.

3 Using a wooden spoon, beat until the mixture starts to thicken. Immediately pour into the prepared pan and cool until set. Cut into squares.

362 ■ COCOA FUDGE WITH PEANUT BUTTER

MAKES 1½ POUNDS

4 cups granulated sugar
2¼ cups evaporated milk or heavy
   cream
¾ cup water
¾ cup Dutch processed cocoa
   powder
1 jar (16 ounces) creamy style
   peanut butter
1 teaspoon chocolate or vanilla
   extract

1 Lightly grease a 13 by 9-inch pan.

2 In a large saucepan, over medium heat, combine the sugar, evaporated milk, water, and cocoa powder. Bring the mixture to boil. Insert a candy thermometer and cook, stirring occasionally, until 244 to 248 degrees. Remove from the heat and cool to 110 degrees.

3 Stir in the peanut butter and the chocolate extract. Using a wooden spoon, beat until

slightly more cooled. Pour into the prepared pan and cool completely until set. Cut into squares.

363 ■ COCOA MINTS

MAKES 2¾ POUNDS
CHILL TIME: *1 hour*

1 cup Dutch processed cocoa
   powder
½ cup butter or margarine, at room
   temperature
1 teaspoon peppermint extract or
   white crème de menthe
½ cup water
2 pounds powdered sugar

1 Line a baking sheet with waxed paper.

2 In a large bowl, using your hands, combine all of the ingredients, kneading until well blended. If extremely thick, add more water, ¼ teaspoon at a time.

3 Between two sheets of waxed paper, roll out the dough to a thickness of ¼ inch. Using a cookie cutter, cut into desired shapes. Place ¼ inch apart on the prepared pan. Chill 1 hour or until firm. Store in an airtight container.

365

366

367

361

362

363

364 ■ COCOA TRUFFLES WITH HAZELNUTS

MAKES 2½ POUNDS
CHILL TIME: *15 hours*

1 pound semisweet chocolate, grated or finely chopped
1½ cups heavy cream
1½ cups hazelnuts, finely ground
¼ cup Dutch processed cocoa powder for dusting hands
1 recipe Dipping Chocolate (see page 186)

1 Melt the chocolate (see page 13). Remove from the heat and place in a medium bowl.

2 In a medium saucepan, over low heat, warm the cream until bubbles start to form around the sides of the pan. Pour the cream into the melted chocolate, stirring until smooth. Stir in 1 cup of the hazelnuts. Cover and let stand at room temperature for 6 to 8 hours.

3 Using a tablespoon or melon baller, scoop up the mixture, and place on waxed paper-lined baking sheets. Cover and chill for 6 hours.

4 Dust your hands with the cocoa powder and roll the truffle centers into small balls. Cover with plastic wrap and chill for at least 6 hours.

5 Make the dipping chocolate.

6 Using a bamboo skewer or a fondue fork, dip the centers into the chocolate, coating completely. Place the truffles on a wax paper-lined baking sheet to cool slightly. Roll the truffles in the remaining ½ cup ground hazelnuts and place on the baking sheet. Chill for 1 hour or until set.

365 ■ COCONUT CHOCOLATE BALLS

MAKES 1½ POUNDS
CHILL TIME: *1 hour*

8 ounces milk chocolate, grated or finely chopped
4 ounces semisweet chocolate, grated or finely chopped
8 ounces flaked coconut
2 cups rice crispy cereal

1 Line a baking sheet with waxed paper.

2 In the top of a double boiler over simmering water, melt the chocolates, stirring until smooth. Remove from the heat. Stir in the coconut and cereal.

3 Butter or oil your hands and roll tablespoons of the mixture into small balls. Place the balls on the prepared pan. Chill 1 hour or until firm.

366 ■ COFFEE-CHIP FUDGE

MAKES 3 POUNDS

3 cups granulated sugar
1 cup milk
½ cup half-and-half
2 tablespoons light corn syrup
2 tablespoons instant espresso powder
Pinch of salt
3 tablespoons butter or margarine
1 teaspoon almond extract
1 cup semisweet chocolate chips
½ cup chopped almonds

1 Lightly grease an 8 or 9-inch square pan.

2 In a large saucepan, over low heat, combine the sugar, milk, half-and-half, corn syrup, espresso powder, and salt. Stirring until smooth, bring to a boil. Insert a candy thermometer and cook, without stirring, until 236 degrees. Remove from the heat. Add the butter and almond extract without stirring and cool to 110 degrees.

3 Using a wooden spoon, beat until the mixture loses it gloss and a small amount dropped from a spoon holds it shape. Stir in the chocolate chips and nuts. Pour into the prepared pan and cool until set. (Do not scrape the sides of the saucepan.) Cut into squares.

367 ■ COQUETIER LE CHOCOLAT

MAKES 8 SERVINGS
CHILL TIME: *30 minutes*

8 ounces semisweet chocolate, grated or finely chopped
8 miniature foil candy cups
¾ cup crème de cacao

1 Place the foil candy cups on a tray and freeze for 10 minutes.

2 Melt the chocolate (see page 13). Remove from the heat. Pour some of the chocolate into each chilled cup. Tilt and move the cups around to coat the sides with chocolate. Freeze for 30 minutes or until hardened.

3 Carefully peel the cup from the hardened chocolate. Serve the chocolate cups filled with crème de cacao. Serve with after dinner coffee.

368 ■ CREAMY CHOCOLATE FUDGE

MAKES 1½ TO 2½ POUNDS
CHILL TIME: *1 hour*

1 jar (7 ounces) marshmallow creme
1½ cups granulated sugar
⅔ cup evaporated milk
¼ cup butter or margarine
¼ teaspoon salt
18 ounces semisweet chocolate, grated or finely chopped
1 cup pecans, finely chopped
1 teaspoon crème de cacao

1 Lightly grease a 13 by 9-inch pan.

2 In a medium saucepan, combine the marshmallow creme, sugar, evaporated milk, butter, and salt. Bring to a boil, over medium heat, and cook for 5

368

364

minutes, stirring constantly. Remove from the heat. Add the chocolate and stir until smooth. Fold in the pecans and crème de cacao. Pour the mixture into the prepared pan and chill for 1 hour, or until firm. Cut into squares.

369 ■ DIPPING CHOCOLATE

MAKES 2 POUNDS

2 pounds semisweet chocolate, grated or finely chopped

1 In the top of a double boiler, over hot, not boiling water, melt the chocolate, stirring constantly until smooth. When the chocolate is melted, insert a chocolate thermometer, immersing the bulb completely. Stir the chocolate frequently, using a rapid circular motion, until 110 degrees. Remove the top of the double boiler. Replace the hot water with cold tap water and replace the top of the double boiler. Stir the chocolate frequently, until the temperature drops to 83 degrees. Be sure to scrape down the sides of the pan as you stir.

2 Remove the top of the double boiler and check the temperature of the water with the thermometer. Add enough hot water, a little at a time, to bring the temperature up to 85 degrees. Wipe the thermometer clean and replace it in the chocolate. The chocolate is now tempered and ready for dipping candies.

3 Dip candies into the chocolate on a bamboo skewer or a fondue fork. Dip each candy deep into the chocolate, using a circular motion. Let the excess chocolate drip off and place the chocolate-coated candy onto a sheet of waxed paper to set. Let stand for 10 minutes, or until the chocolate has hardened completely and can be lifted off the waxed paper.

370 ■ EASY CHOCOLATE FUDGE

MAKES 2½ POUNDS

1 pound semisweet chocolate, grated or finely chopped
1 can (14 ounces) sweetened condensed milk
1¼ cups pecans, chopped
1 teaspoon chocolate extract

1 Lightly grease an 8-inch square pan.

2 In the top of a double boiler over simmering water, combine the chocolate and condensed milk, stirring until smooth. Remove from the heat.

3 Fold in the pecans and chocolate extract. Pour the mixture into the prepared pan and cool until set. Cut into bite-size pieces.

371 ■ EASY CHOCOLATE TRUFFLES

MAKES 5 DOZEN TRUFFLES
CHILL TIME: *3 hours*

12 ounces semisweet chocolate, grated or finely chopped
4 ounces cream cheese, at room temperature
3 cups powdered sugar
1½ teaspoons chocolate extract
Ground almonds for coating

1 Line two baking sheets with waxed paper.

2 Melt the chocolate (see page 13). Remove from the heat.

3 In a large bowl, using an electric mixer on medium speed, beat the cream cheese until smooth. Beat in the powdered sugar, ½ cup at a time. Beat in the melted chocolate and chocolate extract. Cover and chill for 1 hour, or until firm.

4 Pinch off small pieces of the mixture and roll it into 1-inch balls. Roll each truffle in the almonds until well coated. Place on the prepared pans. Chill for 1 to 2 hours, or until serving.

BAKING NOTES: Chopped pecans, cocoa powder, or toasted coconut can also be used to coat the truffles.

372 ■ FRENCH CHOCOLATE

MAKES 50 TO 60 CANDIES
CHILL TIME: *2 hours*

1⅓ cups semisweet chocolate chips
1 cup walnuts, ground
¾ cup sweetened condensed milk
1 teaspoon crème de cacao
Flaked coconut for coating

1 Line a baking sheet with waxed paper.

2 Melt the chocolate chips (see page 13). Remove from the heat. Stir in the walnuts, condensed milk, and crème de cacao. Cool for 5 minutes.

3 Pinch off pieces of the mixture and roll into 1-inch balls. Roll each ball in the coconut until well coated. Place the balls on the prepared pan. Chill for 2 hours before serving.

BAKING NOTES: Chopped walnuts or powdered sugar can also be used to coat the chocolates.

373 ■ FRENCH CHOCOLATE LOGS

MAKES 30 PIECES
CHILL TIME: *1 hour*

CENTERS

⅓ cup heavy cream
8 ounces milk chocolate, grated or finely chopped
4 ounces semisweet chocolate, grated or finely chopped
¾ teaspoon chocolate or vanilla extract

369

FONDANT

¼ cup water
¼ cup almond paste
¼ teaspoon chocolate extract
2 drops peppermint extract
1½ cups powdered sugar (see Baking notes)

TOPPING

1 recipe Dipping Chocolate (see page 186)

1 Line an 8-inch square pan with waxed paper and lightly grease the paper.

2 To make the centers, in a saucepan, over medium heat, warm the cream until bubbles start to form around the sides of the pan. Remove from the heat and cool slightly. Add the chocolates, stirring constantly, until smooth. Add the chocolate extract. Using an electric mixer on medium speed, beat until thickened. Scrape the mixture into the prepared pan and spread evenly. Chill 30 minutes, or until firm. Cut into 2-inch long by ½-inch wide strips.

3 To make the fondant, in a large bowl, combine the water, almond paste, chocolate extract, and peppermint extract. Gradually mix in the powdered sugar to form a smooth dough.

4 To assemble, on a surface lightly dusted with powdered sugar, roll out the fondant to a thickness of ¼ inch. Cut into 2-inch strips, ¾-inch wide. Place the centers on top of the strips of fondant. Wrap the fondant around the centers to form thin logs, pressing to seal the edges. Cut into ½ to ¾-inch slices.

5 Line a baking sheet with waxed paper.

6 Make the dipping chocolate. Dip the slices into the dipping chocolate, coating them completely. Place on the prepared pan and chill 30 minutes until firm.

BAKING NOTES: The amount of powdered sugar will vary. Add enough to form a pastry-like dough.

374 ■ GREGG'S CHOCOLATE

MAKES 1 POUND

8 ounces semisweet chocolate, grated or finely chopped
8 ounces almond bark, grated or finely chopped
½ teaspoon water

1 In the top of a double boiler over simmering water, melt the chocolate and almond bark, stirring constantly until smooth. Stir in the water. The mixture will seize. Continue stirring until the mixture forms a gob.

2 Place the mixture between two sheets of waxed paper and roll out to a thickness of ⅜-inch. Cut into squares while still pliable. Allow to stand at room temperature until firm.

BAKING NOTES: A combination of semisweet chocolate chips and white chocolate chips or chocolate chips and peanut butter chips can also be used. You can also melt the chips separately, and layer one on top of the other before rolling out under the waxed paper. If you use the two layer method, add 1 or 2 drops of peppermint extract to the white chocolate before the water.

372

373

374

370

371

375 ■ HOLIDAY FUDGE

MAKES 3½ POUNDS
CHILL TIME: *1 hour*

2 cups granulated sugar
1 cup heavy cream
¼ cup light corn syrup
2 ounces semisweet chocolate, grated or finely chopped
2 teaspoons chocolate or vanilla extract
1 teaspoon almond extract
1 cup candied cherry halves
1 cup chopped almonds

1 Lightly grease a 9-inch square pan.

2 In a saucepan over low heat, combine the sugar, cream, corn syrup, and chocolate. Bring to a boil, stirring occasionally. Insert a candy thermometer and cook, without stirring, until 238 degrees. Remove from the heat and cool to 110 degrees.

3 Add the chocolate and almond extracts. Using a wooden spoon, beat until thick. Fold in the cherries and almonds. Immediately pour the mixture into the prepared pan and spread evenly. Chill 1 hour, or until firm. Cut into squares.

376 ■ JULEKØNFEKT

MAKES 24 CANDIES
CHILL TIME: *1 hour*

2 cups seedless raisins
1 cup slivered almonds
8 ounces semisweet chocolate, grated or finely chopped

1 Line a 9-inch square pan with waxed paper.

2 Rinse the raisins in hot water, drain, and pat dry with paper towels.

3 Melt 4 ounces of the chocolate (see page 13). Remove from the heat. Stir in the raisins and almonds. Immediately scrape the mixture into the prepared baking pan and spread evenly.

4 Melt the remaining 4 ounces of chocolate. Spread over the top of the mixture in the pan. Cool completely for 1 hour, or until set. Cut into 24 squares.

377 ■ LUSH TEN-MINUTE FUDGE

MAKES 3¼ POUNDS

1⅔ cups granulated sugar
⅔ cup heavy cream or evaporated milk
2 tablespoons butter or margarine
½ teaspoon salt
1½ cups semisweet chocolate chips
1 cup plus 2 tablespoons chopped walnuts
⅔ cup marshmallow creme
1 teaspoon chocolate or vanilla extract

1 Lightly grease an 8-inch square pan.

2 In a large saucepan, over medium heat, combine the sugar, cream, butter, and salt. Bring to a boil and cook for 5 minutes, stirring constantly. Remove from the heat.

3 Add the chocolate chips, 1 cup of the walnuts, the marshmallow creme, and chocolate extract. Beat until the marshmallow creme is blended. Scrape the mixture into the prepared pan and spread evenly. Sprinkle with the remaining 2 tablespoons of walnuts and cool until set. Cut into squares.

378

375

379

376

378 ■ MARSH-MALLOW CHOCOLATE NUT BALLS

MAKES 24 BALLS
CHILL TIME: *1 hour*

2 ounces unsweetened chocolate, grated or finely chopped
1⅓ cups sweetened condensed milk
24 large marshmallows
1 cup chopped almonds for coating

1 Line a baking sheet with waxed paper.

2 In the top of a double boiler over simmering water, melt the chocolate, stirring until smooth. Add the condensed milk and cook for 3 to 5 minutes, or until the mixture thickens.

3 Using a bamboo skewer or a fondue fork, dip the marshmallows in the chocolate mixture, coating completely. Roll in the almonds and place on the prepared pan. Cool for 1 hour, or until set.

379 ■ MEXICAN CHOCOLATE TRUFFLES

MAKES 24 TRUFFLES
CHILL TIME: *2 hours*

COATING

¼ cup unsweetened cocoa powder
1½ teaspoons ground cinnamon

TRUFFLES

4 ounces semisweet chocolate, very finely grated or chopped
⅓ cup powdered sugar
⅓ cup almond paste
1 tablespoon strong brewed coffee
1 teaspoon butter, melted

1 To make the coating, on a small plate, combine the cocoa powder and cinnamon.

2 To make the truffles, mix the chocolate, powdered sugar, almond paste, coffee, and butter until it forms a smooth paste. Using a tablespoon or melon baller, scoop up the mixture and roll it into 1-inch balls. Roll each truffle in the coating mixture until well coated. Place on a waxed paper-lined baking sheet and chill for 2 hours before serving.

BAKING NOTES: For a decorative garnish, drizzle melted white or dark chocolate over the truffles. The truffles can also be made in larger sizes.

380 ■ MINT CHOCOLATE FUDGE

MAKES 1½ TO 2 POUNDS
CHILL TIME: *2 hours*

10 ounces semisweet chocolate, grated or finely chopped
1 can (14 ounces) sweetened condensed milk
2 teaspoons crème de cacao
1 cup white chocolate chips
1 tablespoon peppermint or spearmint schnapps
3 drops green food coloring

1 Line a 9-inch square pan with waxed paper.

2 In a large saucepan, over low heat, melt the semisweet chocolate with 1 cup of the condensed milk, stirring until smooth. Remove from the heat and add the crème de cacao. Scrape half of the mixture into the prepared pan and spread evenly. Chill for 10 minutes. Keep the remaining chocolate mixture at room temperature.

3 Meanwhile, in a medium saucepan, over low heat, melt the white chocolate chips with the remaining condensed milk, stirring until smooth. Remove from the heat and stir in the schnapps and food coloring. Spread this mixture over the top of the chilled chocolate and chill for 10 minutes, or until firm.

4 Spread the remaining chocolate mixture on top of the white chocolate mixture and chill for 2 hours, or until firm. Invert onto a sheet of waxed paper and peel off the waxed paper from the bottom. Cut into bite-size pieces.

BAKING NOTES: Crème de menthe can be used in place of the schnapps.

380

381 ■ MOCHA TRUFFLES I

MAKES 12 TO 16 TRUFFLES
CHILL TIME: *1 hour*

12 ounces semisweet chocolate, grated or finely chopped
1/4 cup butter, at room temperature
1/2 cup coffee liqueur
1/4 cup cocoa powder for coating

1 Melt the chocolate (see page 13). Remove from the heat and transfer to a medium bowl. Using an electric mixer on medium speed, beat in the butter until blended. Beat in the liqueur. Chill 1 hour, or until firm.

2 Using a tablespoon or melon baller, scoop up the mixture and roll it into 1-inch balls. Roll each truffle in the cocoa powder until well coated. Place the truffles in self-sealing plastic bags and freeze until serving.

382 ■ MOCHA TRUFFLES II

MAKES 1½ TO 2 DOZEN TRUFFLES
CHILL TIME: *1 hour*

1¼ cups powdered sugar
3 ounces unsweetened chocolate, finely grated
1/2 cup butter, melted
2 tablespoons coffee liqueur
4 large egg yolks
1/2 cup Brazil nuts, finely ground for coating

1 In a medium bowl, combine the powdered sugar, grated chocolate, butter, and liqueur. Beat in the egg yolks, one at a time. Chill for 1 hour, or until the mixture is firm enough to form into balls.

2 Using a tablespoon or melon baller, scoop up the mixture and roll into 1-inch balls. Roll each truffle in the nuts until well-coated. Place in an an airtight container and chill until serving.

BAKING NOTES: Owing to the raw eggs used in this recipe, keep refrigerated at all times, and for no longer than 1 week.

383 ■ NEEDHAMS

MAKES 5 POUNDS
CHILL TIME: *1 hour*

2 pounds powdered sugar
5½ cups shredded coconut
1 cup hot mashed potatoes
2 teaspoons almond extract
1/2 teaspoon salt

384

385

381

382

2 cups semisweet chocolate chips

4 ounces unsweetened chocolate, grated or finely chopped

1/2 bar paraffin wax, chopped (see Baking notes)

1 Lightly grease a 13 by 9-inch square pan.

2 In a large bowl, combine the powdered sugar, coconut, potatoes, almond extract, and salt, mixing until well blended. Press onto the bottom of the prepared pan. Chill for 1 hour, or until firm.

3 In the top of a double boiler over simmering water, melt the chocolate chips, chocolate, and paraffin.

4 Cut the chilled centers into 2-inch squares. Using a bamboo skewer or a fondue fork, dip the squares into the chocolate mixture, coating completely. Place on the prepared pan and chill until set.

BAKING NOTES: The mashed potatoes should not be seasoned or prepared with butter or milk. Paraffin wax is a consumable wax that works to extend the chocolate, and can be found in any grocery store.

386

384 ■ NEW ORLEANS FUDGE

MAKES 2 POUNDS
CHILL TIME: *1 hour*

1/4 cup butter or margarine

2 cups semisweet chocolate chips

1 can (14 ounces) sweetened condensed milk

1 teaspoon almond extract

Pinch of salt

1/3 cup diced candied cherries

1/3 cup ground pecans

2 tablespoons golden raisins, chopped

1 Lightly grease an 8-inch square pan.

2 In the top of a double boiler over simmering water, melt the butter and chocolate chips, stirring until smooth. Remove from the heat. Stir in the condensed milk, almond extract, and salt, stirring until smooth. Blend in the cherries, pecans, and raisins. Scrape into the prepared pan and spread evenly. Chill for 1 hour, or until firm. Cut into squares.

385 ■ NOUGAT SQUARES

MAKES 1 1/2 POUNDS
CHILL TIME: *1 hour*

3 tablespoons butter or margarine

1 jar (7 ounces) marshmallow creme

4 cups puffed corn cereal

1/2 cup flaked coconut

1/4 cup ground almonds

1/2 teaspoon salt

1 cup semisweet chocolate chips

383

1 Lightly grease a 9-inch square pan.

2 In the top of a double boiler over simmering water, melt the butter with the marshmallow creme, stirring until smooth. Remove from the heat. Add the cereal, coconut, almonds, and salt. Press evenly onto the bottom of the prepared pan.

3 In the top of a double boiler over simmering water, melt the chocolate chips, stirring until smooth. Spread evenly over the top of the mixture in the pan. Chill for 1 hour, or until set. Cut into bars.

386 ■ OLD-FASHIONED CHOCOLATE FUDGE

MAKES 2 TO 2 1/2 POUNDS

2 cups granulated sugar

2/3 cup milk

2 ounces unsweetened chocolate, grated or finely chopped

2 tablespoons light corn syrup

2 tablespoons butter or margarine

1 teaspoon chocolate extract

1 Lightly grease a 9-inch square pan.

2 In a saucepan over low heat, combine the sugar, milk, chocolate, and corn syrup, stirring until smooth. Insert a candy thermometer and cook over medium-low heat until 236 degrees. Remove from the heat, add the butter, and cool to 110 degrees without stirring.

3 Add the chocolate extract. Using a wooden spoon, beat until the fudge loses its glossy appearance or until a small amount dropped from a spoon holds its shape. Pour into the prepared pan and cool until set. Cut into squares.

BAKING NOTES: To increase the number of pieces, use a 13 by 9-inch pan. The fudge will be thinner.

387 ■ OPERA FUDGE

MAKES 2½ POUNDS
CHILL TIME: *1 hour*

3 ounces unsweetened chocolate, grated or finely chopped
1 tablespoon light corn syrup
2 cups granulated sugar
¾ cup heavy cream
½ cup evaporated milk
¾ cup pecans, chopped
1 teaspoon chocolate extract
6 ounces semisweet chocolate, grated or finely chopped

1 Lightly grease a 9-inch square pan.

2 In a saucepan over low heat, melt the unsweetened chocolate and corn syrup, stirring until smooth. Stir in the sugar, cream, and evaporated milk. Insert a candy thermometer and cook, stirring occasionally, until 238 degrees. Remove from the heat and stir in the pecans and chocolate extract. Pour the mixture into the prepared pan and cool slightly.

3 Meanwhile, melt the semisweet chocolate (see page 13). As soon as the fudge starts to harden, spread the melted chocolate over the top. Chill for 1 hour, or until firm. Cut into bite-size pieces.

388 ■ PARISIAN TRUFFLES

MAKES 1½ TO 2 DOZEN
CHILL TIME: *2 hours*

2 ounces semisweet chocolate, grated or finely chopped
½ cup granulated sugar
1 cup hazelnuts, finely ground
⅓ cup water
2 tablespoons butter, melted
1 teaspoon ground cinnamon
1 recipe Dipping Chocolate (see page 186)

1 Line a baking sheet with waxed paper.

2 In the top of a double boiler over simmering water, melt the chocolate, stirring until smooth. Add the sugar and stir until dissolved. Remove from the heat. Stir in the hazelnuts, water, butter, and cinnamon, blending in a slow motion until smooth. Let cool 30 minutes, or until almost solid. Using a tablespoon or melon baller, scoop up the mixture and roll it into 1-inch balls.

3 Make the dipping chocolate.

4 Using a bamboo skewer or a fondue fork, dip the truffles into the dipping chocolate, coating completely. Place on a waxed paper-lined baking sheet. Let cool until set. Chill for 2 hours before serving.

389 ■ PEANUT BUTTER CHOCOLATE FUDGE

MAKES 2½ POUNDS
CHILL TIME: *2 hours*

2 cups peanut butter chips
1 can (14 ounces) sweetened condensed milk
¼ cup butter
½ cup peanuts, chopped
1 cup semisweet chocolate chips

1 Line an 8-inch square pan with waxed paper.

2 In a medium saucepan, over low heat, melt the peanut butter chips, 1 cup of the condensed milk, and 2 tablespoons of the butter, stirring constantly until smooth. Remove from the heat and immediately stir in the peanuts. Spread the mixture evenly in the bottom of the prepared pan.

3 In the top of a double boiler over simmering water, melt the chocolate chips, stirring constantly until smooth. Add the remaining condensed milk and butter and stir until blended. Spread evenly over the peanut butter layer in the pan. Chill for 2 hours, or until firm. Invert onto a sheet of waxed paper and peel off the waxed paper from the bottom. Cut into squares.

390 ■ PEANUT BUTTER CHOCOLATE TRUFFLES

MAKES 1½ TO 2 DOZEN
CHILL TIME: *2 hours and 30 minutes*

½ cup heavy cream
8 ounces milk chocolate, grated or finely chopped
⅓ cup creamy peanut butter
¾ teaspoon coffee liqueur
Cocoa powder for coating

1 In a medium saucepan, over medium heat, bring the cream to a boil. Remove from the heat. Using an electric mixer on low speed, beat in the chocolate until smooth. Stir in the peanut butter and liqueur. Chill for 2 hours, or until thickened.

2 Using a tablespoon or melon baller, scoop up the mixture and roll it into 1-inch balls. Roll each truffle in cocoa powder until well coated. Place on a waxed paper-lined baking sheet. Chill for 30 minutes or until ready to serve.

391 ■ PEANUT MOUND CLUSTERS

MAKES 1½ POUNDS

1 cup creamy peanut butter
6 ounces unsweetened chocolate, grated or finely chopped
6 ounces semisweet chocolate, grated or finely chopped
½ cup flaked coconut
½ cup raisins
1½ cups salted Spanish peanuts
Flaked coconut for sprinkling

1 In the top of a double boiler over simmering water, melt the peanut butter and chocolates, stirring until smooth. Remove from the heat and fold in the coconut, raisins, and peanuts.

2 Drop tablespoonfuls onto a waxed paper-lined baking sheet. Immediately sprinkle coconut over the tops. Let cool until set.

BAKING NOTES: The candies can also be spooned into miniature paper candy cups instead of onto a baking sheet.

392 ■ PECAN CHOCOLATE CLUSTERS

MAKES 24 TO 30 CLUSTERS

1 cup pecan halves
14 ounces caramel candies
1 tablespoon evaporated milk

2 ounces semisweet chocolate, grated or finely chopped
1 ounce milk chocolate, grated or finely chopped

1 Line a baking sheet with waxed paper.

2 Arrange the pecan halves in clusters on the prepared pan.

3 In a small saucepan, over low heat, melt the caramels with the evaporated milk, stirring until smooth. Remove from the heat and cool for 5 minutes, or until the mixture is thick.

4 Melt the semisweet chocolate (see page 13). Remove from the heat and stir in the milk chocolate, stirring until smooth.

5 Spoon teaspoonfuls of the caramel mixture onto each pecan cluster. Top with a spoonful of the melted chocolate and cool slightly. Cover and chill until firm.

BAKING NOTES: It may be necessary to spread the melted chocolate over the pecan clusters. Another method would be to omit the semisweet and milk chocolates and to chill the caramel coated pecan clusters until firm. Coat each cluster with dipping chocolate (see page 186). Place the chocolate-coated clusters on a baking sheet lined with waxed paper to cool until set.

393 ■ POTATO COCONUT FONDANT

MAKES 2¾ POUNDS
CHILL TIME: *30 minutes*

4 ounces semisweet chocolate, grated or finely chopped
1 tablespoon corn syrup
1 cup mashed potatoes
2 cups powdered sugar
1 teaspoon amaretto
2 cups flaked coconut

1 Lightly grease an 8-inch square pan.

2 Melt the chocolate (see page 13). Remove from the heat.

3 In a large bowl, using an electric mixer on medium speed, beat the corn syrup and potatoes until smooth. Beat in the powdered sugar and amaretto. Fold in the coconut. Press the mixture into the prepared pan. Spread the melted chocolate evenly over the top. Chill for 30 minutes, or until firm. Cut into small bite-size pieces.

BAKING NOTES: After these have been cut into pieces, the fondant can be coated with dipping chocolate (see page 186). To dip them in chocolate, omit the semisweet chocolate layer. Dust your hands with powdered sugar, pinch off pieces of the dough, and roll into small balls. Dip each ball into the dipping chocolate. Place the chocolate-covered balls on a wire rack covered with waxed paper and cool until set.

392

391

393

394 ■ POTATO TRUFFLES

MAKES 96 TRUFFLES
CHILL TIME: *4 hours*

2 cups powdered sugar
2 cups flaked coconut
1 cup mashed potatoes
2 teaspoons almond extract
1/2 teaspoon salt
1³/4 cups semisweet chocolate chips
4 ounces unsweetened chocolate, grated or finely chopped
1/2 cup paraffin wax, chopped (see Baking notes)

1 In a large bowl, blend the powdered sugar, coconut, mashed potatoes, almond extract, and salt until thoroughly mixed. Press into a 13 by 9-inch pan. Chill for 2 to 4 hours, or until firm.

2 Meanwhile, in the top of a double boiler over simmering water, melt the chocolate chips, unsweetened chocolate, and wax, stirring until the mixture is smooth and well blended. Remove from the heat.

3 When the potato mixture is chilled, cut into 96 squares. Roll each square into a ball. Using a bamboo skewer or a fondue fork, dip each truffle into the chocolate mixture. Place the truffles on waxed paper and let cool until hardened.

BAKING NOTES: You can also use your fingers to dip the truffles. The truffles can be any size. The squares can also be dipped as is, without forming them into balls. The paraffin wax is used to make the potatoes smoother and easier to work with.

395 ■ ROCKY ROAD CANDY

MAKES 3 TO 3¹/2 POUNDS
CHILL TIME: *2 hours*

8 ounces unsweetened chocolate, grated or finely chopped
4 ounces semisweet chocolate, grated or finely chopped
5 ounces white chocolate, grated or finely chopped
1 can (14 ounces) sweetened condensed milk

2 cups peanut butter chips
1¹/2 cups miniature marshmallows
1¹/2 teaspoons chocolate extract
Pinch of salt

1 Lightly grease a 13 by 9-inch pan.

2 In the top of a double boiler over simmering water, melt the chocolates, stirring until smooth. Remove from the heat and immediately stir in the condensed milk, peanut butter chips, marshmallows, chocolate extract, and salt.

3 Scrape the mixture into the prepared pan and spread evenly. Chill for 2 hours, or until hard. Invert onto a baking sheet and cut into pieces.

396 ■ SCOTCH DROPS

MAKES 1¹/2 POUNDS
CHILL TIME: *1 hour*

6 ounces semisweet chocolate, grated or finely chopped
1 cup butterscotch chips
1 can (7 ounces) salted peanuts, chopped
1 cup puffed rice breakfast cereal

1 In the top of a double boiler over simmering water, melt the chocolate and butterscotch chips, stirring until smooth. Stir in the peanuts and the cereal.

2 Drop by teaspoonfuls onto a waxed paper-lined baking sheet. Chill for 1 hour, or until solid.

BAKING NOTES: The candy can be spooned into miniature paper candy cups instead of onto a baking sheet.

397 ■ SMITH RIDGE FUDGE

MAKES 1¹/2 TO 1³/4 POUNDS

2 ounces unsweetened chocolate, grated or finely chopped
1 cup granulated sugar
1 cup packed light brown sugar
1/2 cup heavy cream
1/4 cup dark molasses
1/4 cup butter, diced
1¹/2 teaspoon vanilla extract

1 Lightly grease an 8-inch square pan.

2 In a saucepan over low heat, melt the chocolate, stirring until smooth. Stir in the sugars, cream, and molasses. Insert a candy thermometer and cook until 238 degrees. Remove from the heat and cool slightly.

3 Add the butter and vanilla extract. Beat with a wooden spoon until the fudge loses its gloss. Pour the mixture into the prepared pan and spread evenly. Let cool until set. Cut into squares.

397

396

394

398 ■ VASSAR FUDGE

MAKES 1 TO 1½ POUNDS

2 ounces unsweetened chocolate, grated or finely chopped
2 cups granulated sugar
1 cup evaporated milk
1 tablespoon butter

1 Lightly grease a 9-inch square pan.

2 In a saucepan over low heat, melt the chocolate, stirring until smooth. Stir in the sugar and evaporated milk. Insert a candy thermometer and cook until 238 degrees. Remove from the heat and add the butter. Set the pan on a wire rack and cool at room temperature until 110 degrees.

3 Using a wooden spoon, beat the mixture until it loses its gloss.   Pour into the prepared pan, and spread evenly. Cool until set. Cut into squares.

BAKING NOTES: For Wellesley Fudge, add 8 ounces of marshmallow creme.

399 ■ WATER FONDANT

MAKES 50 CENTERS
STANDING TIME: *24 hours*

2 cups granulated sugar
Pinch of salt
2 tablespoons light corn syrup
¾ cup boiling water
½ teaspoon vanilla extract

1 In a medium saucepan, over medium heat, combine all of the ingredients. Cook, covered, for at least 3 minutes. Remove the cover, insert a candy thermometer, and cook until 240 degrees. Immediately pour onto a marble slab or cold flat surface. Cool to 110 degrees.

2 Using a metal spatula, work the fondant, using an over-and-under folding motion, until white and creamy. When cool enough handle, knead until smooth. Add the vanilla extract to the center of the fondant and continue kneading until blended. Let stand, uncovered, until cooled to room temperature. Wrap and store in an airtight container for at least 24 hours before using.

BAKING NOTES: To use these centers, dip them in Dipping Chocolate (page 186).

400 ■ WHITE AND BLACK CHOCOLATE FUDGE

MAKES 1½ TO 2 POUNDS
CHILL TIME: *1 hour*

2¼ cups granulated sugar
½ cup butter, melted
⅓ cup evaporated milk or heavy cream
1 jar (7 ounces) marshmallow creme
8 ounces semisweet chocolate, grated or finely chopped
1 cup flaked coconut, toasted

1 Lightly grease an 8-inch square pan.

2 In a medium saucepan, over medium heat, combine the sugar, butter, and evaporated milk. Insert a candy thermometer and cook until 240 degrees, stirring constantly. Remove from the heat. Add the marshmallow creme and chocolate, stirring until smooth. Mix in the coconut. Pour into the prepared pan and chill for 1 hour, or until set. Cut into small or large squares.

401 ■ WHITE CHOCOLATE MARSHMALLOW BARS

MAKES 24 SERVINGS
CHILL TIME: *1 hour*

½ cup chopped pecans
1 tablespoon butter or margarine
1⅓ cups miniature marshmallows
8 ounces white chocolate or almond bark, grated or finely chopped

1 Line an 8 by 4-inch loaf pan with waxed paper, allowing the ends of the paper to extend over the two long sides of the pan.

2 In a small skillet, over low heat, sauté the pecans in the butter for 4 to 5 minutes, or until toasted, stirring constantly. Remove from the heat.

3 Arrange half of the marshmallows in a single layer on the bottom of the prepared pan. Do not crowd the marshmallows or let them touch the sides of the pan.

397

398

400

399

Press the chopped pecans into the spaces between the marshmallows.

4 Melt the white chocolate (see page 13). Pour evenly over the top of the marshmallows in the pan and spread evenly. Gently tap the loaf pan on a flat surface to force the white chocolate to the bottom of the pan. Press the remaining marshmallows evenly into the top of the white chocolate. Chill for 1 hour, or until firm.

5 Using the ends of the waxed paper as handles, lift the candy from the pan. Remove the paper and cut into 24 bars.

402 ■ WHITE CHOCOLATE TRUFFLES

MAKES 1½ TO 2 DOZEN TRUFFLES
CHILL TIME: *2 hours*

12 ounces white chocolate or almond bark, grated or finely chopped
¼ cup butter
⅓ cup heavy cream or evaporated milk
2 cups flaked coconut for coating

1 Place the chocolate in a medium bowl.

2 In a saucepan, over medium heat, melt the butter. Add the cream and bring to a boil. Immediately pour over the white chocolate. Beat until smooth. Chill for 2 hours, or until thickened.

3 Using a tablespoon or melon baller, scoop up the mixture and roll it in to 1-inch balls. Roll each truffle in the coconut until well coated. Store in an airtight container until ready to use.

BAKING NOTES: It is much easier to grate white chocolate or almond bark if it is chilled first. For a variation, after the balls have been rolled in the coconut and chilled thoroughly, they can be coated with dipping chocolate (see page 186).

401

402

Cookies

403 ▪ ALMOND BROWNIE BARS

MAKES 2 DOZEN
BAKING TIME: *50 minutes*

FIRST LAYER

1/2 cup butter or margarine, at room temperature
1 cup ground almonds
1/3 cup granulated sugar
1 cup all-purpose flour

SECOND LAYER

1/4 cup butter or margarine
1 ounce unsweetened chocolate, grated or finely chopped
1/3 cup granulated sugar
1 large egg
3/4 cup all-purpose flour

THIRD LAYER

1 cup almond paste
1/4 cup butter or margarine, at room temperature
1/2 cup granulated sugar
2 large eggs

1 Position a rack in the center of the oven and preheat the oven to 350 degrees. Lightly grease a 9-inch square pan.

2 To make the first layer, in a large bowl, using an electric mixer on medium speed, beat the butter, almonds, sugar, and flour until a crumbly mixture forms. Press evenly onto the bottom of the prepared pan.

3 To make the second layer, in the top of a double boiler over simmering water, melt the butter and chocolate, stirring until smooth. Remove from the heat. Beat in the sugar, egg, and flour until thoroughly blended. Spread evenly over the top of the first layer.

4 To make the third layer, crumble the almond paste into a medium bowl. Using an electric mixer on high speed, beat in the butter, sugar, and eggs. Spread the mixture evenly over the top of the second layer.

5 Bake for 45 to 50 minutes, or until the edges start to pull away from the sides of the pan. The center will be firm. Cool in the pan on a wire rack. Cut into 24 bars.

404 ▪ ALMOND-FLAVORED CHOCOLATE CHIP COOKIES WITH CREAM CHEESE ICING

MAKES 2 TO 3 DOZEN
BAKING TIME: *12 minutes*

COOKIES

1 cup all-purpose flour
1/2 cup ground almonds
1/2 teaspoon baking soda
1/4 teaspoon salt
1/4 cup butter or margarine, at room temperature
1/4 cup granulated sugar
3/4 cup packed light brown sugar
1 large egg
1 tablespoon amaretto
1 teaspoon almond extract
1/2 cup semisweet chocolate chips

ICING

3 cups powdered sugar
3 ounces cream cheese, at room temperature
4 teaspoons amaretto

1 Position a rack in the center of the oven and preheat the oven to 375 degrees. Lightly grease two baking sheets.

2 To make the cookies, combine the flour, almonds, baking soda, and salt.

3 In a large bowl, using an electric mixer on medium speed, beat the butter and sugars until smooth. Beat in the egg, amaretto, and almond extract. Gradually stir in the dry ingredients. Fold in the chocolate chips. Drop the dough by spoonfuls 1 1/2 inches apart onto the prepared pans.

4 Bake for 10 to 12 minutes, or until a light golden color. Transfer to a wire rack to cool, brushing with the icing while the cookies are still warm.

5 Meanwhile, to make the icing, combine all of the ingredients in a medium bowl. Using an electric mixer, on medium speed, beat until smooth. Using a pastry brush, brush each cookie with icing. Cool the cookies completely and brush again with icing.

405 ▪ APRICOT BROWNIES

MAKES 2 DOZEN
BAKING TIME: *15 minutes*

1/4 cup dried apricots, diced
1 tablespoon apricot liqueur
4 ounces semisweet chocolate, grated or finely chopped
4 ounces unsweetened chocolate, grated or finely chopped
2 tablespoons butter or margarine
1/4 cup all-purpose flour
1/4 teaspoon baking powder
Pinch of salt
2 large eggs
3/4 cup granulated sugar
1 cup pecans or hazelnuts, chopped
1 cup white chocolate chips
1/4 cup flaked coconut

1 Place the apricots in a small bowl and sprinkle with the liqueur. Soak for 10 minutes. Drain and reserve the liqueur.

2 Preheat the oven to 350 degrees. Lightly grease a 13 by 9-inch pan.

3 In the top of a double boiler over simmering water, melt the chocolates and butter, stirring until smooth. Remove from the heat.

4 Combine the flour, baking powder, and salt.

5 In a large bowl, using an electric mixer on medium speed, beat the eggs until thick and

403

light-colored. Beat in the sugar and reserved liqueur. Pouring it in a thin stream, beat in the chocolate mixture. Gradually blend in the dry ingredients. Fold in the apricots, pecans, white chocolate chips, and coconut. Scrape the mixture into the prepared pan and spread evenly.

6 Bake for 12 to 15 minutes, or until a cake tester inserted into the center comes out clean. Cool in the pan on a wire rack. Cut into 24 bars.

406 ■ BASIC BROWNIE MASTER MIX

MAKES 14 CUPS BROWNIE MIX
BAKING TIME: *30 minutes*

3 cups all-purpose flour
2 cups unsweetened cocoa powder
1 tablespoon baking powder
2 teaspoons salt
3½ cups vegetable shortening (see Baking notes)
5 cups granulated sugar

405

407

1 To make the brownie master mix: combine the flour, cocoa powder, baking powder, and salt.

2 In a large bowl, using an electric mixer on medium speed, beat the vegetable shortening and sugar until smooth. Gradually blend in the dry ingredients. Store in an airtight container at room temperature until ready to use. This lasts for up to 1 year.

3 To make the brownies, position a rack in the center of the oven and preheat the oven to 350 degrees. Grease a 9-inch square pan.

4 Place 2¾ cups of the Basic Brownie Master Mix in a large bowl. Add 2 beaten large eggs and 1 teaspoon vanilla extract. Using an electric mixer on medium speed, beat until thoroughly mixed.

5 Scrape the mixture into the prepared pan and spread evenly.

6 Bake for 25 to 30 minutes, or until a cake tester inserted into the center comes out clean. Cool in the pan on a wire rack. Cut into 12 bars.

BAKING NOTES: This mix will make 5 single recipes as described above. The vegetable shortening must be of the type that does not need refrigeration. Optional ingredients to mix in are 1 cup chopped walnuts, peanuts, or almonds; ¼ teaspoon mint extract; 1 cup semisweet chocolate chips, white chocolate chips, peanut butter chips, or butterscotch chips.

407 ■ BASIC FUDGE BROWNIES

MAKES 1 DOZEN
BAKING TIME: *20 minutes*

10 tablespoons vegetable shortening
2 tablespoons unsweetened cocoa powder
1 cup granulated sugar
2 large eggs
1 teaspoon vanilla extract
½ cup all-purpose flour

1 Position a rack in the center of the oven and preheat the oven to 350 degrees. Grease a 9-inch square pan.

2 In the top of a double boiler over simmering water, combine the vegetable shortening and cocoa powder, stirring occasionally, until the shortening is melted. Remove from the heat and stir in the sugar. Using an electric mixer on medium speed, beat in the eggs and vanilla extract until well blended. Stir in the flour. Scrape the mixture into the prepared pan and spread evenly.

3 Bake for 15 to 20 minutes, or until a cake tester inserted into the center comes out clean. Cool in the pan on a wire rack. Cut into 12 bars.

BAKING NOTES: When cool, these can be spread with ½ cup Chocolate Glaze I (see page 401) and sprinkled with ¼ cup chopped walnuts before being cut into bars.

408 ■ BITTERSWEET BROWNIES

MAKES 1 DOZEN
BAKING TIME: *25 minutes*

2 ounces unsweetened chocolate, grated or finely chopped
½ cup all-purpose flour
1 teaspoon baking powder
¼ teaspoon salt
½ cup vegetable shortening
¾ cup granulated sugar
2 large eggs
1 teaspoon chocolate or vanilla extract
1½ cups pecans, chopped
1 cup Chocolate Eclair Frosting (see page 398)

1 Position a rack in the center of the oven and preheat the oven to 350 degrees. Grease a 9-inch square pan.

2 Melt the chocolate (see page 13). Remove from the heat.

3 Combine the flour, baking powder, and salt.

4 In a large bowl, using an electric mixer on medium speed, beat the shortening and sugar until fluffy. Beat in the eggs and chocolate extract. Beat in the melted chocolate. Gradually blend in the dry ingredients. Stir in the pecans. Scrape the mixture into the prepared pan and spread evenly.

5 Bake for 20 to 25 minutes, or until a cake tester inserted into the center comes out clean. Cool in the pan on a wire rack.

6 Frost the top of the brownies with chocolate eclair frosting. Cut into 12 bars.

409 ■ BROWN AND WHITE BROWNIES

MAKES 2 DOZEN
BAKING TIME: *15 minutes*

1 tablespoon vegetable shortening
¼ cup granulated sugar
1 large egg
¾ cup milk

½ teaspoon vanilla or almond extract
2 cups packaged sugar cookie mix
⅓ cup chocolate syrup
1 cup white chocolate chips
½ cup semisweet chocolate chips

1 Position a rack in the center of the oven and preheat the oven to 375 degrees. Lightly grease a 9-inch square pan.

2 In a large bowl, using an electric mixer on medium speed, beat the shortening and sugar until fluffy. Beat in the egg. Beat in the milk and vanilla extract. Gradually blend in the cookie mix. Divide the batter between two medium bowls.

3 Beat the chocolate syrup into one bowl of batter. Stir in the white chocolate chips. Spread evenly onto the bottom of the prepared pan.

4 Stir the semisweet chocolate chips into the second bowl. Spread evenly over the top of the brown mixture in the pan.

5 Bake for 12 to 15 minutes, or until a cake tester inserted into the center comes out clean. Cool in the pan on a wire rack. Cut into 24 bars.

410 ■ BROWNIE BARS WITH ALMONDS

MAKES 1 DOZEN
BAKING TIME: *30 minutes*

2 large eggs
1 cup granulated sugar
½ cup vegetable shortening
2 ounces unsweetened chocolate, grated or finely chopped
½ cup semisweet chocolate chips
½ teaspoon chocolate or almond extract
1 cup all-purpose flour
1 cup miniature marshmallows
½ cup almonds, chopped

1 Position a rack in the center of the oven and preheat the oven to 350 degrees. Lightly grease a 9-inch square pan.

2 In a small bowl, using an electric mixer on medium speed, beat the eggs until thick and light-colored. Beat in the sugar.

3 In the top of a double boiler over simmering water, melt the shortening and the chocolates. Remove from the heat and add the egg mixture in a thin steady stream, beating constantly. Gradually blend in the flour. Fold in the marshmallows and almonds. Scrape the mixture into the prepared pan and spread evenly.

4 Bake for 25 to 30 minutes, or until a cake tester inserted into the center comes out clean. Cool in the pan on a wire rack. Cut into 12 bars.

BAKING NOTES: For a variation, substitute 1 cup white or semisweet chocolate chips for the marshmallows. The cooled brownies can be frosted with ½ cup Chocolate Fudge Frosting II before cutting (see page 401).

409

410

414

411 ■ BROWNIE DROP COOKIES

MAKES 1 TO 2 DOZEN
BAKING TIME: *10 minutes*

8 ounces semisweet chocolate, grated or finely chopped
¼ cup all-purpose flour
¼ teaspoon baking powder
¼ teaspoon ground cinnamon
Pinch of salt
1 tablespoon butter or margarine, at room temperature
¾ cup granulated sugar
2 large eggs
½ teaspoon chocolate extract
¾ cup pecans, finely chopped
1 cup Chocolate Glaze (see page 401) (optional)

1 Position a rack in the center of the oven and preheat the oven to 350 degrees. Lightly grease two baking sheets.

2 Melt the chocolate (see page 13). Remove from the heat.

3 Combine the flour, baking powder, cinnamon, and salt.

4 In a large bowl, using an electric mixer on medium speed, beat the butter and sugar until combined. Beat in the eggs. Beat in the chocolate extract. Gradually blend in the melted chocolate. Gradually stir in the dry ingredients. Fold in the pecans. Drop the dough by spoonfuls onto the prepared pans.

5 Bake for 8 to 10 minutes, or until the cookies look dry. Transfer to wire racks to cool. Frost the cookies with chocolate glaze if desired.

412 ■ BROWNIES

MAKES 2 DOZEN
BAKING TIME: *40 minutes*

4 ounces unsweetened chocolate, grated or finely chopped
¾ cup vegetable shortening
2 cups granulated sugar
1 teaspoon vanilla extract
3 large eggs
1 cup all-purpose flour
1 cup walnuts or pecans, finely chopped

1 Position a rack in the center of the oven and preheat the oven to 350 degrees. Lightly grease a 9-inch square pan.

2 In the top of a double boiler over simmering water, melt the chocolate and shortening, stirring until smooth. Remove from the heat. Using an electric mixer on medium speed, beat in the sugar and vanilla extract. Beat in the eggs. Gradually blend in the flour. Fold in the walnuts. Scrape the batter into the prepared pan and spread evenly.

3 Bake for 35 to 40 minutes, or until a cake tester inserted into the center comes out clean. Cool in the pan on a wire rack. Cut into 24 bars.

413 ■ BROWNIES WITH RAISINS AND MARSHMALLOWS

MAKES 1 DOZEN
BAKING TIME: *25 minutes*

½ cup all-purpose flour
½ teaspoon salt
¼ cup vegetable shortening
2 ounces semisweet chocolate, grated or finely chopped
1 cup granulated sugar
1 teaspoon vanilla or chocolate extract
2 large eggs
1 cup raisins (optional)
1 cup miniature marshmallows (optional)

1 Position a rack in the center of the oven and preheat the oven to 325 degrees. Lightly grease an 8-inch square pan.

2 Combine the flour and salt.

3 In a double boiler over simmering water, melt the shortening and chocolate, stirring until smooth. Remove from the heat. Using an electric mixer on medium speed, beat in the sugar and vanilla extract. On high speed, beat in the eggs. Gradually blend in the dry ingredients. Fold in the raisins and marshmallows. Scrape the batter into the prepared pan and spread evenly.

4 Bake for 20 to 25 minutes, or until a cake tester inserted into the center comes out clean. Cool in the pan on a wire rack. Cut into 12 squares.

414 ■ BUTTERMILK BROWNIES

MAKES 3 DOZEN
BAKING TIME: *18 minutes*

BROWNIES

2 cups all-purpose flour
1 teaspoon baking soda
½ teaspoon salt
1 cup butter or margarine
1 cup water
⅓ cup Dutch processed cocoa powder
2 cups granulated sugar
½ cup buttermilk
2 large eggs
1 teaspoon crème de cacao

FROSTING

½ cup butter or margarine
6 tablespoons buttermilk
⅓ cup Dutch processed cocoa powder
½ cup powdered sugar

1 Position a rack in the center of the oven and preheat the oven to 350 degrees. Grease a 15½ by 10½-inch jelly-roll pan.

2 To make the brownies, in a large bowl, combine the flour, baking soda, and salt.

3 In a large saucepan, over medium heat, melt the butter. Add the water and cocoa powder, stirring until smooth. Remove from the heat and stir in the sugar until dissolved. Add the dry ingredients and mix until combined. Beat in the buttermilk, eggs, and crème de cacao. Scrape the mixture into the prepared pan and spread evenly.

4 Bake for 15 to 18 minutes, or until a cake tester inserted into the center comes out clean. Cool in the pan on a wire rack.

5 To make the frosting, in a medium saucepan, over medium heat, melt the butter. Mix in the buttermilk and cocoa powder. Bring to a boil and simmer for 1 minute.

6 In a medium bowl, place the powdered sugar. Pouring it in a thin stream, beat in the cocoa mixture just until mixed. Do not overmix. Cool for 5 minutes at room temperature. Spread the frosting over the top of the brownies. Cut into 36 bars.

415 ■ CHOCOLATE ALMOND BARS I

MAKES 3 DOZEN
BAKING TIME: *25 minutes*

3 cups all-purpose flour
1 cup chopped almonds
2 teaspoons ground cinnamon
1 teaspoon ground cloves
1 teaspoon grated lemon zest
3/4 cup butter or margarine, at room temperature
1¼ cups granulated sugar
2 envelopes premelted unsweetened chocolate (see page 14)
2 large eggs
1 tablespoons cherry liqueur
1 large egg white, beaten, for brushing
Whole almonds for garnish

1 Position a rack in the center of the oven and preheat the oven to 325 degrees. Lightly grease a 15½ by 10½-inch jelly-roll pan.

2 Combine the flour, almonds, spices, and lemon zest.

3 In a large bowl, using an electric mixer on high speed, beat the butter and sugar until fluffy. Beat in the chocolate and eggs, beating until thoroughly blended. Beat in the liqueur. Gradually stir in the dry ingredients. The dough will be very stiff.

4 On a floured surface, roll out the dough into a 15½ by 10½-inch rectangle. Fit the dough into the prepared pan. Brush with the egg white. Using a serrated knife dipped in flour, score the top of the dough into 36 squares. Press an almond into the center of each square.

5 Bake for 20 to 25 minutes, or until a cake tester inserted into the center comes out clean. While still hot, using a serrated knife, cut into squares. Transfer to a wire rack to cool.

BAKING NOTES: If the dough is soft, blend in additional flour, a little at a time. In humid weather, it may not be necessary to use all of the 3 cups flour.

416 ■ CHOCOLATE ALMOND BARS II

MAKES 1½ DOZEN
BAKING TIME: *45 minutes*

CRUST

3/4 cup all-purpose flour
1/2 cup ground almonds
1/3 cup granulated sugar
6 tablespoons butter or margarine

FILLING

1/2 cup granulated sugar
1/3 cup Dutch processed cocoa powder
1/3 cup water
2 tablespoons butter or margarine
1 teaspoon almond extract
Pinch of salt
2 large eggs

411

415

408

404

413

406

412

GARNISH

¹/₄ cup powdered sugar

¹/₄ cup ground almonds

1 teaspoon Dutch processed cocoa powder

1 Position a rack in the center of the oven and preheat the oven to 350 degrees. Lightly grease an 8 or 9-inch square pan.

2 To make the crust, combine the flour, almonds, and sugar. Using an electric mixer on medium speed, cut in the butter until crumbly. Press evenly onto the bottom of the prepared pan.

3 Bake for 25 minutes, or until a cake tester inserted into the center comes out clean. While the crust is baking, make the filling.

4 To make the filling, in a small bowl, combine the sugar and cocoa powder.

5 In a saucepan, over low heat, combine the water and butter, stirring until the butter is melted. Add the cocoa mixture,

stirring until the sugar is dissolved. Remove from the heat and stir in the almond extract and salt. Pour into a medium bowl and cool for 5 minutes. When cooled, beat in the eggs. Pour this mixture over the hot crust.

6 Bake for 20 minutes, or until the filling is set. Cool in the pan on a wire rack.

7 In a cup, combine the ingredients for the garnish. Sprinkle over the top of the baked cookies. Cut into 18 bars.

417 ■ CHOCOLATE ALMOND COOKIES

MAKES 2 DOZEN
BAKING TIME: *20 minutes*
CHILL TIME: *50 minutes*

CRUST

1 envelope premelted unsweetened chocolate (see page 000)

¹/₄ cup butter or margarine

1 large egg

¹/₂ cup granulated sugar

¹/₄ cup all-purpose flour

¹/₄ cup sliced almonds

FILLING

1 cup powdered sugar

2 tablespoons butter or margarine, at room temperature

1 tablespoon evaporated milk or heavy cream

¹/₄ teaspoon almond extract

TOPPING

1 ounce semisweet chocolate

1 tablespoon butter or margarine

1 Position a rack in the center of the oven and preheat the oven to 350 degrees. Lightly grease an 8-inch square pan.

2 To make the crust, in the top of a double boiler over simmering water, melt the chocolate and butter, stirring until smooth. Remove from the heat.

3 In a medium bowl, using an electric mixer on medium speed, beat the egg until thick and light-colored. Beat in the chocolate mixture and sugar. Gradually blend in the flour. Fold in the almonds and mix thoroughly. Scrape the mixture into the prepared pan and spread evenly.

4 Bake for 15 to 20 minutes, or until a cake tester inserted into the center comes out clean. Cool in the pan for 20 minutes.

5 Meanwhile, to make the filling, in a small bowl, blend the powdered sugar, butter, evaporated milk, and almond extract. Spread evenly over the baked crust and chill for 30 minutes.

6 To make the topping, in the top of a double boiler over simmering water, melt the chocolate and butter, stirring until smooth. Drizzle over the top of the filling and chill for 20 minutes. Cut into 24 bars.

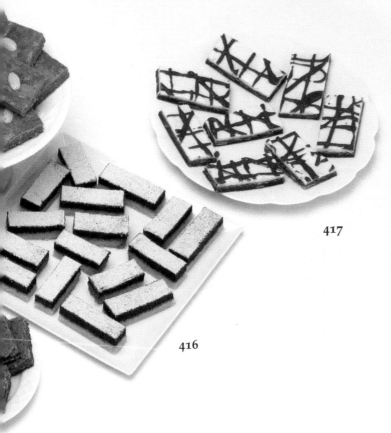

417

418 ■ CHOCOLATE ALMOND DROPS

MAKES 3 TO 4 DOZEN
BAKING TIME: *12 minutes*

1½ cups ground almonds
1 can (14 ounces) sweetened con-
    densed milk
2 envelopes premelted unsweet-
    ened chocolate (see page 14)
2 tablespoons all-purpose flour
1 teaspoon chocolate extract
Pinch of salt

1 Position a rack in the center of
the oven and preheat the oven
to 325 degrees. Lightly grease
and flour two baking sheets.
Place a sheet of waxed paper on
a wire rack.

2 In a large bowl, combine all of
the ingredients. Blend well with
a wooden spoon. Drop the
dough by teaspoonfuls 2 inches
apart onto the prepared pans.

3 Bake for 10 to 12 minutes, or
until a soft dusty color. Carefully remove from the pan and
transfer to the prepared wire
rack to cool.

419 ■ CHOCOLATE APRICOT SPRITZ

MAKES 20 COOKIES
BAKING TIME: *12 minutes*

2 ounces unsweetened chocolate,
    grated or finely chopped
2¼ cups all-purpose flour
¼ teaspoon salt
¾ cup vegetable shortening
½ cup granulated sugar
1 large egg
1 teaspoon almond or hazelnut
    extract
½ cup apricot preserves
½ cup chopped almonds
2 tablespoons granulated sugar

1 Position a rack in the center of
the oven and preheat the oven
to 400 degrees.

2 Melt the chocolate (see page
13). Remove from the heat.

3 Combine the flour and salt.

4 In a large bowl, using an electric mixer on medium speed,
beat the shortening and sugar
until fluffy. Beat in the egg and
almond extract. Beat in the

melted chocolate. Gradually stir
in the dry ingredients.

5 Fill a pastry bag fitted with a
ribbon tip with the dough. Pipe
out four 12½-inch strips onto an
ungreased baking sheet. Spread
a thin layer of apricot preserves
over each strip. Press or pipe
out another strip of dough on
top of the preserves.

6 Combine the almonds and
sugar in a small bowl. Sprinkle
evenly over the tops of the
strips. Cut each strip into five
pieces.

7 Bake for 10 to 12 minutes, or
until a golden color. Transfer to
wire racks to cool.

BAKING NOTES: Almost any kind
of fruit preserves can be used to
fill these cookies.

420 ■ CHOCOLATE BANANA RAISIN COOKIES

MAKES 2 TO 3 DOZEN
BAKING TIME: *40 minutes*

6 ounces semisweet chocolate,
    grated or finely chopped
2 cups plus 2 tablespoons all-
    purpose flour
¼ cup Dutch processed cocoa
    powder
2 teaspoons baking powder
¼ teaspoon baking soda
¼ teaspoon salt
¾ cup butter or margarine, at room
    temperature
½ cup granulated sugar
½ cup packed light brown sugar
1 teaspoon chocolate extract
2 large eggs
1 cup mashed bananas (3 medium)
1½ cups chopped pecans
10 ounces white chocolate or
    almond bark, diced
1 cup golden raisins, chopped

1 Position a rack in the center of
the oven and preheat the oven
to 350 degrees. Lightly grease
two baking sheets.

2 Melt the semisweet chocolate
(see page 13). Remove from the
heat.

3 Combine the flour, cocoa
powder, baking powder, baking
soda, and salt.

4 In a large bowl, using an electric mixer on medium speed,
beat the butter, sugars, and
chocolate extract until fluffy.
Beat in the eggs, one at a time,
beating well after each addition.
Beat in the mashed bananas.
Beat in the melted chocolate.
Gradually blend in the dry
ingredients. Fold in the pecans,
white chocolate, and raisins.
Drop the dough by spoonfuls
1½ inches apart onto the prepared pans.

5 Bake for 18 minutes. Reduce
the oven temperature to 300
degrees and continue baking for
15 to 18 minutes, or until the
tops spring back when gently
touched. Cool on the pans for 5
minutes. Transfer to wire racks
to cool completely.

421 ■ CHOCOLATE BONBON COOKIES

MAKES 3 TO 5 DOZEN
BAKING TIME: *12 minutes*

½ cup all-purpose flour
¼ teaspoon salt
2 tablespoons butter or margarine,
    at room temperature
½ cup granulated sugar
1 large egg
2 tablespoons evaporated milk
1 teaspoon vanilla or chocolate
    extract
⅓ cup Dutch processed cocoa
    powder
1¼ cups walnuts or almonds, finely
    ground, for rolling

1 Position a rack in the center of
the oven and preheat the oven
to 350 degrees. Lightly grease
two baking sheets.

2 Combine the flour and salt.

3 In a large bowl, using an electric mixer on medium speed,
beat the butter and sugar until
light and fluffy. Beat in the egg.
Beat in the evaporated milk and
vanilla extract. Stir in the cocoa
powder. Gradually blend in the
dry ingredients. Drop the dough
by spoonfuls onto the prepared
pans.

4 Bake for 10 to 12 minutes, or
until lightly colored. Roll the hot
cookies in the ground walnuts.
Transfer to wire racks to cool.

422 ■ CHOCOLATE BROWNIES

MAKES 1 DOZEN
BAKING TIME: *35 minutes*

¾ cup all-purpose flour
½ teaspoon baking powder
½ teaspoon salt
2 ounces unsweetened chocolate, grated or finely chopped
⅓ cup butter or margarine
1 cup granulated sugar
1 teaspoon vanilla or chocolate extract
2 large eggs
½ cup walnuts or pecans, chopped

1 Position a rack in the center of the oven and preheat the oven to 350 degrees. Lightly grease a 9-inch square pan.

2 Combine the flour, baking powder, and salt.

3 In the top of a double boiler over simmering water, melt the chocolate and butter, stirring until smooth. Remove from the heat. Using an electric mixer, beat in the sugar and vanilla extract. Beat in the eggs. Gradually blend in the dry ingredients. Fold in the walnuts. Scrape the batter into the prepared pan and spread evenly.

4 Bake for 30 to 35 minutes, or until a cake tester inserted into the center comes out clean. Cool in the pan on a wire rack. Cut into 12 bars.

423 ■ CHOCOLATE BUTTER BALLS

MAKES 2 TO 3 DOZEN
BAKING TIME: *20 minutes*

1 cup ground almonds
⅔ cup all-purpose flour
¼ cup Dutch processed cocoa powder
½ cup butter, at room temperature
3 tablespoons powdered sugar
Powdered sugar for rolling

1 Position a rack in the center of the oven and preheat the oven to 325 degrees.

2 Combine the almonds, flour, and cocoa powder.

3 In a medium bowl, using an electric mixer on medium speed, beat the butter and the 3 tablespoons of powdered sugar. Gradually blend in the dry ingredients. The dough will be stiff. Pinch off pieces of the dough, roll into balls, and place 1 inch apart on an ungreased baking sheet.

4 Bake for 15 to 20 minutes, or until lightly colored. Roll the hot cookies in powdered sugar and transfer to a wire rack to cool. When completely cool, roll in the powdered sugar again.

424 ■ CHOCOLATE BUTTERSCOTCH BARS

MAKES 2 DOZEN
BAKING TIME: *25 minutes*

2½ cups chocolate or vanilla wafer cookie crumbs
¼ cup butter or margarine, melted
2 teaspoons chocolate extract
1 cup flaked coconut
6 ounces semisweet chocolate, grated or finely chopped
1 cup butterscotch chips
1 can (14 ounces) sweetened condensed milk
½ cup pecans or walnuts, chopped

1 Position a rack in the center of the oven and preheat the oven to 350 degrees. Lightly grease a 13 by 9-inch pan.

2 In a medium bowl, combine the cookie crumbs, melted butter, and chocolate extract. Press evenly onto the bottom of the prepared pan. Sprinkle with the coconut, grated chocolate, and butterscotch chips. Pour the condensed milk over the top.

3 Bake for 15 minutes. Sprinkle the pecans over the top and continue baking for 5 to 10 minutes, or until the edges are lightly browned. Cool in the pan on a wire rack. Cut into 24 bars.

418

420

422

424

425 ■ CHOCOLATE CARAMEL BARS

MAKES 2 DOZEN
BAKING TIME: *20 minutes*

CRUST

2 cups all-purpose flour
1 cup packed light brown sugar
1/2 cup butter or margarine
1 cup pecans or almonds, finely
  ground

FILLING

1 cup butter or margarine
3/4 cup packed light brown sugar

TOPPING

2 cups semisweet chocolate chips

1 Position a rack in the center of the oven and preheat the oven to 350 degrees. Lightly grease a 13 by 9-inch pan.

2 To make the crust, in a large bowl, combine the flour and brown sugar. Using a pastry blender, cut in the butter, until the mixture forms coarse crumbs. Press onto the bottom of the prepared pan. Sprinkle the pecans evenly over the top.

3 To make the filling, in a saucepan, over medium heat, combine the butter and brown sugar. Stirring constantly, bring to a boil and cook for 1 minute. Spread evenly over the crust in the pan.

4 Bake for 15 to 20 minutes, or until the surface is bubbly. Sprinkle the chocolate chips over the top. Let stand for 3 minutes. Spread the melted chocolate chips evenly over the top. Cool in the pan on a wire rack. Cut into 24 bars.

BAKING NOTES: White chocolate chips can also be used.

426 ■ CHOCOLATE CARMELITA BARS

MAKES 2 DOZEN
BAKING TIME: *30 minutes*

CRUST

13/4 cups old-fashioned oats
1 cup all-purpose flour
3/4 cup packed light brown sugar
1/2 teaspoon baking soda
3/4 cup vegetable shortening
1 tablespoon coffee liqueur

TOPPING

1 cup caramel dessert topping
1/4 cup all-purpose flour
1 cup pecans, chopped
1 cup semisweet chocolate chips

1 Position a rack in the center of the oven and preheat the oven to 350 degrees. Lightly grease a 13 by 9-inch pan.

2 To make the crust, in a large bowl, combine the oats, flour, brown sugar, and baking soda. Using a pastry blender, cut in the shortening and brandy, until crumbly. Reserve 1 cup. Press the remaining crust mixture evenly onto the bottom of the prepared pan.

3 Bake for 10 minutes. While the crust is baking, make the topping.

4 To make the topping, in a small bowl, combine the caramel topping and flour.

5 Sprinkle the pecans and chocolate chips over the crust. Drizzle with the caramel topping. Sprinkle the reserved 1 cup crust mixture over the top.

6 Bake for 18 to 20 minutes, or until golden brown. Cool in the pan on a wire rack. Cut into 24 bars.

427 ■ CHOCOLATE CHARLIES

MAKES 12 TO 14 DOZEN
BAKING TIME: *12 minutes*
CHILL TIME: *2 hours*

31/4 cups all-purpose flour
1/4 cup Dutch processed cocoa
  powder
1 teaspoon baking soda
1/4 teaspoon ground cinnamon
1/2 teaspoon salt
1 cup vegetable shortening
11/2 cups packed light brown sugar
2 large eggs
1 cup crème de cacao
Semisweet chocolate chips for
  garnish

1 Combine the flour, cocoa powder, baking soda, cinnamon, and salt.

429

430

425

427

2 In a large bowl, using an electric mixer on medium speed, beat the shortening and brown sugar until fluffy. Beat in the eggs. Gradually blend in the dry ingredients, alternating with the crème de cacao. Cover and chill for at least 2 hours.

3 Position a rack in the center of the oven and preheat the oven to 350 degrees. Lightly grease two baking sheets.

4 Fill a pastry bag fitted with a large star tip with the dough. Pipe out stars onto the prepared pans, spacing them 1 inch apart. Place a single chocolate chip into the center of each star.

5 Bake for 10 to 12 minutes, or until a golden brown. Transfer to wire racks to cool.

BAKING NOTES: Chilling the dough keeps the stars from spreading out while baking. White chocolate chips can be used in place of the semisweet chocolate chips. The dough can also be dropped by teaspoonfuls instead of using a pastry bag.

428 ▪ CHOCOLATE CHEESITS

MAKES 3 TO 4 DOZEN
BAKING TIME: *15 minutes*
CHILL TIME: *1 hour*

FILLING

²/₃ cup pitted dates, finely chopped
¹/₂ cup packed light brown sugar
¹/₄ cup water
6 ounces semisweet chocolate, grated or finely chopped

CRUST

1 cup butter or margarine, at room temperature
8 ounces sharp Cheddar cheese, grated
2³/₄ cups all-purpose flour

TOPPING

1 cup Chocolate Glaze II (see page 401)

1 To make the filling, in a saucepan, over low heat, combine the dates, brown sugar, and water. Cook 7 to 10 minutes, or until the dates are soft. Add the chocolate, stirring until melted. Remove from the heat.

2 To make the crust, in a large bowl, using an electric mixer on medium speed, beat the butter and cheese until smooth. Gradually blend in the flour. Cover and chill for at least 1 hour.

3 Position a rack in the center of the oven and preheat the oven to 350 degrees.

4 On a floured surface, roll out the dough to a thickness of ¹/₈ inch. Using a 2-inch round cookie cutter, cut out rounds. Place the rounds 1 inch apart on an ungreased baking sheet. Spread with the date filling and place a second round on top. Pinch to seal the edges, using a pastry wheel or the tines of a fork.

5 Bake for 12 to 15 minutes, or until lightly colored. Transfer to wire racks to cool. Drizzle chocolate glaze over the top before serving.

429 ▪ CHOCOLATE CHEWS

MAKES 2 DOZEN
BAKING TIME: *40 minutes*

¹/₂ cup vegetable shortening
2 ounces unsweetened chocolate, grated or finely chopped
2 large eggs
1 cup granulated sugar
¹/₂ teaspoon almond or hazelnut extract
¹/₂ cup all-purpose flour
1 cup slivered almonds

1 Position a rack in the center of the oven and preheat the oven to 350 degrees. Lightly grease a 13 by 9-inch pan.

2 In the top of a double boiler over simmering water, melt the shortening and chocolate, stirring until smooth. Remove from the heat. Using an electric mixer on medium speed, beat in the eggs, one at a time, beating well after each addition. Beat in the sugar and almond extract. Blend in the flour. Scrape the dough into the prepared pan and spread evenly. Sprinkle the slivered almonds over the top.

3 Bake for 35 to 40 minutes, or until firm to the touch. Cool in the pan on a wire rack. Cut into 24 bars.

430 ▪ CHOCOLATE CHIP ABSOLUTE FAVORITES

MAKES 3 TO 5 DOZEN
BAKING TIME: *12 minutes*
CHILL TIME: *1 hour*

2 cups all-purpose flour
1 teaspoon baking soda
¹/₂ teaspoon salt
1 cup vegetable shortening
¹/₂ cup granulated sugar
³/₄ cup packed light brown sugar
1 large egg
2¹/₂ teaspoons white crème de menthe
1¹/₃ cups semisweet chocolate chips

1 Position a rack in the center of the oven and preheat the oven to 350 degrees. Lightly grease two baking sheets.

2 Combine the flour, baking soda, and salt.

3 In a large bowl, using an electric mixer on medium speed, beat the shortening and the sugars until fluffy. Beat in the egg and crème de menthe. Gradually blend in the dry ingredients. Fold in the chocolate chips. Chill for 1 hour.

4 Drop the dough by spoonfuls 1¹/₂ inches apart onto the prepared pans.

5 Bake for 10 to 12 minutes, or until lightly colored. Transfer to wire racks to cool.

431 ▪ CHOCOLATE CHIP BAR COOKIES

MAKES 2 DOZEN
BAKING TIME: *30 minutes*

2 cups all-purpose flour
1 teaspoon baking powder
¹/₄ teaspoon baking soda
¹/₄ teaspoon salt
1 cup vegetable shortening
1¹/₂ cups packed light brown sugar
2 large eggs
2 tablespoons milk
1 teaspoon vanilla extract
1 cup semisweet chocolate chips

1 Position a rack in the center of the oven and preheat the oven to 350 degrees. Lightly grease a 9-inch square pan.

2 Combine the flour, baking powder, baking soda, and salt.

3 In a large bowl, using an electric mixer on medium speed, beat the shortening and brown sugar until fluffy. Beat in the eggs. Beat in the milk and vanilla extract. Gradually blend in the dry ingredients. Fold in the chocolate chips. Scrape the dough into the prepared pan and spread evenly.

4 Bake for 25 to 30 minutes, or until golden brown. Cool in the pan on a wire rack. Cut into 24 bars.

432 ■ CHOCOLATE CHIP BARS

MAKES 2 DOZEN
BAKING TIME: *20 minutes*

1¼ cups whole wheat flour
½ cup ground walnuts (optional)
1 teaspoon baking powder
⅓ cup butter or margarine, at room temperature
1¼ cups raw sugar
2 large eggs
½ cup semisweet chocolate chips

1 Position a rack in the center of the oven and preheat the oven to 350 degrees. Lightly grease a 9-inch square pan.

2 Combine the flour, walnuts, and baking powder.

3 In a large bowl, using an electric mixer on medium speed, beat the butter and sugar until fluffy. Beat in the eggs. Gradually blend in the dry ingredients. Fold in the chocolate chips. Press the dough onto the bottom of the prepared pan.

4 Bake for 15 to 20 minutes, or until a golden brown color. Cool in the pan on a wire rack. Cut into 24 bars.

BAKING NOTES: These can be baked in a 13 by 9-inch pan, but the cookies will be thinner and drier, so bake for a shorter time.

433 ■ CHOCOLATE CHIP CHEESECAKE BARS

MAKES 2 DOZEN
BAKING TIME: *38 minutes*

CRUST

1½ cups chocolate graham cracker crumbs
2 tablespoons granulated sugar
⅓ cup butter or margarine, melted

FILLING

8 ounces cream cheese, at room temperature
⅓ cup granulated sugar
1 large egg
1 teaspoon chocolate or almond extract
1 tablespoon grated orange zest

TOPPING

1 cup chopped almonds or pecans
1 cup semisweet chocolate chips
⅔ cup flaked coconut

1 Position a rack in the center of the oven and preheat the oven to 350 degrees.

2 In a large bowl, using an electric mixer on medium speed,

428

431

419

421

423

426

beat the graham cracker crumbs, sugar, and melted butter until blended. Press the mixture into an ungreased 13 by 9-inch pan.

3 Bake for 5 to 8 minutes, or until crispy.

4 In a medium bowl, using an electric mixer on medium speed, beat the cream cheese, sugar, egg, chocolate extract, and orange zest until smooth. Spread the mixture evenly over the top of the crust.

5 Bake for 25 minutes.

6 In a small bowl, combine the almonds, chocolate chips, and coconut. Sprinkle over the baked crust and filling.

7 Bake for 5 minutes, or until the topping is melted and spreadable. While still very hot,

use a knife to spread the topping evenly over the cake. Cool in the pan on a wire rack. Cut into 24 bars.

BAKING NOTES: 1/2 cup of golden raisins can be added to the crust mixture.

434 ■ CHOCOLATE CHIP COOKIES

MAKES 6 TO 7 DOZEN
BAKING TIME: *10 minutes*

2¼ cups all-purpose flour
1 (3.4-ounce) package Jell-O Brand chocolate instant pudding mix
1 teaspoon baking soda
1 cup vegetable shortening
¼ cup granulated sugar
¾ cup packed light brown sugar
2 large eggs
1 teaspoon vanilla or chocolate extract
1½ cups semisweet chocolate chips
1 cup walnuts, finely chopped (optional)

1 Position a rack in the center of the oven and preheat the oven to 375 degrees.

2 Combine the flour, pudding mix, and baking soda.

3 In a large bowl, using an electric mixer on medium speed, beat the shortening and sugars until fluffy. Beat in the eggs. Beat in the vanilla extract. Gradually blend in the dry ingredients. Fold in the chocolate chips and walnuts. Drop the dough by spoonfuls 1½ inches apart onto ungreased baking sheets.

4 Bake for 8 to 10 minutes, or until lightly colored. Transfer to wire racks to cool.

435 ■ CHOCOLATE CHIP MANDELS

MAKES 3 TO 4 DOZEN
BAKING TIME: *30 minutes*

3 cups all-purpose flour
3 tablespoons Dutch processed cocoa powder
2 teaspoons baking powder
¼ teaspoon salt
3 large eggs
1 cup canola oil
1 cup granulated sugar
2 cups semisweet chocolate chips

1 Position a rack in the center of the oven and preheat the oven to 350 degrees. Lightly grease a baking sheet.

2 Combine the flour, cocoa powder, baking powder, and salt.

3 In a large bowl, using an electric mixer on medium, beat the eggs until thick and light-colored. Beat in the canola oil. Beat in the sugar. Gradually stir in the dry ingredients. Fold in the chocolate chips.

4 Divide the dough in half and form each half into a log 3 inches in diameter. Place the logs 1½ inches apart on the prepared pan.

5 Bake for 30 minutes, or until golden brown. Cool on the pan for 10 minutes. Cut each log in half lengthwise and cut each half into 1-inch slices. Transfer to wire racks to cool completely.

432

435

434

433

436 ■ CHOCOLATE CHIP NUT BARS

MAKES 1 DOZEN
BAKING TIME: *30 minutes*

1/2 **cup all-purpose flour**
1/2 **teaspoon baking powder**
1/4 **teaspoon salt**
1 **large egg**
1/2 **cup granulated sugar**
1 **teaspoon butter or margarine, melted**
2 **teaspoons hot water**
2/3 **cup walnuts, finely chopped**
1/2 **cup almonds, finely chopped**
1 **cup semisweet chocolate chips**

1 Position a rack in the center of the oven and preheat the oven to 325 degrees. Lightly grease an 8-inch square pan.

2 Combine the flour, baking powder, and salt.

3 In a large bowl, using an electric mixer on medium speed, beat the egg until thick and light-colored. Beat in the sugar. Beat in the butter, water, walnuts, and almonds. Gradually blend in the dry ingredients. Fold in the chocolate chips. Scrape the batter into the prepared pan and spread evenly.

4 Bake for 25 to 30 minutes, or until lightly colored on top. Cool in the pan on a wire rack. Cut into 12 bars.

437 ■ CHOCOLATE CHIP PEANUT LOGS

MAKES 2 DOZEN
CHILL TIME: *30 minutes*

1 **cup semisweet chocolate chips**
1/2 **cup creamy peanut butter**
1/2 **cup peanuts, chopped (optional)**
4 **cups rice crispy cereal**

1 Lightly grease a 9-inch square pan.

2 In the top of a double boiler over simmering water, melt the chocolate chips and peanut butter. Remove from the heat. Blend in the chopped peanuts. Gradually blend in the cereal. Be sure the cereal is well coated with the chocolate mixture.

3 Spread the dough out evenly on the bottom of the prepared pan. Cool in the pan on a wire rack until the mixture hardens slightly. Chill for 30 minutes in the refrigerator.

3 Cut into 24 bars. Roll the bars between your palms to form logs. Wrap individually in waxed paper or plastic wrap and store tightly covered until serving.

BAKING NOTES: This is a great recipe to make with children. Let them roll the logs.

438 ■ CHOCOLATE CHIP SQUARES

MAKES 3 DOZEN
BAKING TIME: *20 minutes*

2 1/4 **cups all-purpose flour**
1 **teaspoon baking soda**
1/2 **teaspoon salt**
1 **cup canola oil**
1/2 **cup granulated sugar**
3/4 **cup packed light brown sugar**
1 **large egg**
2 1/2 **teaspoons white crème de menthe**
1 1/3 **cups semisweet chocolate chips**
1/2 **cup semisweet chocolate chips for topping**

1 Position a rack in the center of the oven and preheat the oven to 350 degrees. Lightly grease a 13 by 9-inch pan.

2 Combine the flour, baking soda, and salt.

3 In a large bowl, using an electric mixer on medium speed, beat the oil and the sugars until smooth. Beat in the egg. Beat in the crème de menthe. Gradually stir in the dry ingredients. Fold in 1 1/3 cups chocolate chips. Scrape into the prepared pan and spread evenly.

4 Bake for 15 to 20 minutes, or until golden colored. Sprinkle the 1/2 cup chocolate chips for the topping over the crust. Let stand for 3 minutes. Spread the melted chocolate chips evenly over the top. Cool in the pan on a wire rack. Cut into 36 bars.

439 ■ CHOCOLATE CHRISTMAS COOKIES

MAKES 2 TO 3 DOZEN
BAKING TIME: *10 minutes*

1 **cup all-purpose flour**
1 **cup whole wheat flour**
1/2 **cup soy flour**
1 **cup Dutch processed cocoa powder**
1/2 **teaspoon baking soda**
1 **teaspoon ground allspice**
Pinch of salt
1 **cup butter or margarine, at room temperature**
2 **cups granulated sugar**
1 **teaspoon chocolate extract**
1 **large egg**
1 **tablespoon crème de cacao**
Cocoa Sugar for dusting (see page 407)

1 Position a rack in the center of the oven and preheat the oven to 400 degrees. Lightly grease two baking sheets.

2 Combine the flours, cocoa powder, baking soda, allspice, and salt.

3 In a large bowl, using an electric mixer on medium speed, beat the butter, sugar, and chocolate extract until light and fluffy. Beat in the egg and crème de cacao. Gradually stir in the dry ingredients.

4 On a floured surface, knead the dough until smooth. Roll out the dough to a thickness of 1/8 to 1/4 inch. Using a 2-inch round cookie cutter or floured glass, cut the dough into rounds. Place 1 inch apart on the prepared pans. Dust the tops with cocoa sugar.

5 Bake for 8 to 10 minutes, or until the cookies look very dry. Do not overbake. Transfer to wire racks to cool.

BAKING NOTES: This recipe can be used to make sandwich cookies. Fill the cookies with Coffee Mocha Icing (see page 408).

440 ■ CHOCOLATE CHUNK COOKIES I

MAKES 1 DOZEN
BAKING TIME: *12 minutes*

9 ounces unsweetened chocolate, grated or finely chopped
3 tablespoons butter
1 teaspoon mocha-flavored instant coffee powder
1/2 cup packed light brown sugar
2 large eggs
1 teaspoon chocolate or vanilla extract
1/3 cup all-purpose flour
1/4 teaspoon baking powder
1 cup pecans, coarsely chopped
1 cup macadamia nuts, whole (optional)
4 ounces semisweet chocolate, diced

1 Position a rack in the center of the oven and preheat the oven to 350 degrees. Lightly grease two baking sheets.

2 In the top of a double boiler over simmering water, melt the unsweetened chocolate and butter, stirring until smooth. Stir in the coffee powder and remove from the heat. By hand, beat in the brown sugar, eggs, and chocolate extract.

3 In a large bowl, combine the flour and baking powder. Using a large spoon, blend in the chocolate mixture, a little at a time. Fold in the pecans, macadamia nuts, and semisweet chocolate. Drop the dough onto the prepared pans to form 12 large mounds, using about 2 tablespoons of dough for each cookie.

4 Bake for 10 to 12 minutes, or until the tops start to crack and the surface is dulled. Cool on the pan for 5 minutes. Transfer to wire racks to cool completely.

441 ■ CHOCOLATE CHUNK COOKIES II

MAKES 3 TO 4 DOZEN
BAKING TIME: *15 minutes*

2 1/4 cups all-purpose flour
1 teaspoon baking soda
1/4 teaspoon salt
1 1/4 cups butter or margarine, at room temperature
3/4 cup packed light brown sugar
1/2 cup granulated sugar
3 large eggs
1 1/2 teaspoons chocolate or vanilla extract
6 ounces semisweet chocolate, diced
6 ounces white chocolate, diced
2 cups chopped pecans or walnuts

1 Position a rack in the center of the oven and preheat the oven to 325 degrees.

2 Combine the flour, baking soda, and salt.

3 In a large bowl, using an electric mixer on medium speed, beat the butter and sugars until smooth. Beat in the eggs and chocolate extract. Gradually stir in the dry ingredients. Fold in the diced chocolates and pecans. Drop the dough by heaping teaspoonfuls, 1 1/2 inches apart, onto ungreased baking sheets.

4 Bake for 12 to 15 minute, or until a light golden color. Transfer to wire racks to cool.

442 ■ CHOCOLATE COATED MACAROONS

MAKES 2 TO 3 DOZEN
BAKING TIME: *25 minutes*
CHILL TIME: *1 hour 10 minutes*

MACAROONS

4 large egg whites
1 1/3 cups granulated sugar
1 1/2 teaspoons almond extract
1/4 teaspoon salt
2 1/2 cups flaked coconut
6 tablespoons all-purpose flour

COATING

4 ounces unsweetened chocolate, grated or finely chopped
4 ounces semisweet chocolate, grated or finely chopped

1 Position a rack in the center of the oven and preheat the oven to 300 degrees. Lightly grease two baking sheets.

2 To make the macaroons, in a saucepan, combine the egg whites, sugar, almond extract, and salt until thoroughly blended. Stir in the coconut and flour. Place over medium heat and cook, stirring constantly, for 5 minutes. Raise the heat to medium-high and cook, stirring constantly, for 4 minutes, or until the mixture is thick and pulls away from the sides of the pan. Immediately transfer to a large bowl and cool for 5 minutes. Cover and chill for at least 10 minutes, or until the dough is cold.

440

437

438

442

3 Drop the dough by teaspoonfuls 1½ inches apart onto the prepared pans.

4 Bake for 20 to 25 minutes, or until a light golden color. Transfer to wire racks to cool completely.

5 To make the coating, in the top of a double boiler over simmering water, melt the chocolates, stirring constantly until smooth. Remove from the heat.

6 Line a baking sheet with waxed paper. Dip the macaroons into the chocolate, coating half of each cookie. Place on the prepared pan. Chill for 30 minutes. When the chocolate has hardened, coat the other half with chocolate and place on the pan to harden. Chill for 30 minutes.

BAKING NOTES: Do not use a skewer to dip the cookies. They will fall off into the chocolate while dipping.

443 ■ CHOCOLATE COCONUT BARS I

MAKES 1 DOZEN
BAKING TIME: *30 minutes*

1½ cups graham cracker crumbs
1 can (14 ounces) sweetened condensed milk
1½ cups flaked coconut
½ cup semisweet chocolate chips

1 Position a rack in the center of the oven and preheat the oven to 350 degrees. Grease a 9-inch square pan.

2 In a large bowl, combine all of the ingredients. Press the mixture evenly onto the bottom of the prepared pan.

3 Bake for 30 minutes, or until golden brown on top. Cool in the pan on a wire rack. Cut into 12 bars.

BAKING NOTES: Chocolate wafer cookies can be substituted for the graham cracker crumbs.

444 ■ CHOCOLATE COCONUT BARS II

MAKES 1 DOZEN
BAKING TIME: *20 minutes*

2½ cups semisweet chocolate chips
1 cup pecan halves
1 cup flaked coconut
½ cup all-purpose flour
2 tablespoons Dutch processed cocoa powder
3 large eggs
1 cup granulated sugar
½ cup butter or margarine, at room temperature
1 teaspoon chocolate extract

1 Position a rack in the center of the oven and preheat the oven to 350 degrees. Lightly grease an 8-inch square pan.

2 Combine 2 cups of the chocolate chips, the pecans, coconut, flour, and cocoa powder.

3 In a large bowl, using an electric mixer on medium speed, beat the eggs until thick and light-colored. Add the sugar and beat until the sugar is dissolved. Add the butter and chocolate extract and beat for 1 minute. Gradually stir in the remaining dry ingredients just until blended. Scrape the mixture into the prepared pan and spread evenly.

4 Bake for 18 to 20 minutes, or until the batter is set but sticky to the touch. Sprinkle the

remaining ½ cup of chocolate chips over the top. Let stand for 3 minutes. Spread the melted chocolate chips over the top. Cool in the pan on a wire rack. Cut into 12 bars.

445 ■ CHOCOLATE AND COCONUT TEA STRIPS

MAKES 64 BARS TOTAL
BAKING TIME: *15 minutes*

1½ cups all-purpose flour
1½ teaspoons baking powder
¼ teaspoon salt
6 tablespoons butter or margarine, at room temperature
¾ cup plus 2 tablespoons granulated sugar
1 large egg
2 tablespoons milk
½ teaspoon vanilla extract
1 ounce unsweetened chocolate, grated or finely chopped
1 teaspoon grated orange zest
¼ cup pecans or walnuts, chopped
⅔ cup flaked coconut

1 Position a rack in the center of the oven and preheat the oven to 375 degrees. Lightly grease two 8-inch square pans.

2 Combine the flour, baking powder, and salt.

3 In a large bowl, using an electric mixer on medium speed, beat the butter and ¾ cup of the sugar until light and fluffy. Beat in the egg. Beat in the milk and vanilla extract. Gradually stir in the dry ingredients. Divide the dough in half and place half in a separate bowl.

443

445

446

447

4 Melt the chocolate (see page 13). Remove from the heat and mix into the dough in one bowl. On a floured surface, roll out the chocolate dough into an 8-inch square and fit it into one of the prepared pans. Sprinkle with 1 tablespoon of the sugar and ½ teaspoon of the orange zest. Set aside.

5 Combine the pecans and coconut. Blend into the dough in the second bowl. On a floured surface, roll out the dough into an 8-inch square and fit into the other prepared pan. Sprinkle with the remaining 1 tablespoon sugar and ½ teaspoon orange zest.

6 Bake both pans at the same time for 10 to 15 minutes, or until firm to the touch. Cool in the pans on wire racks. Cut each pan into 1 by 2-inch strips.

446 ■ CHOCOLATE COCONUT TOFFEE BARS

MAKES 8 TO 10 SERVINGS
BAKING TIME: *30 minutes*

1¼ cups all-purpose flour
⅓ cup Dutch processed cocoa powder
¾ cup butter-flavored vegetable shortening
1 cup powdered sugar
2 tablespoons butter or margarine
1 can (14 ounces) sweetened condensed milk
2 teaspoons chocolate or almond extract
1 cup semisweet chocolate chips
½ cup flaked coconut

1 Position a rack in the center of the oven and preheat the oven to 350 degrees. Lightly grease a 13 by 9-inch pan.

2 Combine the flour and cocoa powder.

3 In a large bowl, using an electric mixer on medium speed, beat the shortening and sugar until fluffy. Gradually blend in the dry ingredients. Press evenly onto the bottom of the prepared pan.

4 Bake for 15 minutes.

5 Meanwhile, in the top of a double boiler over simmering water, melt the butter with the milk until thickened. (It will take about 15 minutes.) Remove from the heat and stir in the chocolate extract. Immediately pour this over the baked crust.

6 Bake for 10 minutes, or until topping is set.

7 Sprinkle the chocolate chips evenly over the top and bake for 3 to 5 minutes, or until the chocolate is melted. Remove from the oven. Using a knife, spread the melted chocolate chips over the top. Sprinkle with the coconut. Cool in the pan on a wire rack. Cut into bars.

447 ■ CHOCOLATE COOKIE KISSES I

MAKES 2 TO 3 DOZEN
BAKING TIME: *40 minutes*

2 ounces unsweetened chocolate, grated or finely chopped
4 large egg whites
¼ teaspoon salt
¼ teaspoon cream of tartar
1 cup granulated sugar
¼ teaspoon almond extract

1 Position a rack in the center of the oven and preheat the oven to 250 degrees. Line two baking sheets with parchment paper.

2 Melt the chocolate (see page 13). Remove from the heat.

3 In a large bowl, using an electric mixer on high speed, beat the egg whites until foamy. Beat in the sugar. Mix in the salt and cream of tartar. Add the almond extract and beat until the mixture forms stiff peaks. Fold in the melted chocolate. Drop the mixture by spoonfuls 1 inch apart onto the prepared pans.

4 Bake for 35 to 40 minutes, or until firm to the touch. Transfer to wire racks to cool.

BAKING NOTES: For crisper kisses, turn the oven off after baking and leave the pan in the oven until the cookies are cool. (Do not open the oven door.)

448 ■ CHOCOLATE COOKIE KISSES II

MAKES 1 DOZEN
BAKING TIME: 14 MINUTES

3 large egg whites
¼ teaspoon salt
⅛ teaspoon cream of tartar
1 cup powdered sugar
⅓ cup crushed saltine crackers
6 ounces semisweet chocolate, grated or finely chopped

1 Position a rack in the center of the oven and preheat the oven to 350 degrees. Line a baking sheet with waxed paper.

2 In a large bowl, using an electric mixer on high speed, beat the egg whites, salt, and cream of tartar until foamy. On low speed, gradually beat in the powdered sugar. Beat until the mixture holds soft peaks. Fold in the cracker crumbs and chocolate. Drop by teaspoonfuls onto the prepared pan.

3 Bake for 14 minutes. Cool for 5 minutes on the pan. Transfer to wire racks to cool completely.

449 ■ CHOCOLATE COOKIES

MAKES 4 TO 5 DOZEN
BAKING TIME: *12 minutes*

1½ cups all-purpose flour
½ cup Dutch processed cocoa powder
1½ teaspoons baking powder
¼ teaspoon salt
½ cup butter or margarine, at room temperature
1 cup packed light brown sugar
1 large egg
½ cup milk
1 tablespoon heavy cream
1 teaspoon vanilla or chocolate extract
¾ cup walnuts, chopped (optional)

1 Position a rack in the center of the oven and preheat the oven to 400 degrees.

2 Combine the flour, cocoa powder, baking powder, and salt.

3 In a large bowl, using an electric mixer on medium speed, beat the butter and brown sugar until fluffy. Beat in the egg. Beat in the milk, cream, and vanilla extract. Gradually blend in the dry ingredients. Fold in the walnuts.

4 On a floured surface, roll out the dough to a thickness of 1/4 inch. Using a 1½-inch round cookie cutter, cut into rounds. Place the rounds 1½ inches apart on ungreased baking sheets.

5 Bake for 10 to 12 minutes, or until firm. Transfer to wire racks to cool.

450 ■ CHOCOLATE CORNUCOPIAS

MAKES 1½ TO 2 DOZEN
BAKING TIME: *10 minutes*

COOKIES

1 cup semisweet chocolate chips
1/2 cup vegetable shortening
1/2 cup granulated sugar
Pinch of salt
1/4 teaspoon ground ginger
1/3 cup light corn syrup
1 cup plus 2 tablespoons all-purpose flour

FILLING

8 ounces cream cheese, at room temperature
2 cups heavy cream
1/2 teaspoon chocolate extract
2 ounces semisweet chocolate, grated or finely chopped

1 Position a rack in the center of the oven and preheat the oven to 350 degrees. Grease two baking sheets.

2 To make the cookies, in the top of a double boiler over simmering water, melt the chocolate chips, stirring until smooth. Stir in the shortening, sugar, salt, and ginger until smooth. Remove from the heat. Using a wooden spoon, blend in the corn syrup and flour. Drop by tablespoonfuls 3 inches apart onto the prepared pans.

3 Bake for 8 to 10 minutes, or until dry-looking. Cool on the pan for 1 to 2 minutes. Remove the cookies and shape into a cornucopia cone by using a cone mold or just rolling into a cone. Lay on a wire rack to cool completely, seam-side down. When the cookies are cool, fill with the cream cheese filling.

4 Meanwhile, to make the filling, using an electric mixer on medium speed, beat the cream cheese until very soft. Add the cream and chocolate extract. Whip on high speed until soft peaks form. Fold in the grated chocolate. In a pastry bag fitted with a medium star tip, pipe the filling into the cookies.

451 ■ CHOCOLATE-COVERED OATMEAL COOKIES

MAKES 3 TO 4 DOZEN
BAKING TIME: *15 minutes*

2½ cups old-fashioned oats
1¾ cups all-purpose flour
1 teaspoon baking soda
1/2 teaspoon salt
1/2 cup butter or margarine, at room temperature
1/2 cup chunky peanut butter
1 cup granulated sugar
1 cup packed light brown sugar
2 large eggs
1/4 cup milk
1 teaspoon almond extract

436

439

441

444

449

448

450

3 ounces semisweet chocolate, grated or finely chopped
1/2 cup golden raisins
1 recipe Dipping Chocolate (see page 186)

1 Position a rack in the center of the oven and preheat the oven to 350 degrees.

2 Combine the oats, flour, baking soda, and salt.

3 In a large bowl, using an electric mixer on medium speed, beat the butter, peanut butter, and sugars until smooth. Beat in the eggs, one at time, beating well after each addition. Beat in the milk and almond extract. Gradually stir in the dry ingredients. Fold in the chocolate and raisins. Drop the dough by tablespoonfuls 2 1/2 to 3 inches apart onto ungreased baking sheets.

4 Bake for 12 to 15 minute, or until dry-looking. Transfer to wire racks to cool.

5 Make the dipping chocolate.

6 When completely cooled, place the cookies on wire racks set over a baking sheet. Spoon the dipping chocolate over the tops of the cookies, letting the

excess chocolate drip off. When the chocolate is firm enough to handle, transfer the coated cookies to a piece of waxed paper to harden.

452 ■ CHOCOLATE CREAM CHEESE BAR COOKIES

MAKES 2 DOZEN
BAKING TIME: *25 minutes*

4 ounces unsweetened chocolate, grated or finely chopped
1 1/2 cups all-purpose flour
1 teaspoon baking powder
Pinch of salt
8 ounces cream cheese, at room temperature
1 1/2 cups packed light brown sugar
1/2 cup butter or margarine, at room temperature
3 large eggs
1 tablespoon chocolate or almond extract
1 cup chopped pecans

1 Position a rack in the center of the oven and preheat the oven to 350 degrees. Lightly grease a 9-inch square pan.

2 Melt the chocolate (see page 13). Remove from the heat.

3 Combine the flour, baking powder, and salt.

4 In a small bowl, using an electric mixer on medium speed, beat 4 ounces of the cream cheese and 1/2 cup of the brown sugar until creamy; set aside.

5 In a large bowl, using an electric mixer on medium speed,

beat the butter and the remaining 4 ounces cream cheese and 1 cup brown sugar until smooth. Beat in the eggs, one at a time. Stir in the melted chocolate and chocolate extract. Gradually blend in the dry ingredients. Fold in the pecans. Scrape half of the batter into the prepared pan and spread evenly. Spread the reserved cream cheese and brown sugar mixture over the top. Spread with the remaining batter.

6 Bake for 20 to 25 minutes, or until a cake tester inserted into the center comes out clean. Cool in the pan on a wire rack. Cut into 24 bars.

453 ■ CHOCOLATE CREAM DREAM BARS

MAKES 3 DOZEN
BAKING TIME: *30 minutes*

CRUST

2 1/2 cups all-purpose flour
2 cups old-fashioned oats
1 1/2 cups packed light brown sugar
1 teaspoon baking soda
1/4 teaspoon salt
1 cup butter-flavored vegetable shortening or margarine

FILLING

2 cups semisweet chocolate chips
1 can (14 ounces) sweetened condensed milk
2 tablespoons butter-flavored vegetable shortening or margarine
2 teaspoons chocolate or vanilla extract
1 cup pecans, finely chopped (optional)

1 Position a rack in the center of the oven and preheat the oven to 350 degrees.

2 To make the crust, in a large bowl, combine the flour, oats, brown sugar, baking soda, and salt. Using a pastry blender, cut in the shortening to make a crumbly mixture. Press 4 cups onto the bottom of an ungreased 15 1/2 by 10 1/2-inch jelly-roll pan. Reserve the remaining crust mixture.

3 To make the filling, in the top of a double boiler over simmering water, melt the chocolate chips, stirring until smooth. Add the condensed milk and shortening and heat thoroughly. Remove from the heat and stir in the chocolate extract and pecans. Immediately pour over the crust in the pan. Sprinkle with the reserved crust mixture.

4 Bake for 25 to 30 minutes, or until a light golden brown color. Cool in the pan on a wire rack. Cut into 36 bars.

BAKING NOTES: For a festive occasion, spread chocolate whipped cream (see page 000) over the bars before serving.

454 ▪ CHOCOLATE CRINKLES

MAKES 3 TO 4 DOZEN
BAKING TIME: *15 minutes*

2 cups all-purpose flour
2 teaspoons baking powder
3 ounces semisweet chocolate, grated or finely chopped
1/2 cup canola oil
1 1/2 cups granulated sugar
1 teaspoon vanilla extract
2 large eggs
1/4 cup milk
Powdered sugar for rolling

1 Position a rack in the center of the oven and preheat the oven to 350 degrees. Lightly grease two baking sheets.

2 Combine the flour and baking powder.

3 Melt the chocolate (see page 13). Remove from the heat.

4 In a large bowl, using an electric mixer on medium speed, beat the oil, sugar, and vanilla extract until smooth. Beat in the eggs, one at a time, beating well after each addition. Beat in the melted chocolate. Beat in the milk. Gradually stir in the dry ingredients.

5 Pinch off walnut-sized pieces of the dough and roll into balls. Roll each ball in powdered sugar and place 1 1/2 inches apart on the prepared pans.

6 Bake for 12 to 15 minutes, or until firm to the touch. Roll in powdered sugar again while still warm. Transfer to wire racks to cool.

455 ▪ CHOCOLATE CRISPY DROPS

MAKES 2 TO 4 DOZEN
CHILL TIME: *1 hour*

1 cup chunky peanut butter
1 cup semisweet chocolate chips
8 cups rice crispy cereal
1 cup butterscotch chips
1/2 cup plain, unsalted peanuts, chopped

1 Line two baking sheets with waxed paper.

2 In the top of a double boiler over simmering water, melt the peanut butter and chocolate chips, stirring until smooth. Add the cereal in one addition and stir until well coated. Remove from the heat and fold in the butterscotch chips. Drop spoonfuls of the mixture onto the prepared pans.

3 Chill for 1 hour, or until firm. Remove from the pans.

456 ▪ CHOCOLATE DATE BARS

MAKES 3 DOZEN
BAKING TIME: *30 minutes*

1 1/4 cups all-purpose flour
3/4 teaspoon baking soda
Pinch of salt
1 1/4 cups dates, pitted and finely chopped
3/4 cup packed light brown sugar
1/2 cup water
1/2 cup butter or margarine
6 ounces semisweet chocolate, grated or finely chopped
2 large eggs
1/2 cup fresh orange juice
1/2 cup milk
1 cup almonds, finely chopped
1 cup Lemon Glaze (see page 413)

1 Position a rack in the center of the oven and preheat the oven to 350 degrees. Lightly grease a 15 1/2 by 10 1/2-inch jelly-roll pan.

2 Combine the flour, baking soda, and salt.

3 In a large saucepan, over low heat, combine the dates, brown sugar, water, and butter. Cook until the dates are soft, about 3 minutes. Remove from the heat and stir in the chocolate. Using an electric mixer on medium speed, beat for 1 to 2 minutes, or until thickened. Beat in the eggs. Stir in the orange juice. Gradually blend in the dry ingredients, alternating with the milk. Fold in the almonds. Scrape the mixture into the prepared pan and spread evenly.

4 Bake for 25 to 30 minutes, or until a cake tester inserted into the center comes out clean, or the mixture pulls away from the sides of the pan. Cool in the pan on a wire rack.

5 Make the lemon glaze. Spread the lemon glaze over the chocolate date bars. Cut into 36 bars.

457 ▪ CHOCOLATE DE LA HARINA DE AVENA BROWNIES

MAKES 2 DOZEN
BAKING TIME: *30 minutes*

3 ounces unsweetened chocolate, grated or finely chopped
1 cup all-purpose flour
1 cup old-fashioned oats
1/2 teaspoon salt
2/3 cup vegetable shortening
1/2 cup granulated sugar
1 cup packed light brown sugar
4 large eggs
2 teaspoons vanilla or chocolate extract
1 cup almonds, finely chopped

1 Position a rack in the center of the oven and preheat the oven to 325 degrees. Lightly grease a 13 by 9-inch pan.

2 Melt the chocolate (see page 13). Remove from the heat.

3 Combine the flour, oats, and salt.

4 In a large bowl, using an electric mixer on medium speed, beat the shortening and sugars until fluffy. Beat in the eggs.

Beat in the vanilla extract and melted chocolate. Gradually stir in the dry ingredients. Fold in the almonds. Scrape the dough into the prepared pan and spread evenly.

5 Bake for 25 to 30 minutes, or until a cake tester inserted into the center comes out clean. Cool in the pan on a wire rack. Cut into 24 bars.

BAKING NOTES: Add 1 cup of raisins to the batter if desired. It is very easy to overbake these brownies, so check frequently near the end of the baking time. These are Mexican wedding cookies.

458 ■ CHOCOLATE DELIGHT BARS

MAKES 1 DOZEN
BAKING TIME: *40 minutes*

CRUST

½ cup butter or margarine, at room temperature
3 tablespoons powdered sugar
2 large eggs yolks (reserve the whites for topping)
1 teaspoon instant coffee powder
1 tablespoon warm water
2 cups all-purpose flour

TOPPING

½ cup semisweet chocolate chips
2 large egg whites
¼ cup granulated sugar
¼ cup almonds, finely ground
¼ cup almonds, chopped, for sprinkling

1 Position a rack in the center of the oven and preheat the oven to 350 degrees. Lightly grease a 9-inch square pan.

2 In a large bowl, using an electric mixer on medium speed, beat the butter, powdered sugar, egg yolks, coffee powder, and water until smooth. Gradually blend in the flour. The mixture will be crumbly. Press the mixture evenly onto the bottom of the prepared pan.

3 Bake for 20 minutes. Remove from the oven. While the crust is baking, make the topping.

4 Meanwhile, to make the topping, melt the chocolate (see page 13). Remove from the heat.

5 In a medium bowl, using an electric mixer on high speed, beat the egg whites until foamy. Beat in the granulated sugar and beat until stiff peaks form. Pouring it in a steady stream, beat in the melted chocolate. Fold in the ground almonds.

6 Spread the topping mixture over the hot crust, sprinkle with the chopped almonds, and bake for 20 minutes longer, or until firm. Cool in the pan on a wire rack. Cut into 12 bars.

459 ■ CHOCOLATE DIPPED HEALTH FOOD COOKIES I

MAKES 2 DOZEN
CHILL TIME: *30 minutes*

3 cups granola
½ cup raisins
½ cup chopped unsalted peanuts
½ cup flaked coconut
¾ cup chunky peanut butter
½ cup light corn syrup
½ cup honey
1 recipe Dipping Chocolate (see page 186)

1 Lightly grease a 13 by 9-inch baking pan.

2 In a large bowl, combine the granola, raisins, peanuts, and coconut.

3 In a saucepan, over medium heat, combine the peanut butter, corn syrup, and honey. Bring to a boil and cook for 1 minute. Remove from the heat. Add to the dry ingredients. Using a wooden spoon, stir until everything is well coated. Press the mixture evenly onto the bottom of the prepared pan. Chill for 30 minutes. Cut into 24 bars.

4 Meanwhile, make the dipping chocolate.

5 Dip the bars into the chocolate, coating half of each bar. Place on a sheet of waxed paper to set. When the chocolate has hardened, dip the other half in the chocolate and place on the waxed paper to set. Individually wrap the bars in waxed paper or plastic wrap and chill until serving.

458

459

454

457

460 ■ CHOCOLATE-DIPPED HEALTH FOOD COOKIES II

MAKES 2 DOZEN
CHILL TIME: *30 minutes*

8 cups quick-cooking oats
1½ cups oat bran
1½ cups golden raisins
1 cup creamy peanut butter
1½ cups crunchy peanut butter
1½ cups honey
1 recipe Dipping Chocolate (see page 186)

1 Lightly grease a 13 by 9-inch pan.

2 In a large bowl, combine the oats, oat bran, and raisins.

3 In the top of a double boiler over simmering water, combine the peanut butters and honey. Remove from heat. Using a wooden spoon, beat until thoroughly blended. Add to the dry ingredients. Using the wooden spoon, mix to make a smooth dough.

4 On a floured surface, using floured hands, knead the dough until smooth. Press the dough evenly onto the bottom of the prepared pan. Chill for 30 minutes. Cut into 24 bars.

5 Meanwhile, make the dipping chocolate.

6 Dip the bars into the chocolate, coating half of each bar. Place on a sheet of waxed paper to set. When the chocolate has hardened, dip the other half in the chocolate and place on the waxed paper to set. Individually wrap the bars in waxed paper or plastic wrap and chill until serving.

461 ■ CHOCOLATE-DIPPED SHORTBREAD

MAKES 16 BARS
BAKING TIME: *30 minutes*

1 cup all-purpose flour
¼ cup rice flour
1 tablespoon mocha-flavored instant coffee powder
1 teaspoon coffee liqueur
6 tablespoons butter or margarine, at room temperature
1 cup Dipping Chocolate (see page 186)

1 Position a rack in the center of the oven and preheat the oven to 325 degrees.

2 In a large bowl, mix all of the ingredients into a smooth, stiff dough, by hand or with an electric mixer. The dough will be very dry. Press the dough onto the bottom of an ungreased 9-inch square pan. Score into 16 squares. Using the tines of a fork, prick each square twice.

3 Bake for 20 to 30 minutes, or until the dough is set and very lightly colored. Cool in the pan on a wire rack for 5 minutes. Transfer to a wire rack to cool completely.

4 Make the dipping chocolate.

5 Cut the squares along the scored lines. Dip half of each bar in the dipping chocolate. Place on waxed paper and cool until the chocolate has hardened.

BAKING NOTES: To increase the yield of this recipe, score each bar into two triangles before baking. When baked and cooled, cut into triangles and dip two of the three corners in the chocolate. The entire square or triangle can be coated in the chocolate; dip first one half and let it harden and then dip the other half.

462 ■ CHOCOLATE DROP COOKIES I

MAKES 4 TO 5 DOZEN

2½ cups old-fashioned oats
½ cup Dutch processed cocoa powder
½ cup butter or margarine
½ cup peanut butter
½ cup evaporated milk
2 cups powdered sugar

1 Line a baking sheet with waxed paper.

2 Combine the oatmeal and cocoa powder.

3 In a large saucepan, over low heat, melt the butter and peanut butter, stirring constantly until smooth. Remove from the heat. Beat in the milk. Gradually beat in the powdered sugar. Gradually blend in the dry ingredients.

4 Drop the dough by spoonfuls onto the prepared pan. Let cool at room temperature until firm.

464

465

460

461

462

463 ■ CHOCOLATE DROP COOKIES II

MAKES 2 TO 3 DOZEN
BAKING TIME: *10 minutes*

2 ounces semisweet chocolate, grated or finely chopped
2 cups all-purpose flour
1/2 cup almonds, finely ground
1/2 teaspoon baking soda
1/2 teaspoon salt
1/2 cup vegetable shortening
1/2 cup packed light brown sugar
1/2 cup granulated sugar
1 large egg
1 teaspoon vanilla or chocolate extract
3/4 cup buttermilk

1 Position a rack in the center of the oven and preheat the oven to 400 degrees. Lightly grease two baking sheets.

2 Melt the chocolate (see page 13). Remove from the heat.

3 Combine the flour, almonds, baking soda, and salt

4 In a large bowl, using an electric mixer on medium speed, beat the shortening and the sugars until fluffy. Beat in the egg. Beat in the vanilla extract. Beat in the buttermilk and melted chocolate. Gradually stir in the dry ingredients. Drop the dough by spoonfuls 1 1/2 inches apart onto the prepared pans.

5 Bake for 8 to 10 minutes, or until firm to the touch. Transfer to wire racks to cool.

464 ■ CHOCOLATE-FILLED CUSHIONS

MAKES 2 TO 3 DOZEN
BAKING TIME: *15 minutes*

CUSHIONS

3 cups all-purpose flour
1/4 teaspoon salt
1 cup butter or margarine, at room temperature
1 cup packed light brown sugar
2 teaspoons chocolate extract
1 1/2 tablespoons milk
1/2 cup Hershey's™ semisweet chocolate candy bar sprinkles
Powdered sugar for rolling

FILLING

1 3/4 cups semisweet chocolate chips
2 tablespoons vegetable shortening
1/4 cup light corn syrup
2 tablespoons crème de cacao
1 teaspoon chocolate extract

1 Position a rack in the center of the oven and preheat the oven to 350 degrees.

2 To make the cushions, combine the flour and salt.

3 In a large bowl, using an electric mixer on medium speed, beat the butter, brown sugar, and chocolate extract until blended. Stir in the milk. Gradually stir in the dry ingredients. Fold in the chocolate sprinkles. Pinch off 1-inch pieces of the dough and roll into balls. Place the balls 1 inch apart on ungreased baking sheets. Press your thumb into the center of each ball to make a deep indentation.

4 Bake for 12 to 15 minutes, or until a light golden color. Roll the hot cookies in powdered sugar. Transfer to a wire rack to cool.

5 Meanwhile, to make the filling, in the top of a double boiler over simmering water, melt the chocolate chips and shortening, stirring until smooth. Stir in the corn syrup and chocolate extract and cook, stirring constantly, for 5 minutes. Do not let the mixture boil. Remove from the heat. Spoon 1/2 teaspoon into the indentation in each cookie. Place on the wire rack and let cool until the filling has set.

465 ■ CHOCOLATE-FILLED OATMEAL BARS

MAKES 3 DOZEN
BAKING TIME: *15 minutes*

CRUST

3 cups quick-cooking oats
2 1/2 cups all-purpose flour
1 teaspoon baking soda
1/4 teaspoon salt
1 1/2 cups peanuts or almonds, chopped

1 cup butter-flavored vegetable shortening
2 cups packed light brown sugar
2 large eggs
1 tablespoon coffee liqueur
1/2 teaspoon instant coffee powder

FILLING

1/2 cup butter-flavored vegetable shortening
2/3 cup Dutch processed cocoa powder
1/2 cup granulated sugar
1 can (14 ounces) sweetened condensed milk
1 1/2 teaspoons chocolate or vanilla extract

1 Position a rack in the center of the oven and preheat the oven to 350 degrees. Lightly grease a 15 1/2 by 10 1/2-inch jelly-roll pan.

2 To make the crust, combine the oats, flour, baking soda, salt, and pecans.

3 In a large bowl, using an electric mixer on medium speed, beat the shortening and brown sugar until fluffy. Beat in the eggs, liqueur, and coffee powder. Gradually blend in the dry ingredients. The dough will be very stiff. Spread 2 cups of the crust mixture evenly onto the bottom of the prepared pan. Reserve the remaining crust mixture.

4 To make the filling, in a large saucepan, over low heat, melt the shortening. Stir in the cocoa powder and sugar. Stir in the condensed milk and cook, stirring frequently, until the mixture is smooth and very thick. Remove from the heat and beat in the chocolate extract.

5 Spread the filling evenly over the crust in the pan. Sprinkle the reserved crust mixture over the top.

6 Bake for 20 to 25 minutes, or until the top is dull and slightly browned. Cool in the pan on a wire rack. Cut into 36 bars.

BAKING NOTES: After the remaining crust mixture is sprinkled over the top, it can be pressed down or left loose.

466 ■ CHOCOLATE-FILLED PINWHEELS

MAKES 4 TO 5 DOZEN
BAKING TIME: *12 minutes*
CHILL TIME: *overnight*

CRUST

2 cups all-purpose flour
1 teaspoon baking powder
1/2 teaspoon salt
3/4 cup butter-flavored vegetable shortening
1 cup granulated sugar
1 large egg
1 tablespoon vanilla extract

FILLING

2 tablespoons butter or margarine
1 cup semisweet chocolate chips
1 cup walnuts, finely ground
1 1/2 teaspoons vanilla extract

1 To make the crust, combine the flour, baking powder, and salt.

2 In a large bowl, using an electric mixer on medium speed, beat the shortening and sugar until fluffy. Beat in the egg. Beat in the vanilla extract. Gradually stir in the dry ingredients. Reserve 2/3 cup of the dough; set aside at room temperature. Wrap the remaining dough in waxed paper and chill for 2 hours.

3 To make the filling, in the top of a double boiler over simmering water, melt the butter and chocolate. Remove from the heat and stir in the walnuts and vanilla extract. Blend in the reserved portion of the dough.

4 On a floured surface roll out the chilled dough to a 16 by 12-inch rectangle. Spread the filling over the dough, spreading it to within 1/2 inch of the edges. Starting on one of the long sides, roll the dough up jelly-roll fashion. Pinch the seam to seal. Cut in half to make two 8-inch logs. Wrap in waxed paper and chill overnight.

5 Position a rack in the center of the oven and preheat the oven to 350 degrees.

6 Slice the logs into 1/4-inch slices. Place the slices 1 1/2 inches apart on ungreased baking sheets.

7 Bake for 10 to 12 minutes, or until lightly colored. Transfer to wire racks to cool.

BAKING NOTES: To decorate, drizzle melted white or dark chocolate over the tops of the cookies after they have cooled. For chocolate mint filling, add a drop or two of peppermint extract.

467 ■ CHOCOLATE FUDGE CHEESECAKE BARS

MAKES 2 DOZEN
BAKING TIME: *25 minutes*
CHILL TIME: *30 minutes*

4 ounces unsweetened chocolate, grated or finely chopped
1 cup butter or margarine
4 large eggs
2 cups granulated sugar
1 teaspoon almond or chocolate extract
8 ounces cream cheese, at room temperature
2 cups all-purpose flour

1 Position a rack in the center of the oven and preheat the oven to 350 degrees. Lightly grease a 13 by 9-inch pan.

2 In the top of a double boiler over simmering water, melt the chocolate and butter, stirring until smooth. Remove from the heat.

3 In a medium bowl, using an electric mixer on medium speed, beat the eggs until thick and light-colored. Beat in the sugar and almond extract just until blended. On low speed, beat in the chocolate mixture, pouring it in a thin stream. Blend in the cream cheese. Gradually blend in the flour. Scrape the mixture into the prepared pan and spread evenly.

4 Bake for 20 to 25 minutes, or until they pull away from the sides of the pan. Cool in the pan on a wire rack. Chill for about 30 minutes. Cut into 24 bars.

468 ■ CHOCOLATE JUMBO COOKIES

MAKES 2 TO 4 DOZEN
BAKING TIME: *15 minutes*

3 cups old-fashioned oats
1 cup all-purpose flour
6 tablespoons Dutch processed cocoa powder
1/2 teaspoon baking soda
1/2 teaspoon salt
1 1/2 cups vegetable shortening
1 1/2 cups granulated sugar
1 large egg
1/4 cup milk
1 teaspoon chocolate extract
1 cup semisweet chocolate chips

1 Position a rack in the center of the oven and preheat the oven to 350 degrees. Lightly grease two baking sheets.

2 Combine the oats, flour, cocoa powder, baking soda, and salt.

3 In a large bowl, using an electric mixer on medium speed, beat the shortening and sugar until fluffy. Beat in the egg. Beat in the milk and chocolate extract. Gradually stir in the dry ingredients. Fold in the chocolate chips. Drop the dough by spoonfuls 2 inches apart onto the prepared pans.

4 Bake for 12 to 15 minutes, or until dry-looking. Transfer to wire racks to cool.

469 ■ CHOCOLATE LEMON DESSERT COOKIES

MAKES 3 TO 4 DOZEN
BAKING TIME: *12 minutes*

1 package (2.9 ounces) Jell-O Brand lemon pudding mix
3 tablespoons cold water
1 ounce semisweet chocolate, grated or finely chopped
1 can (14 ounces) sweetened condensed milk
1 1/2 cups flaked coconut
1 teaspoon vanilla extract

1 Position a rack in the center of the oven and preheat the oven to 350 degrees. Lightly grease two baking sheets.

2 In a saucepan, over low heat, stir the lemon pudding mix, cold water, and chocolate until

smooth. Add the condensed milk and cook for 3 minutes, stirring constantly. Remove from the heat and stir in the coconut and vanilla extract. Drop the dough by spoonfuls onto the prepared pans.

3 Bake for 10 to 12 minutes, or until firm to the touch. Transfer to wire racks to cool

470 ■ CHOCOLATE MACAROONS I

MAKES 1 TO 2 DOZEN
BAKING TIME: *25 minutes*

½ cup ground almonds
2 tablespoons all-purpose flour
Pinch of salt
2 envelopes premelted unsweet-ened chocolate (see page 14)
2 large egg whites
⅓ cup granulated sugar
½ teaspoon chocolate extract
½ teaspoon almond extract

1 Position a rack in the center of the oven and preheat the oven to 325 degrees. Lightly grease and flour two baking sheets.

2 In a large bowl, combine the almonds, flour, and salt. Stir in the chocolate.

3 In a small bowl, using an elec-tric mixer on high speed, beat the egg whites until foamy. Gradually beat in the sugar. Beat until stiff but not dry. Stir one-fourth of the egg whites into the

dry ingredients. Stir in the chocolate and almond extracts. Fold in the remaining egg whites. Drop the dough by spoonfuls 2 inches apart onto the prepared pans.

4 Bake for 20 to 25 minutes, or until crusty. Cool on the pans for 5 minutes. Transfer to a wire rack to cool completely.

471 ■ CHOCOLATE MACAROONS II

MAKES 2 TO 3 DOZEN
BAKING TIME: *12 minutes*

3 ounces semisweet chocolate, grated or finely chopped
1 cup ground almonds
⅔ cup granulated sugar
2 large egg whites

1 Position a rack in the center of the oven and preheat the oven to 325 degrees. Line two baking sheets with parchment paper.

2 Melt the chocolate (see page 13). Remove from the heat.

3 In a medium bowl, using an electric mixer on low speed, beat the almonds with 2 table-spoons of the sugar until com-bined. Add the egg whites and remaining sugar and beat on high speed until blended. Grad-ually blend in the melted choco-late, beating until the mixture is very smooth.

4 Fill a pastry bag fitted with a medium-sized plain tip with the mixture. Pipe out 1-inch rounds on the prepared pans, spacing them 1 inch apart.

5 Bake for 5 minutes. Prop the oven door slightly open and continue baking for 7 minutes longer. Transfer to wire racks to cool completely.

472 ■ CHOCOLATE MARBLE BARS

MAKES 1 DOZEN
BAKING TIME: *45 minutes*

CREAM CHEESE BATTER

6 ounces cream cheese, at room temperature
2 tablespoons butter or margarine, at room temperature
¼ cup granulated sugar
2 tablespoons cornstarch
2 large eggs
½ teaspoon grated lemon zest

CHOCOLATE BATTER

2 ounces semisweet chocolate, grated or finely chopped
¾ cup all-purpose flour
¾ cup granulated sugar
½ teaspoon baking soda
½ teaspoon salt
⅓ cup buttermilk
¼ cup butter or margarine, at room temperature
1 large egg
½ teaspoon chocolate extract

1 Position a rack in the center of the oven and preheat the oven to 350 degrees. Lightly grease a 9-inch square pan.

466

469

472

470

2 To make the cream cheese batter, in a large bowl, using an electric mixer on medium speed, beat the cream cheese and butter until blended. Beat in the sugar and cornstarch until smooth. Beat in the eggs, one at a time, beating well after each addition. Beat in the lemon zest. Pour the mixture into the prepared pan.

3 To make the chocolate batter, melt the chocolate (see page 13). Remove from the heat.

4 In a large mixing bowl, combine the flour, sugar, baking soda, and salt. Using an electric mixer on medium speed, beat in the buttermilk, butter, and melted chocolate until blended. Beat on medium speed for 2 to 3 minutes. Beat in the egg and chocolate extract. Spoon the mixture evenly over the top of the cream mixture already in the baking pan. Using a knife, gently swirl the two mixtures together. Do not overmix.

5 Bake for 40 to 45 minutes, or until a cake tester inserted into the center comes out clean. Cool in the pan on a wire rack. Cut into 12 bars.

473 ■ CHOCOLATE MERINGUES

MAKES 3 TO 4 DOZEN
BAKING TIME: *15 minutes*

6 ounces semisweet chocolate, grated or finely chopped
3 large egg whites
1/2 teaspoon salt
1 cup granulated sugar
1/2 cup ground almonds
1/2 teaspoon chocolate extract
Powdered sugar for rolling

1 Position a rack in the center of the oven and preheat the oven to 350 degrees. Lightly grease two baking sheets.

2 Melt the chocolate (see page 13). Remove from the heat.

3 In a large bowl, using an electric mixer on high speed, beat the egg whites and salt until stiff but not dry. Beat in the sugar. Fold in the almonds, chocolate extract, and melted chocolate.

Drop the dough by teaspoonfuls onto the prepared pans.

4 Bake for 12 to 15 minutes, or until dry-looking. Cool on the pan for 5 minutes. Roll in powdered sugar. Transfer to a wire rack to cool completely.

474 ■ CHOCOLATE MERINGUE STICKS

MAKES 3 TO 4 DOZEN
BAKING TIME: *90 minutes*

1 cup powdered sugar
1/3 cup Dutch processed cocoa powder
5 large egg whites
1/2 cup granulated sugar

1 Position a rack in the center of the oven and preheat the oven to 300 degrees. Line two baking sheets with parchment paper.

2 Combine the powdered sugar and cocoa powder.

3 In a large bowl, using an electric mixer on high speed, beat the egg whites until foamy. On low speed, gradually beat in the granulated sugar. Increase the speed to high and beat until the mixture is stiff but not dry. Gently fold in the dry ingredients, a little at a time, until well incorporated.

4 Fill a pastry bag fitted with a medium-sized plain tip with the mixture. Pipe out 2 1/2 to 3-inch long sticks onto the prepared pans, spacing them 1 inch apart.

5 Bake for 85 to 90 minutes, or until dry-looking. Cool on the pans on wire racks for 10 minutes. Transfer the cookies to the racks to cool completely.

475 ■ CHOCOLATE MINT BARS WITH ALMONDS

MAKES 2 DOZEN
BAKING TIME: *15 minutes*

2 cups all-purpose flour
1/2 teaspoon baking powder
1/2 cup slivered almonds
1 cup mint chocolate chips
8 ounces cream cheese, at room temperature
3/4 cup butter or margarine, at room temperature
3/4 cup granulated sugar
1 teaspoon vanilla extract
1 cup semisweet chocolate chips for garnish
1/2 cup chopped almonds for garnish

1 Position a rack in the center of the oven and preheat the oven to 375 degrees. Grease a 13 by 9-inch pan.

2 Combine the flour, baking powder, almonds, and mint chocolate chips.

3 In a large bowl, using an electric mixer on medium speed, beat the cream cheese, butter, and sugar until blended. Beat in the vanilla extract. Gradually stir in the dry ingredients. Scrape the mixture into the prepared pan and spread evenly.

4 Bake for 12 to 15 minutes, or until a light brown color. Spri-

475

473

477

kle the chocolate chips over the top. Let stand for 3 minutes. Spread the melted chocolate chips evenly over the top. Sprinkle with the chopped almonds and cool completely on a wire rack. Cut into 24 bars.

476 ■ CHOCOLATE NUT COOKIES

MAKES 3 TO 4 DOZEN
BAKING TIME: *15 minutes*

2 ounces unsweetened chocolate, grated or finely chopped
3/4 cup all-purpose flour
1/4 teaspoon salt
1/2 cup vegetable shortening
1 cup granulated sugar
1 teaspoon hazelnut or vanilla extract
1 large egg
3/4 cup hazelnuts or pecans, ground
Powdered sugar for pressing

1 Position a rack in the center of the oven and preheat the oven to 325 degrees. Lightly grease two baking sheets.

2 Melt the chocolate (see page 13). Remove from the heat.

3 Combine the flour and salt.

4 In a large bowl, using an electric mixer on medium speed, beat the shortening, melted chocolate, and sugar until smooth. Beat in the hazelnut extract. Beat in the egg. Gradually stir in the dry ingredients. Fold in the hazelnuts. Drop the dough by spoonfuls 1 1/2 inches apart onto the prepared pans.

476

479

Flatten the cookies with the back of a spoon dipped in powdered sugar.

5 Bake for 12 to 15 minutes, or until firm to the touch. Transfer to wire racks to cool.

477 ■ CHOCOLATE OATMEAL BARS

MAKES 3 DOZEN
BAKING TIME: *30 minutes*

CRUST

3 cups old-fashioned oats
2 1/2 cups all-purpose flour
1 teaspoon baking soda
1 teaspoon salt
1 cup vegetable shortening
2 cups packed light brown sugar
2 large eggs
2 teaspoons vanilla extract

FILLING

2 cups semisweet chocolate chips
2 tablespoons butter or margarine
1 can (14 ounces) sweetened condensed milk
1 cup almonds, chopped
2 teaspoons vanilla extract

1 Preheat the oven to 350 degrees.

2 To make the crust, combine the oats, flour, baking soda, and salt.

3 In a large bowl, using an electric mixer on medium speed, beat the shortening and brown sugar until fluffy. Beat in the eggs and vanilla. Gradually stir in the dry ingredients. Press two-thirds of the crust mixture onto the bottom of an ungreased 13 by 9-inch pan. Reserve the remaining crust mixture.

4 To make the filling, in the top of a double boiler over simmering water, melt the chocolate chips and butter. Add the condensed milk, almonds, and vanilla extract and stir until smooth. Spread the filling evenly over the crust in the pan. Press the remaining crust mixture on the top of the filling.

5 Bake for 25 to 30 minutes, or until firm to the touch. Cool in the pan on a wire rack. Cut into 36 bars.

478 ■ CHOCOLATE OATMEAL COOKIES

MAKES 3 TO 4 DOZEN
BAKING TIME: *12 minutes*

1 cup all-purpose flour
1 cup old-fashioned oats
1/2 teaspoon baking soda
2 ounces unsweetened chocolate, grated or finely chopped
1/2 cup vegetable shortening
1 cup granulated sugar
1 large egg
1 1/2 teaspoons amaretto
1/2 cup almonds or pecans, chopped
Granulated sugar for pressing

1 Position a rack in the center of the oven and preheat the oven to 350 degrees. Lightly grease two baking sheets.

2 Combine the flour, oats, and baking soda.

3 Melt the chocolate (see page 13). Remove from the heat.

4 In a large bowl, using an electric mixer on medium speed, beat the shortening and sugar until fluffy. Beat in the egg. Beat in the amaretto. Stir in the melted chocolate. Gradually blend in the dry ingredients. Fold in the almonds.

5 Pinch off walnut-sized pieces of the dough and roll into balls. Place the balls 1 1/2 inches apart on the prepared pans. Flatten the balls with the bottom of a glass dipped in sugar.

6 Bake for 10 to 12 minutes, or until firm to the touch. Transfer to wire racks to cool.

479 ■ CHOCOLATE PEANUT COOKIES

MAKES 2 TO 3 DOZEN
BAKING TIME: *18 minutes*

1 cup all-purpose flour
3/4 teaspoon baking soda
1/2 cup butter or margarine, at room temperature
1/2 cup creamy peanut butter
1/2 teaspoon chocolate extract
1/4 cup granulated sugar
1/2 cup packed light brown sugar
1 large egg
4 ounces milk chocolate, diced
4 ounces semisweet chocolate, diced
1 cup toasted peanuts

1 Position a rack in the center of the oven and preheat the oven to 350 degrees. Lightly grease two baking sheets.

2 Combine the flour and baking soda.

3 In a large bowl, using an electric mixer on medium speed, beat the butter and peanut butter until smooth. Beat in the chocolate extract and sugars. Beat in the egg. Gradually stir in the dry ingredients. Fold in the chocolates and peanuts. Drop the dough by teaspoonfuls 1½ inches apart onto the prepared pans.

4 Bake for 15 to 18 minutes, or until lightly colored. Cool on the pan for 10 minutes. Transfer to wire racks to cool completely.

BAKING NOTES: These are very fragile cookies and should be handled carefully.

480 ■ CHOCOLATE PEANUT BUTTER SQUARES

MAKES 2 TO 3 DOZEN
CHILL TIME: *30 minutes*

CRUST

2 cups quick-cooking oats
1 cup salted peanuts
2 tablespoons butter or margarine
¼ cup peanut butter
1 jar (7 ounces) marshmallows creme

TOPPING

4 ounces semisweet chocolate, grated or finely chopped
3 tablespoons peanut butter

1 Lightly grease a 9-inch square pan.

2 In a large bowl, using a wooden spoon, combine the oats and peanuts.

3 In the top of a double boiler over simmering water, combine the butter, ¼ cup of the peanut butter, and the marshmallow creme, stirring occasionally until smooth. Pour into the dry ingredients, blending thoroughly. Scrape the mixture into the prepared pan and spread evenly.

4 In the top of a double boiler over simmering water, melt the chocolate and the remaining 3 tablespoons peanut butter, stirring until smooth. Spread evenly over the crust in the pan and chill 30 minutes, or until set. Cut into squares.

481 ■ CHOCOLATE PECAN COOKIES

MAKES 4 TO 5 DOZEN
BAKING TIME: *15 minutes*
CHILL TIME: *2 hours*

1 ounce unsweetened chocolate
¾ cup all-purpose flour
¼ teaspoon salt
½ cup vegetable shortening

455

467

463

478

456

468

471

474

1 cup dark brown sugar
2 large eggs
1 teaspoon rum flavoring
¾ cup pecans, finely ground

1 Melt the chocolate (see page 13). Remove from the heat.

2 Combine the flour and salt.

3 In a large bowl, using an electric mixer on medium speed, beat the shortening and sugar until fluffy. Beat in the eggs, one at a time, beating well after each addition. Beat in the melted chocolate and rum flavoring. Gradually stir in the dry ingredients. Fold in the pecans. Cover and chill for 2 hours.

4 Position a rack in the center of the oven and preheat the oven to 350 degrees. Lightly grease two baking sheets.

5 Drop the chilled dough by spoonfuls 1½ inches apart onto the prepared pans.

6 Bake for 12 to 15 minutes, or until firm to the touch. Transfer to wire racks to cool.

482 ■ CHOCOLATE PEFFERNÜSSE

MAKES 3 TO 4 DOZEN
BAKING TIME: *15 to 20 minutes*
CHILL TIME: *8 hours*

2½ cups all-purpose flour
½ cup chopped almonds
¼ cup finely chopped candied orange or lemon peel
2 tablespoons finely chopped candied citron or glacé cherries
½ teaspoon ground cinnamon
½ teaspoon ground cloves
¼ teaspoon ground allspice
¼ teaspoon ground black pepper
¼ teaspoon salt
3 large eggs
1½ cups granulated sugar
Cocoa Sugar (see page 407) for rolling

1 In a large bowl, combine the flour, almonds, orange peel, citron, spices, pepper, and salt.

2 In a medium bowl, using an electric mixer on medium speed, beat the eggs until thick and light-colored. Beat in the sugar, a tablespoon at a time, until the sugar is completely dissolved. Add to the dry ingredients and mix until blended. Cover tightly with aluminum foil and chill for at least 8 hours.

3 Position a rack in the center of the oven and preheat the oven to 350 degrees. Lightly grease two baking sheets.

4 Dust your hands with flour and break off walnut-sized pieces of the dough and roll into balls. Place the balls 1½ inches apart on the prepared pan.

5 Bake for 15 to 20 minutes, or until the balls are lightly browned. Roll the hot cookies in cocoa sugar. Transfer to a wire rack to cool completely. Roll in the cocoa sugar again.

483 ■ CHOCOLATE PINEAPPLE SQUARES

MAKES 2 DOZEN
BAKING TIME: *45 minutes*

1½ cups all-purpose flour
½ teaspoon baking powder
¼ teaspoon ground allspice
½ teaspoon salt
½ cup Dutch processed cocoa powder
2½ teaspoons butter, melted
1 cup butter-flavored vegetable shortening
2 cups granulated sugar
1 teaspoon chocolate or vanilla extract
4 large eggs
½ cup Macadamia nuts, chopped
1 cup crushed pineapple, drained
1½ cups Chocolate Rum Icing (see page 404)

1 Position a rack in the center of the oven and preheat the oven to 350 degrees. Lightly grease a 13 by 9-inch pan.

2 Combine the flour, baking powder, allspice, and salt.

3 In a small bowl, combine the cocoa powder and melted butter, stirring until smooth.

480

483

482

481

4 In a large bowl, using an electric mixer on medium speed, beat shortening, sugar, and chocolate extract until fluffy. Beat in the eggs, one at a time, beating well after each addition. Stir in the cocoa mixture. Gradually blend in the dry ingredients, mixing just until blended. Fold in the nuts. Remove 1½ cups of the batter and reserve. Scrape the remaining batter into the prepared pan and spread evenly.

5 In a medium bowl, combine the pineapple and reserved batter. Spread over the batter in the pan.

6 Bake for 40 to 45 minutes, or until dry-looking. Cool in the pan on a wire rack. Make the frosting. Frost the top of the cake. Cut into 24 squares.

BAKING NOTES: The cake can also be inverted onto a serving plate and frosted.

484 ■ CHOCOLATE PIXIES

MAKES 2 TO 3 DOZEN
BAKING TIME: *18 minutes*
CHILL TIME: *1 hour*

1½ cups all-purpose flour
1 teaspoon baking powder
¼ teaspoon salt
¼ cup vegetable shortening
2 ounces unsweetened chocolate, grated or finely chopped
2 large eggs
1 cup granulated sugar
¼ cup pecans, chopped
Powdered sugar for rolling

1 Combine the flour, baking powder, and salt.

2 In the top of a double boiler over simmering water, melt the shortening and chocolate, stirring until smooth. Remove from the heat.

3 In a large bowl, using an electric mixer on medium speed, beat the eggs until thick and light-colored. Add the sugar and beat until smooth. Using a wooden spoon, stir in the chocolate mixture. Gradually stir in the dry ingredients, mixing just until blended. Fold in the

pecans. Cover and chill for 1 hour.

4 Position a rack in the center of the oven and preheat the oven to 300 degrees. Lightly grease two baking sheets.

5 Break off walnut-sized pieces of the dough and roll into balls. Place the balls 1½ inches apart on the prepared pans.

6 Bake for 15 to 18 minutes, or until dry-looking. Transfer to wire racks to cool.

BAKING NOTES: For a decorative garnish, press a pecan half into the center of each ball before baking.

485 ■ CHOCOLATE PRETZELS WITH MOCHA FROSTING

MAKES 2 TO 3 DOZEN
BAKING TIME: *20 minutes*
CHILL TIME: *1 hour*

CHOCOLATE PRETZELS

2⅔ cups all-purpose flour
¾ cup granulated sugar
⅓ cup Dutch processed cocoa powder
1 cup less 2 tablespoons butter or margarine
2 large eggs whites
2 teaspoons chocolate extract

FROSTING

4½ ounces unsweetened chocolate, grated or finely chopped
½ cup strong brewed coffee
1 cup Cocoa Sugar (see page 407)
2 tablespoons butter or margarine

1 To make the chocolate pretzels, in a large bowl, combine the flour, sugar, and cocoa powder. Using an electric mixer on medium speed, cut in the butter until crumbly.

2 In a small bowl, using an electric mixer on high speed, beat the egg whites until foamy. Beat in the chocolate extract. Fold the egg whites into the dry ingredients. Wrap and chill for at least 1 hour.

3 Position a rack in the center of the oven and preheat the oven to 375 degrees. Lightly grease two baking sheets.

4 Divide the dough into thirds and work with one-third at a time, keeping the remaining two-thirds in the refrigerator. Form each third of the dough into a log 1½ inches in diameter. Slice into ½-inch pieces. Roll each piece into a pencil-thin rope and twist into a pretzel shape. Place the pretzels on the prepared pans 1 inch apart. Repeat with the remaining dough.

5 Bake for 15 to 20 minutes, or until the pretzels are just starting to turn a golden color. Transfer to a wire rack to cool.

6 To make the frosting, in a medium saucepan, over low heat, melt the chocolate with the coffee, stirring until smooth. Remove from the heat and stir in the cocoa sugar and butter until smooth. Spread the icing on the pretzels and place on a wire rack until firm.

486 ■ CHOCOLATE PUDDING BROWNIES

MAKES 1 DOZEN
BAKING TIME: *30 minutes*

½ cup all-purpose flour
1 package (3.4 ounces) Jell-O Brand chocolate instant pudding mix
½ teaspoon baking powder
¼ teaspoon salt
6 tablespoons vegetable shortening
⅔ cup granulated sugar
2 large eggs
¼ cup milk
1 teaspoon vanilla or chocolate extract
½ cup walnuts or pecans, chopped
Powdered sugar for dusting

1 Position a rack in the center of the oven and preheat the oven to 350 degrees. Lightly grease a 9-inch square pan.

2 Combine the flour, pudding mix, baking powder, and salt.

3 In a large bowl, using an electric mixer on medium speed, beat the shortening and sugar until fluffy. Beat in the eggs. Beat in the milk and vanilla extract. Gradually blend in the dry ingredients. Fold in the walnuts. Scrape the mixture into the prepared pan and spread evenly.

4 Bake for 25 to 30 minutes, or until a cake tester inserted into the center comes out clean. Cool in the pan on a wire rack.

5 Place a paper doily over the top of the cooled brownies. Sprinkle with powdered sugar. Carefully lift off the doily. Cut into 12 bars.

487 ■ CHOCOLATE PUMPKIN COOKIES

MAKES 5 TO 6 DOZEN
BAKING TIME: *15 minutes*

2½ cups all-purpose flour
1 teaspoon baking powder
1 teaspoon baking soda
1½ teaspoons ground cinnamon
1 teaspoon ground nutmeg
¼ teaspoon ground cloves
½ teaspoon salt
½ cup butter or margarine, at room temperature
1½ cups granulated sugar
1 large egg
1 cup solid pack canned pumpkin
1 teaspoon vanilla extract
½ cup chopped almonds
1 cup Hershey's™ Chocolate Shoppe Candy Bar Sprinkles
16 ounces Dipping Chocolate (see page 186)

1 Position a rack in the center of the oven and preheat the oven to 350 degrees. Grease two baking sheets.

2 Combine the flour, baking powder, baking soda, spices, and salt.

3 In a large bowl, using an electric mixer on high speed, beat the butter and sugar until light and fluffy. Beat in the egg, pumpkin, and vanilla extract. Gradually blend in the dry ingredients. Fold in the almonds and chocolate sprinkles. Drop the dough by spoonfuls 1½ inches apart onto the prepared pans.

4 Bake for 12 to 15 minutes, or until lightly colored. Transfer to a wire rack to cool completely.

488 ■ CHOCOLATE RAISIN DROPS

MAKES 2 TO 4 DOZEN
BAKING TIME: *15 minutes*

1 cup all-purpose flour
½ cup walnuts, finely ground
½ teaspoon baking soda
¼ teaspoon salt
½ cup vegetable shortening
½ cup granulated sugar
¼ cup packed light brown sugar
1 large egg
½ teaspoon vanilla extract
¾ cup chocolate-covered raisins

1 Position a rack in the center of the oven and preheat the oven to 350 degrees. Lightly grease two baking sheets.

2 Combine the flour, walnuts, baking soda, and salt.

3 In a large bowl, using an electric mixer on medium speed, beat the shortening and the sugars until fluffy. Beat in the egg. Beat in the vanilla extract. Gradually blend in the dry ingredients. Fold in the chocolate-covered raisins. Drop the dough by spoonfuls 1½ inches apart onto the prepared pans.

4 Bake for 12 to 15 minutes, or until lightly colored. Transfer to wire racks to cool.

489 ■ CHOCOLATE RASPBERRY SWIRL BROWNIES

MAKES 1 DOZEN
BAKING TIME: *25 minutes*

3 ounces unsweetened chocolate, grated or finely chopped
⅓ cup butter or margarine
2 large eggs
1¼ cups granulated sugar
1 teaspoon chocolate extract
¾ cup all-purpose flour
¼ cup raspberry preserves

1 Position a rack in the center of the oven and preheat the oven to 350 degrees. Lightly grease an 8 or 9-inch square pan.

2 In the top of a double boiler over simmering water, melt the chocolate and butter, stirring until smooth. Remove from the heat.

3 In a large bowl, using an electric mixer on medium speed, beat the eggs until thick and light-colored. Beat in the sugar. Beat in the chocolate extract and melted chocolate until thoroughly blended. Gradually blend in the flour. Scrape the mixture into the prepared pan and spread evenly. Drop the preserves by spoonfuls onto the batter in the four corners of the pan. Using a knife, swirl the preserves around to create a marbled pattern. Do not overmix.

484

486

485

489

4 Bake for 20 to 25 minutes, or until a cake tester inserted into the chocolate part comes out clean. Cool in the pan on a wire rack. Cut into 12 bars.

BAKING NOTES: Any flavor preserves can be substituted, but do not use jelly.

490 ■ CHOCOLATE REFRIGERATOR COOKIES I

MAKES 5 TO 6 DOZEN
BAKING TIME: *10 minutes*
CHILL TIME: *4 hours*

2 cups all-purpose flour
1/2 teaspoon baking soda
1/2 teaspoon salt
1/2 cup vegetable shortening
1 cup packed dark brown sugar
1 large egg
2 tablespoons chocolate syrup
2 teaspoons vanilla or chocolate extract

1 Combine the flour, baking soda, and salt.

2 In a large bowl, using an electric mixer on medium speed, beat the shortening and brown sugar until fluffy. Beat in the egg. Beat in the chocolate syrup and vanilla extract. Gradually stir in the dry ingredients. Form the dough into a log 2 inches in diameter. Wrap in waxed paper and chill for 4 hours.

3 Position a rack in the center of the oven and preheat the oven to 400 degrees.

4 Cut the log into 1/4-inch slices. Place the slices 1 inch apart on ungreased baking sheets.

5 Bake for 8 to 10 minutes, or until golden brown. Transfer to wire racks to cool

BAKING NOTES: For a variation, roll the log in chopped nuts before chilling. This dough can be frozen for up to three months.

491 ■ CHOCOLATE REFRIGERATOR COOKIES II

MAKES 7 TO 8 DOZEN
BAKING TIME: *12 minutes*
CHILL TIME: *4 hours*

3 ounces unsweetened chocolate, grated or finely chopped
3 cups all-purpose flour
1 tablespoon baking powder
1/2 teaspoon salt
1 cup vegetable shortening
1 cup granulated sugar
1 large egg
2 teaspoons crème de cacao

1 Melt the chocolate (see page 13). Remove from the heat.

2 Combine the flour, baking powder, and salt.

3 In a large bowl, using an electric mixer on medium speed, beat the shortening and sugar until fluffy. Beat in the egg. Beat in the crème de cacao and melted chocolate. Gradually stir in the dry ingredients. Form the dough into two logs 2 inches in diameter. Wrap in waxed paper and chill for 4 hours.

4 Position a rack in the center of the oven and preheat the oven to 350 degrees.

5 Cut the logs into 1/8-inch slices. Place the slices 1 inch apart on ungreased baking sheets.

6 Bake for 10 to 12 minutes, or until firm to the touch and dry in appearance. Transfer to wire racks to cool.

492 ■ CHOCOLATE ROLL

MAKES 5 TO 6 DOZEN
CHILL TIME: *24 hours*

2 1/4 cups chocolate graham cracker crumbs
1 cup chopped walnuts
1 pound pitted dates, finely chopped
1 pound miniature marshmallows, finely chopped
1 cup heavy cream.
Chocolate graham cracker crumbs for rolling

1 In a large bowl, combine all of the ingredients except the graham cracker crumbs for rolling, and blend. The dough will be sticky. Form the dough into a log 3 inches in diameter. (To make it easier to handle, you can form 2 logs.) Roll in graham cracker crumbs until well coated. Wrap in waxed paper and chill for 24 hours. Slice the log into 1/4-inch slices.

BAKING NOTES: The log can also be rolled in chopped nuts, coconut, chopped chocolate chips, or chocolate bar sprinkles. Serve with chocolate whipped cream (see page 406) on the side if desired.

493 ■ CHOCOLATE RUM BALLS

MAKES 2 TO 3 DOZEN
STANDING TIME: 1 hour

1 1/2 cups chocolate wafer cookie crumbs
1/2 cup powdered sugar
1/2 cup walnuts, finely ground
1/4 cup light corn syrup
4 tablespoons rum
Powdered sugar for rolling

495

490

1 In a large bowl, combine the cookie crumbs, powdered sugar, and walnuts.

2 In a small saucepan, over low heat, warm the corn syrup and rum. Pour into the dry ingredients and mix until thoroughly blended.

3 Pinch off walnut-sized pieces of the dough and roll into balls. Roll each ball in powdered sugar and place on a wire rack. Let stand at room temperature for 1 hour.

4 Roll the balls in the powdered sugar a second time. Store in an airtight container.

494 ■ CHOCOLATE SANDWICH COOKIES

MAKES 2 TO 3 DOZEN
BAKING TIME: *12 minutes*
CHILL TIME: *overnight*

2 cups all-purpose flour
1/4 teaspoon baking soda
1/4 teaspoon allspice
1/4 teaspoon salt
1/2 cup butter or margarine, at room temperature
2/3 cup packed light brown sugar
1 large egg
1/2 teaspoon chocolate or vanilla extract
1 cup semisweet chocolate chips for filling

1 Combine the flour, baking soda, allspice, and salt.

2 In a large bowl, using an electric mixer on medium speed, beat the butter and brown sugar until smooth. Beat in the egg and chocolate extract. Gradually stir in the dry ingredients. The dough will be stiff. Form the dough into a log 3 inches in diameter. Wrap with waxed paper and chill overnight.

3 Position a rack in the center of the oven and preheat the oven to 350 degrees.

4 Cut the chilled log into 1/8-inch slices. Place the slices 3/4 inch apart on an ungreased baking sheet.

5 Bake for 10 to 12 minutes, or until lightly colored. Transfer to wire rack to cool.

6 Meanwhile, melt the chocolate chips (see page 13). Place the cookies bottom-side up, and spread a thin layer of the melted chocolate on half of the cookies. Top with the remaining cookies bottom side down, to form sandwich cookies.

495 ■ CHOCOLATE SHORTBREAD

MAKES 2 TO 2 1/2 DOZEN
BAKING TIME: *25 minutes*

1 1/2 cups all-purpose flour
1/2 cup Dutch processed cocoa powder
1 cup butter, at room temperature
1 cup granulated sugar

1 Position a rack in the center of the oven and preheat the oven to 350 degrees.

2 Combine the flour and cocoa powder.

3 In a large bowl, combine the butter and sugar by rubbing it through your fingers. Gradually blend in the flour and cocoa powder to form a dry dough. On a floured surface, roll out the dough to a thickness of 1/2 inch. Using cookie cutters, cut the dough into shapes, placing the cookies 1 inch apart on an ungreased baking sheet. Pierce

the top of each cookie several times with the tines of a fork.

4 Bake for 20 to 25 minutes, or until the tops are a very light golden brown. Transfer to a wire rack to cool.

BAKING NOTES: Traditionally, shortbread was made by pressing the dough into a baking pan. Later, carved wooden molds with a thistle design in the center were used to make shortbread cookies of varying sizes.

496 ■ CHOCOLATE SPARKLES

MAKES 5 TO 6 DOZEN
BAKING TIME: *10 minutes*
CHILL TIME: *2 hours*

2 ounces semisweet chocolate, grated or finely chopped
2 2/3 cups all-purpose flour
2 teaspoons cream of tartar
1 teaspoon baking soda
1/4 teaspoon salt
1 cup vegetable shortening
1 1/4 cups granulated sugar
2 large eggs
1/2 teaspoon vanilla extract
Granulated sugar for rolling

1 Melt the chocolate (see page 13). Remove from the heat.

2 Combine the flour, cream of tartar, baking soda, and salt.

3 In a large bowl, using an electric mixer on medium speed, beat the shortening and sugar until fluffy. Beat in the eggs. Beat in the vanilla extract and melted chocolate. Gradually stir in the dry ingredients. Cover and chill for 2 hours.

4 Position a rack in the center of the oven and preheat the oven to 400 degrees.

5 Pinch off walnut-sized pieces of the dough and roll into balls. Roll each ball in granulated sugar and place 1 1/2 inches apart on ungreased baking sheets.

6 Bake for 8 to 10 minutes, or until firm to the touch. Transfer to wire racks to cool.

496

493

492

497 ■ CHOCOLATE SPICE DROPS

MAKES 6 TO 7 DOZEN
BAKING TIME: *20 minutes*

2 ounces unsweetened chocolate, grated or finely chopped
3 cups all-purpose flour
1 cup walnuts, finely ground
1 teaspoon baking soda
1 teaspoon ground cinnamon
1 teaspoon ground allspice
1/2 teaspoon ground cloves
1/2 cup butter or margarine, at room temperature
1 1/2 cups granulated sugar
2 large eggs
2/3 cup sour cream
1 cup raisins

1 Melt the chocolate (see page 13). Remove from the heat.

2 Position a rack in the center of the oven and preheat the oven to 350 degrees.

3 Combine the flour, walnuts, baking soda, and spices.

4 In a large bowl, using an electric mixer on medium speed, beat the butter and sugar until light and fluffy. Beat in the eggs, one at a time, beating well after each addition. Beat in the sour cream and melted chocolate. Gradually blend in the dry ingredients. Fold in the raisins. Drop the dough by spoonfuls 1 1/2 inches apart onto ungreased baking sheets.

5 Bake for 15 to 20 minutes, or until golden brown. Transfer to wire racks to cool.

498 ■ CHOCOLATE STARS

MAKES 3 TO 4 DOZEN
BAKING TIME: *30 minutes*

3 large egg whites
1/2 teaspoon cream of tartar
2/3 cup granulated sugar
1/4 cup less 1 teaspoon Dutch processed cocoa powder
1/3 cup ground pecans

1 Position a rack in the center of the oven and preheat the oven to 275 degrees. Line two baking sheets with parchment paper.

2 In a medium bowl, using an electric mixer on high speed, beat the egg whites and cream of tartar until foamy. Beat in the sugar, a tablespoon at a time. Beat until stiff but not dry. Fold in the cocoa powder just until blended. Streaks of cocoa will remain. Do not over mix.

3 Fill a pastry bag fitted with a large star tip with the mixture. Pipe out stars onto the prepared pans, spacing them 1 1/2 inches apart. Sprinkle with the chopped pecans.

4 Bake for 25 to 30 minutes, or until the cookies look crisp and dry. Cool on the pan for 5 to 10 minutes. Remove to a wire rack to cool completely.

499 ■ CHOCOLATE STICKS

MAKES 2 TO 3 DOZEN
BAKING TIME: *12 minutes*

3 ounces unsweetened chocolate, grated or finely chopped
3 cups all-purpose flour
1/2 teaspoon baking soda
1/2 teaspoon salt
2/3 cup butter or margarine, at room temperature
1/2 cup granulated sugar
2 large eggs
1 teaspoon almond extract

1 Position a rack in the center of the oven and preheat the oven to 400 degrees.

2 Melt the chocolate (see page 13). Remove from the heat.

3 Combine the flour, baking soda, and salt.

4 In a large bowl, using an electric mixer on medium speed, beat the butter and sugar until light and fluffy. Beat in the eggs. Beat in the almond extract. Gradually stir in the dry ingredients.

5 Fill a cookie press or pastry bag fitted with a medium-sized plain tip with the dough. Press or pipe 3 1/2 by 1-inch wide strips onto ungreased baking sheets, spacing them 1 inch apart.

6 Bake for 10 to 12 minutes, or until firm to the touch. Transfer to wire racks to cool.

500

501

497

502

500 ■ CHOCOLATE SQUARES

MAKES 2 DOZEN
BAKING TIME: *12 minutes*

2 ounces semisweet chocolate, grated or finely chopped
1¹/₂ cups all-purpose flour
¹/₂ teaspoon baking soda
¹/₄ teaspoon salt
¹/₂ cup vegetable shortening
1 cup packed light brown sugar
1 large egg
1 teaspoon vanilla extract
¹/₂ cup flaked coconut
¹/₂ cup almonds or walnuts, chopped

1 Position a rack in the center of the oven and preheat the oven to 350 degrees. Lightly grease a 13 by 9-inch pan.

2 Melt the chocolate (see page 13). Remove from the heat.

3 Combine the flour, baking soda, and salt.

4 In a large bowl, using an electric mixer on medium speed, beat the shortening and brown sugar until fluffy. Beat in the egg. Beat in the vanilla extract and melted chocolate. Gradually stir in the dry ingredients. Scrape the batter into the prepared pan and spread evenly. Sprinkle the coconut and almonds over the top.

5 Bake for 10 to 12 minutes, or until firm to the touch. Cool in the pan on a wire rack. Cut into 24 bars.

501 ■ CHOCOLATE SUGAR COOKIES

MAKES 5 TO 6 DOZEN
BAKING TIME: *9 minutes*
CHILL TIME: *2 hours*

3³/₄ cups all-purpose flour
1¹/₂ teaspoons baking powder
¹/₂ teaspoon salt
1 cup vegetable shortening
1¹/₂ cups granulated sugar
2 large eggs
2 teaspoons chocolate extract
¹/₄ cup chocolate syrup
Granulated sugar for sprinkling

1 Combine the flour, baking powder, and salt.

2 In a large bowl, using an electric mixer on medium speed, beat the shortening and sugar until light and fluffy. Beat in the eggs. Beat in the chocolate extract and chocolate syrup. Gradually stir in the dry ingredients. Cover and chill for 2 hours.

3 Preheat the oven to 375 degrees. Lightly grease two baking sheets.

4 On a floured surface, roll out half of the dough at a time to a thickness of ¹/₈ inch. Using a 2-inch round cookie cutter, cut the dough into rounds. Place the rounds 1¹/₂ inches apart on the prepared pans. Lightly brush the rounds with water and sprinkle with granulated sugar.

5 Bake for 8 to 9 minutes, or until firm to the touch. Transfer to wire racks to cool.

BAKING NOTES: The dough can also be used for refrigerator cookies. Form the dough into a log 2 inches in diameter, wrap in waxed paper, and chill overnight. Cut in ¹/₄-inch slices and bake as directed.

502 ■ CHOCOLATE SYRUP BROWNIES

MAKES 1 DOZEN
BAKING TIME: *40 minutes*

¹/₂ cup vegetable shortening
1 cup granulated sugar
4 eggs
Pinch of salt
1 cup chocolate syrup
1 cup all-purpose flour
1 cup walnuts or pecans, chopped
1 cup miniature marshmallows (optional)

1 Position a rack in the center of the oven and preheat the oven to 350 degrees.

2 In a large bowl, using an electric mixer on medium speed, beat the shortening and sugar until fluffy. Beat in the eggs, one at a time. Beat in the salt. Beat in the chocolate syrup. Gradually blend in the flour. Fold in the walnuts and marshmallows. Scrape the mixture into an ungreased 9-inch square pan and spread evenly.

3 Bake for 35 to 40 minutes, or until a cake tester inserted into the center comes out clean. Cool in the pan on a wire rack. Cut into 12 bars.

503 ■ CHOCOLATE TOFFEE BARS

MAKES 1¹/₂ DOZEN
BAKING TIME: *25 minutes*

¹/₂ cup butter or margarine, at room temperature
¹/₂ cup packed light brown sugar
1 large egg
1 teaspoon chocolate extract
¹/₂ cup all-purpose flour
¹/₂ cup quick-cooking oats
1 cup semisweet chocolate chips
¹/₂ cup ground pecans

1 Position a rack in the center of the oven and preheat the oven to 350 degrees. Lightly grease and flour a 9-inch square pan.

2 In a large bowl, using an electric mixer on medium speed, beat the butter and brown sugar until fluffy. Beat in the egg and chocolate extract. Gradually stir in the flour and oats. Scrape the mixture into the prepared pan and spread evenly.

3 Bake for 20 to 25 minutes, or until lightly colored. Sprinkle the chocolate chips over the top. Let stand for 3 minutes. Spread the melted chocolate chips evenly over the top. Sprinkle with the pecans and cool completely on a wire rack. Cut into 18 bars.

504 ■ CHOCOLATE TOPPERS

MAKES 3 TO 4 DOZEN
BAKING TIME: *10 minutes*

1¹/₄ cups all-purpose flour
1 cup walnuts, finely ground
¹/₂ teaspoon salt
²/₃ cup vegetable shortening
1 cup granulated sugar
1 teaspoon vanilla extract
1 cup semisweet chocolate chips

1 Position a rack in the center of the oven and preheat the oven to 400 degrees. Lightly grease two baking sheets.

2 Combine the flour, walnuts, and salt.

3 In a large bowl, using an electric mixer on medium speed, beat the shortening and sugar until fluffy. Beat in the vanilla extract. Gradually stir in the dry ingredients.

4 On a floured surface, roll out the dough to a thickness of ⅛ inch. Using a 2-inch fluted round cookie cutter, cut the dough out into rounds. Place the rounds 1 inch apart on the prepared pans.

5 Bake for 8 to 10 minutes, or until firm to the touch. Transfer to wire racks to cool.

6 Melt the chocolate chips (see page 13). Remove from the heat. Place the cookies bottom-side up and spread a thin layer of the melted chocolate on the bottoms of half of the cookies. Top with the remaining cookies, bottom sides down, to form sandwich cookies.

BAKING NOTES: These cookies tend to be dry. This can be remedied by using chocolate buttercream (see page 395) for the filling.

505 ■ CHØKØLADEKAGER

MAKES 3 TO 4 DOZEN
BAKING TIME: *12 minutes*

2¼ cups all-purpose flour
1 teaspoon salt
1 teaspoon baking soda
1 teaspoon warm water
1 cup butter or margarine, at room temperature
¾ cup granulated sugar
¾ cup packed light brown sugar
2 large eggs
1 teaspoon chocolate or vanilla extract
2½ cups semisweet chocolate chips
1 cup chopped walnuts

1 Position a rack in the center of the oven and preheat the oven to 375 degrees. Lightly grease two baking sheets.

2 Combine the flour and salt.

3 In a cup, dissolve the baking soda in the water.

4 In a large bowl, using an electric mixer on medium speed, beat the butter and sugars until smooth. Beat in the eggs, baking soda mixture, and chocolate extract. Gradually stir in the dry ingredients. Fold in the chocolate chips and walnuts. Drop the dough by spoonfuls 2 inches apart onto the prepared pans.

5 Bake for 10 to 12 minutes, or until lightly colored. Transfer to a wire rack to cool.

506 ■ COCOA BARS

MAKES 3 DOZEN
CHILL TIME: *4 hours*

¼ cup butter or margarine, melted
½ cup light corn syrup
1 cup powdered sugar
½ cup Dutch processed cocoa powder
1 cup peanuts, chopped
⅔ cup flaked coconut
4½ cups puffed wheat cereal

1 Lightly grease a 13 by 9-inch pan.

2 In a large bowl, combine the butter, corn syrup, powdered sugar, and cocoa powder. Add the peanuts, coconut, and cereal. Stir until the cereal is well coated. Press onto the bottom of the prepared pan. Place a piece of waxed paper over the top. Weight with dried beans or uncooked rice.

487
491
499
505
488
494
498

3 Chill for at least 4 hours, or until firm. Remove the waxed paper and dried beans. Cut into 36 bars. Wrap the bars individually in waxed paper or plastic wrap.

507 ■ COCOA BROWNIES

MAKES 1 DOZEN
BAKING TIME: *30 minutes*

½ cup vegetable shortening
¼ cup unsweetened cocoa powder
1 teaspoon vanilla or chocolate extract
4 large eggs
1 cup packed light brown sugar
1 cup all-purpose flour
1 cup miniature marshmallows
½ cup walnuts or pecans, chopped

1 Position a rack in the center of the oven and preheat the oven to 350 degrees. Lightly grease a 9-inch square pan.

2 In a large saucepan, melt the shortening. Stir in the cocoa powder and vanilla extract. Remove from the heat.

3 In a medium bowl, using an electric mixer on medium speed, beat the eggs until thick and light-colored. Beat in the sugar. beat in the cocoa mixture, pouring it in a steady stream. Gradually blend in the flour. Fold in the marshmallows and walnuts. Scrape the batter into the prepared pan and spread evenly.

4 Bake for 25 to 30 minutes, or until a cake tester inserted into the center comes out clean. Cool in the pan on a wire rack. Cut into 12 bars.

508 ■ COCOA COOKIES

MAKES 2 TO 3 DOZEN
BAKING TIME: *18 minutes*

1¾ cups all-purpose flour
¼ cup Dutch processed cocoa powder
1 teaspoon baking powder
½ teaspoon salt
¾ cup butter or margarine, at room temperature
¾ cup granulated sugar
1 large egg
1 teaspoon chocolate extract
½ cup chopped pecans
Cocoa Sugar (see page 407) for rolling

1 Position a rack in the center of the oven and preheat the oven to 350 degrees. Lightly grease two baking sheets.

2 Combine the flour, cocoa powder, baking powder, and salt.

3 In a large bowl, using an electric mixer on medium speed, beat the butter and sugar until light and fluffy. Beat in the egg and chocolate extract. Gradually stir in the dry ingredients to make a smooth dough. Fold in the pecans. Pinch off walnut-sized pieces of the dough and roll into balls. Roll each ball in the cocoa sugar and place 1½ inches apart onto the prepared pan. Dip the back of a spoon in the cocoa sugar and flatten each ball with it.

4 Bake for 15 to 18 minutes, or until the cookies are lightly colored. Cool on the pan for 5 minutes. Transfer to a wire rack to cool completely.

506

507

503

504

508

509 ■ COCONUT-CHOCOLATE CHIP COOKIES

MAKES 3 TO 4 DOZEN
BAKING TIME: *15 minutes*

2 cups flaked coconut
2 cups all-purpose flour
3/4 teaspoon baking soda
1 teaspoon salt
1 cup butter or margarine, at room temperature
1 1/3 cups packed light brown sugar
2 large eggs
1 teaspoon chocolate extract
2 cups miniature chocolate chips

1 Position a rack in the center of the oven and preheat the oven to 375 degrees. Lightly grease two baking sheets.

2 Spread the coconut out evenly on a 15 1/2 by 10 1/2-inch jelly-roll pan and toast in the oven for 5 to 10 minutes, or until lightly browned, stirring frequently. Set aside to cool completely on a wire rack.

3 Combine the flour, baking soda, and salt.

4 In a large bowl, using an electric mixer on medium speed, beat the butter and brown sugar until fluffy. Beat in the eggs, one at a time, beating well after each addition. Beat in the chocolate extract. Gradually stir in the dry ingredients. Fold in the toasted coconut and chocolate chips.

Drop the dough by spoonfuls 1 1/2 inches apart onto the prepared pans.

5 Bake for 12 to 15 minutes, or until a golden color. Set aside to cool.

510 ■ CONGO BARS

MAKES 3 DOZEN
BAKING TIME: *25 minutes*

2 1/2 cups all-purpose flour
2 teaspoons baking powder
1/8 teaspoon salt
6 tablespoons butter or margarine, at room temperature
2 1/3 cups packed light brown sugar
3 large eggs
12 ounces semisweet chocolate, grated or finely chopped
1/4 cup walnuts, chopped
1/4 cup almonds, chopped
1/4 cup hazelnuts, chopped
1 cup Chocolate Peanut Butter Frosting (see page 000)

1 Position a rack in the center of the oven and preheat the oven to 350 degrees. Lightly grease a 15 1/2 by 10 1/2-inch jelly-roll pan.

2 Combine the flour, baking powder, and salt.

3 In a large bowl, using an electric mixer on medium speed,

beat the butter and brown sugar until fluffy. Beat in the eggs, one at a time, beating well after each addition. Gradually stir in the dry ingredients, mixing just until moistened. Fold in the chocolate and nuts. Scrape the mixture into the prepared pan and spread evenly.

4 Bake for 20 to 25 minutes, or until the top is lightly colored. Cool in the pan on a wire rack.

5 Make the frosting. Spread the top of the bars with the frosting. Cut into 36 bars.

511 ■ CREAM CHEESE MARBLED BROWNIES

MAKES 2 DOZEN
BAKING TIME: *75 minutes*
CHILL TIME: *overnight*

CAKE

1 1/2 cups all-purpose flour
1 1/2 teaspoons baking powder
1/4 teaspoon salt
12 ounces semisweet chocolate, grated or finely chopped
1 cup butter or margarine
5 large eggs
1 cup granulated sugar
1 3/4 cups packed light brown sugar
1 tablespoon almond or chocolate extract
2 cups chopped almonds

511

510

513

509

512

FILLING

12 ounces cream cheese, at room temperature

5 tablespoons butter or margarine, at room temperature

¾ cup granulated sugar

1½ teaspoons almond or chocolate extract

3 large eggs

1 Position a rack in the center of the oven and preheat the oven to 350 degrees. Lightly grease and flour a 13 by 9-inch pan.

2 To make the cake, combine the flour, baking powder, and salt.

3 In the top of a double boiler over simmering water, melt the chocolate and the butter, stirring until smooth. Remove from the heat.

4 In a large bowl, using an electric mixer on medium speed, beat the eggs just until foamy. Add the sugars and almond extract, beating just until mixed. Beat in the almonds. Beat in the melted chocolate. Gradually blend in the dry ingredients, mixing just until blended. Reserve 2¼ cups of the batter. Scrape the remaining batter into the pan and spread evenly.

5 To make the filling, in a small bowl, using an electric mixer on medium speed, beat the cream cheese and butter until smooth. Beat in the sugar and almond extract. Beat in the eggs, one at a time, beating well after each addition. Slowly pour the filling over the chocolate mixture in the pan.

6 Pour the reserved chocolate mixture slowly over the top of the filling to cover all of the filling. Be sure the filling mixture is totally covered at the sides of the pan. Using a knife, sweep through the mixture to create a marbleized effect. Do not overmix.

7 Bake for 60 to 75 minutes, or until a cake tester inserted into the center comes out clean. Do not overbake. Cool in the pan on a wire rack for 10 minutes. Invert onto a platter, cover with waxed paper, and chill overnight. Cut into 24 bars.

BAKING NOTES: Frost the chilled brownies with ½ cup Chocolate Glaze III (see page 401), if desired.

512 ■ CRÈME DE MENTHE SQUARES

12 TO 16 SQUARES
CHILL TIME: *30 minutes*

BOTTOM LAYER

½ cup butter or margarine

½ cup Dutch processed cocoa powder

½ cup powdered sugar

1 large egg, beaten

1 teaspoon white crème de menthe

2 cups graham cracker crumbs

MIDDLE LAYER

½ cup butter or margarine

⅓ cup green crème de menthe

3 cups powdered sugar

TOP LAYER

¼ cup butter or margarine

1½ cups semisweet chocolate chips

1 To make the bottom layer, in a medium saucepan, over low heat, melt the butter. Add the cocoa powder, stirring until smooth. Remove from the heat and add the powdered sugar, egg, and white crème de menthe. Stir in the graham cracker crumbs. Press the mixture evenly onto the bottom of an ungreased 13 by 9-inch pan.

2 To make the middle layer, in a medium saucepan, over low heat, melt the butter. Remove from the heat and stir in the green crème de menthe. Gradually blend in the powdered sugar. Spread evenly over the bottom layer in the pan.

3 To make the top layer, in the top of a double boiler over simmering water, melt the butter and chocolate chips, stirring until smooth. Spread this mixture evenly over the middle layer. Chill for 30 minutes, or until firm. Cut into 12 to 16 bars.

BAKING NOTES: Owing to the raw egg used in this recipe, it should be kept refrigerated at all times, and for no longer than 3 days.

513 ■ CRUMB COOKIES

MAKES 2 DOZEN
BAKING TIME: *30 minutes*
CHILL TIME: *overnight*

1¾ cups chocolate graham cracker crumbs

1 can (14 ounces) sweetened condensed milk

2 tablespoons honey

2 tablespoons unsweetened apple juice

1 cup chocolate chips

½ cup chopped almonds

1 Position a rack in the center of the oven and preheat the oven to 350 degrees. Lightly grease a 9-inch square pan.

2 In a large bowl, combine all of the ingredients. Lightly press the mixture onto the bottom of the prepared pan.

3 Bake for 25 to 30 minutes, or until the top darkens slightly. Cool in the pan for 5 minutes. Cut into 24 bars. Transfer to a wire rack to cool completely.

514 ■ FANCY BROWNIES

MAKES 2 DOZEN
BAKING TIME: *35 minutes*
CHILL TIME: *30 minutes*

1½ cups all-purpose flour

¾ cup Dutch processed cocoa powder

½ teaspoon baking powder

⅔ cup canola oil

2 cups granulated sugar

½ cup boiling water

2 large eggs

½ cup butterscotch chips

½ cup white vanilla chips

½ cup peanut butter chips

1 Position a rack in the center of the oven and preheat the oven to 350 degrees. Lightly grease a 15½ by 10½-inch jelly-roll pan.

2 Combine the flour, cocoa powder, and baking powder.

3 In a large bowl, using an electric mixer on medium speed, beat the oil and sugar until smooth. Beat in the boiling water. Beat in the eggs, one at a time, beating well after each addition. Gradually blend in the dry ingredients. Fold in the chips. Pour the mixture into the prepared pan.

4 Bake for 30 to 35 minutes, or until a cake tester inserted into the center comes out clean. Cool in the pan on a wire rack. Cover and chill for 30 minutes.

5 Invert the chilled brownies onto a piece of waxed paper. Using cookie cutters, cut into desired shapes.

515 ■ FROSTED BROWNIES WITH NUTS

MAKES 1 TO 2 DOZEN
BAKING TIME: *30 minutes*

BROWNIES

1 cup granulated sugar
1 cup vegetable shortening
4 large eggs
1 cup chocolate syrup
1 cup all-purpose flour

TOPPING

1/3 cup milk
1/2 cup semisweet chocolate chips
1/2 cup walnuts or pecans, chopped

1 Position a rack in the center of the oven and preheat the oven to 350 degrees.

2 To make the brownies, in a large bowl, using an electric mixer on medium speed, beat the sugar and shortening until smooth. Beat in the eggs and chocolate syrup. Gradually beat in the flour. Scrape the mixture into an ungreased 9-inch square pan and spread evenly.

3 Bake for 25 to 30 minutes, or until a cake tester inserted into the center comes out clean. Cool completely in the pan on a wire rack.

4 Meanwhile, to make the topping, in a small saucepan, bring the milk to a boil and simmer for 1 minute. Remove from the heat. Add the chocolate chips and walnuts and stir until blended. Cool slightly. Spread over the baked brownies. Cool in the pan on a wire rack. Cut into 12 bars.

BAKING NOTES: Sprinkle chopped nuts or coconut over the warm topping if desired.

516 ■ FROSTED CHOCOLATE COOKIES

MAKES 3 TO 4 DOZEN
BAKING TIME: *12 minutes*

1½ cups all-purpose flour
5 tablespoons Dutch processed cocoa powder
1 teaspoon baking powder
½ teaspoon baking soda
1 cup packed light brown sugar
½ cup butter, melted
½ cup milk
1 large egg
1 teaspoon crème de cacao
¾ cup walnuts, finely chopped
½ cup Chocolate Frosting III (see page 399)

1 Position a rack in the center of the oven and preheat the oven to 350 degrees. Lightly grease two baking sheets.

2 Combine the flour, cocoa powder, baking powder, and baking soda.

3 In a large bowl, using an electric mixer on medium speed, beat the brown sugar and butter until combined. Beat in the milk, egg, and crème de cacao. Gradually stir in the dry ingredients. Fold in the walnuts. Drop by spoonfuls 1½ inches apart onto the prepared pans.

4 Bake for 10 to 12 minutes, or until dull looking. Transfer to wire racks to cool.

5 Make the chocolate frosting. Spread ½ tablespoon of frosting evenly over the top of each cookie.

515

516

520

519

517 ■ FUDGE COOKIES

MAKES 4 TO 5 DOZEN
BAKING TIME: *12 minutes*

2 cups all-purpose flour
2/3 cup Dutch processed cocoa powder
3/4 teaspoon baking soda
1/4 teaspoon salt
1 cup butter or margarine, at room temperature
1 1/2 cups granulated sugar
2 large eggs
1 teaspoon vanilla extract
1 1/2 cups semisweet chocolate chips

1 Position a rack in the center of the oven and preheat the oven to 350 degrees. Lightly grease two baking sheets.

2 Combine the flour, cocoa powder, baking soda, and salt.

3 In a large bowl, using an electric mixer on medium speed, beat the butter and sugar until light and fluffy. Beat in the eggs, one at a time, beating well after each addition. Stir in the vanilla extract. Gradually stir in the dry ingredients. Fold in the chocolate chips. Drop the dough by teaspoonfuls 1 1/2 inches apart onto the prepared pans.

4 Bake for 10 to 12 minutes, or until golden brown. The cookies will still be soft. Cool on the pans for 5 minutes. Transfer to a wire rack to cool completely.

518 ■ HEALTHY BROWNIES

MAKES 1 DOZEN
BAKING TIME: *20 minutes*

1/4 cup unbleached all-purpose flour
1/4 cup soy flour
1/2 cup walnuts, finely ground
2 tablespoons Dutch processed cocoa powder
1/2 teaspoon salt
1 large egg, separated
1/2 cup canola oil
1 cup packed light brown sugar

1 Position a rack in the center of the oven and preheat the oven to 350 degrees. Lightly grease a 9-inch square pan.

2 Combine the flours, walnuts, cocoa powder, and salt.

3 In a small bowl, whisk the egg white until stiff but not dry.

4 In a large bowl, using an electric mixer on medium speed, beat the oil and brown sugar until blended. Beat in the egg yolk. Gradually blend in the dry ingredients. Fold in the beaten egg white. Scrape the mixture into the prepared pan and spread evenly.

5 Bake for 18 to 20 minutes, or until firm to the touch. Cool in the pan on a wire rack. Cut into 12 bars.

519 ■ JAMAICA COOKIES

MAKES 2 DOZEN
BAKING TIME: *25 minutes*

2 cups all-purpose flour
2 1/2 teaspoons baking powder
1/2 teaspoon salt
2/3 cup butter or margarine, at room temperature
2 1/2 cups packed light brown sugar
3 large eggs
1 teaspoon chocolate extract
1 1/2 cups chocolate chips
1 cup chopped pecans

1 Position a rack in the center of the oven and preheat the oven to 350 degrees. Lightly grease a 13 by 9-inch pan.

2 Combine the flour, baking powder, and salt.

3 In a large bowl, using an electric mixer on medium speed, beat the butter and brown sugar until fluffy. Beat in the eggs one at a time, beating well after each addition. Beat in the chocolate extract. Gradually stir in the dry ingredients. Fold in the chocolate chips and pecans. Press the mixture evenly onto the bottom of the prepared pan.

4 Bake for 20 to 25 minutes, or until a golden color. Cool in the pan on a wire rack. Cut into 24 squares.

520 ■ MANHATTAN STARS

MAKES 5 TO 6 DOZEN
BAKING TIME: *15 minutes*
CHILL TIME: *4 hours*

1/3 cup dried apple chips
1/4 cup water
3 tablespoons packed light brown sugar
2 tablespoons hazelnut liqueur
2 ounces semisweet chocolate, grated or finely chopped
2 1/2 cups all-purpose flour
1/4 teaspoon salt
3/4 cup vegetable shortening
1/2 cup granulated sugar
1 large egg

1 In the container of a blender, place the apple chips, water, brown sugar, and 1 tablespoon of the hazelnut liqueur. Blend on high for 30 seconds, or until the apple chips are diced into small pieces. Pour into a saucepan. Place over low heat and simmer until the mixture is reduced to 1/2 cup. Remove from the heat.

2 Melt the chocolate (see page 13). Remove from the heat.

3 Combine the flour and salt.

4 In a large bowl, using an electric mixer on medium speed, beat the shortening and sugar until fluffy. Beat in the egg and melted chocolate. Gradually stir in the dry ingredients. Fold in the apple mixture. Beat in the remaining 1 tablespoon of hazelnut liqueur. Wrap and chill for at least 4 hours.

5 Position a rack in the center of the oven and preheat the oven to 350 degrees. Very lightly grease two baking sheets.

6 Fill a pastry bag fitted with a large star tip with the dough. Pipe small stars 3/4 inch apart onto the prepared pans. Or, with a large ribbon tip, pipe strips 2 to 3 inches long.

7 Bake for 12 to 15 minutes, or until dry-looking. Transfer to wire racks to cool.

BAKING NOTES: Place a chocolate chip in the center of each star before baking if desired.

521 ■ POPCORN-PEANUT BUTTER-MARSHMALLOW-CHOCOLATE BARS

MAKES 2 DOZEN
CHILL TIME: *30 minutes*

2 quarts freshly popped unsalted popcorn
1½ cups semisweet chocolate chips
1 jar (7 ounces) marshmallow creme
½ cup creamy peanut butter
¼ cup butter or margarine
2 ounces semisweet chocolate, grated or finely chopped

1 Preheat the oven to 200 degrees. Lightly grease a 13 by 9-inch pan.

2 Place the popcorn in a large ovenproof bowl and keep warm in the oven until ready to use.

3 In the top of a double boiler over simmering water, combine the chocolate chips, marshmallow creme, peanut butter, and butter, stirring until smooth. Add to the popcorn. Using a wooden spoon, stir until all of the popcorn is coated. Press onto the bottom of the prepared pan. Place a sheet of waxed paper over the mixture and press firmly.

4 Meanwhile, melt the semisweet chocolate (see page 13). Spread over the popcorn and chill 30 minutes, or until firm. Cut into 24 bars.

522 ■ RED HEARTS WITH CHOCOLATE SPRINKLES

MAKES 1 TO 2 DOZEN
BAKING TIME: *20 minutes*

1 cup all-purpose flour
½ cup pecans, finely ground
2½ tablespoons cornstarch
Pinch of salt
½ cup butter or margarine, at room temperature
⅓ cup granulated sugar
1½ teaspoons grated orange zest
¾ teaspoon almond extract
3 drops red food coloring
⅓ cup Hershey's™ Chocolate Shoppe Candy Bar Sprinkles
Granulated sugar for sprinkling

1 Position a rack in the center of the oven and preheat the oven to 350 degrees. Grease two baking sheets.

2 Combine the flour, pecans, cornstarch, and salt.

3 In a large bowl, using an electric mixer on medium speed, beat the butter and sugar until light and fluffy. Beat in the orange zest, almond extract, and food coloring until thoroughly blended. Gradually blend in the dry ingredients. Fold in the chocolate candy bar sprinkles.

4 On a floured surface, roll out the dough to a thickness of ¼ inch. Using a large heart-shaped cookie cutter, cut out the hearts, placing them 1 inch apart on the prepared pans. Lightly brush each heart with water and sprinkle with granulated sugar.

5 Bake for 15 to 20 minutes, or until firm to the touch. Cool on the pan on a wire rack for 5 minutes. Transfer to the rack to cool completely.

BAKING NOTES: These cookies are ideal for holidays or gift giving. To make them even fancier, use melted white chocolate and pipe a fancy decoration, name, or thought on them.

523 ■ RING OF ERIN COOKIES

MAKES 4 TO 5 DOZEN
BAKING TIME: *10 minutes*
CHILL TIME: *1 hour*

COATING

¾ teaspoon water
4 drops yellow food coloring
2 drops green food coloring
¾ cup finely chopped almonds

COOKIES

1¾ cups all-purpose flour
6 tablespoons Dutch processed cocoa powder
½ teaspoon baking soda
¼ teaspoon salt
½ cup butter or margarine, at room temperature
¾ cup granulated sugar
1 large egg

1 To make the coating, in a small bowl, combine the water and food colorings. Add the almonds and blend well until all the nuts are green.

2 To make the cookies, combine the flour, cocoa powder, baking soda, and salt.

3 In a large bowl, using an electric mixer on medium speed, beat the butter and sugar until light and fluffy. Beat in the egg. Gradually stir in the dry ingredients and shape the dough into two logs 1½ inches in diameter. Roll each log in the green almonds until well coated. Wrap and chill for at least 1 hour.

4 Position a rack in the center of the oven and preheat the oven to 350 degrees. Lightly grease two baking sheets.

5 Cut the chilled logs into ¼-inch slices. Place the slices 1 inch apart on the prepared pans.

6 Bake for 8 to 10 minutes, or until firm to the touch. Transfer to wire racks to cool.

524 ■ ROCKY ROAD BROWNIES

MAKES 2 DOZEN
BAKING TIME: *45 minutes*

4 ounces unsweetened chocolate, grated or finely chopped
1 cup butter or margarine
2 cups granulated sugar
4 large eggs
1 cup all-purpose flour
1 teaspoon chocolate extract
1 cup miniature marshmallows
1 cup semisweet chocolate chips
1 cup chopped pecans

1 Position a rack in the center of the oven and preheat the oven to 350 degrees. Lightly grease an 8 or 9-inch square pan.

2 In the top of a double boiler over simmering water, melt the chocolate and butter, stirring until smooth. Remove from the heat and transfer to a large bowl. Add the sugar, stirring until it is dissolved. Using an electric mixer on medium speed, beat in the eggs, one at a time, beating well after each addition.

Gradually stir in the flour, a little at a time. Stir in the chocolate extract. Fold in the marshmallows, chocolate chips, and pecans. Scrape the mixture into the prepared pan and spread evenly.

3 Bake for 40 to 45 minutes, or until they feel soft but spring back when touched. Cool in the pan on a wire rack. Cut into 24 bars.

525 ■ SPANISH TREATS

MAKES ABOUT 4 DOZEN
BAKING TIME: *30 minutes*

1¼ cups ground almonds
½ cup all-purpose flour
¼ cup Dutch processed cocoa powder
¼ teaspoon salt
2 large eggs
½ cup granulated sugar
2 tablespoons dark rum or crème de cacao
Powdered sugar for dusting

1 Position a rack in the center of the oven and preheat the oven to 350 degrees. Lightly grease and flour a 13 by 9-inch pan. Line with waxed paper and grease the paper.

2 Combine the almonds, flour, cocoa powder, and salt.

3 In a large bowl, using an electric mixer on medium speed, beat the eggs until thick and light-colored. Beat in the sugar, a little at a time. Beat in the rum. Gradually stir in the dry ingredients. Scrape the dough into the prepared pan and spread evenly.

4 Bake for 25 to 30 minutes, or until a cake tester inserted into the center comes out clean. Cool in the pan for 10 minutes.

5 Line a baking sheet with waxed paper and dust with powdered sugar. Invert the cookies onto the pan and peel off the waxed paper. Reinvert onto another baking sheet and cut into 1 by 2-inch strips. Dust with powdered sugar.

526 ■ SUGARLESS BROWNIES

MAKES 1 DOZEN
BAKING TIME: *30 minutes*

¾ cup all-purpose flour
1 teaspoon baking powder
2 ounces unsweetened chocolate, grated or finely chopped
½ cup butter or margarine, at room temperature
3 tablespoons Equal™ sweetener (see Baking Notes)
2 large eggs
½ teaspoon vanilla or chocolate extract
½ cup walnuts or pecans, finely chopped

1 Position a rack in the center of the oven and preheat the oven to 350 degrees. Lightly grease an 8-inch square pan.

2 Combine the flour and baking powder.

3 Melt the chocolate (see page 13). Remove from the heat.

4 In a large bowl, using an electric mixer on medium speed, beat the butter and Equal™ until smooth. Beat in the melted

chocolate. Beat in the eggs. Mix in the vanilla extract. Gradually blend in the dry ingredients. Fold in the walnuts. Scrape the batter into the prepared pan and spread evenly.

5 Bake for 25 to 30 minutes, or until firm to the touch. Cool in the pan on a wire rack. Cut into 12 bars.

BAKING NOTES: Although this recipe was created for diabetics, the brownies can be eaten by anyone on a sugar-restricted diet.

527 ■ SWEET CHOCOLATE CREAM CHEESE BROWNIES

MAKES 1 DOZEN
BAKING TIME: *35 minutes*

BROWNIES

4 ounces semisweet chocolate, grated or finely chopped
¼ cup butter or margarine
½ cup all-purpose flour
½ cup chopped walnuts
2 large eggs
¾ cup granulated sugar
1 teaspoon chocolate extract

FILLING

8 ounces cream cheese, at room temperature
¼ cup powdered sugar
1 large egg

1 Position a rack in the center of the oven and preheat the oven to 350 degrees. Lightly grease and flour an 8-inch square pan.

2 To make the brownies, in the top of a double boiler over simmering water, melt the chocolate and butter, stirring until smooth. Remove from the heat.

525

522

524

526

3 Combine the flour and walnuts.

4 In a medium bowl, using an electric mixer on medium speed, beat the eggs and sugar until light-colored. Beat in the chocolate mixture. Stir in the chocolate extract. Blend in the dry ingredients just until incorporated. Scrape the batter into the prepared pan and spread evenly.

5 To make the filling, in a medium bowl, using an electric mixer on high speed, beat the cream cheese, powdered sugar, and egg until smooth. Using a spoon, drizzle over the top of the chocolate mixture. Using a knife, gently swirl to marbleize.

6 Bake for 30 to 35 minutes, or until a cake tester inserted into the center comes out clean. Cool in the pan on a wire rack. Cut into 12 bars.

BAKING NOTES: Do not overbake or the brownies will be dry.

528 ▪ TOASTED COCONUT COOKIES WITH CHOCOLATE CHIPS

MAKES 3 TO 4 DOZEN
BAKING TIME: *15 minutes*

2 cups flaked coconut
2 cups all-purpose flour
3/4 teaspoon baking soda
Pinch of salt
1 cup butter or margarine, at room temperature
1 1/3 cups packed light brown sugar
2 large eggs
1 teaspoon almond extract
2 cups semisweet chocolate chips

1 Position a rack in the center of the oven and preheat the oven to 375 degrees. Lightly grease two baking sheets.

2 Spread the coconut out evenly on a 15 1/2 by 10 1/2-inch jelly-roll pan and toast in the oven for 5 to 10 minutes, or until lightly browned, stirring frequently. Cool completely on a wire rack.

3 Combine the flour, baking soda, and salt.

4 In a large bowl, using an electric mixer on medium speed, beat the butter and brown sugar until fluffy. Beat in the eggs, one at a time, beating well after each addition. Beat in the almond extract. Gradually blend in the dry ingredients. Fold in the toasted coconut and chocolate chips. Drop the dough by tablespoonfuls 1 1/2 inches apart onto the prepared pans.

5 Bake for 12 to 15 minutes, or until a light golden brown. Set aside to cool.

529 ▪ TOFU BROWNIES

MAKES 2 DOZEN
BAKING TIME: *30 minutes*

BROWNIES

1 1/4 cups all-purpose flour
1 tablespoon baking powder
10 ounces tofu
1 cup granulated sugar
3/4 cup honey
1 teaspoon chocolate extract
3/4 cup canola oil
1 cup Dutch processed cocoa powder
1 cup semisweet chocolate chips
1 cup chopped pecans

FROSTING

1 cup Chocolate Frosting II (see page 399)

1 Position a rack in the center of the oven and preheat the oven to 350 degrees. Lightly grease a 13 by 9-inch pan.

2 Combine the flour and baking powder.

3 In a small bowl, using an electric mixer on high speed, beat the tofu until liquefied. Blend in the sugar, honey, and chocolate extract.

4 In a medium bowl, using an electric mixer on high speed, beat the oil and cocoa powder until blended. Using a wooden spoon, stir in the tofu mixture. Do not overmix. Gradually blend in the dry ingredients just until blended. Fold in the chocolate chips and pecans. Scrape the mixture into the prepared pan and spread evenly.

5 Bake for 25 to 30 minutes, or until a cake tester inserted into the center comes out clean. Cool in the pan on a wire rack.

6 Meanwhile, make the frosting. Spread over the top of the cooled bars. Cut into 24 bars.

521

514

517

518

530 ■ TWO-TONE COOKIES

MAKES 2 TO 3 DOZEN
BAKING TIME: *15 minutes*
CHILL TIME: *2 hours*

LIGHT DOUGH

¾ cup all-purpose flour
½ teaspoon baking soda
½ teaspoon ground nutmeg
Pinch of salt
7 tablespoons butter or margarine, at room temperature
¼ cup granulated sugar
½ cup toasted hazelnuts, chopped

DARK DOUGH

¾ cup minus 2 tablespoons all-purpose flour
3 tablespoons Dutch processed cocoa powder
¼ cup butter or margarine, at room temperature
1 tablespoon powdered sugar
½ teaspoon chocolate extract

1 To make the light dough, combine the flour, baking soda, nutmeg, and salt.

2 In a medium bowl, using an electric mixer on medium speed, beat the butter and sugar until light and fluffy. Gradually stir in the dry ingredients. Mix in the hazelnuts. The dough will be dry.

3 On a floured surface, form the dough into a log. Wrap and chill for 2 hours.

4 Position a rack in the center of the oven and preheat the oven to 350 degrees. Lightly grease two baking sheets.

5 To make the dark dough, combine the flour and cocoa powder.

6 In a medium bowl, using an electric mixer on medium speed, beat the butter, powdered sugar, and chocolate extract until fluffy. Gradually stir in the dry ingredients.

7 To assemble, on a floured surface, roll out the chilled light dough into a long, ¼-inch thick, 3-inch wide rectangle. Fill a pastry bag fitted with a plain tip with the dark dough. Pipe a strip of dark dough, about 1½ inches wide, down the center of the rectangle. Carefully fold the long sides of the rectangle up enclosing the dark dough. Cut into ½-inch diagonal slices. Place the slices ¾ inch apart on the prepared pans.

8 Bake for 12 to 15 minutes, or until lightly colored. Transfer to wire racks to cool.

531 ■ WHITE CHOCOLATE BROWNIES

MAKES 1 DOZEN
BAKING TIME: *30 minutes*

½ cup butter or margarine
8 ounces white chocolate or almond bark, grated or finely chopped
2 large eggs
Pinch of salt
½ cup granulated sugar
½ teaspoon almond extract
1 cup flour

1 Position a rack in the center of the oven and preheat the oven to 350 degrees. Lightly grease an 8-inch square pan. Line with waxed paper and grease the paper.

2 In the top of a double boiler over simmering water, melt the butter and 4 ounces of the white chocolate, stirring until smooth. Remove from the heat.

3 In a large bowl, using an electric mixer on medium speed, beat the eggs and salt until thick and light-colored. Beat in the sugar and almond extract. Beat in melted white chocolate mixture. Gradually stir in the flour. Fold in the remaining 4 ounces grated white chocolate. Scrape the mixture into the prepared pan and spread evenly.

523

527

529

531

530

528

4 Bake for 25 to 30 minutes, or until a cake tester inserted into the center comes out clean. Cool in the pan on a wire rack. Cut into 12 squares.

BAKING NOTES: Serve with Chocolate Sauce III (see page 404) on the side, if desired.

532 ■ WHITE CHOCOLATE CHIP MERINGUES

MAKES 4 TO 5 DOZEN
BAKING TIME: *30 minutes*

3 large egg whites
Pinch of salt
1 cup granulated sugar
1 cup white chocolate chips
2 tablespoons Dutch processed cocoa powder
½ teaspoon praline liqueur

1 Position a rack in the center of the oven and preheat the oven to 275 degrees. Line two baking sheets with parchment paper.

2 In a large bowl, using an electric mixer on high speed, beat the egg whites until foamy. Add the salt and continue beating until stiff peaks form. On low speed, gradually beat in the sugar. Fold in the white chocolate chips, cocoa powder, and praline liqueur. Drop the mixture by tablespoonfuls onto the prepared pans.

3 Bake for 27 to 30 minutes, or until the meringues look dry. Transfer the cookies on the paper to wire racks to cool. When completely cool, peel the cookies off the paper.

BAKING NOTES: Chopped white chocolate or almond bark can be used in place of the white chocolate chips.

533 ■ WORLD-CLASS CHOCOLATE COOKIE

MAKES 1 TO 2 DOZEN
BAKING TIME: *11 minutes*
CHILL TIME: *8 to 12 hours*

1 ounce unsweetened chocolate, grated or finely chopped
7 ounces semisweet chocolate, grated or finely chopped
2 tablespoons butter or margarine
¼ cup all-purpose flour
¼ teaspoon baking powder
Pinch of salt
2 large eggs
¼ cup granulated sugar
2 teaspoons instant espresso powder
½ teaspoon chocolate extract
2 cups chopped pecans
1 cup semisweet chocolate chips

1 In the top of a double boiler over simmering water, melt the unsweetened chocolate, semisweet chocolate, and butter, stirring constantly until smooth. Remove from the heat.

2 Combine the flour, baking powder, and salt.

3 In a medium bowl, using an electric mixer on medium speed, beat the eggs until thick and light-colored. Beat in the sugar and espresso powder. Beat in the chocolate extract. Beat in the melted chocolate mixture. Gradually stir in the dry ingredients, stirring just until blended. Fold in the pecans and chocolate chips.

4 On a piece of waxed paper or plastic wrap, form the mixture into a 12 by 2½-inch strip that is 2 inches thick. (If the mixture is too soft to work with, cover and chill for 15 to 20 minutes to harden slightly.) Cover with waxed paper and chill for 8 to 12 hours.

5 Position a rack in the center of the oven and preheat the oven to 350 degrees. Line two baking sheets with parchment paper.

6 Cut the dough strip into ¾ inch slices. Place the slices on the prepared pans ¾ inch apart. Let stand at room temperature for 30 minutes.

7 Bake for 11 minutes. Cool on the baking sheets on wire racks for 15 minutes. Transfer to wire racks to cool completely before serving.

BAKING NOTES: These cookies will be soft until completely cooled.

532

533

Ice Cream

534 ■ BITTERSWEET CHOCOLATE ICE CREAM

MAKES 2 PINTS
FREEZING TIME: *1 hour*

4 cups heavy cream
1 cup granulated sugar
8 ounces semisweet chocolate, grated or finely chopped
⅔ cup Dutch processed cocoa powder
Chocolate Sauce IV (see page 405) for serving

1 In a saucepan, bring the cream to a boil. Reduce the heat to low, add the sugar, chocolate, and cocoa powder and stir constantly until smooth. Remove from the heat and cool.

2 Pour into an ice cream maker and freeze according to the manufacturer's directions. Transfer the ice cream to an airtight container. Cover and freeze 1 hour, or until firm. Serve with chocolate sauce on the side.

535 ■ CHOCOLATE CANDY BAR ICE CREAM

MAKES 1 QUART

3 tablespoons instant espresso powder
3 tablespoons boiling water
1 cup semisweet chocolate chips
2 large eggs
½ cup granulated sugar
1 teaspoon chocolate extract
1 cup milk
1 cup heavy cream
1 cup Hershey's™ Chocolate Shoppe Candy Bar Sprinkles (York flavor)

1 In the top of a double boiler over simmering water, combine the coffee powder and boiling water. Add the chocolate chips and melt over low heat, stirring constantly until smooth. Remove from the heat.

2 In a large bowl, using an electric mixer on high speed, beat the eggs until thick and light-colored. Beat in the sugar until well blended. Beat in the choco-

3 Pour into an ice cream maker and freeze until almost firm according to the manufacturer's directions. Mix in the candy bar bits and freeze until firm. Serve immediately or transfer to an airtight container. Cover and freeze.

BAKING NOTES: If Hershey's™ Chocolate Shoppe Candy Bar Sprinkles are not available, use 1 cup miniature chocolate chips. Owing to the raw eggs in this recipe, it should be kept frozen at all times. It will keep up to 6 months.

536 ■ CHOCOLATE CHARLOTTE RUSSE

MAKES 4 TO 6 SERVINGS
FREEZING TIME: *3 hours*

1¾ cups heavy cream
1 cup after-dinner mints
4 drops green food coloring
2 dozen ladyfingers
2 ounces semisweet chocolate, grated or finely chopped
Raspberry Sauce (see page 416)

1 In a medium bowl, using an electric mixer on high speed, whip 1 cup of the cream until soft peaks form.

2 In the top of a double boiler over simmering water, melt the mints with the remaining ¾ cup cream, stirring until smooth. Remove from the heat and stir in the food coloring. Fold in the whipped cream. Immediately pour into a 13 by 9-inch pan and freeze for 1 to 2 hours, or until the mixture just starts to set.

3 Meanwhile, line the bottom of a springform pan with waxed paper. Line the sides with ladyfingers. Freeze until ready to use.

4 Remove the cream mixture from the freezer and transfer to a big bowl. Using an electric mixer on high speed, whip until smooth. Fold in the grated chocolate. Pour the mixture into the prepared springform pan and freeze until firm.

5 Remove the side of the springform pan and invert onto a serving plate. Remove the waxed paper. Serve with raspberry sauce and garnish with pansies and mint sprigs.

537 ■ CHOCOLATE CHUNK ICE CREAM

MAKES 1 PINT
FREEZING TIME: *1 hour*

1 large egg, separated
1 cup heavy cream
½ cup granulated sugar
1 teaspoon crème de cacao
3 ounces semisweet chocolate, grated or finely chopped

1 In a small bowl, whisk the egg white until stiff but not dry.

2 In a medium bowl, using an electric mixer on high speed, whip the cream until soft peaks form.

3 In a large bowl, whisk the egg yolk until thick and light-colored. Using a wire whisk, beat in the sugar. Add the crème de cacao and beat well. Fold in

the beaten egg white. Fold in the whipped cream and grated chocolate. Pour into a 9 by 5-inch loaf pan. Cover and freeze for 1 hour, or until firm.

BAKING NOTES: Owing to the raw egg in this recipe, it should be kept frozen at all times. This can be kept up to 6 months.

538 ■ CHOCOLATE DREAM CREAM

MAKES 1½ QUARTS
CHILL / FREEZING TIME: *2 hours*

2 ounces unsweetened chocolate, grated or finely chopped
⅔ cup granulated sugar
2¼ cups heavy cream
2 large eggs, separated
Pinch of salt
1 teaspoon chocolate extract

1 In the top of a double boiler over simmering water, melt the chocolate, stirring until smooth. Add ⅓ cup of the sugar and stir until dissolved. Beat in 1 cup of the cream. Beat in the egg yolks and salt. Cook, stirring constantly, until the mixture thickens slightly and coats the back of a spoon. Remove from the heat and strain into a large bowl. Cover and chill for 1 hour, or until very thick.

2 In a medium bowl, using an electric mixer on high speed, beat the egg whites until foamy. Add the remaining ⅓ cup of sugar and beat until stiff but not dry.

3 In another medium bowl, beat the remaining 1¼ cups cream until soft peaks form. Beat in the chocolate extract. Fold the whipped cream mixture into the egg whites. Fold the mixture into the chilled egg yolk custard. Transfer to an airtight container. Cover and freeze for 1 hour, or until firm.

539 ■ CHOCOLATE HAZELNUT ICE CREAM

MAKES 2½ QUARTS
FREEZING TIME: *80 minutes*

7 ounces semisweet chocolate, grated or finely chopped
6 ounces unsweetened chocolate, grated or finely chopped
⅓ cup water
4 teaspoons instant espresso powder
4 teaspoons hot water
2 cups heavy cream
8 large egg yolks
1 cup granulated sugar
2 cups chopped hazelnuts

1 In the top of a double boiler over simmering water, melt the chocolates with the water, stirring constantly until the mixture is smooth. Remove from the heat.

2 In a large saucepan, over low heat, combine the espresso powder and hot water. Stir in the cream. Cook until bubbles start to form around the sides of the pan. Remove from the heat.

3 In a medium bowl, using an electric mixer on medium speed, beat the egg yolks until thick and light-colored. Add the sugar and beat until thick. Beat in the chocolate and cream mixtures. Transfer to the saucepan. Cook over medium-low heat, stirring constantly, until thick enough to coat the back of a spoon. Do not allow the mixture to boil. Remove from the heat and set the pan in a large bowl filled with ice and water. Stir until the mixture is completely cool. Pour into an airtight container. Cover, stir occassionally, and freeze for 20 minutes, or until firm but not set.

4 Fold in the nuts and freeze 1 hour, or until set hard.

540 ■ CHOCOLATE ICE CREAM I

MAKES 1¾ TO 2 QUARTS
FREEZING TIME: *3 hours*

3 ounces semisweet chocolate, grated or finely chopped
2 cups milk
1 cup granulated sugar
Pinch of salt
4 large egg yolks
2 cups heavy cream
2 teaspoons chocolate extract

1 In the top of a double boiler over simmering water, combine the chocolate, milk, sugar, and salt and stir until the sugar is dissolved and the mixture is smooth. Remove from the heat.

2 In a large bowl, using an electric mixer on medium speed, beat the egg yolks until thick and light-colored. Stir ½ cup of the hot mixture into the egg yolks. Slowly beat the egg yolk mixture into the chocolate mixture in the saucepan.

3 Cook over medium heat, stirring constantly, for 2 to 3 minutes, or until it coats the back of a spoon. Remove from the heat and pour into a clean large bowl. Beat in the cream and the chocolate extract.

4 Pour the mixture into an ice cream maker and freeze according to manufacturer's directions. Transfer to an airtight container. Cover and freeze for 2 to 3 hours, or until firm.

BAKING NOTES: For mint chocolate ice cream, use mint-flavored chocolate chips in place of the semisweet chocolate.

541 ■ CHOCOLATE ICE CREAM II

MAKES 1½ TO 1¾ QUARTS
FREEZING TIME: *1 hour*

3 ounces unsweetened chocolate, grated or finely chopped
3 ounces semisweet chocolate, grated or finely chopped
2 tablespoons boiling water
½ cup granulated sugar
¼ cup water
½ teaspoon cream of tartar

Pinch of salt
4 large egg yolks
3 cups heavy cream
1 tablespoon chocolate extract

1 In the top of a double boiler over simmering water, melt the chocolates, stirring until smooth. Slowly stir in the 2 tablespoons of boiling water. Remove from the heat.

2 In a separate saucepan, over medium heat, combine the sugar, ¼ cup water, cream of tartar, and salt. Bring to a boil, stirring until the sugar is dissolved. Insert a candy thermometer and cook until 238 degrees.

3 Meanwhile, in a large bowl, using an electric mixer on high speed, beat the egg yolks until thick and light-colored. Beating on low speed, add the syrup in a thin stream. Beat in the chocolate mixture. Add the cream and chocolate extract and beat until blended.

4 Pour into a 9 by 5-inch loaf pan. Cover and freeze for 1 hour, or until firm, stirring occasionally.

542 ■ CHOCOLATE ICE CREAM CAKE I

MAKES 8 TO 10 SERVINGS
FREEZING TIME: *8 hours*

3 cups macaroon cookie crumbs
½ cup pecans, finely chopped
6 ounces semisweet chocolate, grated or finely chopped
½ cup butter, melted
1 pint chocolate ice cream, softened
1 pint vanilla or chocolate chip ice cream, softened
2 cups heavy cream
1 teaspoon crème de cacao
½ cup pecans, coarsely chopped

1 In a large bowl, combine the cookie crumbs, pecans, chocolate, and melted butter. Mix until crumbly. Press one-third onto the bottom of a 9-inch springform pan.

2 Spread the softened chocolate ice cream evenly over the top of the crumb mixture. Top with half of the remaining crumb

mixture. Spread with the vanilla ice cream and top with the remaining crumb mixture. Cover and freeze for at least 8 hours, or until serving.

3 To serve, in a large bowl, using an electric mixer on high speed, whip the cream until it thickens. Add the crème de cacao and whip until soft peaks form. Spread the whipped cream over the top of the ice cream cake and sprinkle with the pecans. Remove the side of the pan before serving.

BAKING NOTES: Any flavor combination of ice cream can be used.

543 ■ CHOCOLATE ICE CREAM CAKE II

MAKES 8 TO 10 SERVINGS
FREEZING TIME: *4 hours*

3 cups chocolate wafer cookie crumbs
½ cup chopped pecans
1 cup semisweet chocolate chips
½ cup butter or margarine, melted
1 pint chocolate ice cream, softened
1 pint vanilla ice cream, softened
1 pint heavy cream
Ground pecans for garnish

1 In a large bowl, blend the cookie crumbs, pecans, chocolate chips, and melted butter. Press one-third of this mixture evenly onto the bottom of a 9-inch springform pan.

2 Spread the chocolate ice cream over the crumb mixture and top with half of the remaining crumb mixture. Spread with the vanilla ice cream and top with the remaining crumbs. Cover and freeze for 4 hours.

3 In a medium bowl, using an electric mixture on high, whip the cream until soft peaks form.

4 To assemble, remove the side of the pan and transfer the cake to a serving plate. Frost the top and sides with whipped cream and sprinkle with the pecans.

BAKING NOTES: For a variation, use lime or raspberry sherbet in place of the vanilla ice cream.

544 ■ CHOCOLATE ICE CREAM PIE

MAKES 8 TO 10 SERVINGS
BAKING TIME: *1 hour*
CHILL/FREEZING TIME: *9 hours*

MERINGUE CRUST

¾ cup granulated sugar
2 tablespoons Dutch processed cocoa powder
3 large egg whites
¼ teaspoon cream of tartar
Pinch of salt

CHOCOLATE FILLING

1 package (3.4 ounces) Jell-O Brand chocolate instant pudding mix
¼ cup milk
1 pint chocolate ice cream, softened
½ cup heavy cream
Sliced fresh fruit for garnish

1 Position a rack in the center of the oven and preheat the oven to 275 degrees. Lightly grease a 9-inch pie pan.

2 To make the crust, combine the sugar and cocoa powder.

3 In a medium bowl, using an electric mixer on high speed, beat the egg whites, cream of tartar, and salt until foamy. Sprinkle the dry ingredients over the top and beat until stiff but not dry. Spread the mixture evenly over the bottom and sides of the prepared pan.

4 Bake for 1 hour. Cool in the pan on a wire rack.

5 To make the filling, in a medium bowl, using an electric mixer on medium speed, beat the pudding mix and milk. Add the softened ice cream and beat for 2 minutes. Pour the mixture into the cooled shell and freeze for at least 8 hours.

6 In a small bowl, using an electric mixer on high speed, whip the cream until stiff peaks form. Spread over the top of the pie and freeze for 1 hour. When ready to serve, arrange the sliced fruit over the top of the whipped cream.

545 ■ CHOCOLATE ICE MILK I

MAKES 1½ PINTS
CHILL/FREEZING TIME: *3 hours*

2 cups milk
¾ cup granulated sugar
⅓ cup Dutch processed cocoa powder
½ teaspoon chocolate extract

1 Place a clean plastic freezer container with a cover in the freezer.

2 In the container of a blender, combine 1 cup of the milk, the sugar, and cocoa powder. Blend on high speed for 1 minute. Add the remaining 1 cup milk and chocolate extract and blend on low speed for 1 minute. Pour the mixture into a 9-inch square pan. Cover and refrigerate for 1 to 2 hours, or until a thin frozen crust forms on the top.

3 Return the mixture to the blender and blend until smooth and creamy. Pour the mixture into the chilled container, cover and freeze for 1 hour, or until firm. Serve with fruit sauce on the side.

546 ■ CHOCOLATE ICE MILK II

MAKES 1 QUART
CHILL TIME: *10 hours*

16 ounces semisweet chocolate, grated or finely chopped
3 cups milk

1 In the top of a double boiler over simmering water, melt the chocolate, stirring until smooth. Add ½ cup of the milk and stir until the mixture is smooth. Add the remaining 2½ cups milk. Using a wire whisk, beat for 2 minutes. Cover and cook, stirring occasionally, for 30 minutes. Remove from the heat and set the pan in a large bowl filled with ice and water. Stir until completely cool. Cover and chill for at least 10 hours.

2 Using an electric mixer on high speed, beat for 2 minutes. Pour into an ice cream maker and freeze according to the manufacturer's directions. Serve or transfer to an airtight container. Cover and freeze until serving.

540
541
542
543
544
545
546

547 ■ CHOCOLATE MARSHMALLOW FREEZE

MAKES 1 PINT
CHILL TIME: *1 hour*

1 can (14 ounces) evaporated milk
⅓ cup Dutch processed cocoa powder
¼ cup granulated sugar
¼ cup marshmallow creme
Chocolate Sauce V (see page 405) for serving

1 Measure and reserve ½ cup of the evaporated milk. Place the remaining evaporated milk in a medium bowl and place in the freezer until ready to whip.

2 In a medium saucepan, over low heat, combine the cocoa powder and sugar, stirring until smooth and the sugar is dissolved. Stir in the reserved evaporated milk. Add the marshmallow creme and cook until blended. Remove from the heat and set the pan in a large bowl of ice and water. Stir until completely cool.

3 Using an electric mixer on high speed, beat the chilled evaporated milk until stiff peaks form. Fold in the cocoa mixture and pour into a 9-inch square pan. Cover and freeze for 1 hour, or until firm. Serve with chocolate sauce on the side.

548 ■ CHOCOLATE MINT CREAM PIE

MAKES 8 TO 10 SERVINGS
FREEZING TIME: *1 hour*

COOKIE CRUMB CRUST

1¼ cups chocolate wafer cookie crumbs
¼ cup finely ground hazelnuts
3 tablespoons granulated sugar
6 tablespoons butter or margarine, melted

CHOCOLATE AND VANILLA FILLINGS

1 quart vanilla ice cream, softened
2 tablespoons white crème de menthe
1½ quarts chocolate ice cream, softened

CHOCOLATE TOPPING

1 cup Chocolate Sauce VIII (see page 405)
Fresh mint sprigs for garnish

1 To make the crust, in a medium bowl, combine the cookie crumbs, hazelnuts, and sugar. Using a fork, blend in the melted butter. Press the mixture evenly onto the bottom and sides of a 9-inch pie pan. Cover with waxed paper and weight with dried beans or uncooked rice. Freeze until ready to use.

2 Line a medium bowl (see Baking notes) with plastic wrap, allowing it to hang over the edges.

3 In a medium bowl, using an electric mixer on low speed, combine the vanilla ice cream and crème de menthe. Pour the mixture into the prepared bowl. Cover and freeze for 1 hour, or until firm.

4 Spread the chocolate ice cream evenly over the chilled crust and freeze until firm.

5 Make the chocolate sauce.

6 To assemble, using the edges of the plastic wrap as handles, remove the vanilla ice cream from the bowl. Invert on top of the chocolate ice cream in the pie crust. Remove the plastic wrap. Pour the sauce over the top of the mound of vanilla ice cream and allow the excess to drip down and puddle around the base. Garnish with mint sprigs.

BAKING NOTES: Be sure the diameter of the bowl used to mold the vanilla ice cream is at least 1 inch less than that of the pie plate. This will allow for 1 inch of free space for the chocolate sauce to puddle in.

549 ■ CHOCOLATE MINT ICE CREAM PIE I

MAKES 8 TO 10 SERVINGS
FREEZING TIME: *1 hour*

1 recipe Chocolate Cookie Crumb Crust (see page 267)
1 quart chocolate mint ice cream, softened
1 cup miniature chocolate chips
2 cups Chocolate Fudge Sauce (see page 401)
1 cup Chocolate Syrup I (see page 406)
1 cup heavy cream

1 Make and bake the crust.

2 Spread half of the ice cream over the baked and cooled pie crust. Sprinkle the chocolate chips on the top. Spread the

549

548

547

remaining ice cream over the top. Cover and freeze 1 hour, or until firm.

3 Make the fudge sauce and chocolate syrup.

4 In a medium bowl, using an electric mixer on high speed, whip the cream until soft peaks form.

5 To serve, spread the fudge sauce over the pie. Spread the whipped cream over the sauce. Drizzle with the chocolate syrup.

550 ■ CHOCOLATE ORANGE SORBET

MAKES 2½ CUPS
FREEZING TIME: *24 hours*

1 cup water
⅔ cup granulated sugar
⅔ cup Dutch processed cocoa powder
1 ounce unsweetened chocolate, grated or finely chopped
¼ cup fresh orange juice
2 tablespoons grated orange zest
½ cup Triple Sec
Edible fresh flowers or mint sprigs for garnish
Chocolate wafer cookies for serving

1 In a medium saucepan over low heat, combine the water, sugar, and cocoa powder and stir until smooth. Add the chocolate and stir until melted and smooth. Raise the heat to high. Bring to a boil, stirring constantly, and simmer for 1 minute. Remove from the heat and immediately pour into a medium bowl. Add the orange juice, orange zest, and Triple Sec. Place the bowl in a larger bowl of ice and water. Stir until completely cool. Cover and chill.

2 Pour the mixture into an ice cream maker and freeze according to the manufacturer's directions. Transfer to an airtight container. Cover and freeze for 24 hours before serving.

3 To serve, place a large scoop on a serving dish and decorate with edible fresh flowers or mint sprigs and chocolate wafer cookies on the side.

551 ■ CHOCOLATE PEANUT BUTTER SUNDAE

MAKES 2 SERVINGS

1½ cups fudge ripple ice cream
6 tablespoons Peanut Butter and Honey Sauce (see page 416)
4 teaspoons salted peanuts
2 tablespoons chocolate peanut butter cups candy, diced
2 tablespoons whipped cream

1 Scoop the ice cream into two sundae dishes. Spoon the sauce over the top and sprinkle with the nuts and diced peanut butter cups. Drop a tablespoon of whipped cream on each and serve immediately.

552 ■ CHOCOLATE SHERBET

MAKES 1½ TO 2 QUARTS
FREEZING TIME: *1 hour*

1¾ cups Dutch processed cocoa powder
1 cup granulated sugar
3½ cups skim milk
1 tablespoon chocolate extract
Pinch of salt

1 In medium saucepan, over medium heat, combine the cocoa powder, sugar, milk, chocolate extract, and salt. Bring to a boil. Insert a candy thermometer and simmer until 185 degrees, stirring constantly.

2 Set the pan in a large bowl of ice and water. Stir occasionally until the mixture is completely cool. Pour into a shallow 9-inch pan. Cover and freeze, stirring occasionally, for 1 hour, or until firm.

553 ■ CINNAMON-FLAVORED CHOCO-LATE CHIP ICE CREAM

MAKES 1½ TO 2 QUARTS
CHILL/FREEZING TIME: *2 hours*

1 cup granulated sugar
2 tablespoons all-purpose flour
2 tablespoons butter or margarine, at room temperature
2 teaspoons ground cinnamon
2 cups boiling water
2 cups heavy cream
1 cup semisweet chocolate chips

1 In a large saucepan, over low heat, combine the sugar, flour, butter, and cinnamon. Stir until smooth. Add the boiling water and cook, stirring constantly, until smooth. Remove from the heat and transfer to a medium bowl. Cover and chill for 1 hour.

551

550

552

2 In a large bowl, using an electric mixer on high speed, whip the cream until stiff peaks form. Stir into the chilled mixture. Fold in the chocolate chips and freeze in a 9 by 5-inch loaf pan, stirring occasionally, for 1 hour or until firm.

BAKING NOTES: Any kind of chocolate chips can be used. Chopped almonds or walnuts can also be added.

554 ■ COCOA MOCHA ICE CREAM

MAKES 1½ TO 1¾ QUARTS
CHILL TIME: *1 hour*

2 cups heavy cream
2 cups milk
12 ounces semisweet chocolate, grated or finely chopped
½ cup Dutch processed cocoa powder
6 large egg yolks
⅓ cup light corn syrup
¼ cup granulated sugar
½ cup coffee liqueur
1 teaspoon chocolate extract

1 In a large saucepan, over medium heat, heat the cream and 1 cup of the milk until bubbles start to form around the sides of the pan. Remove from the heat.

2 In the top of a double boiler over simmering water, combine the remaining 1 cup milk, the chocolate, and the cocoa powder and stir until smooth. Remove from the heat. Place in a large bowl.

3 In a large bowl, beat the egg yolks, corn syrup, and sugar until smooth and blended.

4 Pouring it in a thin stream and beating constantly, beat the egg yolks into the hot cream mixture. Cook over medium-low heat, stirring constantly, until the mixture thickens and coats the back of a spoon. Remove from the heat.

5 Beat the hot cream mixture into the chocolate mixture. Stir in the liqueur and chocolate extract. Place the bowl in a larger bowl filled with ice and water and stir until completely cooled. Cover and chill for 1 hour.

6 Pour into an ice cream maker and freeze according to the manufacturer's directions. Serve or transfer to an airtight container. Cover and freeze until serving.

555 ■ CREAMY CHOCOLATE ICE CREAM

MAKES 1 QUART

2 cups plus 2 tablespoons heavy cream
2 ounces unsweetened chocolate, grated or finely chopped
6 large egg yolks
½ cup granulated sugar
¼ cup butter or margarine, at room temperature
½ teaspoon chocolate or vanilla extract

1 In the top of a double boiler over simmering water, combine 1 cup of the cream and the chocolate, stirring constantly until smooth. Remove from the heat. Transfer to a small bowl, cover and chill for 45 minutes or until very thick but not set.

2 In a medium bowl, using an electric mixer on medium speed, beat the egg yolks until thick and light-colored. Beat in ¼ cup of the sugar.

3 In a saucepan, over low heat, combine the remaining 1 cup plus 2 tablespoons cream and ¼ cup sugar. Heat just until simmering. Remove from the heat. Slowly beat half of the cream mixture into the egg yolks. Pour the egg yolk mixture back into the saucepan. Return the pan to

553
556
558
555
554
557

the heat and cook, stirring constantly, until the mixture is thick enough to coat the back of a spoon. Remove from heat and beat in the butter. Strain the mixture through a sieve into a large bowl. Beat in the chilled chocolate mixture and the and chocolate extract. Pour into an ice cream maker and freeze according to the manufacturer's directions. Serve or transfer to an airtight container. Cover and freeze until serving.

556 ■ FRENCH CHOCOLATE ICE CREAM

MAKES 1½ TO 1¾ QUARTS
FREEZING TIME: *8 hours*

4 large egg yolks
2½ cups milk
3 ounces unsweetened chocolate, grated or finely chopped
1 cup granulated sugar
¼ teaspoon salt
1 pint heavy cream
1 teaspoon chocolate extract

1 In a medium bowl, beat the egg yolks until thick and light-colored.

2 In a saucepan, heat the milk until bubbles start to form around the sides of the pan. Add the chocolate and blend until smooth. Remove from the heat. Beat about ½ cup of the hot mixture into the egg yolks. Mix the egg mixture into the saucepan. Add the sugar and salt and stir until the sugar is dissolved.

3 Return to the heat and cook, stirring constantly, until the mixture thickens enough to coat the back of a spoon. Remove from the heat and set the pan in a large bowl of ice and water. Stir until completely cool. Add the cream and chocolate extract. Pour into a 9-inch square pan. Cover and freeze for 8 hours.

557 ■ FROZEN CHOCOLATE

MAKES 1 QUART
CHILL/FREEZING TIME: *3 hours*

3 ounces unsweetened chocolate, grated or finely chopped
3 ounces semisweet chocolate, grated or finely chopped
2 cups water
2 teaspoons instant espresso powder
2 tablespoons crème de cacao
½ teaspoon chocolate extract

1 In a saucepan, melt the chocolates with the water, stirring until smooth. Stir in the espresso powder and bring the mixture to a boil. Simmer, stirring occasionally, for 6 to 7 minutes, or until thickened. Remove from the heat and set the pan in a large bowl of ice and water. Stir until cool. Stir in the crème de cacao and chocolate extract. Cover and chill for at least 2 hours.

2 Pour the mixture into an ice cream maker and freeze according to the manufacturer's directions until the mixture is almost firm. Pour the mixture into an airtight container. Cover and freeze for 1 hour before serving.

BAKING NOTES: Serve the ice cream soft. If it does become hard, let soften in the refrigerator for 1 hour before serving.

558 ■ FROZEN CHOCOLATE ICE CREAM PIE

MAKES 8 TO 10 SERVINGS
FREEZING TIME: *1 hour*

CHOCOLATE GRAHAM CRACKER CRUST
¼ cup butter-flavored vegetable shortening
2 ounces unsweetened chocolate, grated or finely chopped
1 teaspoon coffee liqueur
1 cup chocolate graham cracker crumbs
¼ cup powdered sugar

CHOCOLATE ICE CREAM
3 ounces unsweetened chocolate, grated or finely chopped
3 ounces semisweet chocolate, grated or finely chopped
2 tablespoons boiling water
½ cup granulated sugar
¼ cup water
½ teaspoon cream of tartar
Pinch of salt
4 large egg yolks
3 cups heavy cream
1 tablespoon chocolate extract
Chocolate Whipped Cream (see page 406) and Chocolate Curls (see page 422) for serving

1 Position a rack in the center of the oven and preheat the oven to 350 degrees. Lightly grease a 9-inch pie pan.

2 To make the crust, in the top of a double boiler over simmering water, melt the shortening and chocolate, stirring until smooth. Remove from the heat. Stir in the liqueur.

3 In a large bowl, combine the crumbs and sugar. Mix in the chocolate mixture. Press onto the bottom and up the sides of the prepared pie pan.

4 Bake for 10 minutes. Cool completely on a wire rack. Chill while preparing the ice cream.

5 To make the ice cream, in the top of a double boiler over simmering water, melt the chocolates and the 2 tablespoons boiling water, stirring until the chocolate is melted and smooth. Remove from the heat.

6 In a small saucepan, over medium heat, combine the sugar, ¼ cup water, cream of tartar, and salt. Bring to a boil. Insert a candy thermometer and cook, without stirring, until 238 degrees.

7 Meanwhile, in a large bowl, using an electric mixer on medium speed, beat the egg yolks until thick and light-colored. Beating constantly on low speed, pour in the syrup in a thin stream. Beat in the chocolate mixture. Beat in the cream and chocolate extract. Pour into a freezer-safe glass bowl and freeze for 30 minutes, or until

almost firm, stirring several times.

8 Spread the ice cream over the chilled pie crust. Garnish with chocolate whipped cream and chocolate curls. Freeze until the ice cream is hard before serving.

559 ■ FROZEN CHOCOLATE YOGURT

MAKES 1½ TO 1¾ QUARTS
FREEZING TIME: *30 minutes*

32 ounces chocolate yogurt
1½ cups granulated sugar
⅔ cup Dutch processed cocoa powder
Pinch of salt
2 tablespoons instant coffee powder
1 tablespoon coffee liqueur

1 In a large bowl, combine all of the ingredients, beating until smooth and the sugar is dissolved.

2 Pour into an ice cream maker and freeze according to the manufacturer's directions. Transfer to an airtight container. Cover and freeze for 30 minutes, or until firm.

560 ■ FROZEN YOGURT PIE

MAKES 8 TO 10 SERVINGS
FREEZING TIME: *2 hours*

1¼ cups graham cracker crumbs
1 tablespoon Dutch processed cocoa powder
2 tablespoons butter or margarine, melted
1 pint chocolate or chocolate mint ice cream, softened
1 pint chocolate yogurt
Chocolate Sauce IX for serving (see page 406)

1 In a large bowl, mix the crumbs, cocoa powder, and butter. Press the mixture firmly onto the bottom and sides of a 9-inch pie pan.

2 Spoon the chocolate ice cream over the crust. Spread the yogurt evenly over the top of the ice cream. Cover with waxed paper or plastic wrap

and freeze for 2 hours, or until very firm.

3 Make the chocolate sauce.

4 To serve, remove the pie from the freezer and let stand at room temperature for 15 minutes. Serve with the warm chocolate sauce on the side.

BAKING NOTES: The pie can be kept frozen for up to 1 month before serving.

561 ■ HEAVENLY CHOCOLATE ICE CREAM

MAKES 1½ QUARTS
FREEZING TIME: *1 hour*

1 quart heavy cream
1 cup granulated sugar
3 ounces semisweet chocolate, grated or finely chopped
1 tablespoon chocolate extract
Pinch of salt

1 In a saucepan, heat the cream until bubbles start to form around the sides of the pan. Add the sugar, chocolate, chocolate extract, and salt. Stir constantly until the chocolate is melted and well incorporated into the mixture and the sugar is dissolved. Remove from the heat and set the pan in a large bowl of ice and water. Stir until completely cool.

2 Pour the mixture into an ice cream maker and freeze according to the manufacturer's directions. Serve or transfer to an airtight container. Cover and freeze for 1 hour, or until firm.

562 ■ HOT FUDGE SUNDAE PIE I

MAKES 8 TO 10 SERVINGS
FREEZING TIME: *1½ hours*

Chocolate Cookie Crumb Crust (see page 267)
Hot Fudge Sauce IV (see page 412)
1 quart strawberry ice cream, softened
1 quart chocolate ice cream, frozen
½ cup heavy cream

GARNISH

Maraschino cherries
Chocolate leaves (see page 422)
Chopped almonds

1 Make the pie crust and the hot fudge sauce.

2 To assemble, spread half of the strawberry ice cream over the crust and freeze for 30 minutes. Drizzle half of the fudge sauce over the top and spread with the remaining strawberry ice cream. Freeze for 30 minutes.

3 Using a small ice cream scoop, arrange balls of the chocolate ice cream over the top of the strawberry layer. Drizzle the remaining fudge sauce over the top.

4 In a medium bowl, using an electric mixture on high speed, whip the cream until soft peaks form.

5 Fill a pastry bag fitted with a large star tip with the whipped cream. Pipe rosettes around the chocolate ice cream. Freeze for 30 minutes before serving. Garnish with the cherries and chocolate leaves. Sprinkle the almonds over the top.

563 ■ HOT FUDGE SUNDAE PIE II

MAKES 8 TO 10 SERVINGS
FREEZING TIME: *1 hour*

CRUST

1 recipe Chocolate Hazelnut Crumb Crust (see page 271)

559

CHOCOLATE SAUCE

1 cup granulated sugar

¾ cup Dutch processed cocoa powder

1 teaspoon instant espresso powder

1 cup heavy cream

¼ cup butter or margarine

ICE CREAM FILLING

1 quart chocolate ice cream, softened

1 quart chocolate chocolate chip ice cream, softened

½ cup heavy cream

2 tablespoons granulated sugar

½ cup chopped walnuts for garnish

¾ cup diced fresh cherries or strawberries or whole raspberries for garnish

1 Make and chill the crust.

2 To make the sauce, in a saucepan, over low heat, combine the sugar, cocoa powder, and espresso powder. Add ½ cup of the cream and stir to make a smooth paste. Stir in the remaining ½ cup cream and cook, stirring constantly, until smooth. Stir in the butter and cook for 4 to 6 minutes, or until the butter is melted and the mixture is smooth. Remove from the heat.

3 To assemble the pie, spread half of the chocolate ice cream over the prepared crust. Carefully spoon about half of the warm sauce over the top. Spread the remaining chocolate ice cream over the top of the sauce. Freeze for 1 hour, or until firm.

4 Using a small ice cream scoop, place balls of the chocolate chocolate chip ice cream in a decorative manner over the surface of the pie. Drizzle the remaining sauce over the top.

5 In a small bowl, using an electric mixer on high speed, whip the cream and sugar until stiff peaks form. Fill a pastry bag fitted with a large star tip with the whipped cream. Pipe large and small rosettes into the areas not filled with ice cream. Sprinkle with walnuts. Freeze until ready to serve. Garnish with the fresh fruit just before serving.

BAKING NOTES: Almost any combination of ice cream flavors can be used in this recipe.

564 ■ MOCHA ICE CREAM I

MAKES 1 QUART
FREEZING TIME: *1 hour*

½ cup semisweet chocolate, grated or finely chopped

3 tablespoons instant espresso powder

2 tablespoons boiling water

2 large eggs

½ cup granulated sugar

1 teaspoon chocolate or vanilla extract

2 cups heavy cream

1 tablespoon coffee liqueur

1 cup Hershey's™ Chocolate Shoppe Candy Bar Sprinkles (milk chocolate flavor)

1 In the top of a double boiler over simmering water, melt the chocolate, stirring until smooth. Dissolve the espresso powder in the boiling water and stir into the chocolate. Remove from the heat.

2 In a large bowl, using an electric mixer on medium speed, beat the eggs and sugar until thick and light-colored. Beat in the chocolate mixture and chocolate extract. Beat in the cream. Stir in the liqueur.

560

561

562

563

564

3 Pour into an ice cream maker and freeze according to the manufacturer's directions until almost firm. Fold in the candy bar sprinkles and continue freezing until firm. Transfer to an airtight container. Cover and freeze for 1 hour, or until serving.

BAKING NOTES: To mix in a blender, blend the sugar and eggs on high speed until very thick. Add the chocolate extract and cream and blend on high speed 1 minute. Blend in the melted chocolate mixture. Owing to the raw eggs in this recipe, it should be kept frozen at all times. It will keep up to 6 months.

565 ■ MOCHA ICE CREAM II

MAKES 2½ QUARTS

CUSTARD

6 large egg yolks
1½ cups granulated sugar
2 pints heavy cream
2 tablespoons strong brewed coffee

MOCHA FLAVORING

2 ounces semisweet chocolate, grated or finely chopped
½ cup espresso coffee
¼ cup ground almonds
2 tablespoons ground coffee beans
Chocolate Sauce V (see page 405)

1 In a large bowl, using an electric mixer on medium speed, beat the egg yolks until thick and light-colored. Beat in the sugar. Add the cream and coffee and beat thoroughly until well blended.

2 Pour the mixture into an ice cream maker and freeze according to the manufacturer's directions. While the ice cream is churning, make the mocha flavoring.

3 To make the flavoring, melt the chocolate (see page 13). Remove from the heat and cool.

4 Turn off the ice cream maker and add the melted chocolate. Stir in the coffee, almonds, and coffee beans. Restart the ice cream maker and freeze. Transfer the ice cream to an airtight container. Cover and freeze until ready to serve.

5 Make the chocolate sauce. Serve the ice cream with the warm sauce on the side.

BAKING NOTES: Owing to the raw eggs in this recipe, it should be kept frozen at all times. It will keep up to 6 months.

566 ■ RASPBERRY ICE CREAM PIE

MAKES 8 TO 10 SERVINGS
FREEZING TIME: *1 hour*

CHOCOLATE COOKIE CRUMB CRUST

6 tablespoons butter or margarine, at room temperature
1½ cups chocolate wafer cookie crumbs
2 drops peppermint extract

ICE CREAM FILLING

1 quart vanilla ice cream, softened
1½ quarts raspberry ice cream, softened

CHOCOLATE TOPPING

½ cup granulated sugar
1 tablespoon cornstarch or arrowroot
¼ cup milk
¼ cup heavy cream
6 tablespoons butter or margarine
3 ounces unsweetened chocolate, grated or finely chopped
1 teaspoon crème de cacao

566

1 Position a rack in the center of the oven and preheat the oven to 350 degrees.

2 To make the crust, in a medium bowl, using a pastry blender or two knives scissor fashion, cut the butter into the cookie crumbs to form a crumbly mixture. Stir in the extract. Press onto the bottom and up the sides of a 9-inch pie pan.

3 Bake for 10 minutes. Cool slightly on a wire rack. Freeze until ready to use.

4 To make the filling, line a large bowl with plastic wrap. Scoop the vanilla ice cream into the bowl, packing it firmly. Cover and freeze for 1 hour, or until firm.

5 Spread the raspberry ice cream evenly over the chilled pie crust and freeze.

6 To make the topping, in the top of a double boiler over simmering water, combine the sugar and cornstarch. Stir in the milk, cream, butter, and chocolate. Stir over low heat until the chocolate is melted and the mixture thickens. Remove from the heat. Stir in the crème de cacao and cool to room temperature.

7 To assemble, using the edges of the plastic wrap as handles, lift the vanilla ice cream out of the bowl. Invert on top of the raspberry ice cream. Press down slightly. Remove the plastic wrap. Pour the topping over the mound of vanilla ice cream, allowing it to drip down the sides. Serve immediately.

BAKING NOTES: The pie will keep in the freezer for up to 2 months.

567 ■ WHITE CHOCOLATE ICE CREAM

MAKES 2 QUARTS

2 cups heavy cream
2 cups half-and-half
10 ounces white chocolate or almond bark, grated or finely chopped
8 large egg yolks
²/₃ cup granulated sugar

1 In a large saucepan, over medium heat, warm the cream and half-and-half until bubbles start to form around the sides of the pan. Remove from the heat.

2 Place the white chocolate into a large bowl.

3 In a medium bowl, beat the egg yolks and sugar until thick and light-colored. Pouring it in a thin stream, and beating continually, add the hot milk mixture to the egg yolks. Pour the mixture into an extra-large double boiler or an ovenproof mixing bowl placed over a large saucepan filled with simmering water. Insert a candy thermometer and heat the mixture, stirring constantly, until 170 degrees and it coats the back of a spoon. Remove from the heat and pour over the white chocolate. Stir until the chocolate is melted and the mixture is smooth. Set the bowl in a larger bowl of ice and water. Stir until completely cool. Cover and chill thoroughly.

4 Pour the mixture into an ice cream maker and freeze according to the manufacturer's directions. Transfer to an airtight container. Cover and freeze until firm.

Pies and Tarts

568 ■ ALMOND CRUST

MAKES ONE 9-INCH PIE CRUST
FREEZING TIME: *30 minutes*

1¾ cups almonds, coarsely ground
3 tablespoons butter-flavored vegetable shortening
2 tablespoons light corn syrup

1 Lightly grease a 9-inch pie pan.

2 In a medium bowl, combine the almonds, shortening, and corn syrup. Press the mixture onto the bottom and up the sides of the prepared pie pan. Cover and freeze for 30 minutes, or until ready to fill.

569 ■ AMARETTO MOUSSE PIE

MAKES 8 TO 10 SERVINGS
CHILL TIME: *6 hours*

COCONUT CRUST

2 cups flaked coconut
6 ounces semisweet chocolate, grated or finely chopped
2 tablespoons butter or margarine
1 tablespoon light corn syrup

ALMOND MOUSSE FILLING

2 teaspoons unflavored gelatin
¼ cup amaretto
½ cup sour cream or chocolate yogurt
1½ cups heavy cream
1 cup powdered sugar, sifted twice
¾ cup finely ground almonds
Chocolate Cigarettes (see page 421) for garnish
Ground almonds for garnish

1 Lightly grease a 9-inch pie pan.

2 To make the crust, in a medium bowl, crumble the coconut, breaking apart any clumps.

3 In the top of a double boiler over simmering water, melt the chocolate and butter with the corn syrup, stirring until smooth.

4 Pour the warm chocolate mixture over the coconut. Using two spoons, mix until the coconut is well coated. Press the mixture evenly onto the bottom

and sides of the prepared pie pan. Chill for 1 hour.

5 Meanwhile, to make the filling, in a cup, sprinkle the gelatin over the amaretto and let stand for 1 minute to soften. Set the cup in a saucepan of hot water over low heat and stir until the gelatin is dissolved.

6 In a large bowl, stir the gelatin and sour cream until smooth. Stir in the cream. Using an electric mixer on medium speed, beat in the powdered sugar, a little at a time. On high speed, beat until stiff peaks form. Fold in the almonds. Scrape the mixture into the prepared crust and spread evenly. Garnish with chocolate cigarettes and sprinkle with ground almonds. Chill for 3 to 5 hours, or until firm.

570 ■ ANGEL BREATH PIE

MAKES 8 TO 10 SERVINGS
BAKING TIME: *50 minutes*
CHILL TIME: *8 hours*

MERINGUE CRUST

2 large egg whites
⅛ teaspoon cream of tartar
½ cup granulated sugar
½ teaspoon almond or vanilla extract
Pinch of salt

CHOCOLATE FILLING

5 ounces semisweet chocolate, grated or finely chopped
3 tablespoons hot water
1 cup heavy cream
1 tablespoon chocolate extract

1 Position a rack in the center of the oven and preheat the oven to 300 degrees. Lightly grease a 9-inch glass pie plate.

2 To make the crust, in a medium bowl, using an electric mixer on high speed, beat the egg whites and cream of tartar until foamy. Add the sugar, almond extract, and salt. Continue beating until stiff but not dry. Spread the mixture evenly over the bottom and up the sides of the prepared pie plate.

3 Bake for 45 to 50 minutes, or until the surface is a light golden brown.

4 To make the filling, in the top of a double boiler over simmering water, melt 4 ounces of the chocolate with the water, stirring constantly until smooth. Remove from the heat. Transfer to a large bowl and cool to room temperature.

5 Meanwhile, in a medium bowl, using an electric mixer on high speed, whip the cream until soft peaks form. Add to the chocolate mixture and fold until blended. Stir in the chocolate extract. Scrape the mixture over the top of the baked crust and spread evenly. Sprinkle the remaining 1 ounce grated chocolate over the top. Cover and chill for at least 8 hours before serving.

571 ■ ANGEL'S CHOCOLATE PIE

MAKES 8 TO 10 SERVINGS
CHILL TIME: *1 hour*

1 recipe Chocolate Hazelnut Crumb Crust (see page 271)
4 ounces semisweet chocolate, grated or finely chopped
3 tablespoons water
1 teaspoon chocolate extract
1 cup heavy cream

1 Make and chill the crust.

2 In the top of a double boiler over simmering water, melt the chocolate with the water, stirring constantly until smooth.

569

Remove from the heat. Transfer to a large bowl and cool to room temperature. Stir in the chocolate extract.

3 In a medium bowl, using an electric mixer on high speed, whip the cream until stiff peaks form. Fold into the chocolate mixture. Spoon into the prepared pie crust and chill for 1 hour before serving.

572 ■ BLACK BOTTOM PIE

MAKES 8 TO 10 SERVINGS
BAKING TIME: *15 minutes*
CHILL TIME: *overnight*

PASTRY CRUST

2 cups all-purpose flour
1/2 teaspoon salt
2/3 cup butter-flavored vegetable shortening
5 to 6 tablespoons ice water

CUSTARD FILLINGS

4 large eggs, separated, plus 2 large egg yolks
3 cups milk
1 1/4 cups granulated sugar
2 tablespoons cornstarch
1 1/2 teaspoons almond extract
2 ounces unsweetened chocolate, grated or finely chopped
1 envelope unflavored gelatin
1/4 cup cold water
3 tablespoons crème de cacao
Chocolate Whipped Cream (see page 406) for garnish
Chocolate Curls (see page 422) for garnish

571

1 Position a rack in the center of the oven and preheat the oven to 400 degrees.

2 To make the crust, in medium bowl, combine the flour and salt. Using a pastry blender or two knives used scissor fashion, cut in the shortening until the mixture forms fine crumbs. Sprinkle the water, a little at a time, over the top and mix gently with a fork until the dough is just moist enough to hold together. Form into a ball. Wrap and chill for 1 hour, or until firm.

3 On a lightly floured surface, roll the dough out into a circle 1/4 inch thick. Transfer to a 9-inch pie pan and ease into the bottom and up the sides. Trim the edges and flute if desired. Prick the bottom and sides with a fork.

4 Bake for 15 minutes, or until the golden brown. Cool completely in the pan on a wire rack.

5 To make the fillings, in a medium bowl, beat the 6 egg yolks until thick and light-colored.

6 In a large saucepan, over low heat, combine the milk, sugar, and cornstarch, stirring constantly until the mixture thickens. Remove from the heat. Beat 2 tablespoons of the hot milk mixture into the egg yolks. On low speed, gradually beat the egg yolk mixture into the hot mixture. Return to the heat and cook, stirring constantly, until the mixture coats the back of a spoon. Remove from the heat and stir in the almond extract. Measure 2 cups of the hot custard and place in a small bowl. Add the chocolate and stir until melted and smooth. Pour into the baked pie crust and chill for 1 hour. Transfer the remaining hot custard to a large bowl.

7 In a small saucepan, sprinkle the gelatin over the water. Let stand for 1 minute to soften. Stir into the hot custard. Stir in the crème de cacao. Beat the mixture until thickened.

8 In a large bowl, using an electric mixer with clean beaters on high speed, beat the 4 egg whites until stiff peaks form. Fold into the custard mixture and chill for 15 to 30 minutes, or until just beginning to set. Spoon over the chilled chocolate layer in the crust. Cover and chill overnight. Spread with chocolate whipped cream and garnish with chocolate curls.

573 ■ BLACK FOREST PIE

MAKES 8 TO 10 SERVINGS
FREEZING TIME: *1 hour*

CHOCOLATE COOKIE CRUMB CRUST

6 tablespoons butter or margarine, at room temperature
1 1/2 cups chocolate wafer cookie crumbs

CHOCOLATE CHERRY FILLING

2 ounces semisweet chocolate, grated or finely chopped
1 cup heavy cream
1 jar (7 ounces) marshmallow creme
1 teaspoon crème de cacao
2 tablespoons maraschino cherry juice
1/2 cup maraschino cherries, quartered

1 Position a rack in the center of the oven and preheat the oven to 350 degrees.

2 To make the crust, in a medium bowl, using a pastry blender or two knives scissor fashion, cut the butter into the cookie crumbs to form a crumbly mixture. Press the mixture onto the bottom and up the sides of a 9-inch pie pan.

3 Bake for 10 minutes. Cool on a wire rack. Chill until ready to fill.

4 To make the filling, melt the chocolate (see page 13). Remove from the heat.

5 In a medium bowl, using an electric mixer on high speed, whip the cream until soft peaks form.

6 In a large bowl, beat the marshmallow creme, melted chocolate, and crème de cacao.

Gradually stir in the cherry juice. Fold in the whipped cream and cherries. Pour into the prepared crust and freeze for 1 hour before serving.

574 ■ BLACK RUSSIAN PIE

MAKES 8 TO 10 SERVINGS
CHILL TIME: *8 hours*

CHOCOLATE COOKIE CRUMB CRUST

1½ cups chocolate wafer cookie crumbs
¼ cup butter or margarine, melted
2 tablespoons granulated sugar

FILLING

1 envelope unflavored gelatin
¼ cup cold water
3 large eggs, separated
7 tablespoons powdered sugar
¼ cup Kahlúa
2 tablespoons vodka
½ cup heavy cream

WHIPPED CREAM TOPPING

1 cup heavy cream
3 tablespoons Kahlúa
2 tablespoons powdered sugar

GARNISH

White Chocolate Leaves (see page 422)
Chocolate Curls (see page 422)

1 To make the crust, in a medium bowl, mix the cookie crumbs, butter, and sugar until blended. Press onto the bottom and up the sides of a 9-inch pie pan. Freeze until ready to fill.

2 To make the filling, in a small saucepan, sprinkle the gelatin over the water. Let stand for 1 minute to dissolve. Stir over low heat until completely dissolved. Remove from the heat.

3 In a medium bowl, using an electric mixer on medium speed, beat the egg yolks until thick and light-colored. Beat in 3½ tablespoons of the powdered sugar and continue beating until very thick. Beat in the gelatin mixture until blended. Beat in the Kahlúa and vodka. Set the bowl in a larger bowl filled with ice and water and beat for about

3 to 5 minutes, or until the mixture thickens.

4 In a large bowl, using an electric mixer with clean beaters on high speed, beat the egg whites until foamy. Beat in the remaining 3½ tablespoons powdered sugar. Beat until stiff but not dry. Fold in the egg yolk mixture.

5 In a medium bowl, using an electric mixer on high speed, whip the cream until stiff peaks form. Fold into the egg mixture. Pour into the chilled crust and spread evenly. Chill for at least 8 hours.

6 To make the topping, in a medium bowl, using an electric mixer on high speed, whip the cream until soft peaks form. Add the Kahlúa and powdered sugar and beat until stiff peaks form. Spread over the chilled pie and garnish with chocolate leaves and curls.

BAKING NOTES: Owing to the raw eggs used in this recipe, it should be refrigerated at all times and for no longer than 3 days.

575 ■ CHIPPED CHOCOLATE CHERRY PIE

MAKES 8 TO 10 SERVINGS
CHILL TIME: *2 hours*

CHOCOLATE COOKIE CRUMB CRUST

6 tablespoons butter or margarine, at room temperature
1½ cups chocolate wafer cookie crumbs

CHOCOLATE CHERRY MARSHMALLOW FILLING

1 jar (7 ounces) marshmallow creme
1 cup pecans, finely chopped
½ cup maraschino cherries, finely diced
½ cup milk
½ cup heavy cream
2 ounces semisweet chocolate, grated or finely chopped
Chocolate Curls (see page 422) or Chocolate Leaves (see page 422) for garnish

1 Position a rack in the center of the oven and preheat the oven to 350 degrees.

2 To make the crust, in a medium bowl, using a pastry blender or two knives scissor fashion, cut the butter into the cookie crumbs to form a crumbly mixture. Press onto the bottom and up the sides of a 9-inch pie pan.

574

577

575

3 Bake for 10 minutes. Cool completely on a wire rack.

4 To make the filling, in the top of a double boiler over simmering water, heat the marshmallow creme, pecans, cherries, and milk, stirring until smooth. Remove from the heat. Transfer to a large bowl and cool completely.

5 In a medium bowl, using an electric mixer on high speed, whip the cream until soft peaks form.

6 Fold the grated chocolate and whipped cream into the marshmallow mixture. Pour into the prepared crust and spread evenly. Chill for 2 hours before serving. Garnish with chocolate curls or chocolate leaves.

576 ■ CHOCK FULL OF NUTS CHOCOLATE PECAN PIE

MAKES 8 TO 10 SERVINGS
BAKING TIME: *50 minutes*
CHILL TIME: *1 hour*

1 recipe Pecan Pastry Crust (see page 286)
³/₄ cup granulated sugar
3 tablespoons dark corn syrup
2 ounces unsweetened chocolate, grated or finely chopped
3 tablespoons butter or margarine
1 teaspoon vanilla or chocolate extract
3 large eggs
1 cup pecans, chopped
1 cup pecan halves
Chocolate Whipped Cream (see page 406) for garnish

1 Position a rack in the center of the oven and preheat the oven to 375 degrees.

2 Make and chill the crust.

3 To make the filling, in a medium saucepan, over medium heat, combine the sugar and corn syrup. Bring to a boil and cook for 2 minutes. Remove from the heat. Add the

chocolate and butter and stir until melted and smooth. Beat in the vanilla extract.

4 In a medium bowl, using an electric mixer on high speed, beat the eggs until foamy.

5 Pouring it in a thin stream, mix the chocolate mixture into the beaten eggs. Fold in the chopped pecans. Pour the mixture into the prepared crust.

6 Bake for 45 to 50 minutes, or until set. Cool completely. Arrange the pecan halves over the surface of the pie. Top with chocolate whipped cream.

577 ■ CHOCOLATE ALMOND COCONUT PIE

MAKES 8 TO 10 SERVINGS
BAKING TIME: *10 minutes*
CHILL TIME: *2 hours*

COCONUT ALMOND CRUST

2 tablespoons powdered sugar
2 cups flaked coconut
1 tablespoon cornstarch
1 cup ground almonds
3 tablespoons butter, melted

CHOCOLATE FILLING

4 ounces semisweet chocolate, grated or finely chopped
1 container (8 ounces) whipped topping
Chocolate Curls (see page 422) for garnish
Fresh mint sprigs for garnish

1 Position a rack in the center of the oven and preheat the oven to 350 degrees.

2 To make the crust, in a medium bowl, blend the powdered sugar, coconut, cornstarch, and almonds. Using a spoon, blend in the melted butter, mixing thoroughly. Press the mixture onto the bottom and up the sides of a 9-inch pie pan.

3 Bake for 8 to 10 minutes, or until slightly browned. Cool in the pan on a wire rack.

4 To make the filling, melt the chocolate (see page 13). Remove from the heat. Transfer to a medium bowl and cool to

room temperature. Fold the whipped topping into the cooled chocolate. Spread evenly over the pie crust. Chill for 2 hours. Garnish with chocolate curls and mint sprigs and serve.

578 ■ CHOCOLATE AMARETTO PIE

MAKES 6 TO 8 SERVINGS
CHILL TIME: *4 hours*

1 recipe Almond Crust (see page 258)
¹/₄ cup butter or margarine
¹/₂ cup Dutch processed cocoa powder
1 cup butter or margarine, at room temperature
1¹/₂ cups granulated sugar
¹/₄ cup amaretto
4 large eggs

1 Make and chill the pie crust.

2 To make the filling, in a small saucepan, over medium heat, melt ¹/₄ cup of the butter. Add the cocoa powder and stir until smooth. Remove from the heat.

3 In a large bowl, using an electric mixer on medium speed, beat the butter and sugar until fluffy. Beat in the amaretto. Beat in the warm cocoa powder mixture.

4 In a small bowl, using an electric mixture on medium speed, beat the eggs until thick and light-colored. On low speed, beat the eggs into the butter mixture. Pour into the prepared pie crust. Cover and chill for at least 4 hours, or until serving.

BAKING NOTES: Owing to the raw eggs used in this recipe, it should be kept refrigerated at all times, and for no longer than 3 days.

579 ■ CHOCOLATE BUTTERSCOTCH PIE

MAKES 8 TO 10 SERVINGS
BAKING TIME: *35 minutes*
CHILL TIME: *1 hour*

PASTRY CRUST

2 cups all-purpose flour
1/2 teaspoon salt
2/3 cup butter-flavored vegetable shortening
5 to 6 tablespoons ice water

CHOCOLATE BUTTERSCOTCH FILLING

1 tablespoon butter or margarine
1 cup packed light brown sugar
1 1/2 cups milk
1 package (3.4 ounces) Jell-O Brand chocolate instant pudding mix
1 teaspoon chocolate extract
2 large egg yolks

MERINGUE TOPPING

1 1/4 cups Chocolate Mocha Meringue Topping (see page 402)
Cocoa Sugar (see page 407) for garnish

1 Position a rack in the center of the oven and preheat the oven to 375 degrees.

2 To make the crust, in a medium bowl, combine the flour and salt. Using a pastry blender or two knives scissor fashion, cut in the shortening until the mixture forms fine crumbs. Sprinkle the water over the top, a little at a time, and mix gently with a fork until the dough is just moist enough to hold together. Form into a ball. Wrap and chill for 1 hour, or until firm.

3 On a lightly floured surface, roll the dough out into a circle about 1/4 inch thick. Transfer to a 9-inch pie pan and ease into the bottom and up the sides of the pan. Trim the edges and flute if desired.

4 Bake for 18 to 20 minutes, or until the crust turns a light golden brown. Remove from the oven. While the crust is baking, make the filling.

5 To make the filling, in a medium saucepan, over medium heat, melt the butter. Add the brown sugar and 1 cup of the milk and stir until the sugar is dissolved. Dissolve the pudding mix in the remaining 1/2 cup milk and blend it in. Bring the mixture to a boil. Stir in the chocolate extract and cook, stirring constantly, for 3 minutes. Remove from the heat.

6 In a small bowl, beat the egg yolks. Beat in about 1/2 cup of the hot mixture. Beat the egg yolk mixture back into the saucepan. Pour the mixture into the baked pie crust.

7 Make the chocolate meringue. Spread the meringue over the filling.

8 Bake 10 to 15 minutes, or until the meringue starts to turn a very light brown color. Cool completely on a wire rack. Garnish with cocoa sugar.

580 ■ CHOCOLATE CHERRY TRUFFLE PIE

MAKES 8 TO 10 SERVINGS
CHILL TIME: *4 1/2 hours*

1 recipe Chocolate Pastry Crust (see page 274)
1 3/4 cups heavy cream
8 ounces semisweet chocolate, grated or finely chopped
2 tablespoons cherry liqueur
1 pint fresh cherries, pitted
1/2 cup granulated sugar
Chocolate Curls (see page 422) for garnish

1 Make and bake the crust.

2 In a medium saucepan, warm 3/4 cup of the cream until bubbles start to form around the sides of the pan. Remove from the heat. Add the chocolate and stir until smooth. Cool slightly. Whisk until the mixture thickens. Mix in the liqueur. Spoon several spoonfuls of the mixture into the baked crust. Chill for 30 minutes, or until set. Reserve the remaining chocolate mixture at room temperature.

3 Reserve six of the cherries for garnish. Combine the remaining cherries with the sugar in the container of a blender. Blend on high speed until pureed and the sugar is dissolved. Spread the cherry puree evenly over the top of the chilled chocolate layer. Pour the remaining chocolate mixture over the top of the cherries and swirl gently with a knife. (Do not overmix.) Chill for at least 4 hours.

4 To serve, in a medium bowl, using an electric mixer on high

580

579

582

speed, whip the remaining 1 cup cream until stiff peaks form. Spread over the top of the pie. Garnish with chocolate curls and reserved cherries.

Baking notes: Raspberries, blackberries, or boysenberries can be used in place of the cherries. Use the corresponding flavored liqueur in place of the cherry liqueur. To make the pie more decorative, fill a pastry bag fitted with a large or small star tip with whipped cream and pipe 24 stars over the top of the pie. Quarter the reserved cherries and use the wedges to decorate the whipped cream stars.

581 ■ Chocolate Chestnut Tart

Makes 10 to 12 servings
Baking time: *14 minutes*
Chill time: *10 hours (dough) plus 2 days (filling)*

CHESTNUT MOUSSE FILLING

1½ pounds unsweetened chestnuts (see Baking notes)
1 cup marsala
½ cup granulated sugar
1 teaspoon vanilla extract
½ teaspoon ground cinnamon
2 cups heavy cream

AMARETTO PASTRY CRUST

1½ cups all-purpose flour
3 tablespoons granulated sugar
Pinch of salt
⅓ cup butter or margarine, diced
3 tablespoons amaretto
3 ounces semisweet chocolate, grated or finely chopped
Sliced fresh strawberries for garnish
Grated semisweet chocolate for garnish

1 To make the filling, in a saucepan, over medium heat, combine the chestnuts, wine, sugar, vanilla extract, and cinnamon. Cook, stirring occasionally, for 10 minutes. Increase the heat to high and boil for 2 to 3 minutes, stirring constantly, or until thickened. Remove from the heat and transfer to a blender. Process on high speed for 60 to 90 seconds, or until smooth.

Stop the blender and add ½ cup of the cream. Blend on high speed for 30 seconds. Pour into a medium bowl.

2 In a small bowl, using an electric mixer on high speed, whip 1 cup of the remaining cream until soft peaks form. Fold into the chestnut mixture. Cover and chill for 2 to 3 days.

3 To make the crust, in a large bowl, combine the flour, sugar, and salt. Using a pastry blender or two knives scissor fashion, cut in the butter to form a crumbly mixture. Sprinkle the amaretto over the top and mix with a fork until the dough just holds together. Form the dough into a disk 2 inches thick. Wrap and chill for 8 hours.

4 Lightly grease a 10-inch tart pan with a removable bottom.

5 On a lightly floured surface, roll out the dough into a circle about ¹⁄₁₆ inch thick. Carefully fit the dough into the prepared pan, pressing against the bottom and up the sides. Trim the edges evenly. Prick holes on the bottom with a fork. Chill for 1 to 2 hours. Allow the crust to stand at room temperature for 10 to 15 minutes before baking.

6 Position a rack in the center of the oven and preheat the oven to 400 degrees.

7 Line the tart crust with parchment paper or aluminum foil and fill with pie weights or dried beans.

8 Bake for 8 to 10 minutes, or until the crust is firm. Remove the weights and paper and bake about 3 to 4 minutes, until the crust is golden brown. Cool on a wire rack.

9 Melt the chocolate (see page 13). Remove from the heat and immediately spread over the warm crust and cool completely.

10 Spread the chestnut filling evenly over the baked crust. Chill slightly before serving.

11 To serve, in a small bowl, using an electric mixer on high speed, whip the remaining ½ cup cream until soft peaks form. Spoon mounds of whipped cream over the top. Remove the

side of the tart pan and place on a serving plate. Garnish with sliced strawberries and grated chocolate.

Baking notes: These chestnuts can be found water-packed in a can or jar at any grocery store.

582 ■ Chocolate Chiffon Pie

Makes 8 to 10 servings
Chill time: *2 hours and 30 minutes*

1 recipe Chocolate Pastry Crust (see page 274)

FILLING

¼ cup plus 5 tablespoons milk
1 envelope unflavored gelatin
1 large egg
2 tablespoons granulated sugar
4 ounces semisweet chocolate, grated or finely chopped
¼ teaspoon peppermint extract
½ cup heavy cream
¾ cup crushed ice

TOPPING

3 tablespoons powdered sugar
2 tablespoons Dutch processed cocoa powder
1 cup heavy cream
½ teaspoon crème de cacao
Chocolate Leaves (see page 422) for garnish
Fresh mint leaves for garnish

1 Make and bake the crust.

2 To make the filling, in a cup, sprinkle the gelatin over ¼ cup of the milk. Let stand for 1 minute to soften.

3 In a small saucepan, heat the remaining 5 tablespoons of milk just until simmering. Remove from the heat, add the gelatin mixture, and stir constantly until the gelatin no longer clings to the sides of the pan. Transfer to a medium bowl. Add the egg, sugar, and chocolate, and using an electric mixer on high speed, beat for 3 to 4 minutes, or until very smooth. Beating constantly, add the peppermint extract, cream, and crushed ice. Beat on high speed until the ice is completely melted. Pour into the prepared pie crust and chill for at least 2 hours, or until the filling is set.

4 To make the topping, combine the powdered sugar and cocoa powder.

5 In a medium bowl, using an electric mixer on high speed, whip the cream until soft peaks form. Fold in the dry ingredients. Fold in the crème de cacao. Chill for 30 minutes. Spread the topping over the filling.

6 Just before serving, arrange the mint leaves and chocolate leaves in a decorative arrangement over the pie.

BAKING NOTES: To keep the pie crust from becoming soggy, sprinkle chocolate cookie crumbs in the bottom of the pie crust before adding the filling.

583 ■ CHOCOLATE CHIP NUT PIE

MAKE 8 TO 10 SERVINGS
BAKING TIME: *50 minutes*

1 recipe Chocolate Pastry Crust (see page 274)
½ cup butter or margarine, at room temperature
1 cup granulated sugar
2 large eggs
1 teaspoon crème de cacao
1 cup all-purpose flour
2 cups semisweet miniature chocolate chips
1 cup chopped pecans
Chocolate Whipped Cream (see page 406) for garnish
Chocolate Syrup III (see page 406) for garnish

1 Preheat the oven to 325 degrees.

2 Make and bake the crust.

3 In a large bowl, using an electric mixer on medium speed, beat the butter and sugar until light and fluffy. Beat in the eggs and crème de cacao. Gradually blend in the flour, mixing until very smooth. Fold in the chocolate chips and pecans. Scrape the mixture into the prepared pie crust.

4 Bake for 45 to 50 minutes, or until the filling is set and the crust is a golden color. Cool on a wire rack to room temperature.

5 Make the chocolate whipped cream and spread over the top of the pie. Make the chocolate syrup and drizzle over the whipped cream.

584 ■ CHOCOLATE CHIP PECAN PIE

MAKES 8 TO 10 SERVINGS
CHILL TIME: *1 hour 30 minutes*

PASTRY CRUST

2 cups all-purpose flour
½ teaspoon salt
⅔ cup butter-flavored vegetable shortening
5 to 6 tablespoons ice water

CHOCOLATE CHIP FILLING

3 large eggs
1¼ cups light corn syrup
½ cup granulated sugar
1½ teaspoons chocolate or almond extract
1 cup semisweet chocolate chips
1 cup pecans or almonds, coarsely chopped

1 To make the crust, combine the flour and salt. Using a pastry blender or two knives scissor fashion, cut in the shortening until the mixture forms fine crumbs. Sprinkle the water over the top, a little at a time, and mix with a fork until the dough is just moist enough to hold together. Form into a ball. Wrap and chill for 1 hour, or until firm.

2 On a lightly floured surface, roll the dough out into a circle about ¼ inch thick. Transfer to a 9-inch pie pan and ease into the bottom and up the sides of the pan. Trim the edges and flute if desired.

3 Preheat the oven to 375 degrees.

573

578

570

572

576

4 In a medium bowl, whisk the eggs until foamy. Stir in the corn syrup, sugar, and chocolate extract. Stir in the chocolate chips and pecans. Pour into the prepared pastry crust.

5 Bake for 45 to 50 minutes, or until a cake tester inserted half way into the pie comes out clean. Cool in the pan on a wire rack. Chill in the refrigerator for 30 minutes before serving.

585 ■ CHOCOLATE CHIP PIE

MAKES 8 TO 10 SERVINGS
BAKING TIME: *45 minutes*

1 recipe Chocolate Pastry Crust (see page 274)
2 large eggs
1 cup granulated sugar
1/2 cup all-purpose flour
1/4 cup butter or margarine, melted
1 teaspoon almond extract
6 ounces semisweet chocolate, grated or finely chopped
3/4 cup pecans or almonds, chopped
1/2 cup flaked coconut

1 Position a rack in the center of the oven and preheat the oven to 350 degrees.

2 Make and bake the crust. Remove from the oven. Make the filling while the crust is baking.

3 To make the filling, in a small bowl, beat the eggs until thick and light-colored.

4 In a medium bowl, combine the sugar and flour. Add the beaten eggs and melted butter. Blend in the almond extract. Fold in the grated chocolate, pecans, and coconut. Pour the mixture into the unbaked pie crust.

5 Bake for 30 to 35 minutes, or until firm. Cool completely in the pan on a wire rack.

BAKING NOTES: Coconut Pie Crust (see page 279) can also be used.

586 ■ CHOCOLATE CHUNK PIE

MAKES 8 TO 10 SERVINGS
BAKING TIME: *60 minutes*

1 recipe Chocolate Pastry Crust (see page 274)
1/2 cup all-purpose flour
1/2 cup granulated sugar
1/2 cup packed light brown sugar
8 ounces semisweet chocolate, diced into small cubes
2 large eggs
1 cup butter, melted and cooled
Chocolate Curls (see page 422) for garnish

1 Position a rack in the center of the oven and preheat the oven to 325 degrees.

2 Make and bake the crust. Remove from the oven. Make the filling while the crust is in the oven.

3 To make the filling, combine the flour, sugars, and diced chocolate.

4 In a large bowl, using an electric mixer on medium speed, beat the eggs until thick and light-colored. Stir in the dry ingredients. Stir in the melted butter. Pour the mixture into the baked pie crust.

5 Bake for 55 to 60 minutes, or until a cake tester inserted into the center comes out clean. Do not to overbake. Cool in the pan on a wire rack. Garnish with chocolate curls.

585 586 584 581 583

587 ■ CHOCOLATE COCONUT PIE

MAKES 8 TO 10 SERVINGS
BAKING TIME: *10 minutes*

COCONUT CRUST

Coconut Pie Crust (see page 279)

COCOA CUSTARD

3 large egg yolks
¼ cup cornstarch or arrowroot
1 cup granulated sugar
3 cups milk
6 tablespoons Dutch processed cocoa powder
1 tablespoon butter or margarine
1 teaspoon chocolate or almond extract
¾ cup flaked coconut

MERINGUE TOPPING

2 large egg whites
3 tablespoons granulated sugar
¼ teaspoon chocolate extract
¼ cup flaked coconut for garnish

1 Position a rack in the center of the oven and preheat the oven to 350 degrees.

2 Make and bake the crust.

3 To make the custard, in a large bowl, using an electric mixer on medium speed, beat the egg yolks until thick and light-colored. Beat in the cornstarch and sugar.

4 In a large saucepan, over medium heat, warm the milk until simmering. Remove from the heat. Beat about ½ cup of the hot milk into the egg mixture. Mix the egg mixture into the saucepan. Beat in the cocoa powder and butter. Cook, stirring constantly, until thickened and smooth. Remove from the

heat and stir in the extract. Fold in the coconut. Pour into the baked pie crust.

5 To make the topping, in a large bowl, using an electric mixer on high speed, beat the egg whites until foamy. Add the sugar and whip until stiff peaks form. Stir in the chocolate extract. Spread over the top of the pie. Sprinkle with the shredded coconut.

6 Bake for 10 minutes, or until lightly browned on top. Cool completely on a wire rack.

588 ■ CHOCOLATE COCONUT PIE CRUST

MAKES ONE 9-INCH PIE CRUST
CHILL TIME: *30 minutes*

2 ounces unsweetened chocolate, grated or finely chopped
2 tablespoons butter or margarine
⅔ cup powdered sugar
2 tablespoons hot milk
1⅓ cups flaked coconut

1 In the top of a double boiler over simmering water, melt the chocolate and butter, stirring until smooth. Stir in the powdered sugar and stir until completely dissolved. Stir in the milk.

2 Remove from the heat and mix in the coconut. Press onto the bottom and up the sides of a 9-inch pie pan. Chill for 30 minutes, or until firm.

589 ■ CHOCOLATE COFFEE CREAM PIE

MAKES 8 TO 10 SERVINGS
CHILL TIME: *30 minutes*

CRUST

1 recipe Chocolate Pastry (see page 274)

FILLING

2 cups milk
2 ounces unsweetened chocolate, grated or finely chopped
¼ cup granulated sugar
¼ cup cornstarch
4 large egg yolks
3 tablespoons butter or margarine
1 tablespoon coffee liqueur
1 tablespoon cream sherry
1 recipe Chocolate Whipped Cream (see page 406)

1 Make and bake the crust.

2 To make the filling, in the top of a double boiler over simmering water, heat the milk and chocolate, stirring until the chocolate is melted and the mixture is smooth.

3 In a large bowl, using an electric mixer on medium speed, beat the sugar, cornstarch, and egg yolks until well blended. On low speed, pouring it in a thin stream, beat in 1 cup of the hot milk mixture. Pour the egg mixture into the milk mixture in the double boiler and cook, stirring constantly, until thickened. Stir in the butter until melted. Remove from the heat and stir in the liqueur and sherry. Pour into the baked pie crust. Chill for 30 minutes, or until firm.

4 Make topping according to recipe. Spread topping over chilled pie just before serving.

592

587

590 ■ CHOCOLATE COOKIE CRUMB CRUST

MAKES ONE 9-INCH PIE CRUST
BAKING TIME: *10 minutes*

1½ cups chocolate wafer cookie
    crumbs
¼ cup butter or margarine, at room
    temperature
1 tablespoon chocolate extract

1 Position a rack in the center of
the oven and preheat the oven
to 375 degrees.

2 In a medium bowl, combine
the cookie crumbs, butter, and
chocolate extract. Using your
fingertips, a pastry blender, or a
fork, rub the butter into the
crumbs until thoroughly
blended. Press the mixture into
a 9-inch pie pan.

3 Bake for 8 to 10 minutes, or
until the crust looks dry. Cool
completely on a wire rack.

BAKING NOTES: This crust can be
made with almost any kind of
cookie crumbs.

591 ■ CHOCOLATE CORN FLAKE PIE SHELL

MAKES ONE 9-INCH PIE SHELL
BAKING TIME: *10 minutes*

2 ounces semisweet chocolate,
    grated or finely chopped
1 cup corn flakes cereal, crushed
¼ cup granulated sugar
⅓ cup butter-flavored vegetable
    shortening

1 Position a rack in the center of
the oven and preheat the oven
to 375 degrees.

2 Melt the chocolate (see page
13). Remove from the heat.
Transfer to a medium bowl.

3 Add the cereal, sugar, and
shortening. Using your fingertips, a pastry blender, or a fork,
mash ingredients to form a
crumbly mixture. Press evenly
onto the bottom and up the
sides of a 9-inch pie pan.

4 Bake for 8 to 10 minutes, or
until the crust is firm and looks
dry. Cool completely on a wire
rack. Chill well before using.

592 ■ CHOCOLATE CREAM CHEESE PIE I

MAKES 8 TO 10 SERVINGS
CHILL TIME: *1 hour*
BAKING TIME: *40 minutes*

CREAM CHEESE PASTRY

2 cups all-purpose flour
½ teaspoon salt
⅓ cup butter-flavored vegetable
    shortening
⅓ cup cream cheese
5 to 6 tablespoons ice water

CHOCOLATE FILLING

2½ ounces unsweetened chocolate,
    grated or finely chopped
8 ounces cream cheese, at room
    temperature
1 cup granulated sugar
2 teaspoons chocolate or almond
    extract
2 large eggs

SOUR CREAM TOPPING

1 cup sour cream
2 tablespoons granulated sugar
1 teaspoon chocolate extract
Chocolate candy kisses for garnish

1 Position a rack in the center of
the oven and preheat the oven
to 375 degrees.

2 To make the crust, in a
medium bowl, combine the
flour and salt. Using a pastry
blender or two knives scissor
fashion, cut in the shortening
until the mixture forms fine
crumbs. Cut in the cream
cheese. Sprinkle the water over
the top, a little at a time, and
mix gently with a fork until the
dough is just moist enough to
hold together. Form into a ball.
Wrap and chill for 1 hour, or
until firm.

3 On a lightly floured surface,
roll the dough out into a circle
about ¼ inch thick. Transfer to a
9-inch pie pan and ease into the
bottom and up the sides of the
pan. Trim the edges and flute if
desired. Prick the bottom and
sides with a fork.

4 Bake for 10 minutes. Remove
from the oven. Make the filling
while the crust is baking.

5 To make the filling, melt the
chocolate (see page 13). Remove
from the heat.

6 In a large bowl, using an electric mixer on medium speed,
beat the cream cheese, sugar,
and melted chocolate until combined. Beat in the chocolate
extract. Beat in the eggs, one at a
time, beating well after each
addition. Immediately pour into
the baked crust.

7 Bake for 20 minutes or until
the center is almost set. Remove
from the oven and cool on a
wire rack for 10 minutes while
preparing the topping. Increase
the oven temperature to 425
degrees.

8 To make the topping, in a
small bowl, beat the sour cream,
sugar, and chocolate extract.
Spread this mixture evenly over
the top of the pie.

9 Bake for 10 minutes longer, or
until firm. Cool completely on a
wire rack. Chill until serving.
Garnish with chocolate kisses.

593 ■ CHOCOLATE CREAM CHEESE PIE II

MAKES 8 TO 10 SERVINGS
BAKING TIME: *75 minutes*

1 recipe Pecan Pastry Crust (see
    page 286)
1½ cups granulated sugar
5 tablespoons Dutch processed
    cocoa powder
2 tablespoons all-purpose flour
¼ teaspoon salt
½ cup heavy cream
3 large eggs
3 ounces cream cheese, at room
    temperature
⅓ cup butter or margarine, at room
    temperature
1 teaspoon chocolate extract

1 Position a rack in the center of
the oven and preheat the oven
to 325 degrees.

2 Make the pie crust. Bake for
10 to 15 minutes. Cool on a wire
rack while preparing the filling.

3 To make the filling, combine
the sugar, cocoa powder, flour,
and salt.

4 In a large bowl, using an electric mixer on high speed, whip
the cream for 1 to 2 minutes,
until thickened. Beat in the eggs,
one at a time. Add the cream

cheese, butter, and chocolate extract, and beat until the mixture is smooth. Gradually beat in the dry ingredients. Pour the mixture into the baked pie crust.

5 Bake for 55 to 60 minutes, or until the filling is set. Cool completely in the pan on a wire rack for 30 minutes before serving.

594 ■ CHOCOLATE CREAM PIE I

MAKES 8 TO 10 SERVINGS
CHILL TIME: *1 hour*

CRUST

1 recipe Chocolate Cookie Crumb Crust (see page 267)

CHOCOLATE FILLING

2²/₃ cups milk
3 large egg yolks
3 ounces semisweet chocolate, grated or finely chopped
³/₄ cup granulated sugar
¹/₄ cup cornstarch or arrowroot
1 tablespoon butter or margarine, at room temperature
¹/₄ teaspoon salt
1 teaspoon chocolate extract

WHIPPED CREAM TOPPING

¹/₂ cup heavy cream
6 tablespoons sugar

1 Make and bake the crust.

2 To make the filling, in the container of a blender, combine 1²/₃ cups of the milk, the egg yolks, chocolate, sugar, cornstarch, butter, and salt. Cover and blend on high speed for 10 to 12 seconds. Pour into a medium saucepan. Add the remaining 1 cup milk. Cook over medium heat, stirring constantly, until the mixture thickens. Remove from the heat and add the chocolate extract. Cool slightly. Pour into the baked pie crust. Chill for 1 hour.

3 To make the topping, in a medium bowl, using an electric mixer on high speed, whip the cream and sugar until soft peaks form. Spread over the top of the filling.

595 ■ CHOCOLATE CREAM PIE II

MAKES 8 TO 10 SERVINGS
BAKING TIME: *10 minutes*
CHILL TIME: *30 minutes*

PASTRY CRUST

1¹/₃ cups all-purpose flour
1 teaspoon salt
¹/₃ cup canola oil
3 tablespoons milk

CHOCOLATE CUSTARD

2 egg yolks
²/₃ cup all-purpose flour
³/₄ cup granulated sugar
¹/₂ teaspoon salt
4 ounces unsweetened chocolate, grated or finely chopped
3¹/₂ cups milk
1 tablespoon butter or margarine
1 teaspoon chocolate extract
1 recipe Chocolate Whipped Cream (see page 406)

1 Position a rack in the center of the oven and preheat the oven to 475 degrees.

2 To make the crust, in a large bowl, combine the flour and salt. Pour in the oil and milk. Gently stir with a fork just until just mixed. Form into a smooth ball. Between two sheets of waxed paper, roll out into a 12 to 14-inch circle. Remove the top piece of waxed paper and invert onto a 9-inch pie pan. Remove the waxed paper and ease the dough onto the bottom and up the sides of the pan. Trim and flute the edges. Prick all over with a fork.

3 Bake for 8 to 10 minutes, or until golden brown. Cool completely on a wire rack.

4 To make the filling, in a small bowl, using an electric mixer on high speed, beat the egg yolks until thick and light-colored.

5 Combine the flour, sugar, and salt.

6 In the top of a double boiler over simmering water, melt the chocolate with the milk, stirring until the chocolate is melted and the mixture is smooth. Gradually blend in the dry ingredients. Cook, stirring constantly, until the mixture thickens. Remove from the heat. Stir 2

tablespoons of the hot milk mixture into the egg yolks. Beat the egg yolk mixture into the hot milk mixture. Return to the heat and cook for 2 to 3 minutes, stirring constantly, until the mixture thickens. Remove from the heat, stir in the butter and chocolate extract and cool slightly. Pour into the baked pie crust. Chill for 30 minutes, or until thickened.

7 Meanwhile, make the topping according to recipe.

8 To serve, garnish the pie with dollops of chocolate whipped cream.

596 ■ CHOCOLATE CREAM PIE WITH CHOCOLATE CHIP COOKIE CRUST

MAKES 8 TO 10 SERVINGS
BAKING TIME: *8 minutes*
CHILL TIME: *72 minutes*

CHOCOLATE CHIP COOKIE CRUST

2¹/₄ cups chocolate chip cookie crumbs (25 cookies)
¹/₄ cup butter or margarine, at room temperature

CHOCOLATE CREAM FILLING

1 cup raisins
¹/₄ cup crème de cacao
1 cup half-and-half
1 envelope unflavored gelatin
2 large eggs
¹/₄ cup granulated sugar
8 ounces unsweetened chocolate, grated or finely chopped
1 cup ice cubes
Chocolate Whipped Cream (see page 406) for garnish
Chocolate Curls (see page 422) for garnish

1 Position a rack in the center of the oven and preheat the oven to 375 degrees.

2 To make the crust, in a medium bowl, using a pastry blender or two knives scissor fashion, cut the butter into cookie crumbs. Press the mixture onto the bottom and up the sides of a 9-inch pie pan.

3 Bake for 8 minutes. Cool completely on a wire rack.

4 To make the filling, place the raisins and crème de cacao in a small bowl.

5 In a saucepan, over medium-low heat, warm ²/₃ cup of the half-and-half until bubbles start to form around the sides of the pan. Remove from the heat.

6 Place the remaining ¹/₃ cup of half-and-half in the container of a blender and sprinkle the gelatin over the top. Let stand for 1 minute to soften. Pour in the hot half-and-half and blend on low speed until just blended. Add the eggs, sugar, and 4 ounces of the grated chocolate. Blend on high speed for 30 seconds. Add the ice cubes, two at a time, blending for a few seconds after each addition. When all the ice cubes have been added, blend on medium speed for 1 minute. Chill for 10 to 12 minutes in the blender container.

7 Add the remaining 4 ounces of grated chocolate and process until combined. Pour into the baked crust.

8 Drain the raisins and reserve any crème de cacao for another use. Sprinkle the raisins over the top of the pie and chill for 1 hour, or until firm.

9 Just before serving, spread chocolate whipped cream over the top and garnish with chocolate curls.

BAKING NOTES: Owing to the raw eggs used in this recipe, it should be keep refrigerated at all times, and for no longer than 3 days.

597 ■ CHOCOLATE CREAM PIE WITH TOFFEE CRUST

MAKES 8 TO 10 SERVINGS
CHILL TIME: *30 minutes*

TOFFEE PECAN CRUST

²/₃ cup all-purpose flour
¹/₄ cup pecans or walnuts, finely ground
2 tablespoons light brown sugar
¹/₄ teaspoon salt
¹/₃ cup butter or margarine
2 teaspoons water
1 teaspoon Frangelico

CHOCOLATE CREAM FILLING

²/₃ cup heavy cream
¹/₂ teaspoon crème de cacao
6 ounces semisweet chocolate, grated or finely chopped
1 cup miniature marshmallows
¹/₄ cup evaporated milk
Chocolate-Covered Strawberries (see page 172) for garnish
Whipped cream for serving

1 Lightly grease an 8-inch pie pan.

2 To make the crust, in a large bowl, combine the flour, pecans, brown sugar, and salt. Using a pastry blender or two knives scissor fashion, cut in the butter to make a fine crumbed mixture. Combine the water and Frangelico. Sprinkle over the top and stir with a fork just until the dough holds together. Press evenly onto the bottom and up the sides of the pie pan. Chill while making the filling.

3 To make the filling, in a medium bowl, combine the cream and crème de cacao. Chill.

4 In the top of a double boiler, over simmering water, melt the chocolate, stirring until smooth. Add the marshmallows and stir until melted and smooth. Remove from the heat. Stir in the evaporated milk until dissolved.

5 Using an electric mixer on high speed, whip the chilled cream until stiff peaks form. Fold in the chocolate mixture and pour into the prepared pie crust. Chill for 30 minutes, or until set. Garnish with chocolate-covered strawberries. Serve with whipped cream on the side.

594

596

597

598 ■ CHOCOLATE CREAM PUFF PIE

MAKES 8 TO 10 SERVINGS
BAKING TIME: *1 hour*

CREAM PUFF PASTRY

1 cup water
1/2 cup butter
1/8 teaspoon salt
1 cup all-purpose flour
4 large eggs

CHOCOLATE CUSTARD FILLING

1/2 cup granulated sugar
1/3 cup all-purpose flour
1/4 teaspoon salt
2 cups heavy cream
2 ounces unsweetened chocolate, grated or finely chopped
3 large eggs
1 tablespoon crème de cacao
2 teaspoons chocolate extract
Cocoa Sugar (see page 406) for garnish
Sliced fresh peaches or fresh raspberries for garnish

1 Position a rack in the center of the oven and preheat the oven to 425 degrees. Lightly grease a baking sheet.

2 To make the pastry, in a medium saucepan, bring the water, butter, and salt to a boil. Remove from the heat. Add the flour and stir gently until combined. Return to the heat and cook until the mixture pulls away from the side of the pan and forms a ball. Remove from the heat.

3 Beat in the eggs, one at a time, blending thoroughly after each addition. Scrape the dough onto the prepared baking sheet and spread it out into a circle about 1 inch thick.

4 Bake for 55 to 60 minutes, or until a delicate brown color. Turn off the heat and leave the pastry in the oven for 30 minutes. Cool completely in the pan on a wire rack.

5 To make the filling, in the top of a double boiler over simmering water, combine the sugar, flour, and salt. Add the cream and chocolate and stir until the chocolate is melted and the mixture is smooth. Cook for 3 min-

utes, stirring occasionally. Remove from the heat.

6 In a small bowl, using an electric mixer on medium speed, beat the eggs until thick and light-colored. Pouring it in a thin stream, beat 1/2 cup of the hot chocolate mixture into the eggs. Mix the egg mixture into the saucepan. Cook, stirring constantly, until the mixture thickens to a spreadable consistency. Cool slightly. Stir in the crème de cacao and chocolate extract.

7 To assemble, using a serrated knife, cut the pastry in half horizontally. Place the bottom section on a serving plate and spread with the custard. Replace the top and sprinkle with cocoa sugar. Refrigerate until ready to serve. To serve, cut the cream puff into wedges as you would a pie and serve with fresh fruit on the side.

BAKING NOTES: In place of the chocolate custard, the cream puff can be filled with 1 1/2 cups chocolate whipped cream (see page 406) or chocolate ricotta filling (see page 403).

599 ■ CHOCOLATE FRUIT-TOPPED PIE

MAKES 8 TO 10 SERVINGS
BAKING TIME: *25 minutes*

CRUST

1 recipe Chocolate Cookie Crumb Crust (see page 267)

CUSTARD FILLING

3 large eggs, separated
1 cup granulated sugar
2 cups half-and-half
2 tablespoons coffee liqueur
1/4 teaspoon ground nutmeg
Pinch of salt

WHIPPED CREAM TOPPING

1 cup heavy cream
2 tablespoons granulated sugar

GARNISH

3 fresh strawberries, thinly sliced
1/2 lemon, thinly sliced
1 kiwi fruit, peeled and thinly sliced
6 fresh pansies (see Baking notes)
3 or 4 mint leaves

1 Position a rack in the center of the oven and preheat the oven to 375 degrees.

2 Make and bake the crust. Remove from the oven. Reduce the oven temperature to 325 degrees.

3 To make the filling, in a medium bowl, using an electric mixer on high speed, beat the egg whites until stiff but not dry.

4 In a large bowl, using an electric mixer on medium speed, beat the egg yolks until thick and light-colored. Beating on low speed, add the sugar and half-and-half. Stir in the liqueur, nutmeg, and salt. Fold in the beaten egg whites. Pour into the baked pie crust.

5 Bake for 20 to 25 minutes, or until firm. Cool completely on a wire rack.

6 To make the topping, in a large bowl, using an electric mixer on high speed, whip the cream and sugar until soft peaks form. Spread over the surface of the cooled pie. Arrange the sliced fruit over the topping. Garnish with the pansies and mint leaves.

BAKING NOTES: Other liqueurs can be substituted for the coffee liqueur. The garnish on the top of the pie is entirely edible, including the flowers and leaves.

600 ■ CHOCOLATE FUDGE PIE I

MAKES 8 TO 10 SERVINGS
FREEZING TIME: *30 minutes*

1 recipe Chocolate Cookie Crumb Crust (see page 267)
1 3/4 cups heavy cream
1/4 cup butter or margarine
3 large eggs, separated
1/2 cup packed light brown sugar
1/2 cup pecans or walnuts, finely chopped
1 teaspoon chocolate extract
2 ounces unsweetened chocolate, grated or finely chopped
Sliced fresh bananas for garnish

1 Make and bake the crust.

2 In the top of a double boiler over simmering water, combine

the cream, butter, egg yolks, and brown sugar. Cook, stirring constantly, until the mixture thickens slightly. Stir in the chopped pecans and chocolate extract. Remove from the heat and cool slightly before adding the grated chocolate. Stir until melted and smooth. Transfer to a medium bowl and cool.

3 In a medium bowl, using an electric mixture on high speed, beat the egg whites until stiff but not dry. Fold the egg whites into the cooled chocolate mixture. Pour into the baked pie crust. Freeze for 30 minutes, or until firm. Garnish with sliced bananas.

601 ■ CHOCOLATE FUDGE PIE II

MAKES 8 TO 10 SERVINGS
BAKING TIME: *35 minutes*

PASTRY CRUST

1 cup all-purpose flour
1 tablespoon granulated sugar
1/2 teaspoon salt
1/2 cup chilled butter or margarine, diced
3 tablespoons ice water

FUDGE FILLING

1/2 cup butter or margarine
4 ounces unsweetened chocolate, grated or finely chopped
4 large eggs
1 1/2 cups granulated sugar
1/4 cup buttermilk
1 tablespoon light or dark corn syrup
1 teaspoon chocolate or vanilla extract
1/2 teaspoon ground allspice
1/4 teaspoon salt
Whipped cream for serving

1 To make the crust, in a large bowl, combine the flour, sugar, and salt. Using a pastry blender or two knives scissor fashion, cut in the butter to make a fine crumbly mixture. Add the water and gently stir with a fork until blended. The dough will be very dry and may not hold together.

2 On a lightly floured surface, gently knead the dough until it just starts to hold its shape. Wrap and chill for at least 30 minutes.

3 Position a rack in the center of the oven and preheat the oven to 350 degrees.

4 On a lightly floured surface, roll the dough out into a circle about 1/4 inch thick. Transfer to a 9-inch pie pan and ease onto the bottom and up the sides. Trim the edges and flute if desired. Chill until ready to use.

5 Meanwhile, to make the filling, in the top of a double boiler over simmering water, melt the butter and chocolate, stirring until smooth. Remove from the heat.

6 In a large bowl, using an electric mixer on medium speed, beat the eggs until thick. Beat in the sugar, buttermilk, corn syrup, chocolate extract, allspice, and salt. Pouring it in a thin stream, beat in the chocolate mixture. Pour into the prepared crust.

7 Bake for 30 to 35 minutes, or until a knife inserted into the center comes out clean but damp. Do not overbake. Cool on a wire rack for 30 minutes. Serve with whipped cream on the side.

602 ■ CHOCOLATE HAZELNUT CRUMB CRUST

MAKES ONE 9-INCH PIE CRUST

1 1/4 cups chocolate wafer cookie crumbs
1/4 cup finely ground hazelnuts
3 tablespoons sugar
6 tablespoons butter or margarine, melted

1 In a medium bowl, combine the cookie crumbs, hazelnuts, and sugar. Using a fork, blend in the melted butter. Press the mixture evenly onto the bottom and up the sides of a 9-inch pie pan. Cover with waxed paper, weight with dry beans or pie weights, and freeze until ready to use.

BAKING NOTES: Any kind of nut can be used in place of the hazelnuts.

598

599

600

603 ■ CHOCOLATE LIQUEUR PIE

MAKES 8 TO 10 SERVINGS
CHILL TIME: *1 hour*

1 recipe Coconut Pie Crust (see page 279)
6 ounces semisweet chocolate, grated or finely chopped
1 ounce unsweetened chocolate, grated or finely chopped
2 large eggs, separated, plus 1 large egg yolk
1 cup heavy cream
1/4 cup crème de cacao
Chocolate Curls (see page 422) for garnish

1 Make and bake the crust.

2 In the top of a double boiler over simmering water, melt the chocolates, stirring until smooth. Remove from the heat.

3 In a medium bowl, using an electric mixer on high speed, beat the egg whites until stiff but not dry.

4 In another medium bowl, using an electric mixer on high speed, whip the cream until soft peaks form.

5 In a large bowl, using an electric mixer on medium speed, beat the egg yolks until thick and light-colored. Pouring it in a thin stream, beat in the melted chocolate on low speed. Fold in the beaten egg whites. Fold in the crème de cacao and

whipped cream. Pour the mixture into the baked pie crust and chill for at least 1 hour. Before serving garnish with chocolate curls.

BAKING NOTES: For a garnish variation, substitute chocolate leaves or cones in place of the curls.

604 ■ CHOCOLATE LIQUEUR PIE WITH ALMONDS

MAKES 8 TO 10 SERVINGS
BAKING TIME: *15 minutes*
CHILL TIME: *3 1/2 hours*

CHOCOLATE COOKIE CRUST

6 tablespoons butter or margarine, at room temperature
1 1/2 cups chocolate wafer cookie crumbs

LIQUEUR CUSTARD

1 tablespoon unflavored gelatin
2 cups milk
3 large eggs, separated
1/3 cup granulated sugar
1/8 teaspoon salt
1/2 cup heavy cream
1/4 cup crème de cacao
3 tablespoons semisweet chocolate chips
1/4 cup crème de noyeau
3 tablespoons sliced almonds, toasted

1 Position a rack in the center of the oven and preheat the oven to 325 degrees.

2 To make the crust, in a medium bowl, using a pastry blender or two knives scissor fashion, cut the butter into the crushed cookies to form a crumbly mixture. Press the mixture onto the bottom and up the sides of a 9-inch pie pan.

3 Bake for 15 minutes. Cool on a wire rack. Chill until ready to use.

4 To make the filling, in a cup, sprinkle the gelatin over 1/2 cup of the milk. Let stand for 1 minute to soften.

5 In the top of a double boiler, beat the egg yolks and remaining 1 1/2 cups of milk. Beat in the sugar and salt. Cook over simmering water, stirring constantly, until the mixture thickens slightly. Add the gelatin mixture and stir until dissolved. Remove from the heat and transfer to a medium bowl.   Chill 30 minutes, or until the mixture starts to set.

6 Meanwhile, in another medium bowl, using an electric mixer on high speed, beat the egg whites until stiff peaks form.

7 In another bowl, using an electric mixer on high speed, whip the cream until soft peaks form. Fold in the egg whites.

589

595

601

593

Fold the egg white mixture into the cooled custard. Transfer half of the filling mixture to another bowl. Stir the crème de cacao into one of the bowls and spoon into the baked pie crust. Sprinkle with the chocolate chips. Stir the crème de noyeau into the remaining filling. Spoon this over the first layer and sprinkle with the sliced almonds. Chill for 3 hours, or until ready to serve.

BAKING NOTES: Owing to the raw eggs used in this recipe, it should be kept refrigerated at all times, and for no more than 3 days.

605 ■ CHOCOLATE MOUSSE PIE

MAKES 8 TO 10 SERVINGS
CHILL TIME: *2 hours*

1 recipe Chocolate Pastry Crust (see page 274)
1½ teaspoons unflavored gelatin
1 tablespoon cold water
2 tablespoons boiling water
½ cup plus 1 tablespoon granulated sugar
1¼ cups heavy cream
⅓ cup Dutch processed cocoa powder
1 teaspoon chocolate extract
Chocolate Cutouts (see page 422) for garnish

1 Make and bake the crust.

2 To make the filling, in a cup, sprinkle the gelatin over the cold water. Let stand for 2 minutes to soften. Add the boiling water and stir until the gelatin is completely dissolved.

3 In the top of a double boiler over simmering water, combine ½ cup of the sugar, ½ cup of the cream, the cocoa powder, and chocolate extract. Using an electric mixer on medium speed, beat until the mixture thickens. Remove from the heat and beat in the gelatin mixture. Pour into the baked pastry crust and chill for 2 hours.

4 To serve, in a large bowl, using an electric mixer on high speed, whip the remaining ¾ cup cream and 1 tablespoon sugar until soft peaks form. Spread over the top of the pie. Garnish with chocolate cutouts.

606 ■ CHOCOLATE MOUSSE TARTS

MAKES 12 SERVINGS
BAKING TIME: *12 minutes*
CHILL TIME: *30 minutes*

CHOCOLATE CRUST

2 ounces semisweet chocolate, grated or finely chopped
1 cup all-purpose flour
¼ teaspoon salt
3 tablespoons water

CHOCOLATE CUSTARD FILLING

2 large eggs, separated
1 tablespoon unflavored gelatin
1 cup milk
6 ounces semisweet chocolate, grated or finely chopped
1 cup granulated sugar
1 teaspoon chocolate extract
2 tablespoons powdered sugar

TOPPING

1 cup heavy cream
¼ cup granulated sugar
1 teaspoon crème de cacao
Chocolate wafer cookies for garnish

1 Position a rack in the center of the oven and preheat the oven to 400 degrees. Lightly grease twelve 3-inch muffin pan cups.

2 To make the crust, melt the chocolate (see page 13). Remove from the heat.

3 In a medium bowl, combine the flour and salt. Stir in the melted chocolate. Sprinkle the water over the top. Gently stir with a fork until the dough holds together.

4 On a lightly floured surface, roll out the dough to a thickness of ¼ to ½ inch and cut into twelve 5-inch rounds. Press the rounds into the prepared muffin cups and flute the edges.

5 Bake for 10 to 12 minutes. Cool completely in the pan on a wire rack.

603

605

604

606

6 To make the filling, in a small bowl, using an electric mixer on medium speed, beat the egg yolks until thick and light-colored.

7 In a cup, sprinkle the gelatin over the milk. Let stand for 1 minute to soften.

8 Meanwhile, in the top of a double boiler over simmering water, melt the chocolate, stirring until smooth. Add the milk mixture and stir until smooth and the gelatin is completely dissolved. Add the granulated sugar and chocolate extract, stirring until blended. Stir in the beaten egg yolks. Cook, stirring constantly, until the mixture just starts to thicken. Remove from the heat and beat until slightly set. Cool.

9 In a medium bowl, using an electric mixer on high speed, beat the egg whites until stiff but not dry. Fold in the powdered sugar. Fold the egg whites into the chocolate mixture. Cover and chill 30 minutes, just until set.

10 To make the topping, in a medium bowl, using an electric mixer on high speed, whip the cream until soft peaks form. Fold in the sugar and crème de cacao.

11 To serve, remove the tart shells from the pan. Fill each tart with the custard mixture and top with the whipped cream. Garnish with a wedge of chocolate wafer cookie.

607 ■ CHOCOLATE ORANGE PIE

MAKES 8 TO 10 SERVINGS
CHILL TIME: *8 hours*

1 recipe Coconut Chocolate Pie Crust (see page 279)
2 ounces semisweet chocolate, grated or finely chopped
1 envelope unflavored gelatin
1/2 cup cold water
3 large eggs, separated
Pinch of salt
1 can (6 ounces) frozen orange juice concentrate, thawed
1 jar (7 ounces) marshmallow creme
1/3 cup granulated sugar
Chocolate Whipped Cream (see page 406) for garnish
Orange slices for garnish

1 Make and chill the pie crust as directed.

2 Melt the chocolate (see page 13). Remove from the heat.

3 In a small saucepan, sprinkle the gelatin over the water. Let stand for 1 minute to soften. Over low heat, stir until dissolved. Add the egg yolks and salt and stir for 4 minutes, or until the mixture thickens. Remove from the heat and stir in the orange juice concentrate.

4 In a large bowl, using an electric mixer on low speed, beat the melted chocolate and marshmallow creme until combined. Pouring it in a thin stream, beat the orange juice mixture into the chocolate mixture. Chill until very thick, or until the mixture mounds when dropped from a spoon.

5 In a large bowl, using an electric mixer with clean beaters on high speed, beat the egg whites until stiff but not dry. Beat in the sugar. Fold into the chilled chocolate mixture. Spread evenly in the baked pie crust. Chill overnight. Garnish with chocolate whipped cream and orange slices.

608 ■ CHOCOLATE PASTRY CRUST

MAKES ONE 9-INCH PIE CRUST
BAKING TIME: *8 minutes*

1 cup all-purpose flour
1/4 cup Dutch processed cocoa powder
3 tablespoons sugar
1/4 teaspoon salt
1/2 cup butter-flavored vegetable shortening
1 teaspoon chocolate extract
2 tablespoons ice water

1 Position a rack in the center of the oven and preheat the oven to 400 degrees.

2 In a large bowl, combine the flour, cocoa powder, sugar, and salt. Using a pastry blender or two knives scissor fashion, cut in the shortening until the mixture forms coarse crumbs. Blend in the chocolate extract. Sprinkle the water over the top and mix gently with a fork just until moist enough to hold together.

3 On a lightly floured surface, roll the dough out into a circle 10 inches in diameter and about 1/4 inch thick. Transfer to a 9-inch pie pan and ease into the bottom and up the sides. Trim the edges and flute if desired. Prick all over with a fork.

4 Bake for 8 minutes, or until the crust is slightly firm to the touch and looks dry.

609

607

609 ■ CHOCOLATE PEANUT BUTTER PIE I

MAKES 8 TO 10 SERVINGS
CHILL TIME: *1 hour*

1 recipe Chocolate Cookie Crumb Crust (see page 267)
1 envelope unflavored gelatin
1/4 cup water
1 cup chunky peanut butter
1 cup milk
1/2 cup granulated sugar
1/4 cup chocolate-flavored yogurt
2 large eggs
1/2 cup heavy cream
3 ounces semisweet chocolate, grated or finely chopped
3 ounces unsweetened chocolate, grated or finely chopped

1 Make and bake the crust.

2 In a small saucepan, sprinkle the gelatin over the water. Let stand for 1 minute to soften. Stir over low heat until dissolved. Remove from the heat.

3 In a large bowl, beat the peanut butter, milk, sugar, yogurt, and eggs until well mixed. Pouring it in a thin stream, stir in the gelatin mixture. Pour into the baked pie crust. Chill for 30 minutes, until the filling starts to set.

4 In a saucepan, heat the cream until bubbles start to form around the sides of the pan. Remove from the heat and add the chocolates. Let stand for 3 to 5 minutes to melt the chocolates. Stir until smooth. Pour over the pie and carefully spread the chocolate to the edges with the back of a spoon. Chill 30 minutes, or until firm.

BAKING NOTES: Owing to the raw eggs used in this recipe, it should be kept refrigerated at all times, and for no longer than three days.

610 ■ CHOCOLATE PEANUT BUTTER PIE II

MAKES 8 TO 10 SERVINGS
CHILL TIME: *30 minutes*

CRUST

1 recipe Chocolate Cookie Crumb Crust (see page 267)

PEANUT BUTTER LAYER

1/2 cup creamy peanut butter
1/4 cup butter or margarine, at room temperature
1 1/2 cups powdered sugar

CHOCOLATE LAYER

2 1/3 cups milk
2 tablespoons arrowroot or cornstarch
1 1/2 ounces unsweetened chocolate, grated or finely chopped
1 tablespoon butter or margarine
3 large egg yolks
1 cup granulated sugar
1/2 teaspoon chocolate extract
1/2 cup heavy cream for topping

1 Make and bake the crust.

2 To make the peanut butter layer, in a medium bowl, using an electric mixer on medium speed, beat the peanut butter and butter until smooth. Gradually beat in the powdered sugar until blended. Spread evenly over the baked pie crust.

3 To make the chocolate layer, in a cup, combine 1/3 cup of the milk and the arrowroot.

4 In the top of a double boiler over simmering water, melt the chocolate and butter, stirring until smooth. Stir in the remaining 2 cups milk and stir until smooth. Remove from the heat.

5 In a medium bowl, using an electric mixer on medium speed, beat the egg yolks and sugar until combined. Beat in the arrowroot mixture. Beating continually on low speed, mix in the chocolate mixture. Pour into the saucepan and return to the heat. Cook, stirring constantly in slow circles, until the mixture thickens. Remove from the heat and stir in the chocolate extract. Cool. Pour into the prepared crust and chill for 30 minutes, or until set.

6 In a medium bowl, using an electric mixer on high speed, whip the cream until soft peaks form. Spread over the top of the chilled pie.

611 ■ CHOCOLATE PECAN COCONUT CREAM PIE

MAKES 8 TO 10 SERVINGS
BAKING TIME: *1 hour*

1 recipe Chocolate Corn Flake Pie Shell (see page 267)
4 ounces unsweetened chocolate, grated or finely chopped
1/4 cup butter or margarine
2 large eggs
1 1/2 cups granulated sugar
3 tablespoons cornstarch or arrowroot
1 can (12 ounces) evaporated milk
1 teaspoon chocolate extract
1 cup flaked coconut
1/2 cup pecans or walnuts, very coarsely chopped
2 ounces semisweet chocolate, grated

1 Make the crust, but do not bake.

2 Position a rack in the center of the oven and preheat the oven to 350 degrees.

3 To make the filling, in the top of a double boiler over simmering water, melt the chocolate with the butter, stirring until smooth. Remove from the heat.

4 In a medium bowl, using an electric mixer on high speed, beat the eggs until thick and light-colored. Beat in the sugar and cornstarch. Gradually blend in the chocolate mixture. Slowly stir in the evaporated milk and chocolate extract. Pour into the prepared pie crust. Combine the coconut, pecans, and grated chocolate and sprinkle loosely over the top of the pie.

5 Bake for 55 to 60 minutes, or until the top is lightly browned and puffed. Cool in the pan on a wire rack.

BAKING NOTES: If the top of the pie browns too fast, place a sheet of aluminum foil over the pie for the last 15 minutes of baking.

612 ■ CHOCOLATE PECAN PIE I

MAKES 8 TO 10 SERVINGS
BAKING TIME: *1 hour*

CRUST

1 recipe Low-fat Pastry Shell (see page 284)

FILLING

1½ cups pecans, chopped
1 cup unsweetened chocolate chips
2 large eggs
½ cup light corn syrup
½ cup granulated sugar
¼ cup butter or margarine, melted
Chocolate Whipped Cream (see page 406) for garnish

1 Make the pie crust. Bake for only 3 to 4 minutes.

2 Sprinkle the pecans and chocolate chips over the bottom of a the prepared crust.

3 In a medium bowl, using an electric mixer on medium speed, beat the eggs, corn syrup, and sugar until smooth. Beat in the melted butter until blended. Pour the mixture into the prepared crust.

4 Bake for 60 minutes, or until the filling is firm. Cool on a wire rack for 10 minutes.

4 Meanwhile, make the chocolate whipped cream. Spread over the top of the pie before serving.

BAKING NOTES: Chocolate coconut pie crust (see page 266) can be substituted for the low-fat pastry pie crust.

613 ■ CHOCOLATE PECAN PIE II

MAKES 8 TO 10 SERVINGS
BAKING TIME: *30 minutes*

1 recipe Pecan Pastry Crust (see page 286)
3 ounces unsweetened chocolate, grated or finely chopped
¼ cup butter, melted
4 large eggs
2 cups granulated sugar
½ teaspoon coconut amaretto
1 cup whole pecans
Chocolate Whipped Cream (see page 406) for garnish
Chopped pecans for garnish

1 Make the crust and bake for 8 to 10 minutes, until golden brown.

2 In the top of a double boiler over simmering water, melt the chocolate with the butter, stirring until smooth. Remove from the heat.

3 In a large bowl, using an electric mixer on medium speed, beat the eggs until thick and light-colored. Beat in the sugar. Stir in the chocolate mixture and liqueur.

4 Dust the whole pecans with flour and sprinkle them evenly in the baked pie crust. Pour the filling mixture over the top.

5 Bake for 25 to 30 minutes, or until firm. Cool in the pan on a wire rack.

6 Make the chocolate whipped cream.

7 To serve, fill a pastry bag with whipped cream and pipe a border around the edge of the filling. Pipe a rosette in the center and sprinkle with the chopped pecans.

614 ■ CHOCOLATE PECAN PIE III

MAKES 8 TO 10 SERVINGS
BAKING TIME: *50 minutes*
CHILL TIME: *1 hour*

CREAM CHEESE CRUST

2 cups all-purpose flour
½ teaspoon salt
⅓ cup butter-flavored vegetable shortening
⅓ cup cream cheese
5 to 6 tablespoons ice water

CHOCOLATE PECAN FILLING

2 ounces unsweetened chocolate, grated or finely chopped
2 tablespoons butter
3 large eggs
¾ cup light corn syrup
½ cup granulated sugar
¾ cup pecan halves
Dessert Syrup (see page 409) for garnish
Chocolate Cones (see page 421) for garnish

1 Position a rack in the center of the oven and preheat the oven to 350 degrees.

2 To make the crust, in a medium bowl, combine the flour and salt. Using a pastry blender or two knives scissor fashion, cut in the shortening until the mixture forms fine crumbs. Cut in the cream cheese. Sprinkle the water over the top, a little at a time, and mix gently with a fork until the dough is just moist enough to hold together. Form into a ball. Wrap and chill for 1 hour, or until firm.

3 On a lightly floured surface, roll the dough out into a circle about ¼ inch thick. Transfer to a 9-inch pie pan and press onto the bottom and up the sides. Trim the edges and flute if desired.

4 To make the filling, in the top of a double boiler over simmering water, melt the chocolate and butter, stirring until smooth. Remove from the heat.

5 In a large bowl, beat the eggs until thick and light-colored. Stir in the corn syrup, sugar, and chocolate mixture. Pour into the prepared crust. Place the pecan halves in a ring around the top of the filling.

6 Bake for 40 to 50 minutes, or just until set. Cool completely in the pan on a wire rack. Brush each of the pecan halves with dessert syrup. Arrange the chocolate cones between each of the pecan halves for garnish.

617

BAKING NOTES: Although this recipe calls for pecans, walnuts or any nut that can be cut in half can be used.

615 ■ CHOCOLATE PIE

MAKES 8 TO 10 SERVINGS
CHILL TIME: 5 hours

1 recipe Graham Cracker Crumb Crust (see page 284)
30 large marshmallows
1/2 cup heavy cream
1/2 cup candied cherries, minced
2 ounces unsweetened chocolate, grated or finely chopped
1/2 cup chopped almonds
1 container (4 ounces) whipped topping
Candied cherry halves for garnish

1 Make and bake the crust.

2 In the top of a double boiler over simmering water, combine the marshmallows, cream, and minced cherries and stir until the marshmallows are melted and the mixture is smooth. Remove from the heat. Add the chocolate and stir until melted and smooth. Fold in the chopped almonds. Cool completely.

3 Fold in the whipped topping. Spread the mixture evenly in the prepared crust and chill for 3 to 5 hours before serving. Garnish with candied cherry halves.

615

616 ■ CHOCOLATE PIE SHELL

MAKES ONE 9-INCH PIE SHELL
CHILL TIME: 2 hours

12 ounces semisweet chocolate, grated or finely chopped
2 tablespoons butter or margarine
2 tablespoons granulated sugar

1 In the top of a double boiler over simmering water, melt the chocolate and butter, stirring until smooth. Stir in the sugar until dissolved. Immediately pour the mixture into a 9-inch foil pie pan, tipping and using a spoon to spread the chocolate up the sides. Chill for at least 1 hour, or until firm.

2 Carefully invert the pan onto a plate to remove the chocolate shell. Then reinvert onto a serving plate. Chill for 1 hour, or until ready to fill.

3 Fill with mousse or light custard pie filling.

BAKING NOTES: This pie shell will chip and crack very easily. Let stand at room temperature for at least 30 minutes before serving to soften it. In warmer weather, reduce the time out of the refrigerator.

617 ■ CHOCOLATE PIE WITH CURRANTS

MAKES 8 TO 10 SERVINGS
CHILL TIME: 8 to 10 hours

1 recipe Graham Cracker Crumb Crust # 788 (see page 000)
1/3 cup Grand Marnier
1/2 cup black currants
4 ounces semisweet chocolate, grated or finely chopped
2 tablespoons milk
2 1/4 cups heavy cream
8 ounces cream cheese, softened
1/4 cup granulated sugar
Chocolate Curls (see page 422) for garnish

1 Make and bake the crust.

2 In a small bowl, combine the Grand Marnier and currants.

3 Melt the chocolate (see page 13). Add the milk and stir. Remove from the heat.

4 In a large bowl, using an electric mixer on high speed, whip 1 1/4 cups of the cream until soft peaks form.

5 In a medium bowl, using an electric mixer on medium speed, beat the cream cheese and sugar until smooth. On low speed, beat in the melted chocolate. Fold in the currants and Grand Marnier and blend thoroughly. Fold in the whipped cream. Spread the mixture evenly in the baked crust. Cover and chill for 8 to 10 hours.

6 To serve, in a medium bowl, beat the remaining 3/4 cup cream until soft peaks form. Spread the whipped cream over the top of the pie and garnish with chocolate curls.

618 ■ CHOCOLATE PUDDINEE PIE

MAKES 8 TO 10 SERVINGS
BAKING TIME: 1 hour
FREEZING TIME: 30 minutes
CHILL TIME: 8 hours

COCOA MERINGUE CRUST

3/4 cup powdered sugar
1/4 cup Dutch processed cocoa powder
3 egg whites
1/4 teaspoon cream of tartar

CHOCOLATE FILLING

1 pint chocolate ice cream, softened
1/4 cup milk
1 package (3.4 ounces) Jell-O Brand chocolate instant pudding mix

WHIPPED CREAM TOPPING

1/2 cup heavy cream
1 tablespoon granulated sugar
1 1/2 teaspoons cherry liqueur
8 large strawberries, thinly sliced for garnish
1 large banana, thinly sliced for garnish

1 Position a rack in the center of the oven and preheat the oven to 275 degrees. Lightly grease a 9-inch pie pan.

2 To make the crust, combine the powdered sugar and cocoa powder.

3 In a large bowl, using an electric mixer on high speed, beat the egg whites and cream of tar-

tar until soft peaks form. Gradually blend the dry ingredients into the egg whites and beat until stiff peaks form. Spread evenly over the bottom and up the sides of the prepared pan.

4 Bake for 55 to 60 minutes, or until the crust appears dry. Cool in the pan on a wire rack. Freeze for 30 minutes.

4 To make the filling, in a medium bowl, using an electric mixer on medium speed, beat ice cream, milk, and pudding mix for 1 to 2 minutes, or until very smooth. Pour into the chilled meringue crust. Refrigerate for 8 hours or longer.

5 To serve, in a medium bowl, using an electric mixer on high speed, whip the cream and sugar until thickened. Add the liqueur and beat until soft peaks form. Spread evenly over the top of the chilled pie. Garnish with the sliced fruit.

619 ■ CHOCOLATE PUMPKIN PIE

MAKES 8 TO 10 SERVINGS
CHILL TIME: *4 hours*

1 recipe Graham Cracker Crumb Crust (see page 284)
4 ounces semisweet chocolate, grated or finely chopped
1 cup solid-pack canned pumpkin
1 teaspoon ground cinnamon
1/4 teaspoon ground ginger
1/4 teaspoon ground nutmeg
1/8 teaspoon ground cloves
1 1/2 teaspoons unflavored gelatin
1/2 cup milk
1 jar (7 ounces) marshmallow creme
1 cup heavy cream
Chocolate Sauce III (see page 404) for serving

1 Make and bake the crust, substituting 1 teaspoon almond extract for the vanilla extract.

2 Melt the chocolate (see page 13). Remove from the heat.

3 In a medium bowl, combine the pumpkin and spices.

4 In the top of a double boiler sprinkle the gelatin over the milk. Let stand for 1 minute to soften. Set over simmering water and stir until completely

dissolved. Add the marshmallow creme and stir until smooth. Stir in the melted chocolate. Gradually stir the pumpkin mixture into the marshmallow mixture, a little at a time. Cook just until thickened. Remove from the heat and beat until smooth. Cool for 15 minutes.

5 In a medium bowl, using an electric mixer on high speed, whip the cream until soft peaks form. Fold into the chocolate mixture. Pour into the baked crust. Chill at least 4 hours before serving. Serve with chocolate sauce.

620 ■ CHOCOLATE RUM WAFER PIE

MAKES 8 TO 10 SERVINGS
CHILL TIME: *45 minutes*

1 recipe Chocolate Cookie Crumb Crust (see page 267)
2/3 cup granulated sugar
1/2 cup all-purpose flour
3 large eggs
1/2 cup dark rum
1 1/2 cups milk
1/4 cup black currant preserves
1 cup heavy cream
1/2 teaspoon unflavored gelatin
10 to 12 Chocolate Leaves (see page 422) for garnish

1 Make and bake the crust.

2 Combine the sugar and flour.

3 In a large bowl, using an electric mixer on high speed, beat the eggs until thick and light-colored. Gradually blend in the dry ingredients, alternating with the rum. Pour the mixture into a saucepan over medium heat. Add the milk and cook, stirring constantly, until smooth and very thick. Remove from the heat and cool.

4 Spread the black currant preserves over the bottom of the baked pie crust. Pour the cooled custard over the preserves. Chill for 45 minutes, or until firm.

5 In a small saucepan over medium heat, combine 1/4 cup of the heavy cream with the gelatin, stirring until the gelatin dissolves. Remove from the heat and cool to room temperature.

6 In a medium bowl, using an electric mixer on high speed, whip the gelatin mixture with the remaining heavy cream until stiff peaks form. Spread over the top of the filling and garnish with the chocolate leaves.

621 ■ COCOA PIE I

MAKES 8 TO 10 SERVINGS
BAKING TIME: *8 minutes*
CHILL TIME: *2 hours*

1 recipe Chocolate Pastry Crust (see page 274)
1 cup plus 3 tablespoons granulated sugar
3/4 cup Dutch processed cocoa powder
1/4 cup all-purpose flour
1/2 teaspoon salt
2 cups milk
3 tablespoons butter or margarine
2 large eggs, separated
1 teaspoon chocolate extract

1 Make and bake the crust.

2 In a medium saucepan, over medium heat, combine 1 cup of the sugar, the cocoa powder, flour, and salt. Stir in the milk. Cook, stirring constantly, until the mixture is thick. Remove from the heat. Beat in the butter.

3 In a small bowl, using an electric mixer on high speed, beat the egg yolks until thick and light-colored. Beat in about 1 cup of the hot cocoa mixture. Beat the egg yolk mixture into the saucepan until blended. Stir in the chocolate extract. Pour into the baked pie crust.

4 Position a rack in the center of the oven and preheat the oven to 325 degrees.

5 In a medium bowl, using an electric mixer on high speed, beat the egg whites until foamy. Add the remaining 3 tablespoons sugar and continue beating until stiff peaks form. Spread the meringue evenly over the top of the pie.

6 Bake for 6 to 8 minutes, or until the peaks of meringue start to turn a golden color. Cool completely on a wire rack. Chill for 2 hours before serving.

622 ■ COCOA PIE II

MAKES 8 TO 10 SERVINGS
CHILL TIME: *8 hours*

1 recipe Coconut Pie Crust (see recipe this page)
1 envelope unflavored gelatin
1 cup milk
6 large eggs, separated
1 cup granulated sugar
½ cup Dutch processed cocoa powder
¼ teaspoon salt
1 teaspoon crème de cacao
½ teaspoon cream of tartar
Chocolate cookie crumbs for garnish

1 Make and bake the crust.

2 In a cup, sprinkle the gelatin over the milk. Let stand for 1 minute to soften.

3 Meanwhile, in a medium bowl, using an electric mixer on medium speed, beat the egg yolks until thick and light-colored. Beat in the milk mixture.

4 In the top of a double boiler, combine ¼ cup of the sugar, the cocoa powder, and salt. Gradually blend in the egg yolk mixture. Set over simmering water and cook, stirring constantly, until the mixture thickens slightly. Remove from the heat and stir in the crème de cacao. Chill 30 minutes, or until the mixture thickens and will form mounds when dropped from a spoon.

5 In a large bowl, using an electric mixer on high speed, beat the egg whites and cream of tartar until soft peaks form. On low speed, beat in the remaining ¾ cup sugar. On high speed, beat until stiff peaks form.

6 Gradually fold the chilled custard mixture into the egg white mixture until blended. Pour into the baked crust and chill overnight or until set. Sprinkle with chocolate cookie crumbs.

BAKING NOTES: Owing to the raw egg whites used in this recipe, it should be kept refrigerated at all times, and for no longer than 3 days.

623 ■ COCONUT CHOCOLATE PIE CRUST

MAKES ONE 9-INCH PIE CRUST
CHILL TIME: *30 minutes*

1 ounce unsweetened chocolate, grated or finely chopped
1 ounce semisweet chocolate, grated or finely chopped
6 tablespoons granulated sugar
1 can (3.5 ounces) flaked coconut

1 In the top of a double boiler over simmering water, melt the chocolates, stirring until smooth. Remove from the heat.

2 Stir in the sugar until dissolved. Stir in the coconut. Press the mixture evenly onto the bottom and up the sides of a 9-inch pie plate. Chill 30 minutes, or until ready to use.

624 ■ COCONUT PIE CRUST

MAKES ONE 9-INCH PIE CRUST
BAKING TIME: *10 minutes*

2 cups flaked coconut
2 tablespoons powdered sugar
1 tablespoon cornstarch
3 tablespoons butter, melted

1 Position a rack in the center of the oven and preheat the oven to 350 degrees.

2 In a medium bowl, combine the coconut, powdered sugar, and cornstarch. Stir in the melted butter until thoroughly mixed. Press onto the bottom and up the sides of a 9-inch pie pan.

3 Bake for 8 to 10 minutes, or until the lightly browned. Cool completely on a wire rack.

BAKING NOTES: Use flaked rather than shredded or grated coconut for a finer textured crust. The crust can be tinted with a few drops of food coloring, but take into consideration the color of the filling.

619

620

622

625 ■ CORN FLAKE PIE SHELL

MAKES ONE 9-INCH PIE SHELL
BAKING TIME: *10 to 15 minutes*

1 cup corn flakes cereal, crushed
1/4 cup granulated sugar
1/3 cup butter-flavored vegetable shortening

1 Position a rack in the center of the oven and preheat the oven to 375 degrees.

2 In a medium bowl, combine the corn flakes and sugar. Add the shortening and working by hand, or using a pastry blender form a crumbly mixture. Press evenly onto the bottom and up the sides of a 9-inch pie pan.

3 Bake for 8 to 10 minutes, or until the crust looks dry. Cool completely on a wire rack. Chill before using.

626 ■ CRACKER CRUST CHOCOLATE PIE

MAKES 8 TO 10 SERVINGS
BAKING TIME: *47 minutes*

CRACKER CRUST

3 large egg whites
1/4 teaspoon cream of tartar
Pinch of salt
1 cup granulated sugar
1 1/2 cups saltine cracker crumbs (30 crackers)
1 cup ground pecans or almonds

CHOCOLATE FILLING

1/2 cup butter or margarine
2 ounces unsweetened chocolate, grated or finely chopped
2 large eggs
1 cup granulated sugar
1/4 cup all-purpose flour
2 teaspoons chocolate extract
1 quart chocolate ice cream for serving

1 Position a rack in the center of the oven and preheat the oven to 350 degrees. Lightly grease a 9 or 10-inch glass pie plate.

2 To make the crust, in a large bowl, using an electric mixer on high speed, beat the egg whites, cream of tartar, and salt until foamy. Add the sugar, a few tablespoons at a time, and beat until stiff but not dry. Fold in the cracker crumbs and pecans. Spread the mixture evenly onto the bottom and sides of the prepared pie plate.

3 Bake for 12 minutes, or until a golden brown color. Cool in the pan on a wire rack while making the filling.

4 To make the filling, in the top of a double boiler over simmering water, melt the butter and chocolate, stirring until smooth. Remove from the heat.

5 In a medium bowl, using an electric mixer on high speed, beat the eggs until thick and light-colored. Add the sugar, a little at a time, and beat until very thick. Beat in the flour, melted chocolate, and chocolate extract until smooth and blended. Spread the mixture in the warm crust.

6 Bake for 35 minutes, or until the filling is firm. Cool in the pan on a wire rack. Serve with ice cream on the side.

610

614

618

611

613

627 ■ CRÈME DE MENTHE PIE

MAKES 12 TO 15 SERVINGS
CHILL TIME: *8 hours*

COOKIE CRUST

2 cups crushed chocolate cream-
    filled sandwich cookies
1/4 cup butter-flavored vegetable
    shortening

CRÈME DE MENTHE FILLING

16 ounces cream cheese, at room
    temperature
1 1/2 cups powdered sugar
2 tablespoons crème de menthe
2 cups heavy cream

1 Position a rack in the center of
the oven and preheat the oven
to 350 degrees. Lightly grease a
13 by 9-inch pan.

2 To make the crust, combine
the crushed cookies and shortening to make a crumbly mixture. Press evenly onto the
bottom of the prepared pan.

3 Bake for 5 minutes. Cool completely on a wire rack. Chill
while making the filling.

4 To make the filling, in a large
bowl, using an electric mixer on
medium speed, beat the cream
cheese, 1/4 cup of the powdered
sugar, and crème de menthe
until smooth.

5 In a large bowl, using an electric mixer on high speed, whip
the cream and the remaining 1 1/4
cups powdered sugar until stiff
peaks form. Fold into the cream
cheese mixture. Pour into the
chilled crust. Chill overnight
before serving.

628 ■ EVERYMAN'S FAVORITE PIE

MAKES 8 TO 10 SERVINGS
FREEZING TIME: *1 hour*

CHOCOLATE TOPPING

2 ounces unsweetened chocolate,
    grated or finely chopped
2 ounces semisweet chocolate,
    grated or finely chopped
2/3 cup water
1 cup granulated sugar
6 tablespoons butter or margarine,
    at room temperature
1 teaspoon chocolate extract or
    crème de cacao

CRUST

1 recipe Chocolate Pastry Crust (see
    page 274)

ICE CREAM FILLINGS

1 pint chocolate ice cream, softened
1 pint vanilla ice cream, softened

MERINGUE TOPPING

3 large egg whites
1/8 teaspoon cream of tartar
1/2 cup granulated sugar

1 To make the chocolate topping, in the top of a double
boiler over simmering water,
melt the chocolates with the
water, stirring until smooth.
Add the sugar and stir until dissolved. Remove from the heat
and immediately stir in the butter and chocolate extract until
blended. Transfer to a medium
bowl. Cover and chill while
making the crust.

2 Make and bake the crust.

3 To assemble the pie, spread
the vanilla ice cream in the
baked crust. Spread 1/2 cup of
the topping over the top of the
ice cream. Freeze for 30 minutes.

4 Spread the chocolate ice
cream over the top of the sauce
and top with another 1/2 cup of
the sauce. Freeze for 30 minutes.

621

628

626

627

5 To make the meringue topping, in a medium bowl, using an electric mixer on high speed, beat the egg whites and cream of tartar until foamy. Add the sugar and beat until stiff and glossy. Spread the meringue over the top of the frozen pie so that it touches the edges of the crust.

6 Bake in a 400-degree oven for 1 to 2 minutes, or until the meringue is browned. Serve at once with the remaining chocolate topping as a sauce on the side.

BAKING NOTES: Due to the raw egg whites, keep this pie in the freezer at all times, up to two weeks.

629 ■ FRENCH SILK PIE

MAKES 8 TO 10 SERVINGS
BAKING TIME: *15 to 20 minutes*
CHILL TIME: *2 hours*

PASTRY CRUST

2 cups all-purpose flour
1/2 teaspoon salt
2/3 cup butter-flavored vegetable shortening
5 to 6 tablespoons ice water

CHOCOLATE SILK FILLING

2 ounces unsweetened chocolate, grated or finely chopped
1/2 cup butter or margarine, at room temperature
3/4 cup granulated sugar
2 large eggs
1 teaspoon crème de cacao
Chocolate Whipped Cream (see page 406) for garnish

1 Position a rack in the center of the oven and preheat the oven to 375 degrees.

2 To make the crust, combine the flour and salt. Using a pastry blender or two knives scissor fashion, cut in the shortening until the mixture forms fine crumbs. Sprinkle the water over the top, a little at a time, and mix gently with a fork just until the dough is moist enough to hold together. Form into a ball. Wrap and chill for 1 hour, or until firm.

3 On a lightly floured surface, roll the dough out into a circle about 1/4 inch thick. Transfer to a 9-inch pie pan and ease into the bottom and up the sides. Trim the edges and flute if desired. Line the crust with a piece of aluminum foil and fill with dried beans or pie weights.

4 Bake for 15 to 20 minutes, or until the edges of the crust are golden brown. Remove the foil and beans. Cool completely on a wire rack.

5 To make the filling, melt the chocolate (see page 13). Transfer to a medium bowl. Using an electric mixer on low speed, beat in the butter and sugar. On medium speed, beat in the eggs, one at a time, mixing for 5 minutes after each addition. Beat in the crème de cacao. Pour into the baked crust and chill for 1 hour or until set. Garnish each serving with a dab of chocolate whipped cream.

BAKING NOTES: Owing to the raw eggs used in this recipe, it should be kept refrigerated at all times, and for no longer than 3 days.

630 ■ FROZEN FUDGE PIE

MAKES 8 TO 10 SERVINGS
BAKING TIME: *35 minutes*
FREEZING TIME: *4 hours*

8 ounces semisweet chocolate, grated or finely chopped
1/4 cup boiling water
3/4 cup granulated sugar
4 large eggs
3/4 cup butter-flavored vegetable shortening
1 tablespoon mocha-flavored instant coffee powder
1 tablespoon crème de cacao
1/4 cup all-purpose flour
1 cup pecans, finely chopped
Whipped cream for serving

1 Position a rack in the center of the oven and preheat the oven to 350 degrees. Lightly grease a 9-inch pie pan.

2 In the top of a double boiler over simmering water, melt the chocolate with the water, stir-

ring until smooth. Stir in the sugar, blending until dissolved. Transfer to a large bowl. Using an electric mixer on medium speed, beat in the eggs, one at a time, beating well after each addition. Beat in the shortening, coffee powder, and crème de cacao. Mix in the flour and chopped nuts. Spread the mixture in the prepared pie pan.

3 Bake for 30 to 35 minutes, or until the edges are set. The center will be slightly soft. Cool completely on a wire rack. Freeze for at least 4 hours. Remove from freezer 30 minutes before serving. Top each piece with whipped cream.

631 ■ FUDGE CREAM PIE WITH A GINGER CRUST

MAKES 8 TO 10 SERVINGS
BAKING TIME: *10 minutes*
CHILL TIME: *30 minutes*

GINGERSNAP CRUST

1 1/2 cups gingersnap cookie crumbs
1/4 cup butter or margarine, at room temperature
4 ounces semisweet chocolate, grated or finely chopped
1/4 cup granulated sugar
1/3 cup minus 1 tablespoon water
1 tablespoon ginger liqueur

CHOCOLATE CUSTARD

1/2 cup granulated sugar
1/3 cup all-purpose flour
1/4 teaspoon salt
2 cups heavy cream
2 ounces unsweetened chocolate, grated or finely chopped
3 large eggs
1 tablespoon crème de cacao
2 teaspoons chocolate extract

CHOCOLATE CREAM TOPPING

3 tablespoons powdered sugar
2 tablespoons Dutch processed cocoa powder
1 cup heavy cream
1/2 teaspoon crème de cacao
Grated semisweet chocolate for garnish
Fresh strawberry slices for garnish

1 Position a rack in the center of the oven and preheat the oven to 350 degrees.

2 To make the crust, combine the cookie crumbs and butter. Using your fingertips, rub the butter into the crumbs until blended. Press into an 8 or 9-inch pie pan.

3 Bake for 8 to 10 minutes, or until the crust looks dry. Cool on a wire rack.

4 Meanwhile, in the top of a double boiler over simmering water, melt the chocolate with the sugar and water, stirring until the chocolate is melted and the sugar dissolved. Remove from the heat and stir in the liqueur. Pour this mixture over the pie crust.

5 To make the filling, in the top of a double boiler over simmering water, combine the sugar, flour, and salt. Add the cream and chocolate and stir until the chocolate is melted and smooth. Cook for 3 minutes, stirring occasionally. Remove from the heat.

6 In a small bowl, using an electric mixer on medium speed, beat the eggs until thick and light-colored. Pouring it in a thin stream, beat ½ cup the hot chocolate mixture into the eggs. Mix the egg mixture back into the hot mixture in the saucepan. Return to the heat and cook, stirring constantly, until the mixture thickens. Remove from the heat and cool slightly. Add the crème de cacao and chocolate extract and pour into the prepared crust. Chill 30 minutes, or until set.

7 To make the topping, in a cup, combine the powdered sugar and cocoa powder.

8 In a medium bowl, using an electric mixer on high speed, whip the cream until soft peaks form. Fold in the dry ingredients. Fold in the crème de cacao. Chill before using.

9 To serve, fill a pastry bag fitted with a large star tip with the topping. Pipe a ring around the outer edge of the filling and a cluster of rosettes in the center. In the area between, sprinkle grated chocolate. Place a strawberry slice in the center of each rosette.

632 ■ FUDGE PECAN PIE

MAKES 8 TO 10 SERVINGS
BAKING TIME: *40 minutes*

1 recipe Chocolate Pastry Crust (see page 274)
4 ounces semisweet chocolate, grated or finely chopped
¼ cup butter-flavored vegetable shortening
1 can (14 ounces) sweetened condensed milk
2 large eggs
¼ cup hot water
1 teaspoon almond extract
Pinch of salt
½ cup pecan pieces
Dessert Syrup (see page 409) for garnish

1 Position a rack in the center of the oven and preheat the oven to 400 degrees.

2 Make and bake the crust. Cool on a wire rack. Reduce the oven temperature to 350 degrees.

3 Meanwhile, to make the filling, in the top of a double boiler over simmering water, melt the chocolate and shortening, stirring until smooth. Remove from the heat.

4 In a large bowl, using an electric mixer on medium speed, beat the condensed milk, eggs, hot water, almond extract, and salt until well blended. Beat in the chocolate mixture. Pour into the baked pie crust and top with the pecan pieces.

5 Bake for 35 to 40 minutes, or until the filling is set. Cool on a wire rack. Lightly brush the dessert syrup over the top of the pecans.

632

630

629

633 ■ GRAHAM CRACKER CRUMB CRUST

MAKES ONE 9-INCH PIE CRUST
BAKING TIME: *8 minutes*

1 cup graham cracker crumbs
¼ cup granulated sugar
¼ cup butter or margarine, chilled
1 teaspoon vanilla extract

1 Position a rack in the center of the oven and preheat the oven to 375 degrees.

2 In a medium bowl, combine the crumbs and sugar. Using a pastry blender or your finger-tips, cut or rub the butter into the crumb mixture. Stir in the vanilla extract. Press the mixture onto the bottom and sides of an 8 or 9-inch pie pan.

3 Bake for 8 minutes, or until very lightly browned. Cool completely on a wire rack.

BAKING NOTES: For a chocolate variation, stir in 2 ounces of melted semisweet chocolate after the butter has been cut in and substitute chocolate extract for the vanilla extract.

634 ■ LOW-FAT PASTRY SHELL

MAKES TWO 9-INCH PIE SHELLS
BAKING TIME: *10 minutes*

⅓ cup canola oil
1 tablespoon cider vinegar
2 cups all-purpose flour
½ teaspoon salt
2 to 3 tablespoons ice water

1 Position a rack in the center of the oven and preheat the oven to 425 degrees. Lightly grease a 9-inch pie pan.

2 Combine the canola oil and vinegar.

3 In a large bowl, combine the flour and salt. Using a fork, stir, in the oil and vinegar until crumbly. Sprinkle the water over the top, a little at a time, and mix just until it makes a smooth dough.

4 On a lightly floured surface, roll one half of the dough out into a circle about ¼ inch thick. Transfer to the prepared pie pan and ease into the bottom and up the sides. Trim the edges and flute if desired. Line the crust with a piece of aluminum foil and fill with dried beans or pie weights.

5 Bake for 3 to 4 minutes, or until the crust feels set. Remove the foil and beans. Bake for 7 minutes, or until golden brown.

BAKING NOTES: Wrap remaining pastry shell dough in plastic wrap and place in the freezer for up to six months.

635 ■ LUSCIOUS CHOCOLATE ALMOND PIE

MAKES 8 TO 10 SERVINGS
BAKING TIME: *20 minutes*
CHILL TIME: *9 hours*

ALMOND CRUST

1 cup all-purpose flour
1 cup chopped almonds
1 cup butter or margarine, softened

FLUFFY CREAM CHEESE FILLING

8 ounces cream cheese, at room temperature
1 cup powdered sugar
1 cup whipped topping

CHOCOLATE PUDDING FILLING

2 packages (3.4 ounces each) Jell-O Brand chocolate instant pudding mix
2 cups cold milk
1½ cups whipped topping for garnish
½ cup chopped almonds for garnish

635

637

636

1 Position a rack in the center of the oven and preheat the oven to 325 degrees.

2 To make the crust, in a medium bowl, combine the flour and almonds. Using a pastry blender or two knives scissor fashion, cut the butter into the flour. Press the mixture onto the bottom and sides of a 9-inch glass pie plate.

3 Bake for 20 minutes. Cool completely on a wire rack.

4 To make the cream cheese filling, in a large bowl, using an electric mixer on medium speed, beat the cream cheese until smooth. Beat in the powdered sugar until smooth. On low speed, beat in the whipped topping. Spread evenly over the baked crust.

5 To make the chocolate filling, in a small bowl, using an electric mixer on high speed, beat the pudding mix and milk. Spread over the cream cheese filling. Chill for 1 hour. Fill a pastry bag fitted with a large star tip with the whipped topping and pipe rosettes over the entire surface of the chilled pie. Chill for at least 8 hours before serving. Sprinkle with the chopped almonds.

636 ▪ MERINGUE TARTS WITH CHOCOLATE FILLING

MAKES 8 TO 10 SERVINGS
BAKING TIME: *85 minutes*
STANDING TIME: *8 hours*

MERINGUE TART SHELLS

4 large egg whites
1/2 teaspoon cream of tartar
1 cup powdered sugar

CHOCOLATE MOUSSE FILLING

6 ounces semisweet chocolate, grated or finely chopped
4 large egg yolks
2 tablespoons heavy cream
Chocolate Curls (see page 422) for garnish
Fresh mint sprigs for garnish

1 Position a rack in the center of the oven and preheat the oven to 200 degrees. Line a baking sheet with parchment paper.

2 To make the tart shells, in a large bowl, using an electric mixer on high speed, beat the egg whites and cream of tartar until foamy. Beat in the powdered sugar, a few teaspoonfuls at a time, until the sugar is dissolved. Beat until soft peaks form.

3 Using a 1/3 measuring cup, drop the mixture onto the prepared pan, 1 1/2 inches apart. Using the back of the a spoon dipped in powdered sugar, spread into a nest-shaped 3-inch circle, making a depression in the center of each round.

4 Bake for 85 minutes. Turn off the oven and leave the tart shells in the oven for at least 8 hours.

5 To make the filling, melt the chocolate (see page 13). Remove from the heat.

6 In a medium bowl, using an electric mixer on medium speed, beat the egg yolks and 2 tablespoons cream until thickened. Gradually beat in the melted chocolate. Chill until ready to fill the tarts.

7 To assemble, fill a pastry bag fitted with a large star tip with the filling. Pipe the filling into the meringue tart shells. Garnish each with chocolate curls and a small sprig of mint.

BAKING NOTES: The meringue tarts can be frozen up to 1 week before using. Place in a zip-lock plastic bag, removing as much excess air as possible, and freeze until ready to use. For chocolate tart shells, add 1/3 of the Dutch processed cocoa powder and reduce the powdered sugar to 3/4 cup. Owing to the raw egg yolks used in this chocolate mousse recipe, it should be kept refrigerated at all times, and for no longer than 3 days.

637 ▪ MOCHA FUDGE PIE WITH CHOCOLATE FILLING

MAKES 8 TO 10 SERVINGS
BAKING TIME: *40 minutes*

MOCHA CRUST

1 3/4 cups all-purpose flour
1/3 cup Dutch processed cocoa powder
1/4 cup granulated sugar
Pinch of salt
3/4 cup butter or margarine
1/4 cup cold strong brewed coffee
1/4 cup coffee liqueur

MOCHA WALNUT FILLING

6 ounces semisweet chocolate, grated or finely chopped
6 ounces unsweetened chocolate, grated or finely chopped
2 tablespoons butter or margarine
2/3 cup granulated sugar
2 tablespoons buttermilk
2 teaspoons coffee liqueur
1/2 cup ground walnuts
2 large eggs
Chocolate ice cream for serving

1 Position a rack in the center of the oven and preheat the oven to 350 degrees.

2 To make the crust, in a large bowl, combine the flour, cocoa powder, sugar, and salt. Using a pastry blender or two knives scissor fashion, cut in the butter to make a crumbly mixture. Stir in the coffee. If the mixture seems dry, add the liqueur, a tablespoon at a time. Press the dough evenly onto the bottom and up the sides of a 9-inch pie pan. Freeze until ready to fill.

3 To make the filling, in the top of a double boiler over simmering water, melt the chocolates and butter, stirring constantly until smooth. Remove from the heat. Stir in the sugar, buttermilk, liqueur, walnuts, and eggs and blend thoroughly. Pour into the prepared pie crust.

4 Bake for 35 to 40 minutes, or until the filling is firm. Cool completely on a wire rack. Serve with a scoop of chocolate ice cream on the side.

638 ■ ORANGE CREAM PIE WITH CHOCOLATE SHELL

MAKES 6 TO 8 SERVINGS
CHILL TIME: *150 minutes*
STANDING TIME: *1 hour*

1 recipe Chocolate Pie Shell (see page 277)

FILLING

1 envelope unflavored gelatin
¼ cup water
4 large eggs, separated
½ cup granulated sugar
½ cup fresh orange juice, strained
1 tablespoon grated orange zest
Pinch of salt
1 cup heavy cream
2 tablespoons Triple Sec or Curaçao

1 Make the pie shell recipe. Chill until ready to fill.

2 To make the filling, in a cup, sprinkle the gelatin over the water. Let stand for 1 minute to soften.

3 Meanwhile, in a large bowl, using an electric mixer on medium speed, beat the egg yolks until thick and light-colored. Add ¼ cup of the sugar and beat until creamy. Add the orange juice, orange zest, and salt. Pour the mixture into the top of a double boiler over simmering water. Cook, stirring constantly, until the mixture is thick and smooth. Stir in the gelatin until dissolved. Remove from the heat and cool.

4 In a large bowl, using an electric mixer with clean beaters on high speed, beat the egg whites and salt until stiff but not dry. Fold in the remaining ¼ cup sugar. Fold the egg whites into the egg yolk mixture.

5 In a small bowl, using an electric mixer on high speed, beat the cream until thick. Fold in the Triple Sec. Fold the cream mixture into the egg mixture. Chill for 20 to 30 minutes, or until thickened.

6 To assemble, carefully spread the chilled custard mixture in the chocolate crust and chill for at least 1 hour, or until firm.

7 To serve, let stand at room temperature for 1 hour before cutting to allow the shell to soften.

639 ■ PECAN PASTRY CRUST

MAKES ONE 9-INCH PIE CRUST
CHILL TIME: *1 hour*

1½ cups all-purpose flour
¼ cup pecans, finely ground
¼ teaspoon salt
⅓ cup vegetable shortening
1 to 2 tablespoons ice-cold water

1 Lightly grease a 9-inch pie pan.

2 In a large bowl, combine the flour, pecans, and salt. Using a pastry blender or two knives scissor fashion, cut in the shortening until the mixture forms large coarse crumbs. Sprinkle the water, a little at a time, over the top and mix gently with a fork until the dough is just moist enough to hold together. Chill for 30 minutes.

3 On a lightly floured surface, roll the dough out into a circle about ¼ inch thick. Transfer to the prepared pie pan and press onto the bottom and up the sides. Trim the edges and flute if desired. Chill for 30 minutes, or until ready to use.

640 ■ SCOTCH CHOCOLATE CREAM PIE

MAKE 8 TO 10 SERVINGS
FREEZE TIME: *30 minutes*

Chocolate Hazelnut Crumb Crust (see page 271)
2 cups heavy cream
3 ounces semisweet chocolate, grated or finely chopped
1 ounce unsweetened chocolate, grated or finely chopped
1 cup clover honey
⅓ cup Scotch whisky
1 cup chocolate wafer cookie crumbs for topping
Mint sprigs for garnish
Peeled and thinly sliced kiwifruit for garnish

1 Make the crust. Press the mixture firmly onto the bottom of an 8 or 9-inch springform pan. Freeze 30 minutes, or until ready to fill.

2 In a medium bowl, using an electric mixer on high speed, beat the cream until soft peaks form.

3 In the top of a double boiler over simmering water, melt the chocolates, stirring until smooth. Remove from the heat. Stir in the honey. Beat in the Scotch and ⅓ cup of the whipped cream.

4 Fold the chocolate mixture into the remaining whipped cream. Pour the mixture into the prepared crust and smooth the top. Sprinkle the crushed cookie crumbs evenly over the top.

641

638

Press the crumbs very lightly into the filling. Freeze until the filling is set. To serve, remove the side of the springform pan and cut into wedges.

641 ■ SOUTHERN GENTLEMAN'S PECAN PIE

MAKES 8 TO 10 SERVINGS
BAKING TIME: *80 minutes*

PECAN PASTRY CRUST

1 cup all-purpose flour
3 tablespoons pecans, finely ground
1/4 teaspoon salt
1/3 cup vegetable shortening
1 to 2 tablespoons ice water

CHOCOLATE PECAN FILLING

4 ounces semisweet chocolate, grated or finely chopped
3 tablespoons butter-flavored vegetable shortening
1 teaspoon instant coffee powder
1 cup light corn syrup
1/3 cup granulated sugar
3 large eggs
1 teaspoon coffee liqueur
1 cup pecans, coarsely chopped

COFFEE WHIPPED CREAM TOPPING

1/2 cup heavy cream
1 teaspoon instant coffee powder
1 tablespoon powdered sugar
1/2 teaspoon coffee liqueur
1 cup pecan halves for garnish

1 Position a rack in the center of the oven and preheat the oven to 375 degrees.

2 In a large bowl, combine the flour, pecans, and salt. Using a pastry blender or two knives scissor fashion, cut in the shortening until the mixture forms coarse crumbs. Sprinkle the water over the top, a little at a time, and mix gently with a fork just until moist enough to hold the mixture together. Form into a ball.

3 On a lightly floured surface, roll the dough out into a circle about 1/4 inch thick. Transfer to a 9-inch pie pan and ease onto the bottom and up the sides. Trim the edges and flute if desired.

4 To make the filling, in the top of a double boiler over simmering water, melt the chocolate and shortening, stirring until smooth. Remove from the heat and stir in the coffee powder.

5 In a medium saucepan, over high heat, combine the corn syrup and sugar, stirring until blended and dissolved. Reduce the heat to medium and simmer for 2 to 3 minutes. Remove from the heat. Cool slightly and stir in the chocolate mixture.

6 In a large bowl, using an electric mixer on high speed, beat the eggs until foamy. Beating constantly, add the chocolate mixture. Stir in the coffee liqueur and pecans. Pour into the prepared pie crust.

7 Bake for 45 to 50 minutes, or until the filling is puffed up over the entire surface. Cool completely on a wire rack. Chill in the refrigerator for 30 minutes.

8 To make the topping, in a large bowl, using an electric mixer on high speed, whip the cream until it starts to thicken. Add the coffee powder, powdered sugar, and liqueur. Whip until soft peaks form. Spread over the top of the cooled pie. Garnish with pecan halves.

BAKING NOTES: When preparing the crust, if too much water is used, the pie crust will be tough.

642 ■ SOUTHERN PRIDE PECAN PIE

MAKES 8 TO 10 SERVINGS
BAKING TIME: *40 minutes*
CHILL TIME: *1 hour*

PASTRY CRUST

1 1/4 cups all-purpose flour
1/4 teaspoon salt
1/2 cup butter-flavored vegetable shortening
3 tablespoons ice water

BOURBON PECAN FILLING

3/4 cup light or dark corn syrup
1/4 cup vegetable shortening
3 large eggs
1 cup granulated sugar
1/2 cup semisweet chocolate chips
1/2 cup chopped pecans
3 tablespoons bourbon

1 To make the crust, in a large bowl, combine the flour and salt. Using a pastry blender or two knives scissor fashion, cut in the shortening until the mixture forms coarse crumbs. Sprinkle the water over the top and mix gently with a fork to form a smooth dough. Knead the dough lightly and form into a ball. Sprinkle the ball with flour. Wrap and chill for at least 1 hour, or until firm.

2 Position a rack in the center of the oven and preheat the oven to 350 degrees.

3 On a lightly floured surface, roll the dough out into a circle about 1/8 inch thick. Transfer to a 9-inch pie pan and ease into the bottom and up the sides. Trim the edges and flute if desired. Freeze for 30 minutes, or until ready to fill.

4 To make the filling, in a small saucepan, over medium heat, combine the corn syrup and shortening and stir until smooth. Remove from the heat.

5 In a medium bowl, using an electric mixer on high speed, beat the eggs until thick and light-colored. Add the sugar and beat until dissolved. Beat in the warm corn syrup mixture. Stir in the chocolate chips, pecans, and bourbon. Pour the mixture into the chilled crust.

6 Bake for 35 to 40 minutes, or until the top is a golden brown color. Cool completely on a wire rack.

643 ■ SPECKLED CHOCOLATE PIE

MAKES 8 TO 10 SERVINGS
BAKING TIME: *1 hour*

1 recipe Coconut Pie Crust (see page 279)
2 large eggs
1/2 cup all-purpose flour
1/2 cup granulated sugar
1/2 cup packed light brown sugar
1 cup butter or margarine, at room temperature
1 cup chocolate sprinkles
1 cup pecans, chopped

1 Make and bake the crust.

2 To make the filling, in a large bowl, using an electric mixer on medium speed, beat the eggs until thick and light-colored. Beat on low speed and add the flour and sugars. Beat in the butter. Fold in the sprinkles and pecans. Pour into the prepared crust.

3 Bake for 1 hour, or until firm. Cool completely on a wire rack.

644 ■ TWO-CHOCOLATE CREAM PIE

MAKES 8 TO 10 SERVINGS
BAKING TIME: *22 minutes*

1 recipe Corn Flake Pie Shell (see page 280)

CHOCOLATE CUSTARD AND MERINGUE TOPPING

2²⁄₃ cups milk
¾ cup plus 6 tablespoons granulated sugar
3 large eggs, separated
1 ounce unsweetened chocolate, grated or finely chopped
2 ounces semisweet chocolate, grated or finely chopped
¼ cup cornstarch or arrowroot
1 tablespoon butter, melted
¼ teaspoon salt
1 teaspoon chocolate extract
1 cup Creamy Chocolate Frosting (see page 408) for garnish

1 Position a rack in the center of the oven and preheat the oven to 375 degrees.

2 In a medium bowl, combine the cereal, sugar, and butter. Stir to form a crumbly mixture. Press evenly onto the bottom and up the sides of a 9-inch pie pan.

3 Bake for 8 to 10 minutes, or until the crust looks dry. Cool on a wire rack. Chill well before using.

4 In the top of a double boiler over simmering water, combine 1²⁄₃ cups of the milk, ¾ cup of the sugar, the egg yolks, chocolates, cornstarch, butter, and salt. Cook, stirring constantly, until everything is well blended and thick. Remove from the heat. Stir in the chocolate

extract. Cool slightly. Pour into the baked pie crust.

5 Meanwhile, to make the topping, in a medium bowl, using an electric mixer on high speed, beat the egg whites until foamy. Add the remaining 6 tablespoons of sugar and beat until stiff peaks form. Spread over the top of the filling.

6 Bake for 10 to 12 minutes, or until the meringue is light brown. Cool completely in the pan on a wire rack.

7 Make the frosting. Fill a pastry bag fitted with a fluted tip with the frosting and pipe rosettes around the edge of the pie.

640

631

643

645 ■ WHITE CHOCOLATE PIE

MAKES 8 TO 10
FREEZING TIME: *5 hours*

1 recipe Almond Crust (see page 258)
10 ounces white chocolate, grated or finely chopped
1/3 cup evaporated milk
3 tablespoons butter-flavored vegetable shortening
3 tablespoons crème de cacao
1½ teaspoons white chocolate liqueur or vanilla extract
½ teaspoon almond extract
2 large egg whites
2 tablespoons granulated sugar
1¾ cups heavy cream
1¼ cups frozen raspberries, thawed and drained
Whipped cream for garnish
Chocolate Leaves (see page 422) for garnish

1 Make and chill the crust.
2 To make the filling, in the top of a double boiler over simmering water, melt the chocolate with the evaporated milk and shortening, stirring until smooth. Remove from the heat and immediately set the pan in a bowl filled with water and ice. Cool, stirring occasionally, until thickened. Stir in the crème de cacao, white chocolate liqueur, and almond extract.

3 In a small bowl, using an electric mixer on high speed, beat the egg whites until foamy. Add the sugar and continue beating until stiff peaks form.
4 In a large bowl, using an electric mixer on high speed, whip the cream until stiff peaks form. Pouring it in a thin stream, beat in the chocolate mixture on low speed. Fold in the egg whites. Spread evenly in the chilled pie crust and freeze for 4 to 5 hours, or until frozen. Remove the pie from the freezer 30 minutes before serving.
5 To serve, mound the raspberries in the center of the pie. Garnish with dabs of whipped cream and the chocolate leaves.

BAKING NOTES: Owing to the raw egg whites used in this recipe, after first serving keep frozen at all times.

642

645

644

Puddings

646 ■ AMARETTO CHOCOLATE PUDDING

MAKES 4 TO 6 SERVINGS
CHILL TIME: *2 hours*

1 package (3.4 ounces) Jell-O Brand chocolate instant pudding mix
2 ounces semisweet chocolate, grated or finely chopped
1½ cups milk
2 tablespoons buttermilk
7 tablespoons amaretto
½ cup heavy cream
1 tablespoon granulated sugar
Sliced fresh peeled kiwifruit or strawberries for garnish
Macaroons for serving

1 In a medium saucepan, over low heat, combine the pudding mix, chocolate, milks, and 6 tablespoons of the amaretto and stir constantly until the chocolate is melted and the mixture is smooth. Raise the heat to medium and cook, stirring constantly, until the mixture boils and thickens. Pour into four to six custard cups or ramekins. Chill for 2 hours.

2 In a medium bowl, using an electric mixer on high speed, beat the cream with the sugar and remaining 1 tablespoon amaretto until soft peaks form. Chill until ready to use.

3 To serve, place a dab of whipped cream on top of each cup of pudding and garnish with fresh fruit. Serve with macaroons on the side.

647 ■ AUSTRIAN CHOCOLATE CREAM

MAKES 8 TO 10 SERVINGS
CHILL TIME: *5 hours*

1 envelope unflavored gelatin
¼ cup water
1 cup milk
3 large egg yolks
⅓ cup granulated sugar
5 envelopes premelted unsweetened chocolate (see page 14)
1 cup heavy cream

GARNISH

Chocolate Whipped Cream (see page 406)
Chocolate Curls (see page 422)
Sliced fresh fruit

1 Lightly grease a 1-quart mold or serving dish.

2 In a cup, sprinkle the gelatin over the water. Let stand for 10 minutes to soften.

3 In a medium saucepan, over medium-low heat, combine the milk, egg yolks, and sugar, and cook, stirring constantly, for about 7 minutes, or until thickened. Remove from the heat.

4 Using an electric mixer on medium speed, beat the gelatin into the custard mixture and pour into a large bowl. On low speed, gradually beat in the chocolate. Beat for about 7 to 10 minutes, or until very thick. Cool to room temperature. Cover and chill for 10 to 15 minutes. Do not allow to set completely.

5 In a medium bowl, using an electric mixer on high speed, whip the cream until soft peaks form. Gently fold into the chilled chocolate mixture. Pour into the prepared mold, cover, and chill for at least 4 hours.

6 To unmold, dip the bowl into a large bowl of warm water for 15 to 20 seconds. Dry the bottom of the bowl. Run a knife around the inside edge and invert onto a serving plate. If the pudding does not slip out easily, dip the bowl in the warm water again. Smooth the top and sides with a spatula and chill for at least 1 hour, or until ready to serve. Serve with chocolate whipped cream and garnish with chocolate curls and thin slices of fresh fruit.

648

650

646

647

649

648 ■ BAKED CHOCOLATE CUSTARD

MAKES 4 TO 6 SERVINGS
BAKING TIME: *50 minutes*
CHILL TIME: *30 minutes*

3 cups heavy cream
2 ounces unsweetened chocolate, grated or finely chopped
5 large eggs
1/3 cup powdered sugar
1 teaspoon chocolate extract
Pinch of salt

GARNISH

Chocolate Whipped Cream (see page 406)
Fresh mint sprigs

1 Position a rack in the center of the oven and preheat the oven to 350 degrees. Lightly grease a 1½-quart casserole.

2 In the top of a double boiler over simmering water, combine the cream and chocolate, stirring until the chocolate is melted and the mixture is smooth. Remove from the heat.

3 In a large bowl, using an electric mixer on medium speed, beat the eggs, powdered sugar, chocolate extract, and salt until smooth. Stirring constantly, beat in the hot chocolate mixture. Pour into the prepared casserole. Place the casserole in a roasting pan and place on the oven rack. Pour hot water into the roasting pan until it comes halfway up the sides of the casserole.

4 Bake for 40 to 50 minutes, or until a cake tester inserted into the center comes out clean. Chill for 30 minutes, or until ready to serve. Serve with chocolate whipped cream and garnish with mint sprigs.

649 ■ BAKED CHOCOLATE MOUSSE CAKE

MAKES 16 SERVINGS
BAKING TIME: *50 minutes*
CHILL TIME: *2 hours*

15 ounces semisweet chocolate, grated or finely chopped
2 cups butter or margarine
7 large eggs, separated, plus 7 large egg yolks
3/4 cup granulated sugar
2 teaspoons chocolate extract
1/2 cup fresh raspberries
1 sprig fresh mint

1 Position a rack in the center of the oven and preheat the oven to 300 degrees. Lightly grease a 9-inch springform pan.

2 In the top of a double boiler over simmering water, melt the chocolate and butter, stirring until smooth. Remove from the heat.

3 In a large bowl placed over a pan of hot water, whisk the egg yolks and the sugar until blended. Remove from the pan of water. Using an electric mixer on medium speed, beat until thick and light-colored. Pouring it in a thin stream, beat in the chocolate mixture and chocolate extract on low speed.

4 In a medium bowl, using an electric mixer on high speed, beat the egg whites until stiff peaks form. Gently fold the beaten whites into the chocolate mixture.

5 Pour two-thirds of the batter into the prepared pan. Cover the remaining batter in the bowl.

6 Bake for 45 to 50 minutes, or until a cake tester inserted into the center comes out clean. Cool in the pan on a wire rack. The center will sink and the cake will crack.

7 Using a piece of waxed paper or a very flat plate, press down on the raised portion of the cake to make it level with the sunken portion. Pour the reserved batter over the top. Cover the pan and chill for at least 2 hours. Remove from refrigerator 1 hour before serving.

8 To serve, remove the side of the pan and place the cake on a serving plate. Cut the raspberries in half and arrange on top of the cake. The mint may be used in one piece or the leaves may be removed and placed around the raspberries.

BAKING NOTES: Owing to the raw eggs used in this recipe, it should be kept refrigerated at all times, and for no longer than 3 days.

650 ■ BAKED CHOCOLATE PUDDING

MAKES 6 TO 8 SERVINGS
BAKING TIME: *45 minutes*

6 ounces unsweetened chocolate, grated or finely chopped
6 large eggs, separated
1/2 cup butter, at room temperature
1 cup powdered sugar
1 teaspoon crème de cacao
5 tablespoons arrowroot or cornstarch
1 cup milk
1 cup heavy cream
Kahlúa Cocoa Sauce (see page 413) for serving

1 Position a rack in the center of the oven and preheat the oven to 350 degrees. Lightly grease a 1½-quart casserole dish.

2 Melt the chocolate (see page 13). Remove from the heat.

3 In a large bowl, using an electric mixer on high speed, beat the egg whites until stiff but not dry.

4 In another large bowl, using an electric mixer on medium speed, beat the butter and powdered sugar until fluffy. Beat in the crème de cacao. Beat in the egg yolks, one at a time, beating well after each addition. Pouring it in a steady stream, beat in the melted chocolate on low speed. Combine the arrowroot and milk and stir into the chocolate mixture. Stir in the cream. Fold in the egg whites. Pour into the prepared casserole.

5 Bake for 40 to 45 minutes, or until firm. Cool slightly and serve with Kahlúa sauce.

651 ■ BAKED CHOCOLATE SOUFFLÉ

MAKES 8 TO 10 SERVINGS
BAKING TIME: *1 hour*

2 ounces unsweetened chocolate, grated or finely chopped
2 cups milk
½ cup granulated sugar
⅓ cup all-purpose flour
½ teaspoon salt
4 large eggs, separated
2 tablespoons butter or margarine
2 teaspoons chocolate or vanilla extract
Ganache (see page 410) or whipped cream for serving

1 Position a rack in the center of the oven and preheat the oven to 325 degrees. Lightly grease the bottom of a 2-quart soufflé dish.

2 In a saucepan over low heat, melt the chocolate, stirring until smooth. Stir in 1½ cups of the milk and heat until bubbles start to form around the sides of the pan. Remove from the heat and beat well.

3 In a medium bowl, using an electric mixer on high speed, combine the sugar, flour, and salt. Stir in the remaining ½ cup milk and blend thoroughly until smooth. Pour this mixture into the chocolate mixture in the saucepan. Return to the heat and cook, stirring constantly, for about 6 minutes, until the mixture thickens. Remove from the heat.

4 In a medium bowl, using an electric mixer on medium speed, beat the egg yolks until thick and light-colored. Beat in ¼ cup of the hot chocolate mixture. Beat the egg yolk mixture back into the remaining chocolate mixture in the saucepan. Return to the heat and cook, stirring constantly, for 5 minutes. Remove from the heat and stir in the butter and chocolate extract.

5 In a large bowl, using an electric mixer with clean beaters on high speed, beat the egg whites until stiff peaks form. Pouring it in a thin stream, beat the chocolate mixture into the egg whites on low speed. Pour into the prepared dish and set the dish in a roasting pan. Place on the oven rack and add boiling water until it comes halfway up the soufflé dish.

6 Bake for 1 hour or until a cake tester inserted into the center comes out clean. Serve with ganache or whipped cream on the side.

652 ■ BAKED CHOCOLATE SOUFFLÉ WITH RASPBERRY TOPPING

MAKES 8 TO 10 SERVING
BAKING TIME: *35 minutes*

Cocoa Sugar (see page 407) or granulated sugar for dusting
2 ounces unsweetened chocolate, grated or finely chopped
3 large eggs, separated
½ cup granulated sugar
⅓ cup all-purpose flour
2 tablespoons butter or margarine
1 cup heavy cream
1 teaspoon chocolate extract
Raspberry Sauce (see page 416), warmed

1 Preheat the oven to 350 degrees. Position a rack in the center of the oven. Grease a 1½-quart soufflé dish and dust with cocoa sugar.

2 Melt the chocolate (see page 13). Remove from the heat.

3 In a medium bowl, using an electric mixer on medium speed, beat the egg yolks until thick and light-colored.

4 In a medium bowl, using an electric mixer with clean beaters on high speed, beat the egg whites until stiff but not dry.

5 Combine the sugar and the flour.

6 In a medium saucepan, over low heat, melt the butter. Add the melted chocolate. Add the dry ingredients and stir until smooth. Add the cream and stir until the texture of a thick custard. Remove from the heat.

7 Beat ½ cup of the hot custard into the beaten egg yolks. Stirring constantly, add the egg yolks to the remaining hot custard. Cook, stirring constantly, for 1 to 2 minutes. Remove from the heat and cool to 130 degrees. Fold the beaten egg whites into the custard. Stir in the chocolate extract.

8 Pour the mixture into the prepared soufflé dish and spread evenly. Set in a roasting pan and place on the oven rack. Pour hot water into the roasting pan until it comes halfway up the sides of the soufflé dish.

9 Bake for 35 minutes, or until the top has risen to the rim of the dish and looks very dry. Serve with warm raspberry sauce.

653 ■ BANANA CHOCOLATE PUDDING

MAKES 4 SERVINGS
CHILL TIME: *30 minutes*

1 package (3.4 ounces) Jell-O Brand chocolate instant pudding mix
12 to 15 chocolate wafer cookies
3 ripe medium bananas, sliced
1 cup heavy cream

652

1 Make the pudding according to the package directions. Let stand until slightly thickened.

2 To assemble, place half of the cookies in the bottom of a serving bowl. Place a layer of sliced bananas on the cookies and cover with pudding. Repeat until all of the cookies, bananas, and pudding are used. Chill for 30 minutes, or until ready to serve.

3 To serve, in a medium bowl, using an electric mixer on high speed, whip the cream until soft peaks form. Serve the pudding with the whipped cream on the side.

654 ■ BARRIGA DE FREIRA

MAKES 8 TO 10 SERVINGS

1½ cups granulated sugar
½ cup water
¾ cup finely ground almonds
½ cup dried bread crumbs
3 large eggs
4 ounces unsweetened chocolate, grated or finely chopped
1 cup milk or heavy cream

1 In a medium saucepan, over low heat, combine 1 cup of the sugar and the water. Cook, stirring occasionally, until the sugar is dissolved. Using a pastry brush dipped in cold water, wash down the sugar crystals on the side of the pan. Raise the heat to medium and bring to a boil. Cook, without stirring, for 2 minutes. Remove from the heat and immediately stir in the almonds and bread crumbs. Cover and let stand for 3 minutes.

2 Meanwhile, in a medium bowl, using an electric mixer on medium speed, beat the eggs until thick and light-colored.

3 Stir the beaten eggs into the sugar mixture. Cook over medium heat, stirring constantly, until thickened. Do not allow the mixture to boil. Remove from the heat and transfer to serving bowl.

4 In the top of a double boiler over simmering water, melt the chocolate, stirring constantly until smooth. Stir in the milk and the remaining ½ cup sugar. Cook, stirring constantly, until smooth. Stir into the egg mixture. Cool to room temperature before serving.

655 ■ BITTERSWEET CHOCOLATE MOUSSE

MAKES 4 TO 6 SERVINGS
CHILL TIME: 4 hours

3 large eggs, separated
¾ cup plus 1 tablespoon powdered sugar
5 ounces unsweetened chocolate, grated or finely chopped
¼ cup butter or margarine, at room temperature
3 tablespoons raspberry liqueur
1 teaspoon chocolate extract
3 tablespoons strong brewed coffee
½ cup heavy cream

1 In a small bowl, using an electric mixer on high speed, beat the egg whites until stiff peaks form. Fold in 1 tablespoon of the powdered sugar.

2 Melt the chocolate (see page 13). Remove from the heat and stir in the butter.

3 In the top of a double boiler, blend the egg yolks, the remaining ¾ cup powdered sugar, the raspberry liqueur, and chocolate extract. Using a wire whisk, beat well until the mixture is thick. Place over simmering water and stir constantly for about 5 minutes, or until the mixture is foamy. Remove from the heat. Blend the chocolate mixture into the egg yolk mixture. Beat in the coffee and cool for 5 minutes. Fold the egg whites into the mixture, stirring until completely blended.

4 In a small bowl, using an electric mixer on high speed, whip the cream until soft peaks form. Fold the whipped cream into the chocolate mixture. Spoon the mixture into four to six chilled custard cups or a chilled serving bowl. Chill for 4 hours, or until ready to serve.

BAKING NOTES: Owing to the raw eggs in this recipe, it should be kept refrigerated at all times, and for no longer than 1 week.

653

651

654

655

656 ■ BLACK FOREST PARFAITS

MAKES 4 TO 6 SERVINGS
CHILL TIME: *30 minutes*

3 ounces cream cheese, at room temperature
2 cups minus 2 tablespoons milk
1 package (3.4 ounces) Jell-O Brand chocolate instant pudding mix
1½ tablespoons Kümmel liqueur or Aquavit
½ cup chocolate wafer cookie crumbs
1 can (21 ounces) cherry pie filling
Whipped cream for garnish
Ground hazelnuts for garnish

1 In a small bowl, using an electric mixer on medium speed, beat the cream cheese and ½ cup of the milk until smooth. Beat in the pudding mix and the remaining milk. Add the liqueur and beat for 2 minutes.

2 Spoon half of the mixture evenly into four to six chilled parfait glasses. Sprinkle with chocolate wafer crumbs and cover with the pie filling. Top with the remaining pudding and chill for 30 minutes, or until ready to serve. Garnish with whipped cream and sprinkle with ground hazelnuts.

657 ■ BLENDER CHOCOLATE MOUSSE

MAKES 4 SERVINGS
CHILL TIME: *8 hours*

1 large egg
1 envelope unflavored gelatin
1 tablespoon cornstarch or arrowroot
1 tablespoon cold water
1 cup boiling water
2 tablespoons mocha-flavored instant coffee powder
½ cup ricotta cheese
½ cup skim milk, chilled
2 tablespoons Dutch processed cocoa powder
½ cup granulated sugar
⅛ teaspoon salt

1 In the container of a blender, combine the egg, gelatin, cornstarch, and cold water. Blend for 20 seconds. Add the boiling water and blend for 30 seconds. Add the coffee powder, ricotta cheese, skim milk, cocoa powder, sugar, and salt, and blend for about 1 minute, or until smooth.

2 Pour into four chilled custard cups and chill overnight or until set.

BAKING NOTES: Owing to the raw egg in this recipe, it should be kept refrigerated at all times, and for no longer than 3 days.

658 ■ CHOCOLATE AMARETTO PUDDING CAKE

MAKES 10 TO 12 SERVINGS
CHILL TIME: *1 hour and 30 minutes*

6 ounces semisweet chocolate, grated or finely chopped
½ cup amaretto
2 envelopes unflavored gelatin
½ cup warm water
4 large eggs, separated
⅓ cup granulated sugar
2 cups milk
6 ounces ladyfingers, split in half
2 cups heavy cream
Chocolate Whipped Cream (see page 406) for garnish
Chocolate-Coated Almonds (see page 421) for garnish

1 In a medium saucepan, over low heat, melt the chocolate, stirring until smooth. Stir in the amaretto. Remove from the heat.

2 In another saucepan, combine the gelatin and water. Let stand for 1 minute to soften. Using an electric mixer on medium speed, beat in the egg yolks, sugar, and milk until thickened. Cook over medium-low heat, stirring constantly, until the mixture thickens and coats the back of a spoon. Remove from the heat and stir in the chocolate mixture. Transfer to a large bowl. Cover and chill for 30 minutes, or until thick.

3 Line the bottom of an ungreased 10-inch springform pan with the ladyfingers.

4 In a medium bowl, using an electric mixer on high speed, beat the egg whites until stiff but not dry. Fold the egg whites into the chocolate mixture.

5 In a large bowl, using an electric mixer on high speed, whip the cream until soft peaks form. Fold the whipped cream into the chocolate mixture. Pour over the ladyfingers in the prepared pan. Chill for 1 hour, or until firm.

6 Make the chocolate whipped cream.

7 Remove the side of the springform pan and place the cake on a serving plate. Fill a pastry bag fitted with a large star tip with the chocolate whipped cream. Pipe rosettes around the sides of the cake and press a chocolate-covered almond into the center of each.

659 ■ CHOCOLATE AND CRANBERRY INDULGENCE

MAKES 10 TO 12 SERVINGS
CHILL TIME: *8 hours*

CANDIED CRANBERRIES

1 cup granulated sugar
1 cup water
1½ cups fresh cranberries

CHOCOLATE CUSTARD

1¾ cups heavy cream
4 large egg yolks
¾ cup granulated sugar
12 ounces semisweet chocolate, grated or finely chopped
1 teaspoon chocolate extract
1 cup butter or margarine, at room temperature
1 cup Dutch processed cocoa powder
1 cup chopped pecans
Chocolate Whipped Cream (see page 406)
Edible fresh flowers (see page 22) for garnish

1 Line a 9 by 5-inch loaf pan with waxed or parchment paper.

2 To make the cranberries, place a cake rack on top of a cookie sheet or other shallow pan.

3 In a medium saucepan, over medium heat, combine the sugar and water, stirring until the sugar is dissolved. Bring to a boil and insert a candy thermometer. Boil, without stirring, until 243 degrees. Add the cran-

berries and cook for 3 to 4 minutes, until the berries begin to burst open. Using a slotted spoon, transfer the cranberries to the prepared rack. Discard any remaining syrup.

4 To make the custard, in a small bowl, using an electric mixer on high speed, beat ¾ cup of the heavy cream until soft peaks form.

5 In a saucepan, over medium heat, heat the remaining 1 cup of the cream until bubbles start to form around the sides of the pan. Remove from the heat. Let cool for 5 minutes.

6 In a medium bowl, using an electric mixer on medium speed, beat the egg yolks until thick and light-colored. Pouring it in a thin stream, beat in the hot cream. Return the mixture to the pan and cook over low heat, stirring constantly, for about 6 minutes. The mixture will thicken. Do not allow the mixture to boil. Remove from the heat and immediately add the grated chocolate and stir until smooth. Stir in the chocolate extract.

7 In a large bowl, using an electric mixer on medium speed, beat the butter and cocoa powder until smooth. Gradually beat in the custard, one-fourth at a time. Gradually fold in the whipped cream. Fold in the

cranberries and pecans. Pour the mixture into the prepared pan and spread evenly. Cover and chill for at least 8 hours.

8 Make the chocolate whipped cream.

9 To assemble, unmold the loaf, inverting it onto a serving plate. Remove the waxed paper and smooth the top and sides with a metal spatula dipped in ice-cold water. Spread three-fourths of the chocolate whipped cream evenly over the top and sides of the loaf. Fill a pastry bag fitted with a star tip with the remaining whipped cream and pipe rosettes over the top and around the base. Garnish with edible flowers.

660 ■ CHOCOLATE APPLE PUDDING

MAKES 12 TO 16 SERVINGS
BAKING TIME: *50 minutes*

2 ounces semisweet chocolate, grated or finely chopped
2 cups granulated sugar
1 cup hot water
½ cup crème de cacao
2¼ cups all-purpose flour
2 teaspoons baking powder
1 teaspoon baking soda
1½ teaspoons ground allspice
½ cup butter or margarine, at room temperature
4 cups chopped apples
Chocolate Whipped Cream (see page 406) for serving

1 Position a rack in the center of the oven and preheat the oven to 350 degrees. Lightly grease a 2½-quart casserole dish.

2 In the top of a double boiler over simmering water, melt the chocolate, stirring until smooth. Stir in 1 cup of the sugar, blending until dissolved. Remove from the heat and stir in the hot water and crème de cacao.

3 In a large bowl, combine the remaining 1 cup sugar, the flour, baking powder, baking soda, and allspice. Using a pastry blender or two knives scissor fashion, cut in the butter to make a crumbly mixture. Fold in the apples.

4 To assemble, spread one-third of the apple mixture onto the bottom of the prepared casserole. Pour one-third of the chocolate mixture over the top. Repeat with the remaining apple and chocolate mixtures, ending with the chocolate mixture. Carefully swirl a spoon through the layers until the apple mixture is just moistened.

5 Bake for 45 to 50 minutes, or until thickened.

6 Make the chocolate whipped cream. Serve the pudding warm from the oven topped with the chocolate whipped cream.

BAKING NOTES: Coffee liqueur can be substituted for the crème de cacao.

658

660

656

657

659

661 ■ CHOCOLATE BAVARIAN CREAM I

MAKES 6 TO 8 SERVINGS
CHILL TIME: *5 hours*

1 envelope unflavored gelatin
⅓ cup Dutch processed cocoa powder
3 large eggs, separated
1½ cups milk
6 tablespoons granulated sugar
1 teaspoon chocolate extract
Fresh fruit and sweetened whipped cream for garnish

1 In the top of a double boiler, combine the gelatin and cocoa powder. Whisk in the egg yolks and milk. Set over simmering water and cook over high heat for 4 to 5 minutes, or until thickened and well-blended. Remove from the heat and mix in 2 tablespoons of the sugar and the chocolate extract. Transfer to a large bowl and chill for 1 hour, or until the mixture thickens.

2 Meanwhile, in a large bowl, using an electric mixer on high speed, beat the egg whites until foamy. Gradually sprinkle in the remaining sugar and beat until stiff peaks form. Gently fold the egg whites into the chilled chocolate mixture and pour into a large serving bowl. Chill for at least 4 hours before serving. Garnish with fresh fruit and whipped cream.

BAKING NOTES: Owing to the raw egg whites in this recipe, it should be kept refrigerated at all times, and for no longer than 1 week.

662 ■ CHOCOLATE BAVARIAN CREAM II

MAKES 8 TO 10 SERVINGS
CHILL TIME: *5 hours*

3 large eggs, separated
1½ cups evaporated milk
1 envelope unflavored gelatin
⅓ cup Dutch processed cocoa powder
Pinch of salt
1 teaspoon chocolate extract
1 teaspoon almond extract
¼ cup granulated sugar
Chocolate Syrup II (see page 406) for serving

1 Lightly grease or oil a 7-inch metal mold.

2 In the top of a double boiler, using a wire whisk, beat the egg yolks until thick and light-colored. Beat in the milk. Add the gelatin, cocoa powder, and salt. Set over boiling water and cook, stirring frequently, for 3 to 5 minutes, until the gelatin is dissolved and the mixture is smooth. Remove from the heat and stir in the chocolate and almond extracts. Chill for 1 hour, or until thickened.

3 Meanwhile, in a large bowl, using an electric mixer on high speed, beat the egg whites until foamy. Gradually sprinkle in the sugar and beat until stiff peaks form. Gently fold the egg whites into the chilled mixture and pour into the prepared mold. Chill for 3 to 4 hours, or until set.

4 To unmold, immerse the mold just up to the lip in a larger pan of hot water for 3 seconds. Repeat as needed. Invert onto a serving plate. Serve with chocolate syrup.

BAKING NOTES: Owing to the raw egg whites in this recipe, it should be kept refrigerated at all times, and for no longer than 1 week.

662

664

661

663

665

663 ■ CHOCOLATE BREAD PUDDING I

MAKES 6 SERVINGS
BAKING TIME: *40 minutes*

BREAD PUDDING

2 cups stale, coarse bread crumbs
4 cups milk
1/2 teaspoon ground nutmeg
1/3 cup Dutch processed cocoa
  powder
2 large eggs
2/3 cup granulated sugar
1/2 teaspoon salt

CREAM TOPPING

1/2 cup heavy cream
1/3 cup milk
1 large egg, separated
1/3 cup powdered sugar
1/2 teaspoon chocolate extract

1 Position a rack in the center of the oven and preheat the oven to 250 degrees. Lightly grease an 8-inch square pan or a 6-inch round pudding dish.

2 To make the bread pudding, in a large bowl, combine the bread crumbs, milk, nutmeg, and cocoa powder. Soak for 2 to 3 minutes.

3 Meanwhile, in a small bowl, using an electric mixer on medium speed, beat the eggs, sugar, and salt. Beat in the bread crumb mixture, 1/2 cup at a time, beating well after each addition. Pour the mixture into the prepared pan. Place the pan in a roasting pan and set on the oven rack. Pour hot water into the roasting pan until it comes halfway up the sides of the pan with the pudding.

4 Bake for 35 to 40 minutes, or until set.

5 Meanwhile, to make the topping, in a medium bowl, using an electric mixer on high speed, beat the cream until soft peaks form.

6 In a medium bowl, beat the egg white until stiff but not dry. Beat in the yolk, milk, powdered sugar, and chocolate extract. Fold this mixture into the whipped cream. Serve the bread pudding hot with the topping on the side.

BAKING NOTES: Owing to the raw egg in this topping, it should be kept refrigerated at all times, and for no longer than 3 days.

664 ■ CHOCOLATE BREAD PUDDING II

MAKES 6 SERVINGS
BAKING TIME: *40 minutes*

2 ounces unsweetened chocolate, grated or finely chopped
3 cups milk
2 large eggs, separated
1/2 cup firmly packed brown sugar
1 1/2 teaspoons chocolate extract
3/4 cup plain croutons
1/4 cup granulated sugar
Chocolate Syrup III (see page 406)
  or chocolate sprinkles for
  garnish

1 Position a rack in the center of the oven and preheat the oven to 350 degrees. Lightly grease a 1 1/2-quart casserole dish.

2 In the top of a double boiler over simmering water, melt the chocolate, stirring until smooth. Stir in the milk, blend well, and remove from the heat.

3 In a large bowl, using an electric mixer on medium speed, beat the egg yolks until thick and light-colored. Beat in the brown sugar. Pouring it in a thin stream, beat in the chocolate mixture. Stir in the chocolate extract. Add the croutons and let stand, without stirring, for 10 minutes. Pour into the prepared casserole. Set the casserole in a roasting pan and place on the oven rack. Pour hot water into the roasting pan until it comes halfway up the sides of the casserole.

4 Bake for 25 to 30 minutes, or just until firm. Remove from the oven.

5 Meanwhile, in a medium bowl, using an electric mixer on high speed, beat the egg whites until foamy. Add the granulated sugar and continue beating until stiff peaks form. Spread over the top of the hot pudding and return to the oven for 8 to 10 minutes longer, or until the tips of the meringue turn golden.

Cool in the pan on a wire rack. Drizzle chocolate syrup over the top, or sprinkle with chocolate sprinkles.

665 ■ CHOCOLATE BROWN BETTY

MAKES 6 TO 8 SERVINGS
BAKING TIME: *1 hour*

1/3 cup butter or margarine, melted
2 cups whole-wheat bread crumbs
1/4 teaspoon ground cinnamon
1/4 teaspoon ground nutmeg
1/2 cup granulated sugar
2 cups cored, peeled, and diced
  apples
1/2 cup Chocolate Syrup I (see page
  406)
1 tablespoon water
Juice of 1 lemon
Grated zest of 1 lemon
Chocolate Whipped Cream (see
  page 406) for serving

1 Position a rack in the center of the oven and preheat the oven to 350 degrees. Lightly grease a 9-inch square pan.

2 In a medium bowl, using an electric mixer on low speed, drizzle the melted butter over the bread crumbs while beating. Stir in the spices and sugar. Press one-third of the crumb mixture onto the bottom of the prepared pan. Spread half of the diced apples evenly over the top of the crumbs. Sprinkle half of the remaining crumbs over the apples. Spread the remaining apples over the crumbs and top with the remaining crumbs.

3 Combine the chocolate syrup, water, lemon juice, and zest. Spoon evenly over the top of the mixture in the pan, making sure all portions have been covered.

4 Cover with aluminum foil and bake for 30 minutes. Remove the foil and bake for an additional 30 minutes, or until crust forms on top. Cool in the pan for 15 minutes. Serve with chocolate whipped cream on the side.

BAKING NOTES: Almost any fruit or combination of fruits can be used in place of the apples.

666 ■ CHOCOLATE CHOCOLATE MOUSSE

MAKES 8 TO 10 SERVINGS
FREEZING TIME: *4 hours*

3 ounces unsweetened chocolate, grated or finely chopped
1/3 cup crème de cacao
3/4 cup granulated sugar
Pinch of salt
3 large egg yolks
2 cups heavy cream
1 teaspoon chocolate extract
Fresh mint sprigs for garnish
Sliced orange or peeled, sliced kiwifruit for garnish

1 In the top of a double boiler over simmering water, melt the chocolate, stirring until smooth. Stir in the crème de cacao. Add the sugar and salt and continue to cook, stirring constantly, until the sugar is dissolved and the mixture is smooth. Remove from the heat.

2 Meanwhile, in a large bowl, using an electric mixer on medium speed, beat the egg yolks until thick and light-colored. Pouring it in a thin stream, beat in the chocolate mixture until well blended. Set aside to cool to room temperature.

3 Meanwhile, in a large bowl, using an electric mixer on high speed, whip the cream and chocolate extract until soft peaks form. Fold into the chocolate mixture and pour into a serving bowl. Cover and freeze for 3 to 4 hours or until ready to serve. Remove from the freezer 30 minutes before serving. Garnish with fresh mint and slices of oranges or kiwifruits.

BAKING NOTES: Owing to the raw egg in this recipe, it should be kept refrigerated at all times, and for no longer than 3 days.

667 ■ CHOCOLATE COFFEE CHARLOTTE

MAKES 6 TO 8 SERVINGS
CHILL TIME: *6½ hours*

36 ladyfingers, split
6 ounces semisweet chocolate, grated or finely chopped
2 cups milk
2 teaspoons unflavored gelatin
1/4 cup water
5 large egg yolks
1/4 cup granulated sugar
1 teaspoon chocolate or vanilla extract
3 tablespoon coffee liqueur
1/2 cup heavy cream
Cocoa Sugar (see page 407) for dusting
Chocolate Whipped Cream (see page 406) for garnish
Fresh mint leaves for garnish

1 Line the bottom and sides of a straight-sided 1½- to 2-quart mold with waxed paper. Lightly butter the paper. (Do not use oil or a non-stick spray.)

2 Line the bottom and sides of the mold with ladyfingers, trimming them to fit as needed. The ladyfingers should be fitted as tightly as possible. The tips of the ladyfingers may extend above the mold. Trim if desired or leave the rounded ends. Chill until ready to fill.

3 Melt the chocolate (see page 13). Remove from the heat.

4 In a large saucepan, over medium-low heat, heat the milk until bubbles start to form around the sides of the pan. Remove the from heat.

5 In a small saucepan, sprinkle the gelatin over the water and let stand for 1 minute to soften. Over low heat, stir until the gelatin is completely dissolved. Remove from the heat.

6 In a large mixing bowl, using an electric mixer on medium speed, beat the egg yolks until thick and light-colored. Beat in the sugar. Beating constantly, beat in half of the hot milk. Pour the mixture back into the remaining milk in the saucepan and beat on high speed for 1 to 2 minutes. Return to the heat and cook, stirring constantly, until

the mixture thickens enough to coat the back of a spoon. (Do not allow the mixture to boil.) Strain into a large bowl. Beat in the gelatin and add the chocolate extract. Pouring it in a thin stream, beat in the melted chocolate. Stir in the coffee liqueur. Cover and chill for 30 minutes.

7 Meanwhile, in a medium bowl, using an electric mixer on high speed, beat the cream until soft peaks form. Fold the whipped cream into the chilled chocolate custard mixture. Immediately pour into the pre-pared mold. Cover and chill for 4 to 6 hours.

8 When ready to serve, unmold onto a serving plate. Remove the waxed paper and sift a light coating of cocoa sugar over the top. Fill a pastry bag fitted with a large star tip with the chocolate whipped cream and pipe rosettes around the base of the charlotte. Place a mint leaf on each rosette.

667

666

668 ■ CHOCOLATE CREAM PUDDING

MAKES 6 TO 8 SERVINGS
CHILL TIME: *4 hours*

1¹/₃ cups chocolate graham cracker
   crumbs
¹/₂ cup plus 2 tablespoons packed
   light brown sugar
3 ounces semisweet chocolate,
   grated or finely chopped
1 tablespoon Dutch processed
   cocoa powder
1 teaspoon instant espresso powder
2 cups heavy cream
Chocolate Whipped Cream (see
   page 406) for garnish
Chocolate Curls (see page 422) for
   garnish

1 In a medium bowl, combine
the graham cracker crumbs,
brown sugar, grated chocolate,
cocoa powder, and espresso
powder.

2 In a large bowl, using an electric mixer on high speed, whip
the cream until slightly
thickened.

3 To assemble, pour one-fourth
of the cream into a serving
bowl. Top with one-third of the
crumb mixture. Repeat with the
remaining cream and crumb
mixture. Cover and chill for 4
hours.

4 When ready to serve, serve
with chocolate whipped cream
and chocolate curls on the side.

669 ■ CHOCOLATE CUSTARD I

MAKES 6 SERVINGS
BAKING TIME: *45 minutes*

2 ounces semisweet chocolate,
   grated or finely chopped
1 ounce white chocolate, grated or
   finely chopped
1 cup evaporated milk
¹/₄ cup water
¹/₄ cup crème de cacao
2 tablespoons molasses
Pinch of salt
2 large eggs
Chocolate-Covered Cherries II (see
   page 172) or Chocolate-Covered
   Strawberries (see page 172) for
   garnish

1 Position a rack in the center of
the oven and preheat the oven
to 350 degrees. Lightly grease 6
4-ounce custard cups.

2 In a medium saucepan, over
low heat, melt the chocolates
with the evaporated milk, stirring until smooth. Remove from
the heat. Using an electric mixer
on medium speed, beat in all of
the remaining ingredients
except the garnish, at one time,
beating until the mixture is
smooth and slightly thickened.
Divide the mixture evenly
between the prepared custard
cups and place the cups in a
roasting pan. Place on the oven
rack and pour boiling water into
the roasting pan until it comes
halfway up the sides of the
cups.

3 Bake for 40 to 45 minutes, or
until a cake tester inserted into
the center comes out clean.
Remove the cups from the hot
water and cool on a wire rack.
Serve warm, garnished with
chocolate-covered cherries or
strawberries.

670 ■ CHOCOLATE CUSTARD II

MAKES 8 SERVINGS
BAKING TIME: *90 minutes*
CHILL TIME: *80 minutes*

3 ounces unsweetened chocolate,
   grated or finely chopped
3 ounces semisweet chocolate,
   grated or finely chopped
2 tablespoons butter or margarine
6 large eggs
¹/₂ cup granulated sugar
3¹/₃ cups milk
2 teaspoons chocolate or vanilla
   extract

1 Position a rack in the center of
the oven and preheat the oven
to 350 degrees.

2 Combine the chocolates and
butter in a 1¹/₂-quart casserole
dish and heat in the oven for 3
to 5 minutes. Remove from the
oven and stir until blended.
Chill for 20 minutes, or until the
mixture is just starting to set.
Using a spatula, spread evenly
over the bottom and sides of the
casserole. Chill for 30 minutes.

3 Meanwhile, in a large bowl,
using an electric mixer on
medium speed, beat the eggs
until thick and light-colored.
Add the sugar, milk, and chocolate extract and beat until the
sugar is completely dissolved.
Pour the mixture into the chilled
casserole. Place the casserole in
a roasting pan on the oven rack.
Pour boiling water into the pan
until it comes halfway up the
sides of the casserole.

4 Bake for 80 to 90 minutes, or
until a cake tester inserted into
the center comes out clean.
Remove from the hot water and
chill 30 mintes, or until ready to
serve.

669

670

668

671 ■ CHOCOLATE DATE CUPS

MAKES 6 SERVINGS
BAKING TIME: *45 minutes*

1 package (3.4-ounces) Jell-O Brand
   chocolate instant pudding mix
2 cups plus 3 tablespoons milk
2 large eggs
1/4 cup granulated sugar
1/2 cup dates, pitted and chopped
1/2 cup pecans, chopped
1 teaspoon almond extract
1/2 cup flaked coconut
Whipped cream for garnish

1 Position a rack in the center of the oven and preheat the oven to 325 degrees. Lightly grease 6 4-ounce custard cups or ramekins.

2 In a small bowl, combine the pudding mix and 3 tablespoons of the milk.

3 In a large bowl, using an electric mixer on medium speed, beat the eggs until thick and light-colored. Beat in the sugar, dates, and pecans. Blend in the pudding mixture, almond extract, and the remaining 2 cups milk. Divide the butter evenly between the prepared custard cups and place them in a roasting pan. Place on the oven rack and pour boiling water into the roasting pan until it comes halfway up the sides of the custard cups.

4 Bake for 40 to 45 minutes, or until firm around the edges. Remove the cups from the hot water and sprinkle the coconut over the tops. Cool and serve with whipped cream on top.

672 ■ CHOCOLATE DREAM PUDDING

MAKES 6 TO 8 SERVINGS
CHILL TIME: *30 minutes*

4 ounces unsweetened chocolate,
   grated or finely chopped
4 large eggs, separated
1/2 cup granulated sugar
1/2 cup heavy cream
2 tablespoons crème de cacao
1/4 cup coffee liqueur
Whipped cream for serving

1 Melt the chocolate (see page 13). Remove from the heat. Cool to room temperature.

2 In the top of a double boiler over simmering water, using an electric mixer on medium speed, beat the egg yolks and 1/4 cup of the sugar until smooth and light-colored. On low speed, mix in the melted chocolate. Using a wooden spoon, stir in the cream until the mixture is smooth. Cook, stirring constantly, until the mixture thickens. Remove from the heat and stir in the crème de cacao and liqueur.

3 In a medium bowl, using an electric mixer with clean beaters on high speed, beat the egg whites until they hold their shape. Continue beating on low speed and blend in the remaining 1/4 cup sugar. Fold into the chocolate mixture. Chill 30 minutes, or until set.

4 Spoon the mixture into six to eight chilled custard cups or parfait glasses. Served with whipped cream on the side.

BAKING NOTES: Due to the raw eggs in this recipe, keep refrigerated at all times and no more than 3 days.

673 ■ CHOCOLATE ESPRESSO MOUSSE

MAKES 8 TO 10 SERVINGS
CHILL TIME: *30 minutes*

CHOCOLATE HAZELNUT CRUMBS

1 1/2 cups chocolate wafer cookie
   crumbs
2/3 cup chopped hazelnuts

MOUSSE

2 envelopes unflavored gelatin
1/2 cup granulated sugar
1/4 cup instant espresso powder
2 3/4 cups heavy cream
6 ounces semisweet chocolate,
   grated or finely chopped
6 ounces unsweetened chocolate,
   grated or finely chopped

TOPPING

1 1/2 cups heavy cream
1/4 cup granulated sugar
Chopped hazelnuts for garnish

1 To make the crumbs, combine the cookie crumbs and hazelnuts.

2 To make the mousse, in a medium saucepan, combine the gelatin, 1/2 cup of the sugar, the espresso powder, and 2 3/4 cups of the cream and stir until the sugar is dissolved. Place the pan over low heat and cook, stirring constantly, for about 5 minutes, or until the gelatin is dissolved. Add the chocolates and stir constantly until the chocolate is melted and the mixture is smooth. Remove from the heat. Beat until slightly thickened. Pour into a large bowl. Place into a larger bowl of ice and water and stir until the mixture is cool.

3 To prepare the topping, in another large bowl, using an electric mixer on high speed, beat the 1 1/2 cups cream and 1/4 cup sugar until soft peaks form. Reserve 1/2 cup. Fold into the cool chocolate mixture.

4 To assemble, sprinkle a thin layer of the crumbs onto the bottom of eight to ten custard or dessert cups. Spoon a layer of the mousse over the crumbs. Top with another layer of crumbs and another layer of mousse, continuing in alternating layers until all of the custard and crumbs are used. Chill 30 minutes, or until ready to serve. Garnish with a dab of the reserved whipped cream and a few chopped nuts.

BAKING NOTES: For an especially festive garnish, insert a chocolate mint into the dab of cream or sprinkle with crushed butterscotch candy.

674 ■ CHOCOLATE LIQUEUR CREAM

MAKES 8 TO 10 SERVINGS
CHILL TIME: *2 hours*

4 ounces semisweet chocolate,
   grated or finely chopped
4 large eggs, separated
1/2 cup granulated sugar
1/2 cup heavy cream
4 tablespoons crème de cacao
Whipped cream for garnish

1 In the top of a double boiler over simmering water, melt the chocolate, stirring until smooth. Remove from the heat.

2 In a large bowl, using an electric mixer on medium speed, beat the egg yolks until thick and light-colored. Beat in 1/4 cup of the sugar. Beat in the melted chocolate, blending until no streaks appear. Beat in the cream. Return the mixture to the double boiler and cook over low heat until the mixture has thickened slightly. Remove from the heat.

3 In a medium bowl, using an electric mixer on high speed, beat the egg whites until stiff but not dry. Beat in the remaining 1/4 cup sugar. Fold into the chocolate mixture and fold in the crème de cacao. Cover and chill for at least 2 hours.

4 To serve, spoon into eight to ten dessert cups and garnish with whipped cream.

675 ■ CHOCOLATE MOCHA MOUSSE

MAKES 8 TO 10 SERVINGS
CHILL TIME: *24 hours*

Chocolate Cookie Crumb Crust (see page 276)
1/3 cup amaretto
1 tablespoon unflavored gelatin
4 large egg yolks
1/2 cup granulated sugar
3/4 cup coffee liqueur
8 ounces unsweetened chocolate, grated or finely chopped

4 ounces semisweet chocolate, grated or finely chopped
1 tablespoon instant espresso powder
1/4 cup butter or margarine, at room temperature
1 cup heavy cream
Fresh mint sprigs for garnish
Chocolate Leaves (see page 422) for garnish

1 Make the crust. Press half of the mixture onto the bottom of an 8 or 9-inch springform pan. Cover the remaining crust mixture and set aside at room temperature.

2 In a cup, combine the amaretto and gelatin. Let stand 1 minute to soften.

3 In the top of a double boiler, using a wire whisk, beat the egg yolks and sugar until blended. Stir in the coffee liqueur. Set over simmering water and beat until the mixture starts to thicken. Remove from the heat and stir in the softened gelatin. Set the top of the double boiler in a large bowl of ice and water and beat for about 5 minutes, or until the mixture is room temperature. Remove from the bowl of ice water.

4 In the top of a double boiler over simmering water, melt the chocolates, stirring until smooth. Add the espresso powder and stir until dissolved and smooth. Transfer to a large bowl. Using an electric mixer on medium speed, beat in the butter, a little at a time, blending thoroughly after each addition.

Add the egg yolk mixture and beat until thickened and cooled to room temperature. Set the bowl in the bowl of ice and water and continue beating until the mixture is completely cool.

5 In a medium bowl, using an electric mixer on high speed, whip the cream until soft peaks form. Fold the whipped cream into the cooled chocolate mixture. Pour into the prepared pan and spread evenly. Cover and chill for 24 hours.

6 To serve, remove the side of the springform pan and place the mousse on a serving plate. Sprinkle the reserved crust mixture over the top and press it against the sides of the mousse. Garnish with chocolate leaves and mint sprigs

676 ■ CHOCOLATE MOCHA SOUFFLÉ

MAKES 8 TO 10 SERVINGS
BAKING TIME: *40 minutes*

3 ounces unsweetened chocolate, grated or finely chopped
4 large eggs, separated, plus 1 large egg white
3 tablespoons butter
2 tablespoons all-purpose flour
1 cup milk
1/2 cup granulated sugar
1 tablespoon coffee liqueur
1 teaspoon crème de cacao
Pinch of salt
Whipped cream for garnish

1 Position a rack in the center of the oven and preheat the oven to 350 degrees. Lightly grease and dust with sugar a 1½-quart soufflé dish. Wrap a strip of aluminum foil or parchment paper around the top of the dish so that it extends 2 inches above the rim and tie securely with string.

2 Melt the chocolate (see page 13). Remove from the heat.

3 In a small bowl, using an electric mixer on medium speed, beat the egg yolks until thick and light-colored.

4 In a medium bowl, using an electric mixer with clean beaters on high speed, beat the egg whites until stiff but not dry.

5 In a large saucepan, over medium heat, melt the butter. Stir in the flour to make a roux. Stir in the milk. Cook, stirring constantly, until the mixture is thickened and smooth. Add the sugar and melted chocolate. Mix in the beaten egg yolks and cook, stirring constantly, for 2 to 3 minutes. Remove from the heat and stir in the liqueurs and salt. Fold in the beaten egg whites. Do not overmix. Pour into the prepared baking dish and set the dish in a roasting pan. Set on the oven rack and pour hot water into the roasting pan until it comes halfway up the side of the soufflé dish.

6 Bake for 35 to 40 minutes, or until firm. Remove the foil strip and serve immediately with whipped cream on the side.

BAKING NOTES: For a decorative garnish, just before serving, place an overlapping ring of peeled, thinly sliced kiwifruit, thinly sliced strawberries, or both, on the top of the soufflé.

677 ■ CHOCOLATE MOUSSE

MAKES 8 TO 10 SERVINGS
CHILL TIME: *2 hours*

6 ounces semisweet chocolate, grated or finely chopped
5 tablespoons boiling water
4 large eggs, separated
2 tablespoons Grand Marnier
Pinch of cream of tartar
Chocolate wafer cookie crumbs for garnish

1 Place the chocolate in a blender and process on high speed for 2 to 3 seconds, or until pulverized. Add the boiling water and process on high speed for 2 to 3 seconds to melt the chocolate. Scrape down the sides and bottom of the container. Add the egg yolks and Grand Marnier and process on high speed for 3 to 4 seconds, or until smooth. Pour into a large mixing bowl.

2 In a medium mixing bowl, using an electric mixer on high speed, beat the egg whites until foamy. Add the cream of tartar and continue beating until stiff peaks form. Fold the egg whites into the chocolate mixture.

Spoon into eight to ten individual serving dishes and chill for 2 hours. Sprinkle chocolate cookie crumbs over the top.

BAKING NOTES: Owing to the raw eggs used in this recipe, it should be kept refrigerated at all times, and for no longer than 3 days.

678 ■ CHOCOLATE MOUSSE AU GRAND MARNIER

MAKES 8 TO 10 SERVINGS
CHILL TIME: *4 hours*

2 ounces semisweet chocolate, grated or finely chopped
2 ounces unsweetened chocolate, grated or finely chopped
¼ cup honey
1½ teaspoons instant espresso powder
1½ tablespoons Grand Marnier
1 cup heavy cream

1 In the top of a double boiler over simmering water, melt the chocolates, stirring constantly until smooth. Stir in the honey. Dissolve the espresso powder in the Grand Marnier and stir into the chocolate mixture. Remove from the heat.

2 Add the cream to the chocolate mixture. Using an electric mixer on high speed, beat until

soft peaks form. Immediately pour into a 1-quart serving bowl. Cover and chill for at least 4 hours, or until ready to serve.

BAKING NOTES: This can be made ahead and frozen. Any good liqueur can be used in place of the Grand Marnier. Keep in mind that most of the flavor of this mousse comes from the liqueur, so be sure to use a good one.

679 ■ CHOCOLATE MOUSSE À L' ORANGE

MAKES 8 TO 10 SERVINGS
CHILL TIME: *10 hours*

8 ounces semisweet chocolate, grated or finely chopped
3 tablespoons marshmallow creme
2 tablespoons thawed frozen orange juice concentrate
4 large eggs, separated
1/2 teaspoon cream of tartar
Whipped cream for garnish
Grated orange zest for garnish

1 In the top of a double boiler over simmering water, melt the chocolate, stirring constantly until smooth. Add the marshmallow creme and orange juice concentrate, stirring until blended and smooth. Remove from the heat.

2 In a large bowl, using an electric mixer on high speed, beat the egg whites until foamy. Add the cream of tartar and continue beating until stiff peaks form.

3 In a small bowl, using an electric mixer on high speed, beat the egg yolks until thick and light-colored. Beat in the chocolate mixture. Gently fold into the egg whites, blending thoroughly. Spoon the mixture into eight to ten custard cups or ramekins and chill for 8 to 10 hours before serving. Just before serving top with whipped cream and sprinkle with grated orange zest.

BAKING NOTES: The mousse can also be chilled in a 9 or 10-inch serving bowl. Owing to the raw eggs in this recipe, it should be kept refrigerated at all times, and for no longer than 3 days.

680 ■ CHOCOLATE NUT PUDDING

MAKES 6 TO 8 SERVINGS
BAKING TIME: *30 minutes*

2 ounces unsweetened chocolate, grated or finely chopped
6 large eggs
1 cup granulated sugar
1 cup almonds, finely ground
Pinch of salt
1 teaspoon cherry liqueur
Chocolate or Neapolitan ice cream for serving

1 Position a rack in the center of the oven and preheat the oven to 250 degrees. Lightly grease a 1½-quart casserole dish.

2 Melt the chocolate (see page 13). Remove from the heat.

3 In a large bowl, using an electric mixer on medium speed, beat the eggs until thick and light-colored. On low speed, beat in the sugar, a tablespoonful at a time. Beat in the melted chocolate, almonds, and salt. Fold in the liqueur. Pour the mixture into the prepared casserole.

4 Bake for 20 to 30 minutes, or until firm. Cool slightly. Serve hot over a scoop of chocolate or Neapolitan ice cream.

BAKING NOTES: For a stronger almond flavor, use amaretto in place of the cherry liqueur.

681 ■ CHOCOLATE NUT SOUFFLÉ

MAKES 6 TO 8 SERVINGS
BAKING TIME: *40 minutes*

3 ounces unsweetened chocolate, grated or finely chopped
2/3 cup heavy cream or milk
3 tablespoons butter, at room temperature
3 tablespoons all-purpose flour
1/4 cup granulated sugar
3 large eggs, separated, plus 1 large egg white
3 tablespoons amaretto
3/4 teaspoons almond extract
Pinch of salt
1/2 cup chopped hazelnuts
1/2 cup chopped pecans
Chopped nuts for garnish
Fresh mint sprigs for garnish

Grand Marnier Sauce (see page 411) for serving

1 Position a rack in the center of the oven and preheat the oven to 350 degrees. Lightly grease and dust with sugar a 1-quart soufflé dish. Wrap a strip of aluminum foil or parchment paper around the top of the dish so that it extends 2 inches above the rim and tie securely with string.

2 Melt the chocolate (see page 13). Remove from the heat.

3 In a small saucepan, over medium heat, warm the cream until bubbles start to form around the sides of the pan. Remove from the heat.

4 In a medium saucepan, over medium heat, combine the butter and flour and stir constantly to make a roux. Remove from the heat and stir in the hot cream. Return to the heat and cook for 2 minutes. Remove from the heat and stir in the sugar and melted chocolate.

5 In a medium bowl, using an electric mixer on medium speed, beat the egg yolks until thick and light-colored. Beat in the amaretto and almond extract. Fold in the chocolate mixture just until blended.

6 In a large bowl, using an electric mixer with clean beaters on high speed, beat the egg whites and salt until stiff but not dry. Fold about 1 cup of the egg whites into the chocolate mixture, stirring until white streaks no longer appear. Then fold the chocolate mixture back into the egg whites until blended. Fold in the chopped nuts. Pour into the prepared dish. Place the casserole into a roasting pan and set on the oven rack. Pour boiling water into the roasting pan to a depth of 2 inches.

7 Bake for 35 to 40 minutes, or until firm. Remove from the hot water and cool on a wire rack for 10 minutes. Carefully remove the foil strip and garnish with a sprig of mint and chopped nuts. Serve warm with Grand Marnier sauce on the side.

682 ▪ CHOCOLATE OMELET SOUFFLÉ WITH RASPBERRIES

MAKES 4 TO 6 SERVINGS
BAKING TIME: *15 minutes*

1½ cups raspberries
2 tablespoons powdered sugar
2 tablespoons butter or margarine, at room temperature
4 large eggs, separated
¼ cup granulated sugar
¼ cup Dutch processed cocoa powder
2 tablespoon Triple Sec
Crushed raspberries for garnish

1 Position a rack in the center of the oven and preheat the oven to 375 degrees. Lightly grease a 1½-quart ovenproof soufflé dish.

2 In a small bowl, place the raspberries and crush with the back of a spoon until a paste forms. Combine the crushed raspberries and powdered sugar. Spoon over the bottom of the prepared dish.

3 In a medium bowl, using an electric mixer on medium speed, beat the butter and egg yolks until thick and light-colored.

4 In a medium bowl, using an electric mixer with clean beaters on high speed, beat the egg whites until foamy. Add the granulated sugar, a little at a time, and continue beating until stiff but not dry. Fold in the cocoa powder, a little at a time. Gently fold in the beaten egg yolks. Fold in the Triple Sec. Spread the egg mixture evenly over the top of the raspberries.

5 Bake for 12 to 15 minutes, or until the soufflé is puffy and set. Remove from the oven. Serve with crushed raspberries on the side.

683 ▪ CHOCOLATE PARFAIT I

MAKES 8 SERVINGS
CHILL TIME: *3 hours*

⅔ cup granulated sugar
¼ cup Dutch processed cocoa powder
2 tablespoons cornstarch
2 cups skim milk
1 tablespoon butter-flavored vegetable shortening
1 teaspoon chocolate extract
1 tablespoon grated orange zest
½ cup heavy cream
1 teaspoon crème de cacao
1 orange, sliced paper-thin

1 In a medium saucepan, over medium heat, combine the sugar, cocoa powder, and cornstarch. Stir in the milk. Cook, stirring constantly, until the mixture starts to boil. Remove from the heat. Fold in the shortening and chocolate extract until blended and smooth. Fold in the zest. Pour into a medium bowl and cover with waxed paper or plastic wrap, pressing onto the surface of the mixture. Chill for 3 hours.

2 In a medium bowl, using an electric mixer on high speed, whip the cream until soft peaks form. Fold in the crème de cacao. Fold half of the whipped cream mixture into the chilled pudding.

3 Spoon the pudding, alternating with the remaining whipped cream, into eight chilled parfait glasses. Chill until ready to serve. Garnish with the orange slices.

684 ▪ CHOCOLATE PARFAIT II

MAKES 6 SERVINGS
FREEZING TIME: 1 HOUR

3 ounces unsweetened chocolate, grated or finely chopped
1 cup heavy cream
½ cup butter or margarine, at room temperature
2½ cups powdered sugar
1½ teaspoons chocolate or vanilla extract
2 large eggs
Sliced fresh strawberries for garnish

1 Melt the chocolate (see page 13). Remove from the heat.

2 In a medium bowl, using an electric mixer on high speed, whip the cream until soft peaks form.

682

684

687

683

685

686

3 In a large bowl, using an electric mixer on medium speed, combine the butter, powdered sugar, melted chocolate, and chocolate extract until blended. Beat in the eggs, one at a time, beating well after each addition. Fold in the whipped cream.

4 Divide the mixture between six chilled parfait glasses. Freeze for 1 hour, or until ready to serve. Garnish with sliced strawberries.

BAKING NOTES: Owing to the raw eggs in this recipe, it should be kept refrigerated at all times, and for no longer than 3 days.

685 ▪ CHOCOLATE-PEANUT BUTTER MOUSSE TERRINE

MAKES 8 SERVINGS
FREEZING TIME: *7 hours*

PEANUT BUTTER LAYER

3/4 cup creamy peanut butter
6 ounces cream cheese, softened
2 cups powdered sugar
3 tablespoons heavy cream
2 large egg whites

CHOCOLATE LAYER

3 large egg yolks
8 ounces semisweet chocolate, grated or finely chopped
1 1/2 teaspoons instant espresso powder
2 1/2 tablespoons boiling water

GANACHE TOPPING

2/3 cup heavy cream
5 tablespoons butter or margarine
5 ounces semisweet chocolate, grated or finely chopped

1 Line a 9 by 5-inch loaf pan with plastic wrap.

2 To make the peanut butter layer, in a medium bowl, using an electric mixer on medium speed, beat the peanut butter and cream cheese until smooth. Beat in the powdered sugar and cream.

3 In a small bowl, using an electric mixer on medium speed, beat the egg whites until foamy. Fold into the peanut butter mixture. Pour into the prepared pan and freeze for 1 hour.

4 To make the chocolate layer, in a small bowl, using a wire whisk, beat the egg yolks until blended.

5 In a saucepan over low heat, melt the chocolate, stirring until smooth. Stir in the coffee and boiling water. Add the beaten egg yolks and stir until well blended. Cook until the mixture reaches a boil, lower the heat, and simmer for 2 minutes. Gradually spoon this mixture over the chilled peanut butter layer and freeze for 4 to 6 hours, or until firm.

6 To make the topping, in a small saucepan, over low heat, heat the cream and butter, stirring until the butter is melted. Remove from the heat and add the chocolate. Whisk until smooth. Let stand at room temperature for about 1 hour, or until cool.

7 Invert the loaf pan onto a cake rack and remove the pan and plastic wrap. Pour the topping over the terrine and smooth it along the sides. Transfer to a serving plate.

686 ▪ CHOCOLATE PUDDING

MAKES 8 TO 10 SERVINGS
CHILL TIME: *30 minutes*

16 ounces bittersweet chocolate, grated or finely chopped
1/3 cup chopped pecans
2 tablespoons crème de cacao
4 cups heavy cream
Finely chopped pecans or chocolate sprinkles for garnish

1 In the top of a double boiler over simmering water, melt the chocolate, stirring constantly until smooth. Stir in the pecans and crème de cacao. Remove from the heat.

2 In large bowl, using an electric mixer on high speed, whip the cream until stiff peaks form.

3 Gradually fold the chocolate mixture into the cream. Divide the mixture evenly between eight to ten parfait or dessert dishes. Chill for 30 minutes, or until firm. Before serving, gar-

nish with finely chopped pecans or chocolate sprinkles.

687 ▪ CHOCOLATE PUDDING CAKE

MAKES 8 TO 10 SERVINGS
BAKING TIME: *1 hour*
CHILL TIME: *12 hours*
STANDING TIME: *4 hours*

CRÈME FRÂICHE TOPPING

3 1/2 cups heavy cream
1/4 cup sour cream or buttermilk

CHOCOLATE PUDDING

1 cup all-purpose flour
1 1/4 cups granulated sugar
5 tablespoons Dutch processed cocoa powder
1/2 cup pecans, chopped
2 teaspoons baking powder
1/8 teaspoon salt
1/2 cup milk
2 tablespoons butter or margarine, at room temperature
1 teaspoon chocolate extract or crème de cacao
1/2 cup packed light brown sugar
1 cup water

1 To make the topping, in the container of a blender, combine the cream and sour cream. Blend on high speed for 20 to 30 seconds. Cover and let stand at room temperature for 4 hours. Chill for 10 to 12 hours, shaking the container periodically.

2 Preheat the oven to 325 degrees. Lightly grease an 8-inch springform pan.

3 To make the pudding, combine the flour, 3/4 of the granulated cup sugar, 3 tablespoons of the cocoa powder, the nuts, baking powder, and salt.

4 In a small saucepan, over low heat, warm the milk until bubbles form around the edges. Remove from the heat.

5 In large bowl, using an electric mixer on medium speed, beat the hot milk, butter, and chocolate extract until blended. Gradually blend in the dry ingredients and beat well. Pour the mixture into the prepared pan.

6 In a medium bowl, combine the remaining 1/2 cup granulated sugar, 2 tablespoons cocoa powder, and the brown sugar. Sprinkle this over the top of the batter in the pan. Add the water by slowly pouring it over a spoon held over the top of the batter.

7 Bake for 55 minutes to 1 hour, or until firm. Cool in the pan on a wire rack. Remove the side of the springform pan and transfer the pudding cake to a serving plate, removing it from the chocolate liquid.

8 In a medium bowl, using an electric mixer on high speed, whip the topping until soft peaks form. Spread over the top and sides of the pudding cake. Chill until ready to serve.

688 ■ CHOCOLATE PUMPKIN PUDDING

Makes 4 servings
Chill time: *30 minutes*
Steaming time: *3 hours*

1/2 **cup dried cherries**
1/4 **cup amaretto**
11/2 **cups dried bread crumbs**
1/2 **cup Dutch processed cocoa powder**
1/4 **cup ground almonds**
11/2 **teaspoon ground cinnamon**
1/2 **teaspoon ground nutmeg**
1/4 **teaspoon ground cloves**
Pinch of salt
1 **cup butter or margarine, at room temperature**
1/2 **cup granulated sugar**
11/2 **cups solid pack canned pumpkin**
2 **large eggs**
Grand Marnier Sauce (see page 411) for serving
12 **White Chocolate Leaves (see page 422) for garnish**

1 One day before you make the pudding, place the dried cherries in an airtight container and cover with amaretto.

2 Grease four 1-cup ovenproof pudding dishes or custard cups. Cut four squares of aluminum foil or parchment paper large enough to cover the tops of the pudding dishes.

3 Combine the bread crumbs, cocoa powder, almonds, spices, and salt.

4 In a large bowl, using an electric mixer on medium speed, beat the butter and sugar until light and fluffy. Add the pumpkin and eggs and beat until the mixture is smooth. Beat in the dry ingredients.

5 Drain the cherries, reserving the amaretto for another use. Immediately fold cherries into the pumpkin mixture. Spoon the mixture into the prepared pudding dishes and cover tightly with the foil or paper. (If parchment paper is used, secure it in place with a string.)

6 Place in a steamer or pot with enough water to cover the bottom by 2 inches and cover. Steam over medium-low heat for 3 hours. Cool completely on wire racks without removing the foil covers. Chill 30 minutes, or until ready to serve.

7 Meanwhile, make the Grand Marnier sauce and the white chocolate leaves.

8 To assemble, invert the chilled puddings onto small serving plates. Spoon the sauce over the top and garnish each pudding with three chocolate leaves. Serve with additional Grand Marnier sauce on the side and a glass of the amaretto, if desired.

Baking notes: Fresh or canned cherries will not work in this recipe. The sauce can be prepared with amaretto in place of the Grand Marnier.

689 ■ CHOCOLATE RASPBERRY SOUFFLÉ

Makes 6 servings
Chill time: *30 minutes*

1 **cup fresh raspberries**
2 **tablespoons granulated sugar**
1 **envelope unflavored gelatin**
1/4 **cup boiling water**
2 **large egg whites**
1 **jar (7 ounces) marshmallow creme**
1 **cup heavy cream**
2 **ounces semisweet chocolate, grated or finely chopped**
1/2 **cup whole fresh raspberries for garnish**
Chocolate Curls (see page 422) for garnish

1 Wrap a strip of aluminum foil or parchment paper around the top of a 3-cup soufflé dish so that it extends 2 inches above the rim and tie securely with string.

2 In a small bowl, mash the raspberries. Strain through a sieve into another bowl. Stir in the sugar and let stand for at least 10 minutes.

3 In a cup, sprinkle the gelatin over boiling water and stir until dissolved. Stir into the raspberries and chill until thickened but not set.

4 Meanwhile, in a medium bowl, using an electric mixer on high speed, beat the egg whites until soft peaks form. Gradually add the marshmallow creme, a little at a time, beating until stiff peaks form. Fold the raspberry mixture into the egg whites.

5 In a large bowl, using an electric mixer on high speed, beat the cream until soft peaks form. Fold into the raspberry mixture. Fold in the grated chocolate. Pour the mixture into the prepared soufflé dish and chill 30 minutes, or until firm.

6 To serve, remove the foil strip and garnish with fresh raspberries and chocolate curls.

690 ■ CHOCOLATE RENNET CUSTARD

Makes 4 to 6 servings
Chill time: *1 hour*

1 **rennet tablet**
1 **tablespoon cold water**
1 **ounce semisweet chocolate, grated or finely chopped**
3 **tablespoons hot water**
2 **cups milk**
3 **tablespoons granulated sugar**
1 **teaspoon vanilla extract**

1 In a cup, dissolve the rennet tablet in the cold water.

2 In the top of a double boiler over simmering water, melt the chocolate, stirring until smooth. Stir in the hot water. Add the milk, sugar, and vanilla extract, stirring constantly until lukewarm. (A thermometer should read 120 degrees. Do not allow to become warmer than this.) Remove from the heat and add the rennet mixture and stir for a few seconds.

3 Immediately spoon into four to six dessert glasses and let stand at room temperature until the custard starts to thicken. Chill for 1 hour before serving.

691 ■ CHOCOLATE RUM CRÈME

MAKES 2 SERVINGS
CHILL TIME: *30 minutes*

3 large eggs
Pinch of salt
4 ounces semisweet chocolate, grated or finely chopped
2 tablespoons boiling water
1 teaspoon rum or rum extract

1 In a small bowl, using an electric mixer on medium speed, beat the egg yolks until thick and light-colored.

2 In a medium bowl, using an electric mixer with clean beaters on high speed, beat the egg whites and salt until stiff but not dry.

3 In the top of a double boiler over simmering water, blend the chocolate and water, stirring until smooth. Pouring them in a thin stream, add the egg yolks and beat, using an electric mixer on medium speed. Stir in the rum. Remove from the heat and transfer to a large bowl. Gently fold in the egg whites until streaks no longer appear. Cover and chill 30 minutes, or until set.

BAKING NOTES: Owing to the raw eggs in this recipe, it should be kept refrigerated at all times, and for no longer than 3 days.

692 ■ CHOCOLATE RUM MOUSSE

MAKES 6 TO 8 SERVINGS
CHILL TIME: *3 to 5 hours*

½ cup milk
½ cup heavy cream
2 large eggs, at room temperature
2 tablespoons butter or margarine, at room temperature
6 ounces semisweet chocolate, grated or finely chopped
1 teaspoon rum or rum extract
Chocolate Whipped Cream (see page 406)
Chocolate Curls (see page 422) for garnish

1 Lightly butter six pudding dishes or custard cups.

2 In a medium saucepan, over low heat, warm the milk and cream until bubbles start to form around the sides of the pan.

3 In the container of a blender, combine the eggs, butter, chocolate, and rum. Blend on medium speed until smooth. Add the warm milk and blend for a few seconds until slightly thickened.

4 Pour the mixture into the prepared pudding dishes and chill for 3 to 5 hours, or until firm.

5 When ready to serve, place a dab of chocolate whipped cream on the top of each and sprinkle with chocolate curls.

693 ■ CHOCOLATE SOUFFLÉ WITH CREAM TOPPING

MAKES 6 TO 8 SERVINGS
CHILL TIME: *8 hours*

2 envelopes unflavored gelatin
½ cup plus 2 tablespoons granulated sugar
⅓ cup Dutch processed cocoa powder
2¼ cups skim milk
3 large eggs, separated
½ cup heavy cream
1 teaspoon coffee liqueur
Apricot Rose (see page 420) for garnish
Large Chocolate Curls (see page 422) for garnish

1 Wrap a strip of aluminum foil or parchment paper around the top of a 1-quart soufflé dish so that it extends 2 inches above the rim and tie securely with string.

2 In a medium saucepan, combine the gelatin, ½ cup of the sugar, and the cocoa powder. Stir in the milk, blending until the dry ingredients are dissolved and smooth. Beat in the egg yolks. Over low heat, cook, stirring constantly, until the mixture coats the back of a spoon. Do not let come to a boil. Remove from the heat and immediately pour into a large

bowl. Chill until the mixture is thick and forms mounds when dropped from a spoon.

3 Meanwhile, in a small bowl, whip the cream until soft peaks form. Fold in the liqueur. Blend into the chilled chocolate mixture.

4 In a small bowl, using an electric mixer with clean beaters on high speed, beat the eggs whites until foamy. Add the remaining 2 tablespoons sugar and continue beating until stiff peaks form. Gently fold into the chocolate mixture. Pour into the prepared soufflé dish. Chill for 6 to 8 hours, or until firm. Carefully remove the foil and garnish with an apricot rose and chocolate curls.

BAKING NOTES: Any flavor liqueur can be used in place of the coffee liqueur. To decorate the soufflé, place the apricot rose in the center, and arrange the chocolate curls around it like spokes of a wheel. Owing to the raw egg whites in this recipe, it should be kept refrigerated at all times, and for no longer than 3 days.

694 ▪ CHOCOLATE SOUR DOUGH BREAD PUDDING I

MAKES 4 TO 6 SERVINGS
BAKING TIME: *45 minutes*

3 cups stale sour dough bread, crusts removed, cut into 1/2-inch cubes
2 ounces semisweet chocolate, grated or finely chopped
2 cups milk
3 large egg yolks
1/2 cup granulated sugar
Pinch of salt
1 teaspoon crème de cacao
1 tablespoon golden raisins, finely chopped

1 Position a rack in the center of the oven and preheat the oven to 350 degrees. Lightly grease a 1½ to 2-quart casserole dish.

2 Place the bread in a large mixing bowl.

3 In the top of a double boiler over simmering water, melt the

chocolate with the milk, stirring until smooth. Pour over the bread and let soak for 5 minutes.

4 Meanwhile, in a medium bowl, using an electric mixer on medium speed, beat the egg yolks until thick and light-colored. Stir in sugar, salt, crème de cacao, and raisins. Fold into the bread mixture. Pour into the prepared casserole. Set the casserole in a roasting pan and place on the oven rack. Pour hot water into the roasting pan until it comes halfway up the sides of the casserole.

5 Bake for 40 to 45 minutes, or until firm. Serve the pudding hot or cold.

695 ▪ CHOCOLATE SOUR DOUGH BREAD PUDDING II

MAKES 10 TO 12 SERVINGS
BAKING TIME: *70 minutes*

BREAD PUDDING

1 pound sourdough bread
1/3 cup butter, melted
6 large egg yolks plus 3 large eggs
1 cup granulated sugar
6 ounces unsweetened chocolate, grated or finely chopped
4 cups milk
1 teaspoon crème de cacao
1/2 cup pecans, finely chopped

PECAN CUSTARD SAUCE

1 cup milk
1/2 cup pecans, coarsely chopped
1 teaspoon almond extract
3 large egg yolks
1/4 cup granulated sugar

1 To make the bread pudding, remove the crusts from the bread. Brush each side of the bread with the melted butter. Dice the bread into 3/4 to 1-inch cubes.

2 In a large bowl, using an electric mixer on medium speed, beat the egg yolks until thick and light-colored. Beat in the whole eggs and sugar.

3 In a medium saucepan, over low heat, melt the chocolate, stirring until smooth. Add the milk and stir until blended and smooth. Remove from the heat

and stir in the crème de cacao. Pouring it in a thin stream, beat it into the egg mixture. Add the bread cubes and toss to ensure that each cube is coated. Let stand, stirring occasionally, for at least 1 hour.

4 Meanwhile, to make the sauce, in a medium saucepan, over medium heat, combine the milk and coarsely chopped pecans. Heat just until bubbles start to form around the sides of the pan. Pour into a blender and process for 3 to 5 seconds on medium speed. Cool to room temperature. Strain to remove the nuts. Add enough milk to make 1 cup. Return to the heat and cook just until bubbles start to form around the sides of the pan.

5 In a medium bowl, using an electric mixer on medium speed, beat the egg yolks until thick and light-colored. Beat in the sugar. Pouring it in a thin stream, beat in half of the hot milk mixture. Return to the remaining milk in the saucepan and cook, over medium-low heat, stirring constantly for 2 to 3 minutes, until the mixture thickens enough to coat the back of a spoon. Remove from the heat and cool to room temperature. Strain when cooled and add the almond extract. Cover and chill until ready to use.

694

6 Preheat the oven to 325 degrees. Lightly grease a 9-inch square pan.

7 Pour the cooled bread mixture into the prepared pan, and sprinkle the finely chopped pecans over the top. Set the pan in a roasting pan and place on the oven rack. Pour hot water into the roasting pan until it comes halfway up the sides of the pan with the bread pudding.

8 Bake for 65 to 70 minutes, or until a cake tester inserted into the center comes out clean. Remove from the hot water and cool on a wire rack until room temperature. Serve with the chilled sauce on the side.

BAKING NOTES: A fancy baking dish can be used if serving at the table.

696 ■ CHOCOLATE TRIFLE

MAKES 6 SERVINGS
CHILL TIME: *1 hour*

3 large egg yolks
1½ cups milk
1 cup granulated sugar
¼ cup Dutch processed cocoa
  powder
2½ tablespoons cornstarch or
  arrowroot
Pinch of salt
1 cup half-and-half
1 tablespoon butter or margarine
1 teaspoon almond or chocolate
  extract
10 ladyfingers
2 tablespoons sherry
½ cup heavy cream
1½ cups Raspberry Sauce (see page
  416) for serving

1 In a large bowl, using an electric mixer on medium speed, beat the egg yolks until thick and light-colored.

2 In a medium saucepan, over medium heat, combine the milk, sugar, cocoa powder, cornstarch, and salt, stirring until smooth. Stir in the half-and-half and bring to a boil. Cook, stirring constantly, for 1 to 2 minutes, until thick. Remove from the heat.

3 Pouring it in a thin stream, beat half of the hot milk mixture into the beaten egg yolks. Beat the egg yolk mixture back into the hot mixture in the saucepan. Return to the heat and cook, stirring constantly, just to the boiling point. Remove from the heat. Beat in the butter and almond extract. Cover with a piece of plastic wrap, pressing lightly down onto the custard, and cool.

4 Split the ladyfingers in half lengthwise and sprinkle the flat sides with the sherry. Line the bottom and sides of a 1-quart serving bowl with the ladyfingers with the flat sides facing in. Gently spoon half of the custard mixture over the ladyfingers in the bowl. Pour the remaining custard into the center.

5 In a small bowl, using an electric mixer on high speed, beat the heavy cream until soft peaks form.

6 Spread the whipped cream over the top of the mixture in the bowl. Cover and chill for 1 hour, or until ready to serve. Serve with the raspberry sauce on the side.

BAKING NOTES: An alternate way to assemble the trifle is to spoon the first half of the custard over the ladyfingers lining the bowl and top the custard with a layer of ladyfingers. Then, pour the remaining custard over the ladyfingers. Amaretto can be substituted for the sherry.

697 ■ CHOCOLATE TRIFLE WITH FRUIT

MAKES 8 TO 10 SERVINGS
CHILL TIME: *4 hours*

3 cups milk
⅔ cup granulated sugar
2 tablespoons cornstarch or
  arrowroot
Pinch of salt
2 large eggs
3 ounces unsweetened chocolate,
  grated or finely chopped
3 tablespoons amaretto
12 ladyfingers, split
1 pint fresh strawberries, hulled
  and sliced
1 can (16 ounces) apricot halves,
  drained and sliced
Chocolate Whipped Cream (see
  page 406) for garnish
Sliced strawberries and apricots for
  garnish

1 In a large saucepan, over low heat, heat the milk until bubbles start to form around the sides of the pan. Remove from the heat.

2 In a large bowl, combine the sugar, cornstarch, and salt. Using an electric mixer on medium speed, beat in the eggs, one at a time, beating well after each addition. Pouring it in a thin stream, beat in the hot milk.

3 Return the mixture to the saucepan and cook over low heat, stirring constantly, until smooth and thick. Remove from the heat. Add the chocolate and stir until the chocolate is melted and the mixture is smooth. Stir in the amaretto.

697

695
696

4 To assemble, arrange a layer of the ladyfingers in the bottom of a 1½-quart serving bowl. Top with a layer of the sliced strawberries and apricots. Spread a layer of the custard over the fruit. Repeat until all the fruit and custard are used, ending with a layer of custard. Cover and chill for 4 hours, or until ready to serve. Garnish with chocolate whipped cream and additional strawberries and apricots.

698 ■ CHUNKY CHOCOLATE PUDDING

MAKES 4 SERVINGS
CHILL TIME: *30 minutes*

¼ cup granulated sugar
2 tablespoons cornstarch or arrowroot
¼ teaspoon salt
2 ounces unsweetened chocolate, grated or finely chopped
2 cups milk
½ teaspoon vanilla or chocolate extract
⅓ cup miniature chocolate chips
½ cup Chocolate Syrup I (see page 406) for serving
Edible fresh flowers for garnish

1 Chill four custard cups.

2 Combine the sugar, cornstarch, and salt.

3 In the top of a double boiler over simmering water, combine the chocolate and milk. Cook until the chocolate is melted and the mixture is smooth. Stir in the dry ingredients and cook for 10 minutes, stirring once. Stir in the vanilla extract and cook, stirring constantly, until the mixture thickens. Remove from the heat, cool slightly, and quickly stir in the chocolate chips. Rinse the chilled cups in ice water. Spoon the pudding into the chilled cups. Chill for 30 minutes, or until ready to serve.

4 To serve, drizzle chocolate syrup over four small plates. Decorate with the flowers and invert a pudding into the center of each plate.

699 ■ CIOCCOLATO RESTITUZIONE

MAKES 10 TO 12 SERVINGS
SOAKING TIME: *24 hours*
BAKING TIME: *65 minutes*
STANDING TIME: *2 hours*
CHILL TIME: *1 hour*

½ cup dried cherries
Amaretto for soaking, plus 1 teaspoon
5 cups chocolate graham cracker crumbs
½ cup Dutch processed cocoa powder
¼ cup ground almonds
1½ teaspoons ground cinnamon
½ teaspoon ground nutmeg
¼ teaspoon ground cloves
Pinch of salt
1 cup butter or margarine, at room temperature
½ cup plus ⅔ cup granulated sugar
1½ cups solid pack canned pumpkin
4 large eggs
2 pounds ricotta cheese, drained
2 tablespoons lemon juice

1 Place the cherries in a small bowl and add just enough amaretto to cover them. Cover the bowl and soak at room temperature for 24 hours, or until ready to use. (The cherries will keep for several days.)

2 Position a rack in the center of the oven and preheat the oven to 350 degrees. Lightly grease a 10-inch springform pan. Line the bottom with waxed paper and grease the paper.

3 Combine the graham crackers crumbs, cocoa powder, almonds, cherries, spices, and salt.

4 In a large bowl, using an electric mixer on medium speed, beat the butter and ½ cup of the sugar until light and fluffy. Add the pumpkin and 2 of the eggs and beat until well blended. Add the dry ingredients and blend thoroughly. Spread evenly over the bottom of the prepared pan. Bake for 20 minutes.

5 Meanwhile, drain the ricotta cheese. Transfer to a large bowl. Beat in the lemon juice, 1 teaspoon amaretto, the remaining ⅔ cup sugar, and the remaining

2 eggs. Pour the cheese mixture over the top of the cake.

6 Bake for 45 minutes, or until the edges look dry. The center will still look moist. Turn off the oven and leave the cake undisturbed for at least 2 hours. Chill for 1 hour until set. Remove the side of the springform pan and place the cake on a serving plate.

700 ■ COCOA MOCHA PUDDING

MAKES 8 TO 10 SERVINGS
CHILL TIME: *4 hours*

1 tablespoon instant espresso powder
2 teaspoons chocolate extract or crème de cacao
1½ cups powdered sugar
¾ cup Dutch processed cocoa powder
3 cups heavy cream
Chocolate Syrup III (see page 406) for garnish
Chocolate cookies for serving
Chocolate Whipped Cream (see page 406)

1 In a cup, dissolve the espresso powder in the chocolate extract.

2 Combine and sift twice the powdered sugar and cocoa powder.

3 In a large bowl, combine the espresso mixture, cream, and powdered sugar mixture. Using an electric mixer on medium speed, beat until soft peaks form. Spoon evenly into eight to ten custard or dessert cups and chill for 2 to 4 hours.

699

698

4 To serve, drizzle the top of each pudding with chocolate syrup. Serve with chocolate cookies on the side.

701 ▪ COCOA PUDDING

MAKES 4 TO 6 SERVINGS
CHILL TIME: *30 minutes*

¹/₄ cup Dutch processed cocoa powder
¹/₄ cup arrowroot or cornstarch
6 tablespoons granulated sugar
2 cups milk
1 tablespoon butter or margarine, at room temperature
1 teaspoon crème de cacao
Chocolate cookies for garnish
Fresh mint leaves for garnish

1 In a large bowl, blend the cocoa powder, arrowroot, and sugar. By hand, beat in ¹/₂ cup of the milk, mixing thoroughly until smooth.

2 In the top of a double boiler over simmering water, warm the remaining 1¹/₂ cups milk. Stir in the cocoa mixture until smooth. Cook, stirring constantly, until the mixture thickens. Remove from the heat and stir in the butter and crème de cacao. Spoon the mixture into four to six chilled custard cups or parfait glasses. Chill for 30 minutes, or until ready to serve. Garnish with chocolate cookies and mint leaves.

702 ▪ COFFEE RAISIN FROZEN CHOCOLATE FUDGE

MAKES 8 TO 10 SERVINGS
FREEZING TIME: *1 hour*

¹/₂ cup raisins
¹/₃ cup coffee liqueur
4 ounces semisweet chocolate, grated or finely chopped
3 ounces unsweetened chocolate, grated or finely chopped
1 ounces white chocolate or almond bark, grated or finely chopped
¹/₂ cup butter or margarine, at room temperature
¹/₄ cup Dutch processed cocoa powder
5 tablespoons boiling water
4 large eggs, separated
¹/₃ cup granulated sugar
Pinch of salt
Chocolate Sauce V (see page 405) for serving

1 Combine the raisins and liqueur in an airtight container and cover. Soak the raisins for at least 24 hours.

2 In the top of a double boiler over simmering water, melt the chocolates, stirring until smooth. Remove from the heat.

3 In a cup, blend the cocoa powder and boiling water until smooth. Stir into the melted chocolate.

4 In a large bowl, using an electric mixer on medium speed, beat the egg yolks and butter until thick and light-colored. Beat in the sugar.

5 Beat the chocolate mixture into the egg yolks until smooth. Fold in the raisins and liqueur. Freeze for 1 hour, or until thickened. Do not allow to set.

6 Meanwhile, in a large bowl, using an electric mixer on high speed, beat the egg whites and salt until stiff but not dry. Fold into the chilled chocolate mixture. Cover and freeze until firm. Spoon out the fudge and serve with chocolate sauce on the side.

703 ▪ CRÈME AU CHOCOLAT

MAKES 6 TO 8 SERVINGS
BAKING TIME: *1 hour*

3 cups heavy cream
¹/₃ cup granulated sugar
6 ounces semisweet chocolate, grated or finely chopped
6 large egg yolks
1 teaspoon crème de cacao
¹/₂ cup packed light brown sugar

1 Position a rack in the center of the oven and preheat the oven to 350 degrees.

2 In the top of a double boiler over simmering water, heat the cream until just warm to the touch. Stir in the sugar and chocolate, stirring constantly until the chocolate is melted and the mixture is smooth. Remove from the heat.

701

703

702

700

3 In a large bowl, using an electric mixer on medium speed, beat the egg yolks until thick and light-colored. Pouring it in a thin stream, whisk the chocolate mixture into the egg yolks. Stir in the crème de cacao. Stir in the brown sugar until it dissolves. Strain the mixture though a sieve into a 9 or 10-inch casserole dish. Set the dish in roasting pan and set on the oven rack. Pour boiling water into the roasting pan until it comes halfway up the sides of the casserole dish.

4 Bake for 1 hour, or until set. Remove the casserole dish from the hot water and place in another pan filled with ice cubes or shaved ice and cool completely.

704 ■ DARK VELVET PUDDING

MAKES 6 TO 8 SERVINGS
CHILL TIME: *1 hour*

1 cup heavy cream
4 large eggs, separated
Dash of salt
6 ounces semisweet chocolate, grated or finely chopped
1/4 cup dark buckwheat honey
1/4 cup hot strong brewed coffee
2 tablespoons coffee liqueur
Sponge cake or angel food cake for serving
Chocolate Leaves (see page 422) for garnish

1 In a large bowl, using an electric mixer on high speed, whip the cream until it holds its shape. Chill until ready to use.

2 In a medium bowl, using an electric mixer with clean beaters on high speed, beat the egg whites and salt until stiff peaks form.

3 In the top of a double boiler over simmering water, melt the chocolate with the honey and coffee, stirring until the chocolate is melted and the mixture is smooth. Remove from the heat and transfer to a large bowl. Using an electric mixer on medium speed, beat in the egg yolks, one at a time, beating well after each addition. Beat in

the liqueur. Fold in the beaten egg whites. Fold in the whipped cream. Spoon into a chilled serving bowl or six to eight custard cups. Chill for at least 1 hour, or until ready to serve. Serve with a thin slice of sponge cake or angel food cake on the side and garnish with chocolate leaves.

BAKING NOTES: The pudding can be made a day ahead. Buckwheat honey is a darker color and has a stronger flavor than other honeys. If you cannot find it, any honey will do. Crème de cacao can be substituted for the coffee liqueur. Owing to the raw eggs in this recipe, it should be kept refrigerated at all times, and for no longer than 3 days.

705 ■ DOUBLE CHOCOLATE MOUSSE

MAKES 10 TO 12 SERVINGS
CHILL TIME: *30 minutes*

5 ounces unsweetened chocolate, grated or finely chopped
4 ounces semisweet chocolate, grated or finely chopped
8 large egg yolks
1 1/3 cups granulated sugar
1 quart heavy cream
2 tablespoons coffee liqueur
Seasonal fresh fruit or Chocolate Leaves (see page 422) for garnish

1 In the top of a double boiler over simmering water, melt the chocolates, stirring until smooth. Remove from the heat.

2 In a large bowl, using an electric mixer on medium speed, beat the egg yolks until thick and light-colored. Beat in the sugar. Pouring it in thin steady stream, beat in the melted chocolate on low speed. Fold in the liqueur.

3 In a large bowl, using an electric mixer on high speed, beat the heavy cream until it forms stiff peaks. Fold into the chocolate mixture and blend thoroughly. Pour into a chilled serving dish or spoon into ten to twelve chilled custard cups. Chill for 30 minutes, or until ready to serve. Garnish with fresh fruit or chocolate leaves.

BAKING NOTES: Owing to the raw eggs in this recipe, it should be kept refrigerated at all times, and for no longer than 3 days.

706 ■ EASTER EGG MOUSSE

MAKES 10 TO 12 SERVINGS
CHILL TIME: *5 hours*

4 ounces unsweetened chocolate, grated or finely chopped
1 1/4 cups granulated sugar
4 large eggs, separated
2 cups milk
2 envelopes unflavored gelatin
Pinch of salt
1/4 cup crème de cacao
1/4 cup coffee liqueur
2 cups heavy cream
Coffee Mocha Icing (see page 408) for garnish

1 In the top of a double boiler over simmering water, melt the chocolate, stirring until smooth. Add 1/2 cup of the sugar, stirring until dissolved. Remove from the heat and transfer to a large bowl.

2 In a medium bowl, using an electric mixer on medium speed, beat the egg yolks until thick and light-colored. Beat in the milk.

3 In a medium saucepan, over medium heat, combine the gelatin, 1/4 cup of the sugar, and the salt. Beat in the egg yolk mixture. Stir constantly until the gelatin is dissolved and the mixture starts to thicken. Remove from the heat. Stir in the crème de cacao and liqueur.

4 Add the gelatin mixture to the chocolate mixture and stir until combined. Chill 1 hour, until the mixture mounds when a spoon is drawn through it.

5 Meanwhile, in a medium bowl, using an electric mixer on high speed, whip the egg whites until foamy. Continue beating and add the remaining 1/2 cup sugar, a little at a time. Beat until stiff but not dry.

6 In a large bowl, using an electric mixer on high speed, whip the cream until soft peaks form.

7 Fold the egg whites into the chocolate mixture. Fold in the whipped cream. Pour the mixture into a 10 to 12-cup egg-shaped mold. Chill for 4 hours.

8 Meanwhile, make the mocha frosting.

9 To serve, unmold the mousse egg and place on a serving plate. Fill a pastry bag fitted with a small plain tip with mocha frosting. Pipe designs on the egg.

707 ■ EASY CHOCOLATE MOUSSE

MAKES 8 TO 10 SERVINGS
CHILL TIME: *2 hours*

12 ounces semisweet chocolate, grated or finely chopped
5 large eggs, separated
2 cups heavy cream

1 Melt the chocolate (see page 13). Remove from the heat and cool to room temperature.

2 In a large bowl, using an electric mixer on high speed, beat the egg whites until stiff but not dry.

3 In a medium bowl, using an electric mixer on medium speed, beat the egg yolks until thick and light-colored.

4 In another medium bowl, using an electric mixer on high speed, whip the cream until soft peaks form.

5 Beat the chocolate into the egg yolks until smooth and yellow

streaks no longer appear. Fold in one-third of the egg whites into the chocolate mixture. Fold the chocolate mixture back into the remaining egg whites until streaks no longer appear. Fold in the whipped cream. Spoon the mousse into a large glass serving bowl. Cover and chill for 1 to 2 hours, or until ready to serve.

BAKING NOTES: Owing to the raw eggs in this recipe, it should be kept refrigerated at all times, and for no longer than 3 days.

708 ■ EBONY MOUSSE

MAKES 8 TO 12 SERVINGS
CHILL TIME: *8 hours*

6 ounces semisweet chocolate, grated or finely chopped
4 teaspoons thawed frozen orange juice concentrate
1½ cups heavy cream
1 cup prunes, pitted and chopped
3 large egg whites
3 tablespoons powdered sugar
2 tablespoons grated orange zest, for garnish

1 In the container of a blender, combine the chocolate and orange juice concentrate. Blend on medium speed for 2 to 3 seconds.

2 In a small saucepan, over medium heat, heat ½ cup of the cream until bubbles start to form around the sides of the pan. Pouring it in a thin stream, add the hot cream to the chocolate mixture in the blender and blend on low speed until the chocolate is melted and the mixture is smooth. Pour the mixture into a large bowl. Fold in the chopped prunes.

3 In a medium bowl, using an electric mixer on high speed, whip ¾ cup of the cream until soft peaks form. Fold into the chocolate mixture.

4 In a large bowl, using an electric mixer with clean beaters on high speed, beat the egg whites until stiff but not dry. Beat in the powdered sugar. Fold into the chocolate mixture. Spoon into eight to twelve ramekin dishes. Chill overnight.

5 When ready to serve, in a small bowl, using an electric mixer on high speed, whip the remaining ¼ cup cream until stiff peaks form. Fill a pastry bag fitted with a large star tip with the whipped cream. Pipe large rosettes onto the top of each serving. Garnish with the grated orange zest.

BAKING NOTES: For an alternative garnish, omit the orange zest and place half of a thin orange slice across each rosette and sprinkle with chocolate sprinkles or orange-colored sugar crystals.

706

704

705

707

708

709 ■ ECLAIR PUDDING

MAKES 12 TO 15 SERVINGS
CHILL TIME: *10 hours*

1 box (16 ounces) graham crackers
2 packages (3.4 ounces each) Jell-O Brand chocolate instant pudding mix
3¼ cups plus 3 tablespoons milk
1 cup whipped topping
2 ounces semisweet chocolate, grated or finely chopped
2 teaspoons light corn syrup
2 teaspoons chocolate or almond extract
3 tablespoons butter-flavored vegetable shortening
1½ cups powdered sugar, sifted

1 Lightly grease a 13 by 9-inch pan and line the bottom with some of the graham crackers.

2 In a large bowl, using an electric mixer on low speed, beat the pudding mix and 3¼ cups of the milk for 2 minutes. On low speed, blend in the whipped topping. Pour half of the mixture over the graham crackers. Top with a second layer of graham crackers. Pour the remaining pudding mixture over the graham crackers. Chill for 2 hours.

3 Melt the chocolate (see page 13). Remove from the heat.

4 In a large bowl, using an electric mixer on medium speed, beat the corn syrup, chocolate extract, shortening, powdered sugar, and remaining 3 tablespoons milk. Pouring it in a steady stream, beat in the melted chocolate. Spread this mixture over the chilled pudding. Chill for 6 to 8 hours, or until ready to serve.

BAKING NOTES: This pudding can be made a day or two ahead and kept covered in the refrigerator.

710 ■ ENGLISH CHOCOLATE PUDDING

MAKES 6 SERVINGS
STEAMING TIME: *90 minutes*

2 ounces unsweetened chocolate, grated or finely chopped
½ cup milk
2 tablespoons butter, at room temperature
½ cup granulated sugar
2 large eggs, separated
½ cup bread or cake crumbs
1½ teaspoons chocolate or vanilla extract
Chocolate Custard Sauce (see page 398) for serving

1 Generously grease six ½-cup heatproof molds or one 3-cup mold.

2 In the top of a double boiler over simmering water, melt the chocolate with the milk, stirring until smooth. Remove from the heat.

3 In a medium bowl, using an electric mixer on medium speed, beat the butter and sugar until light and fluffy. Beat in the egg yolks. Beat in the crumbs and chocolate extract. Stir in the chocolate mixture.

4 In a small bowl, using an electric mixer on high speed, beat the egg whites until stiff but not dry. Fold into the chocolate mixture. Divide the mixture evenly between the prepared molds. Cover tightly with aluminum foil. Prick the foil several times.

5 Place in a steamer or pot with enough water to cover the bottom by 2 inches and cover. Steam over medium-low heat for 90 minutes. Cool completely on wire racks without removing the foil covers. Serve with chocolate custard sauce on the side.

BAKING NOTES: Traditionally, the puddings are covered with a piece of cloth and it is tied in place with string. Today, they can be covered with a piece of aluminum foil. Tightly fit the foil over the top of the mold and down the sides. Prick the top of the foil several times with a needle.

711 ■ ESPRESSO MOUSSE WITH NUT BRITTLE

MAKES 8 TO 10 SERVINGS

MOUSSE

2 envelopes unflavored gelatin
¾ cup granulated sugar
4 tablespoons instant espresso coffee
2¾ cups milk
12 ounces semisweet chocolate, grated or finely chopped
1½ cups finely chopped chocolate wafer cookie crumbs, or chocolate graham cracker crumbs
⅔ cup chopped pecans
1½ cups heavy cream

TOPPING

1 cup sugar
½ cup chopped pecans

1 In the top of a double boiler, blend the gelatin, ½ cup of the sugar, the espresso powder, and milk. Let stand 2 minutes. Place over simmering water, stirring constantly until the gelatin is dissolved. Add the chocolate, stirring constantly until smooth. Remove from the heat.

2 Using an electric mixer on high speed, beat well for 2 to 3 minutes. Transfer to a medium bowl. Place into another bowl filled with ice cubes or shaved ice. Stir occasionally until the mixture is thick enough to coat the back of a spoon.

712

709

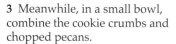

3 Meanwhile, in a small bowl, combine the cookie crumbs and chopped pecans.

4 In a medium bowl, using an electric mixer on high speed, whip the cream and remaining ¼ cup sugar. Reserve ½ cup of the whipped cream and chill. Fold the remaining whipped cream into the chilled chocolate mixture.

5 To assemble, place ½ tablespoon of the cookie crumb mixture into the bottom of each of eight to ten parfait glasses. Add a spoonful of the chocolate mixture to each glass. Add spoonfuls of the crumb mixture, alternating with spoonfuls of the chocolate mixture, until both mixtures are used up. Chill until the chocolate mixture is firm.

6 Meanwhile, to make the brittle, in a saucepan, over medium heat, heat the sugar, stirring constantly, until the sugar melts and turns golden brown. Stir in the chopped nuts and immediately pour onto a greased baking sheet. Chill 15 minutes, or until firm. Break into pieces.

7 To serve, sprinkle the puddings with the pieces of nut brittle.

712 ▪ FROZEN CHOCOLATE MOUSSE CAKE

MAKES 6 TO 8 SERVINGS
FREEZING TIME: *1 hour*

½ **cup graham cracker crumbs**
⅓ **cup almonds, finely ground**
3 **tablespoons granulated sugar**
3 **tablespoons butter or margarine, melted**
1 **pint coffee ice cream, softened**
6 **ounces semisweet chocolate, grated or finely chopped**
2 **large eggs, separated**
1 **cup heavy cream**
3 **tablespoons Crème de Prunelle**
⅓ **cup chopped almonds**

1 Position a rack in the center of the oven and preheat the oven to 350 degrees. Lightly grease an 8-inch springform pan.

2 Combine the graham cracker crumbs, ground almonds, 1 tablespoon of the sugar, and the melted butter. Press the mixture evenly onto the bottom of the prepared pan.

3 Bake for 10 minutes. Cool on a wire rack. Freeze until well chilled.

4 Spoon the ice cream evenly over the crust. Return to the freezer.

5 Melt the chocolate (see page 13). Remove from the heat.

6 Meanwhile, in a small bowl, using an electric mixer on high speed, beat the egg whites until stiff peaks form. Fold in the remaining 2 tablespoons sugar.

711

713

710

7 In a medium bowl, using an electric mixer on high speed, beat ½ cup of the cream until soft peaks form.

8 In a medium bowl, using an electric mixer on medium speed, beat the egg yolks until thick and light-colored. Beat in the melted chocolate and liqueur. Fold in the beaten egg whites. Fold in the whipped cream. Fold in the chopped almonds. Pour the mixture over the top of the ice cream in the springform pan. Cover and freeze for 1 hour, until the mixture is frozen solid.

9 When ready to serve, remove the side of the springform pan and place the cake on a serving plate. In a small bowl, using an electric mixer on high speed, whip the remaining ½ cup cream and spread over the top of the mousse.

BAKING NOTES: Owing to the raw eggs in this recipe, it should be kept refrigerated at all times, and for no longer than 3 days.

713 ▪ FROZEN CHOCOLATE MOUSSE WITH CUSTARD SAUCE

MAKES 8 TO 10 SERVINGS
FREEZING TIME: *8 hours*

2 **tablespoons finely ground almonds**
4 **large eggs, separated**
⅔ **cup granulated sugar**
8 **ounces semisweet chocolate, grated or finely chopped**
1 **cup butter or margarine, at room temperature**
Pinch of salt
Vanilla Custard Sauce (see page 417)

1 Lightly oil an 8-inch square pan. Sprinkle the almonds over the bottom and sides of the pan.

2 In a medium bowl, using an electric mixer on medium speed, beat the egg yolks for about 5 minutes, or until thick and light-colored. Beat in the sugar until blended.

3 In a medium saucepan, over low heat, melt the chocolate,

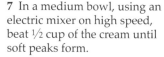

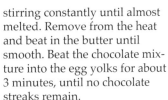

stirring constantly until almost melted. Remove from the heat and beat in the butter until smooth. Beat the chocolate mixture into the egg yolks for about 3 minutes, until no chocolate streaks remain.

4 In a medium bowl, using an electric mixer with clean beaters on high speed, beat the egg whites and salt until stiff but not dry. Using a wooden spoon, stir into the chocolate mixture, a little at a time, blending until no streaks appear after each addition. Pour the mixture into the prepared pan and spread evenly. Cover tightly and freeze for at least 8 hours.

5 Meanwhile, make the custard sauce.

6 To unmold, dip the bottom of the pan into a large pan of warm water for 3 to 5 seconds. Dry the bottom of the pan and immediately invert onto a serving plate. Give the bottom of the pan a light tap with a wooden spoon and the mousse should slide out onto the plate. Serve with the custard sauce on the side.

714 ■ FROZEN CHOCOLATE PARFAITS

MAKES 8 SERVINGS
FREEZING TIME: *8 hours*

CHOCOLATE AND COFFEE CUSTARDS

2/3 cup granulated sugar
1/3 cup water
3 large egg yolks
4 ounces unsweetened chocolate, grated or finely chopped
4 teaspoons instant coffee powder
1 tablespoon coffee liqueur
1 1/3 cups heavy cream

WHIPPED CREAM TOPPING

1/2 cup heavy cream
2 tablespoons granulated sugar
Chocolate coffee bean candies for garnish

1 To make the custard, in a saucepan, over low heat, stir the sugar and water until the sugar is completely dissolved. Insert a candy thermometer and increase the heat to medium. Bring to a boil and simmer, without stirring, for about 5 minutes, until 245 degrees.

2 Meanwhile, in a medium bowl, using an electric mixer on medium speed, beat the egg yolks until thick and light-colored. Pouring it in a thin stream, gradually beat in the hot syrup and beat for about 5 minutes, until the mixture is cool. Pour one-third of the yolk mixture into a small bowl.

3 Melt the chocolate (see page 13). Remove from the heat and immediately beat into the medium bowl with the remaining two-thirds of the yolk mixture.

4 Dissolve the coffee powder in the liqueur and beat into the egg yolk mixture poured into the small bowl.

5 In another medium bowl, using an electric mixer on high speed, whip the cream until soft peaks form. Fold two-thirds of the whipped cream into the chocolate mixture. Fold the remaining whipped cream into the coffee mixture.

6 Spoon half of the chocolate mixture into eight parfait glasses. Spoon all of the coffee mixture over the top of the chocolate mixture in the glasses. Top with the remaining chocolate mixture. Cover with plastic wrap and freeze for at least 8 hours.

7 Meanwhile, to make the topping, in a small bowl, using an electric mixer on high speed, beat the cream and sugar until soft peaks form. Chill until ready to use.

8 One hour before serving, remove the parfaits from the freezer. Remove the plastic wrap

716

714

718

717

715

and top each with a dab of whipped cream. Garnish with chocolate coffee beans.

BAKING NOTES: The chocolate coffee beans can also be crushed and sprinkled over the top of the whipped cream.

715 ■ FROZEN NESSELRODE CHOCOLATE PUDDING

MAKES 6 TO 8 SERVINGS
FREEZING TIME: *2 hours*

3 large egg yolks
1¹/₂ cups half-and-half
1 can (10 ounces) crushed pineapple in juice
³/₄ cup granulated sugar
1 envelope unflavored gelatin
¹/₄ teaspoon salt
1 cup heavy cream
¹/₂ cup golden raisins
2 tablespoons diced maraschino cherries
3 ounces semisweet chocolate, grated or finely chopped

1 In a medium saucepan, using an electric mixer on medium speed, beat the egg yolks until thick and light-colored. Add the half-and-half, pineapple with its juice, sugar, gelatin, and salt and cook over medium-low heat, stirring constantly, for about 5 to 7 minutes, or until slightly thickened. Pour into a shallow pan, cover, and freeze for 2 hours.

2 In a medium bowl, using an electric mixer on high speed, beat the cream until stiff peaks form.

3 Transfer the partially frozen custard to a medium bowl. Using an electric mixer on high speed, beat until smooth. Fold in the whipped cream, raisins, cherries, and grated chocolate. Pour into a 2-quart mold or back into the shallow dish. Cover and freeze until firm. To serve, dip the bottom of the mold into a bowl of warm water for a few seconds. Dry the bottom of the mold and invert onto a serving plate. Or scoop out of the dish and serve in dessert cups.

716 ■ GRAND MARNIER MOUSSE

MAKES 6 TO 8 SERVINGS
CHILL TIME: *2 hours*

1 cup heavy cream
¹/₄ cup granulated sugar
¹/₂ cup fresh orange juice, strained
8 ounces semisweet chocolate, grated or finely chopped
3 large egg yolks
¹/₄ cup Grand Marnier

1 In a medium bowl, using an electric mixer on high speed, whip the cream until soft peaks form.

2 In the top of a double boiler over simmering water, warm the sugar and orange juice. Add the chocolate and stir constantly until it is melted and smooth. Remove from the heat.

3 In a medium bowl, using an electric mixer on medium speed, beat the egg yolks until thick and light-colored. Pouring it in a thin stream, beat in the chocolate mixture on low speed. Fold in the whipped cream and Grand Marnier. Pour into a serving bowl and chill for at least 2 hours, or until ready to serve.

BAKING NOTES: Owing to the raw eggs in this recipe, it should be kept refrigerated at all times, and for no longer than 3 days.

717 ■ HAZELNUT MOUSSE

MAKES 8 TO 10 SERVINGS
CHILL TIME: *3 hours*

10 ounces unsweetened chocolate, grated or finely chopped
8 ounces semisweet chocolate, grated or finely chopped
1 cup Frangelico
4 large eggs, separated, plus 4 large egg whites
1 cup heavy cream
¹/₄ cup granulated sugar
8 large egg whites
Pinch of salt
Pinch of cream of tartar
1 cup hazelnuts, finely ground
Whipped cream for garnish

1 In the top of a double boiler over simmering water, melt the chocolates, stirring until smooth. Gradually stir in the Frangelico. Remove from the heat and cool completely. Beat in the egg yolks.

2 In a medium bowl, using an electric mixer on high speed, beat the cream until thickened. Beat in the sugar 1 tablespoon at a time until soft peaks form.

3 In a large bowl, using an electric mixer on high speed, beat the egg whites and salt until foamy. Add the cream of tartar and beat until stiff but not dry. Fold in the whipped cream. Fold one-third into the chocolate mixture. Fold the chocolate mixture back into the egg white mixture. Fold in the hazelnuts. Pour the mixture into a large bowl and chill for at least 3 hours, or until set.

4 To serve, spoon the mousse into eight to ten serving glasses and top with whipped cream.

BAKING NOTES: Owing to the raw eggs in this recipe, it should be kept refrigerated at all times, and for no longer than 3 days.

718 ■ HUNGARIAN CHOCOLATE BOMBE

MAKES 8 TO 10 SERVINGS
BAKING TIME: *20 minutes*
CHILL TIME: *8 hours*

CHOCOLATE ALMOND CAKE

3 ounces unsweetened chocolate, grated or finely chopped
1 cup all-purpose flour
²/₃ cup ground almonds
6 large eggs, separated
²/₃ cup granulated sugar

CHOCOLATE RAISIN MOUSSE

¹/₃ cup raisins
¹/₄ cup Grand Marnier
12 ounces unsweetened chocolate, grated or finely chopped
2 cups heavy cream
¹/₂ cup powdered sugar
2 tablespoons black currant jelly
¹/₄ cup candied orange peel, diced
Powdered sugar for garnish

1 Position a rack in the center of the oven and preheat the oven to 375 degrees. Lightly grease a 10-inch springform pan. Line the bottom with waxed paper and grease the paper. Lightly flour the pan.

2 To make the cake, melt the chocolate (see page 13). Remove from the heat.

3 Combine the flour and almonds.

4 In a large bowl, using an electric mixer on medium speed, beat the egg yolks until thick and light-colored. Beat in 1/3 cup of the granulated sugar. Add the melted chocolate and beat until very thick.

5 In a large bowl, using an electric mixer with clean beaters on high speed, beat the egg whites until foamy. Add the remaining 1/3 cup sugar and beat until stiff but not dry. Stir one-third of the egg whites into the chocolate mixture. Gradually blend the dry ingredients into the chocolate mixture. Fold in the remaining egg whites and blend thoroughly. Pour the mixture into the prepared pan.

6 Bake for 15 to 20 minutes, or until a cake tester inserted into the center comes out clean. Cool in the pan on a wire rack for 5 minutes. Remove the side of the springform pan and invert the cake onto the wire rack. Remove the waxed paper and cool completely. Using a serrated knife, cut the cake horizontally into three layers.

7 Fit one of the cake layers into the bottom of a 4-quart bowl, bending it a little way up the sides. Cut some of the remaining cake layers into pieces and fit around the sides of the bowl. Reserve any remaining pieces of cake. Cover the bowl and pieces of cake while making the mousse.

8 To make the mousse, in a small bowl, combine the raisins and Grand Marnier. Soak the raisins for 1 hour at room temperature. Drain before adding using.

9 Melt the chocolate (see page 13). Transfer to a large bowl and cool to room temperature.

10 In a large bowl, using an electric mixer on high speed, whip the cream until stiff peaks form. Stir 2 cups of the whipped cream, the powdered sugar, and jelly into the melted chocolate. Fold in the remaining whipped cream. Spoon the mousse into the cake-lined bowl until it is filled halfway. Trim some of the remaining cake into pieces that will fit in an even layer over the mousse. Fold the orange peel and raisins into the mousse and spoon over the top of the cake layer. Top with any remaining cake pieces, cutting to fit if necessary. Cover and chill for at least 8 hours.

11 To serve, invert the bombe onto a large serving plate and sift the powdered sugar over the top.

BAKING NOTES: For a special garnish, place a doily over the top of the bombe and sift the powdered sugar over the doily. Carefully lift off the doily.

719 ■ ICE BOX PUDDING CAKE

MAKES 12 TO 15 SERVINGS
CHILL TIME: *3 hours*

1 package (3.4 ounces) Jell-O Brand chocolate instant pudding mix
1 package (3.4 ounces) Jell-O Brand banana-flavored instant pudding mix
1 box (16 ounces) chocolate graham crackers

1 Prepare each of the pudding mixes as the packages direct.

2 Line the bottom of a 13 by 9-inch baking pan with a layer of graham crackers. Pour in enough of the chocolate pudding to just cover the crackers. Top with another layer of the graham crackers. Top with just enough banana-flavored pudding to cover the graham crackers. Repeat the layers, ending with a layer of pudding. Crush a few graham crackers and sprinkle the crumbs over the top.

Cover and chill for at least 3 hours, or until ready to serve.

720 ■ MOCHA CHOCOLATE BISCUIT PUDDING

MAKES 6 SERVINGS
CHILL TIME: *30 minutes*

2 tablespoons all-purpose flour
1 quart milk
3 ounces semisweet chocolate, grated or finely chopped
1 teaspoon instant espresso powder
6 large eggs
1/2 cup granulated sugar
6 to 8 cookies for garnish
Whipped cream for garnish

1 Line twelve 2-inch muffin cups with paper baking cups.

2 Stir the flour into 2 tablespoons of the milk. Set aside

3 In the top of a double boiler over simmering water, combine the remaining milk, the chocolate, and espresso powder and heat, stirring, until the chocolate is melted and the mixture is smooth. Stir in the flour mixture and cook for 15 minutes, stirring occasionally. Remove from the heat.

4 Meanwhile, in a large bowl, using an electric mixer on medium speed, beat the eggs and sugar until thick and light-colored and the sugar is completely dissolved. Beat in the warm milk mixture. Return the mixture to the double boiler. Cook over medium heat, stirring for about 5 to 7 minutes, or until the mixture is smooth and thick. Remove from the heat and cool to room temperature.

5 Spoon the mixture into the prepared muffin cups and chill 30 minutes, until firm.

6 To serve, remove the puddings from the pan. Garnish each with half of a cookie and a dab of whipped cream.

721 ■ MOCHA CHOCOLATE SOUFFLÉS

MAKES 6 SERVINGS
BAKING TIME: *20 minutes*

CHOCOLATE SOUFFLÉS

1/4 cup Cocoa Sugar (see page 407)
4 ounces unsweetened chocolate, grated or finely chopped
1 cup milk
1/2 cup granulated sugar
3 large eggs, separated, plus 9 large egg whites
2 tablespoons all-purpose flour
1 teaspoon Swiss chocolate almond liqueur

COFFEE CUSTARD SAUCE

1 1/2 cups heavy cream
1 1/2 tablespoons mocha-flavored instant coffee powder
6 large egg yolks
1/4 cup granulated sugar

1 Position a rack in the center of the oven and preheat the oven to 375 degrees. Lightly grease six 1-cup ramekins. Sprinkle generously with the cocoa sugar.

2 To make the soufflés, melt the chocolate (see page 13). Remove from the heat.

3 In a saucepan, over medium heat, combine the milk and 1/4 cup of the sugar and stir constantly until the mixture boils. Remove from the heat.

4 In a medium bowl, using an electric mixer on medium speed, beat the egg yolks until thick and light-colored. Beat in the remaining 1/4 cup sugar. Add the flour and blend just until mixed. Gradually mix in the hot milk and beat for 1 minute. Pour the mixture back into the saucepan.

Bring to a boil, stirring constantly, and cook until thick and smooth. Remove from the heat. Strain the mixture through a sieve into a large bowl. Stir in the liqueur and melted chocolate.

5 In a large bowl, using an electric mixer with clean beaters on high speed, beat the egg whites until soft peaks form. One-third at a time, fold the egg whites into the custard mixture. Spoon into the prepared ramekins. Set the cups in a roasting pan and place on the oven rack. Pour boiling water into the roasting pan until it comes halfway up the sides of the ramekins.

6 Bake for 15 to 20 minutes, or until the soufflés puff up and a cake tester inserted into the center comes out clean. Remove from the hot water.

7 Meanwhile, to make the sauce, in a medium saucepan, over medium heat, heat the cream until bubbles start to form around the sides of the pan. Remove from the heat. Stir in the coffee powder until dissolved.

8 In a medium bowl, using an electric mixer on medium speed, beat the egg yolks until thick and light-colored. Beat in the sugar. Pouring it in a thin stream, beat in the hot cream. Pour the mixture back into the saucepan and cook over low heat, stirring constantly, until thick. Do not allow to boil. Remove from the heat and

immediately strain through a sieve into a small bowl. Cover with plastic wrap and keep warm until ready to use.

9 While still warm, open the top of each soufflé and spoon 3/4 of a teaspoonful of sauce into each pudding. Serve the remaining sauce on the side.

722 ■ MOCHA PUDDING CAKE

MAKES 10 TO 12 SERVINGS
CHILL TIME: *6 hours*

18 ladyfingers, split
1 envelope unflavored gelatin
2 tablespoons coffee liqueur
1 cup semisweet chocolate chips
8 ounces cream cheese, at room temperature
1/2 cup packed light brown sugar
1 teaspoon instant espresso powder
1/2 cup heavy cream
1 1/2 teaspoons chocolate extract
1 1/2 cups Chocolate Whipped Cream (see page 406)
Chocolate Curls (see page 422) for garnish

1 To make the cake, line the bottom and sides of a 9-inch springform pan with the ladyfingers, trimming them to fit as needed.

2 In a cup, sprinkle the gelatin over the liqueur. Let stand for 1 minute to soften. Place the cup in a pan of hot water and stir until the gelatin is dissolved.

719
720
721
722

3 Melt the chocolate chips (see page 13). Remove from the heat and transfer to a large bowl. Using an electric mixer on medium speed, beat in the cream cheese, ¼ cup of the brown sugar, and the espresso powder until blended and smooth. Beat in the gelatin mixture.

4 In a medium bowl, using an electric mixer on high speed, beat the cream until soft peaks form. Add the remaining ¼ cup brown sugar and the chocolate extract and beat until stiff peaks form. Fold the cream into the chocolate mixture. Scrape into the prepared pan. Cover and chill for 5 to 6 hours or overnight, or until set.

5 Meanwhile, make the chocolate whipped cream.

6 To serve, carefully remove the side of the springform pan and place the cake on a serving plate. Drop large dabs of the topping over the cake. Sprinkle with chocolate curls.

723 ▪ MOUSSE AU CHOCOLAT

MAKES 6 SERVINGS
CHILL TIME: *2 hours*

4 ounces unsweetened chocolate, grated or finely chopped
2 ounces semisweet chocolate, grated or finely chopped
2 ounces white chocolate, grated or finely chopped
⅓ cup hot strong brewed coffee
4 large eggs, separated
2 tablespoons coffee liqueur
3 tablespoons granulated sugar
Chocolate Curls (see page 422) for garnish

1 In the top of a double boiler over simmering water, melt the chocolates with the coffee, stirring constantly until smooth. Do not overheat. Remove from the heat.

2 In a medium bowl, using an electric mixer on medium speed, beat the egg yolks until thick and light-colored. Beat in the chocolate mixture. Stir in the liqueur.

3 In a large bowl, using an electric mixer with clean beaters on high speed, beat the egg whites until soft peaks form. Fold in the sugar. Fold in the chocolate mixture until blended. Spoon the mousse into six parfait glasses or a serving bowl. Chill for at least 2 hours, or until ready to serve. Garnish with chocolate curls.

BAKING NOTES: Owing to the raw eggs in this recipe, it should be kept refrigerated at all times, and for no longer than 3 days.

724 ▪ OLD-FASHIONED CHOCOLATE PUDDING

MAKES 6 TO 8 SERVINGS

Chocolate Marshmallow Sauce (see page 402) for serving
1¾ cups granulated sugar
⅔ cup Dutch processed cocoa powder
¼ teaspoon salt
4¾ cups milk
½ cup cornstarch or arrowroot
1 tablespoon butter or margarine
1 tablespoon chocolate extract
1½ teaspoons crème de cacao

1 Make the chocolate marshmallow sauce and chill until ready to serve.

2 In a large saucepan, over medium heat, combine the sugar, cocoa powder, and salt. Using a wire whisk, beat in 3½ cups of the milk. Cook until bubbles start to form around the sides of the pan. Remove from the heat.

3 In a small bowl, combine the cornstarch and remaining 1¼ cups milk, blending until smooth. Stir in 1 cup of the hot mixture and return to the saucepan. Bring to a boil, stirring constantly, and cook for 1 to 2 minutes. Remove from the heat and immediately stir in the butter, chocolate extract, and crème de cacao. Pour into six to eight custard cups. Serve warm with the chilled sauce on the side.

BAKING NOTES: For a festive occasion, garnish each pudding with a chocolate wafer cookie and a small sprig of fresh mint.

725 ▪ PEANUT BUTTER 'N JELLY PUDDING

MAKES 6 SERVINGS
FREEZING TIME: *20 minutes*

1 lime, sliced paper-thin
1 tablespoon granulated sugar
4 cups milk
1 cup peanut butter
1 tablespoon Chocolate Syrup II (see page 406)
2 tablespoons black currant jelly
1 pint chocolate ice cream, softened

1 Chill six glasses in the freezer.

2 Make a cut in each lime slice. Place in a small bowl and sprinkle with the granulated sugar.

3 In a large bowl, using an electric mixer on medium speed, combine the milk, peanut butter, chocolate syrup, and jelly. Beat for 2 minutes. Gently blend in the ice cream. Freeze for 15 to 20 minutes.

4 To serve, using an electric mixture on low speed, beat until smooth. Pour into the chilled glasses and garnish with a slice of lime.

723

725

726 ■ PINEAPPLE CHANTILLY WITH CHOCOLATE SAUCE

MAKES 4 TO 6 SERVINGS

CHOCOLATE ALMOND SAUCE

1 cup Chocolate Syrup III (see page 406)
2 tablespoons sliced almonds
1 tablespoon rum

PINEAPPLE CHANTILLY

1 cup heavy cream
2 tablespoons powdered sugar
2 tablespoons amaretto
1 cup pineapple chunks
1 cup green seedless grapes
1 cup banana slices
2 tablespoons slivered almonds, toasted

1 Chill four to six dessert glasses or a serving bowl.

2 To make the sauce, make the chocolate syrup as directed. Stir in the almonds and rum.

3 To make the chantilly, in a medium bowl, using an electric mixer on high speed, beat the cream and powdered sugar until stiff peaks form. Stir in the amaretto.

4 In a large bowl, combine the pineapple, grapes, bananas, and almonds. Fold the whipped cream into the fruits. Spoon into the chilled glasses or serving bowl and top with the chocolate syrup.

727 ■ PLUM-FLAVORED CHOCOLATE MOUSSE

MAKES 12 SERVINGS
CHILL TIME: *8 hours*

5 ounces semisweet chocolate, grated or finely chopped
3 ounces unsweetened chocolate, grated or finely chopped
½ cup butter or margarine
1 cup Dutch processed cocoa powder
1 cup granulated sugar
¼ cup strong brewed coffee
¾ cup crème de prunelle
¼ cup plum juice
4 large eggs, separated
Pinch of salt

1 In the top of a double boiler over simmering water, melt the chocolates and butter, stirring constantly until smooth. Add the cocoa powder and stir until well blended. Mix in the sugar and coffee. Stir in the crème de prunelle and plum juice. Using an electric mixer on medium speed, beat in the egg yolks, one at a time, until smooth. Pour the mixture into a large bowl.

2 In another large bowl, using an electric mixer with clean beaters on high speed, beat the egg whites and salt until stiff but not dry. Fold into the chocolate mixture until blended. Spoon the mousse into twelve custard cups or ramekins and chill overnight.

BAKING NOTES: Owing to the raw eggs used in this recipe, it should be kept refrigerated at all times, and for no longer than 3 days.

728 ■ POTS AU CHOCOLAT I

MAKES 6 TO 8 SERVINGS
CHILL TIME: *8 hours*

6 ounces semisweet chocolate, grated or finely chopped
¼ cup water
1 tablespoon butter or margarine
3 large eggs, separated
¼ cup cherry liqueur

1 In the top of a double boiler over simmering water, melt the chocolate with the water, stirring until smooth. Remove from the heat and beat in the butter. Using an electric mixer on medium speed, beat in the egg yolks and liqueur.

2 In a medium bowl, using an electric mixer with clean beaters on high speed, beat the egg whites until stiff but not dry. Fold into the chocolate mixture. Pour into six to eight chilled custard cups and chill overnight.

BAKING NOTES: Owing to the raw eggs used in this recipe, it should be kept refrigerated at all time, and for no longer than 3 days.

729 ■ POTS AU CHOCOLAT II

MAKES 10 TO 12 SERVINGS
CHILL TIME: *1 hour*

2 cups heavy cream
8 ounces semisweet chocolate, grated or finely chopped
6 large egg yolks
2 tablespoons coffee liqueur

726

727

728

1 Chill six to eight custard cups or parfait glasses.

2 In the top of a double boiler over simmering water, warm the cream and chocolate, stirring until the chocolate is melted and the mixture is smooth. Remove from the heat.

3 In a medium bowl, using an electric mixer on medium speed, beat the egg yolks until thick and light-colored. On low speed, pour the chocolate mixture in a thin stream into the egg yolks and beat until thoroughly blended and no lumps appear. Stir in the liqueur. Pour into the chilled cups or glasses and chill for at least 1 hour before serving.

BAKING NOTES: Owing to the raw eggs used in this recipe, it should be kept refrigerated at all times, and for no longer than 3 days.

730 ■ POTS DE CRÈME AU CHOCOLAT I

MAKES 8 SERVINGS
BAKING TIME: *45 minutes*
CHILL TIME: *4 hours*

2 cups milk
1 cup candied orange peel
3 ounces semisweet chocolate, grated or finely chopped
2 ounces unsweetened chocolate, grated or finely chopped
6 large egg yolks
2 tablespoons granulated sugar

1 Position a rack in the center of the oven and preheat the oven to 350 degrees.

2 In a small saucepan, over medium heat, bring 1 cup of the milk and the orange peel to a boil. Remove from the heat, cover and let stand for 10 minutes.

3 In the top of a double boiler over simmering water, combine the remaining 1 cup milk and the chocolates, stirring until the chocolate is melted and the mixture is smooth. Remove from the heat and add the hot milk mixture.

4 In a large bowl, using an electric mixer on low speed, beat the egg yolks until foamy. Beat in the sugar until dissolved. Pouring it in a thin stream, beat in half of the chocolate mixture. Gradually stir in the remaining chocolate mixture. Strain the mixture through a sieve into a small bowl.

5 Divide the custard evenly between 8 4-ounce ramekins and place them in a large shallow pan. Set the pan on the oven rack and pour boiling water into the pan to a depth of 1 inch.

6 Bake 40 to 45 minutes, or until a cake tester inserted into the center comes out clean. Remove from the hot water and cool on a wire rack. Chill for 4 hours before serving.

731 ■ POTS DE CRÈME AU CHOCOLAT II

MAKES 4 TO 6 SERVINGS
CHILL TIME: *1 hour*

3 large egg yolks
2 tablespoons powdered sugar
Pinch of salt
1¼ cups heavy cream
6 ounces unsweetened chocolate, grated or finely chopped
1 tablespoon butter or margarine
1 teaspoon crème de cassis

1 Chill a serving bowl or four to six custard cups or parfait glasses.

2 In the top of a double boiler over simmering water, using an electric mixer on medium speed, beat the egg yolks until thick and light-colored. Beat in the powdered sugar and salt. Stir in the cream and cook, stirring constantly, for 5 minutes, or until thick and smooth. Add the chocolate, butter, and crème de cassis and stir constantly until the chocolate is melted and the mixture is smooth and well blended. Spoon into the chilled bowl or cups and chill for at least 1 hour before serving.

732 ■ POTS DE CRÈME AU MOCHA CHOCOLAT

MAKES 12 SERVINGS
BAKING TIME: *30 minutes*

3 cups heavy cream
4 ounces semisweet chocolate, grated or finely chopped
1/3 cup powdered sugar
8 large egg yolks
1 teaspoon crème de cacao
1 teaspoon coffee-flavored liqueur
Chocolate cookie crumbs or whole cookies for garnish

1 Position a rack in the center of the oven and preheat the oven to 325 degrees. Lightly grease twelve 4-ounce ramekins.

2 In the top of a double boiler over simmering water, warm the cream and chocolate, stirring until the chocolate is melted and the mixture is smooth. Stir in the powdered sugar. Remove from the heat.

3 In a large bowl, using an electric mixer on medium speed, beat the egg yolks until thick and light-colored. Pouring in a thin stream, whisk the chocolate mixture into the yolks. Stir in the crème de cacao and coffee liqueur and pour into the prepared dishes. Place the ramekins in a roasting pan and place on the oven rack. Pour hot water into the roasting pan until it comes halfway up the sides of the ramekins.

4 Bake for 25 to 30 minutes, or until the puddings are firm around the outside edges. Remove from the hot water and chill until ready to serve. Garnish with chocolate cookie crumbs or whole chocolate wafer cookies.

733 ■ POUDING AU CHOCOLAT

MAKES 8 SERVINGS
STEAMING TIME: *90 minutes*

1 cup milk
¼ cup granulated sugar
4 ounces unsweetened chocolate, grated or finely chopped
4 large eggs, separated
¼ cup butter, at room temperature
½ cup all-purpose flour
½ teaspoon chocolate or vanilla extract
1 cup chocolate cake crumbs or dried bread crumbs
Chocolate Sauce III (see page 406) for serving

1 Generously grease eight 1-cup pudding molds.

2 In the top of a double boiler over simmering water, warm the milk and sugar. Add the chocolate and stir until it is melted and smooth. Remove from the heat.

3 In a large bowl, using an electric mixer on high speed, beat the egg whites until stiff but not dry.

4 In a another large bowl, using an electric mixer on high speed, beat the egg yolks until thick and light-colored. Beat in the butter and flour. Beat in the chocolate mixture and chocolate extract. Fold in the egg whites.

Stir in the cake crumbs. Pour the mixture into the prepared molds. Cover tightly with aluminum foil and prick the foil several times.

5 Place in a steamer or pot with enough water to cover the bottom by 2 inches and cover. Steam over medium-low heat for 90 minutes. Cool on wire racks without removing the foil covers. Serve warm with chocolate sauce on the side.

BAKING NOTES: This recipe was created in the early 19th century and it was designed for the puddings to be steamed. The pudding can be baked in a water bath, but it is not recommended. For best results, use dried chocolate cake crumbs.

734 ■ SKILLET SOUFFLÉ

MAKES 8 TO 10 SERVINGS
BAKING TIME: *15 minutes*

4 ounces semisweet chocolate, grated or finely chopped
2 tablespoons water
4 large eggs, separated, plus 2 large egg whites
⅓ cup granulated sugar
1 teaspoon mocha-flavored instant coffee powder
1 teaspoon coffee liqueur
Pinch of salt
1 tablespoon butter or margarine
Whipped topping for serving

1 Preheat the oven to 375 degrees.

2 Melt the chocolate (see page 13). Remove from the heat.

3 In a small bowl, using an electric mixer on high speed, beat the 6 egg whites until stiff but not dry.

4 In a large bowl, using an electric mixer on medium speed, beat the 4 egg yolks until thick and light-colored. Beat in the sugar, melted chocolate, coffee powder, liqueur, and salt. Gently fold in the egg whites, a little at a time, blending until no white streaks appear.

5 In an 8 or 9-inch ovenproof skillet, over low heat, melt the butter, swirling it to grease the bottom and sides. Sprinkle with a little granulated sugar and pour in the egg mixture.

6 Bake for 12 to 15 minutes, or until a cake tester inserted into the center comes out clean. Cool in the pan on a wire rack for 10 minutes. Serve from the skillet with whipped topping on the side.

BAKING NOTES: Sprinkle finely ground nuts, flaked coconut, chocolate sprinkles, or a sprinkle of freshly ground nutmeg over the soufflé as soon as it comes from the oven, if desired.

729
731
734
730
732
733

735 ■ SOUFFLÉ FROID AU CHOCOLAT

MAKES 8 TO 10 SERVINGS
CHILL TIME: *3 hours*

1 cup heavy cream
1 envelope unflavored gelatin
3 tablespoons cold water
2 ounces unsweetened chocolate, grated or finely chopped
1/2 cup powdered sugar
3/4 cup granulated sugar
1 teaspoon chocolate extract
Pinch of salt
2 cups heavy cream
Fresh mint sprig for garnish

1 Wrap a strip of aluminum foil or parchment paper around the top of a 1½-quart soufflé dish so that it extends 2 inches above the rim and tie securely with string.

2 In a small saucepan, over medium heat, warm the cream until bubbles start to form around the sides of the pan. Remove from the heat.

3 In a cup, sprinkle the gelatin over the water. Let stand for 1 minute to soften.

4 In a medium saucepan, over low heat, melt the chocolate, stirring constantly until smooth. Stir in the powdered sugar. Gradually stir in the hot cream and heat until bubbles start to form around the sides of the

pan. Do not boil. Remove from the heat and stir in the softened gelatin, granulated sugar, chocolate extract, and salt. Stir until the gelatin is dissolved. Transfer to a large bowl and chill until the mixture just starts to thicken.

5 In a large bowl, using an electric mixer on high speed, beat the cream until soft peaks form. Beat the whipped cream into the chilled chocolate mixture until light-colored and smooth. Pour into the prepared soufflé dish and chill for 2 to 3 hours, or until firm. Carefully remove the foil, garnish with a sprig of mint, and serve.

736 ■ SPICED CHOCOLATE BREAD PUDDING

MAKES 6 SERVINGS
BAKING TIME: *70 minutes*

2½ cups heavy cream
2 ounces semisweet chocolate, grated or finely chopped
2 tablespoons butter or margarine
2 large eggs
3 tablespoons coffee liqueur
1 cup soft white bread, cut into 1/2-inch cubes
2/3 cup granulated sugar
1/2 teaspoon ground cinnamon
1/4 teaspoon ground nutmeg

Pinch of salt
2 teaspoons chocolate extract
Chocolate Whipped Cream (see page 406) for garnish

1 Position a rack in the center of the oven and preheat the oven to 325 degrees. Lightly grease and sugar a 1-quart soufflé dish or casserole dish.

2 In a large saucepan, over medium heat, heat the cream until bubbles start to form around the sides of the pan. Add the chocolate and butter, stirring constantly, until melted and smooth. Remove from the heat and cool.

3 In a small bowl, using an electric mixer on medium speed, beat the eggs until thick and light-colored. Beat in the liqueur.

4 In a large bowl, combine the bread cubes, sugar, spices, and salt. Using a wooden spoon, stir in the cream mixture. Add the chocolate extract. Stir in the egg mixture and pour into the prepared baking dish.

5 Bake for 65 to 70 minutes, or until a cake tester inserted into the center comes out clean.

6 Make the chocolate whipped cream. Serve warm or cold with chocolate whipped cream on the side.

735

737

738

736

739

737 ■ STEAMED CHOCOLATE PUDDING

MAKES 6 TO 8 SERVINGS
STEAMING TIME: *2 hours*

1½ cups all-purpose flour
1 teaspoon salt
½ teaspoon baking powder
3 ounces semisweet chocolate, grated or finely chopped
2 tablespoons butter or margarine, melted
⅔ cup granulated sugar
2 large eggs
1 teaspoon rum
1 cup milk
Rum Sauce for garnish

1 Lightly grease a 1-quart steaming mold with cover.

2 Combine the flour, salt, and baking powder

3 Melt the chocolate (see page 13). Remove from the heat.

4 In a large bowl, using an electric mixer on medium speed, beat the butter and sugar until blended. Beat in the eggs, one at a time, beating well after each addition. Beat in the melted chocolate and rum. Gradually beat in the dry ingredients, alternating with the milk, beginning and ending with the dry ingredients. Pour the mixture into the prepared mold and cover.

5 Place in a steamer or pot with enough water to cover the bottom by 2 inches and cover. Steam over medium-low heat for 2 hours. Cool completely in the mold on wire racks without removing the cover. Can be served hot or cold. Serve with rum sauce.

BAKING NOTES: If a steaming mold isn't available, a 1-quart ovenproof dish can be used with a piece of aluminum foil fitted tightly over the top and tied. Puncture several small holes in the top of the foil.

738 ■ STEAMED CHOCOLATE PUMPKIN AND FRUIT PUDDING

MAKES 7 SERVINGS
STEAMING TIME: *2 hours*
CHILLING TIME: *2 hours*

2 cups dried cherries
Amaretto for soaking
1¾ cups raisins
1 box (1 pound) chocolate graham crackers
2 teaspoons baking soda
1 teaspoon ground cinnamon
½ teaspoon ground nutmeg
½ teaspoon ground cloves
1¼ cups butter or margarine, at room temperature
2 cups packed light brown sugar
6 large eggs
2 cups solid pack canned pumpkin
2 tablespoons lemon or lime juice
2 cups ground almonds
Whipped Hard Sauce (see page 418)

1 Five days before you make the pudding, place the cherries in an airtight container with a lid and fill with amaretto to cover. Cover and let soak in a dark place.

2 Grease seven 1-cup ovenproof glass custard cups.

3 In a small bowl, plump the raisins in hot water to cover for 3 to 5 minutes.

4 In a large bowl, crush the graham crackers. Stir in the baking soda and spices.

5 Drain the cherries and reserve the amaretto for another use. Drain the raisins, discarding the water. Pat the raisins dry with paper towels.

6 In a large mixing bowl, using an electric mixer on high speed, beat the butter and brown sugar until smooth. Beat in the eggs until well blended. Beat in the pumpkin and lemon juice. Stir in the raisins, cherries, and almonds. Gradually blend in the dry ingredients, mixing thoroughly.

7 Spoon the mixture into the prepared cups and cover tightly with aluminum foil. Prick the top of the foil several times with a toothpick. Place in a steamer or pot with enough water to cover the bottom by 2 inches and cover.

8 Steam over medium-low heat for 2 hours. Cool completely in the cups on wire racks without removing the foil covers. Remove the foil and invert the puddings onto a baking sheet and chill for 2 hours. Serve at room temperature with brandy hard sauce.

BAKING NOTES: If the puddings are to be kept for any length of time, place each in an resealable sandwich bag and pour 1 ounce of a flavored liqueur such as amaretto over the top. Seal the bag and keep chilled until ready to serve. The pudding will keep for up to one year.

739 ■ SWISS CHOCOLATE SOUFFLÉ

MAKES 10 TO 12 SERVINGS
BAKING TIME: *1 hour*

4 ounces milk chocolate, grated or finely chopped
2 ounces semisweet chocolate, grated or finely chopped
1 cup milk
¼ cup butter or margarine, at room temperature
5 tablespoons all-purpose flour
4 tablespoons granulated sugar
¼ cup heavy cream
6 large eggs, separated
Pinch of salt
Chocolate Whipped Cream (see page 406) for serving

1 Position a rack in the center of the oven and preheat the oven to 350 degrees. Lightly grease and sprinkle with sugar a 2-quart soufflé dish. Wrap a strip of aluminum foil or parchment paper around the top of the dish so that it extends 6 inches above the rim and tie securely with string.

2 In the top of a double boiler over simmering water, melt the chocolates and milk, stirring until smooth. Remove from the heat.

3 In a medium saucepan, over low heat, cook the butter and flour, stirring to make a roux, for

about 3 minutes. Remove from the heat and stir in the melted chocolate and 2 tablespoons of the sugar. Return to the heat and cook for about 3 to 4 minutes. Remove from the heat and transfer to a large bowl.

4 In a small bowl, using an electric mixer on high speed, beat the cream until soft peaks form.

5 Using an electric mixer on medium speed, beat the egg yolks, one at a time, into the chocolate mixture. Beat in the whipped cream.

6 In a large bowl, using an electric mixer with clean beaters on high speed, beat the egg whites and salt until foamy. Add the remaining 2 tablespoons sugar and beat until stiff but not dry. Fold into the chocolate mixture. Pour the mixture into the prepared dish. Place the dish in a roasting pan and set on the oven rack. Pour boiling water into the roasting pan to a depth of 2½ inches.

7 Bake for 55 minutes to 1 hour, or until the soufflé is golden brown and puffed on top. Remove from the hot water. Cool on a wire rack for 10 minutes. Carefully remove the foil. Serve the soufflé warm with chocolate whipped cream on the side.

740 ■ TWO-CHOCOLATE SOUFFLÉ

MAKES 8 TO 10 SERVINGS
CHILL TIME: *4 hours*

2 ounces unsweetened chocolate, grated or finely chopped
2 ounces semisweet chocolate, grated or finely chopped
5 tablespoons water
2 teaspoons unflavored gelatin
4 large eggs plus 4 large egg yolks
¼ cup granulated sugar
½ cup sliced almonds for garnish
Fresh mint sprig for garnish

1 Lightly oil a 1½-quart soufflé dish. Wrap a greased strip of aluminum foil or parchment paper around the top of the dish so that it extends 5 to 6 inches above the rim and tie securely with string.

2 In the top of a double boiler over simmering water, melt the chocolates with 2 tablespoons of the water, stirring until smooth. Remove from the heat.

3 In a small saucepan, sprinkle the gelatin over the remaining 3 tablespoons water. Let stand for 1 minute to soften. Stir over low heat until completely dissolved. Stir into the chocolate mixture.

4 In the top of a double boiler over simmering water, using an electric mixer on medium speed, beat the eggs and egg yolks until thick and light-colored. Beat in the sugar. Remove from the heat. Beat in the chocolate mixture. Immediately pour into the prepared soufflé dish and chill for at least 4 hours.

5 To serve, carefully remove the foil strip. Sprinkle the top with the sliced almonds and garnish with a sprig of mint.

741 ■ UPSIDE-DOWN CHOCOLATE PUDDING

MAKES 8 TO 10 SERVINGS
BAKING TIME: *35 minutes*

¼ cup butter or margarine
½ cup Dutch processed cocoa powder
1 cup all-purpose flour
¾ cup granulated sugar
3 tablespoons mocha-flavored instant coffee powder
1½ teaspoons baking powder
1 large egg
½ cup milk
1¼ cups boiling water
Chocolate Whipped Cream (see page 406) for garnish

1 Position a rack in the center of the oven and preheat the oven to 350 degrees. Lightly grease a 1½-quart casserole dish.

2 In a small saucepan, over low heat, melt the butter, stirring until smooth. Remove from the heat. Stir in the cocoa until smooth.

3 Combine the flour, ½ cup of the sugar, the coffee powder, and baking powder.

4 In a small bowl, using an electric mixer on high speed, beat the egg until foamy. Beat in the milk. On low speed, beat in the chocolate mixture. Gradually blend in the dry ingredients, a little at a time, blending well after each addition. Pour into the prepared casserole dish.

5 Sprinkle ¼ cup sugar over the batter in the casserole dish. Gently pour the boiling water over the cocoa mixture. Place the casserole dish in a roasting pan and set on the oven rack. Pour boiling water into the roasting pan until it comes halfway up the side of the casserole dish.

6 Bake for 30 to 35 minutes, or until the center springs back when touched. Cool for 15 to 30 minutes. Invert onto a serving plate. To serve, spoon into individual serving dishes and top with chocolate whipped cream.

742 ■ WHITE CHOCOLATE MOUSSE WITH CRÈME FRAÎCHE

MAKES 8 SERVINGS
CHILL TIME: *8 hours*

10 ounces white chocolate or almond bark, grated or finely chopped
¼ cup water
1 envelope unflavored gelatin
2 tablespoons arrowroot or cornstarch
1½ cups milk or heavy cream
3 large eggs, separated, plus 2 large eggs
⅔ cup granulated sugar
3 tablespoons crème de cacao
1 teaspoon chocolate extract
1 cup heavy cream
Crème Fraîche (see page 409) for serving

1 Melt the white chocolate (see page 13). Remove from the heat.

2 Place the water in a cup and sprinkle the gelatin over the top. Let stand for 1 minute to soften.

3 Combine the arrowroot into ¼ cup of the milk.

4 In a large bowl, using an electric mixer on medium speed, beat the egg yolks and eggs until thick and light-colored. Gradually beat in 1/3 cup of the sugar, mixing until dissolved. Beat in the arrowroot mixture.

5 In a medium saucepan, over medium heat, heat the remaining 1 1/4 cups milk until bubbles start to form around the sides of the pan. Remove from the heat. Pouring it in a thin stream, beat the hot milk into the egg mixture. Pour the egg mixture back into the saucepan. Cook over low heat, stirring occasionally, for about 8 to 10 minutes, or until the mixture coats the back of a spoon. Remove from the heat. Stir in the gelatin until dissolved.

6 Stir 1 cup of the hot custard into the melted white chocolate. Stir the white chocolate mixture back into the hot custard, blending thoroughly. Cool slightly. Stir in the crème de cacao and chocolate extract.

7 Meanwhile, in a small bowl, using an electric mixer on high speed, beat the heavy cream until soft peaks form.

8 In a small bowl, using an electric mixer with clean beaters on high speed, beat the egg whites until they just hold their shape. Continue beating on low speed and sprinkle in the remaining 1/3 cup sugar. Fold 1 cup of the custard into the whipped cream. Fold 1 cup of the custard into

the egg whites. Then combine everything in a large bowl and fold gently to incorporate. Pour into a serving bowl. Cover and chill for 6 to 8 hours. Serve with the crème fraîche.

743 ■ WHITE CHOCOLATE SOUFFLÉ

MAKES 10 TO 12 SERVINGS
BAKING TIME: *50 minutes*

4 large eggs
2 ounces white chocolate or almond bark, grated or finely chopped
1/3 cup granulated sugar
2 tablespoons coffee liqueur
1/2 teaspoon almond extract
1 cup heavy cream
1/4 cup butter or margarine, at room temperature
1/4 cup all-purpose flour

1 Position a rack in the center of the oven and preheat the oven to 350 degrees. Lightly grease and dust with sugar a 2-quart soufflé dish.

2 Place the eggs in a small bowl of warm water for 5 to 10 minutes.

3 Meanwhile, in the top of a double boiler over simmering water, melt the chocolate with the sugar and liqueur, stirring constantly until the chocolate is melted and the sugar is dissolved. Remove from the heat and stir in the almond extract.

4 Separate the eggs. In a small bowl, using an electric mixer on

high speed, beat the egg whites until stiff but not dry.

5 In a small saucepan, over medium heat, heat the cream until bubbles start to form around the sides of the pan. Remove from the heat.

6 In a medium saucepan, over medium heat, melt the butter. Add the flour and stir constantly for about 2 to 3 minutes, until well incorporated and the mixture starts to bubble. Remove from the heat. Add the hot cream and beat constantly until thickened. Return to the heat and bring to a boil. Remove from the heat and pour into a large bowl. Using an electric mixer on medium speed, beat in the egg yolks. Beat in the chocolate mixture on low speed. Fold 1/4 cup of the egg whites into the mixture until white streaks no longer appear. Spoon the remaining whites on top of the custard and gently fold in. Scrape the mixture into the prepared baking dish and spread evenly.

7 Bake for 45 to 50 minutes, or until puffed and a cake tester inserted into the center comes out clean. Serve immediately.

BAKING NOTES: Insert the cake tester into the side of the soufflé that has risen above the edge of the dish. The secret to making a successful soufflé is to not deflate the egg whites when folding them into the custard mixture.

740

741

742

743

744 ■ WILD TURKEY AND AMARETTO CHOCOLATE FROZEN SOUFFLÉ

MAKES 8 TO 10 SERVINGS
FREEZING TIME: *14 hours*

WILD TURKEY CHOCOLATE LAYER

¹/₂ cup Wild Turkey (bourbon)
1³/₄ teaspoons unflavored gelatin
3 ounces semisweet chocolate, grated or finely chopped
1 ounce unsweetened chocolate, grated or finely chopped
1 tablespoon butter or margarine
6 large egg yolks plus 3 large eggs, separated
¹/₂ cup granulated sugar
¹/₄ teaspoon chocolate extract
Pinch of salt
Pinch of cream of tartar
1³/₄ cups heavy cream
10 tablespoons Grasshopper liqueur

CHOCOLATE AMARETTO LAYER

¹/₃ cup mint chocolate chips
2 large egg yolks plus 2 large eggs, separated
3 tablespoons granulated sugar
¹/₄ teaspoon almond extract
¹/₄ cup amaretto
Pinch of cream of tartar
Pinch of salt
¹/₂ cup heavy cream
Shaved or grated semisweet chocolate for garnish

1 Wrap a strip of aluminum foil or parchment paper around the top of a 2-quart soufflé dish so that it extends 4 inches above the top of the rim and tie securely with string. Lightly grease the inside of the dish and the foil. Freeze until ready to use.

2 To make the Wild Turkey chocolate layer, place the Wild Turkey in a cup and sprinkle the gelatin over the top. Let stand for 1 minute to soften. Set in a larger bowl of hot water and stir to dissolve the gelatin.

3 In the top of a double boiler over simmering water, melt the chocolates and butter, stirring constantly until smooth. Remove from the heat.

4 In a large bowl, using an electric mixer on medium speed, beat the egg yolks until thick and light-colored. Mix in the sugar, chocolate extract, and salt, and beat for about 4 to 6 minutes, until very thick. On low speed, beat in half of the gelatin mixture. Reserve the remaining gelatin mixture for the second layer, keeping it warm in the hot water until ready to use.

5 In another large bowl, using an electric mixer with clean beaters on high speed, beat the egg whites and cream of tartar until soft peaks form. Gently fold one-fourth of the whites into the yolks, blending until white streaks no longer appear. Fold in the remaining whites.

6 In a medium bowl, using an electric mixer on high speed, beat the cream until it just starts to thicken. Add the Grasshopper liqueur and beat until soft peaks form. Gently fold the cream into the egg mixture. Cover and chill until ready to use.

7 To make the chocolate amaretto layer, melt the chocolate chips (see page 13). Remove from the heat.

8 In a large bowl, using an electric mixer on medium speed, beat the egg yolks and the sugar until thick and light-colored. Add the almond extract and beat for 4 to 6 minutes, until very thick. On low speed, beat in the amaretto and melted chocolate.

9 In small bowl, using an electric mixer on high speed, beat the egg whites, cream of tartar, and salt until soft peaks form. Gently fold into the egg yolk mixture until white streaks no longer appear.

10 In another small bowl, using an electric mixer on high speed, beat the cream just until thickened. Add the remaining gelatin mixture and beat until soft peaks form. Fold into the egg mixture.

11 To assemble, spoon some of the chilled Wild Turkey chocolate mixture into the prepared soufflé dish and spread evenly. Spoon one-fourth of the chocolate amaretto mixture over the top, leaving a border around the edge of the dish. Spoon more of the Wild Turkey chocolate mixture in and spread evenly. Repeat until all of the custard mixtures are used up. The chocolate amaretto mixture should not be visible. Freeze for at least 12 to 14 hours, or until ready to serve.

12 To serve, remove the foil and sprinkle with shaved or grated chocolate.

BAKING NOTES: Owing to the raw eggs used in this recipe, after first use it should be kept refrigerated at all times, and for no longer than 3 days.

744

Quick Breads

745 ■ ALMOND SCONES WITH CHOCOLATE SAUCE

MAKES 10 TO 12 SCONES
BAKING TIME: *17 minutes*

SCONES

2 cups all-purpose flour
¹/₃ cup granulated sugar
1¹/₂ teaspoons baking powder
¹/₂ cup finely ground almonds
¹/₄ teaspoon salt
¹/₃ cup butter or margarine, cubed
¹/₂ cup sour cream or plain yogurt
1 large egg
1¹/₂ teaspoons almond extract

SAUCE

Chocolate Sauce III (see pages 404)

1 Position a rack in the center of the oven and preheat the oven to 400 degrees. Lightly grease two baking sheets.

2 In a large bowl, combine the flour, sugar, baking powder, almonds, and salt. Using a pastry blender or two knives scissor fashion, cut in the butter to make a crumbly mixture.

3 In a medium bowl, using an electric mixer on high speed, beat the sour cream, egg, and almond extract until smooth.

4 Using a pastry blender or two knives, combine the flour mixture and the sour cream mixture and blend to make a soft, sticky dough. Drop the dough by heaping spoonfuls onto the prepared baking sheet, spacing them 2¹/₂ to 3 inches apart.

5 Bake for 15 to 17 minutes, or until golden brown on top. Cool on a wire rack.

6 Meanwhile, make the chocolate sauce.

7 Serve the muffins on individual dishes with the chocolate sauce spooned over the top.

746 ■ BANANA CHOCOLATE CHIP MUFFINS I

MAKES 12 MUFFINS
BAKING TIME: *20 minutes*

1³/₄ cups plus 2 tablespoon all-purpose flour
¹/₃ cup granulated sugar
2 tablespoons Dutch processed unsweetened cocoa powder
1 tablespoon baking powder
1 cup mashed bananas (2 medium)
²/₃ cup canola oil
1 large egg, beaten
1 cup semisweet chocolate chips

1 Position a rack in the center of the oven and preheat the oven to 425 degrees. Line twelve 2³/₄-inch muffin cups with paper baking cups.

2 In a large bowl, combine the flour, sugar, cocoa powder, and baking powder.

3 Blend the bananas, oil, and egg into the dry ingredients, mixing just until blended. Fold in the chocolate chips. Spoon the batter into the prepared muffin cups, filling them three-fourths full.

4 Bake for 15 to 20 minutes, or until a cake tester inserted into the center comes out clean. Remove the muffins to a wire rack to cool completely.

745

746

747

749

748

747 ■ BANANA CHOCOLATE CHIP MUFFINS II

MAKES 12 MUFFINS
BAKING TIME: *25 minutes*

1 cup all-purpose flour
1/2 cup whole wheat flour
1/2 cup oat bran
1/2 cup miniature chocolate chips
2 tablespoons pecans, chopped
1/2 teaspoon baking soda
1/2 cup granulated sugar
1/2 cup water
1/2 cup canola oil
1 large egg
1 cup mashed bananas (2 medium)

1 Position a rack in the center of the oven and preheat the oven to 350 degrees. Lightly grease twelve 2¾-inch muffin cups.

2 Combine the flours, oat bran, chocolate chips, pecans, and baking soda.

3 In a large bowl, using an electric mixer on medium speed, beat the sugar, water, and oil until smooth. Beat in the egg and mashed bananas. Gradually blend in the dry ingredients, mixing just until blended. Spoon into the prepared muffin cups, filling them three-fourths full.

4 Bake for 20 to 25 minutes, or until a cake tester inserted into the center comes out clean. Cool in the pan on a wire rack for 5 minutes. Invert onto the rack to cool completely.

750

748 ■ BANANA CHOCOLATE CHIP MUFFINS WITH PISTACHIO NUTS

MAKES 12 MUFFINS
BAKING TIME: *25 minutes*

2 cups all-purpose flour
4 ounces semisweet chocolate, grated or finely chopped
1/2 cup pistachio nuts, chopped
2 teaspoons baking soda
6 tablespoons butter or margarine, at room temperature
2/3 cup granulated sugar
2 large eggs
1 cup mashed bananas (2 medium)
1 teaspoon crème de cacao
1/4 cup buttermilk

1 Position a rack in the center of the oven and preheat the oven to 350 degrees. Lightly grease twelve 2¾-inch muffin cups.

2 Combine the flour, chocolate, pistachios, and baking soda.

3 In a large bowl, using an electric mixer on medium speed, beat the butter and sugar until light and fluffy. Beat in the eggs, bananas, and crème de cacao. Gradually blend in the dry ingredients, alternating with the buttermilk, blending until the dry ingredients are just moistened. Spoon into the prepared muffin cups, filling them two-thirds full.

4 Bake for 20 to 25 minutes, or until a cake tester inserted into the center comes out clean. Cool in the pan on a wire rack for 5 minutes. Transfer to the rack to cool completely.

749 ■ BANANA LOAF WITH CHOCOLATE CHIPS

MAKES 1 LOAF
BAKING TIME: *50 minutes*

1¾ cups all-purpose flour
3/4 teaspoon baking soda
1¼ teaspoon cream of tartar
1/4 teaspoon ground cinnamon
1/2 cup semisweet chocolate chips
1/2 cup chopped walnuts or almonds
3/4 cup granulated sugar
1/2 cup canola oil

2 large eggs
2 ripe bananas, sliced
1/2 teaspoon banana or vanilla extract

1 Position a rack in the center of the oven and preheat the oven to 350 degrees. Lightly grease and flour a 9 by 5-inch loaf pan.

2 In a large bowl, combine the flour, baking soda, cream of tartar, cinnamon, chocolate chips, and walnuts.

3 In a medium bowl, using an electric mixer on medium speed, beat the sugar, oil, eggs, bananas, and banana extract until smooth. Gradually blend in the dry ingredients. Pour the mixture into the prepared pan.

4 Bake for 45 to 50 minutes, or until a cake tester inserted into the center comes out clean. Cool in the pan on a wire rack for 10 minutes. Invert onto the rack to cool completely.

750 ■ BISHOP'S BREAD

MAKES 2 LOAVES
BAKING TIME: *1 hour*

2 cups all-purpose flour
1 cup granulated sugar
1 tablespoon baking powder
1 teaspoon salt
1/3 cup vegetable shortening
1½ cups orange juice
3 tablespoons canola oil
1 large egg
1 tablespoon grated orange zest
1/2 cup wheat germ
6 ounces semisweet chocolate, grated or finely chopped
1/4 cup golden raisins
1/4 cup candied cherry halves
1/4 cup walnuts, chopped

1 Position a rack in the center of the oven and preheat the oven to 350 degrees. Lightly grease two 9 by 5-inch loaf pans.

2 In a large bowl, combine the flour, sugar, baking powder, and salt. Using fingertips, rub the shortening into the dry ingredients to form a crumbly mixture.

3 In a medium bowl, combine the orange juice, oil, egg, and orange zest. Gradually blend into the dry ingredients. Add

the wheat germ, chocolate, raisins, cherries, and nuts. Divide the mixture between the prepared pans and spread evenly.

4 Bake for 55 minutes to 1 hour, or until a cake tester inserted into the center comes out clean. Cool in the pans on a wire rack for 10 minutes. Invert onto the rack to cool completely.

751 ■ BLACK FOREST CHERRY COBBLER

MAKES 6 TO 8 SERVINGS
BAKING TIME: *25 minutes*

CHERRY FILLING

2 tablespoons packed light brown sugar
2 tablespoons cornstarch or arrowroot
1 can (16 ounces) pitted red cherries
1 teaspoon almond extract
6 to 8 drops red food coloring (optional)
1 cup finely ground almonds (optional)

COBBLER TOPPING

1/2 cup all-purpose flour
2 tablespoons Dutch processed cocoa powder
1 tablespoon packed light brown sugar
3/4 teaspoon baking powder
Pinch of salt
2 tablespoons butter or margarine, at room temperature
1/3 cup evaporated milk or heavy cream
1 teaspoon chocolate or vanilla extract
Chocolate Whipped Cream (see page 406) for serving

1 Position a rack in the center of the oven and preheat the oven to 375 degrees.

2 To make the filling, in a medium saucepan, over medium heat, combine the brown sugar, cornstarch, and cherries and cook, stirring occasionally, until thickened. Remove from the heat and stir in the almond extract, food coloring, and almonds. Immediately pour into an ungreased 1 1/2-quart ovenproof casserole dish.

3 To make the topping, in a large bowl, combine the flour, cocoa powder, brown sugar, baking powder, and salt and blend thoroughly. Using fingertips, rub the butter into the dry ingredients to form a fine, crumbly mixture. Stir in the evaporated milk and chocolate extract. Drop the dough by heaping spoonfuls onto the hot cherry mixture in the casserole dish.

4 Bake for 20 to 25 minutes, or until the topping is golden brown. Cool slightly and serve with chocolate whipped cream on the side.

752 ■ BRUNCH COFFEE RING

MAKES 10 TO 12 SERVINGS
BAKING TIME: *65 minutes*

COFFEE CAKE

2 cups all-purpose flour
1 teaspoon baking powder
1 teaspoon baking soda
1/2 teaspoon salt
1 cup sour cream
1 cup granulated sugar
2 large eggs
1 teaspoon Praline liqueur
1/2 cup semisweet chocolate chips

TOPPING

1/2 cup all-purpose flour
1/2 cup packed light brown sugar
1 1/2 teaspoon Dutch processed cocoa powder
1/4 cup butter or margarine, at room temperature
1/2 cup walnuts or pecans, chopped

1 Position a rack in the center of the oven and preheat the oven to 350 degrees. Lightly grease a 9-inch tube pan.

2 To make the cake, combine the flour, baking powder, baking soda, and salt.

3 In a large bowl, using an electric mixer on medium speed, beat the sour cream, sugar, eggs, and liqueur until combined. Gradually blend in the dry ingredients. Fold in the chocolate chips. Scrape the mixture into the prepared pan and spread evenly.

4 To make the topping, in a medium bowl, combine the flour, brown sugar, and cocoa powder. Using a pastry blender or two knives scissor fashion, cut in the butter to form a crumbly mixture. Blend in the walnuts. Crumble over the batter in the pan.

5 Bake for 1 hour to 65 minutes, or until golden brown and a cake tester inserted into the center comes out clean. Cool in the pan on a wire rack. Remove from the pan and place on a serving plate.

753 ■ CHERRY NUT MUFFINS WITH CHOCOLATE CHIPS

MAKES 12 MUFFINS
BAKING TIME: *25 minutes*
SOAKING TIME: *2 hours*

1/2 cup dried cherries
Boiling water or brandy for soaking
2 cups all-purpose flour
3/4 cup semisweet chocolate chips
1/2 cup granulated sugar
1/2 cup slivered almonds
1 tablespoon baking powder
1 tablespoon grated orange zest
1/2 teaspoon salt
1 cup heavy cream or evaporated milk
1/3 cup canola oil
1/3 cup butter or margarine, at room temperature
1 large egg

752

1 Place the dried cherries in a cup and cover with boiling water or brandy. Let soak for 2 hours.

2 Position a rack in the center of the oven and preheat the oven to 400 degrees. Lightly grease twelve 2¾-inch muffin cups.

3 Drain and chop the cherries. If brandy was used to soak the cherries, reserve for another use. Discard the water.

4 In a large bowl, combine the flour, chocolate chips, cherries, sugar, almonds, baking powder, orange zest, and salt.

5 In a medium bowl, using an electric mixer on medium speed, beat the cream, oil, butter, and egg until blended. Add to the dry ingredients and stir just until blended. Do not overmix. Spoon the mixture into the prepared muffin cups, dividing it evenly.

6 Bake for 20 to 25 minutes, or until a cake tester inserted into the center comes out clean. Cool in the pan on a wire rack for 2 to 3 minutes. Transfer to the rack to cool completely.

BAKING NOTES: For cherry lovers, double the amount of cherries and do not chop them after soaking.

754 ■ CHOCOLATE ALMOND TEA BREAD

MAKES 2 LOAVES
BAKING TIME: *55 minutes*

1¼ cups all-purpose flour
2½ cups whole wheat flour
2¼ teaspoons baking powder
½ teaspoon ground cinnamon
¼ teaspoon ground nutmeg
½ teaspoon salt
¼ cup butter or margarine, at room temperature
⅔ cup granulated sugar
2 large eggs
½ cup milk
¼ teaspoon almond or chocolate extract
½ cup sliced almonds
1 ounce semisweet chocolate, grated or finely chopped

1 Position a rack in the center of the oven and preheat the oven to 325 degrees. Lightly grease two 9 by 5-inch loaf pans.

2 Combine the flours, baking powder, spices, and salt.

3 In a large bowl, using an electric mixer on medium speed, beat the butter and sugar until blended. Beat in the eggs, one at a time, beating well after each addition. Beat in milk and almond extract. Gradually blend in the dry ingredients. Fold in the almonds and grated chocolate. Divide the mixture

between prepared pans and spread evenly.

4 Bake for 50 to 55 minutes, or until a cake tester inserted into the center comes out clean. Cool in the pans on wire racks.

BAKING NOTES: Each loaf makes 9 to 12 servings.

755 ■ CHOCOLATE BABKAS

MAKES 2 LOAVES
BAKING TIME: *35 minutes*
RISING TIME: *2 hours*

DOUGH

2 tablespoons active dry yeast
½ cup warm water (105 to 115 degrees on a thermometer)
⅓ cup granulated sugar
⅔ cup heavy cream, warmed to 105 degrees
3 tablespoons butter or margarine, at room temperature
½ teaspoon chocolate or vanilla extract
Pinch of salt
4½ cups cake flour, sifted twice
2 large eggs plus 1 large egg yolk

COCOA WALNUT FILLING

1 cup powdered sugar
½ cup Dutch processed cocoa powder
1 cup chopped walnuts or almonds

CRUMB TOPPING

⅓ cup powdered sugar
¼ cup all-purpose flour
¼ teaspoon ground allspice
2 tablespoons butter or margarine, at room temperature

ASSEMBLY

2 tablespoons melted butter for brushing
1 large egg white
¼ teaspoon water

1 In a large bowl, blend the yeast and water. Stir in 1 teaspoon of the sugar. Let stand for about 5 minutes, until foamy.

2 Blend in the remaining sugar, cream, butter, chocolate extract, and salt. Using an electric mixer on low speed, blend in 2½ cups of the flour and beat for about 3 to 5 minutes, until smooth and elastic. Beat in the whole eggs, one at a time. Beat in the egg

754

751

753

yolk. Blend in 1½ cups of the flour.

3 On a lightly floured surface, knead the dough for about 12 to 15 minutes, until smooth. (This can also be done in a heavy-duty electric mixer fitted with the dough hook attachment.) Add the remaining flour as necessary to prevent sticking. Place the dough in a large bowl and cover with a towel. Let rise for about 1 hour in a draft-free warm place until doubled in bulk.

4 Meanwhile, to make the filling, in a small bowl, combine the powdered sugar, cocoa powder, and walnuts and mix until well blended.

5 To make the topping, in a small bowl, combine the powdered sugar, flour, and allspice. Using fingertips, rub the butter into the dry ingredients to form a crumbly mixture.

6 Position a rack in the center of the oven and preheat the oven to 350 degrees.

7 On the lightly floured surface, punch the dough down and knead for about 2 to 3 minutes. Invert the bowl over the dough and let rest for 15 minutes.

8 To assemble, divide the dough in half. Roll each half into a rectangle approximately 10 by 20 inches. Brush each with the melted butter. Sprinkle the filling evenly over the buttered areas. Starting with one of the long sides, roll up jelly-roll fashion. Seal the ends and place each roll seam-side down in an

8½ by 4½-inch loaf pan. Cover with a towel and let rise for up to 45 minutes, until almost doubled in bulk.

9 In a small bowl, using an electric mixer, beat the egg white and water until foamy. Brush over the tops of the loaves. Sprinkle evenly with the topping.

10 Bake for 30 to 35 minutes, or until the tops are golden brown. Cool in the pans on wire racks for 10 minutes. Invert onto the racks. Place right side up and cool slightly. Serve warm.

756 ■ CHOCOLATE BANANA BREAD

MAKES 1 LOAF
BAKING TIME: *50 minutes*

½ cup old-fashioned oats
½ cup all-purpose flour
¾ cup whole wheat flour
½ cup Dutch processed cocoa powder
1¼ teaspoons baking powder
½ teaspoon baking soda
½ teaspoon salt
⅓ cup butter or margarine, at room temperature
⅔ cup granulated sugar
2 large eggs
1 cup mashed ripe bananas
2 tablespoons heavy cream or milk
1 teaspoon chocolate or vanilla extract

1 Position a rack in the center of the oven and preheat the oven to 350 degrees. Lightly grease and flour a 9 by 5-inch loaf pan.

2 Place the oats in the container of a blender and blend for 20 seconds or until a fine powder.

3 Combine the oats, flours, cocoa powder, baking powder, baking soda, and salt.

4 In a large bowl, using an electric mixer on medium speed, beat the butter and sugar until light and fluffy. Beat in the eggs, bananas, cream, and chocolate extract. Beat for 2 to 3 minutes, or until the mixture has thickened a little and is very smooth. Gradually blend in the dry ingredients, beating after each addition until smooth. Pour the mixture into the prepared pan.

5 Bake for 45 to 50 minutes, or until a cake tester inserted into the center comes out clean. Cool in the pan on a wire rack for 10 minutes. Invert onto the rack to cool completely.

755

756

757 ■ CHOCOLATE BREAKFAST CAKE WITH CHOCOLATE ALMOND SAUCE

MAKES 10 TO 12 SERVINGS
RISING TIME: *2 hours*
BAKING TIME: *45 minutes*

2½ cups all-purpose flour
1½ cups granulated sugar
1 tablespoon active dry yeast
1 teaspoon baking soda
½ teaspoon salt
2 ounces unsweetened chocolate, grated or finely chopped
1 cup butter or margarine
1 cup milk
¼ cup Dutch processed cocoa powder
3 large eggs
1 cup Chocolate Almond Sauce (see page 395)
¼ cup sliced almonds

1 Lightly grease and flour a 10-inch Bundt pan.

2 Combine the flour, sugar, yeast, baking soda, and salt.

3 In the top of a double boiler over simmering water, melt the chocolate and butter, stirring until smooth. Stir in the milk and cocoa powder until smooth. Remove from the heat.

4 In a large bowl, using an electric mixer, beat the eggs until thick and light-colored. Pouring it in a thin stream, beat in the chocolate mixture. Gradually blend in the dry ingredients just until blended. Pour into the prepared pan. Cover with a towel and let rise for 2 hours, or until an indentation is left in the dough when poked.

5 Meanwhile, make the chocolate almond sauce.

6 Position a rack in the center of the oven and preheat the oven to 350 degrees. Bake the cake for 40 to 45 minutes, or until it sounds hollow when tapped. Cool in the pan on a wire rack for 15 minutes. Invert onto a serving dish. Drizzle the chocolate almond sauce over the top, allowing it to drip down the sides, and sprinkle with sliced almonds. Serve warm.

758 ■ CHOCOLATE CARROT MUFFINS

MAKES 12 MUFFINS
BAKING TIME: *20 minutes*

COCOA CARROT MUFFINS

1½ cups all-purpose flour
1 cup old-fashioned oats
½ cup granulated sugar
½ cup golden raisins
¼ cup Dutch processed cocoa powder
1 teaspoon baking powder
1 teaspoon ground cinnamon
1 cup milk
¼ cup canola oil
1 large egg, beaten
1 teaspoon chocolate or almond extract
1 cup shredded carrots

CREAM CHEESE FROSTING

3 ounces cream cheese
½ cup powdered sugar
1 tablespoon coffee liqueur
½ cup chocolate sprinkles or grated semisweet chocolate for garnish

1 Position a rack in the center of the oven and preheat the oven to 400 degrees. Lightly grease the bottoms of twelve 2¾-inch muffin cups.

2 In a large bowl, combine the flour, oats, sugar, raisins, cocoa powder, baking powder, and cinnamon. Using a large spoon, stir in the milk, oil, egg, and chocolate extract. Do not overmix. Mix only until the dry ingredients are just moistened. Fold in the carrots. Spoon into the prepared muffin cups, filling them about three-fourths full.

3 Bake for 18 to 20 minutes, or until golden brown. Cool in the pan on a wire rack for 5 minutes. Transfer to the rack and cool completely.

4 Meanwhile, to make the frosting, in a small bowl, using an electric mixer on medium speed, beat the cream cheese, powdered sugar, and liqueur until combined. Chill until ready to use.

5 Spread a teaspoonful of frosting on each muffin and garnish with chocolate sprinkles or grated chocolate.

758

757

759 ■ CHOCOLATE CHERRY PECAN MUFFINS

MAKES 12 MUFFINS
BAKING TIME: *25 minutes*

2 cups all-purpose flour
1/2 cup granulated sugar
1 cup Hershey's™ Chocolate Shoppe Candy Bar Sprinkles
1 cup chopped dried cherries
1/2 cup chopped pecans
1 tablespoon baking powder
1/2 teaspoon salt
1 cup milk
1/3 cup canola oil
1/3 cup butter or margarine, melted
1 large egg
12 whole canned pitted cherries

1 Position a rack in the center of the oven and preheat the oven to 400 degrees. Lightly grease twelve 2¾-inch muffin cups.

2 Combine the flour, sugar, candy bar bits, cherries, pecans, baking powder, and salt.

3 In a large bowl, using an electric mixer on high speed, beat the milk, oil, butter, and egg for 2 to 3 minutes, until smooth. By hand, gradually blend in the dry ingredients, mixing just until incorporated. Spoon the mixture into the prepared cups, filling them just about full. Press 1 whole cherry into the center of each muffin.

4 Bake for 20 to 25 minutes, or until a cake tester inserted into the center comes out clean. Cool in the pan on a wire rack for several minutes. Invert onto the rack to cool completely.

760 ■ CHOCOLATE CHIP MUFFINS I

MAKES 12 MUFFINS
BAKING TIME: *20 minutes*

1 large egg
2 tablespoons butter or margarine, melted
1/4 cup granulated sugar
2 ounces semisweet chocolate, grated or finely chopped
1/3 cup plus 1 tablespoon all-purpose flour
Pinch of salt

1 Position a rack in the center of the oven and preheat the oven to 375 degrees. Line twelve 2¾-inch muffin cups with paper baking cups.

2 In a medium bowl, using an electric mixer on medium speed, beat the egg until thick and light-colored. Beat in butter and sugar. Add the chocolate, flour, and salt and blend just until moistened. Spoon the mixture into the prepared muffin cups.

3 Bake for 18 to 20 minutes, or until a cake tester inserted into the center comes out clean. Cool on a wire rack.

761 ■ CHOCOLATE CHIP MUFFINS II

MAKES 12 SERVINGS
BAKING TIME: *25 minutes*

2 cups all-purpose flour
1 cup (6 ounces) Hershey's™ Chocolate Shoppe Candy Bar Sprinkles (milk chocolate)
1 teaspoon baking soda
2 tablespoons grated orange zest
1/2 cup butter or margarine, at room temperature
1¼ cups granulated sugar
2 large eggs
1 cup sour cream or chocolate yogurt
1/4 cup fresh orange juice

759

760

761

762

764

1 Position a rack in the center of the oven and preheat the oven to 375 degrees. Grease twelve 2¾-inch muffin cups.

2 Combine the flour, candy bar bits, baking soda, and orange zest.

3 In a large bowl, using an electric mixer on medium speed, beat the butter and sugar until light and fluffy. Beat in the eggs, sour cream, and orange juice. Add the dry ingredients and mix just until blended. Spoon the mixture into the prepared pan, dividing it equally between the cups.

4 Bake for 25 minutes, or until a cake tester inserted into the center comes out clean. Cool in the pan on a wire rack for 5 minutes. Invert onto the rack to cool completely.

762 ■ CHOCOLATE CHIP SCONES

MAKES 8 TO 12 SCONES
BAKING TIME: *20 minutes*

½ cup buttermilk
1 large egg
1 teaspoon chocolate or vanilla extract
2 cups all-purpose flour
3 tablespoons granulated sugar
2 teaspoons baking powder
¼ teaspoon salt
½ cup butter or shortening
½ cup semisweet chocolate chips

763

1 Position a rack in the center of the oven and preheat the oven to 425 degrees. Lightly grease a baking sheet.

2 In a medium bowl, using an electric mixer on medium speed, beat the buttermilk, egg, and chocolate extract until combined.

3 In a large bowl, combine the flour, sugar, baking powder, and salt. Using a pastry blender or two knives scissor fashion, cut in the butter to form a crumbly mixture. Using a wooden spoon, stir in the buttermilk mixture. Fold in the chocolate chips, mixing until the mixture forms a soft dough.

4 On a lightly floured surface, knead the dough gently for 2 to 3 minutes. Roll out into an 8-inch circle. Using a sharp knife, score 8 to 12 wedges into the surface of the dough. Transfer to the prepared baking sheet.

5 Bake for 18 to 20 minutes, or until the top is golden brown. Cool on the pan on a wire rack for 5 minutes. Cut into wedges, transfer to a serving plate and serve warm.

763 ■ CHOCOLATE CHIP ZUCCHINI BREAD

MAKES 2 LOAVES
BAKING TIME: *1 hour*

2 cups all-purpose flour
1 package (3.4 ounces) Jell-O Brand instant chocolate pudding mix
1 cup semisweet chocolate chips
½ cup shredded coconut
½ cup almonds, chopped
1 teaspoon baking powder
1 teaspoon ground cinnamon
1 teaspoon ground allspice
½ teaspoon salt
3 large eggs
1 cup granulated sugar
½ cup packed light brown sugar
1 cup canola oil
1 tablespoon orange liqueur
2 cups grated zucchini
Powdered sugar for garnish

1 Position a rack in the center of the oven and preheat the oven to 350 degrees. Lightly grease and flour two 9 by 5-inch loaf pans.

2 Combine the flour, pudding mix, chocolate chips, coconut, almonds, baking powder, spices, and salt.

3 In a large bowl, using an electric mixer on medium speed, beat the eggs until thick and light-colored. Beat in the sugars. Beat in the oil and liqueur. Beat in the zucchini. Gradually blend in the dry ingredients. Scrape the mixture into the prepared pans and spread evenly.

4 Bake for 55 minutes to 1 hour, or until a cake tester inserted into the center comes out clean. Cool in the pans on wire racks. Remove from the pans. Dust with powdered sugar.

764 ■ CHOCOLATE COFFEE CAKE

MAKES 10 TO 12 SERVINGS
BAKING TIME: *55 minutes*

½ cup almonds, ground
2½ cups all-purpose flour
1½ cups dried apricots, finely diced
½ cup Dutch processed cocoa powder
2 teaspoons baking powder
1 teaspoon baking soda
¼ teaspoon salt
1 cup vegetable shortening
8 ounces cream cheese, at room temperature
2¼ cups granulated sugar
5 large eggs
1½ teaspoons amaretto
Powdered sugar for dusting

1 Position a rack in the center of the oven and preheat the oven to 350 degrees. Grease a 10-inch Bundt pan. Press half the ground almonds around the side of the pan.

2 Combine the remaining almonds, flour, apricots, cocoa powder, baking powder, baking soda, and salt.

3 In a large bowl, using an electric mixer on medium speed, beat the shortening, cream cheese, and sugar until blended. Beat in the eggs, one at a time, beating well after each addition. Beat in the amaretto. Gradually blend in the dry ingredients just until moistened. Pour the mixture into the prepared pan.

4 Bake for 50 to 55 minutes, or until a cake tester inserted into the center comes out clean. Cool in the pan on a wire rack for 10 minutes. Invert onto the rack to cool completely. Transfer to a serving plate and dust with powdered sugar.

765 ■ CHOCOLATE COFFEE CAKE WITH APRICOTS

MAKES 10 TO 12 SERVINGS
BAKING TIME: 55 minutes

2½ cups cake flour
½ cup Dutch processed cocoa powder
2 teaspoons baking powder
1 teaspoon baking soda
¼ teaspoon salt
1¼ cups dried apricots, diced
2 cups butter-flavored vegetable shortening
8 ounces cream cheese, at room temperature
2¼ cups granulated sugar
5 large eggs
1 cup butterscotch chips

1 Position a rack in the center of the oven and preheat the oven to 350 degrees. Lightly grease a 10-inch Bundt pan.

2 Combine and sift twice the flour, cocoa powder, baking powder, baking soda, and salt. Add the diced apricots.

3 In a large bowl, using an electric mixer on medium speed, beat the shortening and cream cheese until blended. Beat in the sugar. Beat in the eggs, one at a time, beating well after each addition. Gradually blend in the dry ingredients. Fold in the butterscotch chips. Scrape the mixture into the prepared pan and spread evenly.

4 Bake for 50 to 55 minutes, or until a cake tester inserted into the center comes out clean. Cool in the pan on a wire rack for 10 minutes. Invert onto the rack to cool completely.

766 ■ CHOCOLATE COFFEE CAKE WITH CINNAMON APPLE FILLING

MAKES 10 TO 12 SERVINGS
RISING TIME: 2 hours
BAKING TIME: 1 hour

COFFEE CAKE

2 tablespoons active dry yeast
½ cup plus ½ teaspoon granulated sugar
¾ cup warm water (105 to 115 degrees)
5 cups all-purpose flour
½ cup Dutch processed cocoa powder
½ teaspoon salt
½ cup butter-flavored vegetable shortening
½ cup granulated sugar
½ cup milk, warmed to 110 degrees
2 large eggs

APPLE FILLING

2 large apples, peeled, cored, and diced
3 tablespoons butter-flavored vegetable shortening
½ cup pecans, chopped
½ cup packed light brown sugar
¼ cup Dutch processed cocoa powder
1 tablespoon ground cinnamon
½ cup raisins, finely chopped

1 To make the coffee cake, in a small bowl, combine the yeast, ½ teaspoon sugar, and warm water. Cover and let stand until foamy, about 5 minutes.

2 Meanwhile, combine 4 cups of the flour, the cocoa powder, and salt.

3 In a large bowl, using an electric mixer on medium speed, beat the shortening and remaining ½ cup sugar until fluffy. Beat in the milk and eggs. Gradually blend in the dry ingredients to make a smooth soft dough. Beat in the proofed yeast.

4 On a lightly floured surface, blend in the remaining 1 cup flour, kneading until the dough is elastic. Place the dough into a large floured bowl and cover with a towel. Let rise in a warm place for 45 minutes to 1 hour, until doubled in bulk.

5 Meanwhile, to make the filling, in a large saucepan, over low heat, combine the apples, shortening, and pecans and cook, stirring frequently, for 3 to 4 minutes. Remove from the heat and cool slightly. Blend in the brown sugar, cocoa powder, cinnamon, and raisins.

6 Lightly grease a 10-inch springform pan. To assemble, after the dough has risen, punch it down. On a floured surface, roll out to a rectangle about 14 by 20 inches. Spread the apple filling over the dough, leaving a 1-inch border around the edges. Roll the dough up jelly-roll fashion, pinching the edges to seal. Fit the roll into the prepared pan, forming it into a ring. Cover with a towel. Let rise for about 1 hour to 80 minutes, until doubled in bulk.

7 Meanwhile, preheat the oven to 350 degrees.

8 Bake for 1 hour, or until an even light-brown color. Cool in the pan on a wire rack for 10 minutes. Invert onto the rack to cool completely.

BAKING NOTES: An alternate method of baking is to invert the ring of unbaked dough after rising onto a baking sheet and bake as wreath-type coffee cake. The apples can be shredded instead of dicing. Cook them for 2 minutes, then add all of the other filling ingredients, stirring until everything is well blended. This coffee cake makes a delicious dessert when served with chocolate whipped cream (see page 406). Garnish with thinly sliced apples. To prevent discoloration, soak them in lemon juice for 10 minutes before using them and dry them thoroughly.

767 ■ CHOCOLATE CREAM PUFFS

MAKES 12 SERVINGS
CHILL TIME: *2 hours*
BAKING TIME: *35 minutes*

CREAM PUFF PASTRY

1⅓ cups water
1 package (5½ ounces) pie crust
    mix
4 large eggs

CHOCOLATE FILLING

1 package (3.4 ounces) Jell-O Brand
    instant chocolate pudding mix
½ teaspoon instant espresso
    powder
1½ cups milk
¼ cup coffee liqueur
½ cup heavy cream

COCOA TOPPING

⅓ cup Dutch processed cocoa
    powder
2 tablespoons powdered sugar
2½ teaspoons water

1 Position a rack in the center of the oven and preheat the oven to 400 degrees.

2 To make the puffs, in a saucepan, over medium heat, bring the water to a rolling boil. Add the package of pie crust mix and cook, stirring constantly, for 30 seconds, or until the mixture leaves the sides of the pan and forms a ball. Remove from the heat.

3 Using a wooden spoon, beat in the eggs, one at a time, blending until smooth. Using a measuring cup, drop the batter, ¼ cup at a time, onto an ungreased baking sheet, spacing the puffs 2 inches apart.

4 Bake for 30 to 35 minutes, or until a light golden brown color. Immediately cut a slit in the side of each puff and transfer to a wire rack to cool completely. Cover and chill for at least 2 hours.

5 Meanwhile, to make the filling, in a medium saucepan, over medium heat, stir the pudding mix, espresso powder, and milk until combined. Cook, stirring constantly, until the mixture is very thick. Remove from the heat and stir in the liqueur. Cover and chill until cold.

6 In a small bowl, using an electric mixer on high speed, beat the cream until soft peaks form. Fold the cream into the chilled pudding mixture.

7 To assemble, cut the puffs in half horizontally and fill with the chocolate cream mixture. Place on a serving plate.

8 To make the topping, in a cup, blend the cocoa powder, sugar, and water to make a smooth paste. Spoon over the top of each cream puff.

766

767

765

768 ■ CHOCOLATE DATE NUT BREAD

MAKES 2 LOAVES
BAKING TIME: *1 hour*

1½ cups all-purpose flour
½ cup Dutch processed cocoa
  powder
2 teaspoons ground cinnamon
1 teaspoon ground nutmeg
½ teaspoon ground allspice
1 teaspoon baking powder
½ teaspoon baking soda
¼ teaspoon salt
½ cup butter or margarine, at room
  temperature
1 cup granulated sugar
2 large eggs
1 cup buttermilk
1 cup (6 ounces) Hershey's™
  Chocolate Shoppe Candy Bar
  Sprinkles
½ cup dates, pitted and finely
  chopped
½ cup pecans, coarsely chopped
1 recipe Rum Cream Frosting (see
  page 416)

1 Position a rack in the center of
the oven and preheat the oven
to 350 degrees. Grease two 9 by
5-inch loaf pans.

2 Combine the flour, cocoa
powder, spices, baking powder,
baking soda, and salt.

3 In a large bowl, using an electric mixer on medium speed,
beat the butter and sugar until
smooth. Beat in the eggs, one at
a time, beating well after each
addition. In three additions,
beat in the dry ingredients,
alternating with the buttermilk,
beginning and ending with the
dry ingredients, mixing just
until blended. Fold in the candy
bar bits, dates, and pecans.
Divide the mixture between the
prepared pans and spread
evenly.

4 Bake for 55 minutes to 1 hour,
or until a cake tester inserted
into the center comes out clean.
Cool in the pan on a wire rack
for 5 minutes. Invert onto the
rack to cool completely. Chill
until ready to serve.

5 Meanwhile, make the
frosting.

6 Place the cake on a serving
plate. Spread the frosting over
the top and sides of the cake
and slice.

BAKING NOTES: This is a very
fragile cake and tends to fall
apart if not kept well chilled.

769 ■ CHOCOLATE ECLAIRS

MAKES 10 SERVINGS
BAKING TIME: *50 minutes*

**Cream Puff Pastry (see recipe 819,
  page 362)**
**6 ounces semisweet chocolate,
  grated or finely chopped**
½ cup milk
¼ cup granulated sugar
16 marshmallows
⅓ cup pecans, chopped
1 teaspoon crème de cacao
1 cup heavy cream
1 cup Chocolate Eclair Frosting (see
  page 398)

1 Position a rack in the center of
the oven and preheat the oven
to 400 degrees. Line a baking
sheet with parchment paper.

2 Make the cream puff pastry.

3 Fill a large pastry bag fitted
with a large plain tip with the
dough mixture and pipe out ten
3-inch logs onto the prepared
baking sheet, spacing them 2½
inches apart.

770

771

769

768

4 Bake for 45 to 50 minutes, or until the pastry is puffed and golden brown. Transfer to wire racks to cool completely.

5 In the top of a double boiler over simmering water, melt the chocolate, stirring until smooth. Stir in the milk, sugar, and marshmallows. Cook, stirring constantly, until the mixture is smooth. Remove from the heat and stir in the pecans and crème de cacao. Cover and chill.

6 Meanwhile, in a medium bowl, using an electric mixer on high speed, whip the cream until soft peaks form. Gently fold the cream into the chilled chocolate mixture. Chill until ready to use.

7 Make the chocolate glaze.

8 To assemble, cut the eclairs in half horizontally and spoon the filling onto the bottom half of the eclairs. Replace the top and chill until ready to use. To serve, spread the chocolate glaze over the top of the eclairs.

BAKING NOTES: An alternate way to fill the eclairs is to make a small hole in one end of each eclair and use a pastry bag fitted with a small round tip to pipe the cream filling into the eclair.

772

770 ■ CHOCOLATE FUDGE MUFFINS

MAKES 12 MUFFINS
BAKING TIME: *45 minutes*

1½ cups granulated sugar
1 cup all-purpose flour
¼ teaspoon salt
4 ounces semisweet chocolate, grated or finely chopped
1 cup butter-flavored vegetable shortening
4 large eggs, beaten
1 teaspoon crème de cacao

1 Position a rack in the center of the oven and preheat the oven to 300 degrees. Line twelve 2¾-inch muffin cups with paper baking cups.

2 In a large bowl, combine the sugar, flour, and salt.

3 In the top of a double boiler over simmering water, melt the chocolate, stirring until smooth. Add the shortening and stir until melted. Remove from the heat. Beat in the eggs and crème de cacao and mix until cool. Add to the dry ingredients and mix just until blended. Spoon the mixture into the prepared muffin cups, filling them two-thirds full.

4 Bake for 40 to 45 minutes, or until a cake tester inserted into the center comes out clean. Cool in the pan on a wire rack for 5 minutes. Remove to the racks to cool completely.

BAKING NOTES: These are simple little muffins, not the oversized, puffy kind.

771 ■ CHOCOLATE GINGERBREAD

MAKES 12 TO 15 SERVINGS
BAKING TIME: *25 minutes*

2 cups all-purpose flour
2 teaspoons baking powder
¼ teaspoon baking soda
2 teaspoons ground cinnamon
1 teaspoon ground ginger
¼ teaspoon salt
1½ ounces unsweetened chocolate, grated or finely chopped
⅓ cup vegetable shortening
2 large eggs
¼ cup granulated sugar

¼ cup packed light brown sugar
¼ cup dark molasses
½ cup milk
Powdered sugar for garnish

1 Position a rack in the center of the oven and preheat the oven to 350 degrees. Lightly grease a 13 by 9-inch baking pan.

2 Combine the flour, baking powder, baking soda, spices, and salt.

3 In the top of a double boiler over simmering water, melt the chocolate and shortening, stirring until smooth. Remove from the heat. Beat in the eggs, one at a time. Beat in the sugars. Beat in the molasses and milk. Gradually blend in the dry ingredients. Scrape the mixture into the prepared pan and spread evenly.

4 Bake for 20 to 25 minutes, or until a cake tester inserted into the center comes out clean. Cool in the pan on a wire rack. Dust with powdered sugar and cut into squares.

772 ■ CHOCOLATE HOLIDAY BREAD

MAKES 2 LOAVES
RISING TIME: *2 hours*
BAKING TIME: *75 minutes*

2 envelopes active dry yeast
⅔ cup warm water (105 to 115 degrees)
6 cups all-purpose flour
8 ounces semisweet chocolate, grated or finely chopped
1 cup dried cherries
1 cup candied ginger, finely diced
⅔ cup milk
6 tablespoons butter or margarine, at room temperature
½ cup molasses
½ teaspoon salt
3 large eggs
2 tablespoons granulated sugar

1 In a cup, sprinkle the yeast over the water and stir to blend. Set aside.

2 Meanwhile, combine the flour, chocolate, cherries, and ginger.

3 In a medium saucepan, over low heat, heat the milk until bubbles start to form around the sides of the pan. Remove from the heat and stir in the butter, molasses, and salt. Transfer to a large bowl and cool until just warm. Blend in the yeast mixture. Beat in the eggs and sugar, mixing thoroughly. Gradually blend in the flour mixture to make a smooth dough.

4 On a lightly floured surface, knead the dough for about 3 to 4 minutes, until very smooth. Transfer to a large greased bowl and cover with a clean towel. Let rise in a warm place for about 90 minutes to 2 hours, until doubled in bulk.

5 Lightly grease and flour two 9 by 5-inch loaf pans.

6 Punch down the dough, knead lightly, and divide in half. Form each half into a loaf and place in the prepared pans. Cover with the towel and allow to rise for about 45 minutes to 1 hour, until doubled.

7 Position a rack in the center of the oven and preheat the oven to 325 degrees.

8 Bake for 70 to 75 minutes, or until the loaves sound hollow when tapped, and are a golden brown color. Cool in the pans on wire racks for 3 to 5 minutes. Invert onto the racks to cool completely.

773 ■ CHOCOLATE OATMEAL MUFFINS

MAKES 12 MUFFINS
BAKING TIME: *20 minutes*

1¹/₂ cups all-purpose flour
1 cup old-fashioned oats
²/₃ cup granulated sugar
¹/₄ cup Dutch processed cocoa
   powder
1 teaspoon baking powder
1 cup milk
¹/₄ cup canola oil
1 large egg, beaten
1 teaspoon chocolate or vanilla
   extract
¹/₄ cup Cocoa Sugar (see page 407)

1 Position a rack in the center of the oven and preheat the oven to 400 degrees. Lightly grease the bottoms of twelve 2³/₄-inch muffin cups.

2 In a large bowl, combine the flour, oats, sugar, cocoa powder, and baking powder. Stir in the milk, oil, egg, and chocolate extract, mixing just until the dry ingredients are moistened. Do not overmix. Spoon the mixture into the prepared muffin cups, filling them three-fourths full.

3 Bake for 18 to 20 minutes, or until a cake tester inserted into the center comes out clean. Cool in the pan on a wire rack for 5 minutes. Transfer to the rack to cool completely. Sprinkle with cocoa sugar and serve.

774 ■ CHOCOLATE PECAN MUFFINS

MAKES 12 MUFFINS
BAKING TIME: *30 minutes*

1 cup all-purpose flour
1¹/₂ cups pecans, chopped
1 cup vegetable shortening
4 ounces semisweet chocolate,
   grated or finely chopped
1³/₄ cups granulated sugar
1 teaspoon vanilla extract

1 Position a rack in the center of the oven and preheat the oven to 325 degrees. Lightly grease twelve 2³/₄-inch muffin cups.

2 Combine the flour and pecans.

3 In the top of a double boiler over simmering water, melt the shortening and chocolate, stirring until smooth. Remove from the heat and beat in the sugar and vanilla. Gradually blend in

the dry ingredients. Pour the batter into the prepared muffin cups, filling them three-fourths full.

4 Bake for 28 to 30 minutes, or until a cake tester inserted into the center comes out clean. Cool in the pan on a wire rack.

775 ■ CHOCOLATE NUT BREAD I

MAKES 1 LOAF
BAKING TIME: *65 minutes*

3 cups Bisquick™ mix
¹/₂ cup granulated sugar
5 ounces semisweet chocolate,
   grated or finely chopped
¹/₂ cup hazelnuts, chopped
1 large egg
³/₄ cup evaporated milk
¹/₂ cup crème de cacao
¹/₄ cup honey, warmed

1 Position a rack in the center of the oven and preheat the oven to 350 degrees. Lightly grease a 9 by 5-inch loaf pan.

2 Combine the biscuit mix, sugar, chocolate, and hazelnuts.

3 In a large bowl, using an electric mixer on medium speed, beat the egg until thick and light-colored. Beat in the evaporated milk, crème de cacao, and

773

778

775

honey. Gradually blend in the dry ingredients. Pour the batter into the prepared pan.

4 Bake for 60 to 65 minutes, or until a cake tester inserted into the center comes out clean. Cool in the pan on a wire rack for 10 minutes. Invert onto a the rack to cool completely.

776 ■ CHOCOLATE NUT BREAD II

MAKES 1 LOAF
BAKING TIME: *70 minutes*

2 cups all-purpose flour
²⁄₃ cup whole wheat flour
1 cup chopped pecans
¹⁄₂ cup granulated sugar
3 ounces semisweet chocolate, grated or finely chopped
2 teaspoons baking powder
¹⁄₂ teaspoon baking soda
¹⁄₂ teaspoon salt
²⁄₃ cup buttermilk
¹⁄₂ cup Triple Sec
¹⁄₂ cup molasses
2 tablespoons canola oil

1 Position a rack in the center of the oven and preheat the oven to 325 degrees. Lightly grease and flour a 9 by 5-inch loaf pan.

2 In a large bowl, combine the flours, pecans, sugar, chocolate, baking powder, baking soda, and salt.

3 Combine the buttermilk, Triple Sec, molasses, and oil. Using a wooden spoon, blend into the dry ingredients. Do not overmix. Pour into the prepared pan.

4 Bake for 1 hour to 70 minutes, or until a cake tester inserted into the center comes out clean. Cool in the pan on a wire rack for 10 minutes. Invert onto the rack to cool completely.

BAKING NOTES: As an added treat, add ¾ cup diced dried apricots, cherries, or cranberries.

777 ■ CHOCOLATE NUT LOAVES

MAKES 5 MINIATURE LOAVES
BAKING TIME: *40 minutes*

2¼ cups all-purpose flour
1 cup hazelnuts or pecans, chopped
3 tablespoons Dutch processed cocoa powder
1½ teaspoons baking powder
1 teaspoon baking soda
¼ teaspoon salt
1 cup butter-flavored vegetable shortening
2 cups granulated sugar
5 large eggs
1 cup buttermilk
1 tablespoon cider vinegar
2 teaspoons almond or chocolate extract

1 Position a rack in the center of the oven and preheat the oven to 350 degrees. Lightly grease five 5 by 3-inch miniature loaf pans.

2 Combine the flour, hazelnuts, cocoa powder, baking powder, baking soda, and salt.

3 In a large bowl, using an electric mixer on medium speed, beat the shortening and sugar until fluffy. Beat in the eggs, one at a time. Beat in the buttermilk, vinegar, and almond extract. Gradually blend in the dry ingredients. Spoon the mixture into the prepared pans and spread evenly.

4 Bake for 30 to 40 minutes, or until a cake tester inserted into the center comes out clean. Cool in the pans on wire racks.

BAKING NOTES: If you do not have miniature loaf pans, you can use two 9 by 5-inch loaf pans and increase the baking time by 10 to 15 minutes.

778 ■ CHOCOLATE NUT PANCAKES

MAKES 14 TO 16 PANCAKES

1 cup all-purpose flour
1 cup hazelnuts or pecans, finely ground
¹⁄₂ cup Dutch processed cocoa powder
2 teaspoons grated orange zest
1 large egg, separated, plus 2 large egg yolks
1 cup heavy cream
¹⁄₂ cup granulated sugar
¹⁄₄ cup butter or margarine, melted
Cocoa Sugar (see page 407) for garnish

1 Preheat a griddle or skillet over medium heat.

2 Meanwhile, combine the flour, hazelnuts, cocoa powder, and orange zest.

3 In a medium bowl, using an electric mixer on medium speed, beat the 3 egg yolks until thick and light-colored. Beat in the egg white. Beat in the cream and sugar. By hand, stir in the melted butter. Gradually blend in the dry ingredients.

4 Brush the griddle with oil. Using a tablespoon or a measuring cup, pour the batter onto the prepared griddle and cook until the top looks dry. Turn and brown on the other side. Roll the hot pancakes, place on serving plates, and dust with cocoa sugar.

774

777

776

779 ■ CHOCOLATE NUT TEA BREAD I

MAKES 1 LOAF
BAKING TIME: *1 hour*

2 ounces unsweetened chocolate, grated or finely chopped
1½ teaspoons mocha-flavored instant coffee powder
1 cup boiling water
2 cups all-purpose flour
½ cup hazelnuts, chopped
½ cup pecans, finely ground
1 teaspoon baking soda
½ teaspoon salt
¼ cup butter-flavored vegetable shortening
1 cup granulated sugar
1 large egg
1 teaspoon coffee liqueur
Raspberry Sauce (see page 416) for serving

1 Position a rack in the center of the oven and preheat the oven to 350 degrees. Lightly grease a 9 by 5-inch loaf pan.

2 In a small bowl, combine the chocolate, coffee powder, and water and stir until the chocolate is melted and smooth.

3 Combine the flour, nuts, baking soda, and salt.

4 In a large bowl, using an electric mixer on medium speed, beat the shortening and sugar until smooth. Beat in the egg and liqueur. Gradually blend in the dry ingredients, alternating with the chocolate mixture. Scrape the mixture into the prepared pan and spread evenly.

5 Bake for 55 minutes to 1 hour, or until a cake tester inserted into the center comes out clean. Cool in the pan on a wire rack for 10 minutes. Invert onto the rack to cool completely. Chill for 2 hours. Top with raspberry sauce before serving.

780 ■ CHOCOLATE NUT TEA BREAD II

MAKES 1 LOAF
BAKING TIME: *1 hour*

2 cups all-purpose flour
¼ cup walnuts, chopped
¼ cup pecans, chopped
¼ cup Brazil nuts, chopped
1 teaspoon baking soda
½ teaspoon salt
2 ounces unsweetened chocolate, grated or finely chopped
¼ cup butter-flavored vegetable shortening
1 cup granulated sugar
1 large egg
1 cup strong brewed coffee
1½ teaspoons coffee liqueur
Coffee Hard Sauce (see page 408) for serving

1 Position a rack in the center of the oven and preheat the oven to 350 degrees. Lightly grease a 9 by 5-inch loaf pan.

2 Combine the flour, nuts, baking soda, and salt.

3 Melt the chocolate (see page 13). Remove from the heat.

4 In a large bowl, using an electric mixer on medium speed, beat the shortening and sugar until fluffy. Beat in the egg, coffee, and liqueur. Beat in the melted chocolate. Gradually blend in the dry ingredients. Scrape the mixture into the prepared pan and spread evenly.

5 Bake for 55 minutes to 1 hour, or until a cake tester inserted into the center comes out clean. Cool in the pan on a wire rack for 5 minutes. Invert onto the rack to cool completely. Serve with coffee hard sauce on the side.

781 ■ CHOCOLATE OAT SCONES

MAKES 8 SCONES
BAKING TIME: *18 minutes*

1 cup all-purpose flour
¼ cup packed light brown sugar
¼ cup Dutch processed cocoa powder
1½ teaspoons baking powder
¼ teaspoon baking soda
¼ teaspoon salt
3 tablespoons butter or margarine, at room temperature
½ cup old-fashioned oats
½ cup dried cherries or cranberries
2 large eggs
¼ cup buttermilk

1 Position a rack in the center of the oven and preheat the oven to 400 degrees. Lightly grease a baking sheet.

2 In a large bowl, combine the flour, brown sugar, cocoa powder, baking powder, baking soda, and salt. Using a pastry blender or two knives scissor fashion, cut in the butter to form a crumbly mixture. Using a wooden spoon, stir in the oats and cherries. Stir in the eggs and just enough buttermilk to make a smooth, workable dough.

3 On a lightly floured surface, roll the dough out to create an 8-inch round circle. Transfer to the

779

780

781

prepared baking sheet, and using a serrated knife, cut the circle into 8 wedges.

4 Bake for 16 to 18 minutes, or until the wedges look dry and a little crusty and a cake tester inserted into the center comes out clean.

782 ■ CHOCOLATE ORANGE BREAKFAST LOAF

MAKES 1 LOAF
BAKING TIME: *1 hour*

CHOCOLATE ORANGE CAKE

2 ounces unsweetened chocolate, grated or finely chopped
1¾ cups all-purpose flour
¾ teaspoon baking powder
¾ teaspoon baking soda
1 cup butter or margarine, at room temperature
1 cup granulated sugar
1 teaspoon vanilla or orange extract
3 large eggs
1 cup sour cream
1 tablespoon grated orange zest
1 teaspoon chocolate extract

GRAND MARNIER GLAZE

⅓ cup Grand Marnier
3 tablespoons powdered sugar

1 Position a rack in the center of the oven and preheat the oven to 350 degrees. Lightly grease and flour a 9 by 5-inch loaf pan.

2 To make the cake, melt the chocolate (see page 13). Remove from the heat.

3 Combine the flour, baking powder, and baking soda.

4 In a large bowl, using an electric mixer on medium speed, beat the butter and sugar until smooth. Beat in the vanilla extract. Beat in the eggs, one at a time, beating well after each addition. Blend in the dry ingredients. Beat in the sour cream. Place half of the batter in another bowl. Add the orange zest to the first bowl and spread evenly in the bottom of the prepared pan.

5 To the second bowl, add the chocolate extract and the melted chocolate. Spoon the chocolate batter into the pan and gently spread over the orange-flavored batter.

6 Bake for 55 minutes to 1 hour, or until a cake tester inserted into the center comes out clean. Cool in the pan on a wire rack for 5 minutes. Invert onto a wire rack to cool completely.

7 Meanwhile, make the glaze. In a small saucepan, over low heat, combine the Grand Marnier and powdered sugar. Raise the temperature to medium and bring to a boil. Simmer for 1 minute. Remove from the heat and spoon over the top of the cake.

783 ■ CHOCOLATE PANCAKES WITH CINNAMON CANDY WHIPPED CREAM

MAKES 6 TO 8 SERVINGS

COCOA PANCAKES

1 large egg
1 cup milk
¼ cup canola oil
1¼ cups all-purpose flour
6 tablespoons Dutch processed cocoa powder
¼ cup plus 2 tablespoons granulated sugar
2 teaspoons baking powder
¾ teaspoon salt

CINNAMON CANDY WHIPPED CREAM

1½ cups heavy cream
2 tablespoons granulated sugar
1 teaspoon chocolate extract
¼ cup cinnamon candies, crushed

1 Preheat a griddle or skillet over medium-high heat until a drop of water sizzles when dropped onto the pan.

2 Meanwhile, in a small bowl, beat the egg until foamy. Beat in the milk and oil.

3 In a large bowl, combine the flour, cocoa powder, sugar, baking powder, and salt. Gradually blend in the egg mixture just until moistened.

4 Brush the griddle with oil. Spoon about 1½ tablespoons of the batter onto the prepared griddle. Cook until holes start to appear around the edges and the top starts to look dry. Turn and brown on the other side. Do not overcook. Place on wire rack until ready to serve.

5 To make the whipped cream, in a medium bowl, using an electric mixer on high speed, whip the cream, sugar, and chocolate extract until soft peaks form. Fold in the candy until well blended.

6 To serve, place three pancakes on each plate, placing a dab of the whipped cream between each one and an additional dab on the top.

BAKING NOTES: Any flavor of hard candy can be used. The

782

783

candy can be finely crushed into a powder or left in larger pieces. Substitute any liqueur or brandy for the chocolate extract.

784 ■ CHOCOLATE PANCAKES WITH FRUIT

MAKES 4 TO 6 SERVINGS

1/2 cup all-purpose flour
3 tablespoons Dutch processed cocoa powder
3 tablespoons granulated sugar
1/2 cup minus 1 tablespoon evaporated milk
1 large egg
1 tablespoon butter or margarine, melted
1 tablespoon chocolate or vanilla extract
Fresh fruit in season, crushed or chopped for serving
1 cup Coffee Hard Sauce (see page 408) for serving

1 Preheat a griddle or skillet over medium heat.

2 Meanwhile, in a large bowl, combine the flour, cocoa powder, and sugar.

3 In another large bowl, using an electric mixer on medium speed, beat the evaporated milk, egg, butter, and chocolate extract. Gradually blend in the dry ingredients.

4 Brush the griddle with oil. Drop the batter by spoonfuls onto the prepared griddle. Cook until tiny holes appear on the surface. Turn and cook for 20 to 30 seconds longer. Remove the pancakes to a serving plate and keep warm. Repeat until all of the batter is used.

5 Serve with crushed fruit and coffee hard sauce over the top.

BAKING NOTES: Use any fresh fruit that is in season or use a fruit preserve or puree. Do not use canned fruit.

785 ■ CHOCOLATE PECAN DATE LOAF

MAKES 1 LOAF
BAKING TIME: *1 hour*

1 1/2 cups all-purpose flour
1 cup semisweet chocolate chips
1/2 cup dates, pitted and finely chopped
1/2 cup pecans, finely ground
1/4 cup Dutch processed cocoa powder
1 teaspoon baking powder
1/2 teaspoon baking soda
2 teaspoons ground cinnamon
1 teaspoon ground nutmeg
1/4 teaspoon ground cloves
1/4 teaspoon salt
1/4 cup butter or margarine, at room temperature
1 cup granulated sugar
2 large eggs
1 cup buttermilk
Chocolate or Neapolitan ice cream for serving
Fresh mint sprigs for garnish

1 Position a rack in the center of the oven and preheat the oven to 350 degrees. Grease a 9 by 5-inch loaf pan.

2 Combine the flour, chocolate chips, dates, pecans, cocoa powder, baking powder, baking soda, spices, and salt.

3 In a large bowl, using an electric mixer on high speed, beat the butter and sugar until fluffy. Beat in the eggs, one at a time, beating well after each addition. Beat in the buttermilk. Gradually blend in the dry ingredients just until blended. Scrape the mixture into the prepared pan and spread evenly.

4 Bake for 55 minutes to 1 hour, or until a cake tester inserted into the center comes out clean. Cool in the pan on a wire rack for 15 to 20 minutes. Invert onto the rack to cool completely. Cover and chill until ready to serve. Serve with a scoop of ice cream on the side and garnish with a sprig of mint.

BAKING NOTES: For a variation, substitute mint chocolate chips.

784

785

786

786 ■ CHOCOLATE PUMPKIN BREAD I

MAKES 2 LOAVES
BAKING TIME: *75 minutes*

1½ cups all-purpose flour
½ cup pecans or hazelnuts, chopped
¼ cup Dutch processed cocoa powder
¼ cup golden raisins
1 teaspoon baking powder
1 teaspoon baking soda
1 teaspoon ground cinnamon
½ teaspoon ground nutmeg
¼ teaspoon ground cloves
¼ teaspoon ground ginger
¼ teaspoon salt
¼ cup butter-flavored vegetable shortening
¾ cup granulated sugar
¾ cup packed light brown sugar
2 large eggs
¼ cup milk
1 cup solid pack canned pumpkin
1 cup semisweet chocolate chips

1 Position a rack in the center of the oven and preheat the oven to 350 degrees. Lightly grease two 9 by 5-inch loaf pans.

2 Combine the flour, pecans, cocoa powder, raisins, baking powder, baking soda, spices, and salt.

3 In a large bowl, using an electric mixer on medium speed, beat the shortening and sugars until fluffy. Beat in the eggs, milk, and pumpkin. Gradually blend in the dry ingredients, mixing just until blended. Fold in the chocolate chips. Divide the mixture between the prepared pans and spread evenly.

4 Bake for 70 to 75 minutes, or until a cake tester inserted into the center comes out clean. Cool in the pans on a wire rack for 15 minutes. Invert onto the rack to cool completely.

BAKING NOTES: For a variation, substitute 1½ teaspoons ground allspice for all of the above spices.

787 ■ CHOCOLATE PUMPKIN BREAD II

MAKES 1 LOAF
BAKING TIME: *65 minutes*

1½ cups all-purpose flour
½ cup Dutch processed cocoa powder
¼ cup pecans or hazelnuts, chopped
¼ cup raisins or golden raisins, chopped
1 teaspoon baking powder
1 teaspoon baking soda
2 teaspoons pumpkin pie spice
½ teaspoon salt
¼ cup vegetable shortening
¾ cup granulated sugar
¾ cup packed light brown sugar
1 cup solid pack canned pumpkin
2 large eggs
Jam or jelly for serving

1 Position a rack in the center of the oven and preheat the oven to 350 degrees. Lightly grease a 9 by 5-inch loaf pan.

2 Combine the flour, cocoa powder, pecans, raisins, baking powder, baking soda, spices, and salt.

3 In a large bowl, using an electric mixer on medium speed, beat the shortening and sugars until fluffy. Beat in the pumpkin and eggs. Gradually blend in the dry ingredients. Scrape the mixture into the prepared pan and spread evenly.

4 Bake for 1 hour to 65 minutes, or until a cake tester inserted into the center comes out clean.

Cool in the pan on a wire rack for 10 minutes. Invert onto the rack to cool completely. Serve with jam or jelly on the side.

788 ■ CHOCOLATE SCONES

MAKES 8 SCONES
BAKING TIME: *20 minutes*

2 cups all-purpose flour
½ cup almonds, finely chopped
½ cup granulated sugar
¼ cup packed dark brown sugar
2¼ teaspoons baking powder
Pinch of salt
3 ounces unsweetened chocolate, grated or finely chopped
⅓ cup butter-flavored vegetable shortening
⅓ cup milk
1 large egg
1½ teaspoons almond extract
Jam or jelly for serving

1 Position a rack in the center of the oven and preheat the oven to 350 degrees. Lightly grease a 12-inch pizza pan or a baking sheet

2 Combine the flour, almonds, sugars, baking powder, and salt.

3 In the top of a double boiler over simmering water, melt the chocolate and shortening, stirring until smooth. Using an electric mixer on medium speed, beat in the milk until blended and smooth. Remove from the heat and beat in the egg and almond extract.   One-third at a time, blend in the dry ingredients and stir to form a soft dough.

4 On the pizza pan or baking sheet, roll or pat the dough out into a circle 12 inches in diameter and ½-inch thick With a sharp knife, cut the circle into eight wedges.

5 Bake for 18 to 20 minutes, or until a cake tester inserted into the center comes out with a few crumbs clinging to it. Cool on the pan on a wire rack for 5 minutes. Remove to the rack to cool completely. To serve, cut the wedges apart, if necessary, and serve with jam or jelly on the side.

787

788

789 ■ CHOCOLATE STICKY BUNS

MAKES 26 SERVINGS
RISING TIME: *80 minutes*
BAKING TIME: *25 minutes*

CHOCOLATE DOUGH

¾ cup milk
3 tablespoons butter or margarine
2 cups all-purpose flour
⅓ cup granulated sugar
¼ cup Dutch processed cocoa
   powder
1 tablespoon active dry yeast
¼ teaspoon salt
1 large egg

PECAN TOPPING

¼ cup butter or margarine
½ cup packed light brown sugar
½ cup pecans or almonds, chopped

CHOCOLATE FILLING

3 tablespoons butter or margarine
6 ounces semisweet chocolate,
   grated or finely chopped
¾ cup packed light brown sugar
3 tablespoons light corn syrup
1 tablespoon ground cinnamon

1 To make the dough, in a saucepan, over medium heat, heat the milk and 3 tablespoons butter until the butter melts. Insert a candy thermometer and heat until the mixture reaches 110 to 120 degrees. Remove from the heat.

2 In a large bowl, combine the flour, sugar, cocoa powder, yeast, and salt. Beat in the hot milk mixture. Beat in the egg.

3 On a lightly floured surface, knead the dough for 5 to 7 minutes, or until the dough is smooth and elastic. Place in the bowl and cover with a towel. Let rise in a warm place for 20 minutes, or until doubled in bulk.

4 Meanwhile, lightly grease twenty-four 2¾-inch muffin cups.

5 To make the topping, in a small saucepan, combine the butter and ½ cup brown sugar. Cook over low heat until the butter is melted and the sugar is dissolved. Remove from the heat and stir in the pecans.

Spoon the mixture into the prepared muffin cups.

6 To make the filling, in the top of a double boiler over simmering water, melt the butter and chocolate, stirring until smooth. Remove from the heat and cool slightly. Beat in the brown sugar, corn syrup, and cinnamon.

7 After the dough has risen, punch it down and divide in half. On a floured surface, roll each half into an 18 by 9-inch rectangle. Spread each rectangle with half of the chocolate filling, leaving a ¼ to ½-inch border on each side. Starting with one of the long sides, roll up jelly-roll fashion. Moisten the edges with water and pinch together. Using a sharp knife, cut each roll into twelve slices. Place a slice in each of the prepared muffin pans. Cover and let rise for about 1 hour, or until doubled in bulk.

8 Meanwhile, preheat the oven to 350 degrees.

9 Bake for 20 to 25 minutes, or until golden brown. Immediately invert the pans onto wire racks and cool for 15 minutes. Serve warm.

790 ■ CHOCOLATE TEA BREAD

MAKES 1 LOAF
BAKING TIME: *70 minutes*

1¾ cups all-purpose flour
1 cup Dutch processed cocoa
   powder
1 teaspoon baking powder
½ teaspoon baking soda
¼ teaspoon salt
½ cup butter or margarine, at room
   temperature
1⅓ cups granulated sugar
1 teaspoon chocolate extract
2 large eggs
1 cup sour cream or chocolate
   yogurt
Cocoa Sugar (see page 407) for
   garnish

1 Position a rack in the center of the oven and preheat the oven to 350 degrees. Lightly grease and flour a 9 by 5-inch loaf pan.

2 Combine the flour, cocoa powder, baking powder, baking soda, and salt.

3 In a large bowl, using an electric mixer on high speed, beat the butter and sugar until fluffy. Beat in the chocolate extract. Beat in the eggs, one at a time. Beat in the sour cream. Gradually blend in the dry ingredients until well blended. Scrape the mixture into the prepared pan and spread evenly.

4 Bake for 1 hour to 70 minutes, or until a cake tester inserted into the center comes out clean. Cool in the pan on a wire rack for 15 to 20 minutes. Invert onto the rack to cool completely. Sprinkle cocoa sugar over the top.

791 ■ CHOCOLATE TEA CAKE

MAKES 8 TO 12 SERVINGS
BAKING TIME: *30 minutes*

8 ounces unsweetened chocolate,
   grated or finely chopped
¾ cup butter or margarine, at room
   temperature
¾ cup granulated sugar
4 large eggs
½ cup cake flour, sifted twice
2 tablespoons Cocoa Sugar (see
   page 407) for garnish
Whipped cream for serving

1 Position a rack in the center of the oven and preheat the oven to 350 degrees. Lightly grease a 9-inch square pan and line with waxed paper.

2 Melt the chocolate (see page 13). Remove from the heat.

3 In a large bowl, using an electric mixer on medium speed, beat the butter and sugar until fluffy. Beat in the eggs, one at a time, beating well after each addition. Beat in the melted chocolate. Stir in the flour just until moistened. Pour the mixture into the prepared pan.

4 Bake for 28 to 30 minutes, or until a cake tester inserted into the center comes out clean. Cool in the pan on a wire rack for 10 minutes. Invert onto the rack to cool completely.

5 Place the cake on a serving plate, place a square paper doily on top and sprinkle the cocoa sugar over the doily. Carefully lift off the doily. Cut into squares and serve with whipped cream on the side.

BAKING NOTES: Instead of using a doily, you can also make your own stencil by drawing a design on paper and cutting it out.

792 ■ CHOCOLATE WAFFLES I

MAKES 4 TO 6 SERVINGS

1½ cups all-purpose flour
2 teaspoons baking powder
⅛ teaspoon ground cinnamon
¼ teaspoon salt
2½ ounces semisweet chocolate, grated or finely chopped
½ cup butter, melted
1 cup granulated sugar
2 large eggs
1 teaspoon chocolate extract
½ cup evaporated milk
Chocolate Whipped Cream (see page 406) for serving
Chocolate Curls (see page 422) for garnish

1 Preheat a waffle iron.
2 Combine the flour, baking powder, cinnamon, and salt.
3 Melt the chocolate (see page 13). Remove from the heat.
4 In a large bowl, using an electric mixer on medium speed, beat the butter and sugar until blended. Beat in the eggs, one at a time, beating well after each addition. Stir in the chocolate extract and melted chocolate. Gradually blend in the dry ingredients, alternating with the evaporated milk.
5 Spoon the batter into the center of the waffle iron. Close and bake according to the manufacturer's directions. Serve hot, topped with a large scoop of chocolate whipped cream and chocolate curls.

793 ■ CHOCOLATE WAFFLES II

MAKES 4 TO 6 SERVINGS

2 cups all-purpose flour
¼ cup granulated sugar
3 tablespoons Dutch processed cocoa powder
1 tablespoon baking powder
¼ teaspoon salt
1¼ cups milk
¼ cup butter, melted
2 large eggs
1 teaspoon crème de cacao or chocolate extract
Syrup or fruit in season for serving
Whipped cream for garnish

1 Preheat a waffle iron.
2 Combine the flour, sugar, cocoa powder, baking powder, and salt.
3 In the container of a blender, combine the milk, butter, eggs, and crème de cacao and blend for a few seconds. On low speed, gradually blend in the dry ingredients until well mixed.
4 Pour the batter onto the preheated waffle iron, using about ¾ cup for each waffle. Close and bake according to the manufacturer's directions. Serve hot with syrup or fruit in season and garnish with whipped cream.

789
790
791
792
793

794 ■ CHOCOLATE ZUCCHINI BREAD I

MAKES 2 LOAVES
BAKING TIME: *1 hour*

2 ounces unsweetened chocolate, grated or finely chopped
3 cups all-purpose flour
1 cup walnuts, chopped
1 teaspoon baking soda
¹⁄₂ teaspoon baking powder
1 teaspoon ground allspice
¹⁄₄ teaspoon salt
3 large eggs
2 cups granulated sugar
1 cup canola oil
1 teaspoon chocolate extract
2 cups finely grated zucchini
Chocolate Quark Cream Filling (see page 403) for serving

1 Position a rack in the center of the oven and preheat the oven to 350 degrees. Lightly grease two 9 by 5-inch loaf pans.

2 Melt the chocolate (see page 13). Remove from the heat.

3 Combine the flour, walnuts, baking soda, baking powder, allspice, and salt.

4 In a large bowl, using an electric mixer on medium speed, beat the eggs until thick and light-colored. Beat in the sugar, oil, melted chocolate, and chocolate extract. Gradually blend in the dry ingredients. Fold in the zucchini and divide evenly between the prepared pans.

5 Bake for 1 hour, or until a cake tester inserted into the center comes out clean. Cool in the pans on wire racks for 10 minutes. Invert onto the racks to cool completely. Serve with quark cream filling on the side.

BAKING NOTES: Each loaf serves 9 to 12.

795 ■ CHOCOLATE ZUCCHINI BREAD II

MAKES 2 LOAVES
BAKING TIME: *1 hour*

3 cups all-purpose flour
¹⁄₂ cup flaked coconut
¹⁄₂ cup pecans, finely ground
1 package (3.4 ounces) chocolate Jell-O™ instant pudding mix
1 teaspoon baking powder
1 teaspoon baking soda
1 tablespoon ground cinnamon
1 teaspoon salt
3 large eggs
1¹⁄₂ cups granulated sugar
2 teaspoons coffee liqueur
1 teaspoon vanilla extract
1 cup canola oil
2 cups finely grated zucchini
¹⁄₂ cup semisweet chocolate chips
¹⁄₄ cup milk chocolate chips

1 Position a rack in the center of the oven and preheat the oven to 350 degrees. Lightly grease two 9 by 5-inch loaf pans.

2 Combine the flour, coconut, pecans, pudding mix, baking powder, baking soda, cinnamon, and salt.

3 In a large bowl, using an electric mixer on medium speed, beat the eggs until thick and light-colored. Beat in the sugar, liqueur, and vanilla extract. Beat in the oil. Gradually blend in the

797

796

794

798

dry ingredients. Fold in the zucchini and chocolate chips. Divide the mixture evenly between the prepared pans.

4 Bake for 1 hour, or until a cake tester inserted into the center comes out clean. Cool in the pans on wire racks for 10 minutes. Invert onto the racks to cool completely.

BAKING NOTES: This bread is not just for breakfast. Try it as a side dish with dinner or thinly sliced and toasted with a soup or salad.

796 ■ CHOCOLATE ZUCCHINI BREAKFAST BREAD

MAKES 2 LOAVES
BAKING TIME: *75 minutes*

3 cups all-purpose flour
1 teaspoon baking powder
1 teaspoon baking soda
1 teaspoon ground cinnamon
3 large eggs
2 cups granulated sugar
1 cup canola oil
1 tablespoon coffee liqueur
1/2 cup chocolate yogurt or sour cream
2 cups shredded zucchini
6 ounces semisweet chocolate, grated or finely chopped

795

1 Position a rack in the center of the oven and preheat the oven to 350 degrees. Lightly grease two 9 by 5-inch loaf pans.

2 In a large bowl, combine the flour, baking powder, baking soda, and cinnamon.

3 In another large bowl, using an electric mixer on medium speed, beat the eggs and sugar until thick and light-colored. Beat in the oil and liqueur. Beat in the yogurt. Gradually blend in the dry ingredients, just until mixed in. Fold in the zucchini and chocolate chips. Divide the mixture evenly between the prepared pans.

4 Bake for 70 to 75 minutes, or until a cake tester inserted into the center comes out clean. Cool for 5 minutes in the pans on wire racks. Invert onto the racks to cool completely.

BAKING NOTES: Each loaf serves 9 to 12 people.

797 ■ COCOA BREAD

MAKES 1 LOAF
BAKING TIME: *55 minutes*

1 3/4 cups all-purpose flour
1/4 cup Dutch processed cocoa powder
3/4 teaspoon allspice
1/4 teaspoon baking powder
1/8 teaspoon baking soda
1/2 teaspoon salt
2 large eggs
3/4 cup packed light brown sugar
3/4 cup sour cream or chocolate yogurt
1/4 cup butter or margarine, melted
Cocoa Sugar (see page 407) for garnish

1 Position a rack in the center of the oven and preheat the oven to 375 degrees. Lightly grease a 9 by 5-inch loaf pan.

2 Combine the flour, cocoa powder, allspice, baking powder, baking soda, and salt.

3 In a large bowl, using an electric mixer on high speed, beat the eggs until light-colored. Beat in the brown sugar, sour cream, and butter. Gradually mix in the dry ingredients just until blended. Do not overmix. Scrape the mixture into the prepared pan and spread evenly.

4 Bake for 50 to 55 minutes, or until a cake tester inserted into the center comes out clean. Cool in the pan on a wire rack for 10 minutes. Invert onto the rack to cool completely. Sprinkle with cocoa sugar.

798 ■ COCOA MUFFINS WITH BANANAS

MAKES 12 MUFFINS
BAKING TIME: *25 minutes*

1 1/4 cups all-purpose flour
1 cup old-fashioned oats
1/2 cup packed light brown sugar
1/2 cup Dutch processed cocoa powder
1 tablespoon baking powder
1/4 teaspoon baking soda
1 cup mashed bananas (2 medium)
1/2 cup milk
1/3 cup butter-flavored vegetable shortening, at room temperature
1 extra-large egg
1 teaspoon chocolate extract
Cocoa Sugar (see page 407) for dusting

1 Heat the oven to 400 degrees. Lightly grease the bottoms of twelve 2 3/4-inch muffin cups.

2 In a large bowl, combine the flour, oats, brown sugar, cocoa powder, baking powder, and baking soda.

3 In a medium bowl, using an electric mixer on medium speed, beat the bananas, milk, shortening, egg, and chocolate extract until combined. Stir the banana mixture into the dry ingredients, mixing only until the dry ingredients are moistened. Spoon the mixture into the prepared muffin cups, filling them almost full.

4 Bake for 20 to 25 minutes, or until a cake tester inserted into the center comes out clean. Cool in the pan on a wire rack for 5 minutes. Invert onto the rack to cool. Dust with cocoa sugar.

799 ■ CRÊPES WITH CHOCOLATE CREAM FILLING

MAKES 10 TO 12 SERVINGS
CHILL TIME: *2 hours*
BAKING TIME: *12 minutes*

CRÊPE BATTER

1$\frac{1}{2}$ cups milk
$\frac{2}{3}$ cup all-purpose flour
3 large eggs
2 tablespoons butter, melted
$\frac{1}{2}$ teaspoon of salt

CHOCOLATE FILLING

$\frac{3}{4}$ cup heavy cream
2 large egg yolks
$\frac{1}{2}$ cup granulated sugar
1 tablespoon cornstarch or arrowroot
2 ounces unsweetened chocolate, grated or finely chopped
2 tablespoons butter or margarine
2 tablespoons powdered sugar for garnish
Melted butter for brushing pan

1 To make the batter, in a medium bowl, using a wire whisk, combine the milk, flour, eggs, butter, and salt, beating until smooth. Cover and chill for at least 2 hours.

2 Meanwhile, to make the filling, in a small saucepan, over medium heat, heat the cream until steaming hot. Remove from the heat.

3 In a small bowl, using an electric mixer on medium speed, beat the egg yolks until thick and light-colored. On low speed, beat in the sugar and cornstarch. Pouring it in a thin stream, mix in the hot cream and beat until light and fluffy. Pour the mixture into the top of a double boiler and set over simmering water. Cook, stirring constantly, for 15 minutes, or until the mixture is as thick as mayonnaise. Remove

from the heat. Add the chocolate and butter and stir until melted and smooth.

4 To make the crêpes, brush the bottom of a 7-inch crêpe pan and a 10-inch skillet with some of the butter and heat over medium heat. Pour $\frac{1}{4}$ cup of the chilled batter into the crêpe pan and tilt the pan to spread the batter out to the sides of the pan. Cook for about 2 minutes, or until golden brown around the edges. Loosen the crêpe around the edges with a spatula and invert into the hot 10-inch skillet. Cook on the second side for 30 seconds. Slip the crêpe onto a towel covered with waxed paper and cover with a piece of aluminum foil to keep warm. Repeat until the batter is all used up, stacking the crêpes on the towel as they are done.

5 Preheat the oven to 350 degrees. Lightly grease a 13 by 9-inch glass baking dish.

6 Spoon a heaping tablespoon of the chocolate filling across the center of each crêpe and roll it up. Place the filled crêpes seam-side down in the prepared dish.

7 Bake for 10 to 12 minutes, or until just heated through. Remove from the oven, dust with powdered sugar and serve immediately.

800 ■ CRÊPES WITH CHOCOLATE SAUCE

MAKES 12 TO 14 CRÊPES
CHILL TIME: *2 hours*

$\frac{2}{3}$ cup all-purpose flour
1 tablespoon granulated sugar
Pinch of salt
2 large eggs
1$\frac{1}{3}$ cups milk
2 tablespoons butter or margarine, melted
1 tablespoon coffee liqueur
1 cup Chocolate Sauce III (see page 404)
Melted butter for brushing pan
1 cup apricot jam
Fresh pansies for garnish

1 Combine the flour, sugar, and salt.

2 In a large bowl, using an electric mixer on medium speed,

beat the eggs until thick and light-colored. On low speed, beat in the milk. By hand, blend in the dry ingredients. Stir in the melted butter and coffee liqueur. Cover and chill for 2 hours.

3 Meanwhile, make the chocolate sauce.

4 Brush the bottom of a crêpe pan or small skillet with butter and heat over medium heat. Pour about $\frac{1}{4}$ cup of the chilled batter into the pan and use the back of a spoon to spread it out as thinly as possible. Cook for about 1 minute on each side. Transfer to a plate and keep warm.

5 To serve, spread each crêpe with a layer of apricot jam and roll up loosely. Place on serving plates and spoon the chocolate sauce over the top. Garnish with pansies.

BAKING NOTES: Two crêpes can be cooked at once if a large skillet is used.

801 ■ DOUBLE CHOCOLATE MUFFINS I

MAKES 12 MUFFINS
BAKING TIME: *20 minutes*

2 cups all-purpose flour
1$\frac{1}{2}$ cups miniature chocolate chips
$\frac{3}{4}$ cup Dutch processed cocoa powder
1 tablespoon baking powder
$\frac{1}{2}$ cup vegetable shortening
1 cup granulated sugar
1 large egg
1 cup milk

799

1 Position a rack in the center of the oven and preheat the oven to 400 degrees. Lightly grease twelve 2¾-inch muffin cups.

2 Combine the flour, chocolate chips, cocoa powder, and baking powder.

3 In a large bowl, using an electric mixer on medium speed, beat the shortening and sugar until fluffy. Beat in the egg. Beat in the milk. Blend in the dry ingredients, stirring until just moistened. Spoon the batter by spoonfuls into the prepared pan.

4 Bake for 18 to 20 minutes, until browned. Cool in the pan on a wire rack. Remove to the rack to cool completely.

802 ■ DOUBLE CHOCOLATE MUFFINS II

MAKES 12 MUFFINS
BAKING TIME: *20 minutes*

2 cups all-purpose flour
1 teaspoon baking soda
¼ cup butter-flavored vegetable shortening
3 ounces unsweetened chocolate, grated or finely chopped
1 cup granulated sugar

1 cup buttermilk
1 large egg
2 teaspoons chocolate extract
1 cup semisweet chocolate chips

1 Position a rack in the center of the oven and preheat the oven to 400 degrees. Line twelve 2¾-inch muffin cups with paper baking cups.

2 Combine the flour and baking soda.

3 In the top of a double boiler over simmering water, melt the shortening and chocolate, stirring until smooth. Remove from the heat.

4 In a large bowl, using an electric mixer on medium speed, beat the sugar, buttermilk, and egg until very light-colored. Gradually stir in the dry ingredients. Stir in the melted chocolate and chocolate extract. Fold in the chocolate chips. Spoon the mixture into the prepared muffin cups, filling them to the top.

5 Bake for 15 to 20 minutes, or until a cake tester inserted into the center comes out clean. Remove the muffins to a wire rack to cool.

BAKING NOTES: White chocolate chips, peanut butter chips, or butterscotch chips can be substituted for the regular chocolate chips.

803 ■ DOUBLE CHOCOLATE ZUCCHINI BREAD

MAKES 2 LOAVES
BAKING TIME: *1 hour*

2 ounces unsweetened chocolate, grated or finely chopped
2½ cups all-purpose flour
1 cup walnut pieces, chopped
½ cup semisweet chocolate chips
1 teaspoon baking powder
1 teaspoon ground cinnamon
½ teaspoon salt
3 large eggs
2 cups granulated sugar
1 cup canola oil
1 tablespoon crème de cacao
2 cups grated zucchini

1 Position a rack in the center of the oven and preheat the oven to 350 degrees. Lightly grease and flour two 9 by 5-inch loaf pans.

2 Melt the chocolate (see page 13). Remove from the heat.

3 Combine the flour, walnuts, chocolate chips, baking powder, cinnamon, and salt.

4 In a large bowl, using an electric mixer on medium speed, beat the eggs until thick and light-colored. Beat in the sugar and oil. Beat in the crème de cacao and melted chocolate. Beat in the zucchini. Gradually blend in the dry ingredients. Pour the batter into the prepared pans.

5 Bake for 1 hour, or until a cake tester inserted into the center comes out clean. Cool completely in the pan on wire racks.

801

802

803

800

804 ■ FILLED CHOCOLATE BREAKFAST ROLL

MAKES 10 TO 12 SERVINGS
BAKING TIME: *30 minutes*

ROLLS

1 envelope active dry yeast
¼ cup warm water (105 to 110 degrees)
2½ cups all-purpose flour
½ cup Dutch processed cocoa powder
1¼ cups granulated sugar
¼ teaspoon salt
¼ cup butter or margarine, at room temperature
3 large eggs

FILLING

2 ounces unsweetened chocolate, grated or finely chopped
½ cup honey
2 tablespoon Frangelico or amaretto
2 cups ground hazelnuts
½ cup black currants
Grand Marnier Sauce (see page 411) for serving

1 In a cup, sprinkle the yeast over the warm water and set aside.

2 In a large bowl, combine the flour, cocoa powder, sugar, and salt. Using a pastry blender or two knives scissor fashion, cut in the butter. Using an electric mixer on medium speed, beat in eggs, one at a time, beating well after each addition. Blend in the yeast and form a smooth dough. On a lightly floured surface, knead for 2 to 3 minutes. Place in a buttered or floured bowl and let rise for up to 2 hours, until doubled in bulk.

3 Meanwhile, to make the filling, melt the chocolate (see page 13). Remove from the heat. Using an electric mixer on low speed, beat in the Frangelico. Using a spoon or spatula, fold in the hazelnuts and currants until combined.

4 Position a rack in the lower third of the oven and preheat the oven to 375 degrees. Lightly grease a baking sheet or jelly roll pan.

5 On a lightly floured surface, roll out the dough to a thickness of ½ inch. Spread the filling evenly over the dough, leaving a ½-inch border on the edges.

Using a pastry brush, lightly brush the border with water and roll up the dough, jelly-roll fashion. Seal the seam and ends by pinching them together. Place in the center of the prepared baking sheet.

6 Bake for 25 to 30 minutes, or until golden brown. Cool on a wire rack. Serve with Grand Marnier sauce on the side.

805 ■ FUDGE MUFFINS

MAKES 24 MUFFINS
BAKING TIME: *45 minutes*

1 cup all-purpose flour
2 cups pecans, finely chopped
4 ounces unsweetened chocolate, grated or finely chopped
1 cup butter or margarine
4 large eggs
1¾ cups granulated sugar
1 teaspoon almond extract

806

805

804

807

1 Position a rack in the center of the oven and preheat the oven to 300 degrees. Line twenty-four 2¾-inch muffin cups with paper baking cups.

2 Combine the flour and pecans.

3 In the top of a double boiler over simmering water, melt the chocolate and butter, stirring until smooth. Remove from the heat and using a wire whisk, beat in the eggs, one at a time. Beat in the sugar. Beat in the almond extract. Gradually blend in the dry ingredients. Spoon the batter into the prepared muffin cups, filling them about three-fourths full.

4 Bake for 40 to 45 minutes, or until a cake tester inserted into the center comes out clean. Transfer to wire racks to cool.

806 ■ GERMAN SWEET BREAD

MAKES 10 TO 12 SERVINGS
BAKING TIME: *1 hour*

1½ cups all-purpose flour
1 cup oat bran
1 cup chopped almonds
2 ounces semisweet chocolate, grated or finely chopped
½ cup golden raisins
½ cup dried cherries
1 teaspoon baking powder
½ teaspoon salt
½ cup butter or margarine, at room temperature
1⅓ cups granulated sugar
3 large eggs

1 teaspoon chocolate extract
1 cup milk
Powdered sugar for garnish
Shaved chocolate for garnish
Chocolate Syrup II (see page 406) for serving

1 Position a rack in the center of the oven and preheat the oven to 350 degrees. Lightly grease and flour a kugelhopf pan.

2 Combine the flour, oat bran, almonds, chocolate, raisins, cherries, baking powder, and salt.

3 In a large bowl, using an electric mixer on medium speed, beat the butter and sugar until fluffy. Beat in the eggs and chocolate extract. In three additions, blend in the dry ingredients, alternating with the milk, beginning and ending with the dry ingredients. Scrape the mixture into the prepared pan and spread evenly.

4 Bake for 55 minutes to 1 hour, or until a cake tester inserted into the center comes out clean. Cool in the pan on a wire rack for 15 minutes. Invert onto the wire rack to cool completely. Place on a serving plate. Dust with powdered sugar and shaved chocolate. Serve with chocolate syrup on the side.

807 ■ HAZELNUT SCONES

MAKES 8 SCONES
BAKING TIME: *20 minutes*

1 cup all-purpose flour
1 cup whole wheat flour
⅓ cup packed light brown sugar
1½ teaspoons baking powder
½ teaspoon baking soda
¼ teaspoon salt
6 tablespoons butter or margarine
½ cup buttermilk
1 large egg
1½ teaspoons hazelnut liqueur
6 ounces semisweet chocolate, grated or finely chopped
½ cup hazelnuts, chopped
Jam or jelly for serving

1 Position a rack in the center of the oven and preheat the oven to 400 degrees. Lightly grease a baking sheet.

2 In a large bowl, combine the flours, brown sugar, baking powder, baking soda, and salt. Using a pastry blender or two knives scissor fashion, cut in the butter to form a crumbly mixture.

3 In a small bowl, using an electric mixer on medium speed, beat the buttermilk, egg, and liqueur. Gradually blend into the dry mixture, stirring just until moistened. Fold in the grated chocolate and hazelnuts.

4 On a floured surface, roll out the dough to a thickness of ½ inch. Using a 2 to 2½-inch round cookie cutter, cut out as many rounds as possible. Place the rounds on the prepared baking sheet, spacing them 1 inch apart.

5 Bake for 17 to 20 minutes, or until lightly colored. Cool on the pan on a wire rack for 5 minutes. Remove to the rack to cool completely. Serve warm or cold with jam or jelly on the side.

BAKING NOTES: As an alternative, sprinkle with cocoa sugar (see page 407). Or, using dipping chocolate (see page 186), dip half of each scone in chocolate when cool.

808 ■ HAZELNUT SCONES WITH CHOCOLATE SYRUP

MAKES 8 SCONES
BAKING TIME: *20 minutes*

2 cups all-purpose flour
⅓ cup packed light brown sugar
1½ teaspoons baking powder
½ teaspoon baking soda
¼ teaspoon salt
6 tablespoons butter or margarine
½ cup buttermilk
1 large egg
1½ teaspoons chocolate extract
1 cup semisweet chocolate chips
¾ cup chopped hazelnuts
Chocolate Syrup II (see page 406) for serving

808

1 Position a rack in the center of the oven and preheat the oven to 400 degrees. Lightly grease a baking sheet.

2 In a large bowl, combine the flour, brown sugar, baking powder, baking soda, and salt. Using a pastry cutter or two knives scissor fashion, cut in the butter to form a crumbly mixture.

3 In a small bowl, using an electric mixer on medium speed, beat the buttermilk, egg, and chocolate extract. Blend into the dry ingredients, stirring just until moistened. Fold in the chocolate chips and ½ cup of the hazelnuts.

4 Form the dough into a ball and spread into a 9-inch circle on the center of the prepared baking sheet. Sprinkle the remaining ¼ cup nuts over the top. Using a serrated knife dipped in flour, score eight wedges into the surface of the dough.

5 Bake for 18 to 20 minutes, or until the top is a lightly browned. Cut into wedges. Transfer to a wire rack to cool. Serve warm with the chocolate syrup on the side.

809 ■ HOLIDAY PUMPKIN LOAF

MAKES 1 LOAF
BAKING TIME: 70 minutes

1¾ cups all-purpose flour
1 teaspoon baking soda
2 teaspoons ground allspice
¼ teaspoon salt
¼ cup butter-flavored vegetable shortening
1 cup granulated sugar
2 large eggs
¾ cup solid pack canned pumpkin
1 cup semisweet chocolate chips
½ cup Chocolate Frosting VI (see page 400) for serving

1 Position a rack in the center of the oven and preheat the oven to 350 degrees. Lightly grease a 9 by 5-inch loaf pan.

2 Combine the flour, baking soda, allspice, and salt.

3 In a large bowl, using an electric mixer on medium speed,

beat the shortening, sugar, and eggs until fluffy. Beat in the pumpkin. Gradually add the dry ingredients and mix just until blended. Fold in the chocolate chips. Scrape the mixture into the prepared pan and spread evenly.

4 Bake for 1 hour to 70 minutes, or until a cake tester inserted into the center comes out clean. Cool in the pan on a wire rack for 5 minutes. Invert onto the rack to cool completely. Place on a serving plate and drizzle chocolate frosting over the top.

810 ■ LEMON-FLAVORED CHOCOLATE MUFFINS

MAKES 12 MUFFINS
BAKING TIME: 35 minutes

2 cups all-purpose flour
¾ cup semisweet chocolate chips
1 teaspoon baking soda
Grated zest of 1 lemon
½ cup butter or margarine, at room temperature
1¼ cups granulated sugar
2 large eggs
1 cup chocolate yogurt or sour cream
¼ cup fresh lemon juice

1 Position a rack in the center of the oven and preheat the oven to 375 degrees. Lightly grease twelve 2¾-inch muffin cups.

2 Combine the flour, chocolate chips, baking soda, and lemon zest.

3 In a large bowl, using an electric mixer on medium speed, beat the butter and sugar until light and fluffy. Beat in the eggs and yogurt. Beat in the lemon juice. Gradually blend in the dry ingredients, blending just until moistened. Spoon into the prepared muffin cups.

4 Bake 30 to 35 minutes, or until a cake tester inserted into the center comes out clean. Cool in the pan on a wire rack for 10 minutes. Invert onto the rack to cool completely.

811 ■ MARBLEIZED CHOCOLATE LOAF

MAKES 1 LOAF
BAKING TIME: 1 hour

2 ounces unsweetened chocolate, grated or finely chopped
1¾ cups all purpose flour
1 tablespoon grated orange zest
¾ teaspoon baking powder
¾ teaspoon baking soda
1 cup butter-flavored vegetable shortening
1 cup granulated sugar
2 teaspoons chocolate or orange extract
3 large eggs
1 cup chocolate yogurt or sour cream
⅓ cup crème de cacao
Chocolate Icing (see page 402) for serving
Sliced fresh strawberries for garnish
Chocolate Leaves (see page 422) for garnish

1 Position a rack in the center of the oven and preheat the oven to 350 degrees. Lightly grease a 9 by 5-inch loaf pan.

2 Melt the chocolate (see page 13). Remove from the heat.

3 Combine the flour, orange zest, baking powder, and baking soda.

4 In a large bowl, using an electric mixer on medium speed, beat the shortening, sugar, and chocolate extract until fluffy. Beat in the eggs, one at a time,

809

beating well after each addition. Gradually blend in half of the dry ingredients. Beat in the yogurt. Gradually blend in the remaining dry ingredients, alternating with the crème de cacao. Transfer one-fourth of the batter to another bowl. Scrape the remaining batter into the prepared pan and spread evenly.

5 Using an electric mixer on medium speed, beat the melted chocolate into the reserved batter, mixing thoroughly. Spoon this mixture over the top of the batter in the pan. Swirl around with a metal spatula or knife.

6 Bake for 55 minutes to 1 hour, or until a cake tester inserted into the center comes out clean. Cool in the pan on a wire rack for 10 minutes. Invert onto the rack to cool completely.

7 Make the icing. Place the loaf on a serving plate and frost with the icing. Garnish with strawberries and chocolate leaves.

812 ■ MOCHA-FLAVORED SCONES

MAKES 8 TO 10 SCONES
BAKING TIME: *30 minutes*

1³/4 cups all-purpose flour
1/2 cup granulated sugar
2 tablespoons Dutch processed cocoa powder
2¹/2 teaspoons instant coffee powder
1¹/2 teaspoons baking powder
1/2 teaspoon salt
1/3 cup butter or margarine, cubed
1/3 cup buttermilk
1 large egg
1¹/2 teaspoon chocolate extract
Jam or jelly for serving

1 Position a rack in the center of the oven and preheat the oven to 375 degrees. Lightly grease two baking sheets.

2 In a large bowl, combine the flour, sugar, cocoa powder, coffee powder, baking powder, and salt. Using a pastry blender or two knives scissor fashion, cut in the butter to form a crumbly mixture.

3 In a medium bowl, beat the buttermilk, egg, and chocolate extract until blended. Stir into the flour mixture, blending to form a soft sticky dough. Using a measuring cup, drop the dough, 1/2 cup at a time, onto the prepared baking sheets, spacing the scones 4 to 4¹/2 inches apart.

4 Bake for 25 to 30 minutes, until a cake tester inserted into the center comes out clean. Transfer to a wire rack to cool for 5 to 10 minutes. Serve warm with jam or jelly.

BAKING NOTES: The scones can be made larger or smaller if desired.

813 ■ MUD PIE SCONES

MAKES 8 TO 10 SCONES
BAKING TIME: *18 minutes*

2 cups all-purpose flour
1/2 cup packed light brown sugar
1/3 cup Dutch processed cocoa powder
2¹/2 teaspoons baking powder
1/4 teaspoon salt
1/3 cup butter or margarine
1/2 cup chocolate yogurt
1 tablespoon water
1 large egg
1 teaspoon chocolate extract
Jam or jelly for serving

1 Position a rack in the center of the oven and preheat the oven to 375 degrees. Lightly grease two baking sheets.

2 In a large bowl, combine the flour, brown sugar, cocoa powder, baking powder, and salt. Using a pastry blender or two knives scissor fashion, cut in the butter to form a crumbly mixture.

3 In a medium bowl, using an electric mixer on high speed, beat the yogurt, water, egg, and chocolate extract until well blended. Stir into the flour mixture to form a soft sticky dough. Using a measuring cup or large serving spoon, drop the dough onto the prepared baking sheet, spacing the scones 4 inches apart.

811

813

812

810

4 Bake for 16 to 18 minutes, or until a cake tester inserted into the center comes out clean. Transfer to a wire rack to cool for 5 minutes. Serve warm with jam or jelly.

814 ■ ORANGE SCONES

MAKES 8 SCONES
BAKING TIME: *10 minutes*

2 cups all-purpose flour
1/2 cup granulated sugar
2 teaspoons baking powder
1/4 teaspoon salt
1/2 cup butter-flavored vegetable shortening
2 large eggs
2 tablespoons fresh orange juice
2 tablespoons orange liqueur
3 ounces semisweet chocolate, grated or finely chopped
1/2 cup Chocolate Syrup II (see page 406) for serving

1 Position a rack in the center of the oven and preheat the oven to 425 degrees. Lightly grease a baking sheet.

2 Combine the flour, sugar, baking powder, and salt in a large bowl. Using a pastry blender of two knives scissor fashion, cut in the shortening to form a crumbly mixture.

3 In a small bowl, using an electric mixer on medium speed, beat the eggs until thick and light-colored. Beat in the orange juice and liqueur. Gradually stir this mixture into the dry ingredients to form a sticky dough. Fold in the grated chocolate. Form the dough into a ball and place it in the center of the prepared baking sheet. Spread the dough into a circle 12 inches in diameter and 1/2-inch thick. Using a serrated knife dipped in flour, score eight wedges into the surface of the dough.

4 Bake for 8 to 10 minutes, or until a light golden color. Transfer to a wire rack to cool completely. Cut into wedges. Serve with chocolate syrup on the side.

815 ■ ORANGE SCONES WITH CHOCOLATE CANDY BAR SPRINKLES

MAKES 10 TO 12 SCONES
BAKING TIME: *18 minutes*

13/4 cups all-purpose flour
1/3 cup granulated sugar
2 tablespoons Dutch processed cocoa powder
11/2 teaspoons baking powder
1/4 teaspoon salt
1/4 cup butter or margarine, at room temperature
1/2 cup Hershey's™ Chocolate Shoppe Candy Bar Sprinkles
1/4 cup candied orange peel, finely chopped
1 large egg, separated, plus 1 large egg yolk
1/2 cup heavy cream
Jam or jelly for serving

1 Position a rack in the center of the oven and preheat the oven to 400 degrees. Lightly grease a baking sheet.

2 In a large bowl, combine the flour, sugar, cocoa powder, baking powder, and salt. Using a pastry blender or two knives scissor fashion, cut in the butter to form a crumbly mixture. Stir in the candy bar bits and candied orange peel.

814

815

816

817

818

3 In a small bowl, using an electric mixer on medium speed, beat the egg yolks until thick and light-colored. Beat in the cream. Gradually blend into the flour mixture to make a soft dough. Using a measuring cup, drop the batter, 1/4 cup at a time, onto the prepared baking sheet, spacing the scones 1 1/2 inches apart. Using a pastry brush, brush lightly with the egg white.

4 Bake for 15 to 18 minutes, or until a cake tester inserted into the center comes out clean. Do not overbake. Cool on the pan on a wire rack for 5 minutes. Transfer to the rack to cool completely. Serve warm or cold with a jam or jelly on the side.

816 ■ PLUM SCONES WITH PECANS

MAKES 12 SCONES
BAKING TIME: *17 minutes*

2 cups all-purpose flour
1/3 cup packed light brown sugar
1 1/2 teaspoons baking powder
1/4 teaspoon salt
6 tablespoons butter or margarine
1/2 cup chocolate yogurt
1 large egg
2/3 cup chopped plums
1/2 cup chopped pecans
1 1/2 teaspoons chocolate extract

1 Position a rack in the center of the oven and preheat the oven to 400 degrees. Lightly grease a baking sheet.

2 In a large bowl, combine the flour, brown sugar, baking powder, and salt. Using a pastry blender or two knives scissor fashion, cut in the butter to form a crumbly mixture.

3 In a medium bowl, using an electric mixer on low speed, beat the yogurt, egg, plums, pecans, and chocolate extract. Stir into the flour mixture and mix just until blended.

4 Using a measuring cup, drop the mixture, 1/4 cup at a time, onto the prepared baking sheets, spacing the scones 1 1/2 inches apart.

5 Bake for 15 to 17 minutes, or until a cake tester inserted into the center comes out clean. Cool on the pan on a wire rack for 3 to 5 minutes. Transfer to the rack to cool completely.

817 ■ PROFITEROLES WITH CHOCOLATE HAZELNUT ICE CREAM AND CHOCOLATE AND RASPBERRY SAUCES

MAKES 24 PROFITEROLES
BAKING TIME: *30 minutes*
FREEZING TIME: *30 minutes*

2 recipes Cream Puff Pastry (see recipe 819, page 362)
1/2 cup Chocolate Sauce VIII (see page 405)
1/2 cup Raspberry Sauce (see page 416)

ICE CREAM FILLING

3 tablespoons butter or margarine
1 cup ground hazelnuts
1 quart chocolate ice cream, softened

1 Position a rack in the center of the oven and preheat the oven to 425 degrees. Lightly grease two baking sheets.

2 Make the cream puff pastry. Spoon the dough into a pastry bag fitted with a large plain tip. Pipe out twenty-four mounds 2 3/4 to 3 inches in diameter onto the prepared baking sheets, spacing them 2 inches apart.

3 Bake for 25 to 30 minutes, or until the puffs are golden brown. Remove from the oven and immediately cut a small slit in the side of each puff with the tip of a serrated knife. Bake for 3 more minutes. Transfer to a wire rack to cool completely. Cover and chill until ready to use.

4 Meanwhile, make the chocolate sauce and raspberry sauce.

5 To make the filling, in a medium saucepan, over low heat, melt the butter. Stir in the hazelnuts. Remove from the heat. In a large bowl, fold into the ice cream, blending until thoroughly mixed.

6 To assemble, using a serrated knife, cut the puffs in half horizontally, three-fourths of the way through. Spoon a little of the ice cream filling into each of the puffs. Freeze for 30 minutes, until firm or until ready to serve.

7 To serve, spoon a small amount raspberry sauce on top of the ice cream in each puff. Set the puffs on serving plates and spoon a little of the chocolate sauce over the top. Serve with additional chocolate sauce on the side.

818 ■ PUMPKIN MUFFINS WITH CHOCOLATE CHIPS

MAKES 12 MUFFINS
BAKING TIME: *25 minutes*

1 2/3 cups all-purpose flour
1 cup granulated sugar
1 1/2 teaspoons baking powder
1 teaspoon baking soda
1 1/2 teaspoons ground cinnamon
1 teaspoon ground nutmeg
1/2 teaspoon ground cloves
1/4 teaspoon salt
2 large eggs
1 cup solid pack canned pumpkin
1/2 cup butter or margarine, at room temperature
1 cup semisweet chocolate chips

1 Position a rack in the center of the oven and preheat the oven to 350 degrees. Grease and lightly flour twelve 2 3/4-inch muffin cups.

2 Combine the flour, sugar, baking powder, baking soda, spices, and salt.

3 In a large bowl, using an electric mixer on medium speed, beat the eggs until thick and light-colored. Beat in the pumpkin and butter until smooth. Stir in the chocolate chips. Stir in the dry ingredients just until blended. Spoon the mixture into the prepared muffin cups.

4 Bake for 20 to 25 minutes, or until a cake tester inserted into the center comes out clean. Cool in the pan on a wire rack for 2 to 3 minutes. Invert onto the rack to cool completely.

819 ■ RICOTTA CHEESE-FILLED CREAM PUFFS

MAKES 12 SERVINGS
BAKING TIME: *1 hour*

CREAM PUFF PASTRY

1 cup water
½ cup butter or margarine
¼ teaspoon salt
1 cup all-purpose flour
4 large eggs

RICOTTA FILLING

1 pound ricotta cheese
¼ cup granulated sugar
2 ounces semisweet chocolate, grated or finely chopped
3 tablespoons evaporated milk
1 teaspoon chocolate extract

CHOCOLATE FROSTING

Chocolate Eclair Frosting (see page 398)

1 Position a rack in the center of the oven and preheat the oven to 375 degrees. Lightly grease two baking sheets.

2 In a large saucepan, over medium heat, heat the water, butter, and salt until the butter is melted. Raise the temperature to high. Bring to a boil and immediately remove from the heat.

3 Add the flour and return to the heat. Stir for about 1 minute with a wooden spoon until the mixture leaves the side of the pan and forms a ball. Remove from the heat. Beat in the eggs, one at a time, mixing well after each addition. Drop the dough by heaping spoonfuls onto the prepared baking sheets, making twelve mounds spaced 3 inches apart.

4 Bake for 50 minutes. Remove from the oven and immediately cut a small slit into the side of each puff. Return to the oven and bake for 10 minutes or until golden brown. Transfer to a wire rack to cool. Cover and chill until ready to use.

5 To make the filling, in a small bowl, using an electric mixer on high speed, beat the ricotta, sugar, chocolate, 1 tablespoon of the milk, and the chocolate extract. Add the remaining milk, a little at a time, until the consistency of thick mayonnaise. Cover and chill until ready to use.

6 Make the frosting.

7 To assemble, using a small serrated knife, cut the puffs horizontally halfway through, leaving just enough pastry on one side to act as a hinge. Fill each of the puffs with some of the filling. Spread a spoonful of the frosting over the top. Chill for at least 1 hour before serving.

BAKING NOTES: An alternative method of filling the cream puffs is to use a pastry bag. Fill a pastry bag fitted with a large round tip with the filling and pipe it through the slit made in the puffs while baking.

820 ■ SCONES WITH ALMONDS, APRICOTS AND CHOCOLATE CHIPS

MAKES 8 TO 10 SCONES
BAKING TIME: *20 minutes*

2 cups all-purpose flour
⅓ cup granulated sugar
2 teaspoons baking powder
½ teaspoon salt
¼ cup butter or margarine
1 cup chopped almonds
1 cup dried apricots, finely diced
1 cup miniature chocolate chips
½ cup heavy cream or evaporated milk
1 large egg
1½ teaspoons almond extract

819

821

820

1 Position a rack in the center of the oven and preheat the oven to 375 degrees. Lightly grease a baking pan.

2 In a large bowl, combine the flour, sugar, baking powder, and salt. Using a pastry blender or two knives scissor fashion, cut in the butter to form a crumbly mixture. Stir in the almonds, apricots, and chocolate chips and mix until just blended.

3 In a medium bowl, using an electric mixer on high speed, whip the cream, egg, and almond extract. Stir into the flour mixture, blending until the dry ingredients are just moistened.

4 On a lightly floured surface, roll out the dough to a thickness of ½ to ¾ inch, cutting the dough into 3 to 4-inch rounds. Place the rounds on the prepared baking sheet, spacing them 1 inch apart.

5 Bake for 15 to 20 minutes, or until a light golden brown. Transfer to a wire rack to cool for 5 minutes. Serve warm.

821 ■ TRIPLE CHOCOLATE CHUNK SCONES

MAKES 4 TO 6 SERVINGS
BAKING TIME: *25 minutes*

2 cups all-purpose flour
⅓ cup packed light brown sugar
1½ teaspoons baking powder
½ teaspoon baking soda
¼ teaspoon salt
¼ cup butter or margarine
½ cup buttermilk
1 large egg
1½ teaspoons chocolate extract
3 ounces unsweetened chocolate chips
3 ounces milk chocolate chips
3 ounces semisweet chocolate chips
Fruit preserves for serving

1 Position a rack in the center of the oven and preheat the oven to 375 degrees.

2 In a large bowl, combine the flour, sugar, baking powder, baking soda, and salt. Using a pastry blender or two knives scissor fashion, cut in the butter to form coarse crumbs.

3 In a small bowl, using an electric mixer on medium speed, beat the buttermilk, egg, and chocolate extract until blended. Gradually blend in the dry ingredients to form a smooth dough. Work in the chocolate chips.

4 Using a measuring cup, drop the dough, 1 cup at a time, onto an ungreased baking sheet, spacing the scones 2 inches apart.

5 Bake for 20 to 25 minutes, or until a light golden color. Transfer to wire rack to cool. Serve warm with fruit preserves on the side.

822 ■ TRIPLE CHOCOLATE MUFFINS

MAKES 12 MUFFINS
BAKING TIME: *35 minutes*

1 cup all-purpose flour
3 tablespoons Dutch processed cocoa powder
Pinch of salt
1 cup butter or margarine
2 ounces unsweetened chocolate, grated or finely chopped
2 ounces semisweet chocolate, grated or finely chopped
1½ cups granulated sugar
4 large eggs
1 teaspoon crème de cacao
12 pecan halves

1 Position a rack in the center of the oven and preheat the oven to 350 degrees. Lightly grease twelve 2¾-inch muffin cups or line them with paper baking cups.

2 Combine the flour, cocoa powder, and salt.

3 In the top of a double boiler over simmering water, melt the butter and chocolates, stirring until smooth. Remove from the heat and stir in the sugar. Using an electric mixer on medium speed, beat in the eggs, one at a time. Beat in the crème de cacao. Gradually blend in the dry ingredients. Spoon the batter into the prepared muffin cups, filling them to the top. Press a pecan half into each cup.

4 Bake for 30 to 35 minutes, or until a cake tester inserted into the center comes out clean. Remove to wire racks to cool.

BAKING NOTES: It is very easy to overbake these muffins. If you do, they will be dry.

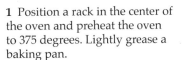

822

823 ■ WHITE CHOCOLATE, CHERRY, AND ALMOND SCONES

MAKES 8 SCONES
BAKING TIME: *20 minutes*

2 cups all-purpose flour
1 cup chopped almonds
1 cup finely chopped dried cherries
1/3 cup granulated sugar
2 teaspoons baking powder
1/4 teaspoon salt
1/4 cup butter or margarine
1/2 cup heavy cream
1 large egg
1 1/2 teaspoons cherry liqueur
1 cup white chocolate chips
Butter for serving

1 Position a rack in the center of the oven and preheat the oven to 375 degrees.

2 In a large bowl, combine the flour, almonds, cherries, sugar, baking powder, and salt. Using a pastry blender or two knives scissor fashion, cut in the butter to form a crumbly mixture.

3 In a medium bowl, using an electric mixer on high speed, whip the cream, egg, and liqueur. Stir into the flour mixture. Stir in the chocolate chips.

4 On a lightly floured surface, with floured hands, knead to form a smooth dough. Form the dough into a ball and spread into an 8 or 9-inch circle on the center of an ungreased baking sheet. Using a serrated knife dipped in flour, score eight wedges into the surface of the dough, cutting only part of the way through.

5 Bake for 15 to 20 minutes, or until light golden brown. Remove to a wire rack and cool slightly. Cut into wedges. Serve warm with butter on the side.

823

Tortes

824 ■ BLACK FOREST CHERRY TORTE

MAKES 10 TO 12 SERVINGS
BAKING TIME: *35 minutes*
CHILL TIME: *30 minutes*

CAKE

1²/₃ cups cake flour, sifted
1 tablespoons Dutch processed cocoa powder
2 teaspoons baking powder
4¹/₂ ounces semisweet chocolate, grated or finely chopped
2 tablespoons kirsch
6 large eggs, separated
³/₄ cup butter or margarine, at room temperature
1¹/₄ cups granulated sugar

WHIPPED CREAM FILLING

2 cups heavy cream
6 tablespoons powdered sugar
¹/₂ cup kirsch
4 cups tart cherries, drained, pitted, and finely chopped

1 Position a rack in the center of the oven and preheat the oven to 350 degrees. Lightly grease and flour two 9-inch round cake pans.

2 Combine the flour, cocoa powder, and baking powder.

3 Melt the chocolate (see page 13). Remove from the heat. Stir in the kirsch.

4 In a medium bowl, using an electric mixer on high speed, beat the egg whites until stiff but not dry.

5 In a large bowl, using an electric mixer on medium speed, beat the butter and sugar until light and fluffy. Beat in the eggs yolks, one at a time. Pouring it in a thin stream, beat in the melted chocolate. Gradually stir in the dry ingredients. Fold in the beaten egg whites. Divide the mixture evenly between the prepared pans.

6 Bake for 30 to 35 minutes, or until a cake tester inserted into the center comes out clean. Cool in the pans on wire racks for 10 minutes. Invert the cakes onto the racks to cool completely.

7 To make the filling, in a large bowl, using an electric mixer on high speed, whip the cream and powdered sugar until soft peaks form.

8 To assemble, using a serrated knife, slice the cake layers in half horizontally. Sprinkle the four layers with the kirsch. Place one of the layers on a serving plate and spread evenly with some of the whipped cream. Sprinkle with cherries. Top with a second cake layer and press down lightly onto the filling. Repeat with the remaining ingredients. Spread whipped cream over the top of the cake to the edge. Chill the torte for 30 minutes before serving.

825 ■ BLACK FOREST TORTE

MAKES 10 TO 12 SERVINGS
BAKING TIME: *90 minutes*
CHILL TIME: *1 hour*

1¹/₂ cups almonds, finely ground
2 tablespoons all-purpose flour
1¹/₄ cups egg whites (about 9 egg whites)
1 cup granulated sugar
6 ounces semisweet chocolate, grated or finely chopped
1 envelope unflavored gelatin
6 tablespoons water
3 cups heavy cream
2 tablespoons Dutch processed cocoa powder

1 Position a rack in the center of the oven and preheat the oven to 250 degrees. Line two baking sheets with parchment paper. Draw three 8-inch circles on the paper (two on one sheet and one on the other).

2 Combine the flour and almonds.

3 In a large bowl, using an electric mixer on high speed, beat the egg whites until stiff but not dry. Beat in ²/₃ cup of the sugar. Fold in the almond mixture. Spoon one-third of the mixture onto each circle and spread evenly, filling in the circles completely.

4 Bake for 85 to 90 minutes, or until set. Remove from the oven and cool slightly on the pan. Peel the paper from the bottom of the circles and transfer to wire racks to cool completely.

824

825

5 Melt 4 ounces of the chocolate (see page 13). Remove from the heat. Immediately spread one-third of the chocolate evenly over each of the three meringue layers. Cool until the chocolate is set.

6 In a small saucepan, over low heat, sprinkle the gelatin over water and let stand for 1 minute to soften. Over low heat, stir constantly until gelatin is dissolved. Remove from the heat and cool slightly. Stir in the remaining 1/3 cup sugar.

7 In a large bowl, using an electric mixer on high speed, whip the cream until soft peaks form. Fold in the gelatin mixture.

8 To assemble, place one meringue layer on a serving plate and spread with one-third of the whipped cream. Top with a second layer and spread with half of the remaining whipped cream. Top with the third layer. Fold the cocoa powder into the remaining one-third of the whipped cream and spread over the top. Sprinkle with the remaining 2 ounces grated chocolate and chill for at least 1 hour before serving.

826 ▪ CHESTNUT TORTE

MAKES 10 TO 12 SERVINGS
BAKING TIME: *30 minutes*
CHILL TIME: *1 hour*

MOCHA SPONGE CAKE

1 cup all-purpose flour
1/4 cup Dutch processed cocoa powder
1 1/2 teaspoons baking powder
1/4 teaspoon salt
4 large eggs, separated
1 cup granulated sugar
1/4 cup strong brewed espresso
1/2 teaspoon coffee liqueur

CHOCOLATE CHESTNUT FILLING

1 can (16 ounces) chestnuts, drained and diced
2 large egg yolks
3 tablespoons Frangelico
2 tablespoons coffee liqueur
1/2 teaspoon almond extract
1/2 cup butter or margarine, at room temperature
3 ounces semisweet chocolate, grated or finely chopped

WHIPPED CREAM FROSTING

2 cups heavy cream
1/2 cup powdered sugar
1/2 cup Dutch processed cocoa powder

1 Position a rack in the center of the oven and preheat the oven to 325 degrees. Lightly grease and flour two 9-inch round cake pans. Line the bottoms with waxed paper and grease and flour the paper.

2 To make the cake, combine the flour, cocoa powder, baking powder, and salt.

3 In a medium bowl, using an electric mixer on high speed, beat the egg whites until foamy. Gradually add the sugar and beat until stiff but not dry.

4 In a large bowl, using an electric mixer on medium speed, beat the egg yolks until thick and light-colored. Beat in the espresso and liqueur. Gradually fold in the egg whites. Fold in the dry ingredients. Divide the mixture evenly between the prepared pans.

5 Bake for 25 to 30 minutes, or until a cake tester inserted into the center comes out clean. Cool in the pans on wire racks for 5 minutes. Invert onto the racks to cool completely. Cover the cake until ready to assemble.

6 Meanwhile, to make the filling, in the container of a blender, combine the chestnuts, egg yolks, Frangelico, coffee liqueur, and almond extract. Blend on high until smooth. Blend in the butter until smooth. Pour into a medium bowl and fold in the grated chocolate. Cover and chill for 1 hour.

7 To make the frosting, in a medium bowl, using an electric mixer on high speed, beat the cream, powdered sugar, and cocoa powder until soft peaks form.

8 To assemble, using a serrated knife, cut each cake in half horizontally to make four layers. Place one of the layers on a serving plate. Spread with one-third of the chestnut filling and place a second layer on top. Continue until all of the chestnut filling

and cake layers are used. Spread the whipped cream topping over the top and sides of the cake.

BAKING NOTES: Owing to the raw egg yolks used in this filling, it should be kept in the refrigerator at all times, and for no longer than 3 days.

827 ▪ CHOCOLATE BANANA TORTE

MAKES 10 TO 12 SERVINGS
BAKING TIME: *8 hours*
CHILL TIME: *4 hours*

MERINGUE LAYERS

3 large egg whites
1 cup granulated sugar

FILLINGS

6 ounces semisweet chocolate, grated
3 tablespoons crème de cacao
3 cups heavy cream
1/4 cup granulated sugar
3 bananas, sliced paper-thin

1 Preheat the oven to 400 degrees. Line two baking sheets with parchment paper. Draw two 9-inch circles on one piece of paper, and one 9-inch circle on the other.

2 To make the layers, in a medium bowl, using an electric mixer on high speed, beat the egg whites until foamy. Gradually add the sugar and beat until stiff but not dry. Fill a pastry bag fitted with a large plain tip with the meringue. Pipe the meringue on parchment paper, starting in the center of each of the drawn circles and continuing in an outward spiral until they are filled with meringue. Place the baking sheets in the oven, turn off the oven, and let dry for at least 8 hours.

3 To make the fillings, in a small saucepan, over low heat, combine the chocolate and crème de cacao, stirring constantly until the chocolate is melted and the mixture is smooth. Remove from the heat.

4 In a medium bowl, using an electric mixer on high speed, beat the cream until soft peaks form. Gradually add the sugar and beat until stiff peaks form.

5 To assemble, place one of the meringues on a serving plate, spread with one-third of the chocolate filling mixture. Spread one-fourth of the whipped cream over the chocolate filling. Arrange half of the banana slices over the top of the cream. Top with a second meringue and repeat the layers of chocolate filling, whipped cream, and bananas. Top with the third meringue and spread the remaining whipped cream over the top. Drizzle the remaining chocolate filling over the top of the cake, first in one direction and then in another. Chill for 3 to 4 hours before serving.

BAKING NOTES: Almost any fruit can be used in place of bananas.

828 ■ CHOCOLATE CHOCOLATE TORTE

MAKES 10 TO 12 SERVINGS
BAKING TIME: *1 hour*

FLOURLESS CHOCOLATE CAKE

8 ounces semisweet chocolate, grated or finely chopped
1¹/₂ tablespoons butter or margarine
5 large eggs
¹/₄ cup granulated sugar
¹/₃ cup dark corn syrup

CHOCOLATE GLAZE

³/₄ cup heavy cream
8 ounces semisweet chocolate, grated or finely chopped
1¹/₂ tablespoons butter or margarine, at room temperature
1¹/₂ tablespoons dark corn syrup
Paper-thin slices of orange for garnish

1 Position a rack in the center of the oven and preheat the oven to 350 degrees. Grease and flour a 9-inch round cake pan and line the bottom with waxed paper or parchment paper. Grease and flour the paper.

2 In the top of a double boiler over simmering water, melt the chocolate and butter, stirring until smooth. Remove from the heat.

3 In a large bowl, using an electric mixer on high speed, beat the eggs and sugar until thick and light-colored. Beat in the corn syrup. Pouring it in a thin stream, beat in the chocolate mixture on low speed. Pour the mixture into the prepared pan.

4 Bake for 1 hour, or until a cake tester inserted into the center comes out clean. Cool in the pan on a wire rack. Invert onto a serving plate.

5 To make the glaze, in a saucepan over low heat, warm the cream for 1 minute. Reduce the heat to low and add the chocolate. Stir constantly until the chocolate is melted and the mixture is smooth. Remove from the heat. Let stand just until cool. Using a wire whisk, beat in the butter and corn syrup. Spread the glaze over the top and sides of the torte. Garnish with orange slices.

829 ■ CHOCOLATE CHRISTMAS TORTE

MAKES 10 TO 12 SERVINGS
BAKING TIME: *35 minutes*

CHOCOLATE PUDDING CAKE

4 ounces unsweetened chocolate, grated or finely chopped
2 cups all-purpose flour
2 packages (3.4 ounces each) Jell-O Brand instant chocolate pudding
¹/₂ teaspoon baking powder
1¹/₄ teaspoons baking soda
¹/₂ teaspoon salt
¹/₄ cup vegetable shortening
2 cups granulated sugar
³/₄ cup chocolate yogurt
1 cup water
2 large eggs
1 teaspoon amaretto

CRÈME DE CACAO FILLING

3 cups powdered sugar
1 cup vegetable shortening
¹/₂ cup milk
1 teaspoon crème de cacao

COCOA FROSTING

¹/₂ cup butter or margarine
3 tablespoons hot water
³/₄ cup Dutch processed cocoa powder
1 large egg
3 cups powdered sugar
¹/₂ teaspoon crème de cacao

1 Position a rack in the center of the oven and preheat the oven to 350 degrees. Lightly grease three 8-inch round cake pans.

2 Melt the chocolate (see page 13). Remove from the heat.

3 Combine the flour, pudding mix, baking powder, baking soda, and salt.

4 In a large bowl, using an electric mixer on high speed, beat the shortening and sugar until fluffy. Beat in the melted chocolate. Beat in the yogurt. Beat in the water. Beat in the eggs and amaretto. Gradually blend in the dry ingredients. Pour the mixture into the three prepared pans.

5 Bake for 30 to 35 minutes, or until a cake tester inserted into the center comes out clean. Cool in the pans on wire racks.

6 To make the filling, using an electric mixer on high speed, beat the powdered sugar and shortening until fluffy. Beat in the milk and crème de cacao until blended.

7 To assemble, place one of the cake layers on a serving plate and spread with half of the filling. Top with a second layer and spread with the remaining filling.

8 To make the frosting, in the top of a double boiler over simmering water, melt the butter with the hot water, stirring until smooth. Stir in the cocoa powder. Beat in the egg. Beat in the powdered sugar. Stir in the crème de cacao. Turn off the

828

heat and leave the top of the double boiler sitting over the warm water. Immediately spread the frosting over the top and sides of the torte.

830 ■ CHOCOLATE CREAM TORTE

MAKES 10 TO 12 SERVINGS
BAKING TIME: *25 minutes*
CHILL TIME: *3 hours*

CHOCOLATE TORTE

4 ounces semisweet chocolate, grated or finely chopped
1 1/2 tablespoons strong brewed coffee
3/4 teaspoon chocolate extract
4 large eggs, separated
Pinch of salt
1/2 cup granulated sugar

CHOCOLATE ALMOND FILLING

2 ounces semisweet chocolate, grated or finely chopped
2 large egg whites
1/4 cup granulated sugar
1 tablespoon amaretto
1/4 cup ground almonds

WHIPPED CREAM TOPPING

1/2 cup heavy cream
1 1/2 teaspoons powdered sugar
1/4 cup ground almonds
1 ounce semisweet chocolate, grated or finely chopped
Melted semisweet chocolate for garnish
6 to 8 Chocolate Leaves (see page 422) for garnish

1 Position a rack in the center of the oven and preheat the oven to 350 degrees. Lightly grease two 8-inch square pans. Line the bottoms of the pans with waxed paper and grease the paper.

2 In the top of a double boiler over simmering water, melt the chocolate with the coffee, stirring constantly until the chocolate is melted and the mixture is smooth. Remove from the heat and stir in the chocolate extract.

3 In a large bowl, using an electric mixer on high speed, beat the egg whites with the salt until foamy. Gradually add the sugar and beat until stiff but not dry.

4 In another large bowl, using an electric mixer on medium speed, beat the egg yolks until thick and light-colored. Stir in the chocolate mixture. Fold in the egg whites, one-third at a time, blending after each addition until white streaks no longer appear. Divide the mixture evenly between the prepared pans.

5 Bake for 20 to 25 minutes, or until a cake tester inserted into the center comes out clean. Cool in the pans on wire racks for 5 minutes. Invert onto the racks to cool completely.

6 Meanwhile, to make the filling, melt the chocolate (see page 13). Remove from the heat.

7 In a large bowl, using an electric mixer on high speed, beat the egg whites until foamy. Gradually add the sugar and beat until stiff but not dry. Fold in the amaretto, almonds, and melted chocolate. Chill until ready to use.

8 To make the topping, in a medium bowl, using an electric mixer on high speed, whip the cream and powdered sugar until stiff peaks form. Fold in the almonds and grated chocolate.

9 To assemble, using a serrated knife, cut the two layers in half horizontally to make four layers. Place one of the layers on a serving plate and spread with one-third of the filling. Top with a second layer. Repeat the layers of cake and filling, ending with the fourth cake layer. Spread the top cake layer with the whipped cream topping. Garnish with a drizzle of melted chocolate and chocolate leaves. Chill for 2 to 3 hours before serving.

BAKING NOTES: An alternative garnish is fresh fruit, such as sliced strawberries, whole raspberries, peeled and sliced kiwifruit, or sliced lemon or orange.

830

831 ▪ CHOCOLATE HAZELNUT TORTE

MAKES 10 TO 12 SERVINGS
BAKING TIME: *45 minutes*

CHOCOLATE HAZELNUT CAKE

8 ounces unsweetened chocolate, grated or finely chopped
6 tablespoons butter or margarine
4 large eggs, separated
1/2 cup powdered sugar
1/2 cup hazelnuts, finely ground
1/4 cup all-purpose flour
1/4 teaspoon amaretto
1/4 teaspoon cream of tartar
Pinch of salt
1/4 cup granulated sugar

CHOCOLATE GLAZE

6 ounces semisweet chocolate, grated or finely chopped
1/4 cup butter or margarine
1 tablespoon dark corn syrup
2 tablespoons apricot liqueur
Apricot Roses (see page 420) for garnish
Chocolate Leaves (see page 422) for garnish

1 Position a rack in the center of the oven and preheat the oven to 375 degrees. Lightly grease and flour an 8-inch springform pan.

2 To make the cake, in the top of a double boiler over simmering water, melt the chocolate and the butter. Stir until smooth. Remove from the heat.

3 In a large bowl, using an electric mixer on medium speed, beat the egg yolks until thick and light-colored. Add the powdered sugar and beat thoroughly. Stir in the melted chocolate, hazelnuts, flour, and amaretto.

4 In a medium bowl, using an electric mixer on high speed, beat the egg whites, cream of tartar, and salt until foamy. Gradually add the granulated sugar and beat until stiff but not dry. Fold one-third into the chocolate mixture until no white streaks appear. Fold in the remaining egg whites. Scrape into the prepared pan and spread evenly.

5 Bake for 40 to 45 minutes, or until a cake tester inserted 1 inch from the edge of the pan comes out clean. Cool in the pan on a wire rack for 10 minutes. Remove the side of the springform pan and place the cake on the rack to cool completely.

6 Meanwhile, to make the glaze, in the top of a double boiler over simmering water, melt the chocolate, stirring until smooth. Stir in the butter and corn syrup until completely blended. Remove from the heat and immediately stir in the apricot liqueur. Cool until thickened and spread over the cooled cake. Place on a serving plate and garnish with apricot roses and chocolate leaves.

832 ▪ CHOCOLATE MERINGUE TORTE

MAKES 10 TO 12 SERVINGS
BAKING TIME: *35 minutes*

1/4 cup Dutch processed cocoa powder
1/4 cup pecan pieces, finely ground
1 tablespoon cornstarch or arrowroot
3 large egg whites
1/8 teaspoon cream of tartar
Pinch of salt
1 teaspoon chocolate extract
3/4 cup plus 2 tablespoons granulated sugar
Chocolate Buttercream (see page 395)
Kahlúa Cocoa Sauce (see page 413)

1 Position a rack in the center of the oven and preheat the oven to 325 degrees. Line two baking sheets with parchment paper and draw two 8-inch circles on each sheet.

2 Combine the cocoa powder, pecans, and cornstarch.

3 In a large bowl, using an electric mixer on high speed, beat the egg whites and cream of tartar until foamy. Add the salt and continue beating until soft peaks form. Gradually add the sugar and beat until stiff but not dry. Gradually fold in the dry ingredients.

4 Spoon the mixture into a pastry bag fitted with a 1/4-inch plain tip. Pipe the meringue onto the prepared pans, starting in the center of each of the drawn circles and continuing in an outward spiral until they are filled with meringue.

5 Bake for 30 to 35 minutes, or until it looks dry. Cool on the pans on wire racks.

6 Make the buttercream and the Kahlúa cocoa sauce.

7 To assemble, place one of the meringue layers on a serving plate and spread with a generous layer of the buttercream. Top with a second meringue layer. Repeat with the remaining meringue layers and buttercream, ending with a layer of buttercream. Drizzle some of the sauce over the top of the cake. Serve with the remaining sauce on the side.

833 ▪ CHOCOLATE NUT PASSOVER TORTE

MAKES 10 TO 12 SERVINGS
BAKING TIME: *35 minutes*
CHILL TIME: *1 hour*
STANDING TIME: 1 HOUR

CHOCOLATE NUT CAKE

1/3 cup golden raisins
2 tablespoons amaretto
1 cup butter or margarine, at room temperature
8 ounces unsweetened chocolate, grated or finely chopped
2 cups chopped walnuts or almonds
1/2 cup matzo meal
5 large eggs plus 2 large egg yolks
1 1/2 cups granulated sugar
1/2 cup kosher liqueur
1 1/2 cups Chocolate Glaze I (see page 401)
White Chocolate Leaves # 639 (see page 422)

1 To make the cake, in a cup, combine the raisins and liqueur. Cover and soak overnight.

2 Position a rack in the center of the oven and preheat the oven to 375 degrees. Grease a 9-inch springform pan. Line the bottom with waxed paper and grease the paper.

3 In the top of a double boiler over simmering water, melt the butter and chocolate, stirring until smooth. Remove from the heat.

4 Combine the walnuts and matzo meal.

5 In a large bowl, using an electric mixer on medium speed, beat the eggs, egg yolks, and sugar until thick and light-colored. Beat in the melted chocolate and liqueur. Fold in the dry ingredients. Drain and fold in the raisins. Scrape the mixture into the prepared pan and spread evenly.

6 Bake for 30 to 35 minutes, or until a cake tester inserted into the center comes out clean. Cool in the pan on a wire rack for 1 hour. Invert onto the rack to cool completely. Remove the waxed paper.

7 Make the chocolate glaze.

8 To assemble, place the cake on a cardboard circle the same diameter as the cake and set on a wire rack over a baking sheet large enough to catch the drippings. Using an icing spatula, spread the sides with the chocolate glaze. Pour the remaining glaze over the top, allowing the excess to drip off the cake. Smooth with a spatula and garnish with white chocolate leaves. Chill for at least 1 hour. Transfer to a serving plate and let stand at room temperature for 1 hour before serving.

834 ■ CHOCOLATE NUT TORTE I

MAKES 10 TO 12 SERVINGS
BAKING TIME: *35 minutes*

CHOCOLATE PECAN CAKE

1$\frac{1}{2}$ cups graham cracker crumbs
1$\frac{1}{4}$ cups pecans, finely ground
6 ounces semisweet chocolate, grated or finely chopped
2 teaspoons baking powder
5 large egg whites
1$\frac{1}{2}$ cups granulated sugar
1$\frac{1}{2}$ teaspoons praline liqueur

MOCHA TOPPING

1 cup heavy cream
1 teaspoon instant espresso powder
12 ounces unsweetened chocolate, grated or finely chopped

1 Position a rack in the center of the oven and preheat the oven to 350 degrees. Grease and flour a 9-inch springform pan.

2 Combine the graham cracker crumbs, pecans, grated chocolate, and baking powder.

3 In a large bowl, using an electric mixer on high speed, beat the egg whites until foamy. Gradually add the sugar and beat until stiff but not dry. Gently fold in the dry ingredients. Fold in the liqueur. Scrape into the prepared pan and spread evenly.

4 Bake for 30 to 35 minutes, or until crusty on the top. Cool in the pan on a wire rack. Remove the side of the springform pan and transfer the cake to a serving plate.

5 Meanwhile, to make the topping, in a medium saucepan, over low heat, combine the cream and espresso powder, stirring until smooth. Add the chocolate and stir constantly until melted. Remove from the heat. Spoon the warm topping over the cake. Cool completely before serving.

BAKING NOTES: The top of the cake will crack while it cools.

835 ■ CHOCOLATE NUT TORTE II

MAKES 16 SERVINGS
BAKING TIME: *35 minutes*

Plain bread crumbs or cake crumbs for dusting
1$\frac{2}{3}$ cups ground walnuts
$\frac{2}{3}$ cup granulated sugar
6 ounces unsweetened chocolate, grated or finely chopped
$\frac{1}{4}$ cup candied orange peel, finely diced
1 tablespoon grated orange zest
5 large eggs, separated, plus 1 large egg white
2 cups Chocolate Whipped Cream (see page 406)
White and dark Chocolate Leaves (see page 422) for garnish

1 Position a rack in the center of the oven and preheat the oven to 375 degrees. Lightly grease a 10-inch springform pan. Dust with very fine bread or cake crumbs.

831

832

833

2 Combine the walnuts, sugar, grated chocolate, candied orange peel, and orange zest.

3 In a large bowl, using an electric mixer on medium speed, beat the egg yolks until very thick and light-colored.

4 In another large bowl, using an electric mixer with clean beaters on high speed, beat the egg whites until stiff but not dry.

5 Fold one-third of the egg whites and the walnut mixture into the egg yolks. Gently fold the remaining egg whites into the egg yolk mixture. Scrape the mixture into the prepared pan and spread evenly.

6 Bake for 30 to 35 minutes, or until a cake tester inserted into the center comes out clean. Cool in the pan on a wire rack. Remove the side of the springform pan and transfer the cake to a serving plate. Cover until ready to assemble.

7 Meanwhile, make the chocolate whipped cream and the chocolate leaves.

8 To assemble, using a serrated knife, cut the cake in half horizontally. Place the bottom layer on a serving plate. Spread with half of the whipped cream. Place the top half in place and spread the remaining whipped cream over the top. Garnish with the chocolate leaves.

BAKING NOTES: Sliced fresh fruit can also be arranged on top as a garnish along with the chocolate leaves.

836 ■ CHOCOLATE NUT TORTEN

MAKES 8 TO 10 SERVINGS
SETTING TIME: *24 hours*

1½ cups butter or margarine, at room temperature
1¼ cups granulated sugar
1 cup honey
1¼ cups ground walnuts or hazelnuts
4 ounces unsweetened chocolate, grated or finely chopped
1 tablespoon Dutch processed cocoa powder
1 tablespoon chocolate extract
6 to 8 6-inch gaufrettes (see Baking notes)

1 In a saucepan over medium heat, combine the butter, sugar, and honey, stirring constantly until the butter is melted and the sugar is dissolved. Bring to a boil and add the walnuts, chocolate, and cocoa powder, stirring until the chocolate is melted. Cook for 4 minutes and remove from the heat. Stir in the chocolate extract and immediately assemble and frost the cake. (The frosting sets up quickly.)

2 Place one gaufrette wafer, design side down, onto a serving plate. Spread ½ cup of the chocolate mixture evenly over the top, leaving a ¼-inch border on each side. Top with another wafer and press lightly into place. Repeat the layers until all of the wafers are used. Spread the remaining chocolate mixture smoothly over the top and sides. Let stand at room temperature for at least 1 day before serving.

BAKING NOTES: The gaufrettes are pastry wafers that are available at stores that carry German products or imported food items. The chocolate mixture sets very quickly. When spreading it on the sides of the torte, spread it from the bottom up for best results.

837 ■ CHOCOLATE ORANGE TORTE I

MAKES 10 TO 12 SERVINGS
BAKING TIME: *1 hour*

¾ cup raisins
Kosher liqueur for soaking
¼ cup matzo cake meal, plus 1 tablespoon for dusting pan
½ cup almonds, very finely ground
4 large eggs, separated
½ cup granulated sugar

827
829
834
825
835

4 ounces unsweetened chocolate, grated or finely chopped
6 tablespoons fresh orange juice, strained
2 tablespoons Sabra liqueur
2 tablespoons grated orange zest
White Chocolate Curls (see page 422)

1 In a small bowl, place the raisins and add the kosher liqueur to cover. Cover tightly and soak for at least 1 hour or overnight. Drain the raisins and reserve the brandy for another use. Finely chop the raisins.

2 Position a rack in the center of the oven and preheat the oven to 350 degrees. Lightly grease the bottom of a 9-inch springform pan and dust with matzo cake meal.

3 Combine the soaked raisins, matzo cake meal, and almonds.

4 In a medium bowl, using an electric mixer on high speed, beat the egg whites until stiff but not dry.

5 In a large bowl, using an electric mixer on medium speed, beat the egg yolks until thick and light-colored. Beat in the sugar. Gradually add the dry ingredients. Fold in the chocolate, orange juice, Sabra liqueur, and 1 tablespoon of the orange

zest. Fold in the egg whites. Scrape the mixture into the prepared pan and spread evenly.

6 Bake for 55 minutes to 1 hour, or until a cake tester inserted into the center comes out clean. Cool in the pan on a wire rack. Remove the side of the springform pan and place on a serving plate. Garnish with the remaining grated orange zest and white chocolate curls.

Baking notes: For a variation, mix in all of the grated orange zest and garnish with paper-thin orange slices arranged in an overlapping circle around the top of the cake. This recipe can be used during the Jewish holiday of Passover.

838 ▪ CHOCOLATE ORANGE TORTE II

Makes 8 to 12 servings
Baking time: *1 hour*

CHOCOLATE ALMOND TORTE

2 cups ground almonds
6 ounces semisweet chocolate, grated or finely chopped
1/4 cup dried bread crumbs
2 tablespoons grated orange zest
1 tablespoon baking powder
1/2 cup butter or margarine, at room temperature
1 cup granulated sugar
7 large eggs, separated
2 teaspoons Triple Sec
Pinch of salt

CHOCOLATE ORANGE GLAZE

1/4 cup powdered sugar, sifted twice
3 ounces semisweet chocolate, grated or finely chopped
2 tablespoons butter or margarine
2 tablespoons fresh orange juice
1 tablespoon Triple Sec

1 Position a rack in the center of the oven and preheat the oven to 350 degrees. Lightly butter an 8-inch springform pan. Line the bottom of the pan with waxed paper and grease the paper.

2 In a large bowl, combine 1¾ cups of the almonds, the chocolate, bread crumbs, orange zest, and baking powder.

3 In a large bowl, using an electric mixer on high speed, beat the butter and 1/2 cup of the sugar until fluffy. Beat in the egg yolks, two at a time, beating well after each addition. Beat in the Triple Sec. Gradually blend in the dry ingredients.

4 In a medium bowl, using an electric mixer with clean beaters on high speed, beat the egg whites and salt until foamy. Gradually beat in the remaining 1/2 cup granulated sugar, a tablespoonful at a time. Beat until stiff but not dry. Fold into the egg yolk mixture, a little at a time, until white streaks no longer appear. Scrape the mixture into the prepared pan and spread evenly.

5 Bake for 55 minutes to 1 hour, or until a cake tester inserted into the center comes out clean. Cool in the pan on a wire rack.

6 To make the glaze, in the top of a double boiler over simmering water, combine the powdered sugar, chocolate, butter, and orange juice and cook, stirring constantly, until the chocolate is melted and the mixture is smooth. Remove from the heat and stir in the Triple Sec.

7 To assemble, remove the side of the springform pan and invert the torte onto a serving plate. Remove the waxed paper and spread the warm glaze over the top and sides. Garnish with the remaining 1/4 cup almonds.

837

838

836

839 ■ GERMAN CHOCOLATE TORTE

MAKES 10 TO 12 SERVINGS
BAKING TIME: *30 minutes*

CHOCOLATE PUDDING CAKE

4 ounces semisweet chocolate, grated or finely chopped
1¾ cups all-purpose flour
1 package (3.4 ounces) Jell-O Brand chocolate instant pudding mix
1 tablespoon baking powder
1 teaspoon salt
½ cup butter or margarine, at room temperature
1¼ cups granulated sugar
2 large eggs
1 cup milk
1½ teaspoons Chocolate Syrup II (see page 406) or commercial brand

COCONUT PECAN TOPPING

1 cup evaporated milk
1 cup granulated sugar
3 large egg yolks
½ cup butter or margarine
1 teaspoon chocolate extract
1 cup flaked coconut
1 cup pecans, finely chopped

1 Position a rack in the center of the oven and preheat the oven to 375 degrees. Lightly grease two 8-inch round cake pans.

2 Melt the chocolate (see page 13). Remove from the heat.

3 Combine the flour, pudding mix, baking powder, and salt.

4 In a large bowl, using an electric mixer on medium speed, beat the butter and sugar until light and fluffy. Beat in the eggs. Beat in the milk and chocolate syrup. Beat in the melted chocolate. Gradually blend in the dry ingredients. Divide the mixture evenly between the prepared pans.

5 Bake for 25 to 30 minutes, or until the cake springs back when lightly touched. Cool in the pans on a wire rack for 5 minutes. Remove from the pans and cool completely on the rack.

6 To make the topping, in the top of a double boiler over simmering water, combine the evaporated milk, sugar, egg yolks, butter, and chocolate extract. Cook for about 12 min-

utes, stirring constantly, until the mixture thickens. Remove from the heat and add the coconut and pecans. Using an electric mixer on medium speed, beat until cool and a spreadable consistency.

7 To assemble, place one of the cake layers on a serving plate and spread with some of the topping. Top with the second cake layer. Spread the remaining topping over the top and sides of the cake.

840 ■ ITALIAN ALMOND TORTE

MAKES 10 TO 12 SERVINGS
BAKING TIME: *25 minutes*

⅔ cup almonds, finely ground
3 ounces unsweetened chocolate, grated or finely chopped
½ cup amaretti or almond wafer cookie crumbs
1 teaspoon baking powder
Pinch of salt
6 large eggs, separated
1 cup granulated sugar
1 teaspoon almond extract
1 teaspoon crème de cacao or chocolate extract
Pinch of cream of tartar
2 cups Chocolate Whipped Cream (see page 406)
Chocolate Curls (see page 422) for garnish

1 Position a rack in the center of the oven and preheat the oven to 350 degrees. Lightly grease and flour two 9-inch round cake pans.

2 In a medium bowl, combine the nuts, grated chocolate, cookie crumbs, baking powder, and salt.

3 In a large bowl, using an electric mixer on medium speed, beat the egg yolks until thick and light-colored. Gradually beat in ¾ cup of the sugar. Beat in the almond extract and crème de cacao.

4 In another large bowl, using an electric mixer on high speed, beat the egg whites and cream of tartar until foamy. Gradually beat in the remaining ¼ cup sugar and beat until stiff but not dry. Fold in the egg yolks, one-

fourth at a time. Fold in the dry ingredients. Divide the mixture evenly between the prepared pans.

5 Bake for 20 to 25 minutes, or until a cake tester inserted into the center comes out clean. Cool in the pans on wire racks for 10 minutes. Invert onto the racks to cool completely.

6 To assemble, using a serrated knife, cut each layer in half horizontally to make four layers. Place one layer on a serving plate and spread with ½ cup of the chocolate whipped cream. Top with a second cake layer. Repeat the layers until all four cake layers are used, ending with a layer of whipped cream. Garnish with chocolate curls.

841 ■ MOCHA CHOCOLATE TORTE WITH CHOCOLATE GLAZE

MAKES 10 TO 12 SERVINGS
BAKING TIME: *30 minutes*

MOCHA PECAN TORTE

4 ounces semisweet chocolate, grated or finely chopped
¼ cup water
1 teaspoon instant espresso powder
Pinch of salt
4 large eggs
½ cup granulated sugar
1 teaspoon chocolate extract
½ cup all-purpose flour
¾ cup chopped pecans or walnuts

CHOCOLATE GLAZE

3 ounces semisweet chocolate, grated or finely chopped
¼ cup light corn syrup
1 tablespoon water

1 Position a rack in the center of the oven and preheat the oven to 350 degrees. Lightly grease and flour a 9-inch springform pan. Line the bottom with waxed paper and grease the paper.

2 In the top of a double boiler of simmering water, combine the chocolate, water, espresso powder, and salt and stir constantly until the chocolate is melted and

the mixture is smooth. Remove from the heat.

3 In a large bowl, using an electric mixer on medium speed, beat the eggs until thick and light-colored. Beat in the sugar until very thick. Beat in the chocolate mixture and the chocolate extract. Gradually blend in the flour. Fold in half of the nuts. Scrape the mixture into the prepared pan and spread evenly.

4 Bake for 25 to 30 minutes, or until a cake tester inserted into the center comes out clean. Cool in the pan on a wire rack for 5 minutes. Remove the side of the springform pan and invert onto the rack to cool completely. Remove the waxed paper and place on a serving plate.

5 To make the glaze, in the top of a double boiler over simmering water, combine the chocolate, corn syrup, and water and cook until the chocolate is melted and the mixture is smooth. Immediately pour over the cake and sprinkle the remaining nuts on the top.

842 ■ MOCHA TORTE

MAKES 16 SERVINGS
BAKING TIME: *25 minutes*
STANDING TIME: *45 minutes*

CAKE

1 cup almonds, very finely ground
2/3 cup granulated sugar
1/4 cup all-purpose flour
4 ounces unsweetened chocolate, grated or finely chopped
4 ounces semisweet chocolate, grated or finely chopped
2/3 cup butter or margarine, at room temperature
8 large eggs, separated
1/3 cup coffee liqueur
1 tablespoon mocha-flavored instant coffee powder
1/2 teaspoon ground nutmeg
3 tablespoons Tia Maria
1 cup Ganache III (see page 410)
1/2 cup Cocoa Glaze (see page 407)
Chocolate Cones (see page 421) for garnish

1 Position a rack in the center of the oven and preheat the oven to 350 degrees. Lightly grease three 9-inch round cake pans. Line the bottoms with waxed paper.

2 Combine the almonds, sugar, and flour.

3 In the top of a double boiler over simmering water, melt the chocolates, stirring until smooth. Remove from the heat

and stir in the butter until blended. Transfer to a large bowl and gradually add the dry ingredients, egg yolks, coffee liqueur, coffee powder, and nutmeg. Using an electric mixer on medium speed, beat until well blended.

4 In a large bowl, using an electric mixer with clean beaters on high speed, beat the egg whites until stiff but not dry. Fold the egg whites, a little at a time, into the chocolate mixture. Pour into the prepared pans.

5 Bake for 20 to 25 minutes, or until a cake tester inserted into the center comes out clean. Cool in the pans on wire racks for 12 minutes. Invert onto the racks to cool completely. While still warm, brush each layer with 1 tablespoon of the Tia Maria.

6 Make the ganache. Whisk until a spreadable consistency.

7 Make the chocolate glaze.

8 To assemble, place one cake layer on a wire rack and spread with half of the ganache. Top with the second layer and spread with the remaining ganache. Top with the third cake layer. Spread a thin layer of the glaze over the top and sides of the cake. Let stand for 30 to 45 minutes.

9 Reheat the chocolate glaze over low heat if necessary. Spread a second layer of glaze over the top and sides of the cake. Place the cake on a serving plate. Garnish with chocolate cones.

840

842

843 ■ PASSOVER NUT TORTE

MAKES 10 TO 12 SERVINGS
BAKING TIME: *30 minutes*

¾ **cup matzo meal**
¾ **cup walnuts, very finely ground**
¼ **cup Dutch processed cocoa powder**
4 **large eggs, separated**
½ **teaspoon salt**
8 **tablespoons granulated sugar**
¼ **cup honey**
¼ **cup fresh orange juice**
¼ **teaspoon ground cinnamon**
1 **tablespoon Cocoa Sugar (see page 407) for garnish**
Raspberry Sauce (see page 416) for serving

1 Position a rack in the center of the oven and preheat the oven to 350 degrees. Lightly grease a 9-inch square pan. Line the bottom with waxed paper.

2 Combine the matzo meal, walnuts, and cocoa powder.

3 In a medium bowl, using an electric mixer on high speed, beat the egg whites and salt until foamy. Add 2 tablespoons of the sugar and beat until stiff but not dry.

4 In a large bowl, using an electric mixer on medium speed, beat the egg yolks until thick and light-colored. Gradually add the remaining 6 tablespoons sugar and beat on high speed for 2 to 3 minutes. Beat in the honey, orange juice, and cinnamon. Gently fold in the egg whites, a little at a time, alternating with the dry ingredients. Spoon the mixture into the prepared pan.

5 Bake for 25 to 30 minutes, or until a cake tester inserted into the center comes out clean. Cool in the pan on a wire rack for 10 to 12 minutes. Invert onto the rack to cool completely. Remove the waxed paper and place on a serving plate. Sift the cocoa sugar over the top. Cut into squares and serve with the sauce on the side.

844 ■ PRINZREGENTEN-TORTE

MAKES 10 TO 12 SERVINGS
BAKING TIME: *30 minutes*
CHILL TIME: *1 hour*

CAKE

3 **cups all-purpose flour**
5 **tablespoons Dutch processed cocoa powder**
½ **teaspoon baking powder**
½ **teaspoon salt**
1½ **cups butter-flavored vegetable shortening**
3 **cups granulated sugar**
5 **large eggs**
1 **cup milk**
1 **teaspoon crème de cacao**

CHOCOLATE FILLING

6 **ounces semisweet chocolate, grated or finely chopped**
½ **cup butter**
2 **large egg yolks**

CHOCOLATE FROSTING

3 **ounces unsweetened chocolate, grated or finely chopped**
2 **large egg whites**
1 **cup powdered sugar, sifted**

1 Position a rack in the center of the oven and preheat the oven to 350 degrees. Lightly grease five 8-inch round cake pans. (If five pans are not available, this may be done in batches.)

2 To make the cake, combine the flour, cocoa powder, baking powder, and salt.

3 In a large bowl, using an electric mixer on medium speed, beat the shortening and sugar until fluffy. Beat in the eggs, one at a time. Beat in the milk and crème de cacao. Gradually blend in the dry ingredients. Pour ¾ cup of the batter evenly into each of the prepared pans.

4 Bake 28 to 30 minutes, or until golden brown and the edges pull away from the sides of the pan. Remove from the pan and cool on wire racks.

843

845

5 To make the filling, in the top of a double boiler over simmering water, melt the chocolate and butter, stirring until smooth. Remove from the heat and cool slightly. Using an electric mixer on medium speed, beat in the egg yolks until the mixture thickens and is a spreadable consistency.

6 To assemble, place one cake layer on a serving plate and spread with some of the filling. Top with a second cake layer, pressing gently to seal in the filling. Repeat until all the cake layers and filling are used up, ending with a cake layer. Chill for 1 hour.

7 To make the frosting, melt the chocolate (see page 13). Remove from the heat.

8 In a medium bowl, using an electric mixer on high speed, beat the egg whites until foamy. Gradually beat in the powdered sugar. Stir in the melted chocolate. Spread over the top of the chilled cake. Chill until ready to serve.

BAKING NOTES: Owing to the raw egg whites used in this frosting, it should be kept refrigerated at all times, and for no longer than 3 days.

845 ■ RASPBERRY TORTE WITH CHOCOLATE SAUCE

MAKES 8 TO 10 SERVINGS
BAKING TIME: *90 minutes*
STANDING TIME: *2 hours*
CHILL TIME: *24 hours*

MERINGUE

1¹/₂ cups powdered sugar
³/₄ cup ground almonds
4 large egg whites
¹/₄ teaspoon cream of tartar
Pinch of salt

RASPBERRY FILLING

6 ounces fresh raspberries
¹/₄ cup powdered sugar
1 tablespoons crème de framboise
   or raspberry extract
1 teaspoon lemon extract
6 large egg yolks
6 tablespoons granulated sugar
1 cup butter or margarine, at room
   temperature

CUSTARD

3 large egg yolks
¹/₂ cup sugar
¹/₄ cup heavy cream
2 tablespoons Grand Marnier or
   Triple Sec liqueur

CHOCOLATE SAUCE

3 ounces semisweet chocolate,
   grated or finely chopped
1 ounce unsweetened chocolate,
   grated or finely chopped
3 tablespoons heavy cream

GARNISH

Raspberry Sauce (see page 416)
Fresh raspberries

1 To make the meringues, position a rack in the center of the oven and preheat the oven to 225 degrees. Line two baking sheets with parchment paper. Using a pencil (not a pen), draw three 8-inch circles on the sheets.

2 Combine ³/₄ cup of the powdered sugar and the almonds.

3 In a medium bowl, using an electric mixer on high speed, beat the egg whites, cream of tartar, and salt until foamy. Reduce the speed to medium speed and beat in the remaining ³/₄ cup sugar, a little at a time. Increase the speed to high and beat until stiff but not dry. Fold in the almond mixture.

4 Using a pastry bag fitted with a large plain tip, pipe out the mixture into the circles on the paper. Start in the center and work in a spiral outward. Continue until all three circles are filled with the mixture.

5 Bake for 90 minutes, turn off the oven, and let stand with the oven door open slightly for at least 2 hours. Remove from the oven and transfer from the paper to a wire rack.

6 Meanwhile, to make the filling, in the container of a blender or food processor, puree the raspberries on high speed. Blend in the sugar, liqueur, and lemon extract. Strain through a sieve to remove any seeds. In the same blender container, blend the egg yolks, sugar, butter, and ¹/₄ cup of the strained

sauce. Process for 3 second on high speed, or until smooth.

7 To make the custard, in a medium bowl, using an electric mixer on medium speed, beat the egg yolks until thick and light-colored. Add the sugar and beat until very thick. Beat in the cream and pour the mixture into a saucepan. Insert a candy thermometer and cook over medium heat, stirring constantly, until 180 degrees and the mixture is thickened and coats the back of a spoon.

8 Remove from the heat and set in a pan of cold water to cool to room temperature. Stir in the Grand Marnier, strain to remove any lumps, and chill until ready to use.

9 Meanwhile, to make the sauce, in the top of a double boiler over simmering water, melt the chocolates, stirring constantly until smooth. Stir in the cream. Immediately spread a thin layer of sauce on the three meringue rounds.

10 To assemble, fill a pastry bag fitted with a large star tip with the raspberry filling. Press a small ring of rosettes around the edge of the chocolate-covered meringues. Arrange one-third of the fresh raspberries in the center and place on a serving plate. Repeat with the other two meringue layers, stacking them one on the other. Cover with plastic wrap and chill for at least 24 hours.

11 To serve, spoon some of the raspberry sauce onto a serving plate and place a piece of the cake on top. Garnish with fresh raspberries.

BAKING NOTES: Owing to the raw egg yolks used in this recipe, it should be kept refrigerated at all times, and for no longer than 3 days.

846 ■ SACHERTORTE

MAKES 10 TO 12 SERVINGS
BAKING TIME: *40 minutes*
CHILL TIME: *30 minutes*

3 ounces unsweetened chocolate, grated or finely chopped
3 ounces semisweet chocolate, grated or finely chopped
³/₄ cup all-purpose flour
¹/₄ cup almonds, very finely ground
³/₄ cup butter, at room temperature
³/₄ cup powdered sugar
6 large eggs, separated, plus 1 large egg white
Pinch of salt
1¹/₂ cups Apricot Glaze (see page 394)
1 cup Chocolate Glaze III (see page 401)
2 Apricot Roses (see page 420) for garnish
5 large Chocolate Leaves (see page 422) for garnish

1 Position a rack in the center of the oven and preheat the oven to 350 degrees. Lightly grease and flour a 9-inch springform pan. Line the bottom with waxed paper.

2 In the top of a double boiler over simmering water, melt the chocolates, stirring until smooth. Remove from the heat.

3 Combine the flour and almonds.

4 In a large bowl, using an electric mixer on medium speed, beat the butter and ¹/₂ cup of the powdered sugar until fluffy. Beat in the egg yolks, one at a time, beating well after each addition. Pouring it in a thin stream, beat in the melted chocolate.

5 In a large bowl, using an electric mixer with clean beaters on high speed, beat the egg whites and salt until foamy. Add the remaining ¹/₄ cup powdered sugar and beat until stiff but not dry. Beat 1 cup of the egg whites into the egg yolk mixture until blended. Gently fold in the remaining egg whites, alternating with the dry ingredients. Scrape the mixture into the prepared pan and spread evenly.

6 Bake for 35 to 40 minutes, or until a cake tester inserted into the center comes out clean. Cool in the pan on a wire rack for 10 minutes. Invert onto the rack to cool completely. Remove the waxed paper.

7 Make the apricot glaze.

8 To assemble, using a serrated knife, cut the cake in half horizontally and place one half, cut side up, on a wire rack set over a baking sheet.

9 Spread the apricot glaze evenly over the top and sides of cake on the rack, allowing the excess to drip down off the cake. Top with the other half, with the cut side facing down. Pour the remaining glaze over the top and sides of the cake and let stand until dry but sticky to the touch.

10 Prepare the chocolate glaze and garnishes. Pour the glaze over the top of the cake, allowing it to drip down the sides and spreading it as thinly as possible. Do not disturb the apricot glaze. Smooth the frosting over the whole cake and chill for 20 to 30 minutes, until set.

11 Spread a second coat of the glaze over the cake to give it a satiny finish. Transfer the cake to a serving plate and garnish with apricot roses and chocolate leaves.

847 ■ SCHWARZWÄLDER KIRSCHTORTE

MAKES 10 TO 12 SERVINGS
BAKING TIME: *20 minutes*

³/₄ cup cake flour, sifted
1 teaspoon baking powder
¹/₂ teaspoon salt
¹/₂ cup butter or margarine, at room temperature
¹/₂ cup granulated sugar
3 large eggs
¹/₂ cup hazelnuts, finely chopped
6 ounces unsweetened chocolate, grated or finely chopped
1 teaspoon vanilla extract
1 cup heavy cream
2 tablespoons honey
¹/₂ cup kirsch
2 21-ounce cans sour cherries, drained and pitted
15 maraschino cherries for garnish
Semisweet chocolate shavings for garnish

1 Position a rack in the center of the oven and preheat the oven to 375 degrees. Lightly grease three 8-inch round cake pans. Line the bottoms with waxed paper and grease the paper.

2 Combine the flour, baking powder, and salt.

3 In a large bowl, using an electric mixer on medium speed, beat the butter and sugar until light and fluffy. Beat in the eggs, one at a time, beating well after each addition. Beat in the hazelnuts, grated chocolate, and vanilla extract. Gradually blend in the dry ingredients. Pour the mixture into the prepared pans.

4 Bake for 18 to 20 minutes, or until a cake tester inserted into the center comes out clean. Cool for 5 minutes in the pans on wire racks. Invert onto the racks and cool completely. Remove the waxed paper.

5 In a large bowl, using an electric mixer on high speed, whip the cream and honey until stiff peaks form.

6 To assemble, using a serrated knife, trim the rounded tops off the cakes. Place one layer on a serving plate. Sprinkle with one-third of the kirsch and spread with one-third of the whipped cream mixture. Arrange half of the sour cherries over the cream. Top with the second layer and press it gently into place. Sprinkle with half of the remaining liqueur, spread with half of the remaining whipped cream, and arrange the remaining cherries on top. Top with the remaining cake layer and spread the remaining whipped cream over the top and sides of the cake. Garnish with the maraschino cherries and chocolate shavings.

848 ■ SWEDISH CHOCOLATE TORTE

MAKES 10 TO 12 SERVINGS
BAKING TIME: *20 minutes*
CHILL TIME: *24 hours*

MERINGUE LAYERS

1 cup ground hazelnuts
1 cup powdered sugar, sifted twice
4 large egg whites
Pinch of cream of tartar

CHOCOLATE FILLING

4 large egg yolks
1/3 cup plus 2 tablespoons granulated sugar
1/3 cup plus 2 tablespoons heavy cream
4 ounces unsweetened chocolate, grated or finely chopped
1/4 cup butter or margarine, at room temperature
1 tablespoon Frangelico liqueur
1 cup heavy cream for garnish
8 large Chocolate Leaves (see page 422) for garnish

1 Position a rack in the center of the oven and preheat the oven to 300 degrees. Line two baking sheets with parchment paper and draw three 8-inch circles on the paper. Lightly grease and flour the paper.

2 Combine the hazelnuts and 1/4 cup of the powdered sugar.

3 In a large bowl, using an electric mixer on high speed, beat the egg whites and cream of tartar until foamy. Gradually add the remaining 3/4 cup powdered sugar and beat until stiff but not dry. Fold in the hazelnut mixture. Spoon one-third of the mixture onto each of the circles and spread evenly, filling in the circles completely.

4 Bake for 15 to 20 minutes, or until a light golden color. Cool on the pan on a wire rack for 5 minutes. Transfer to the rack to cool completely.

5 To make the filling, in a small bowl, using an electric mixer on high speed, beat the egg yolks until thick and light-colored. Beat in the sugar and heavy cream. Pour the mixture into a medium saucepan. Over low heat, stirring constantly, cook for 6 to 8 minutes, until thickened. Remove from the heat. Add the chocolate and stir constantly until melted and smooth. Add the butter and stir until melted. Pour into a small bowl and stir in the Frangelico. Cover and chill until ready to use.

6 To assemble, place one meringue layer on a serving plate and spread evenly with one-third of the filling. Top with the second layer and spread with half of the remaining filling. Top with the third layer and spread with the remaining filling. Cover lightly with paper towels and chill for 24 hours.

7 To make the garnish, in a medium bowl, using an electric mixer on high speed, whip the cream until stiff peaks form. Fill a pastry bag fitted with a medium star tip with the whipped cream. Pipe rosettes around the base of the torte. Pipe a lattice, checkerboard, or swirling design over the top. Garnish with the chocolate leaves and serve.

849 ■ SWISS ALMOND TORTE

MAKES 12 TO 14 SERVINGS
BAKING TIME: *12 minutes*

ALMOND CAKE

6 large eggs, separated
3/4 cup granulated sugar
1 cup almonds, finely ground
1/2 cup all-purpose flour
2 teaspoons amaretto

CHOCOLATE FROSTING

4 ounces unsweetened chocolate, grated or finely chopped
2 large eggs
1 1/2 cups granulated sugar
1 1/2 cups butter or margarine, at room temperature
1 teaspoon almond extract

ASSEMBLY

1/2 cup sliced almonds
1/4 cup apricot preserves
1 teaspoon crème de cacao

1 Position two racks in the oven: one in the top third and the other in the bottom third. Preheat the oven to 375 degrees. Line two 15 1/2 by 10 1/2-inch jelly-roll pans with waxed paper.

2 To make the cake, in a large bowl, using an electric mixer on high speed, beat the egg whites until foamy. Add 1/4 cup of the sugar and beat until stiff peaks form.

846

848

3 In another large bowl, using an electric mixer on medium speed, beat the egg yolks with the remaining ½ cup sugar until thick and light-colored. Add the ground almonds, flour, and amaretto. Fold the beaten egg whites into the egg yolk mixture. Pour half of the batter into each of the prepared pans and spread evenly.

4 Bake for 12 minutes, or until golden brown, switching the pans' positions in the oven after 6 minutes. Immediately invert the cakes and remove the waxed paper. Cut each cake into four 4 by 11-inch strips. Cool the strips on wire racks.

5 To make the frosting, melt the chocolate (see page 13). Remove from the heat.

6 In a medium saucepan, using an electric mixer on medium speed, beat in the eggs and sugar until blended. Cook over low heat, stirring constantly, for 3 minutes. Remove from the heat. Add the melted chocolate, butter, and almond extract and beat until the butter is melted and the mixture is smooth. Cover and chill until a spreadable consistency.

7 To assemble, spread half of the chocolate frosting on seven of the strips of cake. Stack the strips on a serving plate and top with the unfrosted strip of cake. Frost the top and sides with the remaining chocolate frosting. Press the sliced almonds onto the sides of the torte. Mix the apricot preserves and crème de cacao and spread on the top. Chill until ready to serve.

BAKING NOTES: If you only have one 15½ by 10½-inch pan, bake half of the batter at a time, relining the pan with waxed paper and baking the second cake as soon as the first one is out of the pan.

850 ■ THREE-LAYER MERINGUE TORTE

MAKES 10 TO 12 SERVINGS
BAKING TIME: *90 minutes*

1 cup powdered sugar
2 tablespoons cornstarch or arrowroot
6 large egg whites, at room temperature
¼ teaspoon cream of tartar
Pinch of salt
¼ cup granulated sugar
1 teaspoon vanilla or chocolate extract
1½ cups Chocolate Whipped Cream (see page 406)
1½ cups sliced fresh strawberries plus additional for garnish

1 Position a rack in the center of the oven and preheat the oven to 200 degrees. Line two baking sheets with parchment paper and draw three 9-inch circles on the paper. Lightly butter each circle and dust with flour.

2 Combine the powdered sugar and cornstarch.

3 In a large bowl, using an electric mixer on high speed, beat the egg whites, cream of tartar, and salt until foamy. Gradually add the granulated sugar and beat until stiff but not dry. Fold in the dry ingredients. Fold in the vanilla extract. Fill a large pastry bag fitted with a large plain or star tip with the meringue. Pipe the meringue onto the prepared pans, starting in the center of each of the circles and continuing in an outward spiral until they are filled with meringue.

847

839

841

4 Bake for 85 to 90 minutes, or until the meringue is set and lightly colored. Cool on the pans on wire racks for 10 minutes before. Remove to the racks to cool completely.

5 Make the chocolate whipped cream.

6 To assemble, place one of the meringue layers on a serving plate and spread a layer of the chocolate whipped cream on top. Arrange half of the fruit on top of the whipped cream and top with a second meringue layer. Spread with more cream and the remaining fruit. Top with the third layer and mound the remaining whipped cream on top. Garnish with the fresh fruit.

851 ■ TORTA DI CACAO D'ITALIA

MAKES 14 TO 16 SERVINGS
BAKING TIME: *1 hour*

3 1/2 cups all-purpose flour
1/4 cup Dutch processed cocoa powder
1 tablespoon baking powder
1/2 teaspoon salt
1 cup butter or margarine, at room temperature
2 cups granulated sugar
1 teaspoon almond extract
4 large eggs, beaten
1 cup milk
1 teaspoon crème de cacao
2 tablespoons water
1 cup Chocolate Glaze II (see page 401)

1 Position a rack in the center of the oven and preheat the oven to 350 degrees. Lightly grease and flour a 10-inch tube pan.

2 Combine the flour, cocoa powder, baking powder, and salt.

3 In a large bowl, using an electric mixer on high speed, beat the butter, sugar, and almond extract. Add the beaten eggs, a little at a time, beating well after each addition. Beat in the milk and the crème de cacao. Gradually blend in the dry ingredients, alternating with the water. Scrape the mixture into the prepared pan and spread evenly.

4 Bake for 55 minutes to 1 hour, or until a cake tester inserted into the center comes out clean. Cool in the pan on a wire rack for 15 minutes. Invert onto the rack to cool completely.

5 Make the chocolate glaze.

6 Place the cake on a serving plate and pour the glaze over the top.

844

850

849

852 ■ TORTA DI CIOCCOLATA

MAKES 10 TO 12 SERVINGS
BAKING TIME: *25 minutes*

1½ cups all-purpose flour
1 teaspoon baking powder
1 teaspoon salt
1 cup water
½ cup quick-cooking oats
2 tablespoons butter or margarine,
  at room temperature
1 tablespoon amaretto
½ cup granulated sugar
4 large eggs
⅓ cup Dutch processed cocoa
  powder
1½ cups Cocoa Cream Topping
  (see page 406)

1 Position a rack in the center of the oven and preheat the oven to 350 degrees. Lightly grease two 8-inch round cake pans.

2 Combine the flour and baking powder.

3 In a saucepan, over high heat, dissolve the salt in the water and bring to a boil. Add the oats and stir until the liquid returns to a boil. Cover and remove from the heat. Let stand for about 5 minutes, until the liquid is absorbed.

4 In the container of a blender, combine the butter, amaretto, sugar, and eggs. Blend on high speed for 30 seconds, or until smooth. On low speed, blend in the cocoa powder. Pour in the hot cooked oatmeal and blend on high speed for 20 seconds. Stop the blender and scrape down the sides. Beat on high speed for 1 minute, or until the mixture is liquefied. Transfer to a large bowl and blend in the dry ingredients. Divide the batter between the prepared pans.

5 Bake for 20 to 25 minutes, or until a cake tester inserted into the center comes out clean. Cool in the pans on wire racks.

6 Make the cocoa cream topping.

7 To assemble, place one of the cake layers on a serving plate and spread with some of the cocoa cream topping. Top with the second layer and spread the remaining cocoa cream on the top and sides of the torte.

852

851

Miscellaneous Chocolate

853 ■ BISCOTTI WITH MASCARPONE

MAKES 8 SERVINGS
CHILL TIME: *8 hours*

3 large eggs, separated
Pinch of salt
2/3 cup powdered sugar
10 ounces mascarpone cheese (1¼ cups)
¼ cup dark rum
1 package (7 ounces) biscotti
⅓ cup strong brewed coffee
2 tablespoons grated semisweet chocolate

1 In a medium bowl, using an electric mixer on high speed, beat the egg whites and salt until stiff but not dry.

2 In a large bowl, using an electric mixer on medium speed, beat the egg yolks and powdered sugar until thick and light-colored. Add the mascarpone and rum and beat until smooth. Fold in the egg whites.

3 Arrange the biscotti on a shallow serving plate and sprinkle the coffee over the top. Spread the mascarpone mixture evenly over the biscotti. Sprinkle the chocolate over the top. Chill for 8 to 10 hours, or until serving.

BAKING NOTES: Owing to the raw eggs used in this recipe, it should be kept refrigerated at all times, and for no longer than 3 to 5 days.

854 ■ CHICKEN BREASTS WITH ALMONDS, RAISINS, AND CHOCOLATE

MAKES 4 SERVINGS

3 tablespoons all-purpose flour
¼ teaspoon pepper
¼ teaspoon cayenne pepper
Pinch of celery salt
4 skinless, boneless chicken breasts
¼ cup butter or margarine
1 large Bermuda onion, sliced
1 can (28 ounces) crushed tomatoes
½ cup chopped almonds
½ teaspoon ground cinnamon
2 ounces unsweetened chocolate, grated or finely chopped
½ cup golden raisins
4 cups chicken stock
Salt and pepper to taste

1 In a plastic or paper bag, combine the flour, pepper, cayenne pepper, and celery salt.

2 Thoroughly rinse the chicken and pat dry with paper towels. One at a time, place the chicken breasts into the bag with the dry ingredients and shake to coat.

3 In a large skillet, over medium heat, melt the butter. Add the chicken and brown for 3 to 5 minutes, turning once. Remove to a hot plate.

4 In the same skillet, sauté the onions until translucent. Do not allow to brown. Add the tomatoes and cook for 5 minutes. Strain, discarding the liquid. Return the tomatoes and onions to the skillet. Add the almonds, cinnamon, chocolate, raisins, and stock. Season with salt and pepper to taste. Cook for 3 to 5 minutes. Return the chicken to the skillet, cover, and simmer until tender. Place the chicken on a serving plate. Serve the sauce in a bowl on the side.

855 ■ CHOCOLATE APPLE SLICES

MAKES APPROXIMATELY 12 PIECES

3 firm medium apples
1 cup granulated sugar
1 cup honey
1 teaspoon ground cinnamon
½ cup water
8 ounces semisweet chocolate, grated or finely chopped

1 Core and peel the apples. Slice horizontally into ½-inch slices. Place in a bowl of cold water.

2 In a medium saucepan, over medium heat, combine the sugar, honey, cinnamon, and water. Bring to a boil. Simmer for 5 minutes, or until reduced by half.

854

857

858

853

855

856

3 Drain the apples and pat them dry between two paper towels. Drop them into the boiling syrup and cook for 3 to 4, or until they look translucent. Place on a wire rack for 5 minutes, or until cool and dry.

4 To coat the apple slices, melt the chocolate (see page 13). Remove from the heat. Using a bamboo skewer or a fondue fork, dip each apple slice into the chocolate and place on a waxed paper-lined baking sheet. Cool until firm.

856 ■ CHOCOLATE-COATED GINGER

MAKES 1½ POUNDS

8 ounces semisweet chocolate, grated or finely chopped
1 pound crystallized ginger, cut into bite-size cubes

1 Melt the chocolate (see page 13). Remove from the heat.

2 Insert a toothpick into each cube of ginger. Dip the ginger in the chocolate and set on a waxed paper-lined baking sheet to harden. Use as hors d'oeuvres.

859

BAKING NOTES: If many pieces of ginger are to be coated with chocolate, use a flat piece of Styrofoam as a holder for the toothpicks while the chocolate hardens. Skewer each piece of ginger with a toothpick, dip it into the melted chocolate, and insert the other side of the toothpick into the foam.

857 ■ CHOCOLATE-COVERED BANANAS

MAKES 12 SERVINGS

6 medium bananas
1 cup semisweet chocolate chips
2 tablespoons butter or margarine
12 wooden Popsicle™ sticks
½ cup pecans, finely chopped

1 Peel the bananas and cut in half. Insert a wooden stick into the small end and place on a waxed paper-lined baking sheet. Freeze for 2 to 3 hours, or until hard.

2 In the top of a double boiler over simmering water, melt the chocolate chips and butter, stirring until smooth.

3 Dip the frozen bananas into the chocolate and roll in the pecans. Freeze until the chocolate is hard. Serve or wrap in plastic wrap and freeze until serving.

858 ■ CHOCOLATE-FILLED FRENCH TOAST

MAKES 2 SERVINGS

2 slices French bread (each 1 inch thick)
1½ ounces semisweet chocolate, grated or finely chopped
1 large egg
¼ cup milk
1 tablespoon powdered sugar
½ teaspoon chocolate extract
⅛ teaspoon ground cinnamon
1½ tablespoons butter or margarine
Powdered sugar for garnish
Chocolate syrup or ice cream for serving

1 Using a serrated knife, cut the slices of bread in half horizontally, but do not cut all the way through. Lay each slice flat, hold one half of the slice open, and sprinkle the grated chocolate inside. Place in a bowl just large enough to hold both of the slices.

2 In a medium bowl, using an electric mixer on medium speed, beat the egg, milk, powdered sugar, chocolate extract, and cinnamon until the sugar is dissolved. Pour evenly over the bread. Let soak, turning once, until most of the egg mixture is absorbed into the bread.

3 In a medium skillet, over medium-low heat, melt the butter. Add the bread and cook, turning occasionally, for 10 minutes, or until both sides are golden brown. Transfer to warm plates and dust with powdered sugar. Serve with syrup or ice cream.

859 ■ CHOCOLATE FONDUE I

MAKES 8 TO 10 SERVINGS

6 ounces unsweetened chocolate, grated or finely chopped
1½ cups granulated sugar
1 cup heavy cream
½ cup butter or margarine
3 tablespoons crème de cacao or conticream liqueur

1 In a double boiler over simmering water, melt the chocolate with the sugar, cream, and butter. Cook for 10 to 12 minutes, stirring constantly, until the chocolate is melted and the sugar is dissolved. Remove from the heat and stir in the crème de cacao.

2 Transfer to a fondue pot. Serve warm with cubes of bread, cake, or fresh fruit.

BAKING NOTES: If the mixture becomes too thick, stir in 1 tablespoon of milk.

860 ■ CHOCOLATE FONDUE II

MAKES 8 TO 10 SERVINGS

8 ounces semisweet chocolate, grated or finely chopped
²/₃ cup milk
¼ cup granulated sugar
Pinch of cinnamon

1 In the top of a double boiler over simmering water, melt the chocolate with the milk, sugar, and cinnamon, stirring constantly until the chocolate is melted and the sugar is dissolved. Remove from the heat.

2 Transfer to a fondue pot. Serve warm with cubes of bread, cake, or fresh fruit.

BAKING NOTES: If the mixture becomes too thick, stir in 1 tablespoon of milk.

861 ■ CHOCOLATE MERINGUE TART SHELLS

MAKES 8 SHELLS
BAKING TIME: *1 hour*
COOLING TIME: *2 hours*

3 large egg whites, at room temperature
¼ teaspoon cream of tartar
³/₄ cup granulated sugar
1 ounce semisweet chocolate, grated or finely chopped

1 Position a rack in the center of the oven and preheat the oven to 275 degrees. Line a baking sheet with parchment paper.

2 In a medium bowl, using an electric mixer on high speed, beat the egg whites and cream of tartar until foamy. Continue beating and sprinkle in the sugar, a little at a time, and beat until stiff but not dry. Do not underbeat. Fold in the grated chocolate and drop the mixture by ¹/₃ cupfuls onto the prepared pan. Using the back of a spoon dipped in powdered sugar, spread into nest-shaped 3-inch circles, making a depression in the center of each round.

3 Bake for 1 hour. Turn off the oven and leave the tart shells undisturbed for at least 2 hours. Remove from the oven and cool completely.

BAKING NOTES: To serve, fill the tarts with any kind of fruit filling or pudding.

862 ■ CHOCOLATE MOCHA-DIPPED STRAWBERRIES

MAKES 10 TO 12 SERVINGS

2 ounces semisweet chocolate, grated or finely chopped
1 tablespoon strong brewed coffee
2 teaspoons coffee liqueur
10 to 12 very large strawberries with stems intact

1 Wash the strawberries and pat dry with paper towels.

2 In the top of a double boiler over simmering water, melt the chocolate with the coffee and liqueur, stirring until smooth. Remove from the heat.

3 Holding the strawberries by the stems, dip the bottom half of each berry in the chocolate and place on a waxed paper-lined baking sheet. Let cool until hardened. Chill until ready to serve.

863 ■ CHOCOLATE NUT FONDUE

MAKES 6 TO 8 SERVINGS

6 ounces semisweet chocolate, grated or finely chopped
¹/₂ cup granulated sugar
¹/₂ cup milk
¹/₂ cup chunky peanut butter

1 In the top of a double boiler over simmering water, melt the chocolate with the sugar and milk, stirring until smooth. Blend in the peanut butter. Remove from the heat.

2 Transfer to a fondue pot. Serve with marshmallows, cubes of day-old cake, or fresh fruit.

864 ■ CHOCOLATE OMELET

MAKES 1 LARGE OMELET

1 tablespoon butter
5 large eggs
2 tablespoons milk
¹/₂ teaspoon salt
¹/₈ teaspoon white pepper
¹/₂ cup semisweet chocolate chips
2 tablespoons finely chopped pecans

860

861

862

864

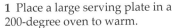

1 Place a large serving plate in a 200-degree oven to warm.

2 Heat a 9-inch skillet over medium heat. Melt the butter in the hot skillet.

3 In a large bowl, beat the eggs, milk, salt, and pepper. Pour into the skillet. When the edges of the eggs start to turn color, sprinkle the chocolate chips and pecans over the surface of the eggs. When the eggs are set, fold the omelet in half and cook for 1 to 2 minutes more. Turn out onto the warmed serving plate and serve.

865 ■ CHOCOLATE PEANUT BUTTER

MAKES 2/3 CUP

5 ounces semisweet chocolate, grated or finely chopped
1/3 cup peanut butter

1 In the top of a double boiler over simmering water, melt the chocolate, stirring until smooth. Remove from the heat and stir in the peanut butter. Transfer to a cup. Cover and chill until ready to use.

BAKING NOTES: Premelted chocolate can also be used.

866 ■ CHOCOLATE PEARS SUPREME

MAKES 6 SERVINGS

2 cans (17 ounces each) pear halves, chilled overnight
1 cup sour cream or chocolate yogurt
1 cup granulated sugar
2 ounces semisweet chocolate, grated or finely chopped
1/4 cup Dutch processed cocoa powder
2 tablespoons crème de cacao
1 teaspoon chocolate or vanilla extract

1 Drain the pears and pat dry with paper towels. Cover and chill until serving.

2 In the container of a blender, combine the sour cream, sugar, chocolate, and cocoa powder. Blend on high speed for 1 minute.

3 Pour the mixture into a medium saucepan. Cook over low heat until the sauce thickens. Remove from the heat and stir in the crème de cacao and chocolate extract.

4 To serve, place the pears into serving bowls. Spoon the warm sauce over the pears and serve.

BAKING NOTES: White crème de menthe works especially well in the sauce.

867 ■ CHOCOLATE PECAN TULIP CUPS

MAKES 8 COOKIE CUPS

1 cup granulated sugar
3/4 cup pecans, finely ground
1/4 cup all-purpose flour
1/4 cup Dutch processed cocoa powder
4 large egg whites
1/2 cup crème de cacao

1 Position a rack in the center of the oven and preheat the oven to 425 degrees. Lightly grease two baking sheets. Have two 6-ounce custard cups ready for shaping the cookies.

2 Combine the sugar, pecans, flour, and cocoa powder.

3 In a large bowl, stir the egg whites and crème de cacao. Gradually stir in the dry ingredients. The batter will be thin. Bake only two cookies at a time. Spoon 2 tablespoons of the batter onto one side of the prepared pan. Using the back of the spoon, spread the batter into a 5-inch circle. Repeat with more batter on the other half of the pan.

863

865

866

867

4 Bake for 7 minutes, or until the cookie just starts to turn golden brown. Using a spatula, immediately lift the cookie off the baking sheet and drape over a custard cup. Press the sides down, molding the cookie over the cup to form a tulip shape. If the cookie starts to harden before you have it shaped, place back in a hot oven for a few seconds. Once the cookie is placed over the custard cup, ruffle the edges with your fingers. If you do not have custard cups, place a paper towel over a soup can, and use that. Cool completely before removing the cookies from the cup. Repeat with the remaining batter. Store in airtight containers in a cool place.

BAKING NOTES: To serve, fill the tulip cups with chopped fruit, ice cream, mousse, or pudding. Garnish with candied flowers and mint leaves.

868 ■ CHOCOLATE RICE PUDDING

MAKES 4 TO 6 SERVING
CHILL TIME: *1 hour*

2 cups milk
1/3 cup long-grain rice, uncooked
3 tablespoons Dutch processed cocoa powder
1/4 cup granulated sugar
1/2 teaspoon chocolate extract
Fresh mint sprigs or peeled, sliced kiwifruit for garnish
Chocolate Sauce III (see page 404) for serving

1 Rinse four to six 4-ounce custard cups or pudding glasses in cold water. Do not dry.

2 In the top of a double boiler over simmering water, combine the milk, rice, and cocoa powder. Cover and cook, stirring occasionally, for 15 to 20 minutes, or until the mixture is quite thick. Add the sugar and stir until dissolved. Remove from the heat and stir in the chocolate extract. Immediately pour the mixture into the prepared custard cups. Chill 1 hour, or until set.

3 Invert the set puddings onto individual dessert plates. Garnish with mint sprigs or thinly sliced kiwifruit. Serve with chocolate sauce on the side.

869 ■ CHOCOLATE ZABAGLIONE PEARS

MAKES 2 SERVINGS

POACHED PEARS

1 cup water
1/3 cup granulated sugar
1/4 cup white crème de cacao
2 large ripe pears, peeled

CHOCOLATE ZABAGLIONE

1 ounce semisweet chocolate, grated or finely chopped
1/4 cup coffee liqueur
3 large egg yolks
4 teaspoons granulated sugar
1 tablespoon chocolate extract
Chocolate Curls (see page 000) for garnish
Candied Rose Petals (see page 420) for garnish

868

871

869

870

1 To make the poached pears, in a medium saucepan, combine the water, sugar, and crème de cacao. Place over medium heat and bring to a boil. Add the pears to the pan, standing them upright. Reduce the heat to low, cover, and cook for about 15 minutes, or until fork tender. Remove from the heat and leave the pears in the syrup, covered, for about 30 minutes. Chill until serving.

2 To make the sauce, in a small saucepan, over low heat, combine the chocolate and liqueur, stirring constantly until the chocolate is melted. Remove from the heat.

3 In another medium saucepan, using an electric mixer on medium speed, beat the egg yolks until thick and light-colored. Beat in the sugar. Place over low heat and cook, stirring constantly, until the mixture thickens slightly. Stir in the chocolate and cook for 1 minute. Remove from the heat and beat until very thick and creamy. Blend in the chocolate extract. (If the sauce is too thin, return to the heat.)

4 To serve, place the pears in dessert dishes. Spoon the warm sauce over the top. Garnish with chocolate curls and rose petals.

872

870 ■ CHØKØLADESUPPE

MAKES 6 TO 8 SERVINGS

6 cups milk
1/4 cup heavy cream
2 ounces unsweetened chocolate, grated or finely chopped
1 1/2 cups plus 2 tablespoons granulated sugar
6 large eggs, separated
1 teaspoon chocolate extract

1 In a large saucepan, over medium heat, warm the milk until bubbles form around the sides of the pan. Remove from the heat.

2 In another large saucepan, over low heat, warm the cream. Add the chocolate and 1/4 cup of the sugar, stirring constantly until the chocolate is melted and smooth. Remove from the heat. Add the hot milk.

3 In a large bowl, using an electric mixer on medium speed, beat the egg yolks until thick and light-colored. Beat in 1 cup of the sugar. Beat in the chocolate extract. Add to the saucepan and return to the heat. Cook, stirring constantly, until thick. Remove from the heat.

4 In a medium bowl, using an electric mixer with clean beaters on high speed, beat the egg whites until soft peaks form. Beating on low speed, sprinkle in the remaining 6 tablespoons sugar. Beat until stiff peaks form.

5 Serve the hot chocolate mixture in bowls. Garnish with a dab of the beaten egg whites on top.

871 ■ CRÈME DE CACAO

MAKES 4 QUARTS
STANDING TIME: *7 days*

2 quarts vodka
1 pound cocoa beans, toasted (see Baking notes)
4 cups water
2 cups granulated sugar
2 tablespoons vanilla extract

1 Using a coffee mill or nut grinder, grind the cocoa beans.

2 In a large container with an airtight cover, combine the ground cocoa beans and liqueur. Cover and let stand in a dark place for at least seven days.

3 In a large saucepan, over high heat, combine the water and sugar. Simmer until reduced by half. Remove from the heat and add the liqueur mixture. Stir in the vanilla extract.

4 Line a sieve with a coffee filter and set over a large bowl. Strain the mixture. Bottle and cork tightly until ready to use.

BAKING NOTES: Cocoa beans can be found in many specialty food stores, and in some supermarkets. To toast the cocoa beans, preheat the oven to 350 degrees. Place the beans on a cookie sheet and toast in the oven for 10 minutes.

872 ■ FROZEN FRUIT BARS

MAKES 6 TO 8 SERVINGS
FREEZING TIME: *2 hours*

1 cup chocolate yogurt
1/2 cup spreadable fruit, such as apricot or peach
8 ounces cream cheese

1 Line an 8 or 9 inch-square pan with plastic wrap, allowing the wrap to hang over the sides of the pan.

2 In the container of a blender, combine all of the ingredients. Cover and blend on high speed until smooth, scraping down the sides if necessary. Scrape the mixture into the prepared pan and spread evenly. Cover and freeze for 2 hours, until firm.

3 Invert onto a serving plate, remove the plastic wrap, and cut into bars.

873 ■ MEXICAN CHILI WITH CHOCOLATE

MAKES 4 SERVINGS

¼ cup canola oil
2 pounds beef chuck, diced
1 pound lean pork, diced
1 medium onion, chopped
2 cloves garlic, minced
1 tablespoon all-purpose flour or corn meal
3 tablespoons chili powder
1 tablespoon ground cumin
1¼ teaspoons salt
1 can (32 ounces) pureed tomatoes or stewed tomatoes
2 ounces unsweetened chocolate, grated or finely chopped
4½ teaspoons granulated sugar
½ teaspoon ground cinnamon

1 In a large skillet, over high heat, heat the oil. Sauté the diced meats in the oil until browned. Transfer to a Dutch oven. Add the onions and garlic to the skillet and sauté until soft. Transfer to the Dutch oven.

2 In a cup, combine the flour, chili powder, cumin, and salt. Sprinkle over the meat the toss to coat.

3 Heat the tomatoes in the skillet for 1 minute. Add to the Dutch oven. Cover and simmer for 2 hours, or until the flavors are combined.

4 Remove from the heat and cool slightly. Add the chocolate, sugar, and cinnamon, stirring until the chocolate is melted and the sugar is dissolved. Serve.

874 ■ MEXICAN KIDNEY BEAN CASSEROLE

MAKES 6 TO 8 SERVINGS
BAKING TIME: *25 minutes*

2 cans (15½ ounces each) kidney beans
¼ cup tomato sauce
½ cup red wine
½ cup chopped onion
1 small clove garlic, crushed
1 teaspoon salt
2 cups diced, cooked chicken
2 ounces unsweetened chocolate, grated or finely chopped
½ cup bread crumbs
Croutons for serving

1 Position a rack in the center of the oven and preheat the oven to 350 degrees. Lightly grease a 2-quart casserole dish.

2 Drain the beans, reserving ½ cup of the liquid. In a small bowl, combine the reserved liquid, tomato sauce, wine, onion, garlic, and salt.

3 Spread the beans evenly on the bottom of the prepared casserole dish. Spread the chicken in a layer over the top of the beans. Sprinkle the chocolate on top of the chicken and pour the tomatoes sauce mixture over the top. Sprinkle with the bread crumbs.

4 Bake for 20 to 25 minutes, or until the mixture is very hot and bubbling. Cool on a wire rack for 2 to 4 minutes before serving. Serve with croutons on the side.

875 ■ MOCHA FILLED CRÊPES WITH CHOCOLATE SAUCE

MAKES 6 TO 8 SERVINGS

CRÊPES

1 cup all-purpose flour
¾ cup milk
¾ cup water
2 large eggs
2 tablespoons granulated sugar
1 tablespoons crème de cacao

875

873

874

MOCHA FILLING

1 teaspoon instant espresso powder
1 tablespoon boiling water
1 tablespoon coffee liqueur
1/2 cup butter or margarine, at room temperature
6 tablespoons powdered sugar, sifted
1 large egg yolk
Chocolate Sauce IV (see page 405)

1 To make the crêpes, in the container of a blender or in a large bowl, combine the flour, milk, water, eggs, sugar, and crème de cacao and blend until smooth. Cover and chill for at least 1 hour.

2 Lightly grease the bottom of an 8-inch crêpe pan or nonstick frying pan. Heat the pan over medium heat. Spread 1/4 cup of the chilled batter evenly on the bottom. The crêpe must be very thin. Cook the crêpe, turning once, until lightly colored on both sides. Stack the cooked crêpes between pieces of waxed paper.

3 To make the filling, in a cup, dissolve the espresso powder in the water. Add the liqueur.

4 In the container of a blender, or in a small bowl using an electric mixer on low speed, beat the butter and sugar until light and fluffy. Beat in the egg yolk and blend thoroughly. Beat in the espresso mixture.

5 Make the chocolate sauce.

6 To assemble the crêpes, spread 1 tablespoon of the filling evenly over the surface of a crêpe and roll up jelly-roll fashion. Spoon a little of the chocolate sauce over the top. Dust with powdered sugar

BAKING NOTES: Owing to the raw egg yolk used in this filling, it should be kept refrigerated at all times, and for no longer than 3 days.

876 ■ PEANUT BUTTER-CHOCOLATE DIP

MAKES 3 1/2 CUPS

1/2 cup creamy peanut butter
2 1/2 cups evaporated milk
1 package (3.4 ounces) Jell-O Brand chocolate instant pudding mix

1 In a medium bowl, using an electric mixer on low to medium speed, beat the peanut butter until smooth. Beat in the evaporated milk. Beat in the chocolate pudding mix. Serve immediately with dry crackers or cookies on the side.

877 ■ POACHED PEARS WITH CHOCOLATE TOPPING

MAKES 8 SERVINGS

8 large fresh pears
1 1/4 cups granulated sugar
2 cups water
1 teaspoon Pear William liqueur or vanilla extract
4 ounces semisweet chocolate, grated
1 tablespoon butter
Chocolate ice cream for serving

1 Peel, core, and slice the pears in half.

2 In a large saucepan, over medium heat, bring the sugar and water to a rolling boil and boil for 5 to 6 minutes. Add the liqueur. Reduce to the heat to low and simmer before adding the pears. Poach the pears until tender. Using a slotted spoon, transfer the pears to a serving platter.

3 Add the chocolate and butter to the hot syrup and heat, stirring constantly, until the chocolate is melted and smooth.

4 To serve, place each pear on a dessert plate. Top with a scoop of chocolate ice cream and spoon the warm syrup over the top.

876

877

878 ■ SPICY CHICKEN WITH FRUIT

MAKES 4 SERVINGS

2 medium apples
2 medium oranges
1 can (10 ounces) unsweetened pineapple chunks
1 frying chicken (4 pounds)
¼ cup all-purpose flour
¼ teaspoon onion powder
¼ teaspoon celery salt
1 tablespoon butter or margarine
¼ cup almonds
1 tablespoon sesame seeds
1 can (32 ounces) peeled plum tomatoes
2 ounces semisweet chocolate, grated or finely chopped
1 tablespoon sugar
1 tablespoon red chili powder
Pinch of ground coriander
2 cups water or chicken broth
Pinch of salt
4 tablespoons Curaçao or Triple Sec

1 Peel, core, and slice the apples and place them in a medium bowl. Peel and separate the oranges into wedges, being sure all of the membranes are removed. Place the oranges with the apples in the bowl. Add the canned pineapple and pour the juice over the fruit.

2 Rinse the chicken and pat dry with paper towels. Cut into serving-size pieces.

3 In a plastic or paper bag, combine the flour, onion powder, and celery salt. One at a time, place the chicken pieces in the bag with the flour and shake to coat.

4 In a large skillet, over medium heat, melt the butter. Add the chicken and lightly brown on both sides.

5 Remove the chicken to a plate. Sauté the almonds and sesame seeds in the skillet until browned. Add the tomatoes, chocolate, sugar, chili, and coriander. Simmer for 6 to 8 minutes, or until the liquid is reduced by half. Remove from the heat.

6 In the container of a blender, place the water, salt, and the sauce mixture from the pan. Cover and blend on high speed until smooth. Add the Curaçao.

7 Return the chicken to the pan, pour the mixture from the blender over the top, cover, and simmer for 30 to 35 minutes, or until the chicken is fork tender.

8 Drain the liquid from the fruit and discard. Add the fruit to the chicken. Cover and cook until the apples are fork tender. Arrange the chicken on a platter with the fruit around it. Pour the sauce over the top and serve.

879 ■ STEWED CHICKEN WITH CHOCOLATE

MAKES 4 SERVINGS
CHILL TIME: 2 hours

1 frying chicken (4 pounds)
½ cup white wine
¼ teaspoon allspice
Salt and pepper to taste
2 cups water
½ cup bread crumbs
2 ounces semisweet chocolate, grated or finely chopped
¼ cup toasted sesame seeds for garnish

1 Thoroughly rinse the chicken and pat dry. Cut into serving-size pieces. In a large bowl, combine the chicken, wine, allspice, salt, and pepper. Cover and marinate in the refrigerator for at least 2 hours.

2 Remove the chicken from the marinade and reserve the marinade. In a large skillet, over high heat, sauté the chicken pieces for 2 minutes on each side. Do not brown.

3 Add the water, bread crumbs, and chocolate to the marinade and pour over the chicken in the skillet. Cover and simmer over low heat for 30 to 35 minutes, or until the chicken is tender. Transfer the chicken pieces to a serving plate and sprinkle sesame seeds over the top. Serve with the sauce on the side.

878

879

Frostings, Icings, and Sauces

880 ■ ALMOND PASTE

MAKES 1½ CUPS
CHILL TIME: *24 hours*

1½ cups powdered sugar, sifted twice
1½ cups almonds, very finely chopped
1 large egg white
1 teaspoon almond extract
¼ teaspoon salt

1 In a medium bowl, combine all of the ingredients. Using an electric mixer on low speed, beat for 4 to 5 minutes, or until a paste forms. Place in an airtight container and chill for at least 24 hours before using.

881 ■ APRICOT GLAZE

MAKES ½ CUP

1 cup apricot preserves

1 In a small saucepan, over medium heat, bring the preserves to a boil. Simmer, stirring occasionally, until the preserves coat the back of a spoon. Strain and cool slightly. Use the glaze to brush over cakes or fresh fruit on the top of cakes and pies.

882 ■ BITTERSWEET CHOCOLATE SAUCE I

MAKES 2 TO 2½ CUPS

8 ounces unsweetened chocolate, grated or finely chopped
¾ cup evaporated milk
1 cup granulated sugar
¼ cup butter, at room temperature
1 tablespoon crème de cacao
2 tablespoons Droste bittersweet liqueur

1 In the top of a double boiler over simmering water, melt the chocolate with the evaporated milk and sugar, stirring until smooth. Remove from the heat and blend in the butter. Cool slightly before stirring in the liqueurs. Serve the sauce hot or cold over desserts.

BAKING NOTES: If Droste Bittersweet isn't available, Choclair, Conticream, or Cheri-Suisse can be used.

883 ■ BITTERSWEET CHOCOLATE SAUCE II

MAKES 2 TO 2½ CUPS

8 ounces unsweetened chocolate, grated or finely chopped
2 cups granulated sugar
⅔ cup evaporated milk
¼ cup butter or margarine, or at room temperature
1 tablespoon chocolate extract

1 In the top of a double boiler over simmering water, melt the chocolate, stirring until smooth. Add the sugar and milk and stir until the sugar is dissolved and completely blended. Remove from the heat and stir in the butter and chocolate extract. Serve the sauce hot or cold.

BAKING NOTES: This sauce is usually very thick and can be thinned with a little water if desired.

884 ■ BITTERSWEET CHOCOLATE SAUCE III

MAKES 1 TO 1½ CUPS

2 teaspoons mocha-flavored instant coffee powder
½ cup boiling water
3 ounces unsweetened chocolate, grated or finely chopped
¼ cup heavy cream
1 cup granulated sugar
1 tablespoon butter or margarine, at room temperature
½ teaspoon chocolate extract

1 In the top of a double boiler over simmering water, dissolve the coffee powder in the boiling water. Stir in the chocolate and heat until melted and smooth. Stir in the cream. Add the sugar and butter and cook until the mixture thickens slightly. Remove from the heat and stir in the chocolate extract. Serve the sauce at room temperature.

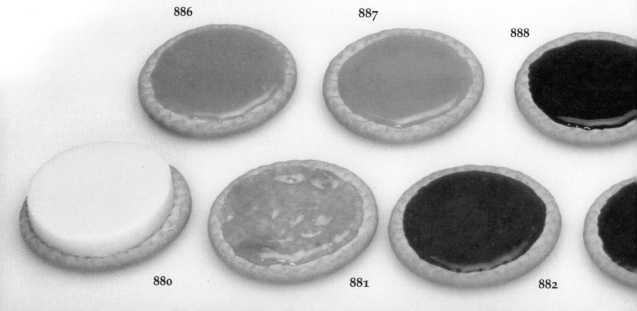

886   887   888

880   881   882

885 ■ BITTERSWEET CHOCOLATE SAUCE IV

MAKES 1 TO 1½ CUPS

3 ounces unsweetened chocolate, grated or finely chopped
½ cup coffee liqueur
¼ cup heavy cream
1 cup granulated sugar
1 tablespoon butter or margarine
1 teaspoon chocolate extract

1 In the top of a double boiler over simmering water, melt the chocolate with the liqueur, stirring until smooth. Stir in the cream. Add the sugar and butter and cook until the sugar dissolves and the mixture thickens slightly. Remove from the heat and stir in the chocolate extract. Serve the sauce at room temperature.

886 ■ BROWN SUGAR SAUCE

MAKES ⅓ CUP

¼ cup water
2 tablespoons granulated sugar
1 tablespoon packed light brown sugar
4½ teaspoons butter

1 In a small saucepan, over low heat, combine the water, sugars, and butter, stirring until the mixture is smooth. Increase the heat to medium-high and bring to a rolling boil.   Remove from the heat and pour the hot sauce over a cake. Let the sauce cool slightly before serving.

887 ■ CARAMEL GLAZE

MAKES ½ CUP

5 tablespoons packed light brown sugar
2 tablespoons butter
2 tablespoons skim milk
1 teaspoon vanilla extract

1 In a small saucepan, combine the brown sugar, butter, and milk. Cook over medium heat, stirring until the mixture comes to a boil. Remove from the heat and stir in the vanilla extract. Pour the glaze over the top of a warm cake, allowing glaze to run down the sides.

888 ■ CHOCOLATE ALMOND SAUCE I

MAKES 1¾ CUPS

1 can (12 ounces) evaporated milk
½ cup granulated sugar
¼ cup Dutch processed cocoa powder
2 teaspoons cornstarch
1 teaspoon almond extract

1 In medium a saucepan, over medium heat, combine the milk, sugar, cocoa powder, and cornstarch, stirring constantly until smooth. Bring to a boil. Remove from the heat.

2 Stir in the almond extract. Using an electric mixer on medium speed, beat until the mixture cools to room temperature. Serve cool or lukewarm. Chill any unused portion in the refrigerator.

889 ■ CHOCOLATE ALMOND SAUCE II

MAKES 1 CUP

2 tablespoons slivered almonds, toasted
1 tablespoons amaretto
1 cup Chocolate Sauce VII (see page 405)

1 In a small bowl, combine all of the ingredients and serve.

890 ■ CHOCOLATE BUTTERCREAM

MAKES 1½ TO 1¾ CUPS

4 ounces semisweet chocolate
1 cup butter or margarine, at room temperature
1 cup powdered sugar
1 tablespoon crème de cacao
¼ cup heavy cream
2 large egg yolks

1 Melt the chocolate (see page 13). Remove from the heat and cool slightly.

2 In a medium bowl, using an electric mixer on medium speed, beat the butter and powdered sugar until light and fluffy. Beat in the crème de cacao. Add the cream and egg yolks. Beat in the chocolate until smooth, streaks no longer appear, and the mixture is of a spreadable consisitancy.

BAKING NOTES: Owing to the raw egg yolks used in this recipe, it should be kept refrigerated at all times, and for no longer than 3 days.

889   890

883   884   885

891 ■ CHOCOLATE COCONUT FROSTING

MAKES 2½ TO 3 CUPS

¾ cup heavy cream
½ cup granulated sugar
⅓ cup coconut liqueur
1 tablespoon cornstarch or arrowroot
1 large egg yolk, beaten
3 ounces unsweetened chocolate, grated or finely chopped
3 ounces semisweet chocolate, grated or finely chopped
2 tablespoons butter or margarine
1⅓ cups flaked coconut
1 cup chopped almonds or pecans
1 teaspoon almond or chocolate extract

1 In a large saucepan, over medium-low heat, combine the cream, sugar, liqueur, cornstarch, and egg yolk, stirring constantly, until well blended and smooth. Cook for 5 to 7 minutes, or until the mixture thickens. Remove from the heat and stir in the chocolates, butter, coconut, almonds, and almond extract. Cool until a spreadable consistency.

892 ■ CHOCOLATE CREAM CHEESE

MAKES ¾ TO 1 CUP
CHILL TIME: 4 hours

3 tablespoons butter or margarine
1 ounces unsweetened chocolate, grated or finely chopped
3 ounces cream cheese, at room temperature
¼ cup powdered sugar
1 teaspoon chocolate extract
2 tablespoons chocolate yogurt

1 In the top of a double boiler over simmering water, melt the butter and chocolate, stirring until smooth. Remove from the heat.

2 In a small bowl, using an electric mixer on medium speed, beat the cream cheese and powdered sugar until smooth. Beat in the chocolate extract. Beat in the chocolate mixture and the yogurt until blended. Cover and chill for 4 hours or until set. Use as a topping on cakes, pies, crackers, donuts, bagels, etc.

893 ■ CHOCOLATE CREAM CHEESE FILLING

MAKES ¾ CUP
CHILL TIME: 30 minutes

3 tablespoons butter or margarine
1 ounce unsweetened chocolate, grated or finely chopped
3 ounces cream cheese, at room temperature
¼ cup powdered sugar
¼ teaspoon chocolate or vanilla extract
2 tablespoons sour cream or chocolate yogurt

1 In the top of a double boiler over simmering water, melt the butter and chocolate, stirring until smooth. Remove from the heat.

2 In a small bowl, using an electric mixer on low speed, beat the cream cheese, powdered sugar, and vanilla extract until smooth.

Beat in the chocolate mixture. Beat in the sour cream. Cover and chill for 30 minutes. Let come to room temperature before using.

BAKING NOTES: Use chilled as a spread on tea breads.

894 ■ CHOCOLATE CREAM CHEESE FROSTING I

MAKES 1½ CUPS

2 ounces unsweetened chocolate, grated or finely chopped
8 ounces cream cheese, at room temperature
2½ tablespoons evaporated milk
2½ cups powdered sugar, sifted twice
Pinch of salt

1 Melt the chocolate (see page 13). Remove from the heat.

2 In a medium bowl, using an electric mixer on medium speed, beat the cream cheese and evaporated milk until smooth. Beat in the powdered sugar, a little at a time, blending well after each addition. Beat in the salt and melted chocolate until smooth.

BAKING NOTES: Use the frosting only on a completely cooled cake.

895 ■ CHOCOLATE CREAM CHEESE FROSTING II

MAKES 1 TO 1¼ CUPS

4 ounces unsweetened chocolate, grated or finely chopped
3 ounces cream cheese, at room temperature
1 tablespoon evaporated milk
½ teaspoon chocolate or vanilla extract
¼ teaspoon salt
1 cup sifted powdered sugar

1 Melt the chocolate (see page 13). Remove from the heat.

2 In a medium bowl, using an electric mixer on medium speed, beat the cream cheese, milk, chocolate extract, and salt until smooth. Beat in the powdered sugar, a little at a time, blending well after each addition. Beat in the melted chocolate until smooth.

896 ■ CHOCOLATE CREAM CHEESE FROSTING III

MAKES 1 CUP
CHILL TIME: *30 minutes*

3 tablespoons butter or margarine
2 ounces unsweetened chocolate, grated or finely chopped
3 ounces cream cheese, at room temperature
¼ cup powdered sugar
¼ teaspoon chocolate extract
2 tablespoons chocolate yogurt or sour cream

1 In the top of a double boiler over simmering water, melt the butter and chocolate, stirring until smooth. Remove from the heat.

2 In a medium bowl, using an electric mixer on medium speed, beat the cream cheese until smooth. Beat in the powdered sugar and chocolate extract. Beat in the melted chocolate and yogurt. Cover and chill 30 minutes until thickened. Let come to room temperature before using.

897 ■ CHOCOLATE CREAM FILLING

MAKES 1 TO 1½ CUPS
CHILL TIME: *30 minutes*

2 ounces semisweet chocolate, grated or finely chopped
3 large eggs
½ cup granulated sugar
1 teaspoon vanilla extract
1 teaspoon cornstarch or arrowroot
¼ cup butter or margarine
½ cup almonds, finely ground

1 In the top of a double boiler over simmering water, melt the chocolate, stirring until smooth. Remove from the heat.

2 In a medium bowl, whisk the eggs, sugar, vanilla extract, and cornstarch until blended. Add the melted chocolate. Cook over simmering water, stirring constantly, until the mixture thickens. Blend in the butter until smooth. Remove from the heat and beat in the ground almonds. Chill 30 minutes before using.

898 ■ CHOCOLATE CUSTARD FILLING

MAKES 2¾ CUPS
CHILL TIME: *30 minutes*

½ cup granulated sugar
⅓ cup all-purpose flour
¼ teaspoon salt
2 cups heavy cream
2 ounces unsweetened chocolate, grated or finely chopped
3 large eggs
1 tablespoons crème de cacao
2 teaspoons chocolate extract

1 In the top of a double boiler, combine the sugar, flour, and salt. Add the cream and chocolate and set over simmering water. Cook, stirring, until the chocolate is melted and the mixture is smooth. Remove from the heat.

2 In a small bowl, using a wire whisk, beat the eggs until thick and light-colored. Pouring it in a thin stream, beat ½ cup of the hot chocolate mixture into the eggs. Pour the egg mixture back into the hot chocolate mixture. Return the double boiler to the heat and cook, stirring, until the mixture thickens and coats the back of a spoon. Remove from the heat and cool slightly before adding the crème de cacao and chocolate extract. Cover and chill 30 minutes before using.

896   892   897   898

899 ■ CHOCOLATE CUSTARD SAUCE

MAKES 2½ TO 3 CUPS
CHILL TIME: *30 minutes*

4 large egg yolks
¼ cup powdered sugar
2 cups milk
⅛ teaspoon salt
2 ounces unsweetened chocolate, grated or finely chopped
1 tablespoon crème de cacao

1 In a medium bowl, using an electric mixer on high speed, beat the egg yolks and sugar until thick and light-colored. Beat in the milk and salt.

2 Place the mixture in the top of a double boiler set over simmering water and cook, stirring frequently, until the mixture thickens and coats the back of a spoon. Remove from the heat and mix in the chocolate until smooth. Stir in the crème de cacao. Cover and chill for 30 minutes.

900 ■ CHOCOLATE DIPPING SAUCE I

MAKES 2 CUPS

1¼ cups evaporated milk
¾ cup granulated sugar
5 ounces unsweetened chocolate, grated or finely chopped
5 ounces semisweet chocolate, grated or finely chopped
2 tablespoons butter or margarine
1 tablespoon coffee liqueur

1 In the top of a double boiler over simmering water, combine the evaporated milk and sugar, stirring constantly, until the sugar is dissolved. Add the chocolates and butter and stir until melted and smooth. Remove from the heat and stir in the liqueur. Use as a dipping sauce for pieces of fresh fruit or cubes of pound cake.

901 ■ CHOCOLATE DIPPING SAUCE II

MAKES 2 CUPS

1 cup heavy cream
¼ cup milk
1½ teaspoons espresso powder
¾ cup granulated sugar
8 ounces semisweet chocolate, grated or finely chopped
2 ounces unsweetened chocolate, grated or finely chopped
2 tablespoons butter or margarine

1 In a saucepan over low heat, combine the cream, milk, and espresso powder. Cook until bubbles start to form around the sides of the pan. Add the sugar and stir until dissolved. Add the chocolate and butter and stir until melted and smooth. Do not allow the mixture to come to a full boil. Remove from the heat. Use as a dipping sauce for pieces of fresh fruit or cubes of pound cake.

902 ■ CHOCOLATE ECLAIR FROSTING

MAKES 1½ TO 1¾ CUPS
CHILL TIME: *30 minutes*

4 ounces unsweetened chocolate, grated or finely chopped
1½ cups sifted powdered sugar
3 tablespoons evaporated milk
2 tablespoons butter or margarine, at room temperature
2 tablespoons light corn syrup
1 teaspoon chocolate extract

1 Melt the chocolate (see page 13). Place in a medium bowl.

2 Add the powdered sugar, evaporated milk, butter, corn syrup, and chocolate extract and beat until smooth. Chill 30 minutes until the frosting is set before using. Spread over the top of eclairs or tortes.

903 ■ CHOCOLATE FILLING

MAKES 1½ TO 2 CUPS
CHILL TIME: *30 minutes*

3 ounces unsweetened chocolate, grated or finely chopped
6 large eggs
1 cup granulated sugar
¾ cup butter or margarine, at room temperature

1 Melt the chocolate (see page 13). Remove from the heat.

2 In the top of a double boiler, using an electric mixer on medium speed, beat the eggs until thick. Mix in the sugar. Set over a pot of simmering water and cook, stirring constantly, for 8 to 10 minutes, or until thickened.

3 Pour the mixture into a large bowl and add the melted chocolate. Beat until cool. Gradually blend in the butter, mixing until smooth after each addition. Chill for 30 minutes, or until a spreadable consistency.

903

904 ▪ CHOCOLATE FROSTING (FOR SUGAR-RESTRICTED DIETS)

MAKES 1 CUP
CHILL TIME: *30 minutes*

2 ounces unsweetened chocolate, grated or finely chopped
¾ cup heavy cream
1 teaspoon Equal™ artificial sweetener
1 teaspoon chocolate or vanilla extract

1 Melt the chocolate (see page 13). Remove from the heat.

2 In a medium bowl, using an electric mixer on high speed, beat the cream until soft peaks form. Beat in the sweetener and chocolate extract. Beat in the melted chocolate until streaks no longer appear. Spread evenly over the top and sides of a cake and chill 30 minutes before serving.

905 ▪ CHOCOLATE FROSTING I

MAKES 1½ CUPS
CHILL TIME: *30 minutes*

4 ounces unsweetened chocolate, grated or finely chopped
3 cups powdered sugar, sifted
4 teaspoons light corn syrup

½ cup heavy cream
3 tablespoons boiling water
4 teaspoons butter or margarine, at room temperature
2 teaspoons chocolate extract

1 Melt the chocolate (see page 13). Place in a large bowl.

2 Using an electric mixer on low speed, beat in the powdered sugar and corn syrup. Blend in the cream and boiling water. Add the butter and chocolate extract and beat until a spreadable consistency. Chill for 30 minutes before using.

906 ▪ CHOCOLATE FROSTING II

MAKES 1¾ CUPS
CHILL TIME: *30 minutes*

½ cup vegetable shortening
½ cup Dutch processed cocoa powder
1 large egg
¼ teaspoon salt
4 cups powdered sugar
⅓ cup milk
1 teaspoon chocolate or vanilla extract

1 In a medium bowl, using an electric mixer on medium speed, beat the shortening, cocoa powder, egg, and salt. Blend in the powdered sugar. Add the milk and chocolate extract and beat until thick and creamy. If the frosting is too thick, add milk, ½ teaspoon at a time. If too thin, add powdered sugar, a tablespoon at a time. Chill for 30 minutes before using.

BAKING NOTES: Owing to the raw egg used in this recipe, it should be kept refrigerated at all times, and for no longer than 3 days.

907 ▪ CHOCOLATE FROSTING III

MAKES 1½ CUPS

3 tablespoons arrowroot or cornstarch
1 cup water
2 ounces unsweetened chocolate, grated or finely chopped
1 tablespoon butter or margarine
1 cup granulated sugar
1 teaspoon chocolate or vanilla extract

1 Dissolve the arrowroot in ¼ cup of the water and blend thoroughly.

2 In the top of a double boiler over simmering water, melt the chocolate and butter, stirring until smooth. Stir in the sugar, arrowroot mixture, and remaining ¾ cup water. Stir constantly until the mixture reaches a spreadable consistency. Remove from the heat and quickly stir in the vanilla extract. Cool slightly before using.

904   905   906   907

900   901   902

908 ■ CHOCOLATE FROSTING IV

MAKES 1½ CUPS

2 ounces semisweet chocolate, grated or finely chopped
½ cup granulated sugar
¼ cup water
4 large egg yolks
½ cup butter or margarine, at room temperature
2 cups powdered sugar
1 teaspoon chocolate extract

1 In the top of a double boiler over simmering water, melt the chocolate with the sugar and water, stirring constantly until smooth. Remove from the heat.
2 In a large bowl, using an electric mixer on medium speed, beat the egg yolks until thick and light-colored. Beat in the chocolate mixture and set aside to cool.
3 Meanwhile, in a small bowl, using an electric mixer on medium speed, beat the butter, powdered sugar, and chocolate extract. Add to the chocolate mixture and beat until thoroughly blended.

BAKING NOTES: Owing to the raw egg yolks used in this recipe, it should be kept refrigerated at all times, and for no longer than 3 days.

909 ■ CHOCOLATE FROSTING V

MAKES 1 CUP

2 ounces unsweetened chocolate, grated or finely chopped
½ cup boiling water
½ cup butter or margarine, at room temperature
2 cups powdered sugar

1 In the container of a blender, combine the chocolate, boiling water, and butter. Blend on medium speed for 2 to 3 seconds, or until smooth. Add 1 cup of the powdered sugar and blend until smooth. Add the remaining 1 cup powdered sugar and blend until creamy.

910 ■ CHOCOLATE FROSTING VI

MAKES 2⅔ CUPS

5 ounces unsweetened chocolate, grated or finely chopped
½ cup butter or margarine, at room temperature
3 cups powdered sugar
2 large egg yolks
½ cup crème de cacao

1 Melt the chocolate (see page 13). Remove from the heat.
2 Using an electric mixer on medium speed, beat in the butter and powdered sugar until blended. Add the egg yolks, one at a time. Add the crème de cacao and beat until a spreadable consistency. If too thick, add water, ½ teaspoon at a time. If too thin, add powdered sugar, a tablespoon at a time.

BAKING NOTES: Owing to the raw egg yolks used in this recipe, it should be kept refrigerated at all times, and for no longer than 3 days.

911 ■ CHOCOLATE FUDGE FROSTING I

MAKES 1¾ TO 2 CUPS

1 cup granulated sugar
1 cup powdered sugar, sifted
1 cup water
1 ounces unsweetened chocolate, grated or finely chopped
1 ounce semisweet chocolate, grated or finely chopped
2 tablespoons light corn syrup
¼ teaspoon salt
2 teaspoons butter or margarine
1 teaspoon chocolate extract

913   914   915   916

908   909   910

1 In a saucepan over low heat, combine the sugars, water, chocolates, corn syrup, and salt, stirring until smooth. Insert a candy thermometer and cook until 285 degrees. Remove from the heat and add the butter, without stirring. Cool until lukewarm 110 degrees. Add the chocolate extract. Using a wooden spoon, beat until a spreadable consistency.

912 ■ CHOCOLATE FUDGE FROSTING II

MAKES 1½ TO 2 CUPS

½ cup butter or margarine
2 ounces unsweetened chocolate, grated or finely chopped
1¾ cups granulated sugar
½ cup heavy cream
1 tablespoon dark corn syrup
1 teaspoon chocolate extract

1 In a saucepan over low heat, melt the butter and chocolate, stirring until smooth. Mix in the sugar, cream, and corn syrup and bring to a boil. Cook for 3 minutes, stirring constantly. Remove from the heat and cool for 7 minutes. Add the chocolate extract and beat until a spreadable consistency.

913 ■ CHOCOLATE FUDGE SAUCE

MAKES 1 TO 1½ CUPS

6 ounces semisweet chocolate, grated or finely chopped
1 tablespoon butter or margarine
¼ cup hot water
¼ cup granulated sugar
¼ cup dark corn syrup
1 teaspoon chocolate extract or crème de cacao

1 In the top of a double boiler over simmering water, melt the chocolate and butter with the water, stirring until smooth. Add the sugar and stir until completely dissolved. Remove from the heat and stir in the corn syrup and chocolate extract. Serve warm.

914 ■ CHOCOLATE GLAZE I

MAKES ½ CUP

2 tablespoons butter or margarine
1 ounce semisweet chocolate, grated or finely chopped
1 cup powdered sugar
1 tablespoon boiling water

1 In the top of a double boiler, melt the butter and chocolate, stirring until smooth. Add the powdered sugar and water and stir until smooth. Cool slightly before using.

915 ■ CHOCOLATE GLAZE II

MAKES ½ CUP

12 ounces semisweet chocolate, grated or finely chopped
6 tablespoons butter or margarine

1 In the top of a double boiler over simmering water, melt the chocolate and butter, stirring until smooth. Remove from heat. Cool slightly and use while still warm.

916 ■ CHOCOLATE GLAZE III

MAKES 1½ TO 2 CUPS

⅔ cup minus 1 tablespoon water
6 tablespoons butter-flavored vegetable shortening
3 tablespoons canola oil
⅔ cup granulated sugar
3 ounces semisweet chocolate, grated or finely chopped
⅓ cup Dutch processed cocoa powder
2 tablespoons coffee liqueur

1 In a medium saucepan, over medium heat, combine the water, shortening, and oil and bring to a boil. Remove from the heat and stir in the sugar, chocolate, cocoa powder, and liqueur and stir until smooth. Using an electric mixer on medium speed, beat for 3 to 4 minutes, or until the mixture starts to thicken. Cool to room temperature before using.

917 ■ CHOCOLATE GLAZE IV

MAKES 1½ TO 2 CUPS

8 ounces unsweetened chocolate, grated or finely chopped
4 ounces semisweet chocolate, grated or finely chopped
6 tablespoons warm water (102 to 115 degrees)

1 In the top of a double boiler over simmering water, melt the chocolates, stirring until smooth. Remove from the heat. Add the water and beat until the consistency of heavy cream. Use at room temperature.

BAKING NOTES: If the glaze is too thick, add water, a teaspoon at a time.

917

911

912

918 ■ CHOCOLATE ICING

MAKES 1 CUP

3/4 cup powdered sugar
5 tablespoons milk
Pinch of salt
4 ounces unsweetened chocolate, grated or finely chopped
1/4 cup butter or margarine
1 teaspoon chocolate or vanilla extract

1 In a large bowl, beat the powdered sugar, milk, and salt until smooth.

2 In the top of a double boiler over simmering water, melt the chocolate and butter, stirring until smooth. Remove from the heat and stir in the chocolate extract. Gradually blend in the powdered sugar mixture. Return to the heat and cook, stirring occasionally, for 30 minutes, or until a spreadable consistency. If the mixture is too thick, add a little more milk. If too thin, cook a little longer. Cool before using.

919 ■ CHOCOLATE LIQUEUR SAUCE

MAKES 1 TO 1 1/2 CUPS

3 ounces unsweetened chocolate, grated or finely chopped
3/4 cup granulated sugar
1/2 cup heavy cream
1 1/2 tablespoons butter or margarine
3 tablespoons crème de cacao
1/2 teaspoon chocolate extract

1 In a saucepan over low heat, melt the chocolate with the sugar, cream, and butter, stirring constantly until the sugar is dissolved and the mixture is smooth. Simmer for 6 minutes. Remove from the heat and add the crème de cacao and chocolate extract, but do not stir for at least 5 minutes. Stir to incorporate and serve hot or cold.

920 ■ CHOCOLATE MARSHMALLOW SAUCE

MAKES 2 CUPS

3 ounces unsweetened chocolate, grated or finely chopped
3 ounces semisweet chocolate, grated or finely chopped
1 1/2 cups powdered sugar, sifted twice
1 cup hot water
1/2 cup marshmallow creme
1 teaspoon chocolate extract

1 In the top of a double boiler over simmering water, combine all of the ingredients and heat until smooth, stirring constantly. Remove from the heat and using an electric mixer on low speed, beat until thick. Serve hot or cold.

BAKING NOTES: 1 cup of miniature marshmallows can be used in place of the marshmallow creme.

921 ■ CHOCOLATE MINT SAUCE

MAKES 3/4 CUP

6 tablespoons heavy cream
20 large chocolate peppermint cream candies

1 In a small bowl, using an electric mixer on high speed, whip the cream until soft peaks form.

2 In the top of a double boiler over simmering water, melt the candies, stirring until smooth. Gently fold the chocolate into the whipped cream just until incorporated. Serve hot over ice cream and sprinkle with chopped nuts.

922 ■ CHOCOLATE MOCHA MERINGUE TOPPING

MAKES 2 1/4 CUPS

1/4 cup powdered sugar
1 1/2 teaspoons cornstarch or arrowroot
1 3/4 teaspoons Dutch processed cocoa powder
1/3 cup granulated sugar
4 large egg whites
1/4 teaspoon salt
Pinch of cream of tartar
1 tablespoon mocha-flavored instant coffee powder

1 Combine and sift the powdered sugar, cornstarch, and cocoa powder.

2 In the top of a double boiler over simmering water, combine the granulated sugar, egg whites, salt, cream of tartar, and coffee powder and stir until smooth and just warm to the touch. Remove from the heat.

3 Using an electric mixer on medium speed, whip until stiff peaks form. Fold in the dry ingredients. Spread evenly over the top of a pie and place in a 450 degree oven for about 5 minutes, until the edges are slightly browned.

BAKING NOTES: The topping can be piped onto the top of the pie with a pastry bag. Use a large star tip and cover the top of the pie with stars.

922

918

923 ■ CHOCOLATE-PEANUT BUTTER FROSTING

MAKES ¾ CUP

1 ounce unsweetened chocolate, grated or finely chopped
¼ cup creamy peanut butter
1½ cups powdered sugar

1 Melt the chocolate (see page 13). Remove from the heat.

2 In a medium bowl, using an electric mixer on medium speed, beat the melted chocolate, peanut butter, and powdered sugar until a smooth, spreadable consistency. Spread the frosting on cakes and brownies.

BAKING NOTES: Premelted chocolate can be used as a substitute for the grated chocolate.

924 ■ CHOCOLATE-PEANUT BUTTER SAUCE

MAKES ¾ CUP

½ cup warm water
⅓ cup granulated sugar
1 tablespoon dark corn syrup
Pinch of salt
1 ounce unsweetened chocolate, grated or finely chopped
¼ cup creamy peanut butter
½ teaspoon chocolate extract

1 In a small saucepan, over medium heat, combine the water, sugar, corn syrup, and salt and bring to a boil. Simmer, stirring constantly, for 3 minutes. Remove from the heat and stir in the chocolate, peanut butter, and chocolate extract. Whisk until the mixture thickens. Serve over ice cream or fruit.

925 ■ CHOCOLATE QUARK CREAM FILLING

MAKES 6 CUPS
CHILL TIME: 1 hour

⅔ cup milk
⅔ cup granulated sugar
3 large egg yolks
¼ cup crème de cacao
2 tablespoons unflavored gelatin
2 cups heavy cream
2 teaspoons granulated sugar
2 cups quark (see Baking notes)

1 In the top of a double boiler over simmering water, combine the milk, sugar, and egg yolks and stir until thickened. Remove from the heat and transfer to a large bowl.

2 Place the crème de cacao in a small saucepan and sprinkle with the gelatin. Let stand for 1 minute to soften. Stir over low heat until completely dissolved. Stir into the egg yolk mixture.

3 In a medium bowl, using an electric mixer on high speed, whip the cream until thick. Beat in the sugar until stiff peaks form. Blend in the quark. Fold the whipped cream mixture into the egg yolk mixture. Chill for 1 hour before using.

BAKING NOTES: To make quark, place 1 pint of large-curd cottage cheese in a blender with ½ teaspoon of salt. Blend on high speed to make a smooth paste. From this point on, anything you want to add will constitute the recipes. Suggestions: strawberries, seedless raspberry jam, caraway seeds, or anise seeds.

926 ■ CHOCOLATE RICOTTA FILLING

MAKES 2 CUPS

1 pound ricotta cheese
¼ cup granulated sugar
1 ounce semisweet chocolate, grated or finely chopped
1 tablespoon grated orange zest
2 teaspoons Campari
1 to 2 tablespoons milk

1 In a medium bowl, using an electric mixer on medium speed, beat the ricotta, sugar, chocolate, orange zest, and Campari until combined. Gradually mix in enough milk until the consistency of a thick custard.

BAKING NOTES: Any orange liqueur can be used in place of Campari.

923   924   925   926

919   920   921

927 ■ CHOCOLATE RUM ICING

MAKES 1½ CUPS

3 ounces semisweet chocolate, grated or finely chopped
5 cups powdered sugar
6 tablespoons dark rum
2 tablespoons crème de cacao

1 Melt the chocolate (see page 13). Remove from the heat. transfer to a medium bowl.
2 Using an electric mixer on medium speed, beat in the powdered sugar and rum. Add the crème de cacao and beat until a spreadable consistency.

928 ■ CHOCOLATE RUM SAUCE

MAKES 1 TO 1½ CUPS

3 ounces unsweetened chocolate, grated or finely chopped
¼ cup coffee liqueur
¼ cup milk
⅔ cup granulated sugar
1 tablespoon butter or margarine
½ cup dark rum
½ teaspoon chocolate extract

1 In the top of a double boiler over simmering water, melt the chocolate, stirring until smooth. Add the liqueur and milk and cook, stirring constantly, for 4 to 5 minutes. Add the sugar and butter and cook until thickened slightly. Remove from the heat and stir in the rum and chocolate extract. Using a wire whisk, beat until cooled to room temperature. Serve the sauce warm or cold.

929 ■ CHOCOLATE SAUCE I

MAKES ½ CUP

2 tablespoons Dutch processed cocoa powder
3 tablespoons granulated sugar
½ cup water
1 teaspoon chocolate extract
2 tablespoons crème de cacao

1 In a small saucepan, combine the cocoa and sugar. Over medium heat, stir in the water and chocolate extract and cook until the mixture thickens. Remove from the heat and stir in the crème de cacao. Let cool before using.

930 ■ CHOCOLATE SAUCE II

MAKES 2 CUPS

½ cup butter or margarine
2 ounces semisweet chocolate, grated or finely chopped
⅔ cup heavy cream
½ cup Dutch processed cocoa powder
½ cup crème de cacao
1 teaspoon chocolate extract

1 In the top of a double boiler over simmering water, melt the butter and chocolate, stirring until smooth. Stir in the cream and cocoa powder. Do not boil. Remove from the heat and cool slightly. Stir in the crème de cacao and chocolate extract.

931 ■ CHOCOLATE SAUCE III

MAKES 2 TO 2¼ CUPS

1 teaspoon cornstarch or arrowroot
¾ cup heavy cream
6 ounces semisweet chocolate, grated or finely chopped
½ cup honey

1 In a small bowl, dissolve the cornstarch in the cream.
2 In the top of a double boiler over simmering water, melt the chocolate with the honey, stirring until smooth. Blend in the cream mixture and cook, stirring, until the sauce is thickened. Cool before using.

927　　928　　929　　930　　931

932 ■ CHOCOLATE SAUCE IV

MAKES ¾ TO 1 CUP

8 ounces semisweet chocolate, grated or finely chopped
¼ cup Grand Marnier
¼ cup water
¼ cup granulated sugar
2 tablespoons grated orange zest

1 Melt the chocolate (see page 13). Remove from the heat.

2 In a small bowl, combine the liqueur, water, sugar, and orange zest, stirring until smooth. Stir into the chocolate mixture.

BAKING NOTES: If Grand Marnier is not available, any orange liqueur can be used. Sabra, a product of Israel that has an orange-chocolate flavor, can also be used.

933 ■ CHOCOLATE SAUCE V

MAKES 1 TO 1½ CUP

1 cup granulated sugar
½ cup water
2 ounces semisweet chocolate, grated or finely chopped
1 teaspoon chocolate extract

1 In the top of a double boiler over simmering water, combine the sugar, water, and chocolate, stirring until smooth. Remove from the heat and stir in the chocolate extract. The sauce will be thin. Cool to room temperature before serving.

934 ■ CHOCOLATE SAUCE VI

MAKES 1 TO 1½ CUPS

¼ cup marshmallow creme
¼ cup Dutch processed cocoa powder
1 tablespoon cornstarch or arrowroot
1 cup milk
1 tablespoon dark corn syrup
2 tablespoons pecans or hazelnuts, finely ground
1 teaspoon chocolate extract

1 In a medium saucepan, over medium heat, combine the marshmallow creme, cocoa powder, and cornstarch, stirring until smooth. Stir in the milk and corn syrup and cook until thickened. Remove from the heat and stir in the pecans and chocolate extract. Cool before using. Serve the sauce over ice cream, mousses, or cakes.

935 ■ CHOCOLATE SAUCE VII

MAKES 2 TO 2¼ CUPS

1 large egg yolk
1 tablespoon powdered sugar
1 teaspoon arrowroot or cornstarch
8 ounces semisweet chocolate, grated or finely chopped
2 cups milk
½ tablespoon Ashanti Gold liqueur

1 In a small bowl, beat the egg yolk, powdered sugar, and arrowroot until thick and light-colored.

2 In a saucepan over low heat, melt the chocolate, stirring constantly until smooth. Stir in the milk. Stir in the egg yolk mixture until blended. Bring to a boil. Simmer for 1 minute. Remove from the heat and stir in the liqueur. Cool to room temperature before serving.

BAKING NOTES: Crème de cacao can be used in place of the Ashanti Gold. For a coffee-flavored sauce, use coffee liqueur.

936 ■ CHOCOLATE SAUCE VIII

MAKES ¾ CUP

1 cup granulated sugar
⅓ cup Dutch processed cocoa powder
¼ teaspoon salt
½ cup warm water
¼ cup light corn syrup
2 tablespoons butter or margarine
1 teaspoon chocolate extract

1 In a medium saucepan, over low heat, combine the sugar, cocoa powder, and salt. Stir in the water and corn syrup until smooth. Insert a candy thermometer and cook until 234 degrees, stirring occasionally. Remove from the heat and stir in the butter and chocolate extract. Serve warm or cold over ice cream, cake, or fresh fruit.

932   933   934   935   936

937 ■ CHOCOLATE SAUCE IX

MAKES 1½ CUPS

4 ounces unsweetened chocolate, grated or finely chopped
1 cup granulated sugar
1 cup heavy cream
½ teaspoon chocolate or vanilla extract

1 In a saucepan over low heat, melt the chocolate, stirring until smooth. Add the sugar and cream and cook, stirring constantly, for 5 to 7 minutes, or until smooth and thick like a custard. Do not allow the mixture to boil. Remove from the heat and stir in the chocolate extract. Serve the sauce hot or cold.

938 ■ CHOCOLATE SYRUP I

MAKES 1½ TO 2 CUPS

5 ounces unsweetened chocolate, grated or finely chopped
1⅓ cups hot water
1 cup granulated sugar
1 teaspoon chocolate extract

1 In the top of a double boiler over simmering water, melt the chocolate with the water, stirring until blended and smooth. Add the sugar and cook for 3 to 5 minutes, or until the sugar is dissolved. Remove from the heat and stir in the chocolate extract. Serve either warm or cold.

939 ■ CHOCOLATE SYRUP II

MAKES 1¼ TO 1½ CUPS

3 ounces unsweetened chocolate, grated or finely chopped
⅔ cup water
½ cup granulated sugar
½ cup light or dark corn syrup
½ teaspoon chocolate or vanilla extract

1 In a saucepan over low heat, melt the chocolate with the water, stirring until smooth and

thick. Stir in the sugar. Bring to a boil and simmer for 2 minutes. Add the corn syrup and return to a boil. Remove from the heat and cool slightly. Stir in the vanilla extract and cool completely.

940 ■ CHOCOLATE SYRUP III

MAKES ½ CUP

1 teaspoon cornstarch or arrowroot
⅓ cup water
1 tablespoon granulated sugar
2 ounces semisweet chocolate, grated or finely chopped
½ teaspoon chocolate or vanilla extract

1 In a cup, dissolve the cornstarch in 1 tablespoon of the water.

2 In the top of a double boiler over simmering water, combine the remaining water and sugar. Add the chocolate and stir constantly until smooth. Add the cornstarch mixture and cook until thickened. Remove from the heat and stir in the chocolate extract. Serve the syrup hot or cold.

941 ■ CHOCOLATE WHIPPED CREAM

MAKES 2 TO 2½ CUPS
CHILL TIME: 30 minutes

3 tablespoons powdered sugar
2 tablespoons Dutch processed cocoa powder
1 cup heavy cream
½ teaspoon crème de cacao

1 In a cup, combine the powdered sugar and cocoa powder.

2 In a medium bowl, using an electric mixer on high speed, whip the cream until soft peaks form. Fold in the dry ingredients. Fold in the crème de cacao. Chill for 30 minutes before using.

942 ■ COCOA CREAM TOPPING

MAKES 1 CUP

1 cup chocolate yogurt
1 tablespoon powdered sugar
2 teaspoons Dutch processed cocoa powder
1 teaspoon crème de cacao
½ teaspoon chocolate extract

1 In a medium bowl, combine all of the ingredients, stirring until smooth. Cover and chill well before using.

943 ■ COCOA FROSTING

MAKES ½ CUP

3 tablespoons Dutch processed cocoa powder
1 cup powdered sugar
½ teaspoon chocolate extract
3 tablespoons coffee liqueur

1 In a small bowl, combine all of the ingredients and whisk until smooth. If the mixture is too thick, add water a few drops at a time. If too thin, add powdered sugar, ½ teaspoon at a time.

943
944
938
937

944 ■ COCOA GLAZE

MAKES 1½ TO 1¾ CUPS

½ cup Dutch processed cocoa
   powder
½ cup granulated sugar
½ cup heavy cream
¼ cup butter or margarine

1 In the top of a double boiler over simmering water, combine all of the ingredients and stir until smooth. Cook for 5 minutes. Remove from the heat and cool for 10 to 15 minutes, or until slightly thickened. Pour over the top of a cake and chill until the glaze hardens.

945 ■ COCOA HONEY FROSTING

MAKES 1½ CUPS

⅓ cup butter-flavored vegetable
   shortening
⅓ cup Dutch processed cocoa
   powder
2 tablespoons milk
2 tablespoons honey, warmed
1 teaspoon chocolate extract
2 cups powdered sugar

1 In a medium bowl, using an electric mixer on medium speed, beat the shortening, cocoa powder, milk, honey, and chocolate extract until blended. Add the powdered sugar and beat until smooth. If too thick, add milk, ½ teaspoon at a time. If too thin, add powdered sugar, a tablespoon at a time.

BAKING NOTES: This recipe makes enough to fill and frost one 8-inch layer or tube cake.

946 ■ COCOA SUGAR

MAKES 1 CUP

1 cup powdered sugar
1 tablespoon Dutch processed
   cocoa powder

1 In a small bowl, combine the powdered sugar and cocoa powder. Use for dusting over baked goods.

947 ■ COCOA SYRUP I

MAKES 1¼ TO 1½ CUPS

1 cup water
½ cup granulated sugar
⅓ cup Dutch processed cocoa
   powder
2 tablespoons butter, at room
   temperature
1 teaspoon vanilla extract

1 In a small saucepan, over medium heat, combine the water, sugar, and cocoa powder. Bring to a boil and cook for 3 minutes. Remove from the heat and stir in the butter until smooth. Cool slightly and stir in the vanilla extract. Chill before using.

948 ■ COCOA SYRUP II

MAKES 2 TO 2¼ CUPS

1 cup Dutch processed cocoa
   powder
1¼ cups granulated sugar
1¼ cups water
1 teaspoon chocolate extract

1 In a heavy medium saucepan, over medium heat, combine all of the ingredients. Bring to a boil and simmer for 3 to 5 minutes, stirring constantly, until smooth. Remove from the heat. Cool slightly and chill before using.

BAKING NOTES: This syrup can be used to make chocolate milk. Stir 2 to 3 tablespoons of the syrup into 1 cup of cold or scalded milk.

945   946   947   948

939   940   941   942

949 ■ COFFEE BUTTERCREAM

MAKES 4 CUPS

3 ounces unsweetened chocolate, grated or finely chopped
9 tablespoons coffee liqueur
1½ cups butter, at room temperature
3 cups powdered sugar, sifted
4 large egg yolks

1 In the top of a double boiler over simmering water, melt the chocolate with the liqueur, stirring constantly until smooth. Remove from the heat and cool.

2 In a medium bowl, using an electric mixer on medium speed, beat the butter and powdered sugar until fluffy. Beat in the egg yolks. Gradually add the chocolate mixture and beat until a spreadable consistency.

BAKING NOTES: Owing to the raw egg yolks used in this recipe, it should be kept refrigerated at all times, and for no longer than 3 days.

950 ■ COFFEE HARD SAUCE

MAKES ½ CUP
CHILL TIME: 30 minutes

¼ teaspoon instant mocha-flavored coffee powder
¼ teaspoon lukewarm water
¼ cup butter or margarine, at room temperature
¾ cup powdered sugar

1 In a small bowl, combine the coffee powder and water. Add the butter. Using an electric mixer on medium speed, beat until blended. Beat in the powdered sugar until smooth. Chill for 30 minutes, or until ready to use.

BAKING NOTES: Hard sauce is really a frosting and is used to dress up plain cakes.

951 ■ COFFEE MOCHA ICING

MAKES 1 CUP

¾ cup powdered sugar
5 tablespoons milk
Pinch of salt
¼ cup butter or margarine
2 teaspoons mocha-flavored instant coffee powder
1 teaspoon chocolate or vanilla extract

1 In a large bowl, mix the powdered sugar, milk, and salt until smooth.

2 In a small saucepan, over low heat, melt the butter with the coffee powder, stirring until smooth. Stir in the vanilla extract. Remove from the heat. Gradually blend in the powdered sugar mixture and set aside. Cook, stirring occasionally, for 30 minutes, or until a spreadable consistency. If too thick, add a little more milk. If too thin, cook a little longer.

952 ■ CREAMY CHOCOLATE CHERRY FROSTING

MAKES 2 CUPS

4 ounces unsweetened chocolate, grated or finely chopped
¼ cup butter or margarine, at room temperature
2 cups powdered sugar
6 tablespoons evaporated milk
1 teaspoon vanilla or chocolate extract
⅛ teaspoon salt
¼ cup maraschino cherries, finely chopped

1 In the top of a double boiler over simmering water, melt the chocolate and butter, stirring until smooth. Remove from the heat and stir in the powdered sugar, evaporated milk, vanilla extract, and salt. Beat until smooth and thick. Stir in the chopped cherries.

953 ■ CREAMY CHOCOLATE FROSTING

MAKES 2½ CUPS

¼ cup all-purpose flour
3 tablespoons Dutch processed cocoa powder
⅔ cup water
⅔ cup granulated sugar
1 large egg
1½ cups heavy cream

1 Combine the flour and cocoa powder.

2 In the top of a double boiler, beat the water, sugar, and egg until combined. Beat in the dry ingredients. Set over simmering water and cook for 20 minutes, or until slightly thickened. Remove from the heat and cool completely.

3 In a large bowl, using an electric mixer on medium speed, whip the cream until stiff peaks form. Beat in the cocoa mixture, pouring in a narrow stream. Chill before using.

952

953

949

950

954 ■ CRÈME CHANTILLY

MAKES 2½ TO 3 CUPS

1 cup heavy cream
2 tablespoons crème de cacao or
    chocolate extract

1 In a small bowl, using an electric mixer on medium speed, whip the cream until soft peaks form. Fold in the crème de cacao. Chill until using. Use the chantilly as a filling or frosting. It can also be used as a topping on puddings and beverages.

BAKING NOTES: To retain the volume of the chantilly longer, soften 1 teaspoon unflavored gelatin in 2 tablespoons water. Warm over low heat until dissolved. Cool slightly and stir into the cream before whipping.

955 ■ CRÈME FRAÎCHE

MAKES 1¼ CUPS
SETTING TIME: *32 hours*

1 cup heavy cream
½ cup sour cream

1 In a large bowl, beat the cream and sour cream until blended. Cover and let stand at room temperature for 8 hours. Line a sieve or strainer with a double layer of cheesecloth.

Add the cream mixture and set over a bowl and cover. Let drain in the refrigerator for 24 hours. Discard the drained liquid. Store the crème fraîche, covered, in the refrigerator for up to 2 weeks. It will become thicker, and should be whipped before using.

956 ■ CUSTARD FILLING

MAKES ¾ TO 1 CUP
CHILL TIME: *30 minutes*

1 large egg
¾ cup skim milk
2 tablespoons powdered sugar
1 tablespoon cornstarch or
    arrowroot
Pinch of salt

1 In a small bowl, beat the egg.
2 In a medium saucepan, over medium heat, combine the milk, powdered sugar, cornstarch, and salt over medium heat. Stir constantly with a wire whisk until thickened and bubbly. Remove from the heat. Beat 2 tablespoons of the hot milk mixture into the beaten egg. Add the egg mixture to the saucepan, whisking constantly. Over medium-low heat, cook, stirring constantly, for 2 minutes. Transfer to a small bowl. Cover and chill 30 minutes, or until using.

957 ■ DESSERT SYRUP

MAKES ⅓ TO ½ CUP

½ cup granulated sugar
2 tablespoons liqueur of choice

1 In a cup, combine the ingredients and mix until smooth. Use a pastry brush to brush over fruit on cakes and pies.

958 ■ DUTCH COCOA FILLING

MAKES 2 TO 2½ CUPS
CHILL TIME: *30 minutes*

¼ cup granulated sugar
3 tablespoons Dutch processed
    cocoa powder
1 tablespoons cornstarch or flour
2 cups heavy cream
1 tablespoon chocolate extract

1 In the top of a double boiler over simmering water, combine the sugar, cocoa powder, cornstarch, and 1 cup of the cream. Cook, stirring constantly, until the mixture thickens. Remove from the heat and stir in the chocolate extract.

2 In a small bowl, using an electric mixer high speed, beat the remaining 1 cup cream until stiff peaks form. Fold half of the chocolate mixture into the whipped cream. Chill 30 minutes before using.

3 To assemble on a cake, spread the remaining half of the chocolate mixture onto the bottom layer of the cake, top with the second layer, and spread the chilled whipped cream portion over the top and sides.

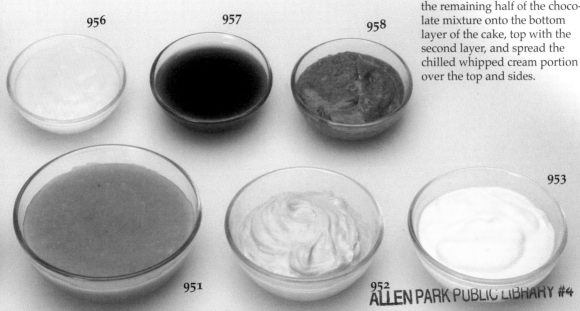

951 · 952 · 953 · 956 · 957 · 958

959 ■ FUDGE FROSTING

MAKES 1 TO 1¼ CUPS

2 ounces unsweetened chocolate, grated or finely chopped
½ cup butter or margarine
1¾ cups granulated sugar
½ cup milk
1 tablespoon light corn syrup
1 teaspoon chocolate extract

1 In a saucepan over low heat, melt the chocolate and butter, stirring until smooth. Stir in the sugar, milk, and corn syrup. Bring to a boil. Boil for 2 to 3 minutes, or until smooth. Remove from the heat and cool for 5 minutes. Add the chocolate extract and using an electric mixer on low speed, beat until a spreadable consistency.

960 ■ FUDGE SAUCE

MAKES 2 TO 2¼ CUPS

1 cup granulated sugar
1 cup light corn syrup
½ cup Dutch processed cocoa powder
½ cup heavy cream
3 tablespoons butter or margarine
½ teaspoon chocolate extract

1 In a large saucepan, over medium heat, combine the sugar, corn syrup, cocoa powder, cream, and butter. Bring to a boil. Cook, stirring constantly, for 3 minutes. Remove from the heat and stir in the chocolate extract. Serve warm or hot.

BAKING NOTES: To reheat, use a double boiler. Any flavor of extract can be used in place of the chocolate extract.

961 ■ GANACHE I

CHILL TIME: 30 MINUTES

VARIATION I
MAKES 4 CUPS

2 pounds semisweet chocolate, grated or finely chopped
3 cups heavy cream

VARIATION II
MAKES 3 TO 3¼ CUPS

27 ounces semisweet chocolate, grated or finely chopped
2¾ cups heavy cream

VARIATION III
MAKES 1¼ CUPS

4 ounces semisweet chocolate, grated or finely chopped
⅓ cup heavy cream

1 In a saucepan over low heat, warm the cream until bubbles start to form around the sides of the pan. Add the chocolate. Remove from the heat and let stand for 2 minutes to melt the chocolate. Stir until the chocolate is completely melted and the mixture is smooth. Transfer to a bowl. If not using the ganache immediately, cool to room temperature, stirring occasionally. Cover and store in the refrigerator.

2 To use the ganache as a glaze, cool slightly. Pour the ganache over the item to be glazed.

3 To whip the ganache for use as a frosting, chill 30 minutes, until the mixture has thickened and is about 50 to 55 degrees. (If it is too cold, it will be too hard to whip.) Using a wire whisk, gently whip the ganache until it is creamy and thick. Do not overmix. Use immediately or the whipped ganache will harden and become difficult to spread.

962 ■ GANACHE II

MAKES 3 TO 3½ CUPS
CHILL TIME: 30 minutes

1 cup heavy cream
8 ounces unsweetened chocolate, grated or finely chopped
7 ounces semisweet chocolate, grated or finely chopped
1¼ cups pecans, finely ground
¼ cup crème de cacao

1 In a saucepan over low heat, warm the cream until bubbles start to form around the sides of the pan. Add the chocolates. Remove from the heat and let stand for 2 minutes to melt the chocolates. Stir until the chocolate is completely melted and the mixture is smooth. Stir in the pecans and crème de cacao. Transfer to a medium bowl.

2 To use the ganache as a glaze, cool slightly. Pour the ganache over the item to be glazed.

3 To whip the ganache for use as a frosting, chill 30 minutes, until the mixture has thickened and is about 50 to 55 degrees. (If it is too cold, it will be too hard to whip.) Using a wire whisk, gently whip the ganache until it is creamy and thick. Do not overmix. Use immediately or the whipped ganache will harden and become difficult to spread.

963 ■ GANACHE III

MAKES 2 CUPS
CHILL TIME: 30 minutes

1½ cups heavy cream
½ teaspoon ground cinnamon
6 ounces unsweetened chocolate, grated or finely chopped
5 ounces semisweet chocolate, grated or finely chopped
1 ounce white chocolate or almond bark

1 In a saucepan over low heat, warm the cream and cinnamon until bubbles start to form around the sides of the pan.

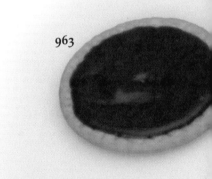

963

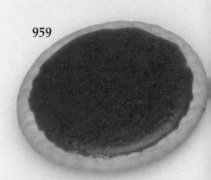

959

Add the chocolates and almond bark. Remove from the heat and let stand for 2 minutes to melt the chocolate. Stir until the chocolate is completely melted and the mixture is smooth. Transfer to a medium bowl.

2 To use the ganache as a glaze, cool slightly. Pour the ganache over the item to be glazed.

3 To whip the ganache for use as a frosting, chill 30 minutes, until the mixture has thickened and is about 50 to 55 degrees. (If it is too cold, it will be too hard to whip.) Using a wire whisk, gently whip the ganache until it is creamy and thick. Do not overmix. Use immediately or the whipped ganache will harden and become difficult to spread.

964 ■ GRAND MARNIER SAUCE

MAKES 1½ TO 1¾ CUPS
CHILL TIME: *30 minutes*

1 cup milk
2 large egg yolks
1 tablespoon granulated sugar
½ cup minus 1½ tablespoons chocolate ice cream
2 tablespoons Grand Marnier

1 In a small saucepan, over medium heat, warm the cream until bubbles start to form around the sides of the pan. Remove from the heat.

2 In a small bowl, using an electric mixer on medium speed, beat the egg yolks until thick and light-colored. Beat in the sugar. Pour the mixture into the top of a double boiler. Place over simmering water and beat in the hot milk, a little at a time. Continue beating 10 to 12 minutes, or until the mixture is thickened. Remove from the heat and stir in the ice cream and Grand Marnier. Pour into a small bowl. Cover and chill 30 minutes before using.

BAKING NOTES: Use chocolate ice cream for a chocolate Grand Marnier sauce.

965 ■ GREEN CRÈME DE MENTHE ICING

MAKES ¾ CUP

¼ cup butter, at room temperature
1½ cups powdered sugar
2 tablespoons green crème de menthe

1 In a small bowl, using an electric mixer on medium speed, beat the butter and ½ cup of the powdered sugar until blended. Beat in the crème de menthe. Beat in the remaining 1 cup of powdered sugar until light and fluffy.

966 ■ HAZELNUT FILLING

MAKES ¾ TO 1 CUP

½ cup hazelnuts, finely ground
½ cup powdered sugar
2 tablespoons butter or margarine, at room temperature
2 tablespoons heavy cream
1 tablespoon amaretto

1 In a medium bowl, combine the hazelnuts and powdered sugar. Using a pastry blender or two knives, cut in the butter. Stir in the cream and amaretto. The mixture should have a spreadable consistency. If too thin, add more powdered sugar, a teaspoonful at a time.

964   965   966

960   961   962

967 ■ HOT FUDGE LIQUEUR SAUCE

MAKES 1¼ CUPS

1 cup packed light brown sugar
½ cup coffee liqueur
¼ cup Dutch processed cocoa powder
1 tablespoon butter or margarine
½ teaspoon chocolate extract

1 In a small saucepan, over low heat, combine the brown sugar, liqueur, and cocoa powder. Bring to a boil and simmer for 4 minutes. Remove from the heat and stir in the butter and chocolate extract. Serve warm over ice cream or other desserts.

968 ■ HOT FUDGE SAUCE I

MAKES 1¼ TO 1½ CUPS

1½ cups granulated sugar
½ cup milk
⅓ cup light corn syrup
2 ounces semisweet chocolate, grated or finely chopped
1 tablespoon butter or margarine
1 teaspoon vanilla or chocolate extract

1 In a saucepan over low heat, combine the sugar, milk, corn syrup, and chocolate, stirring until the mixture is smooth. Insert a candy thermometer and cook, stirring occasionally, until 228 degrees. Remove from the heat and immediately stir in the butter and vanilla extract. Serve hot over ice cream or other desserts.

969 ■ HOT FUDGE SAUCE II

MAKES 1¼ CUPS

1 cup packed light brown sugar
½ cup water
¼ cup Dutch processed cocoa powder
1 tablespoon butter or margarine
½ teaspoon chocolate extract

1 In a small saucepan, over low heat, combine the brown sugar, water, and cocoa powder. Bring to a boil and simmer for 4 minutes. Remove from the heat and stir in the butter and chocolate extract. Serve warm over ice cream or other desserts.

970 ■ HOT FUDGE SAUCE III

MAKES 1¼ CUPS

1 cup granulated sugar
¼ teaspoon baking powder
1½ tablespoons butter or margarine
2½ tablespoons Dutch processed cocoa powder
1 teaspoon chocolate extract
⅔ cup evaporated milk

1 Combine all of the ingredients in the container of a blender. Cover and blend on high speed until smooth. Pour into a medium saucepan. Over medium heat, stirring constantly, bring to a boil. Cook for 2 to 3 minutes, or until the mixture thickens slightly. Remove from the heat. Cool slightly and serve over ice cream or other desserts.

971 ■ HOT FUDGE SAUCE IV

MAKES 1¼ CUPS

1 cup half-and-half
8 ounces semisweet chocolate, grated or finely chopped
½ teaspoon chocolate extract

1 In a saucepan over low heat, warm the cream until bubbles start to form around three sides of the pan. Add the chocolate, stirring until smooth. Cook over low heat, stirring slowly, until the mixture thickens slightly. Remove from the heat and stir in the chocolate extract. Serve hot over ice cream or other desserts.

972 ■ HOT FUDGE TOPPING

MAKES 1¼ CUPS

4 ounces semisweet chocolate, grated or finely chopped
¼ cup butter or margarine
½ cup granulated sugar
⅓ cup heavy cream

1 In the top of a double boiler over simmering water, melt the chocolate and butter, stirring until smooth. Remove from the heat and stir in the cream and sugar until thoroughly blended. Serve warm.

967 968 969 970 971 972

973 ■ KAHLÚA COCOA SAUCE

MAKES 1⅓ CUPS

½ cup water
½ cup Dutch processed cocoa
   powder
½ cup granulated sugar
¼ cup light corn syrup
2 tablespoons Kahlúa
1 teaspoon coffee liqueur

1 In a small saucepan, over medium heat, combine the water, cocoa powder, sugar, and corn syrup. Bring to a boil, stirring constantly. Remove from heat. Stir in the Kahlúa and cool slightly. Stir in the liqueur. Serve warm or cold.

974 ■ LEMON FILLING

MAKES 1½ TO 1¾ CUPS
CHILL TIME: *30 minutes*

1 large egg yolk
1 cup skim milk
½ cup granulated sugar
2 tablespoons cornstarch or
   arrowroot
Pinch of salt
2 tablespoons fresh lemon juice
1 teaspoon grated lemon zest

1 In a small bowl, beat the egg yolk.
2 In a medium saucepan, over medium heat, combine the milk, sugar, cornstarch, and salt. Stirring constantly, cook until the mixture thickens. Remove from the heat. Pouring it in a thin stream, beat 2 tablespoons of the hot mixture into the beaten egg yolk. Stir the egg yolk into the saucepan and blend well. Return the mixture to the heat and cook for 2 minutes. Remove from the heat and cool slightly. Beat in the lemon juice and zest. Cover and chill thoroughly before using, about 30 minutes.

975 ■ LEMON GLAZE

MAKES ½ CUP

½ cup powdered sugar
1 tablespoon water
1 teaspoon fresh lemon juice

1 In a small bowl, combine all of the ingredients and mix thoroughly. Spread over a warm cake.

BAKING NOTES: For a more tart glaze, use lemon extract in place of the lemon juice.

976 ■ LEMON SAUCE

MAKES ½ CUP

½ cup water
3 tablespoons granulated sugar
2 tablespoons cornstarch or
   arrowroot
1 tablespoon fresh lemon juice
1½ teaspoons lemon extract
1 teaspoon butter or margarine
½ teaspoon grated lemon zest

1 In a small saucepan, over low heat, combine all of the ingredients. Increase the heat to medium, and cook, stirring constantly, until the mixture thickens. Remove from the heat and cool before using.

977 ■ MARZIPAN FROSTING

MAKES 1½ CUPS

1 cup almonds, finely ground
1 cup powdered sugar
3 large egg whites
1 teaspoon almond extract

1 Place the almonds and powdered sugar in the container of a blender and blend on high speed for 6 seconds.
2 In a medium bowl, using an electric mixer on high speed, beat the egg whites until stiff peaks form. Beat in the almond mixture. Fold in the almond extract. Use on cakes, cupcakes, or tortes.

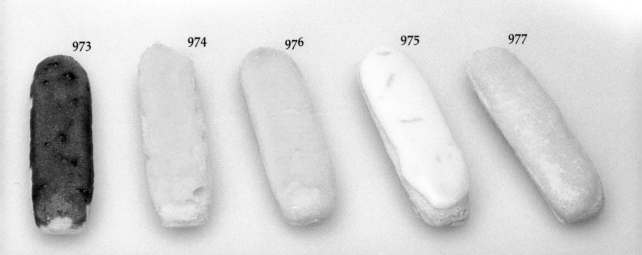

973 974 976 975 977

978 ■ MOCHA COFFEE SAUCE

MAKES 1¼ CUPS

1 cup strong brewed coffee
⅓ cup granulated sugar
3 large egg yolks
1 ounce semisweet chocolate, grated or finely chopped

1 In the top of a double boiler over simmering water, combine all of the ingredients and stir until blended. Raise the heat until the water is simmering and cook, stirring constantly, until the mixture thickens. Remove from the heat and cool to room temperature. Serve over ice cream, fresh fruit, or cake.

979 ■ MOCHA PASTRY CREAM

MAKES 3 CUPS
CHILL TIME: *30 minutes*

2 ounces semisweet chocolate, grated or finely chopped
1 cup heavy cream
1 cup strong brewed espresso
5 large egg yolks
¾ cup granulated sugar
2 teaspoon flour
2 tablespoons heavy cream
1 teaspoon coffee liqueur

1 In the top of a double boiler, over simmering water, melt the chocolate, stirring until smooth. Remove from the heat, add the cream and espresso, and stir until blended.

2 In a small bowl, using an electric mixer on medium speed, beat the egg yolks and sugar until thick and light-colored. Beat in the chocolate mixture. Combine the flour and cream and stir into the mixture.

3 Return the mixture to the top of the double boiler and cook, stirring constantly, until thick and smooth. Strain through a sieve to remove any lumps. Stir in the liqueur. Chill 30 minutes and use as a filling for cream puffs or eclairs.

980 ■ MOCHA WHIPPED CREAM FROSTING

MAKES 2 TO 2½ CUPS
CHILL TIME: *30 minutes*

⅓ cup powdered sugar
¼ cup Dutch processed cocoa powder
1 teaspoon instant coffee powder
1 cup heavy cream

1 Combine the powdered sugar, cocoa powder, and coffee powder.

2 In a large bowl, using an electric mixer on high speed, whip the cream until soft peaks form. Gradually beat in the dry ingredients, a tablespoonful at a time. Chill 30 minutes before using.

981 ■ NEVER FAIL CHOCOLATE FROSTING I

MAKES 1½ CUPS

3 ounces semisweet chocolate, grated or finely chopped
6 tablespoons butter or margarine
1⅓ cups powdered sugar
6 tablespoons evaporated milk or heavy cream

1 In the top of a double boiler over simmering water, melt the chocolate and butter, stirring until smooth. Beat in the powdered sugar and evaporated milk. Remove from the heat and beat until thickened. Cool slightly. Using an electric mixer on medium speed, beat until a spreadable consistency.

981

982

978

979

982 ■ NEVER FAIL CHOCOLATE FROSTING II

MAKES 2½ CUPS

2 cups granulated sugar
½ cup evaporated milk or heavy cream
½ cup butter or margarine
¼ cup light corn syrup
2 ounces unsweetened chocolate, grated or finely chopped
1 teaspoon chocolate extract
⅛ teaspoon salt

1 In a saucepan over low heat, combine the sugar, evaporated milk, butter, corn syrup, and chocolate. Cook until the butter and chocolate have melted, stirring constantly. Bring to a boil. Insert a candy thermometer and cook, stirring occasionally, until 220 degrees. Remove from the heat. Add the chocolate extract and salt and beat until thickened.

BAKING NOTES: This recipe makes enough to fill and frost a three-layer cake.

983 ■ NUT FUDGE SAUCE

MAKES 2 TO 2¼ CUPS

2 ounces semisweet chocolate, grated or finely chopped
1 ounce unsweetened chocolate, grated or finely chopped
2 tablespoons butter or margarine
¾ cup heavy cream
2 cups granulated sugar
1 cup packed brown sugar
1 teaspoon chocolate or almond extract
1 cup ground pecans

1 In the top of a double boiler over simmering water, combine the chocolates, butter, and cream and stir until smooth. Stir in the sugars and cook until the sugar is dissolved and tiny bubbles start to form around the sides of the pan. Remove from the heat and stir in the chocolate extract and ground pecans. Serve over ice cream, cakes, or pies.

984 ■ OLANDESE CACAO SALSA

MAKES 2 CUPS

1 cup heavy cream
¼ cup rose water
1 cup granulated vanilla sugar
1 cup Dutch processed cocoa powder

1 In a medium saucepan, over low heat, bring the cream to a boil. Add the rose water and return to a boil. Simmer for 2 minutes. Transfer to a medium bowl.

2 Using an electric mixer on high speed, beat the cream, sugar, and cocoa powder until smooth. Transfer to a double boiler set over simmering water and cook, stirring occasionally, for about 20 minutes. Strain through a sieve. Serve hot or cold over ice cream, cakes or pies.

983

984

980

985 ■ PARISCRÈME

MAKES 1½ TO 1¾ CUPS
CHILL TIME: *30 minutes*

1½ cups heavy cream
4 ounces semisweet chocolate,
    grated or finely chopped
¼ cup powdered sugar

1 In a medium saucepan, over medium heat, warm the cream until bubbles start to form around the sides of the pan. Remove from the heat. Add the chocolate and stir until smooth. Transfer to a large bowl. Chill thoroughly for 30 minutes until thickened.
2 Add the powdered sugar and whip until soft peaks form.

986 ■ PEANUT BUTTER AND HONEY SAUCE

MAKES 1½ TO 1¾ CUPS
CHILL TIME: *1 hour*

¾ cup creamy peanut butter
¾ cup heavy cream
⅓ cup honey
½ teaspoon vanilla extract

1 In a small bowl, combine all of the ingredients and beat until smooth. Cover and chill 1 hour before using. Let come to room temperature and serve over ice cream or pudding.

987 ■ PEANUT BUTTER FROSTING

MAKES ½ CUP

1½ cups powdered sugar
¼ cup creamy peanut butter

1 In a medium bowl, using an electric mixer on medium-high speed, beat the peanut butter and powdered sugar until smooth. Spread on cakes, brownies, or use as a filling.

988 ■ PLUM FILLING

MAKES ⅔ CUP

¾ pound fresh plums, skinned, pitted, and quartered
½ cup crème de prunelle or port
3 tablespoons powdered sugar

1 In a medium saucepan, over medium heat, combine the plums and crème de prunelle. Cook until the mixture is reduced to 1 cup. Remove from the heat and stir in the sugar. Return to the heat and cook until the mixture is reduced by one-third. Cool slightly before using.

989 ■ RASPBERRY SAUCE

MAKES 1¾ CUPS

¼ cup raspberry liqueur
2 packages (10 ounces each) frozen raspberries, thawed

1 Combine the liqueur and raspberries in the container of a blender. Blend on high speed for 15 to 20 seconds. Strain the mixture through a sieve. Chill until ready to use.

990 ■ RUM CREAM FROSTING

MAKES 2 TO 2¼ CUPS

1 cup heavy cream
3 tablespoons powdered sugar
2 teaspoons dark rum

1 In a medium bowl, using an electric mixer on high speed, whip the cream until it starts to thicken. Gradually beat in the powdered sugar. Beat in the rum. Beat until soft peaks form. Spread over baked goods or use as a topping on fruit.

991 ■ SIMPLE CHOCOLATE FROSTING

MAKES 1 CUP

2 cups powdered sugar
¼ cup Dutch processed cocoa powder
¼ cup butter or margarine
1 large egg white

1 Combine 1 cup of the powdered sugar and the cocoa powder.
2 In a medium bowl, using an electric mixer on medium speed, beat the butter and the remaining 1 cup powdered sugar until light and fluffy. Beat in the egg white. Beat in the cocoa mixture. If the frosting is too thick, add ½ teaspoon of water at a time, beating thoroughly after each addition.

992 ■ STRAWBERRY GLAZE

MAKES ¾ CUP

1 cup fresh strawberries, hulled and mashed
2 tablespoons powdered sugar
2 teaspoons cornstarch or arrowroot

990

985

1 In a medium saucepan, over medium heat, combine the strawberries, powdered sugar, and cornstarch. Stirring constantly, cook until the mixture thickens. Remove from the heat. Cool completely before using.

BAKING NOTES: Raspberries or blueberries can be used in place of the strawberries. Fresh fruit is preferable but frozen fruit that is thawed and well drained can be substituted.

993 ■ TORTEN FROSTING

MAKES 1 TO 1½ CUPS

4 ounces semisweet chocolate, grated or finely chopped
¾ cup water
½ cup granulated sugar

1 In a saucepan over low heat, melt the chocolate with the water and stir until smooth. Blend in the sugar, stirring until dissolved. Bring to a boil. Insert a candy thermometer and cook to 236 degrees. Remove from the heat. Using a wire whisk, beat until a spreadable consistency.

994 ■ VANILLA CUSTARD SAUCE

MAKES 1¾ TO 2 CUPS
CHILL TIME: *30 minutes*

1¾ cups heavy cream
2 tablespoons vanilla extract
4 large egg yolks
¼ cup granulated sugar
1½ teaspoons cornstarch or arrowroot

1 In a small saucepan, over medium heat, warm the cream until bubbles start to form around the sides of the pan. Remove from the heat and add the vanilla extract.

2 In a large bowl, beat the egg yolks until thick and light-colored. Beat in the sugar and cornstarch. Beat in about ½ cup of the hot cream. Beat the egg mixture into the saucepan. Over low heat, cook until the mixture is slightly thickened and coats the back of a spoon (170 to 180 degrees on a candy thermometer). Remove from the heat and strain into a bowl. Cover and chill 30 minutes before using.

BAKING NOTES: This type of sauce is also known as crème Anglaise.

995 ■ VELVET CHOCOLATE FILLING

MAKES 1½ CUP

5 large egg yolks
4 ounces semisweet chocolate, grated or finely chopped
7 tablespoons water
1 tablespoon butter or margarine, at room temperature
1 teaspoon crème de cacao or chocolate extract

1 In a medium bowl, using an electric mixer on medium speed, beat the egg yolks until thick and light-colored.

2 In the top of a double boiler over simmering water, melt the chocolate, stirring constantly until smooth. Stir in the water. Mix in the beaten egg yolks. Beat in the butter. Cook for 5 minutes, or until thick. Remove from the heat and stir in the crème de cacao. Cool until a spreadable consistency before using.

996 ■ WHIPPED HARD SAUCE

MAKES 2½ CUPS
CHILL TIME: *30 minutes*

¾ cup butter, at room temperature
3 cups powdered sugar
1 large egg white
6 tablespoons brandy

1 In a large bowl, using an electric mixer on medium speed, beat the butter and sugar until smooth. Beat in the egg white. Fold in the brandy. Chill for 30 minutes before using.

BAKING NOTES: Owing to the raw egg white used in this recipe, it should be kept refrigerated at all times, and for no longer than 3 days.

997 ■ WHITE CHOCOLATE SAUCE

MAKES 1¼ CUPS
CHILL TIME: *30 minutes*

1 cup heavy cream
3 ounces white chocolate or almond bark, grated or finely chopped

1 In a small saucepan, over low heat, warm the cream until bubbles start to form around the sides of the pan. Add the chocolate and stir constantly until smooth. Remove from the heat. Transfer to a small bowl. Cover and chill 30 minutes before using.

998 ■ WHITE FROSTING

MAKES 2 CUPS

½ cup light corn syrup
¼ cup water
4 large egg whites
1 cup powdered sugar
1 tablespoon vanilla or lemon extract
2 teaspoons butter, at room temperature
1 teaspoon fresh lemon juice

1 In a small saucepan, over medium heat, combine the corn syrup and water. Bring to a boil. Insert a candy thermometer and cook, without stirring, until 234 degrees. Keep the pan covered for the first 3 minutes.

2 Meanwhile, in a medium bowl, using an electric mixer on high speed, beat the egg whites until stiff but not dry. Pouring it in a thin stream, beat in the hot syrup. Beat in the powdered sugar, vanilla extract, butter, and lemon juice. Beat until the mixture is thick and a spreadable consistency.

996

997

998

Garnishes and Decorations

999 ■ APRICOT ROSES

MAKES 1 ROSE
FREEZING TIME: *30 minutes*

7 dried apricot halves
1/2 cup apricot liqueur
Chocolate Leaves (see page 422)

1 In a small bowl, place the apricot halves and pour the liqueur over them. Soak for at least 1 hour.

2 Drain, reserving the soaking liquid for another use. Lightly pat the apricots dry with paper towels. Place one of the halves between two sheets of waxed paper. Using a rolling pin, roll out the half as thinly as possible. Repeat with the remaining apricot halves.

3 To form a flower, roll one of the flattened apricot halves around itself to make a very tight cylinder. To add petals, place another apricot half against the cylinder and pinch at the base to make it stick. Repeat with the remaining apricot halves until a rose in full bloom is formed.

4 Insert a wooden toothpick into the base of the cylinder and trim the bottom of the flower as necessary. Curl the outside tips of each petal. Place on a baking sheet and freeze for 30 minutes, or until firm.

5 Place the rose on a frosted cake and brush the petal tips with water. Dust the rose with coarse granulated sugar or sugar crystals. Arrange chocolate leaves around the flower using small amounts of moist frosting as an adhesive.

BAKING NOTES: For best results, roll out the apricot halves as thinly as possible. Other dried fruits can also be used. Dried peaches make paler-colored roses. Purchased fruit leather can also be used and has the advantage of being paper-thin. Craft books on artificial flower making will have patterns for rose petals that can be used with the fruit leather.

1000 ■ CANDIED ROSE PETALS

YIELD WILL VARY ACCORDING TO THE
SIZE OF THE PETALS (50 TO 150 PETALS)
SOAKING TIME: *10 minutes*
DRYING TIME: *30 minutes*

6 cups rose petals
2 1/2 cups granulated sugar
2 cups water

1 Lightly rinse the rose petals and pat dry on a clean dish towel.

2 In a medium saucepan, over medium heat, combine the sugar and water. Insert a candy thermometer and cook until 270 degrees. Remove from the heat and add the dry rose petals. Leave the petals in the syrup 10 minutes, or until they become almost transparent.

3 Remove the petals with a slotted spoon and place on a wire rack or screen for 30 minutes, or until dry. When the petals have crystallized, store in an airtight container until using.

BAKING NOTES: Use the petals to garnish cakes. These are also edible.

1001 ■ CHOCOLATE BARK

MAKES 3 OUNCES
CHILL TIME: *5 minutes*

3 ounces semisweet chocolate, grated or finely chopped

1 Line a baking sheet with waxed paper.

2 Melt the chocolate (see page 13). Remove from the heat. Pour the chocolate onto the prepared pan and spread out evenly to a thickness of 1/8 inch. Chill for 5 minutes, or until hard.

3 Remove from the refrigerator and shake the paper over the baking sheet as if you were shaking out a towel. This will break the chocolate into strips and slivers.

4 To use, press the chocolate slivers into the top or sides of a cake to give it the appearance of bark.

BAKING NOTES: This garnish works well on rolled cakes to make a Yule log.

999

1000

1001

1002 ■ CHOCOLATE CIGARETTES

MAKES 1 DOZEN CIGARETTES

3 ounces semisweet chocolate, grated or finely chopped

1 Melt the chocolate (see page 13). Remove from the heat and stir constantly until the temperature of the chocolate drops to 88 to 91 degrees.

2 Scrape the chocolate onto a clean, flat surface and spread out into a long 3-inch wide band no thicker than 1/8 inch. Allow to cool until the chocolate is firm but not set. Using a knife, score the chocolate at 3 or 4-inch intervals. Hold a plastic scraper at a 45-degree angle to the chocolate at the first scored line. Push the scraper along, allowing the chocolate to roll up into cigarettes as you go. Carefully transfer the cigarettes to a waxed paper-lined baking sheet and cool to room temperature.

BAKING NOTES: These are actually very easy to make. The first time will be the most difficult, but once you have made one or two cigarettes you will see how easy it is. Work quickly because you only have a few minutes before the chocolate becomes too hard to work with. The broken ones and scraps can be remelted and used again.

1003 ■ CHOCOLATE-COATED ALMONDS

MAKES 1 POUND
CHILL TIME: *30 minutes*

3 ounces semisweet or unsweetened chocolate, grated
3 1/2 cups whole almonds, toasted

1 In the top of a double boiler over simmering water, melt the chocolate, stirring until smooth. Remove from the heat, leaving the top of the double boiler over the pan of hot water.

2 Dip the almonds, one at a time, into the chocolate and place on a waxed paper-lined baking sheet. Chill for 30 minutes, or until set.

BAKING NOTES: Honey-roasted almonds can also be used. The almonds can be hand clustered to form flowers or leaves.

1004 ■ CHOCOLATE CONES

MAKES 1 DOZEN
CHILL TIME: *1 hour*

2 ounces semisweet chocolate, grated or finely chopped
1 teaspoon butter

1 In the top of a double boiler over simmering water, melt the chocolate and butter, stirring until smooth. Remove from the heat.

2 Cut parchment paper or waxed paper into six 4-inch squares. Cut the squares diagonally in half to form triangles. Roll into cones and tape securely. Trim the tops evenly.

3 Place 1 teaspoon of the melted chocolate inside of each cone. Using a small paint brush, brush the chocolate over the inside of the cone, about 1/16 to 1/8 inch thick. Place on a waxed paper-lined baking sheet and chill for 1 hour or until hard. Carefully tear the paper away from the chocolate cones. Place on the baking sheet and chill until using.

BAKING NOTES: These can be used like chocolate cigarettes. Lay them on their sides on the top of a cake. Place crushed nuts or Hershey's™ Chocolate Shoppe Candy Bar Sprinkles inside the cones for added decoration.

1002

1003

1007

GARNISHES AND DECORATIONS ■

1005 ■ CHOCOLATE CURLS

CHILL TIME: *30 minutes*

Semisweet, milk, or white chocolate bars

1 Line a baking sheet with waxed paper.

2 Dip the blade of a sharp vegetable peeler in hot water and wipe dry. Grasp the chocolate with a paper towel so that the heat from your hand does not melt the chocolate. Scrape the vegetable peeler along one of the edges in a downward motion to form tight curls, letting them fall onto the prepared pan. Warm the blade again in hot water, if necessary. Cover and chill the curls 30 minutes, or until using. Use the top of a knife or a pair of tweezers to handle the curls.

BAKING NOTES: There are many ways to make chocolate curls. This method is easiest for the home baker. If the chocolate is too cold, it will form shavings rather than curls. If this happens, warm the surface of the chocolate a little by placing your hand on it. If it is too warm, strips of chocolate rather than curls are formed. A melon baller can also be used. The harder you scrape the chocolate the more open the curl will be.

1006 ■ CHOCOLATE CUTOUTS

MAKES 1 CUP
CHILL TIME: *30 minutes*

1 cup semisweet chocolate chips
2 tablespoons vegetable shortening

1 Line a baking sheet with aluminum foil or parchment paper.

2 In the top of a double boiler over simmering water, melt the chocolate and shortening, stirring until smooth. Pour the mixture onto the prepared pan and spread out to a thickness of ¼ inch. Cool until set but not hardened. The chocolate should not be allowed to harden and become brittle.

3 Use cookie cutters or a stencil and a sharp knife to cut out the desired shapes. Transfer the cutouts to a waxed paper-lined baking sheet ½-inch apart and cool completely. Cover and chill 30 minutes, or until using.

BAKING NOTES: Semisweet chocolate or white chocolate can be substituted for the chocolate chips. When a cookie cutter is not available, draw the design on paper or cardboard and cut out. Use it as a stencil and cut out the shape in the chocolate with a sharp, heavy knife.

1007 ■ CHOCOLATE LEAVES

MAKES 2 DOZEN LEAVES
CHILL TIME: *1 hour*

24 1½-inch long fresh-picked leaves (see Baking notes)
2 ounces semisweet chocolate, grated or finely chopped, OR ½ cup semisweet chocolate chips
1 teaspoon butter
2 ounces almond bark

1 Thoroughly wash the leaves and pat dry with paper towels. Line a baking sheet with waxed paper.

2 In the top of a double boiler over simmering water, melt the chocolate and butter, stirring until smooth. Remove from the heat, leaving the top of the double boiler over the pan of hot water.

3 Using a pastry brush, spread the chocolate on the underside of the leaves, about ⅛ inch thick. Do not coat over the edges or it will be difficult to separate the chocolate from the leaves. Place on the prepared pan and chill for 30 minutes to 1 hour, or until hard.

4 Starting at the stem end, carefully peel the leaves off the chocolate. Place the chocolate leaves on the pan and chill until using.

1004

1005

1006

BAKING NOTES: Not all leaves are safe to use in this recipe. See page 22 for edible plants that are safe to use. For white chocolate leaves, substitute 2 ounces white chocolate or almond bark OR ½ cup white chocolate chips.

1008 ■ CHOCOLATE MINT LEAVES

MAKES 24 LEAVES
CHILL TIME: *1 hour*

24 camellia leaves of assorted sizes
3 ounces mint-flavored semisweet chocolate chips, grated or finely chopped
1 teaspoon vegetable shortening

1 Line a baking sheet with waxed paper. Wash the leaves and pat dry with paper towels.

2 In the top of a double boiler over simmering water, melt the chocolate and shortening, stirring constantly until smooth. Remove from the heat.

3 Using a small pastry brush, spread the chocolate over the underside of the leaves. Do not allow any of the chocolate to drip over the edges or it will be difficult to separate the chocolate from the leaves. Place on the prepared pan and chill for 30 minutes, or until hard.

4 Starting at the stem end, carefully peel the leaves off the chocolate. Place the chocolate leaves on the pan and chill for 1 hour or until using.

1009 ■ HAND MODELING CHOCOLATE

STANDING TIME: *1 hour*

3 ounces semisweet chocolate or white chocolate
4½ teaspoons corn syrup

1 In the top of a double boiler over simmering water, melt the chocolate, stirring until smooth. Add the corn syrup and stir until well blended. Pour the mixture into an airtight container. Cover and let stand at room temperature for at least one hour.

2 Knead the mixture until it forms a workable dough. Use the dough to make flowers, leaves, or other decorations.

BAKING NOTES: The kneading is vital. The chocolate should be worked over and over again until smooth and elastic.

1010 ■ SUGARED ALMONDS

MAKES 1½ CUPS

1¼ cups water
1 cup granulated sugar
2 teaspoons honey
1 teaspoon vanilla extract
1 cup sliced almonds

1 Position a rack in the center of the oven and preheat the oven to 400 degrees.

2 In a medium saucepan, over medium heat, combine the water, sugar, honey, and vanilla extract. Bring to a boil, stirring occasionally, until the sugar dissolves. Add the almonds and simmer, without stirring, for 3 to 5 minutes. Remove from the heat and immediately strain through a sieve. Discard the syrup. Spread the almonds in an even layer on a baking sheet.

3 Bake for 6 to 10 minutes, stirring occasionally, until a light-golden color. Cool and store in an airtight container.

1008

1009

1010

INDEX

Abricotine, 102, 103

All Bran cereal, 167

Allspice, 76, 88, 96, 97, 115, 143, 210, 225, 229, 230, 271, 297, 335, 339, 342, 352, 353, 358, 392

Almond bark, 187, 195, 196, 204, 241, 255, 313, 329, 328, 410, 418, 422

Almond crust, 261, 289

Almond extract, 34, 35, 36, 40, 44, 46, 61, 72, 77, 84, 86, 87, 91, 101, 113, 114, 120, 123, 128, 136, 137, 138, 144, 154, 159, 161, 162, 164, 167, 171, 183, 185, 188, 190, 191, 194, 198, 200, 202, 203, 204, 207, 208, 211, 213, 214, 215, 220, 221, 230, 234, 235, 238, 240, 241, 258, 259, 264, 265, 266, 267, 283, 289, 298, 302, 305, 310, 311, 316, 329, 330, 332, 334, 335, 337, 345, 349, 356, 362, 367, 374, 379, 381, 394, 395, 396, 413, 415

Almond Glaze, 128

Almond paste, 77, 169, 187, 189, 198

Almonds, 34, 35, 45, 46, 58, 59, 62, 69, 74, 76, 78, 86, 93, 109, 114, 118, 120, 123, 130, 135, 135, 140, 143, 161, 166, 168, 171, 173, 178, 183, 185, 186, 188, 189, 191, 198, 200, 202, 203, 204, 205, 206, 207, 208, 210, 216, 217, 219, 221, 222, 223, 225, 227, 231, 234, 235, 238, 239, 252, 254, 258, 261, 264, 265, 272, 277, 280, 284, 295, 305, 308, 312, 317, 319, 323, 327, 328, 332, 333, 334, 335, 337, 339, 349, 350, 357, 362, 364, 366, 369, 370, 372, 373, 374, 375, 377, 378, 379, 384, 392, 394, 395, 396, 397, 413, 421, 423

Almonds, continued

  chocolate-covered, 296

  wafer cookies, 374

Amaretti, 374

Amaretto, 34, 35, 36, 43, 46, 47, 58, 59, 62, 72, 81, 85, 104, 114, 136, 142, 177, 193, 198, 223, 258, 261, 263, 292, 296, 303, 305, 308, 311, 312, 323, 327, 330, 339, 356, 368, 369, 370, 379, 382, 395, 411

  coconut, 276

Ambrosia liqueur, 47

Angel food cake, 314

Apple chips, dried, 237

Apple juice, 235

Apple pie filling, 36

Apples, 36, 49, 297, 299, 340, 384, 392

Applesauce, 37, 115

Apricot glaze, 47, 66, 83, 133, 378

Apricot jam, 354

Apricot liqueur, 38, 102, 103, 132, 198, 370, 420

Apricot preserves, 100, 204, 379, 389, 394

Apricots, 38, 43, 83, 101, 103, 106, 154, 168, 174, 198, 309, 311, 339, 340, 362, 370, 378, 420

Aquavit, 296

Arrowroot, 45, 55, 76, 77, 82, 99, 102, 140, 141, 142, 159, 162, 164, 238, 254, 266, 268, 275, 288, 293, 296, 311, 312, 313, 322, 328, 334, 354, 370, 380, 396, 397, 399, 402, 404, 405, 406, 409, 413, 416, 417

Ashanti Gold liqueur, 405

Baitz Island Cream liqueur, 77

Banana extract, 49, 169, 333

Banana-flavored pudding, 320

Bananas, 38, 49, 50, 204, 270, 277, 294, 323, 332, 333, 336, 353, 367, 385

Beef, chuck, 390

Beets, 35

Berries, 24, 163

Biscotti, 384

Bisquick mix, 344

Bittersweet Chocolate liqueur, 111

Black beans, 52

Bourbon, 136, 287

  Wild Turkey, 330

Brandy, 35, 46, 88, 334, 418

  cherry-, 53, 64

  coffee-flavored, 324

  Hard Sauce, 327

Brazil nuts, 190, 346

Bread, crumbs, 295, 299, 308, 316, 325, 371, 373, 390, 392

  French, 385

  white-, 326

Buttercream frosting, 88

Buttermilk, 34, 35, 44, 53, 54, 56, 57, 69, 77, 78, 84, 94, 97, 99, 101, 102, 104, 106, 107, 108, 113, 114, 118, 124, 125, 127, 131, 132, 141, 142, 146, 147, 148, 153, 155, 156, 159, 161, 168, 201, 219, 221, 271, 285, 292, 307, 333, 339, 342, 345, 346, 348, 355, 357, 359, 363

Butterscotch, 170, 182, 194, 205, 216, 235, 340

Cake crumbs, 316

Camellia leaves, 423

Campari, 150, 403

Caramel, 44, 101, 193

  Glaze, 148

  topping, 206

Caramella liqueur, 171, 173

Cardamom, 46

Carrots, 337

Celery leaves, 129

Celery salt, 384, 392

Cheddar cheese, 207

Cheri-Suisse, 64

Cherries 164, 171, 253, 262, 277, 334, 338, 366, 378

  candied, 175, 183, 188, 191, 277, 333

  chocolate-covered, 121, 301

  dried, 308, 312, 327, 334, 338, 343, 346, 357, 364

  glacé, 37, 58, 64, 68, 225

  maraschino, 26, 35, 53, 59, 105, 124, 172, 252, 259, 260, 319, 378, 408

Cherry extract, 53

Cherry juice, maraschino, 259

Cherry liqueur, 64, 171, 202, 262, 277, 305, 323, 364

  maraschino, 64, 172

Cherry pie filling, 40, 45, 64, 296

Chestnuts, 65, 263, 367

  puree, 65, 123

Chicken, 384, 390, 392

Chicken broth, 392

Chicken stock, 384

Chili powder, 390, 392

Chocolate, 78

  almond sauce, 337

  bittersweet, 124, 307

  cake crumbs, 90, 130, 325

  cake mix, p.47, 70, 119

  candies, 104, 125

  cherry frosting, 153

  chip cookies, 268

  chips, 68, 143, 234, 235, 237, 248, 312, 333, 354, 362

  cigarettes, 74, 136, 258

  coffee bean candies, 318

  cones, 110, 276, 375

  Cookie crumb crust, 163, 248, 252, 275, 278, 303

  Cookies, 279, 312, 313, 324

  Corn flake pie shell, 275

  Cream de Chantilly, 156

  Cream-filled cookies, 281

  curls, 26, 46, 48, 53, 55, 68, 79, 89, 103, 111, 121, 130, 139, 251, 259, 260, 261, 262, 265, 268, 272, 277, 285, 292, 301, 308, 309,

Chocolate, curls, continued
321, 322, 351, 373, 374, 388

  Custard filling, 155

  Custard sauce, 155, 316

  Cutouts, 273

  Dipping, 166, 171, 172, 173, 181, 182, 185, 187, 192, 215, 217, 218, 227

  extract, 25, 26, 27, 28, 32, 34, 35, 36, 38, 39, 43, 44, 48, 50, 52, 53, 54, 55, 56, 57, 58, 60, 61, 62, 63, 64, 65, 66, 67, 68, 73, 74, 75, 76, 78, 79, 80, 82, 83, 84, 85, 86, 87, 88, 94, 95, 96, 97, 99, 100, 101, 102, 103, 104, 105, 106, 107, 110, 112, 113, 114, 116, 118, 120, 121, 122, 123, 124, 125, 128, 131, 133, 134, 135, 137, 138, 141, 142, 146, 147, 148, 149, 150, 151, 152, 153, 155, 156, 158, 159, 160, 163, 166, 167, 168, 171, 173, 174, 175, 176, 178, 180, 181, 182, 184, 186, 187, 188, 191, 192, 194, 199, 200, 201, 204, 205, 208, 209, 210, 211, 212, 213, 214, 215, 216, 219, 220, 221, 222, 223, 225, 226, 227, 228, 229, 231, 232, 233, 234, 235, 237, 238, 239, 240, 241, 242, 244, 245, 246, 247, 249, 250, 251, 252, 253, 258, 261, 262, 264, 266, 267, 268, 270, 271, 272, 273, 274, 275, 278, 280, 281, 282, 288, 293, 294, 295, 296, 298, 299, 300, 301, 306, 307, 311, 312, 316, 321, 322, 325, 326, 328, 330, 334, 335, 336, 337, 339, 344, 345, 347, 348, 350, 351, 352, 353, 355, 357, 358, 359, 361, 362, 363, 369, 370, 372, 374, 380, 385, 387, 388, 389, 394, 395, 396, 397, 398, 399, 400, 401, 402, 403, 404, 405, 406, 407, 408, 409, 410, 412, 415, 417

  filling, 80, 86, 156

Chocolate, continued
  frosting, 34, 35, 36, 44, 53, 54, 56, 57, 60, 72, 78, 82, 87, 94, 99, 112, 113, 119, 121, 136, 137, 140, 146, 159, 199, 225, 234, 236, 240, 288, 342, 358, 362, 370, 378

  glaze, 36, 39, 54, 80, 84, 86, 96, 98, 105, 107, 109, 112, 123, 136, 140, 144, 152, 158, 201, 207, 370, 381

  grated, 26, 29, 137, 143, 146

  Hazelnut crust, 258, 286

  hot-, 94

  Hot fudge sauce, 252

  kisses, 267

  leaves, 48, 55, 63, 64, 65, 75, 78, 89, 93, 102, 103, 110, 118, 119, 137, 154, 252, 260, 263, 278, 289, 303, 308, 314, 358, 369, 370, 371, 378, 379, 420

  Marshmallow sauce, 322

  milk-, 51, 128, 156, 172, 182, 183, 185, 186, 192, 193, 223, 327, 363, 352

  mint-, 156, 222, 330

  Mocha meringue, 262

  Pastry crust, 262, 263, 264, 265, 266, 273, 278, 281, 283

  peanut butter cups, 249

  peppermint candy, 402

  pie shell, 286

  pudding, 25, 34, 42, 45, 64, 88, 118, 119, 158, 209, 226, 247, 262, 277, 284, 292, 294, 296, 302, 316, 320, 339, 341, 352, 368, 374, 391

  Quark cream filling, 156, 352, 403

  Ricotta Filling, 130

  rum icing, 97

  Rum sauce, 49, 104

  sandwich cookies, 146

  sauce, 123, 128, 244, 248, 252, 254, 278, 313, 325, 332, 354, 361, 388, 391, 395

  semisweet, 28, 29, 31, 34, 35, 36, 38, 39, 42, 43, 45, 46, 49, 50, 52, 53, 55, 57,

Chocolate, semisweet, continued

58, 59, 60, 61, 62, 63, 65,
67, 68, 71, 74, 75, 78, 79,
81, 82, 83, 84, 85, 86, 87,
89, 93, 95, 96, 97, 98, 100,
101, 102, 103, 106, 107,
109, 110, 111, 114, 115,
116, 110, 120, 121, 122,
123, 126, 129, 130, 131,
133, 136, 137, 139, 140,
141, 142, 146, 147, 148,
150, 151, 152, 154, 156,
157, 158, 159, 160, 164,
166, 167, 168, 169, 170,
171, 172, 173, 174, 175,
176, 177, 178, 179, 180,
181, 182, 185, 186, 187,
188, 189, 190, 191, 192,
193, 194, 198, 200, 201,
203, 204, 205, 206, 207,
208, 209, 210, 211, 212,
213, 214, 215, 216, 217,
219, 220, 221, 222, 223,
224, 229, 231, 232, 234,
235, 236, 237, 238, 239,
240, 242, 244, 245, 246,
247, 249, 250, 251, 252,
253, 254, 258, 259, 260,
261, 262, 263, 264, 265,
267, 268, 269, 272, 273,
274, 275, 277, 278, 279,
281, 282, 283, 285, 286,
287, 288, 292, 293, 296,
297, 300, 301, 302, 303,
304, 305, 307, 308, 309,
310, 313, 314, 315, 316,
317, 319, 320, 321, 322,
323, 324, 325, 326, 327,
328, 330, 332, 333, 334,
335, 337, 338, 339, 342,
343, 344, 345, 348, 349,
350, 351, 352, 353, 355,
357, 358, 360, 361, 362,
363, 366, 367, 368, 369,
370, 371, 373, 374, 375,
376, 377, 378, 384, 385,
386, 387, 388, 391, 392,
395, 396, 397, 398, 400,
401, 402, 403, 404, 405,
406, 410, 412, 414, 415,
416, 417, 420, 421, 422
shaved, 156, 357
sprinkles, 63, 109, 110, 137,
167, 176, 227, 238, 244,
253, 287, 299, 307, 337,
338, 342, 360
syrup, 25, 26, 27, 28, 29, 30,
50, 51, 53, 78, 80, 91, 99,

Chocolate, syrup, continued

125, 128, 132, 134, 141,
145, 200, 228, 231, 236,
248, 264, 298, 299, 312,
322, 323, 357, 360, 374,
385
unsweetened, 24, 28, 31,
34, 35, 38, 39, 43, 44, 45,
46, 47, 50, 52, 53, 54, 55,
57, 59, 60, 63, 65, 68, 69,
72, 73, 74, 76, 77, 82, 84,
86, 87, 88, 92, 93, 94, 95,
99, 101, 108, 111, 112, 113,
114, 116, 118, 119, 122,
125, 128, 129, 131, 134,
135, 136, 138, 140, 143,
146, 147, 148, 149, 150,
152, 153, 155, 156, 157,
158, 160, 164, 166, 167,
168, 169, 170, 174, 175,
176, 177, 178, 179, 181,
182, 189, 190, 191, 192,
193, 194, 195, 198, 199,
200, 201, 202, 203, 204,
205, 207, 211, 212, 213,
215, 216, 220, 221, 223,
224, 226, 227, 228, 230,
238, 239, 242, 245, 246,
249, 250, 251, 254, 259,
261, 266, 267, 286, 270,
271, 272, 275, 276, 277,
279, 280, 281, 282, 285,
286, 288, 292, 293, 294,
295, 299, 300, 301, 302,
303, 304, 305, 306, 310,
311, 312, 313, 314, 316,
318, 319, 321, 322, 323,
324, 325, 326, 328, 330,
337, 343, 346, 347, 349,
350, 352, 354, 355, 356,
358, 363, 368, 370, 371,
372, 373, 374, 375, 376,
377, 378, 379, 384, 385,
389, 390, 394, 395, 396,
397, 398, 399, 400, 401,
402, 403, 404, 406, 408,
410, 415, 421
wafer cookies, 40, 46, 49,
63, 76, 81, 89, 123, 126,
159, 205, 228, 246, 248,
249, 254, 259, 260, 267,
268, 270, 271, 272, 273,
286, 294, 296, 302, 304,
316
white, 42, 59, 63, 65, 68, 76,
77, 78, 79, 82, 83, 84, 108,
109, 110, 136, 138, 144,
157, 161, 162, 163, 189,

Chocolate, continued

194, 195, 196, 198, 200,
204, 211, 241, 242, 255,
289, 301, 308, 313, 322,
328, 329, 364, 370, 371,
373, 410, 418, 422, 423.
See also Heath Bars™
Chocolate liqueur, white, 289
Chow mein noodles, 182, 183
Chrysanthemums, 59
Cinnamon, 25, 27, 32, 36, 37,
44, 49, 73, 74, 76, 78, 82,
87, 88, 89, 90, 96, 97, 102,
105, 113, 114, 129, 130,
135, 143, 148, 154, 159,
163, 189, 192, 201, 202,
206, 225, 227, 230, 249,
263, 278, 299, 308, 312,
326, 327, 333, 335, 337,
339, 340, 342, 343, 347,
348, 349, 350, 351, 352,
353, 355, 361, 376, 384,
385, 386, 390, 410
stick, 31
Citron, candied, 143, 225
Cloves, 27, 49, 76, 78, 87, 96,
105, 129, 202, 225, 227,
230, 278, 308, 312, 327,
348, 349, 361
Club soda, 145
Cocoa, 24, 25, 27, 29, 30, 31,
32, 34, 35, 36, 37, 38, 39,
40, 44, 45, 49, 54, 56, 58,
59, 61, 62, 64, 66, 67, 69,
71, 72, 73, 76, 77, 79, 80,
83, 85, 86, 87, 88, 89, 92,
93, 94, 95, 96, 97, 100,
101, 102, 104, 105, 106,
107, 108, 109, 110, 111,
113, 114, 115, 116, 120,
121, 123, 124, 126, 127,
128, 129, 131, 132, 136,
138, 139, 140, 141, 142,
143, 146, 147, 148, 149,
151, 152, 153, 154, 158,
159, 160, 164, 166, 173,
177, 179, 181, 182, 183,
184, 185, 189, 190, 192,
199, 201, 202, 203, 204,
205, 206, 209, 210, 212,
213, 218, 219, 220, 222,
225, 226, 229, 230, 232,
233, 235, 236, 237, 238,
239, 240, 241, 242, 244,
247, 248, 249, 250, 252,
253, 261, 263, 266, 267,
273, 274, 277, 278, 279,

Cocoa, continued

282, 285, 296, 298, 299,
301, 306, 307, 308, 309,
311, 312, 313, 322, 323,
328, 332, 334, 335, 336,
337, 339, 340, 341, 342,
344, 345, 346, 347, 348,
349, 350, 351, 353, 354,
356, 359, 360, 363, 366,
367, 368, 370, 372, 376,
381, 382, 387, 388, 395,
399, 401, 402, 404, 405,
406, 407, 408, 409, 410,
412, 413, 414, 415, 416

beans, 389

syrup, 26

Cocoa cream topping, 67,
101, 129, 382

Cocoa frosting, 110, 151

Cocoa glaze, 132, 375

Cocoa honey frosting, 47

Cocoa Sugar, 45, 49, 50, 65,
67, 68, 73, 92, 103, 138,
143, 147, 154, 169, 176,
210, 225, 226, 233, 234,
262, 270, 294, 300, 321,
344, 345, 350, 353, 376

Coconut, 49, 95, 101, 106,
107, 124, 136, 150, 159,
161, 167, 171, 181, 185,
186, 190, 191, 193, 194,
195, 196, 198, 205, 208,
211, 212, 213, 217, 220,
231, 232, 240, 258, 261,
265, 266, 275, 279, 302,
339, 352, 374, 396

Chocolate pie crust, 274,
279

extract, 28

liqueur, 30, 396

milk, 28

pie crust, 266, 272, 287

Coffee, 24, 26, 27, 29, 69, 74,
82, 83, 104, 106, 107, 109,
110, 127, 130, 136, 137,
147, 150, 189, 226, 254,
285, 295, 314, 322, 323,
346, 369, 384, 386, 414

beans, 254

espresso-, 30, 46, 63, 89,
108, 176, 185, 242, 244,
245, 251, 253, 254, 301,
302, 303, 304, 307, 312,
316, 320, 321, 341, 367,
371, 374, 391, 398, 414

Coffee, continued

hazelnut-flavored, 88

Hard sauce, 35, 346, 348

mocha-flavored, 49, 55, 58,
66, 81, 82, 88, 108, 116,
136, 211, 218, 282, 296,
325, 328, 346, 375, 394,
402, 408

powder, 24, 25, 30, 31, 32,
59, 62, 65, 69, 96, 108,
131, 138, 143, 149, 155,
217, 219, 252, 287, 318,
321, 414

Coffee liqueur, 24, 27, 32, 38,
42, 48, 54, 59, 60, 61, 62,
63, 66, 69, 71, 73, 76, 81,
82, 83, 87, 88, 92, 95, 96,
104, 106, 108, 110, 111,
117, 122, 123, 124, 125,
127, 131, 132, 134, 136,
137, 143, 149, 169, 177,
190, 192, 206, 218, 219,
250, 251, 252, 253, 266,
270, 285, 287, 300, 302,
303, 309, 313, 314, 318,
321, 322, 323, 325, 326,
329, 337, 341, 346, 352,
353, 354, 359, 367, 375,
386, 388, 391, 395, 398,
401, 404, 406, 408, 412,
413, 414

Coffee mocha icing, 92, 96,
138

Cola beverage, 26

Coloring, food. *See* Food
coloring

Conticream liqueur, 385

Cookies, 320

Coriander, 392

Corn cereal, puffed, 191

Cornflakes, 171, 267, 280, 288

Cornmeal, 31, 390

white, 166

Cottage cheese, 109, 163

Crackers, saltine, 213, 280

Cranberries, 152, 296, 346

Cream

chocolate whipped, 24, 26,
47, 56, 63, 65, 68, 89, 94,
97, 111, 115, 120, 135, 251,
259, 261, 264, 266, 268,
274, 276, 282, 292, 293,
296, 297, 299, 300, 301,
309, 311, 321, 326, 327,

Cream, chocolate whipped, continued

328, 334, 351, 371, 374,
380

heavy, 24, 26, 27, 28, 29, 30,
32, 34, 35, 36, 38, 39, 40,
42, 45, 46, 48, 55, 57, 61,
62, 63, 64, 65, 67, 69, 70,
71, 76, 77, 79, 83, 85, 88,
89, 92, 93, 98, 100, 102,
103, 108, 114, 117, 121,
124, 127, 131, 132, 134,
135, 137, 139, 142, 143,
146, 148, 149, 150, 151,
152, 162, 166, 167, 168,
169, 171, 172, 173, 174,
175, 176, 177, 180, 181,
182, 184, 185, 186, 188,
192, 194, 195, 196, 213,
214, 228, 244, 245, 246,
247, 248, 249, 250, 251,
252, 253, 254, 255, 258,
259, 260, 262, 263, 267,
268, 269, 270, 272, 273,
275, 277, 278, 281, 282,
285, 286, 287, 289, 292,
293, 294, 295, 296, 299,
300, 301, 302, 303, 304,
305, 306, 307, 308, 309,
311, 312, 313, 314, 315,
316, 317, 318, 319, 321,
323, 324, 326, 327, 328,
329, 330, 334, 335, 336,
341, 342, 345, 347, 354,
360, 362, 364, 366, 367,
368, 369, 371, 377, 378,
379, 385, 389, 394, 395,
396, 397, 398, 399, 401,
403, 402, 404, 406, 407,
408, 409, 410, 411, 412,
414, 415, 416, 418

light, 61, 105, 143, 177, 203

whipped, 26, 30, 64, 73, 76,
102, 160, 249, 269, 271,
289, 282, 294, 296, 298,
302, 303, 305, 319, 320,
350, 351

Cream cheese, 35, 36, 39, 40,
43, 44, 46, 57, 62, 69, 81,
82, 89, 91, 106, 107, 108,
109, 110, 111, 117, 118,
123, 125, 126, 135, 137,
147, 150, 163, 164, 173,
186, 198, 208, 214, 215,
220, 221, 222, 235, 239,
267, 276, 277, 281, 284,
296, 307, 321, 337, 339,
340, 389, 396, 397

Cream cheese, continued
frosting, 105
Cream puff pastry, 342, 361
Creamer, non-dairy, 30
Crème de banana, 49
Crème de cacao, 24, 25, 27,
28, 30, 31, 32, 48, 52, 53,
56, 63, 67, 69, 74, 76, 84,
87, 88, 90, 92, 94, 95, 98,
102, 106, 109, 110, 111,
112, 118, 119, 120, 124,
125, 126, 127, 139, 143,
148, 150, 152, 153, 158,
164, 166, 167, 168, 169,
170, 174, 175, 179, 182,
183, 185, 186, 189, 201,
206, 210, 219, 228, 236,
239, 245, 246, 251, 254,
259, 263, 264, 268, 269,
270, 272, 273, 279, 281,
282, 289, 293, 297, 300,
301, 302, 303, 306, 307,
310, 312, 313, 314, 322,
324, 328, 333, 342, 343,
344, 351, 355, 358, 363,
367, 368, 374, 376, 379,
381, 385, 387, 388, 390,
394, 395, 397, 398, 400,
401, 402, 403, 404, 406,
409, 410, 417
Crème de cassis, 324
Crème de fraises, 127
Crème de framboise, 93, 181,
377
Crème de menthe, 26, 75, 281
green, 37, 125, 126, 177,
235, 411
white, 156, 184, 207, 210,
235, 248
Crème de menthe, green
icing, 118
Crème de noyeau, 272
Crème de prunelle, 88, 114,
138, 149, 317, 323, 416
Crème Fraîche, 66, 328
Croutons, 299, 390
Cumin, 390
Curaçao, 286, 392
Currants, 163, 356
black, 92, 277
black jelly, 319, 322
black preserves, 278
Custard filling, 43, 56

Dates, 34, 67, 70, 113, 154,
160, 207, 216, 228, 302,
342, 348
Dessert Glaze, 68
Dessert Syrup, 102, 139, 276,
283
Droste bittersweet liqueur,
394
Egg
whites, 31, 36, 37, 38, 42,
45, 48, 66, 71, 75, 79, 95,
99, 109, 120, 121, 122,
131, 135, 138, 156, 161,
162, 167, 173, 178, 183,
202, 211, 213, 217, 221,
222, 226, 230, 242, 247,
258, 266, 277, 280, 281,
285, 289, 303, 305, 307,
308, 315, 319, 321, 325,
335, 366, 367, 369, 370,
371, 376, 377, 378, 379,
380, 386, 387, 394, 402,
413, 416, 418
yolks, 37, 46, 58, 59, 69, 71,
74, 76, 77, 82, 93, 124,
132, 135, 136, 149, 150,
162, 190, 217, 245, 246,
250, 251, 254, 255, 259,
262, 266, 268, 272, 275,
285, 292, 293, 296, 300,
303, 307, 310, 311, 313,
314, 318, 319, 321, 323,
324, 328, 335, 338, 345,
354, 360, 367, 370, 374,
376, 377, 379, 388, 391,
395, 396, 398, 400, 403,
405, 408, 411, 413, 414,
417
Eggs, 25, 30, 34, 35, 36, 37, 38,
39, 40, 42, 43, 44, 45, 46,
47, 49, 50, 51, 52, 53, 54,
55, 56, 57, 58, 59, 60, 61,
62, 63, 64, 65, 66, 67, 68,
69, 70, 72, 73, 74, 75, 76,
77, 78, 79, 80, 81, 82, 83,
84, 85, 87, 88, 89, 90, 91,
92, 93, 94, 95, 96, 97, 98,
99, 100, 101, 102, 103,
104, 105, 106, 107, 108,
109, 110, 111, 112, 113,
114, 115, 116, 117, 118,
119, 120, 121, 122, 123,
124, 125, 126, 127, 128,
129, 130, 131, 132, 133,
135, 136, 137, 139, 140,
141, 142, 143, 144, 145,
146, 147, 148, 149, 150,

Eggs, continued
151, 152, 153, 154, 155,
156, 157, 158, 159, 160,
161, 162, 163, 164, 181,
198, 199, 200, 201, 202,
203, 204, 205, 206, 207,
208, 209, 210, 211, 212,
213, 214, 215, 216, 219,
220, 221, 223, 225, 226,
227, 228, 229, 230, 231,
232, 233, 234, 235, 236,
237, 238, 239, 240, 241,
242, 244, 245, 253, 259,
260, 261, 263, 264, 265,
267, 268, 270, 271, 272,
273, 274, 275, 276, 278,
279, 280, 282, 283, 285,
286, 287, 288, 293, 294,
295, 296, 298, 299, 301,
302, 303, 304, 305, 306,
308, 309, 310, 311, 312,
313, 314, 315, 316, 317,
319, 320, 321, 322, 323,
325, 326, 327, 328, 329,
330, 332, 333, 334, 335,
336, 337, 338, 339, 340,
341, 342, 343, 344, 345,
346, 347, 348, 349, 350,
351, 352, 353, 354, 355,
356, 357, 358, 359, 360,
361, 362, 363, 364, 366,
367, 368, 369, 370, 371,
372, 373, 374, 375, 376,
378, 379, 381, 382, 384,
385, 386, 389, 390, 397,
398, 399, 408, 409
Equal sweetener, 239, 399
Extracts. See almond extract,
cherry extract, chocolate
extract, coconut extract,
hazelnut extract, lemon
extract, orange extract,
peppermint extract,
raspberry extract, rum
extract, vanilla extract
Flowers, edible, 60, 62, 77, 85,
118, 249, 296, 312
Foil candy cups, 185
Fondant, 166
Food coloring, 81, 93, 103,
114, 189, 238, 244, 334
Frangelico liqueur, 151, 269,
319, 356, 367, 379
Fruit, 60, 74, 96, 102, 108, 118,
119, 128, 131, 247, 292,
298, 314, 348, 351
candied, 34, 58, 59, 169

Fruit, *continued*

    spreadable, 389

Fruit cocktail, 39

Fudge frosting, 142

Galliano liqueur, 71

Ganache, 74, 113, 118, 132, 137, 139, 294, 375

Garlic, 390

Gaufrettes, 372

Gelatin, unflavored, 71, 125, 258, 259, 260, 268, 272, 273, 274, 275, 278, 279, 286, 292, 296, 298, 300, 302, 303, 308, 309, 314, 316, 319, 321, 326, 328, 330, 366, 403

Ginger, 73, 105, 214, 278, 343, 349

    candied, 343

    crystallized, 385

Ginger liqueur, 282

Gingersnaps, 282

Graham crackers, 35, 38, 50, 116, 135, 163, 181, 235, 252, 277, 278, 284, 316, 317, 371

    chocolate, 62, 83, 110, 118, 208, 228, 235, 251, 301, 312, 316, 320, 327

Grand Marnier, 26, 45, 100, 121, 123, 277, 304, 319, 347, 377, 405, 411

    Sauce, 56, 305, 308, 356

Granola, 217

Grapefruit juice, 70

Grapes, 323

Grasshopper liqueur, 330

Half-and-half, 24, 76, 185, 255, 270, 311, 319, 412

Hazelnut extract, 51, 74, 82, 123, 204, 207, 223

Hazelnut filling, 133

Hazelnut liqueur, 51, 65, 168, 237, 357

Hazelnuts, 26, 59, 65, 68, 74, 82, 84, 85, 92, 95, 116, 118, 137, 142, 143, 168, 176, 177, 185, 192, 198, 223, 234, 241, 245, 246, 248, 271, 296, 302, 305, 319, 344, 345, 346, 349, 356, 357, 361, 357, 370, 372, 378, 379, 405, 411

Heath Bars™, 54

Honey, *continued*

Honey, 27, 31, 51, 70, 75, 76, 92, 128, 130, 143, 175, 177, 183, 217, 218, 235, 240, 286, 304, 344, 356, 372, 376, 378, 384, 404, 407, 416, 423

    comb, 171

    buckwheat-, 314

Ice cream

    cherry, 64

    chocolate, 24, 25, 26, 27, 28, 32, 36, 38, 39, 79, 88, 120, 128, 158, 159, 246, 247, 248, 252, 253, 277, 280, 281, 285, 305, 322, 348, 361, 385, 391, 411

    chocolate chip, 246, 253

    chocolate mint, 248, 252

    coffee, 317

    fudge, 159

    fudge ripple, 38, 249

    Neapolitan, 305, 348

    pistachio, 36

    raspberry, 254

    strawberry, 120, 252

    vanilla, 246, 248, 254, 281

Jam, 349, 357, 359, 360

Jelly, 349, 357, 359, 360

Kahlúa, 42, 59, 111, 260, 413

Kahlúa Cocoa Sauce, 112, 134, 293, 370

Kidney beans, 390

Kirsch liqueur, 65, 77, 366, 378

Kiwi, 25, 35, 37, 55, 111, 125, 135, 150, 270, 286, 292, 300, 388

Kosher liqueur, 370, 372

Kümmel liqueur, 296

Ladyfinger cookies, 148

Ladyfingers, 244, 296, 311, 321

Leaves, edible, 62, 422

Lemon extract, 38, 99, 147, 377, 413, 418

Lemon filling, 72, 153

Lemon glaze, 153, 216

Lemon juice, 38, 56, 58, 70, 97, 99, 109, 130, 151, 160, 163, 299, 312, 327, 358, 413, 418

Lemon peel, candied, 130, 143, 225

Lemon pudding, 220

Lemon zest, 70, 97, 144, 148, 202, 221, 299, 358, 413

Lemonier liqueur, 109

Lemons, 55, 270

Lime juice, 327

Limes, 125, 161, 322

Liqueur, 409 *See various liqueurs*

Macadamia nuts, 131, 180, 211, 225

Macaroons, 246, 292

Mandarino liqueur, 144, 151

Mango, 110

Marsala, 138, 149, 263

Marshmallows, 27, 30, 80, 84, 97, 133, 174, 189, 194, 195, 200, 201, 228, 231, 233, 238, 269, 277, 322, 342

    creme, 55, 133, 175, 179, 185, 188, 191, 195, 224, 238, 248, 259, 260, 274, 278, 305, 308, 402, 405

Marzipan, 177

Mascarpone cheese, 384

Matzo meal, 370, 372, 376

Mayonnaise, 134, 138

Milk, 24, 25, 26, 27, 28, 29, 31, 32, 44, 45, 47, 49, 50, 54, 55, 58, 62, 64, 68, 71, 73, 74, 75, 76, 80, 81, 82, 84, 85, 86, 87, 88, 95, 96, 98, 101, 104, 105, 109, 110, 118, 120, 122, 128, 129, 131, 133, 142, 144, 158, 159, 160, 161, 169, 175, 185, 191, 200, 207, 212, 213, 214, 216, 219, 220, 226, 236, 244, 246, 247, 250, 251, 254, 259, 260, 262, 263, 266, 268, 272, 273, 275, 277, 278, 279, 284, 288, 292, 293, 294, 295, 296, 298, 299, 300, 301, 302, 303, 305, 307, 308, 310, 311, 312, 313, 314, 316, 320, 321, 322, 324, 325, 327, 328, 336, 337, 338, 340, 341, 342, 343, 344, 347, 349, 350, 351, 353, 354, 357, 368, 374, 376, 381, 385, 386,

Milk, continued
388, 389, 390, 398, 399, 402, 403, 404, 405, 407, 408, 410, 411, 412

condensed, 30, 44, 114, 123, 167, 170, 171, 176, 179, 181, 182, 186, 189, 191, 192, 194, 204, 205, 213, 215, 219, 220, 223, 235, 283

evaporated, 39, 42, 55, 58, 61, 63, 67, 76, 77, 101, 102, 103, 124, 134, 138, 141, 146, 150, 173, 174, 175, 184, 185, 188, 192, 193, 195, 196, 203, 204, 218, 248, 269, 275, 289, 298, 301, 334, 344, 348, 351, 362, 374, 391, 394, 395, 396, 397, 398, 408, 412, 414, 415

powdered, 30, 152, 176, 183

skim, 164, 249, 296, 306, 309, 395, 409, 413

Mint, candy, 81, 244
sprig, 25, 26, 27, 28, 32, 35, 46, 74, 81, 85, 106, 114, 127, 150, 161, 244, 248, 249, 261, 263, 285, 286, 293, 300, 303, 305, 312, 326, 328, 348, 388

Mocha frosting, 45, 139, 147, 151, 158, 161, 314

Molasses, 73, 96, 105, 194, 301, 343, 345

Non-dairy creamer. *See* Creamer, non-dairy

Nutmeg, 25, 27, 30, 32, 36, 49, 76, 84, 87, 88, 102, 105, 129, 130, 227, 241, 270, 278, 299, 308, 312, 326, 327, 335, 342, 348, 349, 361, 375

Nuts, 78, 146, 182, 305 *See various nuts*

Oat bran, 218, 333, 357

Oats, 104, 106, 115, 140, 179, 206, 214, 215, 216, 218, 219, 220, 223, 224, 231, 336, 337, 344, 346, 353, 382

Okolehao liqueur, 28

Onion, 384, 390
powder, 392

Orange extract, 347, 358

Orange juice, 87, 103, 145, 163, 172, 178, 181, 216, 249, 274, 286, 305, 315, 319, 333, 338, 360, 373, 376

Orange liqueur, 85, 339, 360

Orange marmalade, 121

Orange peel, candied, 130, 143, 151, 225, 319, 324, 360, 371

Orange zest, 46, 49, 70, 87, 90, 103, 121, 139, 148, 151, 163, 178, 208, 212, 238, 249, 286, 305, 306, 315, 333, 334, 338, 345, 347, 358, 371, 373, 403, 405

Oranges, 90, 104, 123, 274, 300, 306, 368, 392
mandarine, 132

Pansies, 244, 270, 354

Papaya, 28, 100, 180

Paraffin wax, 191, 194

Pastry Shell, low-fat, 276

Peaches, 25, 135, 270
spreadable, 389

Peanut butter, 43, 85, 170, 179, 184, 192, 193, 194, 210, 214, 216, 217, 218, 223, 224, 235, 238, 275, 307, 322, 386, 387, 391, 403, 416

Peanut Butter and Honey Sauce, 249

Peanuts, 170, 171, 179, 182, 192, 193, 194, 210, 216, 217, 219, 223, 224, 232, 249

Pear William liqueur, 391

Pears, 387, 388, 391

Pecan Pastry crust, 261, 267, 276

Pecans, 39, 44, 51, 59, 60, 68, 70, 76, 82, 84, 86, 87, 92, 95, 97, 99, 106, 107, 110, 116, 118, 120, 123, 124, 127, 128, 137, 140, 150, 154, 158, 161, 162, 173, 177, 178, 179, 182, 185, 186, 191, 192, 193, 195, 198, 199, 201, 204, 205, 206, 208, 211, 212, 215, 223, 225, 226, 230, 231, 233, 236, 237, 238, 239, 240, 242, 246, 260, 261, 264, 265, 269, 270, 275,

Pecans, continued
276, 280, 282, 283, 286, 287, 296, 302, 305, 307, 310, 316, 333, 334, 338, 340, 342, 344, 345, 346, 348, 349, 350, 352, 356, 361, 363, 370, 371, 374, 385, 386, 387, 396, 405, 410, 415

Pepper, black, 225, 384, 392
cayenne, 384
white, 143, 386

Peppermint candies, 180

Peppermint extract, 26, 75, 80, 81, 135, 184, 187, 254, 263

Peppermint oil, 166

Peppermint schnapps, 32, 75, 80, 81, 189

Pine nuts, 130

Pineapple, 28, 159, 225, 319, 323, 392
candied, 180
juice, 28

Pistachio nuts, 76, 86, 127, 142, 144, 145, 148, 151, 178, 333

Pistachio pudding, 145

Plum juice, 323

Plums, 75, 114, 138, 149, 361, 416

Popcorn, 180, 238

Popsicle sticks, 385

Pork, 390

Port wine, 75, 114, 416

Potatoes, mashed, 87, 129, 158, 181, 190, 193, 194

Praline liqueur, 242, 334, 371

Preserves, 122, 363

Prunes, 88, 315

Puffed rice cereal, 194

Pumpkin, 89, 227, 278, 308, 312, 327, 349, 358, 361

Pumpkin pie spice, 89, 349

Raisins, 49, 59, 76, 102, 130, 181, 188, 191, 193, 201, 204, 215, 217, 218, 227, 230, 268, 310, 313, 319, 327, 333, 337, 340, 349, 357, 370, 372, 384

Raspberries, 56, 93, 163, 181, 253, 270, 289, 293, 306, 308, 377, 416

Raspberry extract, 169, 377
Raspberry jam, 93
Raspberry liqueur, 93, 118, 163, 295, 416
Raspberry preserves, 46, 123, 227
Raspberry sauce, 72, 86, 87, 117, 156, 244, 294, 311, 346, 361, 376, 377
Rennet tablet, 308
Rice cereal, 170
Rice flour, 218
Rice Krispies, 170, 185, 210, 216
Rice, 388
Ricotta cheese, 127, 148, 150, 151, 296, 312, 362, 403
Rose petals, 420
    candied, 388
Rum, 25, 29, 94, 109, 181, 228, 239, 278, 309, 323, 327, 384, 404, 416
    extract, 154, 309
    flavoring, 225
Rum cream frosting, 87, 342
Sabra liqueur, 373
Sauerkraut, 148
Seltzer water, 24, 26
Sesame seeds, 392
Sherry, 266, 311
Shortbread cookies, 137
Sour cream, 34, 35, 40, 43, 46, 47, 50, 52, 54, 63, 81, 91, 95, 108, 110, 113, 115, 121, 124, 126, 128, 131, 136, 137, 150, 151, 152, 163, 230, 258, 267, 307, 332, 334, 338, 347, 350, 353, 358, 387, 396, 397, 409
    -chocolate icing, 53
Sour milk, 53, 153
Sourdough bread, 85, 310
Sourdough starter, 152
Soy flour, 210, 237
Spearmint schnapps, 189
Sponge cake, 56, 314
Sprinkles, 139. See also Chocolate sprinkles
Strawberries, 42, 43, 56, 67, 102, 115, 120, 123, 127, 162, 172, 253, 263, 270, 277, 282, 292, 306, 311, 358, 380, 386, 416

Strawberries, continued
    chocolate-covered, 43, 82, 121, 269, 301
Strawberry glaze, 43, 104
Sugar cookie mix, 200
Sweetener, nonnutritive, 230, 399
Swiss chocolate almond liqueur, 321
Syrup, 351
Tía Maria liqueur, 135, 375
Tofu, 240
Tomatoes, crushed, 384
    plum-, 392
    pureed, 390
    sauce, 390
    stewed, 390
Topping, whipped, 24, 26, 64, 118, 125, 261, 277, 284, 325
Triple Sec, 97, 100, 144, 249, 286, 306, 316, 345, 373, 377, 392
Vanilla chips, 235
Vanilla custard Sauce, 317
Vanilla extract, 27, 28, 31, 34, 35, 36, 38, 39, 42, 44, 48, 52, 55, 56, 57, 58, 63, 66, 67, 71, 72, 74, 76, 77, 78, 80, 82, 84, 85, 87, 90, 91, 94, 96, 97, 99, 100, 101, 103, 104, 106, 107, 110, 112, 113, 114, 116, 118, 120, 122, 124, 125, 128, 131, 133, 136, 137, 141, 142, 146, 147, 149, 150, 151, 152, 153, 156, 158, 159, 160, 161, 162, 163, 168, 171, 174, 175, 176, 178, 180, 184, 186, 188, 194, 195, 199, 200, 201, 204, 205, 207, 209, 211, 212, 213, 215, 216, 219, 220, 222, 223, 226, 227, 228, 229, 231, 232, 233, 237, 239, 250, 253, 258, 261, 263, 271, 284, 289, 294, 300, 301, 306, 308, 312, 316, 325, 333, 334, 335, 336, 339, 344, 348, 352, 347, 378, 380, 387, 389, 391, 395, 396, 397, 399, 402, 406, 407, 408, 412, 416, 417, 418, 423

Vanilla sugar, 415
Vanilla wafers, 111, 123, 182, 205
Vinegar, 64
    cider, 40, 57, 73, 101, 109, 134, 159, 164, 284, 345
    white, 56, 59, 135
    wine, 64
Violet sugar, 151
Violets, 151
    candied, 151
Vodka, 42, 260, 389
Walnuts, 26, 36, 38, 49, 59, 68, 72, 76, 84, 87, 90, 97, 99, 106, 107, 118, 119, 124, 128, 129, 136, 140, 152, 158, 159, 160, 161, 171, 174, 175, 176, 178, 182, 186, 188, 201, 204, 205, 208, 209, 210, 211, 212, 213, 220, 226, 227, 228, 230, 231, 232, 233, 234, 236, 237, 239, 253, 269, 270, 275, 285, 333, 334, 335, 346, 352, 355, 370, 371, 372, 374, 376
Watercress, 129
Wheat cereal, puffed, 232
Wheat germ, 333
Wheat flour, 49, 68, 208, 210, 333, 335, 336, 345, 357
Whiskey, 30, 129, 286
White chocolate liqueur, 289
White chocolate sauce, 112, 157
White sugar icing, 76
Wine, red, 390
    white, 392
Yeast, 335, 337, 340, 343, 350, 356
Yogurt, chocolate, 40, 46, 47, 51, 54, 63, 67, 95, 108, 110, 111, 112, 116, 121, 136, 137, 252, 258, 275, 338, 350, 353, 358, 359, 361, 368, 387, 389, 396, 397, 406
    plain, 35, 43, 81, 91, 110, 113, 115, 126, 128, 131, 150, 151, 332
Zucchini, 102, 116, 339, 352, 353, 355